The **Rough Guide** to

Bulgaria

written and researched by

Jonathan Bousfield and Dan Richardson

with additional contributions from

Matt Willis, Mihaela Nikolova, Kim Burton and Nick Nasev

NEW YORK • LONDON • DELHI

www.roughguides.com

Contents

◀◀ Mesta valley ◀ Shiroka Lûka village

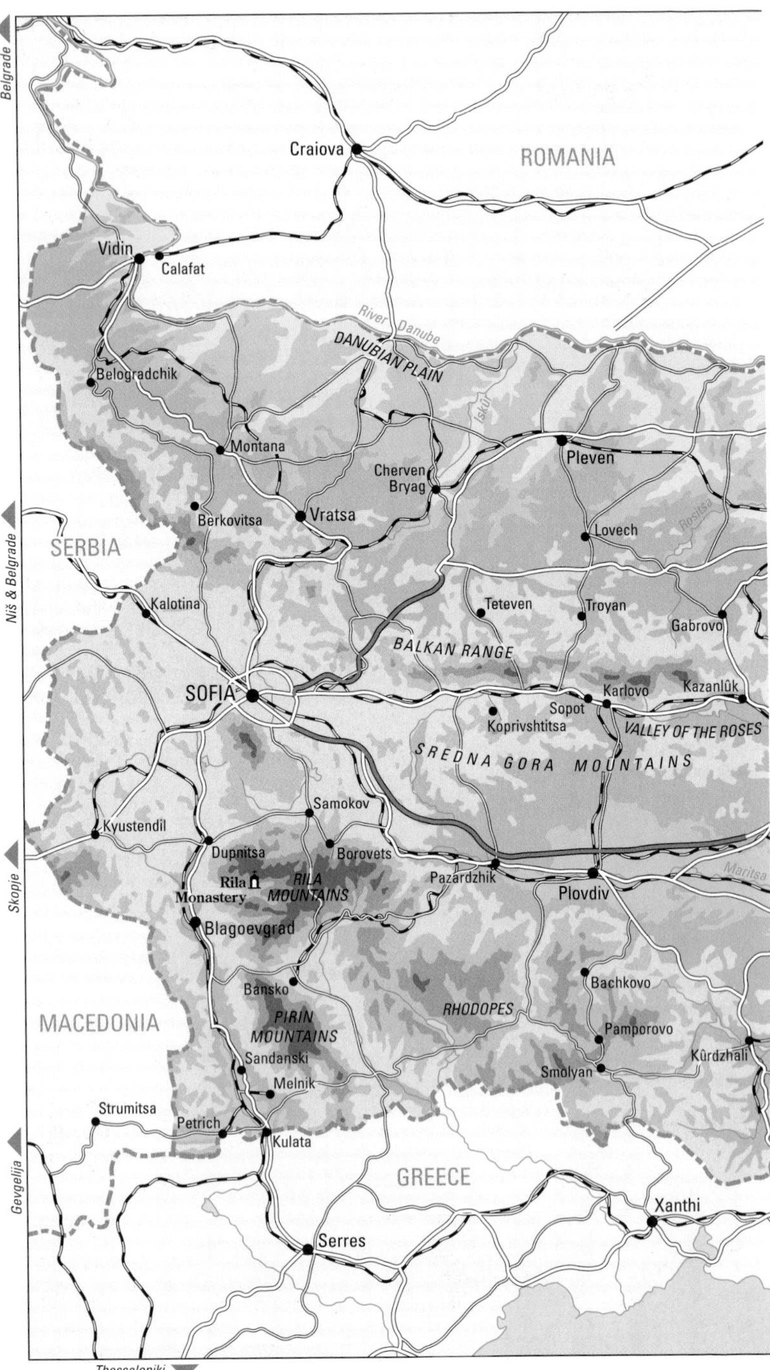

Belgrade
Craiova
ROMANIA
Vidin
Calafat
River Danube
DANUBIAN PLAIN
Belogradchik
Iskûr
Montana
Pleven
Cherven Bryag
Berkovitsa
Vratsa
Lovech
Rositsa
SERBIA
Niš & Belgrade
Kalotina
Teteven
Troyan
Gabrovo
BALKAN RANGE
SOFIA
Karlovo
Kazanlûk
Sopot
Koprivshtitsa
VALLEY OF THE ROSES
SREDNA GORA MOUNTAINS
Samokov
Kyustendil
Dupnitsa
Borovets
Skopje
Rila Monastery
RILA MOUNTAINS
Pazardzhik
Plovdiv
Maritsa
Blagoevgrad
Bansko
Bachkovo
PIRIN MOUNTAINS
RHODOPES
MACEDONIA
Pamporovo
Sandanski
Kûrdzhali
Smolyan
Melnik
Strumitsa
Petrich
Kulata
Gevgelija
GREECE
Xanthi
Serres
Thessaloniki

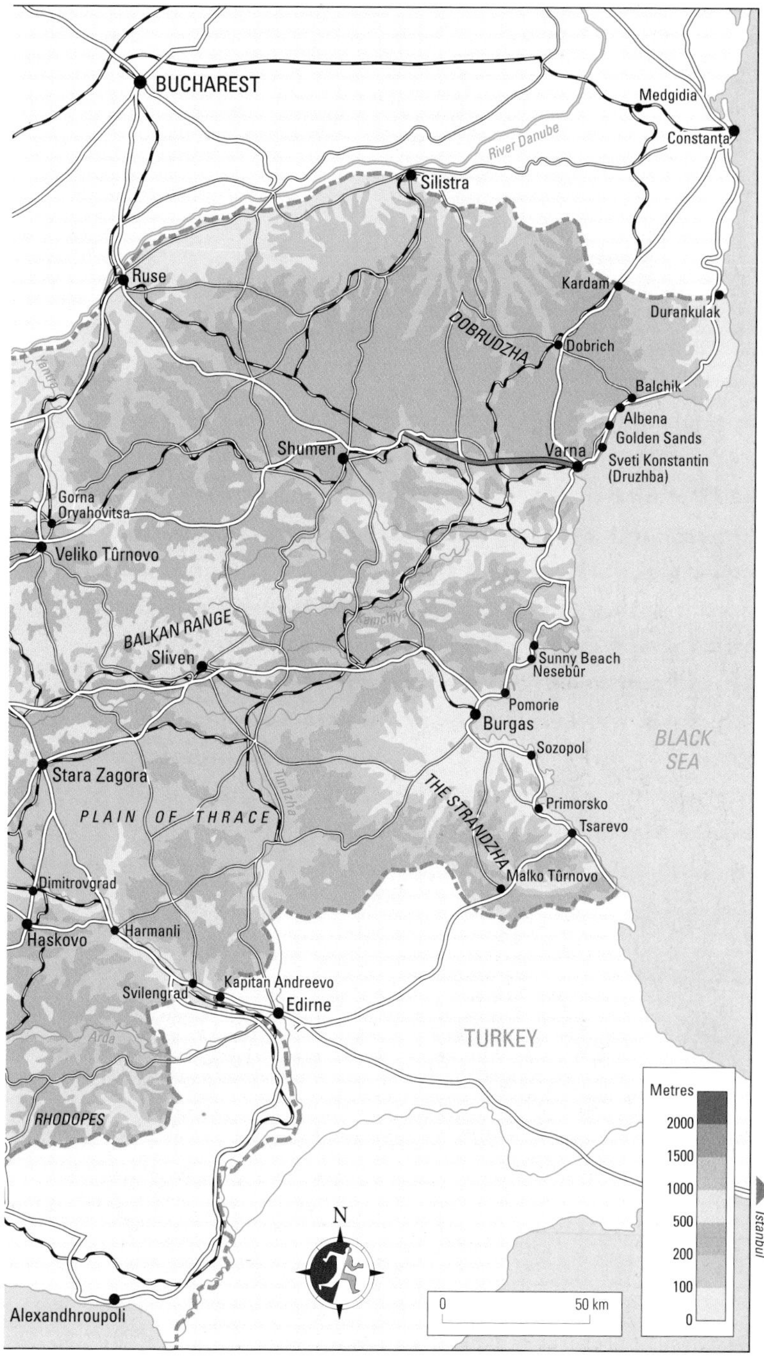
BUCHAREST
Medgidia
Constanţa
River Danube
Silistra
Ruse
Kardam
Durankulak
DOBRUDZHA
Dobrich
Yantra
Balchik
Albena
Golden Sands
Shumen
Varna
Sveti Konstantin
(Druzhba)
Gorna
Oryahovitsa
Veliko Tûrnovo
Kamchiya
BALKAN RANGE
Sliven
Sunny Beach
Nesebûr
Pomorie
Burgas
Sozopol
BLACK
SEA
Stara Zagora
Tundzha
THE STRANDZHA
PLAIN OF THRACE
Primorsko
Tsarevo
Malko Tûrnovo
Dimitrovgrad
Harmanli
Haskovo
Kapitan Andreevo
Svilengrad
Edirne
Arda
TURKEY
Metres
2000
1500
1000
500
200
100
0
RHODOPES
Istanbul
N
0
50 km
Alexandhroupoli

Introduction to Bulgaria

In many ways Bulgaria is one of the success stories of the Balkans; a politically stable democracy on the threshold of EU membership, it also harbours one of the fastest-growing tourist industries in Europe. Yet despite the soaring popularity of its seaside resorts, Bulgaria remains a little-known destination with a great deal to discover: much of the country is like an open-air museum of Balkan culture, with beautifully decorated churches, fine mosques, wonderfully preserved rustic villages and a great deal of enduring folklore. The mountainous interior makes it one of the top hiking destinations of Europe, while over on the Black Sea coast, the white-sand beaches are just as magnificent in reality as they look in the tourist brochures.

The Bulgarians themselves have long been frustrated by their country's lack of a clearly defined image abroad. Heirs to one of Europe's great civilizations, and guardians of Balkan Christian traditions, they have a keen sense of national identity distilled by centuries of turbulent history. In a constantly repeating cycle of grandeur, decline and national rebirth, successive Bulgarian states have striven to dominate the Balkan peninsula before succumbing to defeat and foreign tutelage, only to be regenerated by patriotic resistance to outside control.

The Bulgarian nation was formed in the seventh and eighth centuries when the **Bulgars**, warlike nomads from central Asia, assumed the leadership of Slav tribes in the lower Danube basin and took them on a spree of

It's in the countryside rather than the cities that the real rewards of inland travel are to be found

conquest in southeastern Europe. The resulting **First Bulgarian Kingdom**, after accepting Orthodox Christianity as the state religion, became the centre of Slavonic culture and spirituality before falling victim to a resurgent **Byzantine Empire** in the eleventh century. Recovery came a century later when the local aristocracy broke free from Constantinople and restored past glories in the shape of the **Second Bulgarian Kingdom**. However, the rise of Ottoman power in the fourteenth century ushered in the 500-year-long period of *Tursko robstvo* or "**Turkish bondage**", when the achievements of the medieval era were extinguished. Bulgarian art and culture recovered during the nineteenth-century **National Revival**, and the emergence of a potent revolutionary movement prepared the ground for Bulgaria's eventual **Liberation** in 1878, achieved with the help of Russian arms. However, Europe's other Great Powers conspired to limit the size of the infant state at the Berlin Congress of 1878, the first of a series of betrayals which denied Bulgarian claims to a territory which had long been considered an integral part of the historical Bulgarian state, **Macedonia**. In the twentieth century alone, Bulgaria went to war three times (in the Balkan Wars of 1912–13, World War I and World War II) to try and recover Macedonia, only to be defeated on each occasion. By 1945 it seemed like a country that had somehow missed out on its destiny, and rapidly turned in on itself during the subsequent deep sleep of Communism.

▲ Bar in Plovdiv

Fact file

- Bulgaria is a country of 7.9 million people located in the extreme southeastern corner of Europe, sharing borders with Romania, Yugoslavia, Macedonia, Greece and Turkey.
- Roughly 85 percent of the population is made up of Bulgarians, who speak a Slavic language akin to Russian and Serbo-Croat, and practise the Orthodox Christian faith.
- There is also a sizeable Muslim population (13 percent of the total), comprising both Pomaks (Bulgarians who converted to Islam from the sixteenth century onwards) and ethnic Turks. Bulgaria also plays host to as many as 500,000 Gypsies or Roma, many of whom represent the poorest segment of the population.
- Much of Bulgaria's industry collapsed, along with the Communist system that developed it, after 1989, and the country is nowadays known for natural products such as fruit, vegetables, wine and yoghurt – along with tobacco, a mainstay of the rural south.
- Bulgaria's Black Sea coast was earmarked for intensive tourist development as early as the 1960s, although recent years have seen attempts to encourage village tourism and hiking holidays in the country's mountainous interior.

Today, while undoubtedly more open to the outside world and more visitor-friendly than ever before, Bulgaria remains a country in transition. Back in the momentous winter of 1989, it looked as if it was dragging its feet on the road to democracy while others forged ahead. The Communist Party ditched a few of the old guard, changed its name to the Socialist Party and promptly won the first multiparty elections for more than forty years, remaining the country's most coherent political force until the elections of April 1997, when the SDS took over. Despite stabilizing the economy, the SDS failed to stamp out corruption, and was swept aside four years later by a new movement, the NDSV, centred around the former tsar of Bulgaria, **Simeon of Saxe-Coburg-Gotha**. Such changes of regime have had little impact on the main currents of government policy, with the transition to a fully functioning market economy, integration into the Western alliance and membership of the EU (slated for 2007) remaining the key themes.

With private enterprise and the entrepreneurial spirit bringing a new energy to Bulgaria's streets, locals are quick to

▼ Communist Party medals

▲ Freshly picked roses

point out that the move towards capitalism has meant poor conditions for many. Full employment and job security are things of the past, and the new business culture is riddled with corruption and organized crime. While these problems shouldn't affect your enjoyment of an invigorating and little-experienced culture, it's a good idea to remain sensitive towards such issues.

Where to go and when

Bulgaria has a continental climate, with long, hot, dry summers and – in the interior at least – bitterly cold winters. July and August can be oppressively hot in the big cities, and a little crowded on the Black Sea coast – elsewhere, you won't have to worry about being swamped by fellow visitors. Using public transport is reasonably easy

The mountains

The topography of inland Bulgaria is characterized by a series of dramatic mountain chains, which together offer some of the most exciting and varied hiking opportunities in Europe. The Pirin mountains, in the southwest, are the wildest, most picturesque range in Bulgaria, with 45 peaks over 2590m, deep valleys, karstic massifs and numerous glacial lakes. Immediately to the north, the Rila mountains are characterized by magnificent coniferous forests and alpine scenery abloom with wildflowers all year; here Mount Musala, at 2925m above sea level, stands as the highest peak in the Balkan peninsula. Both these ranges abut the Rhodopes, arguably the loveliest range in Bulgaria, with a mixture of pine forests, crags, highland meadows and villages of stone houses. All three ranges are crisscrossed by well-maintained, well-marked paths, with a network of mountain huts, or *hizhi*, providing basic but cosy accommodation.

▲ Pirin mountains

Folk festivals

Traditional folk music is still very much alive in Bulgaria, and is celebrated in numerous festivals across the country, especially in summer. The biggest bashes of them all are the Koprivshtitsa festival, which attracts performers from all over Bulgaria, and Pirin Sings (*Pirin Pee*), which concentrates on the rich folkloric traditions of the southwest. Both festivals feature an organized programme on a series of stages, as well as a host of unofficial performances by village musicians gathered around the festival fringes, making these occasions more like medieval fairs than modern cultural manifestations. Traditionally, both take place only every four or five years, but such is their popularity and importance that smaller, scaled-down versions of the main events are now organized annually. In addition, there's a whole host of local festivals in villages right around the country, often using traditional feast days such as St Elijah's Day (*Ilinden*) or the Assumption (*Golyama Bogoroditsa*) as an excuse for a day or two of dancing and drinking – ensuring that you stand a good chance of catching something whichever part of the country you're in year-round.

throughout the year, although the highest cross-mountain routes will be closed during the coldest months.

Bulgaria's most obvious urban attractions are **Sofia**, a set-piece capital city whose centre was laid out by successive regimes as an expression of political power; and the second city **Plovdiv**, home to what is arguably the finest collection of nineteenth-century architecture in the Balkans. Both are increasingly cosmopolitan places, offering a range of street cafés and nightlife opportunities in short supply elsewhere in the country. They each form important cultural centres, being well endowed with museums and galleries, and are good bases from which to visit the rest of the interior.

Yet it's in the countryside rather than the cities that the real rewards

▲ Autumn forest, Rila Mountains

Monasteries

During five centuries of Ottoman rule, Bulgarian national traditions were kept alive by its monasteries, which had been centres of Bulgarian-language learning since the Middle Ages. Often hidden away in mountain valleys – both for defensive reasons, and because of the tranquillity thereby offered to hermits – the monasteries went on to provide the populace with both spiritual and political leadership during the nineteenth-century upsurge of patriotic feeling known as the National Revival. For today's visitor, the monasteries offer a unique atmosphere of sanctity and peace, as well as the chance to peer inside some wonderfully decorated churches. Rila, Troyan and Bachkovo are the three most-visited foundations, welcoming a steady stream of pilgrims all year round and attracting crowds of celebrants on major saints' days.

▲ Troyan monastery

of inland travel are to be found. You'll come across some of Europe's finest highland scenery in the **Rila**, **Pirin**, **Balkan**, **Sredna Gora** and **Rhodope mountain ranges**, whose valleys harbour the kind of **bucolic villages** which have all but disappeared in Western Europe. Many of them are time-consuming to reach by public transport, but if traditional architecture and goat-thronged, cobbled alleys appeal, any effort will be rewarded. While the villages of **Bansko**, **Koprivshtitsa** – a living memorial to the 1876 April Rising – and **Melnik** have the best tourist facilities, more rustic out-of-the-way spots such as **Brûshlyan**, **Kovachevitsa** and **Zheravna** are also well worth seeking out. In addition, the highland regions display Bulgaria's rich spiritual traditions in the shape of its many **monasteries**: **Bachkovo**, **Rila**, **Rozhen** and **Troyan** are the big four, although any number of smaller foundations make worthwhile destinations. Also in the mountains, a burgeoning winter tourist industry is taking shape in resorts such as **Bansko**, **Borovets** and **Pamporovo**, although the latter two are purpose-built package resorts which lack the charm of the former. Snow is thick on the ground from late November through to mid-March, and in summer the mountain resorts are taken over by climbers and ramblers.

Much of the country is like an open-air museum of Balkan culture

Body language

A shake of the head means yes and a nod means no according to local custom but natives sometimes shake or nod their head in the "usual" way when talking with foreigners. Bulgarians are tolerant of misunderstandings over gestures, but it must be disconcerting for them to have a chat with someone who constantly nods "no, no". Anyone waving at you is probably signalling "come here" or "step inside", not "goodbye".

However, most foreign visitors still make a beeline for the **Black Sea**, formerly the summer playground of the entire Eastern Bloc. That said, big purpose-built resorts like **Sunny Beach** and **Golden Sands** tend to be rather characterless and isolating: though package tours based at these resorts present a cheap and easy way of getting to Bulgaria, it's best to steer clear of them once you arrive. The main resort-city of **Varna** is the liveliest place along the coast, while small peninsula settlements like **Nesebûr** and **Sozopol**, though crowded in August, provide traditional fishing-village architecture as well as enticing stretches of sand. Indeed, beaches are on the whole magnificent, especially in the south, and private enterprise is more developed here than anywhere else in the country, ensuring a plentiful supply of private rooms and good seafood restaurants. Although the climate remains mild all the year round, the Black Sea becomes deserted outside the main tourist season (June–Sept), when many attractions and hotels shut up shop.

Elsewhere, although few places are geared up to cater to Western-style, consumer-oriented tourism, the rugged highlands that cut across the centre of the country are the best places to explore the heartland of Bulgarian history and culture. The crafts towns and monasteries of the central Balkan Range were the places where Bulgarian culture recovered during the nineteenth-century National Revival, and are easily explored from the

▲ Man tending flock, the Dobrudzha

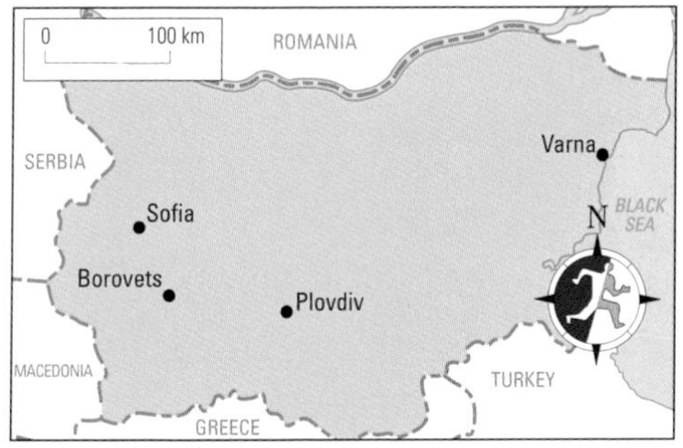

dramatically situated, citadel-encrusted town of **Veliko Tûrnovo**, medieval capital of the Second Bulgarian Kingdom. **Shumen**, main town of the northwest, is dour in comparison, but allows access to the remains of the Bulgarian state's first two capitals, **Pliska** and **Preslav**. Between the Balkan Range and the **Sredna Gora**, with its countless reminders of Bulgaria's nineteenth-century struggles against Turkish oppression, lies the **Valley of the Roses**, lined by a string of historic market towns and home to Bulgaria's renowned rose harvest in late May.

Average temperatures

	Jan	Feb	Mar	Apr	May	June	July	Aug	Sept	Oct	Nov	Dec
Borovets												
°F	30	33	41	48	59	65	71	74	61	54	42	33
°C	-1	1	5	9	15	19	22	23	16	12	6	1
Plovdiv												
°F	33	34	44	54	62	73	74	76	65	55	45	36
°C	1	3	7	12	17	23	23	24	19	13	8	3
Sofia												
°F	30	33	41	51	60	66	73	75	61	54	42	33
°C	-1	1	5	10	15	19	23	24	16	12	6	1
Varna												
°F	36	43	43	54	62	70	75	74	68	60	49	39
°C	3	6	6	12	17	22	24	23	20	16	10	4

30 things not to miss

It's not possible to see everything that Bulgaria has to offer in one trip – and we don't suggest you try. What follows is a selective taste of the country's highlights: outstanding monasteries and churches, vibrant festivals, spectacular mountainscapes, and even good things to eat and drink. It's arranged in five colour-coded categories, so that you can browse through to find the very best things to see, do and experience. All highlights have a page reference to take you into the guide, where you can find out more.

01 Sunflower fields Page **195** • Every summer, the fields of the Balkan Range are bathed in sunflowers, a dazzling sight as you're driving by.

02 Bachkovo monastery Page **354** • Bulgaria's second-largest monastery is beautifully set in the Rhodope mountains, and boasts equally dazzling frescos.

03 Revolutionary spirit Pages **302** & **304** • Visit the birthplace-museums of nineteenth-century freedom-fighters like Vasil Levski (Karlovo) or Hristo Botev (Kalofer).

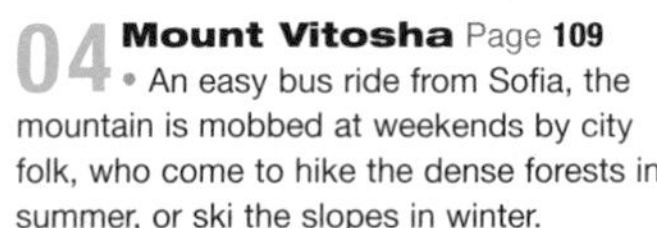

04 Mount Vitosha Page **109** • An easy bus ride from Sofia, the mountain is mobbed at weekends by city folk, who come to hike the dense forests in summer, or ski the slopes in winter.

05 Trigrad Gorge Page **366** • This spectacular gorge lies deep in the Rhodope mountains and is the site of the stupendous Devil's Throat (Dyavolsko gûrlo) cave.

06 The Shipka Pass Page **312** • Pay your respects at the Freedom Monument, where Bulgarian and Russian forces resisted a huge Turkish army in 1877.

07 Yoghurt Page **53** • Available everywhere, Bulgarian yoghurt (*kiselo mlyako*) is renowned for its health-giving properties. Try it with *banitsa*, a delicious flaky pastry, for a typical Bulgarian snack.

08 Orthodox Easter Page **63** • A rewarding time to be in Bulgaria: after midnight Mass on Easter Saturday, celebrants flood out onto the streets bearing candles symbolizing the Resurrection, before smashing specially painted eggs.

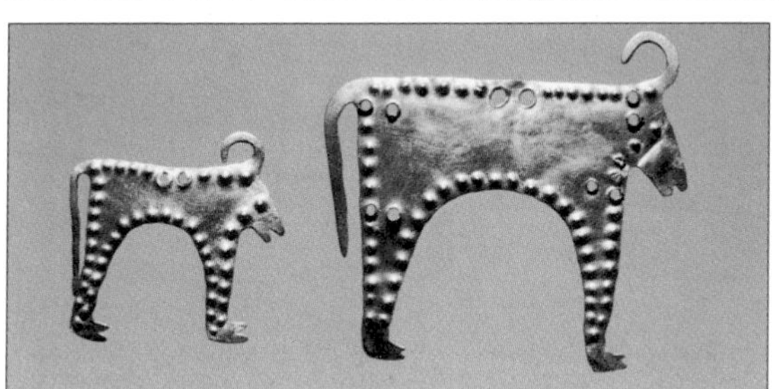

09 Varna Archeological Museum Page **390** • The Black Sea town of Varna is home to an outstanding museum of Thracian artefacts and Roman-era funerary sculpture.

10 **Birdwatching** Pages **222**, **376** & **420** • Bulgaria is a paradise for ornithologists, particularly the unspoilt areas of Srebûrna, Madzharovo and the lakes around Burgas.

11 **Rila Monastery** Page **136** • The most-visited monastic foundation in the country – a hoard of miracle-working relics and icons in its beautifully decorated church draws pilgrims year-round.

12 Nesebûr Page **413** • The rich Byzantine-Bulgarian civilization that thrived here in the late Middle Ages is still visible in Nesebûr's narrow streets and numerous churches.

14 A night in Bansko Page **150** • Restaurants in the village of Bansko cater to crowds of Sofia folk at Eastertime and in high summer, with their famous grilled food and live folk music.

13 Church of the Nativity, Arbanasi
Page **255** • An awe-inspiring example of the spiritual culture retained by the Bulgarians even at the height of the Ottoman occupation.

15 Kukeri Page **158** • The *kukeri* – local men in animal costumes and grotesque masks – drive away evil spirits with orgiastic dances. In most areas, *kukeri* rites take place in January, though the Easter event at Eleshnitsa is one of the most memorable folk festivals in Bulgaria.

16 Apocalyptic art Pages **136**, **239** & **257** • Check out nineteenth-century artist Zahari Zograf's horrific Last Judgement images at the monasteries of Rila, Troyan and Preobrazhenski.

17 Sozopol Page **425** • This ancient fishing village attracts a steady stream of day-trippers, but even in high summer there's still space to escape the crowds.

18 Beach-hopping Page **434** • The southern Black Sea coast is lined by vast stretches of white sand, best of all at Sinemorets.

19 Beach bars Page **398** • In summer impromptu beach bars set up below the Sea Gardens in Varna, and all along the Black Sea coast.

20 The Feast of the Assumption (Golyama Bogoroditsa) Pages **239**, **354** & **111** • August 15 is a big deal here, marked by processions and services at any church associated with the Holy Virgin. Head especially for the monasteries at Troyan, Bachkovo or Dragalevtsi.

21 Veliko Tûrnovo Page **243** • Perched above the twisting River Yantra, this ancient city is home to the vast fortified complex of Tsarevets, capital of the country's thirteenth-century tsars.

22 Thracian tombs Pages **279** & **310** • Bulgaria's ancient inhabitants' burial mounds often preserve richly decorated interiors – the best can be seen in Sveshtari and Kazanlûk.

23 Kopriv-shtitsa Page **289** • This highland village is renowned for its role in the April Rising of 1876, when local revolutionaries heroically failed to unseat the occupying Ottoman powers.

24 Belogradchik Page **193** • Remote Belogradchik rewards a visit with its surrounding landscape of outlandish rock formations.

25 Lazaruvane Page **63** • Across Bulgaria St Lazarus's Day (the day before Palm Sunday) sees young girls dressing up in folk costumes to perform dances in honour of the coming spring.

26 **The Old Quarter, Plovdiv** Page **341** • Many of the houses in this nineteenth-century quarter of town have been restored, with exquisitely carved wooden ceilings and fanciful wall paintings inside.

27 Melnik Page **165** • The walk from this ancient wine-making village over the mountains to Rozhen Monastery takes you through a strange landscape of pyramid-shaped rock formations.

28 Tombul Dzhamiya, Shumen Page **272** • A major spiritual centre for the Turks of the northwest, the Tombul Dzhamiya is the outstanding example of the country's Ottoman-built mosques.

29 Aleksandûr Nevski Church, Sofia Page **101** • The capital's most striking edifice, built in Byzantine–Moscovite style, with an opulently decorated interior.

30 Heritage villages Pages **162**, **364**, **265** & **324** • Many of Bulgaria's villages preserve the kind of stone- or timber-built farmhouses which have largely died out elsewhere in the Balkans. A number have been spruced up or rebuilt with tourism in mind – Kovachevitsa, Shiroka Lûka, Bozhentsi and Zheravna are four of the most evocative.

Basics

Basics

Getting there

The easiest way to reach Bulgaria is by air, with direct flights from the UK and indirect flights from North America and Australasia. Travelling overland from Britain is a long haul, and you'll save little, if anything, by taking the train, although with an Inter Rail or Eurail pass you can take in Bulgaria as part of a wider European trip; buses, on the other hand, can cost less than half the price of the plane, though the trip is arduous. Other possible options from Britain include picking up a discounted flight to Athens, Thessaloniki, Istanbul or Budapest and continuing by land; or driving, a journey of at least 2400km, best covered over three days or more.

Air fares always depend on the **season**. Peak times for flights to Bulgaria are mid-December to early March, June–August, and around the Easter holidays; at these times be prepared to book well in advance. Fares drop during the "shoulder" seasons (May & Sept); and you'll get the best prices during the low season (mid–March & April excluding Easter, Oct to mid-Dec)). Note also that flying at weekends ordinarily adds around £20–30/ US$36–54 to the round-trip fare; prices quoted below assume midweek travel.

You can often cut costs by going through a **specialist flight agent** – either a consolidator, who buys up blocks of tickets from the airlines and sells them at a reduced price, or a **discount agent**, who in addition to dealing with discounted flights may also offer special student and youth fares and a range of other travel-related services such as travel insurance, rail passes, car rental, tours and the like. Some agents specialize in **charter flights**, which may be cheaper than anything available on a scheduled flight, but departure dates are fixed and withdrawal penalties are high. For Bulgaria, you may well find it cheaper to pick up a **package deal** and use it as a springboard for independent travel.

Booking flights online

Many airlines and discount travel websites offer you the opportunity to book your tickets **online**, cutting out the costs of agents and middlemen. Good deals can often be found through discount or auction sites, as well as through the airlines' own websites.

Online booking agents

ⓦ **www.cheapflights.co.uk** (in UK & Ireland), ⓦ www.cheapflights.com (in US), ⓦ www.cheapflights.ca (in Canada), ⓦ www.cheapflights.com.au (in Australia). Flight deals, travel agents, plus links to other travel sites.

ⓦ **www.cheaptickets.com** US and UK discount flight specialists.

ⓦ **www.expedia.co.uk** (in UK), ⓦ www.expedia.com (in US), ⓦ www.expedia.ca (in Canada). Discount air fares, all-airline search engine and daily deals.

ⓦ **www.hotwire.com** Bookings from the US only. Last-minute savings of up to forty percent on regular published fares.

ⓦ **www.lastminute.com** (in UK), ⓦ www.au.lastminute.com (in Australia & New Zealand). Offers good last-minute holiday package and flight-only deals.

ⓦ **www.opodo.co.uk** Popular and reliable source of low air fares from the UK.

ⓦ **www.priceline.co.uk** (in UK), ⓦ www.priceline.com (in US). Name-your-own-price website that has deals at around forty percent off standard fares. You cannot specify flight times (although you do specify dates) and the tickets are non-refundable, non-transferable and non-changeable.

ⓦ **www.skyauction.com** (bookings from the US only). Auctions tickets and travel packages using a "second bid" scheme. The best strategy is to bid the maximum you're willing to pay, since if you win you'll pay just enough to beat the runner-up regardless of your maximum bid.

ⓦ **www.travelocity.co.uk** (in UK), ⓦ www.travelocity.com (in US), ⓦ www.travelocity.ca (in Canada). Destination guides, hot web fares and best deals for car rental, accommodation and lodging.

Ⓦ **www.travelshop.com.au** Australian website offering discounted flights, packages, insurance, online bookings.
Ⓦ **www.zuji.com.au** Australian site detailing destination guides and hot fares.

Flights from the UK and Ireland

Both British Airways and Bulgaria Air (the Bulgarian national carrier) offer daily **direct flights to Sofia** – the former from London Heathrow, the latter from London Gatwick – and the journey takes just over three hours. A low-season return booked well in advance can cost as little as £120 – in busy periods this can rise to £250.

Discount flight agents sometimes sell seats on the Bulgaria Air or BA London–Sofia service for a slightly cheaper price than the airline itself, but are more likely to offer special deals on **indirect flights** with other carriers, such as CSA via Prague, Malev via Budapest, Alitalia via Rome or Milan, Lufthansa via Frankfurt or Air France via Paris. These are particularly worth considering if you live outside London: Lufthansa and CSA use Manchester and other UK airports, while Alitalia offers services from Dublin. Tickets for non-direct flights can cost as little as £150/€210, but are more often in the £230–280/€320–400 range.

Package-tour operators may have a few discounted tickets on **charter flights** to Sofia or Plovdiv in winter, or coastal destinations such as Varna in summer. However these are rarely advertised in the press or online. You'll have to contact operators direct to find out what's on offer; Balkan Holidays is the obvious place to start. Package operators are also more likely to fly from regional airports as well as London ones.

You could also fly to another destination in **southeast Europe**, such as Budapest, Bucharest, Istanbul, Athens or Thessaloniki, and continue to Bulgaria overland. Flights to Bucharest, Istanbul and Thessaloniki can be as expensive as those to Sofia, but budget tickets to Budapest are available from easyJet, Wizzair and Skyeurope; easyJet also flies to Athens.

Airlines

Aer Lingus Ireland Ⓣ0818/365 000, Ⓦwww.aerlingus.ie. Flights from Dublin to Budapest.
Air France UK Ⓣ0870/142 4343, Ireland Ⓣ01/605 0383, Ⓦwww.airfrance.co.uk. Flights from UK airports to Sofia via Paris.
Alitalia UK Ⓣ0870/544 8259, Ireland Ⓣ01/677 5171, Ⓦwww.alitalia.com. Dublin to Warsaw via Rome; London Heathrow to Sofia via Milan.
Austrian Airlines UK Ⓣ0845/601 0948, Ⓦwww.aua.com. London to Sofia via Vienna.
Bulgaria Air UK Ⓣ020/7637 7637, Ⓦwww.balkanair.co.uk. Daily services from London Gatwick to Sofia.
British Airways UK Ⓣ0845/773 3377, Ireland Ⓣ0141/222 2345, Ⓦwww.britishairways.com. Direct flights from London Heathrow to Sofia daily.
CSA UK Ⓣ0870/444 3747, Ⓦwww.czechairlines.co.uk. London, Manchester or Birmingham to Sofia via Prague.
easyJet UK Ⓣ0870/600 0000, Ⓦwww.easyjet.com. Flights from Bristol, London Gatwick, Luton and Newcastle to Budapest; from London Gatwick and Luton to Athens.
Lufthansa UK Ⓣ0845/773 7747, in Ireland Ⓣ01/844 5544, Ⓦwww.lufthansa.com. Flights from various British and Irish airports to Sofia, with a connection in Frankfurt or Munich.
Malev UK Ⓣ020/7439 0577, Ⓦwww.malev.hu. London Stansted to Sofia via Budapest.
SkyEurope UK Ⓣ020/7365 0365, Ⓦwww.skyeurope.com. Flights from London Stansted to Budapest.
Tarom UK Ⓣ020/7224 3693, Ⓦwww.tarom.ro. Flights from London Heathrow to Bucharest.
Turkish Airlines UK Ⓣ 020/7766 9300, Ⓦwww.turkishairlines.com. To Istanbul from London Heathrow or Manchester, with onward connections to Sofia.
Wizzair Ⓣ+36 1 470 9499, Ⓦwww.wizzair.com. Daily flights from Luton or Liverpool to Budapest. Note that the call centre is in Hungary.

Flight and travel agents

Balkans Travel UK Ⓣ020/7687 2053, Ⓦwww.balkanstravel.co.uk. Bulgarian cheap flight specialist.
Bridge the World UK Ⓣ0870/444 7474, Ⓦwww.bridgetheworld.com. Specializing in round-the-world tickets, with good deals aimed at the backpacker market.
East European Travel Centre UK Ⓣ020/7637 0555. Flight bargains to Bulgaria and elsewhere in the Balkans.

ebookers UK ⓣ0870 010 7000, ⓦwww.ebookers.com; Ireland ⓣ01/488 3507, ⓦwww.ebookers.ie. Low fares on an extensive selection of scheduled flights.

Joe Walsh Tours Ireland ⓣ01/241 0800, ⓦwww.joewalshtours.ie. General budget fares agent.

Lee Travel Ireland ⓣ021/277 111, ⓦwww.leetravel.ie. Flights and holidays worldwide.

McCarthy's Travel Ireland ⓣ021/270 127, ⓦwww.mccarthystravel.ie. General flight agent.

North South Travel UK ⓣ01245/608 291, ⓦwww.northsouthtravel.co.uk. Friendly, competitive travel agency, offering discounted fares worldwide – profits are used to support projects in the developing world, especially the promotion of sustainable tourism.

Premier Travel Northern Ireland ⓣ028/7126 3333, ⓦwww.premiertravel.uk.com. Discount flight specialists based in Northern Ireland.

STA Travel UK ⓣ0870/160 0599, ⓦwww.statravel.co.uk. Worldwide specialists in low-cost flights and tours for students and under-26s, though other customers are welcome.

Top Deck UK ⓣ020/7244 8000, ⓦwww.topdecktravel.co.uk. Long-established agent dealing in discount flights.

Trailfinders UK ⓣ020/7938 3939, ⓦwww.trailfinders.com; Ireland ⓣ01/677 7888, ⓦwww.trailfinders.ie. One of the best-informed and most efficient agents for independent travellers.

USIT Northern Ireland ⓣ028/9032 7111, Republic of Ireland ⓣ01/602 1904, ⓦwww.usit.ie. Student and youth specialist for flights and trains.

Package deals

The main advantage of **package holidays** to Bulgaria is their low cost. Flight-plus-accommodation deals are often cheaper than the price of a scheduled air fare alone, and even the most independent of travellers should consider the package option. Although in theory they tie you down to staying in one or two centres, there's nothing to stop you absenting yourself for a few days and indulging in a little exploration of your own. The most popular packages are beach holidays on the Black Sea coast, or winter skiing trips in highland resorts. The **season** for summer packages runs from mid-May to late September, peaking in the first two weeks of August. The winter season runs from December to March, peaking in mid-February.

There are also a number of other options: Balkan Holidays arranges numerous **two-centre trips**, combining coastal and mountain resorts, Bulgarian and Romanian, or Bulgarian and Turkish destinations, as well as fly-drive holidays with pre-booked accommodation. Balkan Holidays and Regent can arrange **city breaks** in Sofia, tailoring a flight-plus-accommodation deal to your needs. If you'd rather travel with a group, **tours** covering the highlights of Bulgaria in eight to ten days are a good option; operators such as Bales, Balkan Holidays and Worldwide Adventures Abroad offer trips in the £1000–1500 per-person range.

Beach holidays

The drawback to package holidays on the Black Sea coast is the nature of the principal **resorts**. The purpose-built complexes are often over-large and some distance from the nearest town or village, ensuring that you experience little of Bulgarian life. Beaches, however, are generally spotless, and coastal waters warm, clean and safe. **Sunny Beach** (Slûnchev bryag) and **Golden Sands** (Zlatni pyasûtsi) are the biggest (and most soulless) of the complexes, chock full of restaurants, bars and discos, while **Albena** is almost as huge but rather more stylish, with excellent sports facilities. **Sveti Konstantin** is smaller, surrounded by woodlands and coves, while villa complexes and holiday villages such as **Dyuni** or **Elenite** will appeal to those in search of something more tranquil. You could also stay in the attractive fishing ports of **Nesebûr** and **Sozopol**, either in a hotel or an apartment.

Balkan Holidays is the main tour operator offering summer beach packages. Peak-season prices for holidays in Sunny Beach, Golden Sands and Albena hover around £400–550 for one week, £550–650 for two, though prices can be £100 lower in May and September. For a hotel in Sveti Konstantin or a self-catering studio at Elenite, you're likely to pay £550–650 for seven nights. Apartments in Nesebûr and Sozopol cost about £400 per person for seven days in high season, dropping to £350 at other times.

Skiing holidays

From December to March, Balkan Holidays, First Choice, Neilson and Crystal all offer one- and two-week **winter holidays** at the Rhodope resort of Pamporovo, where British tourists make up about 75 percent of the foreign guests, and Borovets in the Rila Mountains, where they account for a staggering ninety percent. Bansko in the Pirin range is more international but only on offer from Balkan Holidays and Neilson, while Malyovitsa in the Rila Mountains and Mount Vitosha outside Sofia aren't featured at all.

While **skiing** rules, **snowboarding** is increasingly popular at the three main resorts. The **cost** of the packages depends on the date (Christmas, New Year and mid-February are the most expensive times), the type and standard of accommodation (hotel or chalet), and fees for lessons, equipment and lift passes. Expect to pay £350–450 for seven nights at Borovets or Pamporovo, plus an additional £60–70 for equipment rental.

Mountain and lake holidays and hiking

From May to September the three resorts become centres for **mountain and lake holidays**: packages combining guided walks, entertainments and optional excursions – which can be a good way to indulge in some independent travel as well. Though large operators like Crystal used to feature Bulgaria, the only firm that currently does is Balkan Holidays, with diverse packages based on Pamporovo, Borovets and/or Bansko, with Sofia, Melnik, Plovdiv or Varna as bolt-on extras. While the possibilities for walking are equally good at all three resorts, Bansko and Pamporovo have more to offer in terms of public transport than Borovets does, and Bansko itself has more charm and historic interest than the other two put together.

Despite great opportunities for serious **hiking** in the Rila, Pirin and Rhodopes, the only UK tour operator featuring Bulgaria at present is Exodus – though Interchange can arrange individual itineraries and there are several reliable companies in Bulgaria that welcome direct bookings by email (see "Outdoor activities and ecotourism", p.66).

Specialist holidays

Birdwatching is the fastest growing sector of Bulgarian tourism; in Britain alone, half a dozen firms run ornithological tours to the same sites every spring or autumn, when bird migrations peak (see "Birdwatching" on p.67 for sites and species, and Ⓦwww.free-living.com for tour details). Since some do only one trip a year, it's vital to book well ahead. The amenities can be fairly basic despite the cost (from £995 for ten days), but you can be sure of fantastic bird life and expert guides.

Cultural tours, accompanied by expert lecturers, are offered by ACE Study Tours and Andante. While Melnik, Rila, Plovdiv and Koprivshtitsa invariably feature on the itineraries, other sites vary. These tours are slightly pricier than birdwatching ones, but the amenities are superior.

If your heart is set on a particular activity-based or special-interest holiday not offered by any of the UK-based companies, consider booking your own flight to Sofia and asking a Bulgarian specialist agent to tailor your trip (see "Specialist operators in Bulgaria" below).

Tour operators

ACE Study Tours Ⓣ01223/835055, Ⓦwww.study-tours.org. Two-week study tours of monasteries and natural beauty spots.

Andante Travels Ⓣ01722/713800, Ⓦwww.andantetravels.co.uk. Ten-day lecture tours taking in ancient archeological sites and medieval monasteries.

Avian Adventures Ⓣ01384/372013, Ⓦwww.avianadventures.co.uk. Eight-day birdwatching tour of the Black Sea coast and Danube wetlands.

BTCV Tours Ⓣ01302/572244, Ⓦwww.btcv.org.uk. Summer and autumn ornithology tours, with an emphasis on nature conservation areas.

Bales Worldwide Ⓣ0870/241 3208, Ⓦwww.balesworldwide.com. Upmarket eleven-day cultural tours incorporating all the historic highlights.

Balkan Holidays Ⓣ0845/130 1114, independent travel Ⓣ020/7543 5569, Ⓦwww.balkanholidays.co.uk. Wide range of beach, skiing and mountain and lake holidays; multi-country tours (Bulgaria with Romania or Turkey); plus flight-only deals and special-interest tours for independent travellers.

Balkania Travel Ⓣ020/7237 7616, Ⓦwww.bbfs.org.uk. Travel arm of the British-Bulgarian Friendship Society, offering birdwatching, cultural and other special-interest tours led by local experts.

Birdwatching Breaks Ⓣ01381/610495, Ⓦwww.birdwatchingbreaks.com. Eight-day ornithology tours with expert guides.

Crystal Holidays ⓣ0870/405 5047, ⓦwww.crystalski.co.uk. Ski packages to Borovets and Pamporovo.

Exodus ⓣ0870/240 5550, ⓦwww.exodus.co.uk. Ten-day Rhodope Mountains tour incorporating easy hikes.

First Choice ⓣ0870 /850 3999, ⓦwww.firstchoice.co.uk. Ski packages to Borovets and Pamporovo.

Inghams ⓣ020/8780 4433, ⓦwww.inghams.co.uk. Ski packages to Borovets and Pamporovo.

Limosa Holidays ⓣ01263/578143, ⓦwww.limosaholidays.co.uk. Offers an eleven-day birdwatching tour featuring the Rhodopes, Black Sea coast and Danube wetlands.

Naturetrek ⓣ01962/733051, ⓦwww.naturetrek.co.uk. Eight-day spring and autumn birdwatching tours, plus summer tours concentrating on mountain flora and butterflies.

Neilson ⓣ0870/333 3356, ⓦwww.neilson.co.uk. Ski packages to Borovets and Bansko.

Ornitholidays ⓣ01794/519445, ⓦwww.ornitholidays.co.uk. Eight days' birdwatching in the autumn.

Ramblers Holidays ⓣ01707/331133, ⓦwww.ramblersholidays.co.uk. Two-week mountains-and-monasteries tour covering the Rila and Pirin regions.

Regent Holidays ⓣ0117/921 1711, ⓦwww.regent-holidays.co.uk. Tailor-made holidays from a long-standing eastern Europe specialist.

Worldwide Adventures Abroad ⓣ0114/247 3400, ⓦwww.adventures-abroad.com. Eight-day highlights-of-Bulgaria tour, or two-week trips combining Bulgaria and Romania.

Specialist operators in Bulgaria

Lyuba Tours 1164 Sofia, ul. Tsanko Tserkovski 22, ⓣ+359 2 963 3343, ⓦwww.lyubatours.com. Specialist in one- and two-day, small-group excursions from Sofia (check the website for current schedule), focusing on folk celebrations, archeology, and rural areas that are difficult to get to independently. Can also fix up tailor-made itineraries for individuals and groups.

Pandion 1407 Sofia, ul. Cherni Vrŭh 20A ⓣ+359 2 963 0436, ⓦwww. birdwatchingholidays.com. All-inclusive trips with a birdwatching theme.

Zig-Zag/Odysseia-In 1000 Sofia, bul. Stamboliiski 20-V ⓣ+359 2 980 5102, ⓦwww.zigzag.dir.bg. Bulgaria's leading adventure tourism agency, offering all kinds of individual and group hiking tours, reservations in private hotels in Sofia, mountain huts, rural hotels, monasteries and village homestays.

Flights from the US and Canada

There are no direct flights to Bulgaria from the USA or Canada, nor any Bulgaria Air offices in either country, but other airlines offer **indirect flights to Sofia** via a European airport, and discount travel companies can create round-trip itineraries involving two, three or even four different carriers. The permutations are virtually endless, as even slightly altering your flight dates can greatly affect what's on offer, but you're very unlikely to get an onward connection to Sofia the same day, so an overnight stopover has to be factored into your cost-benefit analysis.

Some of the best **fares** to Sofia from east-coast USA and Canada are offered by European airlines such as LOT (flying from New York, Chicago or Toronto via Warsaw), CSA (from New York, Washington or Toronto via Prague), Malev (from New York and Toronto via Budapest) or Austrian Airlines (from New York or Washington via Vienna). Flying from central or west-coast USA, you're much more likely to be offered a combination of airlines and more than one change of plane en-route. Given all that, the following return fares are only examples of what you might find online or by calling discount travel companies. Fares from New York can be as little as US$650 in low season, rising to US$1100 in high season; from Los Angeles US$1200 in low season and US$1750 in high season. Flying from Toronto you'll be paying anything from Can$2500 to Can$3000 depending on season.

The choice of **package tours** to Bulgaria available in the US or Canada is limited, and they are often priced as **land-only**, excluding the cost of air fares from the US to Sofia or a starting point like London. Compare what's on offer from tour operators in Britain (see opposite) and search for a transatlantic flight yourself, and you could get a better deal.

Airlines

Air Canada ⓣ1-888/247-2262, ⓦwww.aircanada.com. Flights from most Canadian airports to a major European hub, with onward connections to Sofia.

Air France US ⓣ1-800/237-2747, ⓦwww.airfrance.us; Canada ⓣ1-800/667-2747,

Ⓦ www.airfrance.com/ca. Flights from New York and Montreal to Sofia with a stopoff in Paris.

Alitalia US Ⓣ 1-800/223-5730, Canada Ⓣ 1-800/361-8336, Ⓦ www.alitalia.com. Flights to Sofia from Atlanta, Boston, New York and Toronto, with a change of plane in Rome or Milan.

Austrian Airlines US Ⓣ 1-800/843-0002, Canada Ⓣ 1-888/817-6666, Ⓦ www.aua.com. Flights from New York and Washington to Sofia via Vienna.

British Airways US Ⓣ 1-800/247-9297, Canada Ⓣ 1-800/668-1059, Ⓦ www.ba.com. Flights to Sofia from a number of North American cities, via London.

CSA US Ⓣ 1-877/359-6629, Canada Ⓣ 416/363-3174, Ⓦ www.czechairlines.com. Flights to Sofia from New York, Washington and Toronto via Prague.

LOT US Ⓣ 1-800/223-0593, Canada Ⓣ 1-800/668-5928, Ⓦ www.lot.com. Flights from New York, Chicago and Toronto to Sofia via Warsaw.

Lufthansa US Ⓣ 1-800/645-3880, Canada Ⓣ 1-800/563-5954, Ⓦ www.lufthansa-usa.com. Flights from Montreal and various other North American cities to Sofia, via Frankfurt or Munich.

Malev Ⓣ 1-800/223-6884 or 212/566-9944, Ⓦ www.malev.hu. Flights from New York and Toronto to Budapest, with onward connections to Sofia.

United Airlines Ⓣ 1-800/241-6522 (domestic flights), Ⓣ 1-800/538-2929 (international flights), Ⓦ www.united.com. One- or two-stop flights from most American cities to Sofia, with the European leg of the journey operated by Lufthansa.

Virgin Atlantic Airways Ⓣ 1-800/862-8621, Ⓦ www.virgin-atlantic.com. Flights from Los Angeles, Miami, New York and Washington to London, with onward connections to Sofia.

Discount travel companies

Airtech Ⓣ 212/219-7000, Ⓦ www.airtech.com. Standby seat broker; also deals in consolidator fares and courier flights.

Educational Travel Centre Ⓣ 1-800/747-5551 or 608/256-5551, Ⓦ www.edtrav.com. Student/youth discount agent.

Pekao International Travel and Tours Ⓣ 1-800/387-0325 or 416/588-1988, Ⓦ www.pekao-canada.com. Flight agent and tour company operating charter flights from Toronto and Edmonton to eastern Europe.

SkyLink US Ⓣ 1-800/AIR-ONLY or 212/573-8980, Canada Ⓣ 1-800/SKY-LINK, Ⓦ www.skylinkus.com. Consolidator.

STA Travel US Ⓣ 1-800/781-4040, Canada Ⓣ 1-888/427-5639, Ⓦ www.statravel.com. Worldwide specialist in independent travel; also student IDs, travel insurance, car rental, train passes and so on.

Student Flights Ⓣ 1-800/255-8000 or 480/951-1177, Ⓦ www.isecard.com. Student/youth fares, student IDs.

TFI Tours Ⓣ 1-800-745-8000 or 212/736-1140, Ⓦ tfitours.com. Consolidator.

Travel Avenue Ⓣ 1-800/333-3335, Ⓦ www.travelavenue.com. Full-service travel agent that offers discounts in the form of rebates.

Travel Cuts Canada Ⓣ 1-800/667-2887, US Ⓣ 1-866/246-9762, Ⓦ www.travelcuts.com. Canadian student travel organization with branches nationwide.

Travelers Advantage Ⓣ 1-877/259-2691, Ⓦ www.travelersadvantage.com. Discount travel club; annual membership fee required (currently US$1 for three months' trial).

Tour operators

Adventure Center Ⓣ 1-800/228-8747, Ⓦ www.adventurecenter.com. Five-day winter hiking tour, "snow-shoeing" around Vitosha and Rila mountains.

Adventures Abroad US Ⓣ 1-800/665 3998, Canada Ⓣ 1-800/665 3998, Ⓦ www.adventures-abroad.com. Eight-day tour featuring Plovdiv, Troyan, Rila, Veliko Tŭrnovo, Arbanassi and Shipka, plus a little hiking, starting and ending in Sofia.

Barker's European Tours Ⓣ 1-888/307-9145, Ⓦ www.barkereurotours.com. Two-week tours covering the cultural and historical highlights.

Balkan Travel & Tours Ⓣ 212/594 900 or 888/SOFIA 88, Ⓦ www.balkan-travel.com. Various seven- and ten-day tours to the major historical sights, and tailor-made arrangements for individual tourists.

Dovetail Birding Ⓣ 1-877/881-1145, Ⓦ www.dovetailbirding.com. Web resource that lists birdwatching holidays in Bulgaria, most of which depart from London in the UK.

Elderhostel Ⓣ 877/426 8056, Ⓦ www.elderhostel.org. Two-week art and history tour for senior travellers.

Quest Tours and Adventures Ⓣ 1-800/621 8687, Ⓦ www.romtour.com. Seven-day tours of Bulgaria, and two-week Romania-Bulgaria combinations from a specialist operator.

Flights from Australia and New Zealand

There are no direct flights from Australia or New Zealand to Bulgaria, and anyway, travellers from down under usually visit it as part of a wider European trip. Many airlines offer **one-stop** flights from Sydney to European cities from which there are onward flights to Sofia – though you might not get a same-day connection. However, many of the cheaper deals offered by booking agents involve **two-stop** flights, calling at a major Asian hub to pick up a flight to Europe and then an onward connection to Sofia. Typical prices from Sydney are AUS$1900 for a two-stop flight in low season, rising to AUS$2500 for a one-stop flight in high season.

A handful of travel agents offer ten-day and two-week tours of Bulgaria, and can also help in fashioning tailor-made itineraries to your requirements.

Airlines

Aeroflot Australia ⓣ 02/9262 2233, ⓦwww.aeroflot.com.au. Flights from Sydney, Adelaide, and Brisbane to Sofia, with at least two stopoffs en route.
Air France Australia ⓣ02/9244 2999, ⓦwww.airfrance.com/au. One- and two-stop flights from Australia to Sofia via Paris.
Austrian Airlines Australia ⓣ1800/642 438, ⓦwww.aua.com. From Melbourne and Sydney to Sofia via Vienna.
Air New Zealand NZ ⓣ0800/737 000, ⓦwww.airnz.co.nz; Australia ⓣ13/24 76, ⓦwww.airnz.com.au. Daily flights from Auckland to London via Los Angeles, then onward connections to Sofia.
British Airways Australia ⓣ02/8904 8800, NZ ⓣ09/356 8690, ⓦwww.ba.com. Daily flights to London from Sydney, Melbourne or Perth, with onward connections to Sofia.
Cathay Pacific Australia ⓣ13/17 47, ⓦwww.cathaypacific.com/au; NZ ⓣ09/379 0861, ⓦwww.cathaypacific.com/nz. Flights from Australia and New Zealand to Hong Kong, with onward connections to major European hubs then Sofia.
Lufthansa Australia ⓣ1300/655 727, ⓦwww.lufthansa-australia.com. Flights from Australia to Frankfurt with onward connections to Sofia.
Malaysia Airlines Australia ⓣ13/26 27, NZ ⓣ0800/777 747, ⓦwww.malaysiaairlines.com.my. Flights from Melbourne to a European hub via Kuala Lumpur, with onward connections to Sofia.
Qantas Australia ⓣ13/13 13, NZ ⓣ0800/808 767, ⓦwww.qantas.com.au. Flights from Sydney (with connections from New Zealand) to a European hub with onward connections to Sofia.

Travel agents

Flight Centre Australia ⓣ13/31 33, ⓦwww.flightcentre.com.au; NZ ⓣ0800/243 544, ⓦwww.flightcentre.co.nz.
Passport Travel Australia ⓣ03/9867 3888, ⓦwww.travelcentre.com.au.
STA Travel Australia ⓣ1300/733 035, ⓦwww.statravel.com.au; NZ ⓣ0508/782 872, ⓦwww.statravel.co.nz.
Trailfinders Australia ⓣ1300/780 212, ⓦwww.trailfinders.com.au.
travel.com.au and **travel.co.nz** Australia ⓣ1300/130 482, ⓦwww.travel.com.au; NZ ⓣ0800/468 332, ⓦwww.travel.co.nz.

Tour operators

Adventures Abroad Australia ⓣ1800/147827, NZ ⓣ0800/800 434, ⓦwww.adventures-abroad.com. Eight-day highlights-of-Bulgaria tour; or two-week trips combining Bulgaria and Romania.
Eastern Eurotours Australia ⓣ1800/242 353 or 07/5526 2855, ⓦwww.easterneurotours.com.au. Flights, hotel accommodation, city breaks and guided tours.
Gateway Travel Australia ⓣ02/9745 3333, ⓦwww.russian-gateway.com.au. Eastern European specialist offering flights and packages.
Kompas Holidays International Australia ⓣ617/3222 3307, ⓦwww.kompasnet. Runs many tours in eastern Europe.

By rail from the UK and Ireland

You're unlikely to save any money travelling to Bulgaria by train; the chief reason for doing so is to visit other countries as well. The most direct **train routes** to Bulgaria involve heading across France, then though Italy, Slovenia, Croatia and Serbia (Dieppe–Paris–Milan–Venice–Zagreb–Belgrade–Sofia) or through Belgium and Germany before picking up the same route (Ostende–Brussels–Munich–Zagreb–Belgrade–Sofia). Slightly longer though equally rewarding alternatives take in Hungary (Paris/Brussels–Budapest–Belgrade–Sofia) or both Hungary and Romania (Paris/Brussels–Budapest–Bucharest–Sofia).

Travelling **via Budapest** in Hungary makes sense because it's the nearest point to Sofia to which you can buy a ticket in Britain; the city makes a great stopover; and there's a daily train to Belgrade and Sofia from Budapest's Keleti Station. Bear in mind however that trains in Serbia tend to be grubby and uncomfortable and that lone foreign travellers are often targeted by petty thieves on overnight trains – booking a sleeping compartment or travelling with companions will ease your security worries. Depending on delays at border crossings, the journey from Budapest to Sofia takes 17–24 hours. Bring food, drinks and toilet paper for the duration, plus warm clothing if you're travelling from October to May (the carriages are often unheated).

A longer way of reaching Bulgaria is to travel **across Romania** on the Balkan Express from Budapest, entering Bulgaria at the northern town of Ruse. The highlight of the two-and-a-half-day journey is the spectacular crossing of the Carpathian mountains at PetroŞani in Romania, around dawn. The same general advice goes as on the Belgrade route.

Perhaps the most roundabout train route to Bulgaria is London–Paris–Milan–Brindisi, followed by a ferry to Patras in **Greece**, from where you can continue to Sofia via Athens and Thessaloniki by train or bus (one or two of each daily).

Citizens of the EU, USA, Canada, Australia and New Zealand don't need **transit visas** to travel through Croatia, Serbia and Romania; citizens of other countries should check with the relevant embassies before they leave home.

Buying tickets

At present, it's impossible to buy a through ticket from London to Sofia or reserve seats for the last leg of the journey until you reach Budapest, but don't rule out the future possibility of online bookings on Hungarian or Bulgarian railways if their websites improve. Meanwhile, Rail Europe sells tickets to **Budapest**. Getting there from London takes 25 hours by the quickest route, aboard Eurostar to Paris and then a sleeper via Munich or Vienna (both take about 19 hours). A standard second-class **return ticket,** including Eurostar, costs around £250; tickets have two to three months' return validity, and stopovers are allowed so long as you stick to the prescribed route. If you're over 60, it's worth buying a Rail Europe Senior card, which gives a 25 percent **discount** on the regular fare. Otherwise, you'd get better value with some kind of rail pass (see below).

Once in Budapest, it is easy to buy an **onward ticket to Bulgaria** at the MÁV International Bookings office, VI, Andrassy út 36; expect to pay about £55/€80 if you travel via Serbia, and £70/€100 via Romania.

Rail passes

If you're planning to visit Bulgaria as part of a more extensive trip around Europe, it may be worth buying a **rail pass**. Bulgaria is covered in the Inter Rail pass scheme, which is available to European residents. Non-European residents can make use of the Eurail pass (which doesn't cover Bulgaria but does include most of the countries which you might travel through en route) and the Eurail Selectpass (which covers Bulgaria and neighbouring countries).

All these passes can be bought at Rail Europe in the UK; Eurail passes are available from selected agents in North America and Australia (see opposite for details).

Inter Rail

Inter Rail passes are available from any major UK train station or youth/student travel office; the only restriction is that you must have been resident in a European country for at least six months. They come in over-26 and (cheaper) under-26 versions, and cover 29 European countries (including Turkey and Morocco), grouped together in eight zones. As Bulgaria is in Zone H (along with Romania, Serbia and Montenegro, and Macedonia) you'll need the one-month "global" pass (£415/€559; £295/€399 for under-26s) to get there from Britain or Ireland. Inter Rail passes do not include travel between Britain and the Continent, although Inter Rail pass holders are eligible for discounts on rail travel in the UK and on cross-Channel ferries.

Eurail

Non-European residents qualify for the **Eurail Pass**, which must be purchased before arrival in Europe (or from Rail Europe in London if you were unable to get it at home). Note however that it is only likely to pay for itself if you plan to travel widely before reaching Bulgaria, since travel within Bulgaria itself is not included in the pass (Greece is the only one of its neighbours to be included). The Eurail Youthpass (for under-26s) costs US$382 for fifteen consecutive days, US$495 for 21 days and US$615 for one month; if you're 26 or over you'll have to buy a first-class pass, available in fifteen-day (US$558), 21-day (US$762) and one-month increments (US$946). A Eurail **Flexipass** allows you to stagger your rail travel over a longer period: ten days of travel over a two-month period costs US$451 (under 26) or US$694 (over 26); fifteen days of travel over two months weighs in at US$594 (under 26) or US$914 (over 26). If you're planning to travel around southeastern Europe, it's possible to buy a Eurail **Selectpass** covering Bulgaria, Serbia and Montenegro, Romania, Greece and Hungary, covering a number of time periods from five days upwards. However, at US$456 for five days (US$296 for under-26s) they're unreasonably expensive, and purchasing one of these passes will work out more costly than buying individual tickets in the countries themselves.

Rail contacts

In the UK and Ireland

Ⓦwww.interrailnet.com Official Inter Rail website, with full details of passes, prices and discounts available with Inter Rail.

Ⓦwww.seat61.com Compendious guide to rail travel in Europe compiled by committed enthusiasts. The information provided is vastly superior to anything provided by the official sites, and there are links to online ticket agencies.

Rail Europe UK Ⓣ08705/848 848, Ⓦwww.raileurope.co.uk. Through ticketing on most European routes; also agents for Inter Rail and Eurostar, and sells Eurodomino/Freedom passes.

Trainseurope UK Ⓣ0900/195 0101, Ⓦwww.trainseurope.co.uk. Tickets from the UK into Eastern Europe, plus Inter Rail and other individual country passes.

In the US and Canada

Eurail Ⓦwww.eurail.net. Eurail and Eurail Select passes

Europrail International Canada Ⓣ1-888/667-9734, Ⓦwww.europrail.net. European rail passes.

Rail Europe US Ⓣ1-877/257-2887, Canada Ⓣ1-800/361-RAIL, Ⓦwww.raileurope.com. Agent for Eurail and other passes, including Eurodomino/Freedom.

In Australia and New Zealand

Cit World Travel Australia Ⓣ02/9267 1255 or 03/9650 5510, Ⓦwww.cittravel.com.au. Agents for Eurail and other European passes.

Rail Plus Australia Ⓣ1300/555 003 or 03/9642 8644, Ⓦwww.railplus.com.au. European rail passes.

Trailfinders (see p.33). All Europe passes.

By bus from the UK and Ireland

Although there are no direct buses from Britain or Ireland to Bulgaria, it's possible to travel to **Sofia via Frankfurt** on a weekly coach operated by Eurolines – though the whole trip takes about 48 hours. With tickets costing £212 return (with five-percent reductions for the under-26s and over-60s) it's unlikely to be much cheaper than travelling by plane. You might save money by travelling with a London-based Bulgarian company such as Balkan Horn, which operates a twice-weekly London–Sofia–Varna service for £70 single, £100 return.

Although several other bus operators run services to Sofia from elsewhere in Europe (all major cities in Germany, plus Vienna, Prague and Budapest), the near impossibility of finding out schedules or reserving seats from Britain means that you could well spend days waiting for a connection.

Citizens of the EU, USA, Canada, Australia and New Zealand don't need **transit visas** to travel through Croatia, Serbia and Romania; citizens of other countries should check with the relevant embassies before they leave home.

Useful timetable publication

The red-covered **Thomas Cook European Timetables** details schedules of over 50,000 trains in Europe, as well as timings of over 200 ferry routes and rail-connecting bus services. Available from branches of Thomas Cook, it is updated and issued every month; the main changes are in the June edition (published end May) with details of the summer European schedules, and October (published end Sept) for the winter schedules; some have advance summer/winter timings also.

Approaching from Turkey

By contrast, it's quite simple to reach Bulgaria from Turkey. Several Turkish bus operators run six or seven daily **services from Istanbul** to Plovdiv, Sofia, Varna, Burgas and elsewhere in Bulgaria. Prices on the Istanbul–Sofia route hover around €25 each way. Numerous travel agents in the central Sultanahmet district of town can reserve seats; otherwise head for west Istanbul's main bus station at Topkapi, where most of the bus operators have offices. Bear in mind, however, that Bulgarian–Turkish border crossings are usually clogged up with East European bus parties travelling to or from the Bosphorus, and long queues at the frontier (a wait of 5–8 hours is not uncommon) ensure that this option can be long, tedious, and difficult to timetable. Services from **other towns** in western Turkey such as Edirne, Bursa, Gebze and Yalova run to Plovdiv and Kûrdzhali.

Bus contacts

Eurolines UK ⓣ0870/514 3219, ⓦwww.eurolines.co.uk; Ireland ⓣ01/836 6111, ⓦwww.eurolines.ie. Tickets can also be purchased from any Eurolines or National Express agent (ⓣ0870/580 8080, ⓦwww.nationalexpress.co.uk or ⓦwww.gobycoach.com).
Balkan Horn UK ⓣ020/7630 1252, ⓦwww.balkanhorn.com.

By car from the UK and Ireland

Unless you're planning to travel all over Eastern Europe, it would be quixotic to drive to Bulgaria, given the difficulties involved and the high risk of car theft in Balkan countries. If Bulgaria is your main goal, you'd be better off flying and renting a car once you're there. If you do decide to drive it's important to plan ahead. The RAC website (ⓦwww.rac.co.uk) is a good source of detailed directions.

Once across the Channel, the fastest route is via Nuremberg (Germany), Graz (Austria), Maribor (Slovenia), Zagreb (Croatia) and Belgrade (Serbia). Allowing for overnight rests, it takes at least three days to drive the 2400km (1527 miles) from London to Sofia, assuming that things go okay at the many border crossings. Once beyond Croatia, expect the roads to be bad and don't travel at night, especially on the final leg down to the Dimitrovgrad/Kalotina crossing on the Bulgarian border. The alternative, even more arduous route is through Romania (2552km), via Arad–Timisoara–Calafat and then a ferry across the Danube to Vidin.

A longer but more pleasant approach through Europe is **via Italy and Greece**, catching a car ferry to the Greek mainland and driving northwards to Bulgaria. Besides the pleasure of driving through Italy and Greece, this route reveals the similarities and differences between Aegean and Pirin Macedonia and has the advantage of good roads and magnificent scenery for much of the way to Sofia past such prime attractions as Melnik, Bansko and Rila Monastery.

Remember that you'll need an **international driving licence**, available from the motoring organizations in your home country for a small fee, together with an international Green Card from your insurance company. For more on driving around Bulgaria, see p.46.

Crossing the Channel

Heavy competion between companies means that it's always worth shopping around: fares on catamarans operated by SpeedFerries.com from Dover to Boulogne can be as low as £50 return for a family car and passengers provided you book well in advance; Hoverspeed catamarans to Ostend cost around £129–189 return for up to five adults and a car depending on season. Travelling by Eurotunnel costs £180–299 for two adults and a car.

Channel crossing contacts

Eurotunnel UK ⓣ0870/535 3535, ⓦwww.eurotunnel.com. Drive-on drive-off shuttle trains from Folkestone to Coquelles near Calais (35–45min). Fares vary widely; it's cheaper to travel between 10pm and 6am, during the week, and outside July and August.
Hoverspeed UK ⓣ0870/240 8070, ⓦwww.hoverspeed.co.uk. Dover to Calais and Ostend.
P&O North Sea Ferries UK ⓣ08701/129 6002, ⓦwww.ponorthseaferries.com. Hull to Rotterdam and Zeebrugge.
P&O Stena Line UK ⓣ0870/600 0600, ⓦwww.posl.com. Dover to Calais.
Sea France UK ⓣ0870/571 1711, ⓦwww.seafrance.com. Dover to Calais.
SpeedFerries.com UK ⓣ0870/220 0570, ⓦwww.speedferries.com. Dover to Boulogne.
Stena Line UK ⓣ0870/570 7070, ⓦwww.stenaline.co.uk. Harwich to Hook of Holland.

Red tape and visas

All visitors to Bulgaria require a full (not visitors') passport, although citizens of most Western countries no longer need a visa to enter the country. However, as the rules change every year, it's wise to check with a Bulgarian embassy or consulate, whatever your nationality.

Citizens of the UK, Ireland, Australia, New Zealand, Canada and the USA are all allowed to enter the country **without a visa** for a stay of thirty days within a six-month period. Nationals of EU countries other than Ireland and the UK are entitled to visit Bulgaria visa-free for ninety days within a six-month period. Once your thirty or ninety days expire, you either have to leave Bulgaria, or apply for an **extension visa** at the local police station (*politseiski uchastûk*, or *Ministerstvo na vûtreshni raboti – MVR*, мвръ) The latter process involves lots of queuing, paperwork, misunderstandings (people in police stations rarely speak English) and a €100 fee. If you need further advice, contact your embassy (*posolstvo*) in Sofia (see p.120 for a full list). If you're planning to visit Bulgaria more than once within a six-month period, then consider applying to your local Bulgarian embassy (see opposite) for a **multiple-entry visa** which costs anything from £41/€57 for three months to £81/€113 for a whole year).

Registering with the police

All visitors to Bulgaria are **required to register** as a foreigner (*registratsiya na chuzhdentsi*) within 48 hours of arrival. If you're staying in a hotel, campsite, hostel or private room rented through an agency, then the job of registration should be done for you by your hosts. If you are staying with friends, or renting a private room unofficially, then you have to register yourself, by showing up at the local police station with your passport, your host, and your host's ID documents. Either way, you should be provided with a dated registration slip which you should keep with you at all times, ready to surrender it to passport control upon leaving the country.

In practice, however, many visitors end up unregistered; either because hotels are ignorant of the regulations, or because individual hosts simply can't be bothered with the hassle. This shouldn't be a cause of major worry: border guards rarely check the registration slips of short-stay tourists with Western passports (nationals of other countries are much more likely to be targeted by overzealous officials). If you've been in the country for more than a couple of weeks, however, the lack of any registration slips at all may land you in serious trouble (and get you a large fine) at the border, and you'd be well advised to check into a reputable hotel or two in order to get some.

Bulgarian embassies and consulates

Usual opening hours are Mon–Fri 9.30am–noon.

Australia 4 Carlotta Rd, Double Bay, Sydney, NSW ⓣ02/9327 7581, ⓔbulcgsyd@bigpond.com.

Britain 186–188 Queen's Gate, London SW7 5HL ⓣ0870/060 2350, ⓦwww.bulgarianembassy.org.uk.

Canada 325 Stewart St, Ottawa, Ontario N1K 6K5 ⓣ613/789 3215, ⓔmailmn@storm.ca.

Greece 33A Stratigou Kallari St, Athens ⓣ1/647 8105.

Ireland 22 Burlington Rd, Dublin 4 ⓣ1/660 3229, ⓔbgemb@eircom.net.

New Zealand No representation; visa applications should be made through the Bulgarian consulate in Australia (see above) or via local travel agents.

Turkey Ataturk bulvari 124, Kavakli dere, Ankara ⓣ312/426 7455, ⓕ 427 3178; Amhet Adnan Saygun cad. 44, Ulus–Levant, Istanbul ⓣ212/281 0115, ⓔbulgconsul@superonline.com.

US 1621 22nd St N W, Washington DC 20008 ⓣ202/387 0174, ⓦwww.bulgaria-embassy.org.

Health

No inoculations are required for travel in Bulgaria, although anybody planning to spend a lot of time walking in the mountains ought to consider being inoculated against tickborne encephylitis. Most visitors suffer nothing worse than diarrhoea or sunburn, so stock up on preparations like Diocalm before you leave home, and protect yourself with a good sunscreen. While salads and fresh fruit are quite safe, it's risky to eat grilled snacks in provincial restaurants with a slow turnover. Tap water is safe to drink in all parts of the country.

Minor complaints can be solved at a pharmacy or **Apteka**, but if you require a doctor (*lekar*) or dentist (*zûbolekar*) head for the nearest **Poliklinika** or health centre, whose staff might speak English, German or French, and will almost certainly understand Russian. Urgent cases go to **hospitals** (*bolnitsa*) courtesy of the *bûrza pomosht* or ambulance service (Ⓣ150 in most towns, service free), and emergency treatment is free of charge although you must pay for **medicines**. Although Bulgarian physicians are well trained and competent, the equipment, facilities, auxiliary staff and aftercare in hospitals falls well below the standards to which Westerners are accustomed, so it's best to fly home in the case of anything serious.

Bear in mind that many pharmacies are not as widely stocked as those at home, so you should **bring** with you a supply of razor blades, favoured brands of contraceptives and tampons, not to mention any specific medication that you require.

Bulgaria has a strong tradition of **herbal medicine** (though none, curiously, of homeopathy), and most towns will have a *Bilkova apteka* or herbal pharmacy offering a wide range of natural remedies. However, you'll need to speak Bulgarian, or enlist the help of a native speaker, if you want to understand what you're being offered.

Cyrillic checklist: health

Pharmacy	аптека
Health centre	поликлиника
Herbal pharmacy	билкова аптека
Hospital	болница

Insurance

Although emergency health care (but not the cost of medicines) is free of charge in Bulgaria, you'd do well to take out an insurance policy before travelling to cover against theft, loss and illness or injury. Before paying for a new policy, however, it's worth checking whether you are already covered: some all-risks home insurance policies may cover your possessions when overseas, and many private medical schemes include cover when abroad. In Canada, provincial health plans usually provide partial cover for medical mishaps overseas, while holders of official student/teacher/youth cards in Canada and the US are entitled to meagre accident coverage and hospital inpatient benefits. Students will often find that their student health coverage extends during the vacations and for one term beyond the date of last enrolment.

After exhausting the possibilities above, you might want to contact a specialist travel insurance company, or consider the travel insurance deal we offer (see box below). A typical travel insurance policy usually provides cover for the loss of baggage, tickets and – up to a certain limit – cash or cheques, as well as cancellation or curtailment of your journey. Most of them exclude so-called dangerous sports unless an extra premium is paid. Many policies can be chopped and changed to exclude coverage you don't need – for example, sickness and accident benefits can often be excluded or included at will. If you do take medical coverage, ascertain whether benefits will be paid as treatment proceeds or only after return home, and whether there is a 24-hour medical emergency number. When securing baggage cover, make sure that the per-article limit – typically under £500 – will cover your most valuable possession. If you need to make a claim, you should keep receipts for medicines and medical treatment, and in the event you have anything stolen, you must obtain an official statement from the police.

Rough Guides travel insurance

Rough Guides Ltd offers a low-cost travel insurance policy, especially customized for our statistically low-risk readers by a leading British broker, provided by the American International Group (AIG) and registered with the British regulatory body, GISC (the General Insurance Standards Council). There are five main Rough Guides insurance plans: **No Frills** for the bare minimum for secure travel; **Essential**, which provides decent all-round cover; **Premier** for comprehensive cover with a wide range of benefits; **Extended Stay** for cover lasting four months to a year; and **Annual Multi-Trip**, a cost-effective way of getting Premier cover if you travel more than once a year. Premier, Annual Multi-Trip and Extended Stay policies can be supplemented by a "Hazardous Pursuits Extension" if you plan to indulge in sports considered dangerous, such as scuba diving or trekking. For a policy quote, call the Rough Guides Insurance Line: toll-free in the UK ⓣ0800/015 09 06 or ⓣ+44 1392 314 665 from elsewhere. Alternatively, get an online quote at ⓦwww.roughguides.com/insurance

Costs, money and banks

Bulgaria always was a relatively cheap country for tourists and, despite the shift to a market economy, most of life's essentials cost considerably less here than they do in the West. The outlook is less bright for Bulgarians themselves, whose living standards have been eroded by inflation, and who count themselves lucky if they earn £35/€50/US$60 a week.

While visitors to big cities or package resorts could probably subsist on a mixture of **bank cards** and **travellers' cheques**, anyone planning to travel around the country – especially in rural areas – will need to carry the bulk of their funds in **cash** (preferably euros, in a mixture of high and low denominations). To minimize the security risk, always carry your funds in a discreet moneybelt worn under your clothing.

Costs

Despite price rises and comparatively high **costs** in Sofia, Plovdiv and along the coast, the **essentials** remain inexpensive. If you're camping and buying food in local markets, you can live on £15/€21/US$27 a day. Staying in modest hotels or private rooms and eating out regularly, £25–30/€35–42/US$45–54 should be sufficient, while on a daily budget of £50/€70/US$90 or above you can enjoy a very good life, staying in mid-range hotels and taking taxis everywhere. Only if you require business-class accommodation will you need more than that.

The most unpredictable factor is the cost of **accommodation**, which varies from region to region, as well as depending on the facilities, age and ownership of the place in question. Private rooms and B&Bs can cost anywhere from £4/€5.60/US$7 to £15/€21/US$27 per person and hotels are equally variable, with two-star places costing from £10/€14/US$18 per person, three-star hotels from £20/€28/US$36 per person, and four- and five-star establishments from £50/€70/US$90 per person. There is less variation in the cost of hostels, mountain huts and campsites (all £4–7/€5.60–10/US$7–13 per person), but their standards vary even more.

Once you've sorted out a bed for the night, your remaining daily costs can be very low. Public **transport** is cheap, with flat fares of about £0.30/€0.40/US$0.50 on most urban transport and inexpensive rates on intercity buses and trains: travelling second-class by train, you can cross the entire country from east to west for £10/€14/US$18, though international services to neighbouring countries are another matter (see p.34). Providing you avoid deluxe hotel restaurants, **eating** should likewise prove economical. An average evening meal with drinks will set you back £6–12/€8.40–17/US$11–22, less if you stick to standard local food such as simple grills and salad. **Drinking** Bulgarian wine or spirits (about £3/€4.20/US$5.40 and £5/€7/US$9 a bottle respectively) will hit your liver harder than your wallet, and snatching a quick cup of coffee or a sandwich won't set you back more than about £1/€1.40/US$1.80.

Most **museums** and tourist attractions charge foreigners about five times the amount paid by the natives, and with rates averaging £1–2/€1.40–2.80/US$1.80–3.60, and a few places charging as much as £4/€5.60/US$7.20, they can become a significant expense if you're on a very low budget.

Currency

The Bulgarian currency is the **lev** (plural leva), which is divided up into 100 stotinki.

Cyrillic checklist: money and banks

Bank	банка
Hard currency	валута
Exchange	обмяна

In response to the runaway inflation of the 1990s, the currency reform of 1999 knocked three noughts off the value of the lev (so that 1000 old leva became 1 new lev), and you should bear in mind that pre-1999 notes and coins are no longer legal tender. Try and familiarize yourself with the new notes as soon as possible, thereby minimizing the risk of being fobbed off with old ones in exchange bureaux or market stalls. Notes come in denominations of 200, 100, 50, 20, 10, 5, 2 and 1 leva; while coins come in denominations of 2 and 1 leva, and 50, 20, 10, 5, 2 and 1 stotinki. The lev is pegged to the euro and, minor fluctuations aside, remains relatively stable against Western currencies. At the time of writing £1 buys you roughly 2.80Lv, €1 buys 1.95Lv, and US$1 buys 1.45Lv.

Although almost all goods and services can be paid for in leva, **hard currency** (known as *valuta*) is often required when buying international bus and airline tickets. In the case of hotels, however, although they may quote prices in euros, many prefer payment in the leva equivalent.

Banks and exchange

The lev is not a fully convertible currency and is largely unavailable in banks outside Bulgaria. Inside Bulgaria, you can **change** money in banks, tourist offices, at reception desks of the bigger hotels, and at private exchange bureaux. There's usually a slight difference in the **rates** offered, with private bureaux offering the most generous terms, providing you avoid the ones on main streets and well-touristed thoroughfares. Hotels offer the worst exchange rates, and should be avoided unless absolutely necessary.

Bulbank is the biggest of the high street **banks**, with branches in most Bulgarian towns. **Opening hours** are usually Monday to Friday 9am–4pm. **Private exchange bureaux** are usually open until 5 or 6pm (longer in summer), and sometimes 24 hours. Wherever you change money, it makes sense to request a **receipt** (*smetka*) – which can, in theory, enable you to re-exchange surplus leva for hard currency at the frontier before leaving, but don't depend on it. You can usually buy US dollars and euros (and, on occasion, sterling) from bureaux with your excess leva, but the exchange rate may be disadvantageous.

The black market

The realistic exchange rates now available in banks and private bureaux have all but demolished the appeal of the **black market** to visitors, but the demand for hard currency among Bulgarians remains strong. "Freelance" moneychangers may well offer you a slightly higher rate than the best of the exchange bureaux, but it's best to resist the temptation – the vast majority of them are either performing a sleight-of-hand trick or offering you a wad of now worthless pre-1999 leva.

Travellers' cheques and credit cards

While it's a sensible precaution to carry a percentage of your funds in the form of **travellers' cheques**, they are certainly not convenient for everyday use, except in Sofia and the coastal and ski package resorts. Elsewhere you'll be lucky to find a private exchange that will touch them, and even banks can be reluctant to accept any but the particular brand to which they're affiliated. Moreover, the only firm with affiliates in Bulgaria which can issue replacements for **lost or stolen** travellers' cheques is **American Express** (c/o Megatours, ul. Vasil Levski 21, Sofia; Ⓣ02/988 4953, Ⓔmegatours@techno-link.com). If you can't find a branch of Bulbank (which accepts any brand bearing the Eurocard or Mastercard logo), a three- or four-star hotel is your best bet for changing cheques. In holiday resorts, be prepared for a **commission** charge of up to five percent.

Credit cards can be used to pay for car rental, and at top–notch restaurants and hotels in the major cities and resorts, but can only be used throughout most of Bulgaria as a means of obtaining cash from an ATM. You can in theory get **cash advances** in leva with Eurocard, Access, Visa, Diners Club and Mastercard, but most banks are still either inequipped to deal with the procedure or simply can't be bothered. Again, Bulbank is likely to be able to handle transactions more efficiently than other banks. Almost all cards can also be used to get cash from **ATMs**, which are relatively plentiful in city centres but much rarer out in the sticks.

Information, maps and websites

Bulgaria lacks a network of national tourist offices, and the job of promoting the country as a tourist destination is now handled by the trade sections of Bulgarian embassies abroad. Although often far from visitor-friendly or clued up about tourism, these are usually happy to supply booklets designed to whet your appetite. Another source of information is the Internet (see "Useful websites" below), although Bulgaria is less well served with up-to-date websites than most other European destinations.

Information in Bulgaria

Inside Bulgaria, **tourist information offices** in the Western European or North American sense are still in their infancy, and although the Ministry of Trade and Tourism operates an information centre in Sofia (the clumsily named National Information and Publicity Centre; see p.83), the state budget is inadequate to support a network of offices throughout the country. A smattering of tourist offices does exist in the Pirin, Stara planina and western Rhodope regions, but they're for the most part dependent on EU grants for survival, suffer frequent staff shortages, and rarely keep to their advertised working hours.

Privately run **travel agencies** often stick a "tourist information" sign outside the door to attract custom, and although they can arrange rooms, excursions or other services, they're often unwilling or unable to provide unbiased information.

Useful websites

Ⓦ **www.abvg.net** Enthusiast-run virtual guide to Bulgaria – more quirky than the commercial sites.
Ⓦ **www.beachbulgaria.com** Resort profiles of Black Sea coastal towns, with hotel listings and an online booking facility.
Ⓦ **www.bgben.co.uk** Site of London-based Bulgarian newspaper including useful English-language summaries.
Ⓦ **www.discover-bulgaria.com** Best of the tourist information-plus-online booking sites, with plenty of interesting feature content.
Ⓦ **www.hotelsbulgaria.com** Online hotel booking facilities, with news of cheap last-minute deals, although it concentrates on upmarket places rather than the budget end of things.
Ⓦ **www.hotels-in-bulgaria.com** Online accommodation bookings across Bulgaria.
Ⓦ **www.levski.bg** Latest news on Bulgaria's best-supported football team. You can also check on the fortunes of their main cross-town rivals at Ⓦ **www.cska.bg**, or access a round-up of results in general on Ⓦ **www.bulgarian-football.com**.
Ⓦ **www.novinite.bg** Day-to-day news delivered in a lively style by the Sofia Press Agency. An entertaining way of keeping in touch with political events.
Ⓦ **www.sofiacityguide.com** Online guide to the capital with useful practical tips and a limited smattering of listings. Check out also its second-city site Ⓦ **www.plovdivcityguide.com**.
Ⓦ **www.sofiaecho.com** Site belonging to Sofia's English-language weekly newspaper. Best source of info and analysis on politics and business news, accompanied by lifestyle and travel articles.
Ⓦ **www.spellintime.fsnet.co.uk** British-Bulgarian performing arts group with a stimulating set of pages devoted to Bulgarian folklore and mythology.
Ⓦ **www.travel-bulgaria.com** Reliable and up-to-date information on destinations around the country.

Maps

If you can read the Cyrillic alphabet, the best **general map** of Bulgaria is the 1:500,000 road map (*Pûtna karta*) published by Kartografiya in Sofia, and sold on street stalls or at petrol stations throughout the country. If not, you should buy Kümmerly and Frey or Freytag and Berndt's 1:1,000,000 **combined map** of Romania and Bulgaria before leaving home, as either is preferable to the English-language maps sold in Bulgaria.

The availability of **town plans** (*plan-ukazatel*) is less predictable, although a new series of city maps produced by Domino covers most urban areas in the country and can usually be found in newspaper kiosks and bookshops in the cities covered (although it might be dificult finding a map of Varna in Plovdiv, and vice versa). Kartografiya publishes a map of Sofia that marks public transport routes and is available in Bulgarian and English versions.

If you're going walking in the mountains it pays to compare the various **hiking maps** available in Sofia from bookshops or from travel agencies like Zig-Zag/Odysseia-In (see p.84). The Bulgarian Tourist Union (BTS; БТС) publishes series on the Rhodopes, Stara planina, Rila and Pirin ranges, whose accuracy depends on when they were last updated (between 1993 and 1997), and at worst can lead hikers into uncomfortable, if not hazardous, situations. Kartografiya's 1:55,000 maps of the Rila and Pirin mountains are a step in the right direction, if not wholly reliable, while the recent 1:65,000 map of the Troyan Balkan range (available from tourist offices in Gabrovo, Tryavna and Troyan) is absolutely accurate, having been drawn up by the mountain rescue service, using military survey charts.

Map outlets

In the UK and Ireland

Stanfords 12–14 Long Acre, London WC2E 9LP ⓣ020/7836 1321; 29 Corn St, Bristol BS1 1HT ⓣ0117/929 9966; 39 Spring Gardens, Manchester M2 2BG ⓣ0161/831 0250; ⓦwww.stanfords.co.uk.
Blackwell's Map and Travel Shop 53 Broad St, Oxford OX1 3BQ ⓣ01865/793550, ⓦwww.blackwell.co.uk.
The Map Shop 30a Belvoir St, Leicester LE1 6QH ⓣ0116/2471400, ⓦwww.mapshopsleicester.co.uk.
National Map Centre 22–24 Caxton St, London SW1H 0QU ⓣ020/7222 2466, ⓦwww.mapsnmc.co.uk.
National Map Centre Ireland 34 Aungier St, Dublin ⓣ01/476 0471, ⓦwww.mapcentre.ie.
Newcastle Map Centre 55 Grey St, Newcastle upon Tyne, NE1 6EF ⓣ0191/261 5622.
The Travel Bookshop 13–15 Blenheim Crescent, W11 2EE ⓣ020/7229 5260, ⓦwww.thetravelbookshop.co.uk.

In the US and Canada

Book Passage 51 Tamal Vista Blvd, Corte Madera, CA 94925 ⓣ1-800/999-7909, ⓦwww.bookpassage.com.
Distant Lands 56 S Raymond Ave, Pasadena, CA 91105 ⓣ1-800/310-3220.
Elliot Bay Book Company 101 S Main St, Seattle, WA 98104 ⓣ1-800/962-5311, ⓦwww.elliotbaybook.com.
Globe Corner Bookstore 28 Church St, Cambridge, MA 02138 ⓣ1-800/358-6013, ⓦwww.globecorner.com.
Map Link Inc 30 S La Patera Lane, Unit 5, Santa Barbara, CA 93117 ⓣ1-800/962-1394, ⓦwww.maplink.com.
Rand McNally ⓣ1-800/333-0136, ⓦwww.randmcnally.com. Around thirty stores across the US; dial ext 2111 or check the website for the nearest location.
World of Maps 1235 Wellington St, Ottawa, Ontario K1Y 3A3 ⓣ1-800/214-8524, ⓦwww.worldofmaps.com.

In Australia and New Zealand

Mapland 372 Little Bourke St, Melbourne ⓣ03/9670 4383, ⓦwww.mapland.com.au.
The Map Shop 6 Peel St, Adelaide ⓣ08/8231 2033, ⓦwww.mapshop.net.au.
Mapworld 173 Gloucester St, Christchurch ⓣ03/374 5399, ⓦwww.mapworld.co.nz.

Getting around

The lack of investment in public transport over the past 15 years has left it in a sorry state, with semi-derelict stations, run-down vehicles and demoralized staff, and although private bus companies have taken up the slack on major routes, the state-owned network has drastically contracted. While transport remains cheap it is also slow, a failing compounded by Bulgaria's mountainous terrain and climatic extremes (which rapidly degrade tarmac), with train journeys between the north and south being particularly prone to roundabout routes and changes. Bear in mind, too, that schedules are designed to fit in with the working day. There may be several departures in the early morning, then nothing until mid-afternoon, with nothing at all on Sundays.

The fragmentation of the transport system is reflected in the **timetables** (*razpisanie*) in train and bus stations, which used to be on a clearly legible board but are nowadays often merely scribbled on a piece of paper stuck to the window of the ticket office. Usually, arrivals (*pristigane*) are listed on one side, and departures (*trûgvane* or *zaminavane*) on the other. To make things harder for travellers, the schedules of private buses are unlikely to be posted at all, and it's impossible to buy a national train timetable: in addition, any timetables that do exist are invariably in **Cyrillic**. To make things easier we've included a list of town names in Cyrillic at the beginning of each chapter, and a rundown of regional transport under the "Travel Details" at the end of each chapter.

By train

Bulgarian State Railways (*BDZh*) can get you to most towns mentioned in this book, although trains are very slow by Western standards and delays are common on the longer routes. Intercity (*intersiti*) and express (*ekspresen vlak*) services only operate on the main trunk routes, but on everything except the humblest branch lines you'll find so-called rapid (*bûrz vlak*) trains. Use these rather than the snail-like *pûtnicheski* (пътнически; literally "passenger train", but meaning "slow" in this context) services unless you're planning to alight at some particularly insignificant halt. Generally speaking, intercity services are the only ones which carry a buffet car, so if travelling on another type of train, make sure you have enough food

Cyrillic checklist: getting around

Bulgarian State Railways	БДЖ	Couchettes	кушет
		Sleepers	спален вагон
Timetables	разписание	Left luggage office	гардероб
Departures	тръгва (abbreviated to Тр) or заминаване	Bus station	автогара
		Filling station	бензиностанция
Arrivals	пристигане (Пр)	Petrol	бензин
Tickets	билети	Motoring map	пътна карта
National train timetable	пътеводител	Street	ул.
		Square	пл.
Intercity service	интерсити	Boulevard	бул.
Express service	експресен влак	Suburb	кв.
Rapid service	бърз влак	Block	бл.
Slow service	пътнически влак		

and drink to survive the journey. On timetables, the four types of services are indicated by the **abbreviations** ИС, Еб, Б and П; express services are usually lettered in red. A **reservation** (*zapazeno myasto*; about 1Lv in addition to the basic ticket price) is compulsory on intercity and express services, and advisable for all other trains if you're travelling on summer weekends. You might find yourself paying a hefty surcharge if you board a train without one.

Though a **national timetable** (*pûtevoditel*) is extremely useful for frequent train travellers, the chances of obtaining one are slim, as they're snapped up immediately after publication each May. If you do get hold of a copy, note that trains running on a particular day only are indicated by a number in a circle (for example, 1 = Monday, 2 = Tuesday, and so forth). International services are printed in the Roman alphabet, rather than Cyrillic.

Long-distance/overnight trains have a wagon with reasonably priced **couchettes** (*kushet* кушет) and/or **sleepers** (*spalen vagon*). At the time of writing you can travel from Sofia to Varna by sleeper for under 40Lv, which probably works out cheaper than a night's accommodation. In order to secure a bed on the train, you need to reserve a day or two in advance, and, if possible, at least a week in advance in July or August.

Commonly, a single sign halfway down the platform is all that identifies a **station** (*gara*). If you're sitting at the back, you won't see this until the train starts up again, so try to sit up front. Most stations have a **left-luggage office** (*garderob*); in the large ones you may need to complete a form before stowing your gear.

Passes

Unless you've already bought a rail pass (see p.34) in order to get to Bulgaria, buying a train pass to travel around the country makes little sense. Indeed, the only one currently on offer is the **Eurodomino/Freedom Pass**, which must be bought before you travel and allows for three, five, seven or ten days' travel within any given month, but its cost (a seven-day pass will cost £76/€106/US$137 first class, £54/€75/US$97 second class or £42/€59/US$76 for under-26s second class) will almost certainly exceed what you'd spend on fares without a pass – especially given that many destinations in Bulgaria can only be reached by bus.

Eurodomino/Freedom passes are available from Rail Europe in the UK and North America; see p.35 for contact details.

Buying tickets

Bulgaria's main **intercity routes** are very busy in summer and at weekends throughout the year. It is wise – if not always essential – to **book** a day or two in advance; otherwise you'll probably have to spend the journey standing in the carriage corridor. In many large towns, it's possible to buy **tickets** (*bileti*) and make advance reservations from **railway booking offices**, listed in the appropriate places in the Guide. Tickets can also be bought at the station just before travel (in out-of-the-way places, a ticket window will only open a few minutes before the train is due). If you arrive at a station too late to queue up and buy a ticket, you can **pay on the train** itself – with a surcharge of thirty to forty percent.

International tickets

International tickets are handled by a separate organization, the Rila Agency, whose main office is in Sofia at ul. General Gurko 5 (☎02/987 0777). Although cities like Sofia and Ruse have international ticket counters in the stations – so you can buy a ticket immediately before travel if you're pressed for time – more often, Rila offices are located some distance away from stations, and you'll need to make sure you buy your ticket well in advance. We've given addresses where appropriate in the Guide.

Generally speaking, **prices** of tickets to Romania, Hungary and other former Eastern Bloc countries are quite reasonable (at the time of writing, a one-way ticket from Sofia to Bucharest costs about 55Lv), but increase significantly if travelling to hard currency countries like Greece or Turkey, where fares are comparable with those in the West.

By bus

In many parts of Bulgaria it's necessary – or easier – to travel by **bus** (*avtobus* or, colloquially, *reis*), especially in the Rhodopes and the Pirin, where few of the attractions are accessible by train. Each town of any size has a bus station (*avtogara*), or sometimes two, as buses operated by private companies may use another depot (often just a parking lot); in cities, this duplication can result in three or four terminals (as detailed in the Guide). Since the buses run by **private companies** are usually newer than the vehicles owned by municipalities, they tend to be more comfortable and faster, particularly if the route follows a highway through the lowlands rather than mountain roads. The drawback is that information on schedules is harder to obtain as few companies post timetables, so that you may have to ask at several kiosks to get the full picture. In some cases the vehicles are **minibuses** (*mikrobusi*), and leave as soon as they're full.

Tickets

As a general rule, tickets are sold until five minutes before departure, although it's advisable to buy them an hour or two in advance if travelling on a route serving major towns – especially during summer or at weekends. Note that if you're catching a **bus that originates elsewhere**, tickets are only sold when the bus arrives, in which case you need to queue outside the shuttered ticket hatch. *Tova li e gisheto za bileti za...?* means "Is this where I get tickets to...?" (remember that a shake of the head means "yes" and a nod "no"). On **rural routes**, tickets are often sold by the driver rather than at the terminal. If you're aiming for a campsite or monastery along a bus route, ask the driver for the *spirkata za kampinga* (or *manastira*), or call *Spri!* (Stop!) as it hoves into sight.

City buses

On **urban transport** – trams and buses in Sofia, buses and trolleybuses everywhere else – there's usually a **flat fare** (seldom more than 0.50Lv) on all routes. In Sofia, **tickets** are bought beforehand and then punched in a machine on board, so it's sensible to buy a bunch of ten tickets (from street kiosks next to tram and bus stops) as soon as you arrive. Fare dodgers pay a spot fine. Elsewhere in Bulgaria, tickets are sold by an on-board conductor. Routes are sometimes displayed on each bus stop (*spirka*) together with the times of the first and last services, but many of these signs are so old that it's best to check with the locals before jumping aboard. In some regions, private companies operate, so on a few routes you'll encounter a plethora of different coloured buses and minibuses, identifiable only by a scribbled route number posted in the windscreen.

International buses

A plethora of private companies offer **international bus services** connecting Bulgaria's main towns and cities with neighbouring countries and further afield. As you'd expect, the main point of departure is Sofia – whence you can reach any country in Southern and Central Europe – but there are also several regional towns where you can pick up a bus to Turkey, Greece, Albania or the former Yugoslavia. Tickets are priced in leva or euros, but you can pay in most currencies at the prevailing rate of exchange. Details appear in the relevant section of the Guide.

By taxi

Providing you don't get ripped off, **taxis** are a reasonably priced and useful way of getting around in towns and cities, or reaching places that aren't accessible by public transport. All licensed taxis are metered, and generally charge about 0.40Lv initially, plus 0.40Lv per kilometre thereafter during the day (twice as much at night), except for taxis on the Black Sea coast, whose rates are three to four times higher (though city taxis in Varna and Burgas charge normal rates). The minority of taxi drivers out to take advantage of foreigners tend to hang around airports, major train stations and city centre hotels, so it's best to go looking for a taxi elsewhere if you have the option. We've given phone numbers of some reputable taxi firms in the relevant sections of the Guide, though it is unlikely that anyone on the other end of the line will speak English.

By car

Foreigners may drive in Bulgaria using their national **driving licence** (though, should you stay longer than six months, it must be translated and legalized), but most of the neighbouring countries require an international licence. It is obligatory to have third-party **insurance** plus a "Green" or "Blue" card – the latter can be bought at the frontier. Entering Bulgaria, your vehicle will be registered with a special **"visa tag"** or *carnet de passage* which must be presented on leaving – a rule intended to prevent foreigners from selling their cars. As **car theft** is endemic and Bulgaria is a major transit route for stolen vehicles, drivers bringing their own car should be sure to carry their log book (and make photocopies of it), their driving licence and *carnet de passage*, and take every precaution against the documents and the vehicle being stolen. Use guarded parking lots wherever possible, and never leave vehicles on side streets unless fitted with wheel locks and immobilizers.

Fuel, maps and signs

Petrol (*benzin*) in Bulgaria – slightly cheaper than in Britain and Western Europe, and slightly more expensive than in the USA – can sometimes be hard to find. Although you'll find **filling stations** (*benzinostantsiya*) on the main road exits from most large towns, and spaced 30–40km apart along the highways, they're few and far between once you get off the beaten track, so fill up wherever you can. Octane values aren't always what is stated on the pump, so higher capacity engines may make plinking noises, while fuel injection vehicles sometimes have problems with dirty petrol purchased at out-of-the-way stations. The most reliable sources are the 24-hour stations run by Shell and BP, which occupy prime sites on **principal routes**. Filling stations are often marked on the Cyrillic-script **motoring maps** (*pûtna karta*) available from bookshops and street stalls.

Names signposted along the highways appear in both alphabets, and although the system of transliteration is slightly different from the one used in this book, they're recognizably similar. Other **road signs** are basically identical to those employed in the West.

Roads, traffic and speed limits

Roads in Bulgaria tend to be inconsistently numbered (some highways carry two or three designations), and even trunk routes (marked in red on maps) have the same bumpy, potholed surfaces as the minor roads (indicated in yellow.) There are stretches of **dual carriageway** (*magistrala*) between Sofia and Plovdiv (on which the first **tolls** in the country were introduced in 1996), and between Sofia and Pravets, but travel is pretty slow going elsewhere. If following the main Sofia–Burgas, Sofia–Varna, Sofia–Vidin, Sofia–Kulata or Plovdiv–Kapitan Andreevo routes, expect to be stuck behind long files of slow-moving freight **traffic** for large stretches of the journey. Traffic on other routes can be very light, but a combination of poor road manners and abysmal surface quality should prevent you from getting anywhere quickly. Potholes, farm carts and wandering animals make it unsafe to drive **after dark**.

In urban areas buses have the right of way and parking is restricted to specified spots. **Speed limits** in built-up areas (60kph), on the open road (80kph), and highways (120kph) are reduced to 50kph, 70kph or 100kph for minibuses or cars with caravans or trailers.

Accidents, fines and theft

Mountainous Bulgaria has lots of hairpin bends, and in rural areas it's important to watch out for farm animals and carts. Motorists are legally obliged to report **accidents** and, in case of injury, render assistance where appropriate while waiting for the police (*Politsiya*). **Spot fines** for trivial offences are common practice; the police have been known to abuse this by demanding payment in dollars and pocketing the cash. Requests for a receipt might put a stop to this – or make things worse. In the event of arrest, insist on being allowed to contact your embassy (see Sofia "Listings" for addresses). **Drinking and driving** is absolutely prohibited, punishable with a heavy fine or imprisonment. Note that **flashing the lights** of your car does not mean "I am prepared to give way to you" but "get the hell out of my way".

In the event of being in an accident or having your car stolen, the **bureaucratic procedures** are nightmarish. You will need a police report (which can take 2–3 days) that must be taken to the local prosecutor's office for stamping (involving another delay), and then be stamped by the local customs office, which may insist that the document is authorized by the regional office in another town. All this is done in Bulgarian, so unless you're lucky enough to find an official who speaks English, there is also the cost of hiring an interpreter to consider, not to mention accommodation costs and other related expenses for the duration. If the vehicle was brought into Bulgaria you won't be allowed to leave the country without it, even if the car is a total write-off.

Car rental

Car rental can be arranged through Avis, Budget Europcar and Hertz offices in Sofia and other major cities. Most Bulgarian travel agents act as representatives for one of these firms or one of their domestic equivalents. You'll also find car rental desks in the lobby of each town's principal hotel. The cars offered by the big Western firms (which average at about 140Lv/€70/£50/US$90 a day for a Golf or equivalent) are better maintained than the wonky Ladas leased by the smaller Bulgarian outfits (which often work out three times cheaper, but may have to be pushed back to the rental office in question).

You may find it cheaper to **book direct in advance** from your home country with one of the major car rental companies (see below for contacts), or take advantage of some of the pre-booked car rental deals offered by the package-holiday companies. Booked through a package company, a week with unlimited mileage in a Fiat Cinquecento can cost as little as 500Lv/€250/£180/US$320 on the coast and 600Lv/€300/£215/US$390 in the ski resorts. For insurance and driving licence regulations see p.46.

Another option is to rent a car **with a driver**, relieving you of the worries associated with road use in a strange country. Any of the rental firms can oblige, or, if you have Bulgarian friends, it's relatively easy to find someone to drive you around for a negotiable sum. Making arrangements unofficially – or even with a regular taxi driver – you can probably get a car with a driver for 100Lv/€50/£35/US$65 a day, plus petrol costs and any expenses incurred if an overnight stay is required.

International car rental agencies

UK

Avis ⓣ08700/100 287, ⓦwww.avis.co.uk;
Budget ⓣ08701/539170, ⓦwww.budget.co.uk.
Europcar ⓣ0870/607 5000, ⓦwww.europcar.co.uk.
Hertz ⓣ0870/844 8844, ⓦwww.hertz.com.
Holiday Autos ⓣ0870/400 0099, ⓦwww.holidayautos.co.uk.

Ireland

Avis Northern Ireland ⓣ028/9024 0404, Republic of Ireland ⓣ01/605 7500, ⓦwww.avis.ie.
Budget Republic of Ireland ⓣ0906/627711, ⓦwww.budget.ie.
Europcar Northern Ireland ⓣ028/9442 3444, Republic of Ireland ⓣ01/614 2800, ⓦwww.europcar.ie.
Hertz Republic of Ireland ⓣ01/676 7467, ⓦwww.hertz.com.
Holiday Autos Republic of Ireland ⓣ01/872 9366, ⓦwww.holidayautos.ie.

US and Canada

Avis US ⓣ1-800/331-1084, Canada ⓣ1-800/272-5871, ⓦwww.avis.com.
Budget ⓣ1-800/527-0700, ⓦwww.budget.com.
Europcar ⓣ1-877/940-6900, ⓦwww.europcar.com.
Hertz US ⓣ1-800/654-3001, Canada ⓣ1-800/263-0600, ⓦwww.hertz.com.

Australia

Avis ⓣ13/63 33, ⓦwww.avis.com.au.
Budget ⓣ1300/362 848, ⓦwww.budget.com.au.
Europcar ⓣ1300/131 390, ⓦwww.deltaeuropcar.com.au.
Hertz ⓣ13/30 39, ⓦwww.hertz.com.

New Zealand

Avis ⓣ09/526 5231 or 0800 655 111, ⓦwww.avis.co.nz.
Budget ⓣ0800 283 438, ⓦwww.budget.co.nz.
Hertz ⓣ0800 654 321, ⓦwww.hertz.com.

By air

There's little in the way of a domestic air network, with flights from Sofia to Varna (and, in summer, Sofia to Burgas) operated by Hemus Air (ⓦwww.hemusair.bg) being the only services currently available. Given the length of the bus or train journey (6–8hr), the one-hour flight to Varna or Burgas is worth considering, even though at around 200Lv return it works out five times more expensive.

Accommodation

Accommodation in Bulgaria is currently in a state of flux, with many former state-owned hotels still trying to find their feet in a market economy, and a burgeoning number of new private places. While the choice of accommodation is undeniably wider than at any time in the past, standards and prices vary far more than previously, and you can no longer get an idea of what a hotel is like purely from its star rating (if it has one). In addition, things are changing all the time – generally for the better, but not always so.

Hotels

Hotels in Bulgaria come in all shapes and sizes, but can essentially be divided into two groups: those that were run by the state during Communist times, and those which were built by private individuals or enterprises from 1990 onwards. How much choice you have depends very much on where you are: in the cities and holiday resorts there'll be a reasonable spread of different types of hotel, whereas in provincial towns without a tourist tradition there may well be one, decaying, former state-run hotel on the main square, and nothing else for miles.

Mostly built in utilitarian, concrete high-rise style, most of the former state-run, **pre-1990 places** have now been sold off – although the companies that now run them don't always have enough money to reinvest in their upkeep and refurbishment, with a consequent decline in the standard of comfort. The main exceptions to this rule are in the big cities and holiday resorts, where those hotels which attract a significant turnover of foreign guests have received substantial injections of cash and have been refitted to Western standards – leaving Bulgarian holidaymakers to make do with the tatty unrenovated establishments nearby.

Some pre-1990 hotels are known as **rest homes** (*pochivna stantsiya* or *pochiven dom*), many of which were owned by trade unions and factories for the use of their workers, and are now open to all-comers. Many are no more than frugal holiday camps, but those built for the Communist *nomenklatura* can be quite palatial – the former Politburo ones at Primorsko and Sandanski, especially.

Meanwhile, hundreds of **new hotels** have opened in the main cities and resorts, along highways and in historic highland villages. These are often small, family-run establishments rather like B&Bs, although you'll also find sumptuous places on the Black Sea coast and in mountain resorts, and a growing number of smart business-oriented hotels in the big cities. All of these tend to be cleaner, friendlier and more attractive than the older, ex-state hotels.

As a consequence of all this, there is little or no consistency in how **rates** are calculated. In most of Bulgaria, the going rate for a simple en-suite room with no additional frills is 50–60Lv. Expect to pay double this amount in Sofia, Plovdiv, or in major holiday centres. Rooms with a functioning TV cost a few extra dollars; while a double with modern furnishings and minibar could set you back anywhere between 80 and 200Lv. Even hotels that have business-class pretensions, without necessarily providing the requisite levels of comfort, will try and get away with

Cyrillic checklist: accommodation

Accommodation bureau	квартирнобюро
Hotel	хотел
Private rooms	частни квартири
Hostel	туристическа спалня
Mountain hut	хижа
Rest home	почивна станциа or почивен дом
Campsite	къмпинг

nearer the latter figure. Some hotels charge on a per-person basis (which may or may not include breakfast), regardless of whether you occupy a single or a double; others will give solo travellers a double room and charge them a hefty proportion of the full double price. Acceptance of **credit cards** is unpredictable: smart places in cities or on the coast excepted, most places prefer **cash**.

It's **seldom** necessary to make reservations, other than during festivals or at popular rustic retreats such as Kovachevitsa in July or August. Although we've given phone numbers throughout the Guide, the odds of getting a hotel receptionist who speaks English aren't good except in big cities or resorts; however, faxes and emails sent in English will probably be translated and acted upon.

The adoption of the international **star rating system** (from one star up to five) has proceeded in fits and starts in Bulgaria; many hotels either don't display a star rating, or invent one to suit their aspirations. As a new private two-star hotel is often much cosier than an old three-star block, the system is in any case fairly irrelevant, and it's safer to base your assumptions on the age of places. Hotels built in Communist times tend to conform to a few models. Postwar one-star places are gloomy warrens with shared facilities in the corridor and a sink in the room if you're lucky, while two-star hotels of the 1950s and early 1960s are mid-rise prefab blocks of matchbox rooms with en-suite bathrooms and erratic plumbing, where the only amenity that can be taken for granted is a bar. Three-star hotels built in the 1970s and 1980s tend to be high-rise or cuboid blocks with overblown lobbies and restaurants and cheesy basement nightclubs, while four- and five-star hotels usually feature similar facilities, but in a more luxurious style and managed with efficiency.

Private hotels are largely unclassified by the official star system, and in many cases simply make one up for display purposes. Most run to en-suite bathrooms, and the ritzier ones to cable TV and minibars. Though shoddier efforts are already showing their age, the majority are comfortable, clean and well looked after by owner-managers who have sunk their savings into the venture and have every reason to make it succeed. Most places have a small taverna and summer garden, and some have saunas, solariums, fitness centres or even swimming pools.

Another factor worth considering is the time of year. In the old one- and two-star hotels, hot water may only be available in the morning and evening, which is rarely a problem at the height of summer but can be a real pain in winter, when rooms in even three-star establishments may be poorly heated. If travelling at this time of year, it's a good idea to opt for a family hotel or a private room (see below), where the provision of basic comforts can be taken for granted.

Private rooms

Private rooms (*chastni kvartiri*) are available in Sofia, Plovdiv, Ruse, Varna and a number of other tourist destinations, especially along the coast or in picturesque highland villages. They're bookable through local tourist offices, **accommodation bureaux** (*kvartirno byuro*), and private or cooperative firms that specialize in renting out rooms – addresses are given in the Guide. Even when the bureaux are closed (from early September onwards in smaller coastal towns), you can often find a room **unofficially**, by asking around. If you stay in someone's home you're meant to **register with the police** within 48 hours. While agencies

Accommodation price codes

All accommodation in this book has been categorized according to the following price codes. The prices quoted are for the cheapest double room in high season. Accommodation prices in Bulgaria are often quoted in euros, although you can pay in local currency.

- ❶ under 30Lv/€15
- ❷ 30–50Lv/€15–25
- ❸ 50–70Lv/€25–35
- ❹ 70–90Lv/€35–45
- ❺ 90–120Lv/€45–60
- ❻ 120–150Lv/€60–75
- ❼ 150–200Lv/€75–100
- ❽ 200–300Lv/€100–150
- ❾ over 300Lv/€150

should register you automatically, few hosts take these formalities seriously, putting you in the position of being an illegal alien for the duration of your stay (not always as dire as it sounds; see p.37).

The size and quality of private rooms varies enormously (it's rarely possible to inspect the place first), but they are always clean. Spacious rooms in nice old houses seem to be the rule in smaller resorts such as Sozopol and Nesebûr on the coast, and Koprivshtitsa inland, while in the cities private rooms are almost invariably situated in apartment buildings. They are often let by pensioners, who find it hard to afford repairs but keep things tidy. In mountain areas the houses can be warm and cosy or ramshackle and primitive, depending on the wealth of the owner. While some are **B&Bs**, the majority are not, though few landladies will refuse to provide breakfast for a few dollars extra.

Prices vary according to where you are. Expect to pay 40Lv for a double room and 32Lv for a single in Sofia, 20Lv per person almost everywhere else.

Campsites, hostels, mountain huts and monasteries

While most towns of interest once had a **campsite** (*kamping*) on their outskirts, many have now closed down or face an uncertain future, and it is only on the coast and at Pamporovo and Rila that they are still going strong. Most of these charge around 8–10Lv to pitch a tent, and also have two-person **bungalows** available for rent at around 20Lv a night. Note that many campsites close down in early September, as soon as the summer rush has slackened. **Camping rough** is illegal and punishable with a fine.

In Sofia, Plovdiv and Varna there's a handful of small but welcoming backpacker-oriented **hostels**, charging about 20Lv for a comfortable bunk. Elsewhere the only hostel accommodation is provided by a remaining handful of basic, old-fashioned "tourist dormitories" (*turisticheska spalnya*) which lurk in the backstreets of many a provincial town. In some, you'll be offered a bunk in a large, twenty-bed dorm; in others you may be in a two- or four-bed room. Prices range from 10–15Lv per person; contact the Bulgarian Tourist Union (Bûlgarski Turisticheski Sûyuz), 1000 Sofia, bul. Vasil Levski 75 (☎02/873409) for details.

In highland areas favoured by hikers there are scores of **mountain huts** (*hizhi*), some primitive, others more like comfortable hotels. Costs at all but the most expensive will rarely come to more than 10–15Lv per night. Upon arrival you may have to wait for the custodian to turn up before being allocated a bed. You can **reserve** beds in some parts of the country through local tourist offices or Zig-Zag/ Odysseia-In in Sofia (see p.84).

The larger of Bulgaria's **monasteries** traditionally accommodated guests in their cells, but closed their doors to Westerners in the early 1980s. Nowadays it's up to the individual monastery to decide, with popular ones such as Rila, Troyan and Bachkovo allowing foreigners to stay for 10–30Lv per person. The rooms are usually quite spartan, with a washbasin and maybe some form of heating, but no hot water.

Eating and drinking

Bulgaria is stuffed full of vegetable plots and orchards, and fresh fruit and vegetables are half the secret of Bulgarian food. In the villages, almost all the food comes straight from the land and is organic or free range, as few people can afford pesticides or chemical fertilizers. In the towns, however, 45 years of collectivized agriculture and catering have conspired to impose a certain conformity on restaurants, and the high quality and range of cooking you'll experience as a guest in a Bulgarian home is still rarely reflected in the country's eating establishments.

Grilled meat dishes predominate everywhere, and, despite the wide range and quality of the vegetables available, **vegetarians** may well be frustrated by the lack of animal-free options. Though the newer restaurants tend to offer more variety, menus remain pretty unimaginative, with a limited choice of dishes on offer. There is, however, an increasing variety of **street food** available, although traditional Bulgarian pastries and snacks are often a bit too stodgy and greasy for Western tastes.

In big towns and coastal resorts, **food shops** (*hranitelni stoki*) are reasonably well stocked with useful domestic picnic ingredients such as fresh bread, cheese (*kashkaval Vitosha* is made from cow's milk; *kashkaval Balkan* from ewe's milk), sausages (*pastûrma* is a spicy beef salami; *sudzhuk* a flat home-cured sausage), smoked leg of ham (*pushen but*) and dairy products, as well as tinned goods, packet soups, conserves and chocolates imported from Greece or Turkey. In rural areas, food shops are much more sparsely provisioned, with shelves lined with jars of Bulgarian jam, packets of dry biscuits, and little else. Instant **coffee** is usually vile, and **tea** is either Chinese or herbal, so it's wise to bring both if you're planning on self-catering.

Fresh fruit and veg is best bought in the outdoor **markets** (*pazar*) which you'll find in most towns and villages. Here smallholding peasants from the outlying districts sell whatever produce is currently in season, as well as herbs, nuts, sunflower seeds, dried fruit and pulses. Many towns also have old-style, municipally run **indoor markets** (*hali*), though these tend to be sad, half-abandoned affairs with little to offer. Ad hoc street stalls often sell foreign produce such as bananas, coffee and chocolate. City-centre **bakeries** tend to produce fresh bread (*hlyab*) throughout the day. In smaller towns and villages, shops selling bread stand empty for much of the day, until an arbitrarily timed delivery attracts queues of shoppers.

Breakfasts, snacks and street food

Traditionally, food was eaten in the fields or pastures, or consumed on returning home

Cyrillic checklist: eating and drinking

Breakfast/snack	закуски	Skara-bira	скара-бира
Bread	хляб	Restaurant	ресторант
Supermarket	магазин на самообслужване	Vegetarian restaurant	вегетариански ресторант
Food shop	хранителни стоки	Self-service restaurant	експресресторант
Outdoor market	пазар	Folk restaurant, inn	хан ханче
Indoor market	хали	Mehana, tavern	механа
Café	кафене	Café-bar/*kafe-aperitiv*	кафе-аперитиф
Patisserie/ *sladkarnitsa*	сладкарница		

– which meant subsisting on bread, cheese, vegetables and fruit throughout the day until an evening meal of stew or grilled meat. Nowadays, people eat rather less frugally, but the habit of picking up a bite to eat in the morning and continuing to nibble at **snacks** throughout the day still remains. In general, the best advice is to keep an eye out for signs advertising *zakuski*, a generic term meaning either breakfast or any daytime snack.

In towns and cities, a typical **breakfast** tends to consist of an espresso coffee and a cigarette, followed by another round of the same if one still feels any hunger. Few restaurants, except for fast-food or self-service places, open for breakfast, and the most convenient places to pick up snack food are the stalls and kiosks that tend to congregate around main thoroughfares, train and bus stations. You can also pick up a pastry from a **patisserie** (see next column), to be washed down with one of two traditional breakfast drinks: yoghurt (*kiselo mlyako*), or *boza*, a browny-coloured millet drink that tastes like liquidized breakfast cereal.

The most common **Bulgarian snack food** is *banitsa* (often referred to by its diminutive form, *banichka*, or known in some areas as *byurek*), a flaky pastry filled with cheese or, on occasion, meat. At its best, the *banitsa* is a delicious light bite, although it's invariably quite stodgy by the time it reaches the streets. *Mlechna banitsa* (literally "milk *banitsa*") is a richer, sweeter version made using eggs and dusted with icing sugar, while the *Rhodopska banitsa*, found only in the Rhodopes, is more like a soufflé filled with cheese.

Equally popular is the *kifla*, a small bread roll usually made from slightly sweetened dough and with a vein of marmalade running through the middle, although you will probably encounter more savoury variants, filled either with cheese (*sûs sirene*), or a small hot-dog-type sausage (*s krenvirsh*). Similar is the *sirenka*, a small bread bun with a cheese filling. Other favourites among street vendors are *ponichki*, deep-fried lumps of dough, not unlike doughnuts, and *palachinki* or pancakes, usually stuffed with cheese.

Street stands also sell grilled snacks, which are the likeliest cause of an upset stomach for travellers. *Kebapcheta* are wads of mincemeat (traditionally a combination of lamb, pork and veal, although the precise mix depends on what's available) served with a hunk of bread; *kyufte* is the same in meatball form; while *nadenitsa* is a spicy sausage. In autumn and winter, vendors emerge peddling corn on the cob (*tsarevitsa*), and throughout the year incorrigible snack-munchers can find solace in the *fûstûtsi*, or roast nuts, and *semki*, sunflower seeds, sold everywhere in paper cones.

All these traditional snacks are rivalled in popularity by **hot dogs**, **hamburgers** and **pizzas**, which, with a few honourable exceptions, tend to be revolting. The hot dogs are of doubtful composition and gristly consistency; hamburgers often amount to a slice of luncheon meat on a tepid bun, smothered in ketchup; while pizzas are typically rubbery slices with inferior Bulgarian cheese, ham and fish substituted for mozzarella, salami and anchovies. The same goes for open (usually toasted) **sandwiches** (*sandvichi*), sold at many kiosks, cafés and bars. Typical toppings are *kashkaval*, a hard, Cheddar-like cheese; *salam*, an unappetizing slice of pinkish, pork-based meat; *kayma*, a mincemeat paste; *shunka*, ham; or *kombiniran*, a mixture of two or more of the above. Never order any of them without first inspecting what's on offer.

Cakes and **pastries** are sold throughout the day in a **patisserie** or *sladkarnitsa*. Many of Bulgaria's sweet dishes were originally imported from the Middle East by the Turks – the syrupy *baklava* (referred to in some establishments as a *triguna*), the nut-filled *revane*, and the gooey rich *kadaif* being the most common. Turkish Delight (*lokum*) and *halva* are also firm favourites. Betraying a more Central European ancestry are the variety of cakes (*torta*) on offer, with butter-cream (*maselna*), fruit (*frukti*) or chocolate (*shokoladova*) filling. *Garash*, a layered chocolate cake, is the most widely available. Ice cream – *sladoled* – is sold everywhere on the streets in summer.

Restaurants and meals

Although **restaurants** (*restorant*) vary widely in terms of decor and service, it's rare to find any cuisine but Bulgarian outside of Sofia, and the **range of dishes** can be pretty limited – in some cases the waiter will merely rattle through a list of what's on that evening. Higher prices in top-notch restaurants don't necessarily imply a wider choice – merely a better quality of meat. Restaurants are usually **open** between about 11am and 11pm, although many close for a few hours in the afternoon. It's very difficult to get food after 11pm outside big city hotels or package resorts, and in provincial towns you'll be lucky to find anywhere open after 10pm.

The growth in new private places has largely put paid to the former dominance of hotel restaurants, which used to be a focus for the social life of the local elite in provincial towns, but are now mostly sad and soulless affairs. New restaurants catering to the nouveaux riches usually offer slightly more exotic menus than you'll find at the Communist-era restaurants in National Revival-period mansions in Plovdiv or Sozopol, where the food and service often fail to match the setting. As a rule though, you'd do better in a **mehana** or taverna, which concentrates on grills, salads and other traditional staples, and usually has tables outdoors and music in the evening. A **han** or **hanche** – literally an "inn" – is likewise usually decorated in the folk style and features traditional cooking, while **skara-bira** are a lower form of culinary life serving little more than beer and kebabs and, in rural areas at least, traditionally a male-only preserve. In towns, you'll also find **self-service** restaurants (*ekspres-restorant*), which are invariably cheap, but often with reason.

With the exception of deluxe hotel restaurants in the capital, none of these places will **cost** the earth, and providing you avoid imported drinks, the bill should be very modest indeed: in most cases, a three-course meal for two, with a bottle of wine, will rarely exceed 30Lv, except in Sofia, Plovdiv and the coastal resorts, where you can expect to pay 40–50Lv for the same.

What to eat

If you're looking for nothing more than a quick and inexpensive stomach-filler, most restaurants serve filling **soups** accompanied by copious amounts of bread. *Bob*, a spicy bean soup, *shkembe chorba* or tripe soup, and *tarator*, a cold soup made from yoghurt and cucumber, are the three most common varieties.

Salads in Bulgaria are usually eaten as a starter, or as the accompaniment to a stiff

Vegetarians in Bulgaria

Traditional Bulgarian cuisine excels in **vegetable dishes**; the snag is trying to find places that serve them. Vegetarian restaurants (*vegetarianski restorant*) used to exist in most major towns, but began to lose their appeal in the mid-1980s as supplies of agricultural produce from the countryside deteriorated. Most of them were privatized and turned into something else.

Standard menus usually include an omelette (*omlet*), either with cheese or mushroom filling, along with *kashkaval pane*, hard cheese fried in breadcrumbs or batter; *kartofi s sirene*, french fries with grated white cheese; *sirene po shopski*, cheese baked in an earthenware pot with a spicy tomato sauce; and *pûlneni chushki*, peppers stuffed with cheese. One popular meatless dish is *mishmash*, scrambled eggs with chopped peppers and tomatoes; and there's also a vegetarian version of the oven-baked stew *gyuvech* (ask for *posten gyuvech*), although in many cases this turns out to be the same thing as *mishmash*. Any of these would suffice as a main meal; otherwise you're limited to choosing from vegetable side dishes, which are less widely available. If you're lucky, you may encounter fried courgettes (*pûrzheni tikvichki*); aubergines (*patlidzhan*) covered in yogurt (*s kiselo mlyako*); peppers stuffed with egg and cheese and fried in breadcrumbs (*chushka byurek*); eggs fried on spinach (*pûrzheni yaitsa s pyure ot spanak*); or potato purée (*pyure ot kartofi*). The spiciest dish is *kyopoolu* – mashed aubergine with garlic and chilli.

When in doubt, use the phrase *postno yadene* (literally "fasting food") to ensure that you receive something that's genuinely meat-free.

See pp.505–507 of Contexts for a list of food and dishes you'll find on a menu.

aperitif, rather like *meze* in Turkey. Most common are those formed from the following vegetables, whether singly or in combination: cabbage (*zele*), tomatoes (*domati*), cucumber (*krastavitsi*) and peppers (*piperki* or *chushki*). A *meshana salata* (mixed salad) consists of cucumbers, peppers and tomatoes; a *shopska salata* is the same topped with grated white cheese, while a *selska salata* comes with a few additional slices of boiled egg. Two yogurt-based salads are *mlechna salata* (like *tarator* but thicker, with nuts) and *snezhanka* (pickled cucumbers covered in yoghurt). Other oft-encountered starters are *pûrzheni chushki*, baked peppers; *lukanka*, a spicy salami-like sausage; and *sudzhuk* – all of which make an excellent accompaniment to a round of drinks.

Mainstay of any Bulgarian restaurant menu are the grilled meats, of which *kebapcheta* and *kyufte* (see "Breakfast, snacks and street food", p.52) are the most common. More substantial are chops (*pûrzhola* or *kotlet*), or fillets (*file* or *kare*), which are invariably *teleshko* (veal) or *svinsko* (pork). Main courses may be served with a set *garnitura* (usually fries and the occasional vegetable), although sometimes you'll find these items listed individually on the menu and will have to order them separately (always ask about this; otherwise you may end up being served a slab of meat and nothing else). In the grander restaurants the main course will be accompanied by potatoes (*kartofi*) and a couple of vegetables, as well as bread: sometimes a *pitka* or small bread bun, or more rarely a *simitla*, a glazed bun made from chickpea flour. Lower down the scale, you may just get fried potatoes (*pûrzheni kartofi*) and a couple of slices of bread. You're usually expected to specify how many slices (*filiiki*) you want.

Mehanas and touristy folk-style restaurants are the likeliest places to get **traditional Bulgarian dishes** baked and served in earthenware pots. The best known is *gyuvech* (which literally means "earthenware dish"), a rich stew comprising peppers, aubergines, and beans, to which are added either meat or meat stock. *Kavarma*, a spicy meat stew (often pork), is prepared in a similar fashion, and tastes something like Hungarian goulash. Two other traditional recipes which you may come across are *sarmi*, cabbage leaves stuffed with rice and mincemeat; and *imam bayaldi*, aubergine stuffed with all manner of vegetables, meat and herbs – a Turkish dish, whose name translates as "the priest burst", found in the south of the country.

Finally, along the coast and around the highland lakes and reservoirs there's fish (*riba*) – most often fried or grilled, but sometimes in a soup or stew – and nearly always of a higher standard than the meat dishes. Most coastal snack bars and restaurants offer *tsatsa* or *popche*, small white fish which are deep fried in batter and served with fries; and *skumriya* (mackerel), delicious when grilled. *Skumriya na keramidi* (literally "mackerel on a tile"), is baked in an earthenware container, usually with a rich tomato sauce. In parts of the Rhodopes and Pirin you'll also find mountain trout, as well as calamari, shark and other *riba ot Byaloto More* (fish from the White Sea, as Bulgarians call the Aegean).

Drinking

Private enterprise has vastly increased the number of **places to drink**, and all town centres now have a healthy sprinkling of **kiosks** serving coffee, soft drinks and basic snack food, usually with plastic chairs and tables on the adjoining pavement. Some of them serve beer, vodka, and other strong drinks, and stay open well after nightfall, but for the most part they're a daytime, fairweather phenomenon. A more traditional venue is the **sladkarnitsa**, a Bulgarian version of the Central European café, many of which serve cakes as well as alcohol.

Evening drinking tends to take place in restaurants (where it's quite common for tables to be monopolized by drinkers rather than diners), or in the vast number of **café-bars** operating under the generic title of *kafe-aperitiv*. Some are no more than a converted garage or basement room, though many of them – in Sofia, Plovdiv and along the coast in particular – compare favourably with anything found in the average Western European town. Here you can get the full range of domestic alcoholic and non-alcoholic drinks, as well as imported spirits and canned beers, and all kinds of cocktails in the flashier places.

Coffee can be excellent or vile, so it pays to look before ordering. If they've got a machine behind the counter, you can order a *kafe espresso* or a *kapuchino* with reasonable confidence and maybe feel emboldened to ask if they also do *turska* (Turkish coffee) or *Viensko kafe* (Viennese coffee), which comes with a dollop of ice cream on top. If not, you risk getting a revolting brew from some kind of instant coffee under the generic title of *neskafe*, or *nes*. Coffee is often drunk in tandem with a glass of **juice** (*sok*), usually a pretty artificial cocktail of citrus fruits – *naturalen sok* (natural fruit juice from a bottle or packet) or *fresh* (freshly squeezed juice) usually costs more. Delicious domestically produced fruit juices (*nektar*, or *fruktovi sok*) are sometimes sold bottled in supermarkets and food shops, but rarely appear in cafés or bars. **Tea** (*chay*) is available in most cafés; specify *cheren chay* or black tea unless you want some herbal concoction.

Other *bezalkoholni* (non-alcoholic) choices include *gazirana voda* (gaseous mineral water), or international beverages such as Coca Cola, Pepsi, Fanta and Sprite.

Bulgarian wine

From having an insular **wine** industry before World War II, Bulgaria has muscled its way into the forefront of the world's export market, specializing in robust red wines of basic but solid quality. Tried and tested grapes like Cabernet Sauvignon and Merlot have been planted in different regions (such as Pomorie, Haskovo, Asenovgrad or Suhindol), under whose name they're sold with phenomenal success abroad. Inside Bulgaria there's a greater variety and more differentiation between the various blended wines, all of which cost less than 10Lv a bottle in supermarkets and *mehanas*.

Among the **reds** are full-bodied Cabernet; heavier, mellower Melnik and Gûmza; rich, dark Mavrud; and the smooth, strawberry-flavoured Haskovski Merlot. Sweet Pamid, first grown by the Thracians and verging on rosé, is blended with Mavrud to produce Trakiya, or with Melnik wine to make Pirin, while Madara is obtained from concentrated Gûmza and Dimyat grapes (a similar mix is used for the more acidic Tûrnovo). Asenovgradski Mavrud and the red Muscatel Slavyanska are both dessert wines.

The sweeter **whites** are preferable to Dimyat unless you like your wine very dry. Of these, Karlovski and Rilski Misket (Muscatels) and Tamyanka are widely available, but the golden-coloured Evksinograd is much harder to find. Of the dry whites, Traminer Han Krum is the one to look for, while Preslav is a decent **rosé**.

In wine-growing areas, many tavernas and restaurants offer **home-made** wine (*domashno vino*), often straight from the cask (*nalivno*). There is never a problem ordering by the glass (*chasha*).

Spirits

Native **spirits** are highly potent and cost little more than 12Lv a bottle. They are drunk diluted with water in the case of *mastika* (like ouzo in Greece or raki in Turkey), or downed in one, Balkan-style, in the form of *rakiya*, or brandy. *Slivova rakiya* is made from plums, Kaisieva *rakiya* from apricots, and grozdova from grapes – *Pomorska rakiya* is the best example of the latter. *Rakiya* is always accompanied by a soft drink and a salad or appetizer. Vodka is also widely drunk: domestic brands like *Tsarevets* are the cheapest, although Russian and Scandinavian brands are widely available. Imported whisky is cheaper than in the West, but much of it is counterfeit (*mente*). Buy it from the bigger outlets, and avoid stuff sold by the smaller kiosks and street traders.

In bars and restaurants spirits are sold by the gram. *Pedeset grama* (50g or 5cl) is roughly equivalent to a British double measure, *sto grama* (10cl) a quadruple. You'll see plenty of men downing *sto grama* at 11am, or even earlier.

Beer

Bulgarian **beer** (*bira*) is pretty unexciting but perfectly drinkable. The most popular brands are *Zagorka* from Stara Zagora, *Astika* from

Haskovo and *Kamenitza* from Plovdiv, all of which are lager-type beers. While *Pirin*, brewed in Blagoevgrad and available in the southwest, and *Plevensko Pivo* from the northern town of Pleven, also have a following, true drinkers sniff at *Ariana* from Sofia. A 50cl bottle of regular *Kamenitza*, *Astika* or *Zagorka* rarely costs more than 3Lv in a bar or restaurant, while the slightly stronger, 33cl "export" bottles will set you back about 4–5Lv. Imported German, Austrian, Czech or Danish beers are also widely available, at about twice the price. An increasing number of bars offer **draught beer** (*nalivna bira*) as well as bottled – either Bulgarian or an imported brand.

Communications

In recent years Bulgaria's telephone system has improved and expanded rapidly, while the postal service, although slower to modernize, also functions reasonably efficiently. Email is gaining ground, particularly amongst those Bulgarians involved in tourism or other international concerns, and the number of Internet cafés is on the increase.

Post offices and mail

Most **post offices** (*poshta*) are open from 8.30am to 5.30pm from Monday to Saturday, although those in the larger towns tend to open an extra thirty minutes or so either side. It's not always easy to identify the right counter (*gishe*) to queue up at; look for signs advertising the sale of *marki* (stamps) or the despatch of *pisma* (letters) and *koleti* (parcels). **Stamps** are best bought at the post office, although **envelopes** (*plikove*) are sold at street kiosks. Mail can take seven to ten days to reach Britain and two to three weeks to the US; less than half that time if you send it *bûrza* (express) or *vûzdushna* (airmail). It's reasonably cheap to send **parcels** home from Bulgaria, although items have to be brought into the post office and a customs declaration filled out before being wrapped up on the premises.

Poste restante services are available at the major post office in every sizeable town. Mail can be claimed by showing your passeport (ask *Ima li pisma za mene* – is there any mail for me?), and letters should be addressed писма до поискване, централна поща, followed by the name of the town. Letters from Western Europe generally take around a week to arrive in Bulgaria, those from North America two weeks, and Bulgarian postal officers are apt to misfile or return mail to the sender if it's not claimed immediately, so don't hold high hopes for poste restante communications.

When writing **letters to Bulgaria**, remember that the postcode and name of the town comes first, the street and number second, and the name of the addressee last: eg. 9000 Varna, ul. Nevazhna 40, Mr Hristo Stoichkov.

Cyrillic checklist: communications

Post office	поща	Letters	писма
Poste restante	писма до поискване	Envelopes	пликове
Express mail	бърза	Parcels	колети
Air mail	въздушна	Telephone	телефон
Stamps	марки	Phonecard	фонкарта

Phones

Although Bulgaria's **telephone system** has greatly improved in recent years, it remains patchy. Because investment has been concentrated on business communications, international and trunk calls are often easier than local ones, especially using the new public telephones taking **phonecards** (*fonkarta*). These can usually be found in post offices, hotel lobbies and major public buildings such as cultural centres and concert halls. There are two systems, using separate phones and non-interchangeable cards, **Bulfon** (whose phones are orange) and **Betkom** (with blue phones). It's best to carry both cards as you never know which system will be available (in some towns one has a monopoly). You can use them to make any kind of direct-dial call for the same cost as you'd pay in a telephone office or private house. Phonecards are sold at post offices and many shops and kiosks.

In the absence of a cardphone you'll have to fall back on the **telephone offices** (*telefon*, телефон) attached to post offices, where you are assigned a cabin and pay for your call afterwards. The telephone section is usually open longer than other parts of the post office, often as late as 11pm in major cities and 24 hours in Sofia. As most hotels levy extortionate surcharges on **international calls**, you'll almost always save money by going through a phone office instead.

GSM **mobile phones** can be used almost everywhere in Bulgaria save for mountain valleys, although you should contact your network to ensure that your **international roaming** facility is activated (often entailing the payment of a hefty deposit) before you travel.

Calling home from abroad

One of the most convenient ways of phoning home from abroad is via a **telephone charge card**. Using access codes for the particular country you are in and a PIN number, you can make calls from most hotel, public and private phones that will be charged to your own account. Since most major charge cards are free to obtain, it's certainly worth getting one, at least for emergencies; enquire first though whether Bulgaria is covered, and bear in mind that rates aren't necessarily cheaper than calling from a public phone.

In the **UK and Ireland**, British Telecom (Ⓣ0800/345 144, Ⓦwww.payphones.bt.com/callingcards) will issue the BT Charge Card free to all BT customers, which can be used in 116 countries; AT&T (dial Ⓣ0800/890 011, then 888/641 6123 when you hear the AT&T prompt to be transferred to the Florida Call Centre, free 24hr) has the Global Calling Card; while NTL (Ⓣ0500/100 505) issues its own Global Calling Card, which can be used in more than sixty countries abroad, though the fees cannot be charged to a normal phone bill.

In the **USA and Canada**, AT&T, MCI, Sprint, Canada Direct and other North American long-distance companies all enable their customers to make credit-card calls while overseas. Call your company's customer service line to find out if they provide service from Bulgaria, and if so, what the toll-free access code is. Calls made from overseas will automatically be billed to your home number.

In **Australia and New Zealand**, telephone charge cards such as the Telstra Telecard (Ⓣ1800/038 000), Optus Calling Card (Ⓣ1300/300 937) in Australia, and Telecom NZ's Calling Card (Ⓣ04/801 9000) can be

International telephone codes

To **dial abroad direct from Bulgaria**, first use the international code listed below and then the STD (area) code, remembering to omit the initial 0.
UK Ⓣ0044
Ireland Ⓣ00353
US & Canada Ⓣ001
Australia Ⓣ0061
New Zealand Ⓣ0064

To **call Bulgaria from abroad**, use the following international access codes, followed by the area code (omitting the initial 0) and the local number.
From the UK & Ireland Ⓣ00359
From the US & Canada Ⓣ0113 59
From Australia & New Zealand Ⓣ0011359

used to make calls from abroad, which are charged back to a domestic account or credit card.

Email

One of the best ways to keep in touch while travelling is to sign up for a free Internet email address that can be accessed from anywhere, for example YahooMail or Hotmail – accessible through ⓦwww.yahoo.com and ⓦwww.hotmail.com. Once you've set up an account, you can use these sites to pick up and send mail from any Internet café, or hotel with Internet access. In Bulgaria, Internet cafés (most are called "clubs", although this doesn't mean that you have to be a member to use them) are now a common sight in the big cities, and rarely cost more than 2Lv an hour to use, although connection times can be slow.

ⓦwww.kropla.com is a useful website giving details of how to plug your laptop in when abroad, phone country codes around the world, and information about electrical systems in different countries.

The media

English-language newspapers and magazines are not widely available in Bulgaria, although you may find recent copies of *Time*, *Newsweek*, the *Financial Times* and the *Herald Tribune* on the bigger newsstands in Sofia, Plovdiv and Varna. English tabloids appear regularly at the package resorts along the coast, and in Sofia there's an English-language weekly paper called *The Sofia Echo*, which is an excellent source of local news and comment, and carries a handy supplement listing cultural events in the capital.

The Bulgarian press

The collapse of censorship after November 1989 and the disappearance of turgid propaganda organs such as the former party newspaper *Rabotnichesko Delo* ("Workers' Deeds") have resulted in a lively domestic media scene. The two principal **daily newspapers** are 24 Часа (*24 Chasa*, "24 Hours") and Труд (*Trud* or "Work"), tabloids that mix news reporting with racy articles about Hollywood starlets or the antics of the Bulgarian mafia. Although politically independent, they're overwhelmingly conservative-nationalist, rather than liberal, in tone. Of the "serious" dailies, Дневник (*Dnevnik*, "Journal") is reasonably impartial and carries a smattering of cultural and lifestyle features, although it doesn't command as much respect as the weekly Капитал (*Kapital*, "Capital"), which used to be a purely business title, but now supplies the in-depth political analysis and arts coverage that other publications largely lack.

A gaggle of lesser periodicals have emerged to offer a hitherto forbidden diet of celebrity gossip, lurid crime stories, and improbable tales of the paranormal, prime among which is Блясък (*Blyasûk*, "Glitter"), which basically rehashes stories from the Western tabloids.

The only glossy lifestyle monthlies with any real life, style or indeed intelligence are Егоист (*Egoist*) and Едно (*Edno*, "One"), both of which are snazzy, Sofia-based surveys of what's new in music, film and fashion.

TV and radio

Bulgaria's single state **TV channel**, Kanal 1, is augmented by a handful of private stations, all of which peddle a similar diet of talk shows and phone-ins, imported soap operas and action movies, and next to nothing in the way of domestically produced drama. In addition, **cable** and **satellite TV** have caught on in a big way, to the extent that many hotels and bars feature the likes of CNN, MTV and Eurosport, while in the ethnic Turkish regions, household dishes point towards Turkey.

The best way to catch up on news is the **BBC World Service** on short wave (available on the following frequencies, depending on the time of day: MHz 15.07, 12.09, 9.41, 6.18) or in Sofia on VHF (91MHz).

Holidays, festivals and entertainment

With the collapse of Communism, several ideological holidays have disappeared from the Bulgarian calendar to be replaced by traditional Orthodox festivals such as Easter and Christmas. In addition, there's an increasing observance of local festivals and saints' days, marked by the holding of special services, feasting, or simply by lighting candles next to an icon of the appropriate saint. Though traditional folk customs are still observed by many people, when it comes to entertainment tastes are much the same as in the West.

Festivals

In Communist times virtually all festivals were organized and funded by the state under the auspices of the Party, and "unofficial" events such as religious pilgrimages were firmly discouraged. Today, there are almost no ideological constraints but little money either, so that while the diversity of festivals is far greater, there's less certainty of them actually taking place, particularly in the case of events that require major funding. For lovers of **classical music and ballet**, the major events remain the **Sofia Music Weeks** (late-May to late-June), the **March Music Days** in Ruse, the international **chamber music** festival in Plovdiv (mid-June), and the **symphonic music** festival in Haskovo (end of Oct). In addition, there's whatever is featured during the **Varna Summer** (mid-June to mid-Aug), Sozopol's **Apollonia Festival** (beginning of Sept) or the **Trakiisko lyato** in Plovdiv (early Aug) – though none of these three is exclusively devoted to classical music.

While you can also hear some **jazz** during the Varna Summer and Apollonia Festival, a better bet is one of the **international festivals** in Haskovo (Sept or early Oct), Ruse (late Oct), Blagoevgrad or Sofia (both in Nov). Though big names from the West are thin on the ground, top performers from Bulgaria, neighbouring Balkan states and the former Soviet Union often play there, and the general standard of musicianship is high. The best in Bulgarian **drama** can be seen at the **Theatre Days** in Blagoevgrad (Bulgaria's equivalent of the Edinburgh Festival) – though you obviously need to understand Bulgarian to enjoy it to the full.

For dedicated all-night club kids, there are tons of outdoor **rave parties** in the summer, although none have yet established themselves as regular annual events – you'll have to look out for posters or rely on local knowledge to find out what's happening.

Folklore festivals

Bulgaria's **folklore festivals** vary enormously in size and character, from parades of floats through the streets, to gatherings on highland meadows, or a few musicians playing on the village square while everyone dances the *horo*. While the **Rose Carnival** at Kazanlûk in the Valley of the Roses (early June) is fairly cheesy, you're bound to enjoy some of the acts at the **international festivals** in Burgas and Plovdiv in August, featuring dance troupes from all over Europe and the Near East.

A more distinctly Bulgarian event is the **Koprivshtitsa Folklore Festival**, the largest gathering of traditional singers and musicians, held every five years (the next is due in 2010), although a smaller version occurs annually (in August). Other highland music festivals include the annual **Rozhenski sûbor** at Rozhen in the Rhodopes, and **Pirin Pee** (Pirin Sings; see p.155) at the Predel Pass (both in Aug) – the largest gatherings of musicians from the Rhodopes and Pirin regions. In the summer, throughout the Pirin and Rhodope regions (and sometimes in Sofia, Plovdiv and other major cities), a plethora of civic and festive events commemorating the **Ilinden** uprising of 1903 take place on two separate dates a week apart, depending on whether it is pegged to the Old or New Style calendar (see below).

While descendants of refugees from Aegean Thrace celebrate their roots at the **Gathering of the Beautiful Trakiya** in Haskovo (May) and the **Thracian Festival** at Madzharovo (Sept), **Macedonian**, **Pomak** and **Vlach** traditions are celebrated in the Rhodope villages of Dorkovo (first Sun in Aug) and Zabûrdo (Aug 15), and there's a festival of **Gypsy music** in Stara Zagora (late June or early July). Another, spectacular manifestation of Bulgarian folk culture is the **kukeri processions** of mummers in nightmarish costumes, carrying flaming torches throughout the streets of Razlog, Sandanski, Pernik and Petrich on New Year's Eve and January 1. In Blagoevgrad the processions take place as early as December 25, while in Shiroka Lûka they don't appear until March.

Nor does the list of festivals end there, for many of the events above incorporate aspects of religious or agricultural rites which are interwoven with customs and traditions that still feature prominently in Bulgarian life. We've listed the festivals specific to particular places separately from the saints' days that are widely observed at churches, but not worth going out of your way to attend. Those festivals scheduled to take place every two or three years are entirely subject to getting enough funding.

National holidays and specific events

You'll find shops, banks and restaurants closed on major **national holidays**, although the occasional café, exchange bureau or provision shop may open up in big cities or resorts.

Jan 1 New Year's Day
March 3 Liberation of Bulgaria (anniversary of San Stefano)
Easter Sunday (see below)
Easter Monday (see below)
May 1 Labour Day
May 24 Day of Slavonic Education and Culture
September 6 Unification Day
September 22 Independence Day
Dec 25 Christmas Day

Specific events

Events occuring on the cusp of two months are listed under the earlier date.

January

Kukeri processions in Razlog, Sandanski, Pernik and Petrich (New Year's Eve/Jan 1).
Yordanovden celebrations at Koprivshtitsa and Kalofer (Jan 6).
Christmas (Old Style) celebrated by female carol singers at Dobûrsko (Jan 6/7).
Festival of orchestral music in Plovdiv (early Jan).

February

Trifon zarezan celebrated in Melnik, Sandanski, and other wine-growing areas (Feb 1 or 14).

March–April

Kukeri at Shiroka Lûka (first weekend in March) and Eleshnitsa (Easter Sunday).
March Music Days Classical music festival in Ruse (last two weeks in March).
Todorovden Horse races at Koprivshtitsa, Dobrinishte and Katarino near Razlog (first Sat of Lent).
Day of my town festival in Sandanski (end April).
Easter Nationwide church services on Thursday and Saturday night, a Great Easter Concert in Bansko, and Kukeri rites at Eleshnitsa (Easter Monday).
Lazarovden Lazaruvane displays in the City Garden, Stara Zagora, and Dragalevtsi (Sat before Palm Sunday).
Theatre Days in Blagoevgrad (late April/early May).
Young Poets Festival in Haskovo (late April/early May).

May

Procession of icons from Bachkovo Monastery to Ayazmoto (25 days after Easter Sunday).
Gergyovden Sacrifices and feasting at Chiprovtsi, Slatolin (near Montana) and the Monastery of St George near Hadzhidimovo (outside Gotse Delchev). Also Muslim/Christian gatherings at Ak Yazula Baba Tekke near Obrochiste, and Demir Baba Tekke near Sveshtari (May 6).
Measuring of the Milk festivals in Rhodope highland villages (May 21).
Celebration of Bansko Traditions in Bansko (May 17–24).
Classial Guitar Festival in Gotse Delchev (late May).
Gathering of the Beautiful Trakiya Thracian folklore festival in Haskovo (last weekend in May).
Sofia Music Weeks Festival of classical music and ballet (late May to late June).

Festival of Humour and Satire in Gabrovo (every 2 or 3 years).
Trakia Pee Thracian folk music festival in Stara Zagora (last week of May or first week of June).

June

Macedonian Folk Songs festival in Blagoevgrad (every two or three years)
Rockers' Festival (classic cars and bikes) off the highway between Pazardzhik and Plovdiv.
Fire-dancing at Bûlgari in the Strandzha (June 4 or nearest weekend).
Karlovo Rose Festival with folk music and parades (first Sat in June).
Kazanlûk Rose Festival with music, dancing and carnival floats (first Sun in June).
Chamber music festival in Plovdiv (mid-June).
Folklore and crafts displays at Etûra, near Gabrovo (June 24).
Gypsy music festival in Ayzama Park, Stara Zagora (late June or early July).
Varna Summer Festival of classical music, folklore and jazz (mid-June to mid-Aug)

July

Ilinden (New Style) Services at churches and monasteries named after St Elijah, and civic events throughout the Pirin region. Also a Christian/Muslim gathering at Demir Baba Tekke, near Sveshtari (July 20 or the last Sun in July).
Macedonian sûbor at Rozhen, near Melnik (last weekend in July).

August

Ilinden (Old Style) Ilindenski sûbor at Popovi Livadi near Gotse Delchev (Aug 2 or nearest weekend); Ilinden bagpipe festival at Gela near Shiroka Lûka (first Sun in Aug).
Pirin Pee folklore festival at the Predel Pass in the Pirin Mountains.
Folklore festival (Macedonian, Pomak and Vlach) at Dorkovo (first Sun in Aug).
Trakiisko lyato classical, pop and folk music, and an international folklore festival in Plovdiv (early Aug).
Folk music festival in Koprivshtitsa (Aug 15 or nearest weekend).
Golyama Bogoroditsa Parade of icons at Troyan, Rozhen, Rila and Bachkovo monasteries (Aug 15).
Folk music festival at Zabûrdo (Aug 15).
Karakachani festival (folk music and feasting) at the Blue Rocks outside Sliven (third weekend in Aug).
Birthday of St John of Rila celebrated at Rila Monastery (Aug 18).
Dûnovisti gathering at the Seven Lakes in the Rila Mountains (Aug 19–28).
Golyama Bogoroditsa Celebrated everywhere where there's a church dedicated to the Virgin, with big parades at the monasteries of Troyan and Bachkovo (Aug 29).
Gypsy festival at Osikovitsa near Botevgrad (nearest weekend to Aug 29).
International festival of folk music in Burgas (late Aug).
Rozhenski sûbor folklore festival at Rozhen in the Rhodopes (last weekend in Aug).
Milk Festival at Smilyan in the Rhodopes (last weekend in Aug).

September

Thracian Festival of music, dancing and wrestling in Madzharovo (first week in Sept).
Apollonia Festival classical, jazz, rock and theatre festival (first 7–10 days of Sept).
Balklan Folklore Festival in Blagoevgrad (every 2 or 3 years).
Pirin Folklore Festival in Sandanski (second weekend in Sept).
Malka Bogoroditsa Parade of icons at Rozhen Monastery (Sept 8).
Krûstovden pilgrimage to Krûstova gora (Sept 14).
Jazz Festival in Haskovo (late Sept or early Oct).

October

Autumn Festival in Blagoevgrad.
Bansko Day Massed male choirs in Bansko (Oct 8).
Gotse Delchev Day in Gotse Delchev (Oct 18).
Wine harvest festival in Melnik (Oct 18).
Feast day of St John of Rila celebrated at Rila Monastery (Oct 19).
International Jazz Forum in Ruse (last week of Oct).
Symphonic Music Festival in Haskovo (end of Oct).

November

International Jazz Festival in Blagoevgrad
International Jazz Festival in Sofia (second week in Nov).

December

Kukeri rites in Blagoevgrad (Dec 25)

Seasonal rites and religious festivals

Most traditional Bulgarian festivals relate to different stages of the agricultural year and are rooted in paganism, but the pantheon of Orthodox saints and holy days imparts a Christian framework to the seasonal calendar. Although the nearest most tourists get to this cycle of **rural celebrations** is a glimpse of festive costumes in museums, a surprising number of customs are still upheld and can be witnessed if you're in rural areas at the right time. Given that many are scheduled around **Orthodox festivals**, it's unfortunate for visitors that Bulgarians themselves are often confused over whether these should be dated by the Old or New Style calendar, and the rule varies from place to place for no apparent reason. To confuse things further, the major **Islamic festivals** observed by Bulgarian Muslims follow a separate calendar, but several popular feasts fall on Orthodox holy days and are attended by Christians as well.

Seasonal rites

In Christian areas, the festive calendar begins with **New Year's Day** or St Basil's Day – also known as *survaki* – when young children go from house to house offering New Year wishes to the householders by slapping them on the back with a *survaknitsa* – a bunch of twigs adorned with brightly coloured threads and dried fruit. In some villages in southwestern Bulgaria, New Year's Day is also marked by processions of villagers wearing animal masks, a ritual similar to those performed on *Kukerov den* (see below).

In wine-producing areas, vines are pruned and sprinkled with wine for good luck and casks of young wine from last year's harvest are broached on St Tryphon's Day, **Trifon zarezan** (Feb 1 in some places, Feb 14 in others). A more widespread festival associated with the start of the agricultural year in arable or pastoral regions is **Kukerov den**, the Day of the *kukeri*, on the first Sunday before Lent. Processions are led through the village by dancing, leaping men dressed up in animal costumes and grotesque masks, augmented by a girdle of goat or sheep bells and extravagantly tasselled trousers. In urban centres such as Razlog, Petrich and Pernik, the festival is conflated with *survaki* and held on New Year's Eve or New Year's Day.

The advent of spring, **Baba marta** (literally, "Granny March"), is celebrated on March 1, when peasant households embark on a round of spring-cleaning – symbolically sweeping the winter months away. On the same day people present each other with **martenitsa**, good-luck charms made of red and white woollen threads with tassels or furry bobbles on the end, that are worn until the sighting of the first migrating stork or budding bush (when the charms are hung on its branches). **Todorovden**, or St Theodor's Day, on the first Saturday of Lent, is still marked by horse races in Koprivshtitsa, Dobrinishte and Katarino, while another more widespread springtime fertility rite is **lazaruvane** which takes place on St Lazar's Day, or **Lazarovden** (the Saturday before Palm Sunday), when village maidens considered fit for marriage perform ritual dances, songs and games. **Gergyovden**, St George's Day (May 6), is an occasion for sacrificing and roasting sheep, to celebrate the end of spring.

The coming of summer is traditionally marked by the feast day of **SS Konstantin and Elena** (May 21 by the New Style calendar, May 4 by the Old). Many pastoral Rhodope villages hold a festival known as the **Measuring of the Milk** or *Predoi*, intended to ensure good milk yields for the rest of the year, which includes the practice of milking a ewe so that the milk dribbles through the wedding ring of a young bride before falling into the pail; while in a few remote villages in the Strandzha hills, they go in for the ancient pagan custom of **fire-dancing** barefoot on hot coals.

Other church holidays tend to coincide with the changing of the seasons. **St Marina's Day** (July 17) has always been a popular

Easter

The **Orthodox Easter** occurs roughly a week later than in Western Europe, and its exact timing varies from year to year. Certain other festivals (chiefly Lent) and saints' days are also timed in relation to Easter, rather than occurring on a fixed date. The dates for the next few years are:

2006 April 23
2007 April 8
2008 April 27
2009 April 19

midsummer feast day, and Enyovden, the birthday of St John the Baptist (June 24), is still regarded as the best time to pick medicinal herbs. The beginning of autumn is marked by the major religious festival of *Golyama Bogoroditsa* (see opposite). While Melnik and other wine-growing areas rejoice in their harvest on October 18, elsewhere, the end of the farming year is traditionally celebrated on St Demitrius' Day, **Dimitrovden** (Oct 26).

Orthodox festivals

While the majority of Bulgarians who profess to be Christians may not fast or pay much attention to saint's days, they're sure to attend at least one of the high festivals such as Easter, the Feast of the Assumption or Christmas, while those with a strong commitment abstain from meat and even dairy products over **Lent**.

On Palm Sunday (*Tsvetnitsa* or *Varbnitsa*), people everywhere buy willow branches and hang them up at home in preparation for the **Easter** services in churches on Thursday night (the eve of Good Friday) and Saturday night (the eve of Easter Sunday). At the latter the priest emerges from behind the iconostasis at midnight bearing a candle symbolizing the Resurrection; the congregation light their own candles from this and file outside to walk around the church three times. Painted eggs (prepared by families beforehand) are then knocked together and eaten; the first egg to be made is always painted red to symbolize the blood of Christ and put aside – either to be buried in the fields to ensure fertility or kept in the home to bring good luck. On Easter Sunday married couples traditionally visit the best man at their wedding and have roast lamb for lunch.

Lamb is also on the menu for the **Golyama Bogoroditsa**, or Feast of the Assumption of the Virgin, which occasions big gatherings at any church or monastery dedicated to her, picnics in the grounds of the Dragalevski and Lopoushanski monasteries, and a parade of icons at Troyan and Bachkovo. The feast is generally observed on its New Style date (Aug 15), but Christian Gypsies celebrate it according to the Old Style calendar (Aug 29). **Malka Bogoroditsa**, the Feast of the Birth of the Virgin, is also marked in both calandars, by a parade of icons at Rozhen Monastery (Sept 8) and services at Sandanski's Church of SS Kozma and Demyan (Sept 16).

Of the many other saints' days in the Orthodox calendar, three engender particularly impressive crowds and spectacles: the birthday (Aug 18) and feast day (Oct 19) of **St John of Rila** at the Rila Monastery; and the pilgrimage to **Krûstova gora** on the eve of **Krûstovden** (Sept 14). The mountaintop shrine of Krûstova Gora is Bulgaria's chief pilgrimage site (see p.357) and attracts New Age cultists as well as mainstream Christians.

Orthodox saints' days

Where there are two dates below, it is because the saint's day is celebrated either on the date in the Old Calendar or on the date in the New Calendar, or sometimes both.

Yordanovden (Jordan Day) Jan 6
Trifon Zarezan (St Tryphon's Day) Feb 14
Todorovden (St Theodor's Day) First Sat of Lent
Lazarovden (St Lazar's Day) Sat before Palm Sunday
Gergyovden (St George's Day) May 6
SS Cyril and Methodius May 11
SS Konstantin and Elena May 4 and May 24
Ilinden (St Elijah's Day) July 20 and Aug 2
Golyama Bogoroditsa (Feast of the Assumption) Aug 15 and Aug 29
St John of Rila (birthday) Aug 18
Malka Bogoroditsa (Birth of the Virgin) Sept 6 and Sept 16
Krûstovden (Day of the Holy Cross) Sept 14
St John of Rila (feast day) Oct 19
Dimitrovden (St Demetrius' Day) Oct 26
Arhangelovden (Archangels Michael and Gabriel) Nov 8
Nikulen (St Nicholas' Day) Dec 6
Koleda (Christmas) Dec 25 and Jan 6

Muslim festivals

Since the Islamic calendar is lunar, dates of festivals tend to drift backwards eleven days each year relative to the Gregorian calendar, but as the start of Ramadan depends on the visibility of the new moon at Mecca and elsewhere, it is impossible to predict the dates of the Sheker bayram holiday, at the end of Ramadan, or the Kurban bayram, with total accuracy – so these dates are only approximate.

Sheker bayram	**Kurban bayram**
November 3–5 2005	January 10–13 2006
October 23–25 2006	December 31–January 2 2006–7
October 12–14 2007	December 20–23 2007
30 September–2 October 2008	December 8–11 2008

Christmas (*koleda*) is a family and neighbourly affair which most people celebrate on December 25 according to the Gregorian calendar, though traditionalists do so on January 6/7 by the Old calendar, and those who can afford it might even celebrate both. A traditional practice in villages is the *koleduvane*, whereby young men go from house to house singing carols under the leadership of a *stanenik*, charged with the baking of a specially decorated loaf of bread which the singers take with them on their rounds.

In olden times, the pagan New Year rites of *survaki* were followed by an affirmation of Christianity called **Yordanovden**, celebrating Christ's baptism in the River Jordan. Once widespread throughout the Balkans, this involved casting a wooden cross into a river, which local lads dived in to retrieve, while their elders collected bottles of water blessed by the priest. Given the state of Bulgaria's rivers, it's probably for the best that this ritual is nowadays only performed at Koprivshtitsa in the Sredna gora (Jan 6).

Muslim festivals

Bulgaria's Muslim minority is no less observant of **Islamic festivals**, converging on mosques and holy sites in order to celebrate the more important holidays. If you're in Bulgaria at the right time, these gatherings can be observed in Sofia and Plovdiv, or towns in areas of Muslim settlement, such as Shumen, Razgrad and Dobrich in the north; Pazardzhik, Kûrdzhali, Haskovo and Momchilgrad in the south.

During **Ramadan** (*Ramazan*), the month of daylight abstention from food, water, tobacco or sexual relations, cafés and restaurants still open for business, and the degree to which the fast is observed varies from individual to individual, but everyone enjoys the three-day **Sheker bayram** (Sugar Holiday) at the end of Ramadan, celebrated with family get-togethers and the giving of presents and sweets to children. Another major event is the **Kurban bayram** (Festival of the Sacrifice), which is marked by the ritual slaughter of sheep and goats, feasting and dancing.

Outdoor feasts are an important aspect of Muslim culture in Bulgaria, and one that is shared by their Christian compatriots. Many people from both faiths come to picnic and enjoy themselves at localities revered by Muslims (usually a dervish mausoleum, or *Tekke*). Happily for everyone, the Aliani festival of **Hidrelez** at the beginning of summer coincides with the Orthodox feast of Gergyovden (May 6). Foreigners are welcome to attend, but anyone squeamish about animal slaughter should stay away. Bulgarian Muslims are not averse to drinking alcohol on these occasions.

Entertainment

Most Bulgarians have little spare money, and the range of **entertainment** on offer reflects this. Thanks to past state subsidies most provincial towns have a **theatre** and most big cities an **opera house**, but their programmes have been curtailed in recent years – though financial cut-backs have had less effect on **puppet theatre** (*Kuklen teatûr*, куклен театър a popular art form with children.

Although Bulgaria is renowned for its **folk music**, visitors are only likely to see it performed in three situations: at folklore festivals (see p.60); by regional ensembles such as the Pirin Song and Dance troupe; or as part of the entertainments laid on for package tourists. If young Bulgarians listen to folk music at all, it tends to be the pop-folk crossover music known as **chalga** – a mish-mash of Greek, Serbian and Turkish styles which dominates the playlists of national radio stations and small-town discos alike. Although a new generation of ear-bending DJs are beginning to spring up in urban clubs, locally produced rock or rap is generally dire, and regular gig venues are few and far between, although Sofia has a few live music bars, and the capital sometimes plays host to foreign bands.

Football

No list of entertainments in Bulgaria would be complete without a mention of the country's favourite sport, **football**. Teams in the premier division ("A" Grupa) usually play on Sunday afternoons, although some of the big matches take place on Saturdays. Tickets are generally dirt cheap and sold at booths outside the grounds on the day of the match. Due to Bulgaria's harsh winters, the football **season** (mid-Aug to mid-May) is interrupted by a two-month break in January and February. Most Bulgarian stadia are dilapidated, uncovered affairs with rickety bench seating, though the top clubs have installed plastic bucket-seating to meet UEFA safety guidelines.

While CSKA Sofia and Levski Sofia remain the most successful and popular **teams**, in recent seasons powerful private sponsors have done much to ensure high league positions for Lokomotiv Plovdiv and Liteks Lovech. Matches between these clubs are always big occasions, as are any derbies involving teams from the capital (CSKA, Levski, Lokomotiv and Slavia).

Matches involving the Bulgarian national team (fourth in the World Cup in 1994, but largely ineffectual ever since) are the only ones for which advance purchase of tickets, from the stadium box office, is advisable. **International matches** are usually held at the Vasil Levski Stadium in Sofia, or in Burgas.

If you can decipher Cyrillic script, the daily sports papers *7 Dni Sport* and *Meridian Match* are the best sources of football **information**, and carry full details of British and other European league matches in their Monday editions.

Outdoor activities and ecotourism

While Bulgaria is well known for its skiing (see p.29 for details), few foreigners realize its potential for activities such as hiking, climbing and caving, nor the country's wonderful natural history. Bulgaria's mountains and lowlands are incredibly rich in wildlife – especially flora and birds – as the country has features of both the Balkan and Mediterranean ecosystems, and is visited by hundreds of migratory species. Whilst many people may prefer to book a tour through a specialist operator abroad (see p.30), it's perfectly possible to arrange adventure and ecotourism trips through various agencies in Bulgaria.

Hiking

Hiking was first popularized in Bulgaria in the late nineteenth century, when it had patriotic connotations. During Communist times it was regarded as an ideal activity for citizens, and a network of trails and huts (*hizhi*) was created throughout the mountains. Though not as well signposted as they could be, the hundreds of trails can be combined in an almost infinite variety of routes. The main hiking areas are the Pirin and Rila national parks, the central and western Rhodopes, and the Stara planina.

The **Pirin Mountains** (p.146) are the wildest, most picturesque range in Bulgaria, with 45 peaks over 2590m, deep valleys, karstic massifs and more than 200 glacial lakes, mainly in the northern part of the range, which has the finest panoramic views. Further north, the **Rila Mountains** (p.132) include the highest peak in the Balkan peninsula and Bulgaria's greatest monastery, and are characterized by magnificent coniferous forests and alpine scenery, abloom with wildflowers all year. Here too there are many lakes, including a cluster that attracts sun-worshippers. Both ranges abut the **Rhodopes** (p.351), which are lower, but arguably the loveliest range in Bulgaria, with a mixture of pine forests, crags, highland meadows and villages of stone houses, not to mention the fantastic caves and birdlife around the Trigrad Gorge.

In the **Stara planina** or Balkan Range (p.224), the fir-clad heights of the northwest are relatively uncharted, but their ill-marked trails reward the efforts of those with time to spare. Villages such as Berkovitsa and Chiprovtsi provide the best access to higher altitudes. The central Stara planina between the Valley of the Roses and the Danubian plain has better maintained trails, and is best approached from Karlovo in the south or Cherni Osam and Apriltsi in the north.

If you're planning to go hiking independently you should visit Zig-Zag/Odysseia-In in Sofia (see p.84) first, to stock up on hiking maps (see p.43) and advice; they can also book accommodation in some areas. If you don't fancy heading off on your own, you could hire a guide from Zig-Zag/Odysseia-In or through tourist offices in the Pirin and Rhodopes – expect to pay 60Lv/€30 a day plus expenses.

Climbing and caving

Bulgaria's mountainous terrain means that the opportunities for **climbing** are practically limitless. The most popular areas with mountaineers and rock-climbers are Mount Malyovitsa (p.146) in the Rila Mountains; the karst region to the north of Mount Vihren (p.156) in the Pirin range; the Iskûr Gorge (p.182), Vratsa (p.183) and Belogradchik (p.193) in the Stara planina; and the Blue Rocks outside Sliven (p.320).

Of the hundreds of **caves** in Bulgaria (mostly in the Stara planina and western Rhodopes), a dozen have been fitted with walkways and lighting and opened to the public. The most famous are the Magura Cave (p.194), with its prehistoric paintings; the Yagodina Cave, with its stalactites and cave pearls, and the awesome Devil's Throat near Trigrad (p.366). Scores of others that are equally spectacular are only known to Bulgarian cavers, who welcome contacts with their foreign counterparts.

Though no foreign operator runs climbing or caving package tours, individuals can go climbing **with a guide** from Zig-Zag/Odysseia-In for 60–80Lv/€30–40 per person per day – plus expenses and equipment rental (if required). Otherwise your most useful local caving contact is the Bulgarian Federation of Speleologists, 1040 Sofia, bul. Vasil Levski 75 (ⓣ02/987 8812, ⓦwww.speleo.bg.com).

Mountain-biking

Mountain-biking is slowly catching on in Bulgaria, especially in the Pirin, Rhodopes and Stara planina, where you can rent bikes from hotels in Bansko and Pamporovo and tourist offices in Apriltsi, Gabrovo, Teteven, Troyan and Tryavna. From a climatic standpoint, mid-June to late September is the ideal time for biking in the Pirin, while in the Rhodopes it's feasible until mid-October. Though there are plenty of dirt roads and tracks, the challenge is to find a locality with a mixture of mountainous, undulating and flat terrain, where you can get above the tree-line for a panoramic view – such as the area between Pamporovo and Trigrad. Trails are less developed in the Stara planina, but there are several places in the region where routes have been marked by the Stara Planina Tourist Association (see p.224 for details).

Birdwatching

Bulgaria is great for **birdwatching**, being a nesting ground for most European species in spring (May–June) and on the migratory path of many Asian ones in autumn (Sept to mid-Oct), totalling around 400 species in all. There's plenty to see at any time, owing to the diversity of ecological niches and the fact that farmers use fewer pesticides and insecticides than in Western Europe. Though birdlife can be seen anywhere, the richest concentrations are in the Rhodope Mountains, along the Black Sea coast and the floodplain of the River Danube.

In the **Rhodopes**, the Trigrad Gorge (see p.366) is notable for Pallid swifts, Crag martins, Pot-bellied dippers and, above all, the rare, elusive Wallcreeper, while the local caves harbour six types of bat. Although eagles, hawks and falcons can be seen all over the highlands, the best sites for observing raptors are in the Arda Gorge near Madzharovo (see p.376), which boasts rare Eastern and Imperial eagles, Egyptian, Black and Griffon vultures, Black storks, Blue Rock thrushes, Chukars, Nuthatches and Barred, Orphean and Olivaceous warblers.

The **Black Sea coast** has an even greater variety of birdlife, especially during the great autumn migration, when flocks of raptors fly over the lakes and marshes around Burgas (see p.420), which teem with Black and White storks, Marsh harriers and Mediterranean gulls, while Black-winged stilts and avocets feed in the lagoons and terns fish offshore. In spring, the salt-pans and reed-marshes sustain White and Dalmatian pelicans, Great White and Little egrets, Bearded and Penduline tits, Red-necked Phalarope and Broad-billed sandpipers. Cape Kaliakra (see p.407) is likewise good for observing birds of passage (larks, pipits, wagtails, wheatears and warblers besides larger migants like storks and buzzards), while in spring you'll see Alpine swifts, Pied wheatears and the rare Finch's wheatear (found nowhere else in Europe). On Lake Durankulak (see p.410), Spanish sparrows breed in the nests of storks and there's a small nesting colony of Paddyfield warblers. Pygmy cormorants are also around in September, along with Ruddy and Ferruginous shelducks (the latter an endangered species).

In spring, especially, another major site is **Lake Srebûrna** (p.220) on the Danube floodplain, which is frequented by around eighty migratory species and has a nesting colony of Dalmatian pelicans. Its rich variety of wildfowl includes "Wheezing" Penduline tits, egrets, several kinds of warblers, and seventy types of heron. Black- and Red-necked grebes attend their floating nests, and Whiskered and White-winged Black terns drift on the open water. Further west the lowlands are home to Pygmy cormorants, Glossy ibises and Marsh harriers.

For **information** on all these sites, contact the Bulgarian Society for the Protection of Birds, which can recommend local guides and advise on all matters ornithological.

Wildlife organizations in Bulgaria

Bulgarian Society for the Protection of Birds (BDZP) ⓣ02/971 5855, ⓦwww.bspb.org. The national ornithological society, with affiliates around the country.

Bulgarian Biodiversity Foundation ⓣ02/980 4131, ⓦwww.bsbcp.org. Coordinates numerous regional projects throughout Bulgaria, including those at the Poda Nature Reserve outside Burgas (see p.420), and numerous others along the Black Sea coast.

Conservation Centre ⓣ03720/280 or 304, ⓦwww.geocities.com/niccer_bg. Runs the vulture reserve in the Arda gorges near Madzharovo (see p.376).

Le Balkan ⓦwww.lebalkan.com. Coordinates projects aong the northern Black Sea coast around Shabla and Kavarna.

Balkani Wildlife Society ⓣ02/963 1470, ⓦwww.balkani.org. Federation of Bulgarian NGOs involved with nature conservation.

Zoology, botany and geology

Aside from birds, Bulgaria's fauna includes most of the Balkan and Mediterranean **reptiles** (over fifty species) and **mammals**. Mountainous areas are the habitat of bears, boars, wolves, wild cats, deer, foxes and badgers, while jackals can be found in the Strandzha, and otters and coypu in the coastal wetlands. However they are all pretty reclusive, so you shouldn't expect to see too much in the course of walking in these areas – aside from **butterflies** and moths, of which Bulgaria boasts some 1100 species. Of more recherché interest are the 75 species of **cave fauna**, including eight kinds of bats.

Bulgaria's flora is extremely diverse due to the three types of climate (continental, Mediterranean and steppe) within its borders.

Almost a third of the country is covered in **trees**, with conifers (Corsican, Scots, Macedonian and white pine, fir, spruce and juniper) predominating in the high mountains of the Pirin, Rila and western Rhodopes, and deciduous trees (oak, beech, hornbeam, elm, ash, hazel and lime) in the Stara planina, Sredna gora and Strandzha. The Rila, Pirin and Rhodopes are especially rich in **wildflowers**, **herbs** and **fungi**, including some species that became extinct elsewhere in Europe centuries ago and others that are unique to Bulgaria, such as *Astragalus physocalyx*, *Glycyrrhiza glabra*, *Haberlea rhodopensis*, *Prunus laurocerasus*, *Ramondia sorbica*, *Rheum rhaponticum* and *Rhododendron ponticum*.

If geology is your passion, Bulgaria is great for **rock formations and minerals**. The Pirin range has some spectacular glacial and karstic features, while the Rhodopes abound in odd rock formations such as the Miraculous Bridges (see p.359), the Stone Wedding and others in the Kûrdzhali region (see p.375); fantastic caves like the Devil's Throat near Trigrad (see p.366); and all kinds of gemstones and crystals. In northern Bulgaria the finest rockscapes are at Belogradchik (see p.193), Vratsa (see p.183), the Iskûr Gorge (see p.182) and outside Sliven (see p.303).

Museums, churches and mosques

Bulgaria's museums and art galleries were quite well provided for by a postwar state eager to instil in its inhabitants a strong sense of history and a pride in national culture. Civic pride comes into it too: every town in the country was determined to display at least some evidence of its contribution to Bulgarian history, whether in the shape of a small archeological museum, a restored nineteenth-century house, or the former home of a famous revolutionary. Religious monuments fared less well: while the most prestigious of them were paraded as examples of Bulgarian achievement, the vast majority were allowed to fall into neglect and disuse. Since 1989, however, Orthodox and Muslim communities have spent a lot of money on returning churches and mosques to their former glory.

Museums

Most towns and cities have a central **History Museum** or *Istoricheski muzei*, (bigger centres will also have an **Archeological Museum**, *Arheoloshki muzei*), designed to showcase the achievements of the ancient Thracians, the medieval Bulgarian empires, and the struggles of the Bulgarian people to overcome Turkish oppression. The style is often didactic, relying on sequences of texts and photographs past which schoolchildren slowly file; English-language translations are extremely rare. In addition, presentation is old-fashioned, and budgetary problems often mean that museums aren't properly lit, but the wealth of Neolithic and Thracian artefacts make a visit worthwhile.

The same may be said of Bulgaria's outstanding **Ethnographic Museums** (*Etnografski muzei*), where rural traditions are faithfully documented with an array of folk costumes and craft implements – although Bulgarian texts explaining their use are rare, and English-language translations virtually nonexistent. Localities of particular ethnographic importance have been preserved, either whole or in part, as **heritage villages** or museum towns (Old Plovdiv, Tryavna, Nesebûr and Sozopol are just four examples). Buildings falling within such an *arhitekturen rezervat* are carefully reconstructed according to traditional building methods, and the best examples of vernacular architecture are often opened to the public as a *Kûshta-muzei*, or **House-Museum**.

Opening hours and entrance fees

The most frustrating aspect of Bulgarian museums is their failure to observe their own **opening hours**. Although the officially advertised working hours of all Bulgaria's tourist attractions are quoted in the Guide, they should always be taken with a pinch of salt. In much of Bulgaria, financial hardships, staff shortages and a general lack of customers ensure that most museums close earlier than posted, take longer lunch breaks, or simply don't bother opening at all. Many museums devoted to historical personalities or important cultural figures may open during the academic year to cater for parties of schoolchildren, before closing their doors over the summer. That said, most of the museums in well-visited places such as Sofia, Plovdiv and Koprivshtitsa can be relied upon to open as advertised. The same applies to museums on the Black Sea coast during the summer season, although things become much more unpredictable from September through to June. Generally speaking, **opening hours** are Tuesday to Sunday, between 8am and noon and from 2pm to 5.30pm, although many work from Monday to Friday and close for the weekend. Big museums in Sofia, Plovdiv and Varna tend to do without the break for lunch, and may stay open until 6 or 7pm during the summer.

Entrance fees for foreigners are higher than those for Bulgarian citizens, but rarely exceed 5Lv unless you're visting a particularly high-profile attraction. A **student card** usually secures reductions. Many museums offer a *beseda* or **guided tour** with commentary for an extra charge, though there's a fairly slim chance of finding an English-speaking member of staff (French or Russian speakers may have better luck).

Cyrillic checklist: museums

History Museum	исторически музей
Ethnographic Museum	етнографски музей
Archeological Museum	археолошки музей
House-Museum	къща-музей
Guided tour	беседа

Churches and monasteries

During the Communist period, **religious buildings** considered to be of particular architectural or cultural importance were removed from church control and taken under the state's wing. Although their transformation into "museums" was at odds with their spiritual purpose, this policy did ensure that large amounts of cash were channelled into their restoration and upkeep. Now that ecclesiastical properties have been returned to the ownership of the Bulgarian Orthodox Church, many historical churches and chapels, previously used as exhibition halls or tourist attractions, have become places of worship again, but lack funds for repairs and can only afford to do the work slowly, which may entail long periods of closure.

Another reason why you'll find the doors of many churches firmly shut is general unease about crime, with many priests fearing for their precious icons and only opening up just before services. The morning liturgy – which commemorates the Last Supper – begins at 8 or 9am, and there may also be an evening service at 5 or 6pm; both usually take about one and a half hours. As Bulgarians often wander in halfway through to savour a few moments of prayer before crossing themselves and departing, you shouldn't feel embarrassed about doing the same. The period between about 4 and 5pm, just before the evening service, tends to be the best time for looking around. There are no hard and fast rules regarding what to wear in a Bulgarian church, although bare arms for females, and bare legs for males, are often regarded as a sign of disrespect.

The gates of **monasteries** tend to be open to all-comers from dawn until dusk. The more famous monasteries, among them Rila, Troyan, Bachkovo and Dryanovo, are used to receiving visitors all year round, and you can wander through the galleried monastery courtyards more or less at will. Some of the smaller foundations, however, will only have a handful of monks or nuns in residence, so you may again discover that churches and chapels within the monastic precinct are locked. Somebody will probably open up, though, if you show persistent interest.

Mosques

Five hundred years of Turkish occupation left Bulgaria with some of the finest **Islamic architecture** in the Balkans. Prestige mosques (such as the *Tombul dzhamiya* in Shumen) were restored and opened to the public by the Communist authorities, but the vast majority suffered as a result of the government's anti-Turkish policies. Many were left to slide into disrepair while others were demolished – especially during the mid-1980s, when the so-called "Regeneration Process" (see p.478) was at its height. Surviving mosques in Muslim areas have now been returned to the Islamic community and many Pomak villages that were formerly forbidden from building their own mosques are now doing so. Outside of purely Muslim areas, mosques are rarely open other than at prayer times due to acts of racist vandalism or the theft of kilims and other valuables, which are spirited across the border to be sold to dealers in Istanbul.

Architecture and etiquette

The basic **layout** of a mosque is a carpet-covered square with a *mihrab* cut into the eastern end facing Mecca; from this niche the *imam* or priest leads the congregation in prayer, the women grouped behind the men on a balcony or behind a low balustrade. Because the Islamic faith prohibits reproduction of the human form, the richest mosques tend to be covered in passages from the Koran and non-figurative decoration of tiles and ornamented plaster. Visitors are allowed in mosques but should observe certain **proprieties**: shoes must be removed before entering, women have to cover their heads, arms and legs, and you may be asked to leave a small donation. Using the Islamic greeting *salaam aleikum* (Peace be upon you) will be appreciated as a courteous gesture, and you should avoid walking in front of someone who is kneeling in prayer, as it is considered very rude.

Police, trouble and sexual harassment

Despite an increase in theft, corruption and mafia-style organized crime over the last fifteen years, Bulgaria still feels an unthreatening country in which to travel, and most tourists will have little or no contact with the Bulgarian police (*Politsiya*, Полиция). However, everyone is required to carry ID at all times, so it's a good idea to keep your passport on you, together with your registration slip, should you have one (see p.37) to satisfy any policeman making a casual check.

There are a few basic common-sense rules to follow if you want to avoid the attention of the Bulgarian police. **Camping rough** is not recommended, and driving with any quantity of **alcohol** in the blood whatsoever is strictly forbidden and carries stiff penalties. Given Bulgaria's position on the overland route to Turkey and beyond, an equal lack of mercy is shown to anyone caught in possession of **drugs**, for whom years in jail are likely.

Most of the negative stories concerning the Bulgarian police relate to **crossing the border** to or from Turkey or Former Yugoslavia, where cops and customs officials are notorious for extorting cash. Over the past couple of years society has become much more aware of the abuses committed by those in uniform, but it will take some time before all the bad habits of the past are abandoned.

Crime and the police

Bulgaria's **crime rate** has mushroomed since the collapse of the totalitarian system, engendering a great deal of fear and insecurity among the law-abiding majority. While mafia killings make headlines, however, small-time thieves are much more likely to pose a hazard to visitors. Again, a few common-sense precautions will help you avoid trouble: display cameras as little as possible, never leave your valuables in your room, and keep large sums of cash in a moneybelt, out of sight. Don't travel without insurance (see p.39), and be sure to make a photocopy of your passport. If you do have anything stolen, go to the police immediately, and get a report detailing the things you've lost.

Petty theft is most widespread on the coast, where the police are so blasé about it that they take an age to fill out a report, and may even demand payment for doing so. The average Black Sea thief isn't only interested in grabbing your money or your camera, but also items of clothing such as trendy T-shirts and replica football kits. In Sofia and Plovdiv, **pickpockets** are more of a problem, especially in the capital at night, around the *Sheraton Hotel*, Central Station and city centre underpasses. When travelling around Bulgaria, don't fall asleep on train journeys and try to book a couchette or sleeper if you're travelling overnight – it's always more secure than the (often unlit) regular carriages. Foreign embassies also advise visitors not to accept any food or drink from strangers in case it is drugged.

Car theft is endemic, with foreign cars and 4WD vehicles particularly sought after. It's always worth paying to park in a guarded lot (*ohranen parking*), and avoid leaving your vehicle on the street unless it's equipped with immobilizers and wheel locks. Never leave anything of value on display, wherever you park. If your car is stolen, the ensuing hassles can take up to a week to sort out. Because details of your car are written into your passport, you can't leave the country without it unless you obtain letters from (in turn) the police, customs and the public prosecutor.

If you're unfortunate enough to be **arrested** yourself, wait until you can explain matters to someone in English if at all possible (misunderstandings in a foreign language can only make things worse), and then request that your **consulate** be notified (see p.120, Sofia "Listings" for addresses). Note that while consulates can be helpful in some respects, they will never lend cash to nationals who've run out or been robbed.

One aspect of Bulgarian crime you're bound to become aware of, but unlikely to be directly affected by, is the growth of mafia-style organizations operating drug-smuggling networks and **protection rackets**. Almost as dangerous are the (outwardly legitimate) insurance and security firms who use hired muscle to enforce their rule. Whether working legally as bodyguards or illegally as mafia heavies, these bodybuilders and ex-sportsmen (known as **bortsi**, or "wrestlers" to the locals) are instantly recognizable from their short-cropped hair, big biceps, mobile phones and fast foreign cars. Their excess of brawn over brain makes them the butt of many jokes, but they are widely resented and feared. Never argue with a *borets*: most people, including the police, are so scared of them that they'll rarely intervene on your behalf.

Sexual harassment

Modern feminism has made few inroads into what is a predominantly patriarchal society, and **women** travelling alone in Bulgaria can expect to encounter stares, comments and sometimes worse from macho types. Reports of women on overnight international trains experiencing harrassment from sleeping-car attendants and other passengers are on the rise, so it's wise to have a travelling companion if at all possible. Generally, however, Bulgarian men tend to be quite gallant, and it's largely the arrogant nouveaux riches who are prone to sexist excesses. Local women deal with unwanted attentions with a firm display of indifference, and this should be enough to cope with most situations – if not, holler *Pomosht!* (Help!) or *Politsiya!*

Directory

Addresses Like everything else in Bulgaria, addresses are normally written in the Cyrillic alphabet. In the text of the Guide, they're transcribed into Roman script according to the system explained in "Language", on p.501. The most common abbreviations are ул. (*ul.*) for "street" (*ulitsa*), пл. (*pl.*) for "square" (*ploshtad*) and, бул. (*bul.*) for *bulevard*, although these designations are omitted altogether when the meaning is clear from the context. In large towns, you also see the abbreviation; ж.к. (zh.k) for "housing estate". The street number of a building is given after the name of the street. Addresses in the high-rise suburbs (*kvartal*, abbreviated to *kv*, кв) include the building number (*blok*, shortened to *bl*, бл), a letter denoting the entrance (*vhod*), Roman numerals signifying the floor (*etazh*), and finally the number of the apartment itself.

Children Many package deals offer child reductions, with the most suitable of the Black Sea destinations for kids being Albena, Golden Sands and Rusalka; elsewhere in Bulgaria don't expect much in the way of child-oriented facilities. While baby food and disposable nappies are available in shops, it's best to bring a supply of your preferred brand. More positively, Bulgarians dote on children, and they are seldom made to feel unwelcome in restaurants or hotels – though few adults see anything amiss in smoking right next to babies.

Cigarettes Tobacco is a major crop in Bulgaria, so smoking is almost a patriotic duty. The range of *tsigari* on offer in street kiosks varies from place to place, so while you can find imported (or counterfeit) Marlboro, Rothmans and Camel on sale in Sofia or Varna for around 3–4Lv a packet, you may have problems getting even Bulgarian brands, such as Victory or Byal Sredets, in the villages. Smoking is theoretically prohibited in public buildings (notably train and bus terminals), and in many self-service restaurants and patisseries, but elsewhere, smokers rule. Matches are called *kibrit*.

Contraceptives Although condoms are available from pharmacies, supermarkets and some street kiosks, you can't always rely on finding your preferred brand – so it's wise to bring some from home. This advice most definitely applies to all other forms of contraception.

Drugs Bulgaria is a major route for narcotics – mostly Turkish heroin, sent overland to Albania and thence by sea to Italy. The effects of this trade on Bulgarian society have been fairly slight so far, but in cities like Plovdiv, Sofia and Varna, drugs are now used to an extent that would have been inconceivable in Communist times. Penalties for possession are extremely severe and Bulgarian prisons are just as bad as in *Midnight Express*, so you would be mad to have anything to do with drugs here.

Electricity 220 volts AC. Round two-pin plugs are used, so bring an adaptor.

Gay life The mere idea of homosexuality raises hackles in what is essentially a conservative and patriarchal society, and whilst gay issues are beginning to be discussed in the media, homosexuals still tend to keep a low profile. While homosexual acts between men over the age of 21 are not officially illegal, there are heavy restrictions on vague things like "scandalous homosexuality" or "homosexual acts leading to perversions" – which basically means that the authorities have the right to arrest you for any homosexual act. Young, urban educated Bulgarians increasingly display tolerance and understanding on issues of sexuality, however, and there's a small but growing number of gay-friendly clubs and bars in Sofia and several other cities. Several Bulgarian gay and lesbian websites have English-language content: Ⓦwww.bulgayria.com is an excellent source of listings information and travel advice, while Ⓦwww.bgogemini.org and Ⓦwww.queer-bulgaria.org are more oriented towards social and campaigning issues.

Laundry Laundrettes (*peralnya*, пералня), let alone dry cleaners (*himichesko chistene*, имическо чистене), are exceedingly rare in Bulgaria, and are usually found in distant suburban housing estates where travellers are unlikely to go. At the larger hotels, it's possible to have cleaning done on the premises, but this can be quite costly. The longer you spend in the country, therefore, the more likely you are to be washing your smalls in the hotel sink.

Left luggage Most train stations have a left-luggage office or *garderob* (гардероб); in the larger towns these will be open 24hr. Bus stations will usually have a *garderob* as well, but opening times are more restricted and staff take more frequent breaks (*pauza* or *pochivka*). To store each item of baggage should cost no more than a few cents.

Naturism was once forbidden on the Black Sea's beaches, and the sight of naked foreigners being bundled into police cars provided frequent amusement for the locals. Topless bathing is now pretty much *de rigueur* among young Bulgarian holiday-makers, and nude sunbathing quite common on the quieter beaches. "Official" nudist beaches are yet to be established, although each Black Sea resort has a stretch of sand where naturism is tolerated. Generally speaking, it's acceptable to strip off anywhere on the coast providing you find a quiet cove, or a relatively isolated stretch of beach situated a discreet distance away from the main family sunbathing areas.

Photographic supplies Internationally known brands of colour print film are widely available in most big towns and along the coast, and a growing number of photo shops will develop films in one or two hours. More specialized items, such as decent black-and-white film, film for transparencies and camera batteries, can be difficult to find outside Sofia, so it's best to stock up before leaving home.

Prostitution Most hotels of three stars or above have prostitutes hanging around the lobby and bar, who proposition solo male travellers. They often work in tandem with thieves and it's not unusual for clients to be mugged or have their room turned over. For drivers, it's worth noting that some motels along the truck routes to Greece and Turkey are little more than bordellos (called *publichen dom*, or "public house" in Bulgarian, should anybody try to warn you off).

Shopping hours Big city shops are generally open Monday to Friday from 8.30am (or earlier) until 6pm (or later, in the case of neighbourhood stores); on Saturdays they close at 2pm. In rural areas and small towns, a kind of unofficial siesta may prevail between noon and 3pm.

Snakes Of the two kinds of poisonous snakes in Bulgaria, the most venomous is the nose-horned viper (*Vipera ammodytes*, locally known as *pepelanka*). Although vipers instinctively shun contact with humans, you should avoid going barefoot, turning over rocks or sticking your hands into dark crevices anywhere off the beaten track.

Superstitions Bulgarians regard putting your handbag on the floor as a sure sign that you'll lose all your money, while seeing a spider in the house or laying out extra cutlery by mistake means that you'll have a guest. When buying flowers for somebody, make certain there's an odd-number of blooms; even-numbered bouquets are for funerals.

Time Two hours ahead of GMT, seven hours ahead of EST. Bulgarian Summer Time lasts from the beginning of April to the end of September.

Toilets Public toilets (*toaletni*, тоалетни) are found at all train stations, most bus stations, and in central parks in towns. They're usually quite appalling, despite the presence of a caretaker or cleaner, to whom you pay a small fee (*taksa*) on entering. Many toilets will clog if you put paper down them, so take the hint if a wastebasket is provided. *Mûzhe* (Мъжеъ or М) are men; *zheni* (Жениъ or Ж) or *dami* (Дами, Д) are women.

Water (*voda*) is safe to drink from all taps and drinking fountains, though bottled mineral water is also widely available.

Guide

Guide

1

Sofia

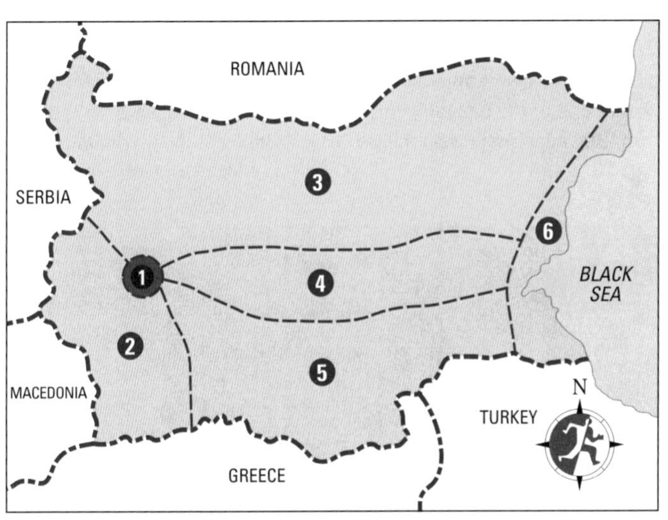

CHAPTER 1 Highlights

* **The Aleksandûr Nevski church** The capital's prime ecclesiastical monument – a magnificent neo-Byzantine confection intended to symbolize Bulgarian–Russian friendship. **See p.101**
* **The National History Museum** An outstanding collection of archeological treasures, and a great introduction to Bulgarian history as a whole. **See p.108**
* **Boyana Church** The vibrant frescoes in this outwardly unassuming structure constitute one of the masterpieces of Bulgarian medieval art. **See p.109**
* **Sofia synagogue** Lovingly restored centrepiece of a recently spruced-up part of pre-World War I Sofia, and a fitting memorial to one of the capital's most historically important communities. **See p.96**
* **Zhenski pazar** A vastly popular central market, where you can pick up everything from fresh vegetables to the kitchen sink. **See p.98**
* **Zlatni mostove** Scramble around the huge boulders of the so-called Stone River, or launch an assault on the Cherni vrûh peak, Mount Vitosha's highest point. **See p.109**

△ Guards of the Presidential Office, Sofia

1

Sofia

According to its motto, **SOFIA** "grows but does not age" (*raste no ne staree*): a tribute to the mushrooming suburbs occupied by one-tenth of Bulgaria's population, and a cryptic reference to its ancient origins. Although various Byzantine ruins and a couple of mosques attest to a long and colourful history, little else in the city is of any real vintage. Sofia's finest architecture post-dates Bulgaria's liberation, when the capital of the infant state was laid out on a grid pattern in imitation of Western capitals – although the peeling stucco of its turn-of-the-twentieth-century buildings lends an air of dilapidation to the capital's wide, tree-shaded boulevards.

Cyrillic place names

Sofia	СОФИЯ
Aleko	АЛЕКО
Boyana	БОЯНА
Dragalevtsi	ДРАГАЛЕВЦИ
Kremikovtsi	КРЕМИКОВЦИ
Simeonovo	СИМЕОНОВО
Vitosha	ВИТОША
Zlatni mostove	ЗЛАТНИ МОСТОВЕ
Bul. Knyaginya Mariya Luiza	БУЛ. КНЯГИНЯ МАРИЯ ЛУИЗА
Bul. Stamboliiski	БУЛ. СТАМБОЛИИСКИ
Bul. Tsar Osvoboditel	БУЛ. ЦАР ОСВОБОДИТЕЛ
Bul. Vitosha	БУЛ. ВИТОША
Ploshtad Sveta Nedelya	ПЛОЩАД СВЕТА НЕДЕЛЯ
Ploshtad Aleksandûr	ПЛОЩАД АЛЕКСАНДЪР
Batenberg	БАТЕНБЕРГ
The Largo	ЛАРГОТО
Tsentralna Gara	ЦЕНТРАЛНА ГАРА
Ul. G. S. Rakovski	УЛ. Г. С. РАКОВСКИ
Bul. Aleksandrov	БУЛ. АЛЕКСАНДРОВ
Ul. Pirotska	УЛ. ПИРОТСКА
Ploshtad Narodno Sûbranie	ПЛОЩАД НАРОДНО СЪБРАНИЕ
Ploshtad Aleksandûr Nevski	ПЛОЩАД АЛЕКСАНДЪР НЕВСКИ
Ul. Graf Ignatiev	УЛ. ГРАФ ИГНАТИЕВ
Avtogara Sofia	АВТОГАРА СОФИЯ
Avtogara Poduyane	АВТОГАРА ПОДУЯНЕ
Avtogara Ovcha Kupel	АВТОГАРА ОВЧА КУПЕЛ
Avtogara Yug	АВТОГАРА ЮГ

The mixture of chaos and decay which characterizes most of Sofia's points of arrival makes it an unwelcoming city for first-time visitors. However once you've settled in and begun to explore, you'll find Sofia surprisingly laid-back for a capital city. Hardly a great European metropolis brimming with fine sights, the place comes into its own on fine spring and summer days, when the downtown streets and their pavement cafés begin to buzz with life. The close historical relationship between Bulgaria and Russia reveals itself in the capital's public buildings, foremost of which is the **Aleksandûr Nevski church**, a magnificent Byzantine–Muscovite confection. The neighbouring streets harbour a modest collection of museums and galleries – enough to justify a day or two's sightseeing. Urban pursuits can be easily combined with the outdoor recreational possibilities offered by verdant **Mount Vitosha**, just 12km south of the centre. Also on the fringes of the city, the medieval frescoes at the **Boyana Church** and **Kremikovtsi monastery** make essential viewing for anyone interested in Orthodox art. Sightseeing apart, things can seem low-key here for those with sophisticated cosmopolitan tastes: entertainment for many in Sofia still revolves around an evening promenade in one of the city's parks, followed by a coffee in a nearby café, and haute cuisine

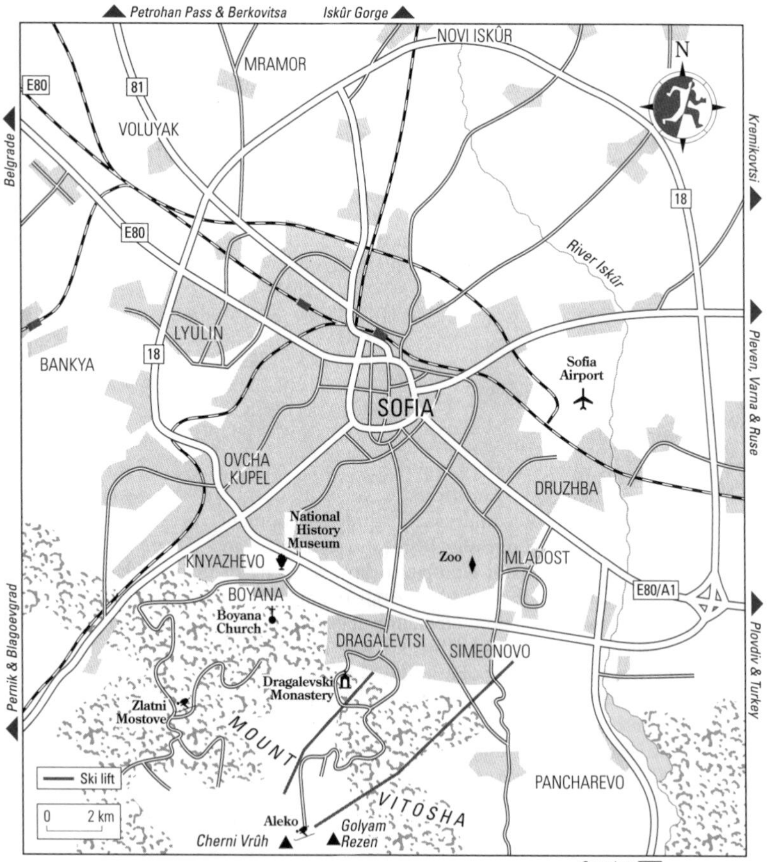

has never been one of Bulgaria's fortes. Nightlife is improving, however, with a host of new bars and clubs giving the city a raw, hedonistic edge on spring and summer nights – plus there's lots of drama and serious music, especially during the **Sofia Music Weeks**, which take place each June.

Some history

Sofia's first inhabitants were the **Serdi**, a Thracian tribe who settled here some 3000 years ago. Their Roman conquerors named it Serdica, a walled city that reached its zenith under Emperor Constantine in the early fourth century AD. Serdica owed its importance to the position it occupied on the *diagonis*, the Roman road that linked Constantinople with modern Belgrade on the Danube, providing the Balkans with its main commercial and strategic artery. However, the empire's foes also used the road as a quick route to the riches of Constantinople, and Serdica was frequently under attack – most notably from the Huns, who sacked the city in the fifth century. Once rebuilt by the emperor Justinian, Serdica became one of the Byzantine Empire's most important strongpoints in the Balkans.

Migrating Slavs began to filter into the city in the seventh century, becoming the dominant force in the region after Serdica's capture by the Bulgar Khan Krum in 809. The city continued to flourish under the Bulgarians, although few medieval cultural monuments remain, save for the thirteenth-century **Boyana Church**. Renamed Sredets by the Slavs (and subsequently Triaditsa by the Byzantines), the city became known as Sofia sometime in the fourteenth century, most probably taking its name from the ancient **Church of Sveta Sofia** (Holy Wisdom) which still stands in the city centre. Five centuries of Ottoman rule began with the city's capture in 1382, during which time Sofia thrived as a market centre, though little material evidence of the Ottoman period remains save for a couple of **mosques**.

Economic decline set in during the nineteenth century, hastened by earthquakes in 1852. Sofia was a minor provincial centre at the time of the Liberation in 1878, when defeat of the Ottoman Empire by Russian forces paved the way for the foundation of an independent Bulgarian state. Sofia was chosen to become the new capital of the country in preference to more prestigious centres (such as Tûrnovo in central Bulgaria) because of its geographical location: situated on a wide plain fringed by mountains, Sofia combined defensibility with the potential for future growth. It was also thought that it would occupy a central position in any Bulgarian state which included (as was then hoped) Macedonia. The Bulgarians were keen to stamp their identity on the city right at the outset. Mosques were demolished or turned to other uses, and 6000 of the city's Turks chose to emigrate. Sofia underwent rapid development after 1878, although progress sometimes sat uneasily beside backwardness and poverty. The Czech historian and educationalist Konstantin Jireček – one of many foreign experts brought in to help run the new state – dubbed Sofia *boklukopolis* ("trashville") in recognition of its chaotic post-Liberation appearance. However foreign observers were on the whole impressed by the way in which the Bulgarians speedily improvised a capital city out of nothing. "I had expected a semi-barbaric Eastern town," remarked Frank Cox, the *Morning Post*'s Balkan correspondent in 1913, "but I found a modern capital, small but orderly, clean and well-managed . . . but oh, so deadly dull." Despite its increasing prosperity, Sofia didn't experience much of a *belle époque*, save for the lavish palace balls presided over by the mercurial Tsar Ferdinand, and the weekly dances at the military club.

The city experienced more frenetic growth during the post-World War II era of "socialist construction", and a veneer of Stalinist monumentalism was added to the city centre in the shape of buildings like the **Party House**, a stern-looking expression of political authority. Sofia's rising population was housed in the endless high-rise suburbs (places with declamatory names like Mladost – "Youth", Druzhba – "Friendship", and Nadezhda – "Hope") that girdle the city today.

The factories that used to employ the inhabitants of these suburbs went into a steep decline during the 1980s and collapsed totally in the 1990s, leading to high unemployment and a drop in living standards. However Sofia has coped with the transition from Communism to capitalism better than most Bulgarian towns. New businesses are springing up all the time (though many go bust just as quickly), jobs are easier to come by here than elsewhere, and the population has been swelled by migrants from provincial towns blighted by economic stagnation. Sofia's city council has made small but significant steps in turning the capital into a city fit for EU membership (an event which is expected to transpire some time before the end of the decade), re-paving central sidewalks and providing key central buildings with a much-needed facelift. Even so, much about contemporary Sofia remains strange or surprising: walking through the quiet, under-lit streets at night often makes you feel as if you're in a small provincial town rather than a million-strong urban sprawl. No less unsettling to the first-time visitor is the visible presence of a large stray **dog** population in Sofia's downtown streets. Nobody knows how many of these beasts are currently roaming the city – estimates range from 30,000 to 50,000. Although

The Shops

The majority of Sofia's inhabitants are of **Shop descent** – the Shops being the original peasant population from the surrounding countryside who have migrated to the city in vast numbers over the past hundred years. Although you can still tell a Shop by his or her accent, which is flatter than standard Bulgarian – they say *desno* instead of *dyasno* for "right", *levo* instead of *lyavo* for "left" – the other ethnographic features that made them a distinct group a century ago have now all but disappeared.

At the time of the Liberation many Shops – especially those living around the foothills of Mount Vitosha – still lived in an extended family community known as a **zadruga**, an arrangement once common to the entire South Slav area. In a zadruga, several married brothers and cousins pooled their lands and lived together under the rule of a *domovladika* (literally "head of the household"), who would apportion tasks and look after the accounts. *Zadruga* members tended to specialize in different jobs (one may be a miller, one an innkeeper, another a priest, and so on) in order to keep the community self-sufficient. The growth of Sofia disrupted the traditional rural economy, signalling the end of the *zadruga* system. It was perhaps the sudden impact of urbanization that earned the Shops a reputation for being the nation's heaviest drinkers. Writing in the 1880s, the Czech observer Konstantin Jireček remarked that "Sofia is the one area of the country where you can actually see drunken Bulgarians on a regular basis". Indeed the expression "to drink like in Sofia" was in common use in late nineteenth-century Bulgaria.

Some of the villages around Sofia still preserve age-old **Shop Lenten customs**. Voluyak, 10km northwest of Sofia on the Berkovitsa road, still celebrates the Dzhamala festival (forty days before Easter on odd-numbered years), when a camel (actually a wooden sled dressed in skins) is hauled through the streets before being symbolically killed and returned to life again, in what is essentially a Dionysiac death-and-rebirth ritual of ancient origins. The neighbouring village of Mramor is the Sofia district's main centre for celebrations linked with Todorovden (St Theodore's day, the first Saturday of Lent), when people from all over the Shop area congregate – usually bringing their horses and carts – for a day of feasting and carousing.

pretty docile during the day, the dog packs become territorial at night, when lone pedestrians can become the victims of massed barking, or worse. Potentially more dangerous, however, are the four-legged brutes acquired by suburban Sofians to act as guard dogs or status symbols.

Arrival

Sofia airport, 10km east of town, is connected to the centre by bus #84 (every 15-20min), which runs to Orlov most (see p.105); or the much more unpredictable minibus #30, which drops off outside the Tzum shopping mall (see p.95). On leaving the international arrivals terminal, head to the right for about 100m to find the **bus stop**, where there's also a small kiosk selling tickets for the bus (see p.84) – if you're catching the minibus you must pay the driver direct. Both buses run between about 7am and 11pm.

Riding into town with a reputable **taxi** firm such as OK Supertrans shouldn't set you back more than 12-15Lv, although unscrupulous drivers may charge unsuspecting foreigners two or three times that amount. Uttering the odd word of Bulgarian or appearing to know where you're going always helps.

By train

Trains arrive at the Central Station (*Tsentralna gara*), a concrete barn twenty minutes' walk north of the city centre. Trams #1 and #7 will take you from the station forecourt to ploshtad Sveta Nedelya, within easy reach of accommodation bureaux, central hotels and the important sights. The station is a target for wide boys and pickpockets at night, so you'd be well advised to book into accommodation rather than attempting to sleep rough in the waiting rooms. For details on **leaving Sofia by train**, see "Moving on from Sofia" on p.120.

By bus

Most inter-city services arrive at the brand-new **Tsentralna Avtogara** just east of the Central Station on bulevard Knyaginya Mariya Luiza. However several services from provincial towns still use a ring of smaller bus stations in the suburbs: some buses from points north and northeast of Sofia use the **Avtogara Poduyane** (sometimes referred to as Avtogara Iztok) terminal on ulitsa Todorini Kukli (bus #75 runs from here to Orlov most; otherwise head one block north from the station and cross to the opposite side of bulevard Vladimir Vazov to catch trolleybus #1 to bul. Vasil Levski); buses from the southwest use **Ovcha Kupel**, halfway down bulevard Tsar Boris III (take tram #5 to the Palace of Justice or *Sûdebna palata* in the city centre, or tram #19 to the Central Station); buses from the southeast use the **Yug** terminal, on bulevard Dragan Tsankov, beneath the overpass known as Nadlez Dûrvenitsa just beyond the *Hotel Moskva* (tram #2 takes you from Nadlez Dûrvenitsa to the central ul. Graf Ignatiev).

International services either use the Tsentralna Avtogara or the Trafik-Market bus park in front of the Central Station. For details on **leaving Sofia by bus**, see p.120.

Information

Getting official information about Sofia can be difficult. The **National Information and Publicity Centre**, at pl. Sveta Nedelya 1 (*Tsentûr za* *natsionalna informatsiya i reklama*; Mon–Fri 9am–5pm; ⓣ02/987 9778, ⓦwww.bulgariatravel.org), doesn't always have the answers to specific queries about the capital, though the staff are English-speaking and friendly. They also have a limited amount of information and brochures on other parts of Bulgaria. More useful is the commercial travel agent **Zig Zag Odysseia-in**, bul. Stamboliiski 20 (entrance round the corner on ul. Lavele; Mon–Fri 9am–6.30pm, plus Sat & Sun in summer 9am–5pm; ⓣ02/980 5102, ⓦwww.zigzag.dir.bg), which specializes in independent travel, and offers accommodation bookings in Sofia and throughout Bulgaria, advice on rural tourism and hiking, and has a good selection of maps for sale. Staff charge a hefty 5Lv consultation fee, but this is deducted from the price of any accommodation you book through them.

You'll find several reasonable **city maps**, most featuring public transport routes, on sale at newsstands and street stalls. For **listings**, the monthly English-language brochure *Sofia City Info Guide* (free from big hotels – try the lobby of the *Sheraton* if you can't find one elsewhere; or available online at ⓦwww.sofiacityguide.com) has comprehensive details of what's on in town as well as advice for new arrivals in the city. There's also a weekly English-language **newspaper**, the increasingly authoritative *Sofia Echo* (ⓦwww.sofiaecho.com; available from central newsstands), which offers good cultural listings as well as up-to-date coverage of Bulgarian politics and business news.

City transport

Sofia is a surprisingly well-organized city when it comes to **getting about**. An extensive bus, trolleybus and tram network extends to just about everywhere you're likely to want to go, and inexpensive taxis fill the gaps. **Public transport** is cheap and reasonably efficient, with intertwining networks of buses (*avtobus*), trolleybuses (*troleibus*) and trams (*tramvai*). Some cross-town routes are operated by privately owned **minibuses** (*marshrutki*), which are faster than regular buses. A single **metro line** runs from central Sofia to the western suburb of Lyulin – but as no hotels or tourist attractions lie along its route, you're unlikely to use it. Most services run from about 4am until 11.30pm.

The main problem for visitors, however, is lack of information: while some bus and tram stops are well marked, others are merely corroded metal poles displaying no information about which services call there or how often. Always be prepared to ask the locals, and buy a good city map if possible.

There's a flat fare on all urban routes (currently 0.50Lv), and **tickets** (*bileti*) for buses, trolleys and trams can be bought from street kiosks or, sometimes, from the driver. All tickets must be punched on board the vehicle: inspections are frequent and there are spot fines for fare-dodgers. Officially, you're supposed to buy an extra ticket for each large item of baggage, but in practice this is rarely enforced – except on buses to and from the airport, where inspectors deliberately pick on foreigners on the grounds that they're less likely than the locals to put up an argument. If you're staying in Sofia any length of time, a one-day ticket (*karta za edin den*; 2Lv) or a five-day ticket (*karta za pet dena*; 10Lv) is a sound investment, but can only be bought from kiosks. Tickets are not valid in minibuses, for which you must pay the driver (around 0.50Lv flat fare).

Taxis aren't particularly expensive, charging the equivalent of 0.30-0.40Lv per km until 10pm, 0.50-0.60Lv per km after that. There's a taxi rank at the northern end of bulevard Vitosha; otherwise vehicles hang around at most big intersections. You can order them by phone (try OK Supertrans ⓣ02/973 2121), but don't expect to get through to an English-speaker. Sofia taxi drivers don't always have a detailed knowledge of their own city, and clients are usually expected to supply directions themselves. The overcharging of foreigners is fairly endemic, and there's little you can do to prevent this except check that meters are working and be firm with obvious transgressors. It's a good idea to stick to reputable firms like OK Supertrans, though if you're staying in Sofia for any length of time you're unlikely to escape without being ripped off at least once.

Accommodation

In general, you'll find yourself paying more in Sofia than elsewhere in the country for a decent place to stay, with the majority of the high-rise socialist-era **hotels** charging rates out of proportion to the level of service they provide. The number of establishments offering international business standards, however, is on the increase, and prices are comparable with those in Western Europe. There's also a number of small **family-run pensions**, offering comfortable rooms at reasonable prices, in the city centre, and they're very well established in outlying village suburbs like Simeonovo and Dragalevtsi. The emergence of a new breed of privately run, backpacker-friendly **hostels** has widened the range of accommodation available to budget travellers. The Zig-Zag/Odysseia-In agency (see opposite) can organize beds in cheap hotels and hostels; it also has its own two- or three-person apartment (❸).

A **private room** is still one of the best-value ways of getting a place close to the action, although the quality of accommodation varies considerably. Rooms are usually clean, but often the decor hasn't changed since the 1950s. Centrally located private rooms can be booked through Almatour, bul. Stamboliiski 27 (Mon–Fri 9am–5pm, Sat 9am–4pm; ⓣ02/986 5691, ⓦwww.almatour.net) for 40Lv a double (32Lv for single occupancy), with reductions for stays of longer than three nights. Best of the smaller agencies is the Markela bureau, ul. Ekzarh Yosif 35 (Mon–Fri 9am–5pm; ⓣ02/980 4925, ⓦwww.markela.hit.bg), which has doubles for 39Lv, singles for 27Lv.

With the Vrana campsite 10km east of town on the main Plovdiv road increasingly gone to seed, **camping** isn't really an option.

Hostels

Hostels are a relatively new phenomenon in Sofia, and none of those listed below have been around long enough to be regarded as permanent fixtures – try and ring in advance before turning up. All are located in converted apartment buildings and staying in one can feel a bit like crashing at a friend's flat. Accommodating places on the whole, they can fill up quickly in summer, putting pressure on both staff and facilities.

Hostel Mostel ul. Denkoglu 2 ⓣ0889 223 296 or 0888 643 294, ⓦwww.hostelmostel.com. Welcoming place with pastel decor, offering bright six- to ten-person dorms with pine bunks and plenty of locker space, plus double rooms in a nearby apartment block. Kitchen, washing machine, reasonably large social area and a generous breakfast. Dorms 20Lv per person, floor space 10Lv (breakfast not included), doubles ❸

Hostel Sofia ul. Pozitano 16 ⓣ02/989 8582, ⓔhostelsofia@yahoo.com. Cramped but cosy place housed on the second storey of a downtown apartment building. Friendly staff, free use of kitchen, and breakfast included. Book in advance if you can. 18Lv per person; reductions for stays longer than two nights.

Kervan ul. Rositsa 3 ⓣ02/983 9428 or 0888 374 369, ⓦwww.kervanhostel.com. North of the

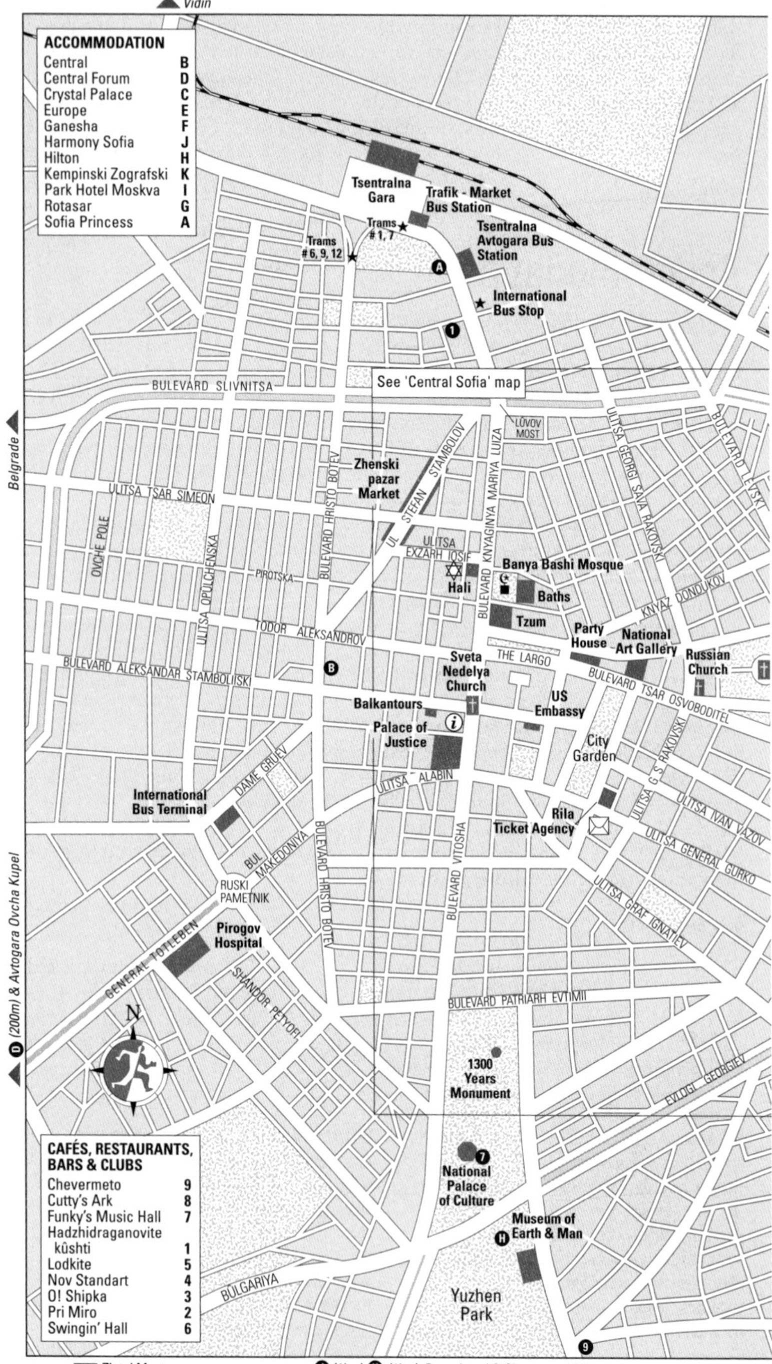
Vidin
ACCOMMODATION
Central B
Central Forum D
Crystal Palace C
Europe E
Ganesha F
Harmony Sofia J
Hilton H
Kempinski Zografski K
Park Hotel Moskva I
Rotasar G
Sofia Princess A
Tsentralna Gara
Trafik - Market Bus Station
Trams # 1, 7
Trams # 6, 9, 12
Tsentralna Avtogara Bus Station
International Bus Stop
See 'Central Sofia' map
BULEVARD SLIVNITSA
LŬVOV MOST
Belgrade
ULITSA GEORGI SAVA RAKOVSKI
BULEVARD LEVSKI
Zhenski pazar Market
UL. STEFAN STAMBOLOV
BULEVARD KNYAGINYA MARIYA LUIZA
ULITSA TSAR SIMEON
OVCHE POLE
ULITSA OPULCHENSKA
BULEVARD HRISTO BOTEV
PIROTSKA
ULITSA EXZARH IOSIF
Hali
Banya Bashi Mosque
Baths
Tzum
KNYAZ DONDUKOV
TODOR ALEKSANDROV
BULEVARD ALEKSANDAR STAMBOLIISKI
Party House
National Art Gallery
Russian Church
Sveta Nedelya Church
THE LARGO
BULEVARD TSAR OSVOBODITEL
US Embassy
Balkantours
Palace of Justice
City Garden
ULITSA G. S. RAKOVSKI
DAME GRUEV
ULITSA ALABIN
International Bus Terminal
Rila Ticket Agency
ULITSA IVAN VAZOV
ULITSA GENERAL GURKO
BUL MAKEDONIYA
BULEVARD VITOSHA
RUSKI PAMETNIK
ULITSA GRAF IGNATIEV
Pirogov Hospital
GENERAL TOTLEBEN
SHANDOR PETYOFI
BULEVARD PATRIARH EVTIMII
D (200m) & Avtogara Ovcha Kupel
N
1300 Years Monument
EVLOGI GEORGIEV
CAFÉS, RESTAURANTS, BARS & CLUBS
Chevermeto 9
Cutty's Ark 8
Funky's Music Hall 7
Hadzhidraganovite kûshti 1
Lodkite 5
Nov Standart 4
O! Shipka 3
Pri Miro 2
Swingin' Hall 6
National Palace of Culture
Museum of Earth & Man
BULGARIYA
Yuzhen Park
Zlatni Mostove
J (1km), K (1km), Dragalevtsi & Simeonovo

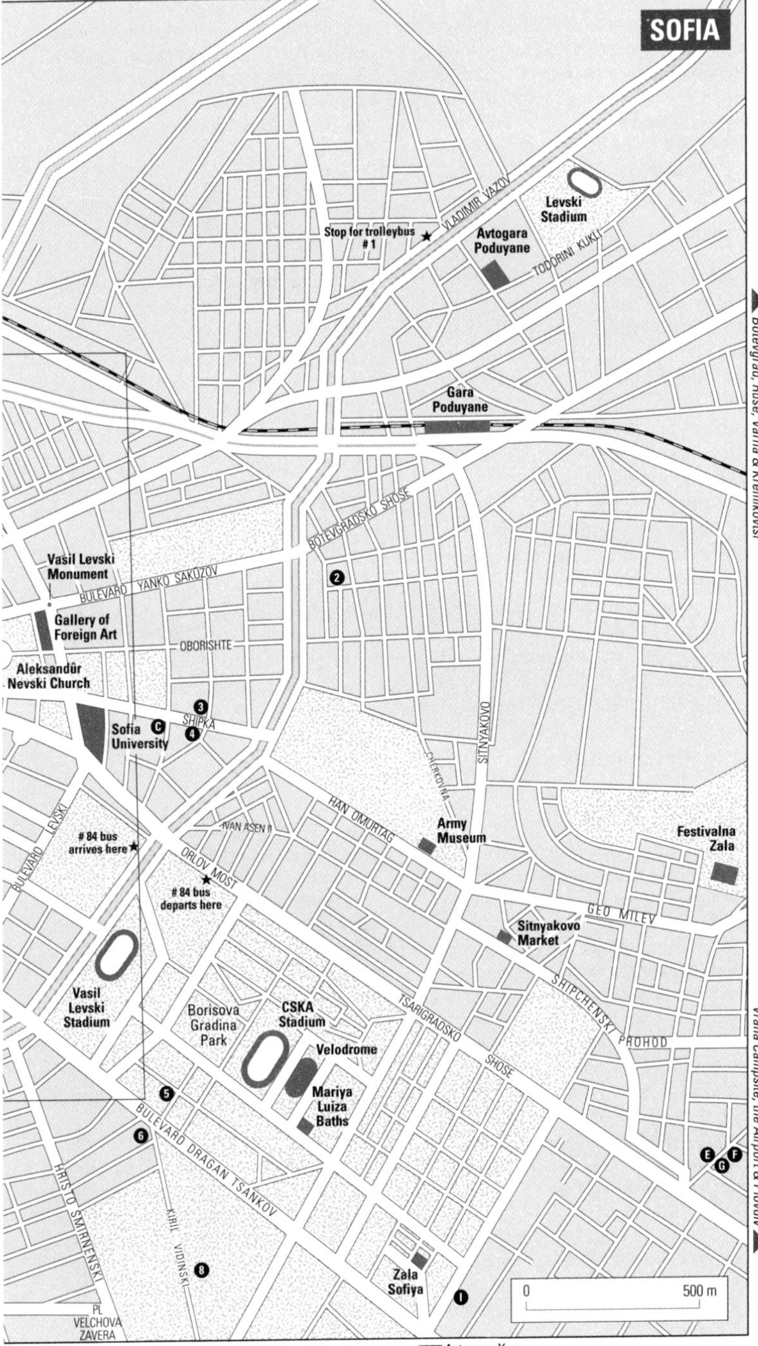
SOFIA
Stop for trolleybus # 1
VLADIMIR VAZOV
Avtogara Poduyane
Levski Stadium
TODORINI KUKLI
Gara Poduyane
BOTEVGRADSKO SHOSE
Vasil Levski Monument
BULEVARD YANKO SAKŬZOV
Gallery of Foreign Art
OBORISHTE
Aleksandŭr Nevski Church
SHIPKA
Sofia University
CHERKOVNA
SITNYAKOVO
HAN OMURTAG
IVAN ASEN II
Army Museum
Festivalna Zala
BULEVARD LEVSKI
84 bus arrives here
ORLOV MOST
84 bus departs here
GEO MILEV
Sitnyakovo Market
SHIPCHENSKI PROHOD
Vasil Levski Stadium
Borisova Gradina Park
CSKA Stadium
Velodrome
TSARIGRADSKO SHOSE
Mariya Luiza Baths
BULEVARD DRAGAN TSANKOV
HRISTO SMIRNENSKI
KIRIL VIDINSKI
Zala Sofiya
PL VELCHOVA ZAVERA
0
500 m
Zoo
Avtogara Yug
Botevgrad, Ruse, Varna & Kremikovtsi
Vrana Campsite, the Airport & Plovdiv

Aleksandûr Nevski church, a thoughtfully decorated place with hardwood floors and warm textiles, with six-bed dorms and double rooms. Very small kitchen and breakfast area. Laundry service for a few extra leva. Dorms 20Lv per person, doubles ❸

Usually We Spend Our Time In The Garden (aka "Art Hostel") ul. Angel Kûnchev 21A ⓣ02/987 0545, ⓦwww.art-hostel.com. Easy-going hostel complete with art gallery, chill-out room, resident DJs, film projections – and a relaxing garden. Only fourteen beds so ring in advance. Traditional Bulgarian yoghurt-and-pastry breakfast included, and kitchen available. 20Lv per person.

Hotels

Your choice of **hotel** will depend a great deal on how much you are prepared to pay in order to be near the heart of things. Places within walking distance of the centre tend to charge Western European prices without offering anything like the same degree of service, and budget alternatives are usually best avoided: the cheap hotels between the train station and the city centre are, for the most part, little more than seedy flop houses renting out rooms by the hour. The smaller family-run hotels tend to be comfortable and moderately priced, but they have limited space and can fill up quickly, so it's advisable to make **reservations** in advance.

Many of the best family-run establishments are in the southern village–suburbs of **Simeonovo** and **Dragalevtsi**. Neither village is particularly attractive, and the journey into central Sofia by public transport involves at least one change. However, they do provide easy access to Mount Vitosha, and the hotels here offer good standards of comfort and service at prices which compare favourably to those in central Sofia. To get to Simeonovo, take tram #2 or #19 to Velchova Zavera (the first stop after emerging from the park), then take bus #67 to the end of the line; otherwise catch tram #12 to the Hladilnika terminus, followed by bus #98. Dragalevtsi can be reached by taking tram #12 to Hladilnika, then bus #93 or #98. For Vladaya, south of town on the main Pernik road, you'll need your own transport.

Central Sofia

Art'Otel ul. Gladston 44 ⓣ02/980 6000. Comfortable downtown three-star with modern fittings and thick carpets, although rooms have showers not bathtubs, and – despite the name – there's no art on display that you would tolerate in your own living room. Ask for a north-facing room with a balcony and you'll get excellent city-centre views. ❼

Baldzhieva ul. Tsar Asen 23 ⓣ02/981 1257 or 987 2914. Relatively small, privately owned hotel in a nicely refurbished town house just one block west of bul. Vitosha. Some rooms have old-style brown colour schemes and slightly worn furnishings, others have bright new decor and a/c. All come with shower and TV. ❻

Balkan Sheraton pl. Sveta Nedelya 5 ⓣ02/981 6541, ⓔsofia.sheraton@luxurycollection.com. Dependable five-star occupying a prime site on the city's central square. Pretty much what you would expect from the chain, this is a long-standing favourite with the business community. The *Sheraton*'s two restaurants are consistently given high marks by Bulgarian food critics. ❾

Central Forum bul. Tsar Boris III 41 ⓣ02/981 2364, ⓦhttp://central-hotel.com. Socialist-era concrete-lump hotel nicely renovated to make a comfortable business choice. Regular rooms are small but very amenable with TV, a/c, modern shower and even (teabag-toting Brits take note) an electric kettle. Pricier "luxe" rooms have bathtubs, and there are also some two-room suites. ❽

Crystal Palace ul. Shipka 14 ⓣ02/948 9489, ⓦwww.crystalpalace-sofia.com. Upscale, chintzy five-star in an old Art-Nouveau town house enhanced (some would say desecrated) with contemporary glass-and-steel additions. Located in a leafy street behind the university – one of Sofia's most desirable residential areas. Doubles from €180. ❾

Grand Hotel Sofia ul. General Gurko 1 ⓣ02/811 0800, ⓦwww.grandhotelsofia.bg. Superbly central five-star with liveried doormen, fully equipped, spacious rooms decked out in chintz, and a gym and a sauna on site. Doubles from €170. ❾

Hilton bul. Bûlgariya 1 ⓣ02/933 5000, ⓦwww.hilton.com. High standards of service and comfort, within walkable distance of the town centre, located just behind the National Palace of Culture (NDK). Indoor pool on site. Ask about weekend discounts. Doubles from €200. ❾

Iskûr ul. Iskûr 11B ⓣ02/986 6750, ⓔhoteliskar@dir.bg. Unpretentious downtown hotel with a nice family-run feel. Most rooms come with en-suite shower and TV although there are a few cheaper ones with shared facilities. Breakfast costs extra. ❸–❹

Light ul. Veslets 37 ⓣ02/917 9090 or 917 9013, ⓦwww.hotellight.com. Modern building in a relatively quiet, cobbled street a stone's throw from the centre. Contemporary design-showroom furnishings provide a welcome dash of style. ❽

Maya ul. Trapezitsa 4 ⓣ02/989 4611. Small family-run pension on the second floor of an apartment block opposite the Largo. There's only a handful of rooms, but they're spacious affairs with settees, fridge and cable TV. ❹

Niky ul. Neofit Rilski 16 ⓣ02/952 3058, ⓔniky-92@internet-bg.net. Totally renovated place in a converted apartment block just off the main bul. Vitosha. Basic doubles are small but neat and tidy with modern showers and a/c; bigger apartment-style rooms have a kitchenette and en-suite bath. ❻–❽

Pop Bogomil ul. Pop Bogomil 5 ⓣ02/903 7865, ⓔhotelpopbogomil@dir.bg. Friendly family-run place on a quiet downtown street. Rooms are small and loudly decorated but otherwise neat and cosy with modern fittings and TV, some with bathtubs, others with shower. Generous breakfast for a few extra leva. ❸

Radisson SAS pl. Narodno Sûbranie 4 ⓣ02/933 4334, ⓦwww.sofia.radissonsas.com. Modern hotel opposite the Bulgarian National Assembly, offering comfortable business-standard rooms, many boasting excellent views of the square. Decent if expensive top-floor restaurant. Doubles from €200. ❾

Slavyanska Beseda ul. Slavyanska 3 ⓣ02/980 1303, ⓕ981 2523. Tolerable mid-range choice, well placed for central Sofia's major sights, but lacking in both character and attentive staff. Worth considering if other places in this price category are full. ❻

Sofia Princess bul. Knyaginya Mariya Luiza 131 ⓣ02/933 8888. Six-hundred-room high-rise located near the main train and bus stations – hardly an upmarket area of town, but an easy walk into the centre. Rooms are decorated to four-star standard but it's the hugely popular hotel casino that's the main attraction. ❽

Sveta Sofia ul. Pirotska 18 ⓣ02/981 2634 or 983 5033, ⓦwww.svetasofia-alexanders.com. Converted nineteenth-century town house on a busy pedestrianized shopping street, offering small but welcoming rooms with contemporary furnishings, neutral colours and showers – "luxe" rooms with bath cost extra. It's noisy at weekends due to wedding parties. ❺

Outside the centre

Europe ul. Liditse 1 ⓣ02/970 1500, ⓦwww.hotel-europe-bg. Modern, medium-sized hotel in the Geo Milev quarter, 4km southeast of the centre and conveniently placed for the southern end of the Borisova gradina park. Rooms feature relaxing lemony-orange decor with TV, minibar, a/c and shower. Take bus #213 or #313 from the train station, or bus #84 from the airport, and get off at the *Hotel Pliska* stop. ❼

Ganesha ul. Al. Humboldt 26 ⓣ02/971 3815, ⓦwww.hotelganesha-bg.com. A converted apartment block on a suburban street, midway between the city centre and the airport. The neat rooms have en-suite shower, satellite TV and a small balcony. Directions as for the *Europe*. ❹

Harmony Sofia bul. Arsenalski 4 ⓣ02/866 1261, ⓦwww.hotels-harmony.com. Small and intimate hotel with tidy modern rooms, all with en-suite shower, minibar and satellite TV. There's a covered swimming pool next door, and the city centre is a dull but unstrenuous twenty-minute walk away. Tram #6 from the Central Station or the NDK to the end of the line. ❻

Kempinski Zografski bul. Dzheims Bauchûr 100 ⓣ02/969 2222, ⓦwww.kempinski.bg. Decent high-rise business choice, featuring a multitude of restaurants and sports facilities. The only drawback is that it's 2.5km south of the centre. In 1980, Pope John Paul II's would-be assassin, Mehmet Ali Agca, stayed in room 911 under the name of "Yogander Singh". Take tram #12 from the Central Station or ul. Graf Ignatiev. Doubles from €170. ❾

Park Hotel Moskva ul. Nezabravka 25 ⓣ02/971 1024, ⓦwww.parkhotelmoskva.com. Old-fashioned, socialist-era high-rise affair much patronized by tour groups. Nice wooded location on the fringes of

Borisova gradina, 4km southeast of the centre. Tram #2 from pl. Sveta Nedelya. ❻

Rotasar ul. Lidice 1 ⓣ02/971 4571, ⓔsarhotel@technolink.com. Smallish suburban hotel with an intimate ambience, 4km southeast of the centre. Rooms are decked out in warm reds and blues, all with fridge, TV and a/c. Some come with shower, others with bathtub. There are a couple of three- to four-person suites suitable for families or groups. Directions as for the *Europe*. ❹

Simeonovo and Dragalevtsi

Accommodation in Simeonovo and Dragalevtsi is marked on the map on p.110.

Atlantik ul. 19-ta 2 ⓣ02/961 3400, ⓕ961 2132. Large modern hotel adorned with mock castle towers. All rooms come with comfortable furnishings, small but clean bathrooms and TV. Breakfast included. There's a restaurant on the top floor with panoramic views of the city below. ❺

Castle Hrankov ul. Krusheva Gradina 33 ⓣ02/948 9489, ⓔcastle_hrankov@yahoo.com. Modern hotel complete with medieval-style turrets just off the main road from Dragalevtsi to Simeonovo. Notorious bastion of nouveau-riche luxury – Hollywood movie stars filming at the nearby Boyana cinema studios usually stay here. Indoor and outdoor pools. ❼

Darling ul. Yabûlkova Gradina 14 ⓣ02/967 5018. Ten-room pension in an angular modern house, just east of the village square. Neat, bright en-suites with satelliteTV, some with tiny balconies. Breakfast costs a few leva extra. ❸

Jasmin Simeonovsko shose 126 ⓣ02/969 8555, ⓦwww.jasminhotel.com. Family-run place occupying a pair of buildings straddling the main road into Simeonovo, with a small open-air swimming pool and en-suite rooms, all with satellite TV. Breakfast is included in the price, and there's a good restaurant attached. ❺

Traders ul. Bozhur 18 ⓣ02/961 3407 or 961 3408. Large, new and very plush hotel with bright modern rooms, each with bath, TV and fridge. Breakfast included. ❺

The City

The heart of Sofia fits compactly within the irregular octagon formed by the city's inner ring road. Most of the sights are found inside this **central area** within easy walking distance of each other, and the grid-like pattern of streets radiating outwards from the main point of reference, **ploshtad Sveta Nedelya**, makes orientation relatively easy. It's a good idea to sample the area around Sveta Nedelya first, before embarking on a trip to the set-piece **public buildings** and **squares** to the east. Within striking distance are the refreshing open spaces of the city's main **parks**, a brisk walk or tram ride away from the centre. Expeditions to **Mount Vitosha** and the **suburbs** nestling in its foothills require more time and reliance on public transport.

Around ploshtad Sveta Nedelya

Ploshtad Sveta Nedelya – Sveta Nedelya square – stands at the historical centre of Sofia and still serves as its hub, straddling the capital's principal north–south thoroughfare and providing easy access to the main business and sightseeing districts – such as they are. The square elongates to join **bulevard Vitosha**, the city's main shopping street, to the south, while to the north the *Balkan Sheraton* hotel and the Tzum shopping mall guard the entrance to the broad street-cum-square known as **the Largo**, main route to the tourist attractions of east central Sofia. On the far side of the Largo, **bulevard Knyaginya Mariya Luiza** heads north towards the main train station, passing the city's principal mosque, synagogue and public bath buildings on the way.

The Church of Sveta Nedelya

Trams rattle round a paved island that bears the **Church of Sveta Nedelya**. Standing upon the former site of Serdica's chief crossroads, the current structure is the much-rebuilt successor to a line of churches that has stood here since medieval times. During the Ottoman period it was known as the Church of Sveti Kral – the "Blessed King" – on account of the remains of the medieval Serbian monarch, Stefan Urosh, kept here since the fourteenth century, when Sofia briefly fell under Serbian rule. In 1925 it almost claimed another king, when Communist insurgents detonated bombs during a funeral mass, killing 123 people but failing to harm their intended victims, Tsar Boris III and his cabinet. Nowadays Sveta Nedelya is second only to the Aleksandûr Nevski memorial church (see p.101) in importance as a city-centre place of worship. It's the venue of choice for society weddings on Saturdays, and is the scene of particularly well-attended services on Thursdays, when special prayers are intoned to ward off black magic and the evil eye.

Inside, the broad dome hovers above a vast chamber paved with slabs of smooth marble, bordered on each side by vigorous modern frescoes. The shrouded relics of Stefan Urosh are kept in a wooden chest directly to the right of the iconostasis – it's sometimes opened for serious pilgrims if there's a priest in attendance. It's a popular prayer site among women who believe that health problems can be cured by leaving a plastic bag containing their underclothes in the chest for 24 hours.

The Church Historical Museum and the Chapel of Sveta Petka Paraskeva

On the southern side of the square, an ochre building with attractive red and green tiling houses both the Theology Faculty and, on the first floor, the **Church Historical Museum** (Mon–Fri 9am–noon & 2–5pm; 3Lv), a collection of icons, ceremonial priestly robes, bejewelled crosses and incense holders. The best of Bulgaria's religious art is found elsewhere – notably in the National History Museum (see p.108), or the crypt of the Aleksandûr Nevski memorial church, see p.101) – and the display here does little more than fill in the gaps. Highlights include two sixteenth-century icons (a *Virgin and Child* and a *Crucifixion*) from the Black Sea town of Sozopol (see p.425), which remained an important icon-painting centre throughout the Ottoman occupation; and some *pafti* (women's belt buckles) engraved with the forms of saints Dimitûr and George.

Round the corner as you head east along ulitsa Sûborna, a low door leads down into the subterranean **Chapel of Sveta Petka Paraskeva**, a medieval foundation now dwarfed beneath turn-of-the-twentieth-century buildings. Built in the thirteenth century by Tsar Kaloyan as a palace chapel, it's central Sofia's most atmospheric church, crammed with daytime shoppers muttering prayers or planting candles next to the icons. Alongside icons of Sveta Petka herself are powerful depictions of warrior–saints George, Dimitûr and Mina (a fourth-century Egyptian known in the West as Menas), powerful personifications of spiritual strength in the face of adversity which have long been important to Balkan Christians. Special prayers and requests for divine intervention are scribbled onto slips of paper, which are then posted into a box which sits beside the icon of St Mina.

Bulevard Vitosha

The silhouette of Mount Vitosha surmounting the rooftops is the first thing you see on **bulevard Vitosha**, which stretches south from ploshtad Sveta Nedelya. Its foothills are hazy beyond the boulevard's tram wires, the vanishing point of parallel lines of greyish buildings, most of which date from the inter-war years.

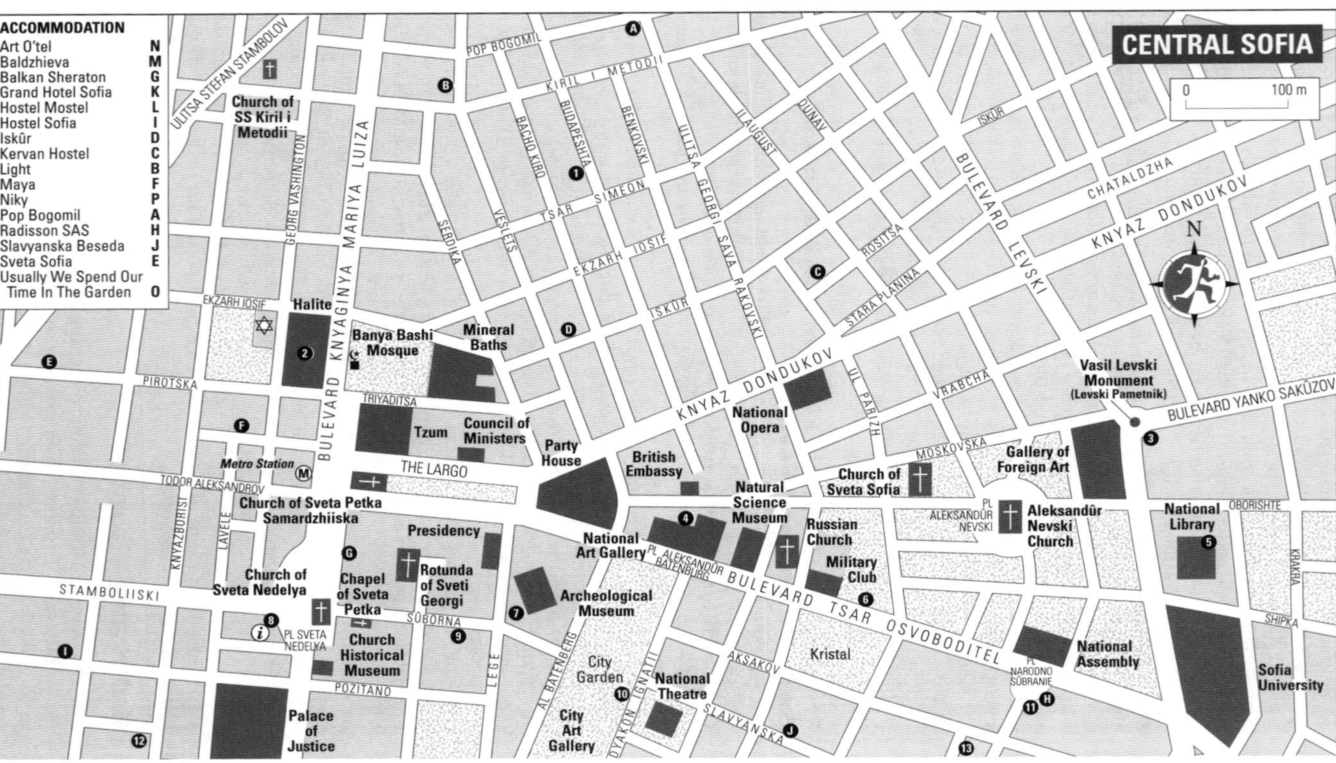
CENTRAL SOFIA
0
100 m
N
ACCOMMODATION
Art O'tel N
Baldzhieva M
Balkan Sheraton G
Grand Hotel Sofia K
Hostel Mostel L
Hostel Sofia I
Iskûr D
Kervan Hostel C
Light B
Maya F
Niky P
Pop Bogomil A
Radisson SAS H
Slavyanska Beseda J
Sveta Sofia E
Usually We Spend Our Time In The Garden O
Church of SS Kiril i Metodii
Halite
Banya Bashi Mosque
Mineral Baths
Tzum
Council of Ministers
Party House
Metro Station
THE LARGO
Church of Sveta Petka Samardzhiiska
Presidency
Church of Sveta Nedelya
Chapel of Sveta Petka
Rotunda of Sveti Georgi
Church Historical Museum
Palace of Justice
Archeological Museum
National Art Gallery
British Embassy
National Opera
Natural Science Museum
Russian Church
Military Club
Church of Sveta Sofia
Gallery of Foreign Art
Aleksandûr Nevski Church
Vasil Levski Monument
(Levski Pametnik)
National Library
National Assembly
Sofia University
Kristal
City Garden
National Theatre
City Art Gallery
ULITSA STEFAN STAMBOLOV
POP BOGOMIL
KIRIL I METODII
BUDAPESHTA
BACHO KIRO
BENKOVSKI
ULITSA GEORGI SAVA RAKOVSKI
II AUGUST
DUNAV
ISKÛR
BULEVARD LEVSKI
CHATALDZHA
KNYAZ DONDUKOV
TSAR SIMEON
EKZARH IOSIF
SERDIKA
VESLETS
GEORG VASHINGTON
BULEVARD KNYAGINYA MARIYA LUIZA
ROSITSA
STARA PLANINA
UL PARIZH
VRABCHA
MOSKOVSKA
BULEVARD YANKO SAKÛZOV
OBORISHTE
KRAKRA
SHIPKA
PIROTSKA
TRIYADITSA
TODOR ALEKSANDROV
KNYAZBORISI
LAVELE
STAMBOLIISKI
SÛBORNA
PL SVETA NEDELYA
POZITANO
LEGE
AL BATENBERG
DYAKON IGNATII
AKSAKOV
SLAVYANSKA
PL ALEKSANDÛR BATENBURG
BULEVARD TSAR OSVOBODITEL
PL ALEKSANDÛR NEVSKI
PL NARODNO SÛBRANIE

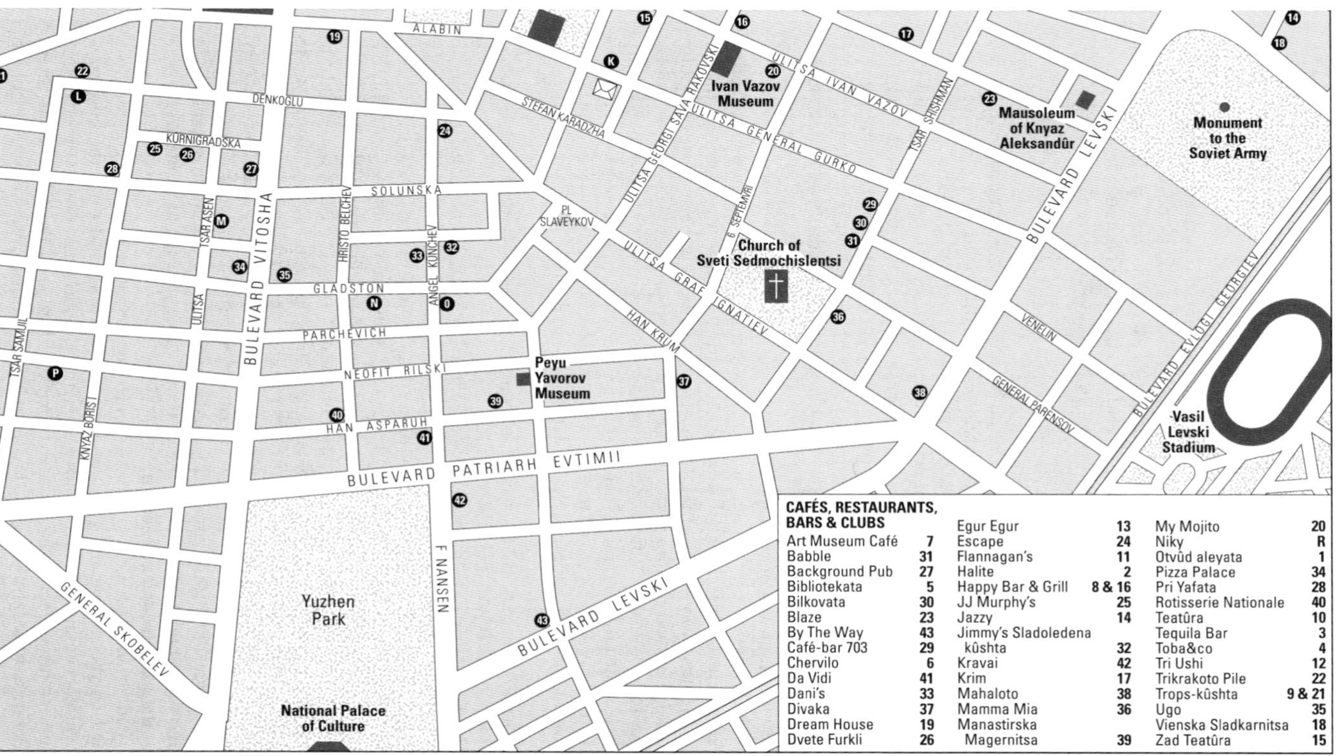

ALABIN
DENKOGLU
KÛRNIGRADSKA
STEFAN KARADZHA
ULITSA GEORGI SAVA RAKOVSKI
Ivan Vazov Museum
ULITSA IVAN VAZOV
ULITSA GENERAL GURKO
TSAR SHISHMAN
Mausoleum of Knyaz Aleksandûr
BULEVARD LEVSKI
Monument to the Soviet Army
SOLUNSKA
TSAR ASEN
BULEVARD VITOSHA
HRISTO BELCHEV
ANGEL KUNCHEV
PL SLAVEYKOV
6 SEPTEMVRI
Church of Sveti Sedmochislentsi
ULITSA GRAF IGNATIEV
GLADSTON
ULITSA
TSAR SAMUIL
PARCHEVICH
HAN KRUM
VENELIN
BULEVARD EVLOGI GEORGIEV
NEOFIT RILSKI
Peyu Yavorov Museum
GENERAL PARENSOV
KNYAZ BORIS I
HAN ASPARUH
Vasil Levski Stadium
BULEVARD PATRIARH EVTIMII
F NANSEN
GENERAL SKOBELEV
Yuzhen Park
BULEVARD LEVSKI
National Palace of Culture
CAFÉS, RESTAURANTS, BARS & CLUBS
Art Museum Café 7
Babble 31
Background Pub 27
Bibliotekata 5
Bilkovata 30
Blaze 23
By The Way 43
Café-bar 703 29
Chervilo 6
Da Vidi 41
Dani's 33
Divaka 37
Dream House 19
Dvete Furkli 26
Egur Egur 13
Escape 24
Flannagan's 11
Halite 2
Happy Bar & Grill 8 & 16
JJ Murphy's 25
Jazzy 14
Jimmy's Sladoledena kûshta 32
Kravai 42
Krim 17
Mahaloto 38
Mamma Mia 36
Manastirska Magernitsa 39
My Mojito 20
Niky R
Otvûd aleyata 1
Pizza Palace 34
Pri Yafata 28
Rotisserie Nationale 40
Teatûra 10
Tequila Bar 3
Toba&co 4
Tri Ushi 12
Trikrakoto Pile 22
Trops-kûshta 9 & 21
Ugo 35
Vienska Sladkarnitsa 18
Zad Teatûra 15

Lined with some of the capital's more stylish shops, Vitosha is an invigorating street to stroll along, although there's little in the way of specific sights save for the monumental cast-iron lions guarding the neo-Egyptian facade of the **Palace of Justice** (*Sûdebna palata*), at its northern end.

Just round the back of the Palace of Justice, on the corner of ulitsas Alabin and Lavele, lurks one of Sofia's least-known attractions, the **Museum of the Interior Ministry** (*Muzeum na MVR*; Mon–Fri 9am–12.30pm & 1.30–5.30pm; free). Changing displays on the history of law, order and police procedure usually feature a fair proportion of grisly crime-scene photographs – definitely not recommended for the young and the squeamish.

The Largo

On the north side of ploshtad Sveta Nedelya, a major crossroads marks the beginning of **the Largo**, traditionally one of the major showpieces of post-war Sofia, not least because of the political symbolism embodied in its most imposing edifice: the Communist Party headquarters. Flanked on three sides by severely monumental buildings, this elongated plaza was built on the ruins of central Sofia, which had been pulverized by British and American bombers in the autumn of 1944. Its yellow-painted stones are the start of a kilometre-long stretch of bright yellow cobbles which, leading through ploshtad Aleksandûr Batenberg and along bulevard Tsar Osvoboditel, forms a kind of processional way linking many of the capital's key sights.

The Largo's western side, from where the dead-straight **bulevard Todor Aleksandrov** blazes a trail towards the distant suburbs, was once dominated by a gargantuan statue of V.I. Lenin. Its place has now been filled by a lofty pedestal topped by a be-robed female figure, who presides over the busy streets like some celestial traffic warden. Intended as an allegory of wisdom (the city itself most probably got its name from an old church dedicated to Sveta Sofia or "Holy Wisdom"; see p.101), the statue was erected in 2000 to serve as a new, non-ideological symbol of the post-Communist capital.

The Rotunda of Sveti Georgi and the Church of Sveta Petka Samardzhiiska

On the south side of the Largo, the *Hotel Balkan Sheraton* casts its sombre wings around a courtyard containing Sofia's oldest church, the fourth-century **Rotunda of Sveti Georgi** (summer 8am–7pm, winter hours are variable due to lack of heating; donation requested). Outwardly dour, with a red brick exterior, the church within holds some incandescent frescoes under the dome. Most of them, including the central image of Christ the Pantokrator and the surrounding frieze of 22 prophets, are fourteenth century, but many of the frescoes below are much older. Another ring of prophets dates from the twelfth century, when Bulgaria was under Byzantine control, and some ninth-century floral designs, in the northern niche, date from the First Bulgarian Empire, when the newly Christianized state subjected unwilling aristocrats to mass baptisms in this very church. You can scramble around some remains of Roman-era Sofia in the plaza behind the church.

Pedestrians scurry down into the underpass which links the Largo's southern and northern sides, and also gives access to **Serdika station** – the busy city-centre terminus of Sofia's brand-new metro. Hogging attention in the adjoining subterranean plaza is the weathered brick and stone of the **Church of Sveta Petka Samardzhiiska**, girded with concrete platforms, its tiled rooftop poking above street level. Originally built in the fourteenth century, the church gained the epithet *samardzhiiska* in the nineteenth century, when it was adopted by the Saddlers' Guild as their private chapel. Despite conscientious restoration, the surviving sixteenth-century frescoes are now patchy and difficult to see, but you can make out portraits of several bearded and haloed figures, one of which is St John of Rila, medieval Bulgaria's leading holy man.

The northern side of the Largo is dominated by a large postwar structure that houses the Council of Ministers (Bulgaria's cabinet) and the **Tzum shopping mall**, three stories of boutiques, cafés and banks occupying the premises of the now-defunct TsUM (WEV), a state-owned department store once the pride of Communist-era Sofia.

The Party House

Of the buildings surrounding the Largo, the white, colonnaded supertanker of the **Party House**, or *partiinyat dom*, is by far the most arresting structure. Nowadays providing office space for members of the Sûbranie (Bulgaria's parliament), it was originally built in the 1950s to accommodate the office of the Communist Party's Central Committee – and featured in a popular joke: A man cycles up to the building and leans his bike against it, whereupon a policeman shouts, "Hey! You can't leave that there, a high Soviet delegation is due to arrive any minute." "That's okay," replies the cyclist, "I'll chain it up".

After November 1989, public pressure mounted to have the Communists evicted from the building: initially without much result. In August 1990 anti-Communist demonstrators, enraged by the continuing presence of an enormous **red star** above the roof, despite a decree from the National Assembly ordering the removal of Communist iconography from all public buildings, attempted to torch it. The Party was finally ejected in early 1992, after which the House served briefly as a cinema before assuming its current function.

Immediately in front of the Party House, another pedestrian subway contains substantial remnants of the **Istochna porta** – the eastern gate of the Roman city of Serdica. Now surrounded by huge chunks of concrete, the bulging defensive towers which once stood guard on each side of the gate are still visible, different courses of brickwork pointing to later Byzantine and medieval Bulgarian rebuildings.

North of the Largo: the Banya Bashi mosque and the mineral baths

North of the Largo, **bulevard Knyaginya Mariya Luiza** was the "most horrible street in Europe" for Arthur Symons when he was here in 1903, a "kind of mongrel East" existing "between two civilizations … a rag-heap for the refuse of both". Though it has been considerably cleaned up since then you can see what he was getting at, if only in the dilapidated mixture of buildings that line the northerly sections of the street. However the southern end is marked by one of the most graceful ensembles of buildings in the city, most eye-catching of which is the **Banya Bashi mosque**: a "Sultan-style" edifice with one large dome and a single minaret, built in 1576 by Hadzhi Mimar Sonah, who also designed the great mosque at Edirne in Turkey. In 1960, Bernard Newman noted "scarcely enough Turks in Sofia to make up a congregation", and in subsequent years the mosque fell into disuse as the Communist regime turned against the country's Muslim population. Now it is once again open for worship, the discreet call of the muezzin occasionally wafting above the heads of bemused city-centre shoppers.

As its name suggests, the mosque stands near Sofia's **mineral baths**, which occupy a stately mock-oriental building overlooking the rear of the park.

Derelict for many years, it's in the process of being restored with money donated by the EU, and will one day house the Museum of Sofia, which currently has nowhere to exhibit its vast collection. The square of park lodged between the mosque and the baths has a slightly scruffy feel, although it has long been one of the capital's prime strolling grounds and meeting points. In the interwar years it was notorious as the place where freelence hitmen used to assemble in the hope of landing a well-paid armed robbery or assassination job. Nowadays people lounge on benches gossiping and spitting sunflower seeds or fragments of *kebapcheta*, or come with jugs to collect mineral water from public taps.

Halite, the synagogue and the Zhenski pazar

Facing the mosque is the market hall or **Halite** (daily 7am–midnight), an elaborate pre-World War I structure crowned by a clock tower, recently reopened to the public after years of neglect. Inside, a glass roof held up by cast-iron pillars stretches above two storeys of stalls selling clothes, booze, and a mouth-watering range of local delicatessen products. A couple of salad bars and canteen-style eateries make this a good place to stop off for food between sightseeing.

Immediately to the west lies the **Sofia synagogue** (Mon–Fri 9am–5pm, Sat 9am–1pm; ring the bell and wait for the caretaker to emerge), a fanciful structure seemingly upheld by its dome, which might have been conceived by a Moorish

Bulgaria's Jews

There are currently approximately 5000 Jews in Bulgaria (around half of whom live in the capital), the meagre remnants of what was historically a much larger community. Their presence in the country dates from at least the tenth century, although the most significant increase in Jewish numbers came about at the tail end of the fifteenth century, when the **Sephardic community** expelled by the Christian monarchs of Spain were resettled throughout the Levant and the Balkans by the considerably more tolerant Islamic rulers of the Ottoman Empire. Speaking the Ladino language (a mixture of medieval Spanish and Portuguese), the new arrivals established trading colonies in Bulgarian towns such as Nikopol, Ruse and elsewhere, although it was **Sofia** that became their cultural and social centre.

Bulgaria is one of the few European countries in which there seems to be no tradition of popular anti-Semitism. Even during the struggle to free Bulgaria from the Ottoman yoke, when Greeks and Turks were frequently perceived as national enemies, Jews managed to retain their status as respected members of the Bulgarian community. Jewish leaders dissuaded the Ottoman authorities from setting fire to Sofia in the aftermath of the Russo-Turkish war of 1877, something that wasn't forgotten by Bulgaria's post-independence leaders.

Things changed for Bulgaria's Jews (a community that by now numbered some 48,000) in February **1940**, when Tsar Boris III appointed a pro-Nazi government under rabid anti-Semite Bogdan Filov, in the hope of forging an alliance with Hitler's Germany. Filov immediately set about introducing descriminatory legislation, closing down Jewish cultural institutions in January 1941, and forcing Jews to wear the yellow star in September 1942.

Uniquely in eastern Europe, however, the bulk of Bulgaria's Jews were saved from the Holocaust. Neither the sitting government nor Tsar Boris III can take much credit for this; they would have passively accepted Nazi plans to murder their Jewish subjects had not public opinion prevented them from doing so. In January **1943** the Bulgarian government responded to German demands for the deportation of Balkan Jews by promising to hand over 20,000 Jews from Bulgarian-occupied Thrace and

Leonardo with a premonition of airships. Designed in 1909 by Friedrich Gruenanger, the Viennese architect also responsible for the Bulgarian Orthodox Church's Theology Faculty (see p.91), the synagogue was intended to symbolize the Jewish contribution to the country's burgeoning capital, blending in with the nearby mosque, market hall and bath house to create an impressive assemblage of downtown buildings. Tsar Ferdinand's presence at the opening ceremony was a clear demonstration of how much the Jewish community – which made up one fifth of the capital's population at the time – was valued by the regime. Until World War II Sofia's Jews occupied an overcrowded maze of narrow streets that stretched from here along what is now the Largo to the east. The area was turned to rubble by Allied bombing, although the vast majority of Sofia's Jews survived the war (see box below), emigrating to Palestine in large numbers in the late 1940s. The synagogue's superbly restored interior is dominated by an enormous brass chandelier weighing over 2000kg, which hangs from a broad octagonal dome. Much of the ceiling space around it is painted to resemble a blue, star-filled sky, all framed by flowing, Art-Nouveau-inspired friezes.

On the southern side of the synagogue, the pedestrianized **ulitsa Pirotska** darts westwards past nineteenth-century apartment blocks, nowadays colonized by clothes boutiques and electrical goods stores. Tastefully cobbled, and with flowerbeds and cast-iron lampstands running down the middle, it's one of central Sofia's more attractive shopping streets.

Macedonia. On discovering that there were only 11,000 Jews from this source, they decided to make up the shortfall by rounding up Jews from Bulgaria proper. Jewish community leaders in Kyustendil complained to their MP, Dimitûr Peshev, who began to rally support for the Jews among his parliamentary colleagues. Fearing a back-bench revolt, Prime Minister Filov went ahead with the deportation of the Jews from Macedonia and Thrace – all of whom perished in the death camps – but backed down from the other deportations, opting instead to intern Bulgaria's own Jews within the country itself.

Sensing that they enjoyed widespread popular sympathy, Jewish leaders in Sofia organized a mass protest on May 24. The demonstration didn't save them from internment, but it succeeded in alerting Bulgarian public opinion to their predicament. A wide cross-section of Bulgarian society supported the Jews: intellectuals wrote letters of protest on their behalf, and Orthodox priests expressed grave concerns about their treatment. The government henceforth remained deaf to German demands for further deportations, and the vast majority of Bulgarian Jews survived the war, returning to their homes after the Communist coup d'état of September 1944.

Communist Bulgaria presented something of a paradox to many Jews. On one hand the new order was welcomed, because it placed all citizens on an equal footing whatever their race. On the other hand, religious institutions of all kinds were persecuted, and Jews were encouraged to abandon their traditional beliefs in favour of state-sponsored atheism. Faced with the choice of staying in Bulgaria or emigrating to the new Jewish homeland in Palestine, the vast majority of Jews chose the latter, 90 percent of them leaving the country between 1948 and 1951. Those who remained were able to retain a sense of Jewish identity, although their religious and community life was now placed under the aegis of a single state-controlled organization. The latter was dissolved in 1990 and replaced by **Shalom**, a nongovernmental cultural organization which has made great strides in the revival of Jewish traditions, and the renewal of contacts with Bulgarian Jews throughout the world.

The junction of Pirotska and ulitsa Stefan Stambolov marks the southern extent of the **Zhenski pazar** or Women's Market, an intensely crowded affair where you can find everything from fruit and vegetables to fake designer-label tracksuits and car parts. Peasants from the surrounding countryside arrive here early each morning to sell their produce, and it's one of the few places in Sofia where the pulse of the Balkans of old can still be felt. Beyond lies one of Sofia's **older quarters**, with rutted cobblestones and low houses built around courtyards: a far cry from the modern housing estates that girdle the town.

East of the Largo: the National Archeological Museum

At the eastern end of the Largo, on the corner of ulitsa Lege, stands an ivy-clad nine-domed building, formerly the *Buyuk Djami* or "Big Mosque", dating from 1494, and now housing the **National Archeological Museum** (Tues–Sun 10am–6pm; 5Lv). Bulgaria's most valuable treasures are concentrated in the National History Museum (see p.108), but the attractively arranged Thracian and Roman finds on display here deserve a brief visit. Numerous individual items stand out, such as an eighth-century BC bronze figurine of a stag found at Sevlievo near Pleven, and there are plentiful Greek and Roman finds from around the country. Most famous of these is the **Stela of Anaxander**, a sixth-century BC gravestone from the ancient Greek colony of Apollonia (now Sozopol) on the Black Sea coast. Upstairs, past a copy of the enigmatic Madara Horseman (see p.274), there's an extensive collection of frescoes plucked from crumbling church walls throughout Bulgaria.

On the opposite side of ulitsa Lege from the museum stand the offices of Bulgaria's president, guarded day and night by soldiers clad in comic-opera nineteenth-century uniforms. Sightseers sometimes pause to observe the **changing of the guard**, which takes place on the hour.

Ploshtad Aleksandûr Batenberg

If the Bulgarian Communist Party had a soul it would doubtless still hover over the cobbled expanse of **ploshtad Aleksandûr Batenberg**, formerly ploshtad Deveti Septemvri or 9 September square – where major anniversaries were celebrated with **parades**. These took place on May 1 and September 9 (the date of the Communist coup in 1944), and featured a familiar repertoire of Communist spectacle: red-scarved Young Pioneers, brigades of workers bearing portraits of their leaders, mass callisthenics, and floats carrying tableaux symbolizing the achievements of socialist construction. The anniversary of the Bolshevik Revolution (Nov 7) was marked by soldiers goose-stepping and armoured vehicles grinding across the plaza in emulation of mightier parades in Moscow. Militia cordons kept the uninvited at a distance (events were televised nationwide), and the regimented proceedings – known as "spontaneous demonstrations of the people" during the Stalinist era – were a tiresome obligation for many participants. "We have seen so many of these demonstrations which humiliate human dignity, where normal people are expected to applaud some paltry mediocrity who has proclaimed himself a demigod and condescendingly waves to them from the heights of his police inviolability", wrote dissident writer Georgi Markov (criticisms like these eventually cost Markov his life, taken by a Bulgarian agent wielding a poisoned umbrella in 1978).

Hastily renamed "Democracy Square" after November 1989, the square soon reverted to its original prewar title, honouring the young German aristocrat who was chosen to be the newly independent country's first monarch in 1878. As an idealistic 22-year-old, Aleksandûr had volunteered to fight alongside Bulgaria's Russian liberators during the War of Independence, yet it was his loss of Russian backing in 1886 – when Bulgaria declared union with Eastern Roumelia without first securing the approval of her big Slav brother – that brought his six-year reign to a premature close.

The National Art Gallery and the Ethnographic Museum

Stretching along the northern side of the square is the former royal palace, which was once so dilapidated that Tsar "Foxy" Ferdinand had to sleep under scaffolding to prevent the roof falling in on him. The palace began life as the Ottoman *Konak* where national hero Vasil Levski (see p.302) was tortured prior to his execution, before having the current Neoclassical facade tacked onto it by Ferdinand's predecessor, Knyaz Aleksandûr. Inside is the **National Art Gallery** (Tues–Sun 10.30am–6pm; 3Lv), a fairly uninspiring collection that reveals how dependent on Western models Bulgarian painting has been. The works that stand out are those which heavily exploit the nostalgia for folk styles and motifs: notably Tsanko Lavrenov's pictures of Old Plovdiv, and the near-naive canvases of fellow Plovdivite Zlatyu Boyadzhiev. The fusion of modern art and folk art which characterizes the work of Bulgaria's most influential twentieth-century painter, Vladimir Dimitrov-Maistor (see p.130), is represented by several stylized pictures of peasant girls. Suffused with the aura of Orthodox icon paintings, they're good examples of Dimitrov-Maistor's attempts to attach a mystical quality to his depictions of Bulgarian rural life.

Housed in the same building is the **Ethnographic Museum** (Tues–Sun 10am–5.30pm; 3Lv), harbouring a multicoloured array of costumes, carpets and domestic knick-knacks from all over the country, accompanied by English-language texts. Much of the museum is taken up by high-profile themed exhibitions (there's usually a new one every year), while part of the ground floor is given over to Sofia's best-stocked souvenir shop (see "Shopping"; p.119).

The south side of the square and the City Garden

On major Communist anniversaries party leaders used to take the salute from atop an austere white mausoleum on the southern side of the square, built to house the embalmed body of **Georgi Dimitrov**, the first leader of the People's Republic of Bulgaria (see box overleaf). Once one of the top "tourist" sights in the capital – with reverential citizens filing through antiseptic corridors guarded by goose-stepping sentries wearing red-braided tunics and plumed hats – the mausoleum stood empty for ten years following the removal of Dimitrov's corpse in July 1990, before finally being demolished by the right-of-centre SDS government. The spot is now occupied by a rather lacklustre arrangement of flowers and shrubs, around which paths lead to the tree-shaded lawns and well-tended flowerbeds of the **City Garden** (*Gradskata gradina*), favoured preserve of chess-playing senior citizens and office workers on their lunch break. Several fountains splash opposite the **Ivan Vazov National Theatre**, a handsome Neoclassical edifice, which provides a welcome contrast to the sombre ministerial buildings on either side. Decked out in red, white and gold, it features Gobelin tapestries and Panagyurishte hangings inside. In spring and summer, the pavement immediately in front of the theatre is taken over by a vast outdoor bar. At the southern end of the park, ulitsa General Gurko is home to the **City Art Gallery** (Tues–Sat 10am–6pm, Sun 11am–5pm; free), with changing exhibitions of contemporary Bulgarian paintings and sculpture.

Georgi Dimitrov (1882–1949)

Both a distinguished antifascist campaigner and one of the twentieth century's great villains, **Georgi Dimitrov** still casts an ambiguous shadow over modern Bulgaria. Born into a humble background, he was a teenage apprentice printer when he converted to Communism, and, with characteristic nerve, doctored the speeches of reactionary MPs before they went to press – the prelude to a lifelong militant career. He organized Party cells, unions, strikes and propaganda inside Bulgaria, emigrating to Moscow after the failure of the September Uprising of 1923. Once in the Soviet Union he rose quickly through the ranks of the Comintern or Communist International, and it was while on Comintern business in Berlin that he was arrested by the Nazis on March 9, 1933, and charged with instigating the Reichstag fire. The subsequent show trial in Leipzig became an international *cause célèbre*, with Dimitrov (despite months of maltreatment by the Gestapo) conducting his own defence and succeeding in making Herman Goering, his prosecutor, appear to be both a liar and a fool. This, and the international attention the trial had received, ensured his acquittal in February 1934. He again took refuge in Moscow, and managed to survive Stalin's purges by betraying fellow Bulgarians also exiled in the USSR. Loyalty to Stalin managed to win him the post of secretary-general of the Comintern in 1935, where he became implicated even further in the liquidation of East European Communists who didn't quite fit into the Soviet leader's plans.

During World War II Dimitrov masterminded the Bulgarian Communist Party's strategy of infiltrating and subverting the antifascist opposition, returning to the country himself in November 1945. He was prime minister from 1946 until his death in 1949, presiding over a period of intense social change: sweeping nationalization and industrialization proceeding hand-in-hand with the ruthless crushing of all political opposition. Under Dimitrov's leadership thousands of Bulgarians were brutally killed, and countless others packed off to concentration camps, in a near-genocidal attempt to rub out the Bulgarian bourgeoisie. Dimitrov was elevated to the level of secular saint following his death, and his embalmed body put on public display in a purpose-built mausoleum in the centre of Sofia. In July 1990 his remains were quietly removed and buried in plot 212 of the Sofia city graveyard, next to his mother. The mausoleum was demolished ten years later.

Bulevard Tsar Osvoboditel and around

Bulevard Tsar Osvoboditel heads out of ploshtad Aleksandûr Batenberg's eastern end, an attractive thoroughfare partially lined with chestnut trees. The **Natural Science Museum**, at no. 1 (daily 10am–5pm; 2Lv), was founded in 1889 by Knyaz Ferdinand I, himself a keen butterfly collector, and presents a thorough cataloguing of Bulgarian and worldwide wildlife, both stuffed and pickled. Tanks containing live snakes and lizards line the stairs, domestic grass snakes vying for attention with central American geckos, pythons and anacondas. At teatime, live rodents are lowered into the tanks of the larger reptiles. There's also a small gift shop selling minerals and fossils. Immediately beyond the museum, the **Russian church** is an unmistakeable, zany firecracker of a building with an exuberant exterior of bright yellow tiles, five gilded domes and an emerald spire, concealing a dark, candlewax-scented interior. Officially dedicated to St Nicholas the Blessed, the church was built in 1913 at the behest of a Tsarist diplomat, Semontovski-Kurilo, who feared for his soul to worship in Bulgarian churches, which he believed to be schismatic.

Towards National Assembly Square

Continuing eastward along bulevard Tsar Osvoboditel you come to a small square of greenery known popularly as **Kristal**, after the café that shelters on its southern flank. Opposite the park on the northern side of the boulevard is the recently spruced-up Neoclassical facade of the **military club**, once the centre of post-Liberation Bulgaria's high society, and the place where the Zveno (a radical political group that attracted young right-wing officers) hatched several conspiracies in the interwar years.

Bulevard Tsar Osvoboditel opens out into ploshtad Narodno sûbranie – **National Assembly Square**. On the northern side stands a cream building housing the *Narodno sûbranie* itself – Bulgaria's **National Assembly**, the facade of which bears the motto *sûedinenieto pravi silata* (unity is strength). Directly opposite, a semicircular plaza encloses the Monument to the Liberators, which gives pride of place to a statue of the *Tsar Osvoboditel*, or "Tsar Liberator" himself, Alexander II of Russia.

Ploshtad Aleksandûr Nevski

The area immediately north of bulevard Tsar Osvoboditel is dominated by **ploshtad Aleksandûr Nevski**, another of Sofia's set-piece squares, an expanse of greenery and paving stones (overlaying what was, in Roman times, the necropolis of Serdica) overlooked by the twinkling domes of the Aleksandûr Nevski memorial church. Entering the square from the western end, however, you first encounter the brown brick **Church of Sveta Sofia**. Dating from late Roman times, but much rebuilt after numerous invasions and earthquakes (the last one in 1858), the church still follows the classic Byzantine plan of a regular cross with a dome at the intersection. It was turned into a mosque by the Ottomans, and locals believed that it was haunted nightly by the ghost of Constantine the Great's daughter Sofia, supposed founder of the first church to stand on this site. An air of calm reigns in the gracefully simple interior, layers of Byzantine brickwork giving some idea of the church's vintage. Around the back an engraved boulder marks the **grave of Ivan Vazov** (p.103), who requested that he be buried amid the daily life of his people; you'll notice his statue, seated with book in hand, in a park nearby. Set beside the southern wall of the church is the Tomb of the Unknown Soldier, flanked by two recumbent lions.

Immediately opposite Sveta Sofia, shielded by trees, a beige building sporting a stripe of brightly coloured ceramic tiles houses the Bulgarian Orthodox Church's **Holy Synod**, a fine example of the melding of Byzantine and Art-Nouveau styles which characterized so many of the public buildings thrown up at the beginning of the twentieth century. In 1992 the Synod was the scene of controversy when reformist priests raided the building, ejecting those loyal to the sitting patriarch, whom they accused of having been a docile servant of the Communists. The Bulgarian Church has been split into hostile camps ever since.

The Aleksandûr Nevski memorial church

One of the finest pieces of architecture in the Balkans and certainly Sofia's crowning glory, the **Aleksandûr Nevski memorial church** honours the 200,000 Russian casualties of the 1877–78 War of Liberation, particularly the defenders of the Shipka pass. Financed by public subscription and built between 1882 and 1924 to the designs of St Petersburg architect Pomerantsev, it's a magnificent structure, bulging with domes and half-domes and glittering with 18lb of gold leaf donated by the Soviet Union in 1960. Within the cavernous interior, a white-bearded God glowers down from the main cupola, an angelic sunburst covers the central vault, and as a parting shot a *Day of Judgement* looms above the exit. Expressive frescoes lacking the stiffness of Byzantine portraiture depict episodes from the life of Christ in rich tones, and the grandeur of the iconostasis is enhanced by twin thrones with columns of onyx and alabaster.

Orthodox congregations stand or kneel during services, although the weak and the elderly traditionally lean or sit on benches round the side. The church's capacity of 5000 is ample for daily **services** (usually in the morning at around 9.30am, and in the evening at about 5pm), which can be spectacular affairs, rich with incense, candlelight and sonorous chanting.

The **crypt**, entered from the outside, contains a superb **collection of icons** (daily except Tues 10.30am–12.30pm & 2–6.30pm; 5Lv) from all over the country. They're mostly eighteenth- and nineteenth-century pieces, but look out for some medieval gems from the coastal town of Nesebûr, home to a prolific icon-painting school, and source of the oldest icon on display here, a serene, white-bearded St Nicholas. Other highlights include a fourteenth-century wood-carved bas-relief from Sozopol showing saints George and Dimitûr riding together against some common foe. The horsemen are regarded as brother-saints in the Balkans, not least because their feast days (May 6 for George, October 26 for Dimitûr) play an important ritual role in marking the beginnings of the summer and winter cycles in the agricultural year. They're often pictured together in Bulgarian art, with St George invariably riding a white steed (symbolizing spring), Dimitûr a red one (symbolizing autumn).

The National Gallery of Foreign Art

An imposing gallery on the northeastern edge of the square houses the **National Gallery of Foreign Art** (daily except Tues 11am–6pm; 3Lv; Ⓦ www.ngfa.icb.bg), an international art collection largely based on the donations of rich Bulgarians living abroad (and the occasional foreigner – Robert Maxwell was one early benefactor). The ground floor contains a sizeable collection of Indian miniatures, manuscripts and sculpture. Next door, a series of ninteenth-century Burmese wall hangings overlook a crowd of wooden Buddhas, including one gilt example sitting cross-legged on the backs of three elephants. Upstairs, second-division French artists take up a lot of space, although there are a couple of Delacroix sketches, a small Picasso etching (*The Visions of Count d'Orgas* from 1966), and a mesmerizing *Lucifer* by turn-of-the-twentieth-century German symbolist Franz von Stück. In the basement (not always open), Thracian gravestones from an ancient necropolis excavated nearby surround a reconstructed mortuary chapel dating from late Roman times.

Ulitsa G. S. Rakovski and around

Central Sofia's southeastern quarter is one of the inner city's liveliest areas, full of office workers and shoppers during the day, theatregoers and restaurant patrons in the evening. The area's main thoroughfares are **ulitsa G.S. Rakovski**, a workaday street lined with office blocks, and **ulitsa Graf Ignatiev**, which is the capital's most important shopping district after bulevard Vitosha. Government buildings and residential houses mingle in the quiet streets in between, along with a couple of worthwhile literary museums.

The Ivan Vazov House-Museum

Three blocks south of bulevard Tsar Osvoboditel, on the corner of ulitsas Rakovski and Vazov, is the **Ivan Vazov House-Museum** (Tues & Sun 1–7pm,

Thurs 1–5pm, Fri & Sat 9am–5pm; 3Lv), where Bulgaria's greatest novelist lived from 1895 until his death in 1921. Most of the rooms are decked out in early nineteenth-century wallpaper and traditional Bulgarian floor coverings, making this one of the few places in town where the atmosphere of the old, post-Liberation Sofia still reigns. Downstairs a words-and-pictures display details the main events of Vazov's life, from childhood in Sopot (see p.300) through exile in Odessa (where he wrote *Under the Yoke*, the epic novel of nineteenth-century Bulgarian life) to old age in Sofia: the dining room where he suffered a fatal heart attack is preserved in its original state. Period rooms upstairs include the writer's study, where visitors are greeted by the stuffed remains of Vazov's beloved dog, Bobi. The unfortunate hound was run over by a tram just outside the house before being whisked off to the taxidermist by Vazov's youngest brother Boris.

Peyu Yavorov (1878–1914)

Man of action, poet and charismatic loner, **Peyu Kracholov** was born in the dusty provincial backwater of Chirpan. At the age of 16, he was forced by an unsympathetic father to abandon his studies and take up work as a telegraph operator. It was in the post offices of provincial towns like Sliven and Pomorie that the introverted **Yavorov** started to write the sombre, romantic symbolist poetry for which he became famous. Changing his name to Yavorov because it sounded more earthy (Yavor means "sycamore tree"), he was instantly received into Sofia's literary world, hung out with all the major writers of the day (including Vazov, who championed his work), and became editor of the top literary magazine *Misûl*. A star while still in his twenties, Yavorov nevertheless yearned for more than the salon-bound cultural life of the capital. Tiring of his youthful passion for socialism, he threw himself into the struggle to free Macedonia from the Ottoman Empire, fighting as a guerrilla in the mountains and writing a biography of the movement's leader, Gotse Delchev (see p.160). The death of Delchev and the failure of the Ilinden Uprising (see p.468) in 1903 left Yavorov disillusioned, but he continued to serve as an unofficial ambassador for the Macedonian cause, and returned to the fray as a *voyvoda* (guerilla leader) in the Balkan Wars, liberating the Aegean town of Kavala from Ottoman rule in 1912.

Yavorov's other great passion was writing love poetry to the two women with whom he had obsessive affairs. The first was Mina Todorova, teenage daughter of Petko Todorov, a fellow member of the *Misûl* circle. Despite being an ardent admirer of Yavorov's writings, Todorov was horrified by the idea of having a penniless revolutionary poet as a son-in-law. Banned from seeing her, Yavorov wrote Mina love letters in verse, offering them to *Misûl* for publication at the same time. Mina died of tuberculosis in 1910, and it was at her graveside in Paris that Yavorov struck up a friendship with the next object of his affections, Lora Karavelova. The daughter of former prime minister Petko Karavelov (and niece of the Bulgarian revolutionary Lyuben Karavelov), Lora was one of Sofia's most modern, emancipated women, and she and Yavorov soon became the city's favourite intellectual couple. They married almost immediately, but Lora found Yavorov – already wed to Macedonia and his own writing – a distant, difficult companion. By early 1913 Lora was convinced (probably without reason) that Yavorov was having an affair with Dora Konova, the fiancée of a friend. They argued, and Lora threatened to shoot herself. Whether intentionally or not, the gun went off. Yavorov was tried for her murder – and speedily acquitted, despite the popular feeling that he was the guilty party. Abandoned by his friends and living in extreme poverty, Yavorov then turned a gun on himself, but at the first attempt lost only his eyesight. A few months later, at his second attempt, he succeeded in taking his life.

The Museum of Peyu Yavorov

Continuing south along ulitsa Rakovski you soon come to the **Museum of Peyu Yavorov** in a Secession-style house at no. 136 (Tues & Sun 1–7pm, Thurs 1–5pm, Fri & Sat 9am–5pm). One of the most compelling figures in Bulgarian literature (see box p.103), Yavorov lived in a modest first-floor flat here for eleven months in 1913. Among the period furniture and traditional rugs are some evocative personal effects, such as the knife and binoculars given to him by Macedonian freedom fighters Gotse Delchev and Yane Sandanski respectively. Quite by chance, the photographs of Yavorov and wife Lora which hang in the sitting-room have been separated by a large crack which has recently appeared in the wall – a poignant reminder of their tragic end.

Ulitsa Graf Ignatiev

Cutting across ulitsa Rakovski is **ulitsa Graf Ignatiev**, a partially pedestrianized thoroughfare lined with shops, and named after the Russian count (and grandfather of Canadian novelist, Michael Ignatiev) who served as Russian ambassador to Constantinople in the 1870s, and persuaded Tsar Aleksandûr to support Bulgarian liberation. The western half of Graf Ignatiev runs through ploshtad Slaveikov, a vast open-air **book market** where Bulgarian translations of the latest Western bestsellers are eagerly snapped up by local readers. Running southeast from the junction with ulitsa Rakovski, the street runs past the city centre's main fruit and veg market. Near here, in the small garden beside the intersection with ulitsa Tsar Shishman stands the **Church of Sveti Sedmochislentsi**, literally the "Holy Seven", referring to Cyril, Methodius and their followers, the seven saints who brought Christianity to the Slavs. It was built on the site of the so-called "Black Mosque", an edifice which served as Sofia's main prison immediately after the Liberation. Prisoners used to sell handmade trinkets to passing city folk in order to pay for their food. British barrister James A. Samuelson bought a belt made of beads from a prisoner on death row in 1887, "for which" he wrote, "I, of course, gave him a trifle".

The inner ring road and beyond

Girdling the city centre is the broad sweep of Sofia's **inner ring road**, built in imitation of the wide boulevards of other European capitals such as Paris, Vienna and Budapest. There's little of architectural interest along its length, save for a scattering of monuments and buildings around the eastern end of ploshtad Aleksandûr Nevski and bulevard Tsar Osvoboditel. A hundred metres north of the Nevski church, at the intersection with Yanko Sakûzov, stands the weathered stone **Vasil Levski Monument** (*Levski pametnik*), marking the spot where the "Apostle of Freedom" (see p.302) was hanged by the Ottoman authorities in 1873.

From there it's a brief stroll south to **Sofia University**, the country's most prestigious educational establishment. Founded a decade after the Liberation, it was named after Kliment Ohridski, a pupil of saints Cyril and Methodius, who as ninth-century bishop of Ohrid in western Macedonia had an important impact on the flowering of Slav culture. Not previously known for their radicalism, Sofia's students were at the heart of demonstrations in June 1990 protesting at the alleged unfairness of Bulgaria's first post-Communist elections. Barricades went up in front of the university, provoking fears that Bulgaria's nascent democracy would descend into confrontation, but government concessions to the opposition prevented any real violence.

Continuing along bulevard Levski from the university, you reach the **mausoleum of Knyaz Aleksandûr Batenberg** (Mon–Fri 9am–noon & 2–5pm), occupying a small park at the corner of ulitsa Slavyanska. Despite being deposed in 1886 and living in exile in Graz until his death in 1893, Bulgaria's first post-Liberation ruler always wanted to be buried in Sofia, and his successor Ferdinand obliged by having the mausoleum erected in his honour. It took so long to build, however, that Aleksandûr's corpse spent five years in the Rotunda of Sveti Georgi before finally taking up residence here. A neo-Baroque cupola-topped structure holds his plain marble sarcophagus, draped with a Bulgarian flag, but other than a couple of military tunics, worn by the prince when visiting front-line troops in the Serb-Bulgarian war of 1885, there's little to see.

Immediately opposite the mausoleum stands the towering **Monument to the Soviet Army**, erected in honour of the "liberation" of Bulgaria in 1944. Although allied to Nazi Germany during World War II, the Bulgarians always shrank from declaring war on the Soviet Union, mindful of the long tradition of Russo–Bulgarian friendship. The Soviets, however, regarded Bulgaria as ripe for conquest, and despite the Bulgarian government's readiness to change sides as the war neared its end, the Red Army invaded anyway. Centrepiece of the monument is a Red Army soldier flanked by a worker and a peasant woman with a child, an archetypal symbol of Bulgaro–Soviet friendship which used to feature in monuments and propaganda billboards throughout the land. Nowadays it serves as the backdrop to the antics of skateboarders, who practise manoeuvres on the flagstoned area between the monument and the main road to the north.

Orlov most and Borisova gradina (Freedom Park)

Just east of the monument, the modest dribble of the River Perlovska is spanned by **Orlov most** or Eagle Bridge, crowned with four ferocious-looking birds of prey. Set amid weeping willows, the bridge marks the spot where Bulgarian prisoners of war – released from Ottoman prisons in Anatolia – were greeted by their compatriots just after the Liberation. The returning heroes had been bestowed with the nickname of "the eagles" ("*orlite*"), and the bridge has borne their name ever since. From here the main highway to Plovdiv (formerly bul. Lenin, it has now reverted to its original name of Tsarigradsko shose) heads southeast, flanked on one side by Sofia's largest park, **Borisova gradina** (literally "Boris' Garden", although many locals still use its Communist-era name, *Park na svobodata* or "Freedom Park"). Partially influenced by St James' Park in London, it was laid out during the reign of Tsar Boris III, and harbours a rich variety of flowers and trees, becoming more densely wooded the further southeast you go. With its lily ponds, bandstands and crisscrossing paths, it's an ideal place for an aimless stroll. In recent years the park has become an important centre of Sofia nightlife, with brash outdoor bars pumping out the kind of ear-splitting music that isn't always appreciated by denizens of the residential districts on either side. Many consider the bars to be a social nuisance, and their continued presence here remains uncertain. A more permanent aspect of the park is its importance to football fans – both the Bulgarian national team and the club side CSKA play in big, bowl-shaped stadia which loom up from among the trees.

The Army Museum

A short walk east of Borisova gradina (or a ride on tram #20 from the centre), occupying a compound on the corner of ulitsas Han Omurtag and Cherkovna, the **Army Museum** (Wed–Sun 9am–5pm; 10Lv), is an essential stopoff for anyone interested in military history. Two halls of exhibits bring together weaponry and uniforms from the 130-year history of the Bulgarian army, although the real highlight is the fearsome array of hardware ranged outside. Highlights include

△ Apartment building, Sofia

T34s, MiG fighter jets, and one of the warhead-bearing SS23 missiles formerly stored in silos south of Sofia.

Yuzhen Park and the NDK

On summer evenings city-centre office workers, shoppers and youngsters pour down bulevard Vitosha to **Yuzhen Park** (literally, "Southern Park") to drink coffee or stroll between increasingly weed-choked flowerbeds. Outshining Borisova gradina as an evening parade ground for the city's youth, the park also holds two structures symbolizing Bulgaria's achievements.

The **Thirteen Hundred Years Monument** is boldly (some say hideously) modernist: huge wrench-shaped blocks emerging from a pit that represents centuries of servitude, garnished with anguished-looking figures (one of whom, it's rumoured, bears the features of former Party leader Todor Zhivkov). Although the lettering stuck to the side of the monument is beginning to fall off, you can just about make out nineteenth-century freedom fighter Vasil Levski's maxim: "We are in time and time is in us" ("We transform it and it transforms us" he continued, to clarify the message).

At the top end of the park, the gleaming **NDK** or National Palace of Culture (*Natsionalen Dvorets na Kulturata*) rears up like a spaceship come to earth. Covering an area of 17,000 square metres, the complex contains concert halls, congress facilities, office space, discos and a subterranean arcade packed with clothes stalls selling cheap T-shirts and jeans. The building was originally built to commemorate Lyudmila Zhivkova, daughter of Todor Zhivkov, who died of a brain tumour while still in her thirties. Lyudmila was a powerful figure, running the ministry of culture like a personal fiefdom, but her interest in eastern religions and her efforts to promote Bulgarian culture abroad made her quite popular among Bulgarian intellectuals. But the most telling aspect of the NDK was its colossal cost, and with this in mind, Sofians invented a sarcastic pun on its initials, which can also stand for "another hole in the belt".

Beyond the NDK, the neat pedestrian-only Lovers' Bridge (so-called because smoochy teenagers lounge around here on warm summer nights) leads over bulevard Bûlgariya and into the southern stretches of the park – which largely consist of overgrown patches of grass traversed by badly maintained pathways. There's not much point in venturing further, unless you're staying in the nearby *Hilton* hotel, or you're keen to investigate the geological exhibits in the **Museum of Earth and Man** (*Muzei na Zemyata i Horata*; Tues–Sat 10am–6pm; 2Lv) at bul. Cherni vrûh 4. Housed in a former armoury, it's a worthy but dull display of the world's minerals and the techniques used to mine them; most striking are the enormous quartz crystals of varying hues crowding the main hall.

The Zoopark

Of all Sofia's city-bound attractions, the **Zoopark** (daily 9am–5pm; 5Lv), 3km southeast of Yuzhen Park, is the only one you can't really walk to from the centre. While the large complex of concrete compounds has seen better days, and many of its cages stand empty, there are enough beasts on display to make a visit worthwhile if zoos are your thing. The tigers, leopards and bears (the latter occupying a large pit at the zoo's western gate) are currently the biggest draws. There are several alfresco cafés inside the zoo, but not much in the way of substantial food, and there is very little shade, particularly at the height of summer.

To get to the zoo, catch tram #2 from ulitsa Graf Ignatiev to ploshtad Velchova Zavera (the first stop after emerging from the park), and change to bus #67 (get off at the second stop) or #102, which terminates at the zoo's eastern gate.

Boyana

Seven kilometres southwest of central Sofia, **BOYANA** is an affluent village suburb lying in the shadow of Mount Vitosha (see opposite). For decades it has been the favoured retreat for Sofia's elite, a process speeded up by the economic changes of the 1990s, when a new class of nouveaux riches moved in to build villas and flats. Most of Boyana's luxury dwellings are hidden away behind high fences in the narrow lanes on the western side of the village, and the centre of the settlement isn't particularly attractive. The village's importance to sightseers, however, is guaranteed by the presence of the **Boyana Church**, whose unique medieval frescoes are once again accessible to the public after many years of restoration; and the **National History Museum**, which was moved to Boyana from its previous home (the Palace of Justice; see p.94) in 2000.

The National History Museum

Occupying a former government palace beside the Okolovrûshten pût, a dusty highway which marks the northern boundary of Boyana, the **National History Museum** (daily 9.30am–5.30pm; 10Lv) is Bulgaria's most worthwhile assemblage of ancient and medieval artefacts. The decision to move one of the city's key attractions out to Boyana was a controversial one, not least because it makes it less likely that large numbers of tourists will make their way out to visit it. However it's well worth the trip if you're in any way interested in the nation's history, and its new home – an opulent residence once used by Zhivkov and his cronies – seems tailor-made for such a prestigious display. On the minus side, English-language labelling is almost nonexistent, and many of the museum's most valuable exhibits are frequently sent abroad to star in touring exhibitions – making it difficult to predict precisely what will be on display at any one time.

Getting to the museum is straightforward: bus #63 from bulevard Totleben passes the museum access road; otherwise catch trolleybus #2 from opposite Sofia University to the final stop, walk straight ahead and cross Okolovrûshten pût, then walk left for 200m to find the access road. There's a simple café inside the museum, but no other facilities within reasonable walking distance, so it's best to catch a bus or taxi onwards to the Boyana church once you've looked around.

Ancient artefacts

Stairs lead up from the main entrance to Hall 1, which contains artefacts left by various Neolithic cultures between the seventh and third millennia BC – including stone **goddess figures** found near Varna and inscribed with rams, birds, chevrons, labyrinths and other motifs associated with the Great Earth Mother. Hall 2 contains the great gold and silver hoards associated with the **Thracians**, who inhabited the eastern Balkans during the pre-Christian era. Most eye-catching of these is the golden treasure of Panagyurishte, a collection of eight *rhyta* (drinking vessels) and one *phiale* (a kind of plate) made by Greek artisans of the Dardanelles area and imported into Thrace by a wealthy chieftain. Each *rhyton* is designed in the shape of an animal's head, with mythological scenes shown in relief around the side. One amphora-shaped *rhyton* features handles in the form of centaurs and a procession of naked warriors round the main body of the vessel.

Further artefacts and jewellery from the Thracian period include a series of fourth-century BC horse trappings found at Letnitsa near Lovech: small silver plaques with gilded images of mythical beasts and a hunter on horseback.

Rather like a modern cartoon strip, the plaques appear to tell a story common to many European cultures: that of a horse-riding hero who slays a serpent in order to win the heart of a maiden and deliver the kingdom from famine. The Thracians were particularly keen on heroic horsemen (see p.391), a fondness that is reflected in the modern Orthodox Church's reverence for saints such as George and Dimitûr.

Bulgarian treasures

Hall 3 is probably the most disappointing part of the museum: the bas-reliefs, ceramics, silverware and frescoes illustrating the artistic heights attained during the medieval era are mostly replicas of items kept elsewhere in Bulgaria. Things pick up in Hall 4, designed to show how the Bulgarian Church kept national culture alive during five centuries of Ottoman rule, which whisks you through the various schools of **icon painting** that flourished in rural Bulgaria throughout the Ottoman period, and contains several examples of the **frescoes** that decorated Bulgarian monasteries. An early example is the sixteenth-century *Last Judgement* from the Church of the Nativity in Arbanasi, in which true believers are transported to a paradise stocked with exotic beasts while the ungodly are suspended over fires or have spikes inserted in their backsides. Equally outstanding is the *Wheel of Life* by Zahari Zograf, the nineteenth-century artist who did more than most to weld the Byzantine traditions of icon painting with the folk art of the Bulgarian peasantry.

Hall 5 covers Bulgarian history from the establishment of an independent Bulgarian state in 1878 to the end of World War II with a non-chronological jumble of photographs and artefacts. Most people will find something enjoyable here – whether the generous collection of military uniforms, or the theatre posters and opera costumes from interwar Sofia – although it's too badly captioned and confused to make much sense of.

Boyana Church

Two kilometres south of the National History Museum, just above Boyana's village square, a small garden surrounds the ivy-covered **Boyana Church** (April–Dec Tues–Sun 9am–5pm; Jan–March Tues–Sat 9am–5pm; 10Lv, plus 5Lv for English-language commentary), home to a justly famed set of medieval frescoes, largely executed in 1259. With their realism and rejection of the Byzantine style, these anticipate the work of Giotto, which heralded the beginning of the Italian Renaissance. As well as biblical themes, the unknown artist drew on contemporary life for inspiration: clothing the saints in medieval Bulgarian dress and setting garlic, radishes and bread – the peasants' staples – on the table in the *Last Supper*. Perhaps the finest portraits are those of Boyana's patrons, Desislava and Sebastocrator Kaloyan (depicted holding the church in the customary fashion), and the haloed figures of the king and queen, Konstantin Asen and Irina.

Visitors are only admitted to the church in small groups, and are only allowed to spend ten minutes inside – a measure designed to protect the frescoes from sudden changes in temperature and humidity. Should you require more time, you can always study the replicas of the frescoes housed in the nearby **museum** (same times; 2Lv), where you can also watch an English-language video (for an additional 2Lv) about the history of the church.

Mount Vitosha

A wooded mass of granite 19km long by 17km wide, **MOUNT VITOSHA**, whose foothills begin some 7km from the city centre, is very much a part of

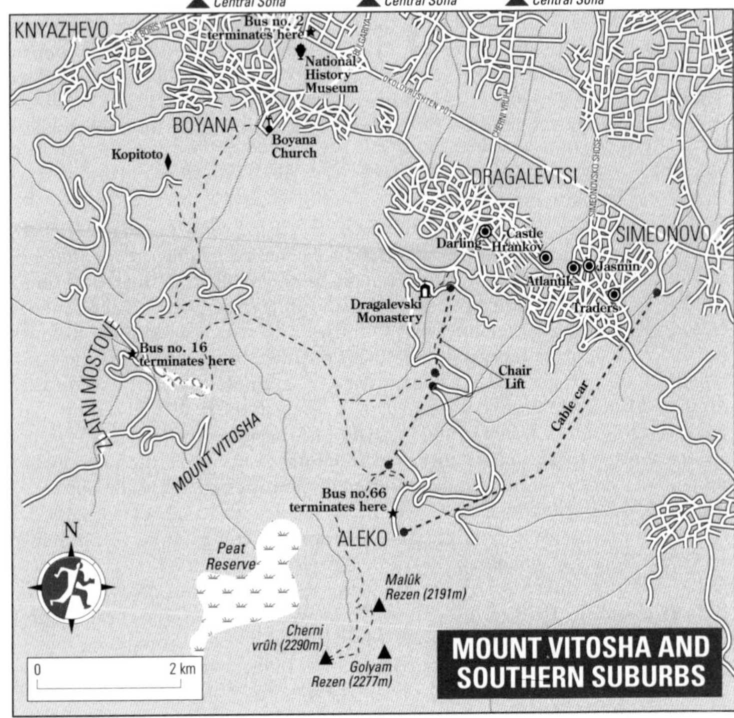

the capital and is the source of its pure water and fresh breezes. *Sofiantsi* come here to picnic, gather wild herbs and berries, savour magnificent views or to ski, and the ascent of its highest peak, **Cherni vrûh**, has become a traditional test of stamina for hikers. Vitosha's two main recreation centres, connected to the city by asphalt road, are **Aleko**, just above the treeline and within easy reach of the summit, and **Zlatni mostove**, on the wooded western flanks of the mountain. Both give access to Cherni vrûh; Aleko is the closer, but the longer ascent from Zlatni mostove takes you through more varied terrain.

Routes from central Sofia to Vitosha pass through the villages (suburbs, really) nestling beneath its foothills: **Dragalevtsi**, with an attractive wood-shrouded monastery just above it, and **Simeonovo** are the starting points for the ski lifts to Aleko. Neither of the above villages, however, are worthy stopoffs in their own right: despite their status as exclusive suburbs for Sofia's post-Communist nouveaux riches, they remain drab, uninspiring little places overshadowed by the glory of the mountain above.

Skiing is possible on Vitosha from late December through to mid-March, with Aleko providing access to the principal pistes. There's a small winter resort here with three hotels, where you can enquire about equipment rental and sign up for ski schools. However, Aleko currently doesn't feature in any of the package holiday brochures, and independent travellers interested in skiing on Vitosha would probably be better off staying in the small hotels in the village suburbs of Simeonovo and Dragalevtsi below, from where they can ascend the mountain by ski lift.

Getting to Vitosha

Public transport to Mount Vitosha is fairly straightforward, with buses for Dragalevtsi, Simeonovo and Aleko starting from the **Hladilnika** terminus on Sofia's southern outskirts, at the end of tram route #9. After disembarking from the tram, head through a small bazaar area and turn left: buses for Vitosha destinations depart from stands 300m away at the end of the street. You can take bus #66 straight to Aleko or head instead for the Aleko-bound lifts at Dragalevtsi and Simeonovo. Which one you choose will largely depend on what day it is: both the Dragalevtsi chair lift and Simeonovo gondola only definitely work at weekends and during school holidays, and can't be relied upon the rest of the time. In addition, they're usually closed for maintenance in May and October. From the Hladilnika terminus, bus #64 goes to Dragalevtsi village then Boyana Church every twenty to thirty minutes; bus #66 goes to Aleko approximately every thirty minutes; bus #93 goes to the Dragalevtsi chair lift every thirty minutes, but only when the chair lift is running; bus #98 goes to Dragalevtsi village and Simeonovo village every twenty to thirty minutes; and bus #122 goes to the Simeonovo gondola every thirty to forty minutes, but only when the gondola is running.

Buses for Zlatni mostove leave from the **Ovcha Kupel** bus station southwest of the city centre, on the main road to Pernik, Blagoevgrad and Greece. To get there, take tram #5 from behind the Palace of Justice (or *Sûdebna palata*) and travel eleven stops until you see the grubby concrete bus station buildings on your right. From here, bus #61 goes to Zlatni mostove (Mon–Sat 3 daily; Sun 8 daily), and bus #62 goes to Kopitoto (Mon–Sat 2 daily; Sun 5 daily).

In addition, you can get to Simeonovo village on bus #67 (every 20–30 min) from **ploshtad Velchova Zavera** (on tram route #2).

As a rule, there are more buses to Vitosha on Sundays than on other days of the week, especially if you're aiming for Zlatni mostove. **Journey times** from Sofia to any of the Mount Vitosha destinations take between thirty minutes and an hour, depending on the traffic and weather conditions. Sofia public transport tickets and travelcards are valid for all the above services except for buses #61, #62 and #66, for which separate tickets must be bought from kiosks at the relevant terminals.

Dragalevtsi and Simeonovo

Arriving in **DRAGALEVTSI**, 3km south of the Hladilnika terminus, you'll either be dropped in the centre of the village or at the **Dragalevtsi chair lift** (1.50Lv each way to Aleko), some thirty minutes' walk above the village square. Ascending to Aleko via the **Bai Krûstyo** middle station in about twenty minutes, the lift offers excellent views of Sofia stretched out on the plain to the north. An asphalt path winds up from the Dragalevtsi lift station to **Dragalevtsi monastery**, a peaceful spot enshrouded by beech woods which serves as the summer residence of the Bulgarian patriarch. There's a fourteenth-century church – the only part of the original monastery that remains – and cells around its leafy courtyard, which during the nineteenth century sheltered the revolutionary Vasil Levski. The monastery comes alive on August 15, the **Feast of the Assumption** (*Uspenie Bogorodichno* or more colloquially *Golyama Bogoroditsa*), when families from far and wide spend the day picnicking in the grounds or praying to the Virgin, the monastery's patron.

From Dragalevtsi, you can catch bus #98 to **SIMEONOVO**, the next village-suburb to the east, and terminus of the **Simeonovo gondola** (3Lv each way to Aleko), which gives great views of the Sofia plain. For details of accommodation in Simeonovo and Dragalevtsi, see p.90.

Aleko

Some twenty minutes beyond Dragalevtsi, bus #66 arrives at **ALEKO**, an expanding **winter sports centre** with three hotels (the *Prostor*, *Moreni* and *Shtastlivetsa*), and a range of pistes to suit all grades of skiers. During the summer, the area is packed with weekending *Sofiantsi* enjoying picnics or taking advantage of the numerous hiking possibilities that radiate outwards from the *Shtastlivetsa Hotel*, the area's central point of reference. The resort takes its name from nineteenth-century writer Aleko Konstantinov (see p.204): in 1895, back in the days when hill-walking was an expression of patriotic love for the country rather than mere recreation, Konstantinov led a party of three hundred idealistic Bulgarians (Ivan Vazov was an enthusiastic participant) in an assault on Vitosha's highest point, Cherni vrûh – a climb that marked the beginning of alpine pursuits in Bulgaria.

The chair lift from Aleko to Stenata, the crag which overlooks Aleko, usually works on summer weekends. If not, it's quite easy to scramble up there in thirty to forty minutes. From here, you can see the 2290m **Cherni vrûh** ("black peak") straight ahead, a clump of rocks surrounded by a grassy plateau – an easy fifteen-minute hike.

Zlatni mostove

From Sofia's Ovcha Kupel bus station, buses #61 and #62 ascend through the forests that cloak the western shoulder of Vitosha. Bus #62 forks left to wind its way up to the **Kopitoto** area on a spur of the mountain, where there's a TV mast, a rather snooty hotel-restaurant and numerous woodland walks, while bus #61 carries on to **Zlatni mostove** ("golden bridges"). This area of mixed deciduous and evergreen forest is centred around the so-called **Stone River**, a ribbon of huge boulders running down the mountainside that was once the moraine of an ancient glacier. Beneath the boulders burbles a rivulet that used to attract gold-panners, hence the locality's name. Tracks lead from the bus stop in all directions, past trade union-owned rest homes and small shacks selling drinks and snacks. The most popular walking route is a well-signed, medium-difficulty ascent of Cherni vrûh, taking two to three hours. The path leads up the side of the Stone River, passing the Kumata and Konyarnika huts before emerging above the treeline onto a boggy plateau. From here the path runs alongside a protected area known as the **Peat Reserve** (*Torfen rezervat*) – a squelchy wilderness area covered with wildflowers in spring – before climbing up towards Cherni vrûh.

Kremikovtsi

Twenty kilometres northeast of Sofia, nestling in a crook of the Balkan mountains, the village of **KREMIKOVTSI** is home to one of western Bulgaria's most charming ecclesiastical attractions, the fourteenth-century **monastery of St George**. Occupying a spur of a fir-shrouded hill overlooking the village, the original monastery church lurks in a small courtyard, dwarfed by a more modern church built at the beginning of the twentieth century. The original church's interior is covered with vibrant frescoes dating from the 1500s, evidence that wealthy Bulgarian nobles were spending considerable sums of money on religious art even at the height of the Ottoman occupation. A picture of St George, seated on a throne and using a dragon as a footrest, straddles the archway leading through to the naos, the inner sanctum of the church. The naos itself is dominated by a rendition of the Virgin Mary behind the altar, arms outstretched in a protective gesture. Look out, too, for a niche on the right bearing another portrayal of St George, this time riding his horse and planting a spear in the dragon's throat.

The best time **to visit** the monastery is at the weekend or on one of the big feast days, as the nun who unlocks the church for visitors can be difficult to track down at other times. The monastery attracts most visitors on St George's Day (*Gyergyovden*, May 6), although it also gets pretty busy on other big holidays, notably Assumption (*Golyama Bogoroditsa*, August 15) and the Birth of the Virgin (*Malka Bogoroditsa*, September 8). Note that there's nowhere to eat or drink in the village, save for a couple of rudimentary cafés, so bring your own supplies.

Getting to Kremikovtsi

Tram #22 runs from Knyaz Dondukov to the Avtogara Iztok in the north-eastern suburbs (on some signs Avtogara Iztok is called "Avtostantsia Iztok", to differentiate it from Avtogara Poduyane, which is sometimes also misleadingly referred to as Avtogara Iztok by locals), where you change to **bus** #117. The bus passes the sprawling Kremikovtsi steelworks before entering Kremikovtsi village: get off at the village library (*chitalishte*), a two-storey concrete building where the bus veers off to the right. Instead of following the route of the bus, bear left uphill through the village, and the monastery is about thirty minutes' walk; you should be able to pick out the church's cupola and bell tower on the hillside ahead.

If you're **driving**, head out of Sofia along Botevgradsko shose for about 10km, then turn left to Kremikovtsi at the KAT (traffic police) checkpoint.

Eating

While none of Sofia's restaurants could be classed as truly outstanding, you'll at least find a greater choice here than anywhere else in the country. Mainstream restaurants aiming at modern European cuisine tend to be disappointing, and you would be better off sticking to the increasing number of establishments rediscovering the virtues of **traditional Bulgarian cooking**. Many of these restaurants feature live music – usually an inoffensive mixture of folk and international easy-listening. There are also a number of **foreign-cuisine** restaurants which, although few would pass muster in their homelands, add to the variety. Decent, inexpensive Chinese restaurants are thick on the ground, especially in the streets just west of the centre around the Zhenski pazar. Summer brings out the best in the city, when places with outdoor seating remain packed well into the evening.

For a quick daytime bite, the many **fast-food** joints around the Banya Bashi Mosque and along bulevard Vitosha serve *kyofteta*, *kebapcheta* and other indigenous dishes. You'll find a bigger choice of snacks and light meals in the city's cafés, most of which serve light lunches and an appetizing range of sweets.

The **market** on ulitsa Graf Ignatiev, alongside the Sveti Sedmochislentsi church, is the handiest place to pick up fresh fruit and veg. Well-stocked supermarkets include Oazis, in the basement of the Tzum shopping mall (Mon–Fri 8.30am–8.30pm, Sat 8.30am–7.30pm); and Billa, just behind the *Central Forum* hotel at ul. Sofiiski Geroi 4 and bul. Bûlgariya 55 (Mon–Sat 8am–9pm, Sun 9am–5pm).

Cafés and snack food

Art Museum Café corner of ul. Sûborna and ul. Lege. Lunch amid the Thracian tombstones in a very pleasant patio café at the back of the Archeological Museum. Salads, pasta and other light meals.

Dani's ul. Angel Kûnchev 16. Deli-style café just off bul. Vitosha serving up generous soups, salads and sandwiches washed down with thirst-quenching home-made lemonade. Pricier than average but worth it.

Dream House ul. Alabin 50A. First-floor vegetarian café-restaurant perched above a certain burger franchise, offering a satisfying range of soups, tofu-based dishes, and Bulgarian standards such as fried aubergines with yoghurt and peppers stuffed with cheese.

Dvete Furkli ul. Kûrnigradska 14. Small daytime café and cake shop just off bul. Vitosha. It's one of the best of the central cafés, with great-quality cakes and good service.

Halite corner of bul. Knyaginya Mariya Luiza and ul. Ekzarh Yosif. Covered market containing numerous snacking possibilities; with a pizza- and kebab-oriented food court on the top floor, a branch of *Trops-kûshta* (see below) in the basement, and several bakeries and salad bars in between.

Jimmy's Sladoledena kûshta ul. Angel Kûnchev 9. Mecca for ice cream (both eat-in and take-out), as well as the usual coffee-and-cake café fare.

Kravai ul. Frityof Nansen 1, on the northeastern corner of Yuzhen Park. Simple Chinese eatery – pull up a stool or take away. Open 24hr.

Trops-kûshta ul. Sûborna 11 & ul. Alabin 22. Excellent-value self-service restaurant offering tasty Bulgarian standards such as *musaka*, *bob* (bean soup), and *pûrzheni chushki* (baked peppers), as well as meat-free and salad options. Daily till 9pm.

Vienska sladkarnitsa/Wiener konditorei Orlov most. Excellent coffee and sumptuous cakes in stylish surroundings, opposite the Soviet war memorial.

Restaurants

For most visitors, eating in a restaurant is relatively cheap, especially if you stay out of deluxe hotels and avoid imported drinks; even in the topnotch establishments, a three-course meal with drink rarely exceeds 30–45Lv/€14–21 per person. Most restaurants open from about 11am until 11pm, with some closing one day a week, often Sunday. We've included telephone numbers below for those restaurants where reservations are a good idea at weekends.

Central Sofia

All the restaurants listed below are marked on the Central Sofia map (pp.92–93).

Background Pub bul. Vitosha 14. Small courtyard bar–restaurant which does decent Bulgarian food. Occasional live music in the evenings.

Divaka ul. 6 Septemvri 41a ⓣ02/986 6971. Lively, informal place serving up superb Bulgarian meat-dominated dishes, excellent salads and decent sweets – all at very reasonable prices. Always full. There's another branch at ul. Gladston 54 (ⓣ02/989 9543).

Da Vidi ul. Angel Kûnchev 36. Upscale but not-too-formal restaurant featuring floor-to-ceiling windows, minimalist decor and an eclectic choice of Mediterranean dishes, including some exquisitely prepared fish.

Egur Egur ul. Dobrudzha 10 ⓣ02/989 3383. Popular Armenian restaurant with plush seats, formal service but only slightly higher-than-average prices. The English-language menu guides you round the exotically flavoured lamb stews and wonderfully tasty vegetarian side dishes. Big international wine list.

Happy Bar & Grill corner of bul. Stamboliiski and pl. Sveta Nedelya. Home-grown chain decked out in international, fun-restaurant style, with fairly standardized chicken-and-chips options, and some traditional Bulgarian dishes. There's another branch at ul. G. S. Rakovski 145.

Krim ul. Slavyanska 17 ⓣ02/981 0666. Grand old restaurant that's been a popular place since Communist times. Upmarket food, including the occasional Russian speciality, served in a nineteenth-century mansion. There's a nice garden, and live music on summer evenings. The only minus point is the unpredictable service.

Manastirska Magernitsa ul. Han Asparuh 67 ⓣ02/980 3883. Plushly decorated town house with a large outdoor terrace, a few steps east of the main bul. Vitosha. Huge range of traditional Bulgarian dishes including all the grilled-meat favourites, and a host of vegetarian side orders that can be grouped together to provide a sumptuous beast-free feast.

Mahaloto bul. Vasil Levski 47. Imaginative mix of traditional Bulgarian grilled meats and modern European cuisine, served up in an attractive brick cellar. Outdoor tables in summer.

Mamma Mia ul. Tsar Shishman 39. Cheap and reliable restaurant with traditional Bulgarian fare downstairs, pizzas upstairs, and a terrace on the roof. Open late.

Niky ul. Neofit Rilski 16. Grill restaurant set in a fancy garden (complete with water features) behind the hotel of the same name. A simple but effective menu of pork and chicken standards.

Pizza Palace bul. Vitosha 34. Probably the best of the city-centre pizzerias, with acceptable if not-quite-Italian food and attentive staff; it's busy, with a fast turnover.

Pri Yafata ul. Solunska 28 ⓣ02/980 1727. Authentic Bulgarian food in rooms decked out in traditional textiles and nineteenth-century knick-knacks. Popular with tourists and prone to over-crowding at the weekend, but a reliable place for quality food nevertheless.

Rotisserie Nationale ul. Neofit Rilski 40 ⓣ02/980 1717. This atmospheric cellar-like restaurant has a good reputation and offers a classy international menu. One of the few places in Sofia to serve a decent T-bone steak. Reserve in advance and dress smartly to avoid the sneers of the doorman.

Trikrakoto Pile ul. Denkoglu 3. Friendly, intimate place in one of the backstreets west of bul. Vitosha, offering umpteen different chicken recipes and a great range of salads.

Ugo corner of bul. Vitosha and ul. Gladston. Fast and satisfying pizzas from one of the more reliable central outlets. There's another branch at ul. Neofit Rilski 68.

Zad Teatrû ul. Ivan Vazov 6. A nineteenth-century house with a tree-shaded garden just behind the National Theatre (hence the name), offering a mixture of Bulgarian and international cuisine but with high-quality grilled fare predominating: the steaks and fish dishes are excellent. Great cakes too.

Out of the centre

All restaurants listed below are marked on the Sofia map (pp.86–87).

Chevermeto bul. Cherni vrûh 31 ⓣ02/963 0308. Folk-styled restaurant in the basement of the *Hotel Hemus*, 2km south of the centre, offering traditional food and colourful rural furnishings. However it's the live performances by folklore groups that constitute the main attraction.

Hadzhidraganovite kûshti ul. Kozlodui 75. Ethnographic-themed restaurant in the back-streets between the centre and the Central Station, with an ensemble of traditionally furnished rooms representing different areas of Bulgaria. Pretty much everything from the Bulgarian culinary repertoire is on the menu; and the list of *rakiyas* is long and appetizing. Folk music most nights.

Nov Standart ul. Shipka 34. Large, minimally decorated bar-restaurant next to the Russian cultural centre east of town, popular with younger diners due to its combination of fast food, filling pastas and hearty steaks. Loudish music and big-screen TVs help to set the atmosphere.

O! Shipka ul. Shipka 11 ⓣ02/449288. Justifiably popular pizzeria east of the centre serving up cheap and filling pizzas in a brightly decorated interior or big garden.

Otvûd aleyata, zad shkafa ("Beyond the alley, behind the cupboard") ul. Budapeshta 31 ⓣ02/983 5545 or 983 5581. Upmarket place hidden away in residential streets northeast of the centre, with pleasant garden seating and Art-Nouveau touches inside. The food is a mixture of modern European and traditional Bulgarian, with excellent sweets.

Pri Miro ul. Mûrfi (i.e "Murphy") 34 ⓣ02/943 7127. Popular Serbian restaurant 3km east of the centre in the Oborishte district (take a taxi). The repertoire of mincemeat rissoles and *pljeskavice* (Serbian burgers) is expertly done and goes down a treat with traditional garnishes such as *ajvar* (pepper and aubergine purée). There's sometimes live music in the large garden at weekends.

Drinking

Drinking in Sofia is a round-the-clock activity, with numerous cafés and kiosks doling out coffee, juice and alcohol during the day, and bars and pubs pulling in punters during the night-time hours. Many of the latter close at around

11pm–midnight, although there are plenty of late-opening bars or discos for those who want to continue until the early hours. Spring and summer bring out the best in the drinking scene, when café life moves out onto the pavements, and alfresco bars and beer pavilions (some of which are open 24hr) emerge in numerous city-centre locations – the City Garden and the area of Yuzhen Park around the NDK are good places to look.

Cafés and bars

Babble ul. Tsar Shishman 22. Groovily furnished drinkerie that looks like a 1960s science fiction movie. DJs spin plastic at weekends. Tucked in a courtyard behind Bilkovata (see below).

Bilkovata ul. Tsar Shishman 22. A buzzing, smoky cellar with decent music and a young crowd. Packed beer garden in summer. The name refers to the *bilkovata apteka* ("herbal pharmacy") that used to stand here.

Blaze ul. Slavyanska 36. Snazzy bar in the streets behind the university with cutting-edge dance music on the sound system and a cool, trendsetting clientele. Usually open until the small hours.

By the Way ul. G. S. Rakovski 166. Big, brash, busy café-bar that pulls a regular after-work crowd and keeps on going till the early hours.

Café-bar 703 ul. Tsar Shishman 24. Popular city-centre bar near the church of Sveti Sedmochislentsi, with dark red decor and a couple of cosy snugs.

Flannagan's *Radisson Hotel*, pl. Narodno Sûbranie 4. Roomy Celtic theme pub which doubles as a dining venue, on the ground floor of the *Radisson* hotel. Popular with movers and shakers due to its position immediately opposite the Bulgarian parliament, it frequently packs out with busily networking expats.

J. J. Murphy's ul. Kûrnigradska 6. The best of Sofia's "Irish" pubs by far, with lively laid-back atmosphere, decent bar-food menu, and European soccer games on the big screen. A place to avoid if you don't like mingling with expats.

Lodkite southwestern side of Borisova gradina, near bul. Dragan Tsankov. Wonderful outdoor bar set in a former children's playground, favoured by students and young professionals. DJs spin either mainstream dance music or something totally weird.

My Mojito ul. Ivan Vazov 12. Dark, cosy and rather stylish corner in which to while away a lengthy evening. DJs playing different styles of music on different nights draw a wide range of discerning arty types.

Toba&co ul. Moskovska 6. Relaxing bar occupying a semicircular summer pavilion built onto the back of the royal palace. Nice place to linger over speciality teas or coffees during the daytime, although the decibel level moves up a notch in the evenings, when there may well be DJs.

Teatûra ul. Dyakon Ignatii. Vast summer-only outdoor bar opposite the National Theatre, drawing a fair proportion of the city's beautiful things and staying open well into the early hours.

Tequila Bar bul. Yanko Sakûzov 2. First-floor bar with a terrace overlooking the Vasil Levski monument, packed with hedonistically inclined young Sofians on weekend evenings. Not much point turning up before midnight.

Sofia's gay scene

Sofia's gay scene was a purely underground phenomenon until recently, and although the number of bars and clubs is on the increase, addresses have a tendency of changing from one year to the next – property-owners don't always like giving long-term leases to nightlife ventures that might draw scandalized protests from the neighbours. You could do worse than try *George*, a laid-back and friendly bar at ul. Lavele 17 (no sign outside, so follow the sound of music); or *Spartakus*, a mixed gay/straight club in the underpass on the corner of bulevards Tsar Osvoboditel and Vasil Levski. For latest information on the gay scene, check Ⓦ www.bulgayria.com.

Entertainment

Sofia's real forte is **drama, ballet and classical music**, all of which are of a high standard and very inexpensive. **Youth culture** is less prevalent, although it is beginning to make its presence felt. Cultural listings are usually to be found in the back pages of the daily press or in weekly mini-magazines like *Edna Sedmitsa v Sofia* ("One Week in Sofia") and *Programata* ("The Programme"), both of which are given away free in trendy bars. Otherwise **information and tickets** for most high-culture venues are available from the Concert Bureau at bul. Tsar Osvoboditel 2 (Mon–Fri 8am–noon & 3–7pm), or in the NDK centre. You can also get information on theatres and concerts by telephoning ⓣ171, but don't bank on getting a foreign-language speaker.

The most popular form of entertainment for many locals is the **cinema** – and the flood of (subtitled) American movies sweeping the country means that you won't have any problems understanding the dialogue. The *Sofia Echo* has weekly cinema listings. Multipleks, underneath the NDK centre (ⓣ02/951 5101), is a modern multi-screen affair with decent sound; other decent city-centre cinemas include Levski, bul. Yanko Sakûzov 30 (ⓣ02/846 7171); and Europa Palace, ul. Alabin 35 (ⓣ02/987 0707).

Theatre

Plays are, naturally, performed in Bulgarian, so not knowing the language is a distinct drawback, but the general standard of performances can make a visit to the theatre rewarding.

Dramatichen Teatûr Sofia bul. Yanko Sakûzov 23A. Big productions and musicals.

Kuklen Teatûr ul. General Gurko 14. Stunningly designed shows by a highly regarded puppet theatre, with daytime performances for children and occasional evening shows of adult-oriented drama.

Malûk Gradski Teatûr "zad kanala" bul. Yanko Sakûzov 25. The best place to see modern works in a small, intimate auditorium, next door to the Dramatichen Teatûr Sofia.

Mladezhki Teatûr pl. Narodno Sûbranie. Youth theatre, with consistently good avant-garde productions.

Naroden Teatûr Ivan Vazov ul. Dyakon Ignatii 1A. Works by eminent Bulgarians and classical writers performed by the national theatre company.

Sûlza i Smyah ul. Slavyanska 5. The oldest professional theatre company in Sofia, dating from 1892, and maintaining a reputation for challenging drama.

Satirichen Teatûr Aleko Konstantinov ul. Stefan Karadzha 26. The place to go for comedy and cabaret.

Teatralna Rabotilnitsa Sfumato ul. Dimitûr Grekov 2 ⓦhttp://sfumato.info. Award-winning experimental theatre group with a reputation for producing challenging, unmissable pieces. Based 2km east of the centre in the suburb of Poduyane.

Music

The National Palace of Culture, or **NDK** (ⓣ02/916 2368), is the venue for many of the bigger symphonic concerts or operatic productions; otherwise **symphonic music** can be heard at the Zala Bûul, Aksakov 1 (ⓣ02/987 7656), which hosts performances by the Sofia Philharmonic in the main auditorium, chamber concerts and solo recitals in the chamber hall. The traditional home of **opera and ballet** is the Narodna Opera, bul. Dondukov 58 (ⓣ02/877011). The Stefan Makedonski State Musical Theatre, bul. Panayot Volov 3 (ⓣ02/442321), tends to concentrate on lighter operetta and musicals. **Festivals** to look out for are the **Sofia Music Weeks** (late May to late June), featuring international soloists and ensembles; the **Music Evenings** (early Dec), concentrating on the best native classical musicians; and the November **Jazz Festival**. Festival events take place in the NDK and in the Zala Univerziada, ul. Shipchenski prohod 2 (tram #20 from the Levski monument).

Clubs and live music

There's a growing club scene in Sofia, offering a wide range of DJ-driven music, although venues go in and out of fashion from one year to the next. Regular gig venues devoted to new music are a rarity in Sofia, although plenty of bars and clubs feature cover bands. Information on what's on is hard to come by, although the *Sofia Echo* (see p.84) publishes lists of mainstream clubs, and usually gives you some idea of what kind of music to expect. Otherwise a quick perusal of *Edna Sedmitsa v Sofia* or *Programata* (see p.117) will provide a few hints as to what's currently hip. Entrance fees rarely exceed 5Lv.

Bulgarian pop stars, and the occasional Western act who can be bothered to make the trip, play in the NDK or in the large multipurpose halls such as Zala Universiada, ul. Shipchenski prohod 2.

Backstage bul. Vasil Levski 100. Roomy disco–bar, with live bands playing jazz or pop/rock covers, and a billiard room at the back.

Bibliotekata in the basement of the National Library, corner of bul. Vasil Levski and ul. Oborishte Ⓦwww.bibliotekata.com. Big, brash and enjoyable club with commercial dance music, frequent live rock bands, and a sushi bar.

Chervilo bul. Tsar Osvoboditel 8. Most enjoyable of the city-centre discos, with up-to-the-minute mainstream dance music at weekends, and different styles – Latin, retro or Britpop – on other nights of the week. The action spreads out onto the terrace in summer, when it's more like an elite, pay-to-enter pavement café than a club.

Cutty's Ark Borisova gradina. Access from ul. Mitropolit Kiril Vidinski. Legendary open-air disco doling out the best in techno and house. Foreign DJs sometimes fly in to play at special events.

Escape ul. Angel Kûnchev 1. Centrally located home-from-home for techno-heads.

Funky's Music Hall pl. Bûlgariya 1. Big, enjoyable bar round the back of the NDK, offering a regular diet of live jazz acts and rock-pop cover bands.

Jazzy ul. San Stefano 33 Ⓦwww.be-jazzy.hit.bg. Stylish subterranean bar offering different branches of DJ culture on different nights. Located near Bulgarian National TV's main studios and popular with media types.

O! Shipka ul. Shipka 11. Cosy candle-lit cellar club beneath the pizza restaurant of the same name (see p.115), hosting regular gigs by local indie and metal bands. Look for posters around town or pick up a schedule on the door.

Swingin' Hall bul. Dragan Tsankov 8. Buzzing suburban bar housed in a sequence of cosy cellar-like chambers. Clientele ranges from arty students to business types. Live music (usually pop/rock or jazz) on two stages.

Tri Ushi ul. Tri Ushi Ⓦwww.triushi.com. Unmarked basement club in an alleyway just off ul. Knyaz Boris I, hosting punk, house and reggae nights – which tend to be advertised by word-of-mouth only, so ask around or check the website.

Football

Sofia has two **football teams** with a mass following. Levski, originally the Interior Ministry (that is, the police and the secret services) team, have been the most successful in recent years, winning a string of first division championships. Their home is the Stadion Georgi Asparuhov, northeast of the city centre on Todorini kukli (trolleybus #1 from bul. Levski). Levski's bitter rivals are the Bulgarian Army club CSKA, who play at Stadion CSKA in the middle of the Borisova gradina park. The capital's two other clubs are Slaviya, who are based at Sporten Kompleks Slaviya just behind the Ovcha Kupel bus station (tram #5 from behind the Palace of Justice), and Lokomotiv, whose ground is on bulevard Rozhen in the northwestern suburb of Nadezhda (tram #12 from the train station). Matches involving the national side, as well as derby matches between Levski and CSKA, take place at the Vasil Levski stadium at the western end of Borisova gradina. **Tickets** for regular league games (rarely costing more than 3Lv or so) are usually sold at turnstiles on the day of the match. For international fixtures, buy tickets from the stadium box office as far in advance as possible.

Shopping

Most of Sofia's high-street stores are located around the bulevard Vitosha, bulevard Stamboliiski, ulitsa Graf Ignatiev area, although it's the Tzum shopping mall, at the western end of the Largo, which has the biggest range of fashionable clothes, luxury goods and souvenirs.

The main fruit, vegetable and bric-a-brac **market** is Zhenski pazar on ulitsa Stefan Stambolov. There are also good fruit and veg markets on ulitsa Graf Ignatiev; at Rimska stena, just south of the city centre on ulitsa Hristo Smirnenski; and, best of all, Sitnyakovo, 2km southeast of the centre on ulitsa Shipchenski prohod (tram #20 from Knyaz Dondukov).

Souvenirs

Ethnographic Museum pl. Aleksandûr Batenberg. The museum shop (head past the ticket office and turn right) has the city's biggest choice of woodcarving, embroidery, woollen kilims and folk CDs.

pl. Aleksandûr Nevski Long line of open-air stalls selling paintings, reproduction icons, antiques, lace and embroidery.

Tchu kilim ul. G.S. Rakovski 38. Small shop near the opera house selling high-quality carpets from Chiprovtsi.

Traditzia bul. Vasil Levski 36 Ⓦ www.traditzia.bg. Artisans' outlet selling ceramics, kilims and other handiwork. Higher-than-average prices, but probably worth it for the quality of craftsmanship on offer.

Books

Orange ul. Graf Ignatiev. Three-storey multimedia store offering stationery, CDs, DVDs, and lots of books – including a smattering of English-language paperbacks.

pl. Slaveykov Huge outdoor book market with a multitude of stalls. Good place to root around for Bulgarian-English dictionaries, large-format art books, and the occasional English-language novel.

Shipka 6 ul. Shipka 6. Headquarters of the Bulgarian Artists' Union, with a brace of bookstores on the ground floor – good place to pick up lavish books about art and architecture.

Music

Bulgarian Composers' Union ul. Ivan Vazov. Beside the National Theatre. Big choice of classical, folk and jazz CDs, as well as sheet music and some traditional musical instruments.

Gega ul. Solunska 49. Retail outlet of the Gega record company. Stocks many contemporary Bulgarian folk CDs.

Dukyan Meloman ul. 6 Septemvri 7A. A basement-bound treasure-trove of jazz and world music CDs (including plenty of Bulgarian folk), plus boxfuls of second-hand vinyl.

Listings

Airlines Aeroflot, ul. Oborishte 23 Ⓣ 02/943 4489; Air France, ul. Sûborna 5 Ⓣ 02/980 6150; Alitalia, ul. Graf Ignatiev 40 Ⓣ 02/981 6702; Austrian Airlines, bul. Vitosha 41 Ⓣ 02/981 2424 or 980 2323, Ⓦ www.aua.com; British Airways, bul. Patriarh Eftimii 49 Ⓣ 02/954 7000, Ⓦ www.ba.com;

Moving on from Sofia

If you're **flying** out of Sofia, call ⓣ02/7932 3211 for flight information; bus #84 runs every ten to fifteen minutes from the Orlov most to the airport, 10km east of town. A full list of airline addresses and telephone numbers appears below and on previous page.

When leaving Sofia **by train**, remember that tickets for lines covering the northern half of Bulgaria (including the routes to Lom, Vidin, Ruse and Varna) are sold on the ground floor of the station; all others in the basement. The system of platform numbering is incredibly confusing (each platform is also divided into *iztok* – eastern – and *zapad* – western – sections, referred to as *i* or И and *z* or З respectively on the departures board), so allow plenty of time to catch your train. Beware, also, of pickpockets, beggars and con merchants who offer to help you onto your train, then make aggressive demands for money. To beat the queues, you can make advance bookings at the **Transport Service Centre**, or TsKTON, in the basement shopping arcade below the NDK (Mon–Fri 7am–7.30pm, Sat 7am–2.30pm; domestic ⓣ02/658402, international ⓣ02/657186). The same office handles bookings for sleeper services, as well as selling tickets for international trains. International tickets can also be bought from a counter in the Central Station or from the Rila Bureau, ul. General Gurko 5 (Mon–Fri 7am–7.30pm, Sat 7am–6.30pm; ⓣ02/987 0777 or 987 5742).

Some **inter-city buses** can be booked in advance from the TsKTON office (see above), although in most cases you'll have to trek out to the relevant bus station in order to buy a ticket. The most important of these is the**Tsentralna Avtogara** on bulevard Knyaginya Mariya Luiza, where a confusing array of private companies sell tickets from booths in the main departure hall – fortunately there's an integrated timetable and an English-speaking information desk. A few services still use bus stations in suburban Sofia – Avtogara Poduyane, Avtogara Ovcha Kupel and Avtogara Yug – which serve different out-of-town regions: see "Travel Details" below for an idea of which one to head for. To get to **Avtogara Poduyane** (destinations to the north and northeast) on ulitsa Todorini Kukli, take bus #75 from Orlov most, or trolleybus #1 from bulevard Levski. For **Avtogara Ovcha Kupel** (destinations to the southwest) take tram #5 from behind the Palace of Justice, and get off at the eleventh stop, or take tram #19 from the train station for **Avtogara Yug** (destinations to the southeast), on bulevard Dragan Tsankov, catch tram #2 from ploshtad Sveta Nedelya or ulitsa Graf Ignatiev, alighting at the stop called Nadlez Dûrvenitsa, just beyond the *Park-Hotel Moskva* (the bus station is immediately beneath you).

The majority of **international buses** use the **Tsentralna Avtogara**, although a few depart from the **Trafik-Market bus park** outside the Central Station, where numerous international bus firms keep their offices.

Bulgaria Air, at the airport ⓣ02/937 3243, ⓦwww.air.bg; Czech Airlines, ul. Sûborna 9 ⓣ02/981 5408; Hemus Air, ul. Gladston 32 ⓣ02/981 8330, ⓦwww.hemusair.bg; JAT, ul. Dyakon Ignatii 1 ⓣ02/988 0419; KLM, ul. Uzundzhovska 14 ⓣ02/981 9910; LOT, bul. Stamboliiski 27A ⓣ02/987 4562; Lufthansa, ul. Sûborna 9 ⓣ02/980 4101; Olympic, bul. Stamboliiski 46 ⓣ02/981 4545; Swiss, ul. Angel Kûnchev 1 ⓣ02/980 4459; Turkish Airlines, ul. Sûborna 11A ⓣ02/980 3957.

Airport information ⓣ02/937 2211.

American Express Megatours, bul. Vasil Levski 21 ⓣ02/988 4953.

Car rental Avis, bul. Vitosha 3 ⓣ02/981 1082, at the airport ⓣ02/738023; Sixt, ul. General Gurko 10 ⓣ02/950 5220; Europcar, bul. Stamboliiski 34 ⓣ02/988 8686, and at the airport ⓣ02/720157; Hertz, bul. Vasil Levski 47 ⓣ02/980 0461, and at the airport ⓣ02/791447.

Currency exchange There's no shortage of cash-only exchange bureaux in central Sofia, although be warned that those on the main strip (bul. Knyaginya Mariya Luiza and bul. Vitosha) tend to offer rip-off rates, and you'll get a better deal in the side streets on either side. For travellers' cheques and credit card advances, Bulbank on pl. Sveta Nedelya, is the most reliable bank.

Embassies and consulates Albania, ul. Krakra 10 ⓣ02/946 1222; Australia, ul. Trakiya 37 ⓣ02/946 1334; Denmark, bul. Dondukov 54

Ⓣ02/980 0830; Greece, ul. San Stefano 33 Ⓣ02/946 1027; Hungary, ul. 6 Septemvri 57 Ⓣ02/963 1135; Macedonia, ul. Frederik Zholiyo Kyuri 17 Ⓣ02/870 1560; Netherlands, ul. Oborishte 15 Ⓣ02/816 0300; Romania, bul. Sitnyakovo 4 Ⓣ02/971 2858; Russia, bul. Dragan Tsankov 28 Ⓣ02/963 0912; South Africa, ul. Al. Gendov 1 Ⓣ02/971 3425; Sweden, ul. Alfred Nobel 4 Ⓣ02/930 1960; Turkey, bul. Vasil Levski 80 Ⓣ02/935 5500; UK, ul. Moskovska Ⓣ02/933 9222; USA, Sûborna 1 Ⓣ02/937 5100: consular section at Kapitan Andreev 1; Serbia and Montenegro, ul. Veliko Tûrnovo 3 Ⓣ02/946 1633. Irish citizens should contact their nearest embassy (in Budapest, Hungary Ⓣ00361/302 9600, Ⓕ302 9599) to find out which English-speaking embassy in Sofia is currently looking after their interests.

Hiking and camping equipment Stenata, ul. Tsar Samuil 63 Ⓦwww.stenata.com.

Hospitals The city's main casualty department is at Pirogov Emergency Hospital, opposite the Rodina hotel, at bul. General Totleben 21 (Ⓣ02/954 9468). For an ambulance call Ⓣ150.

Internet There's an increasing number of Internet cafés in the city centre: try the one on the ground floor of the NDK (by the entrance on the eastern side of the building next to the box office or *bileten tsentûr*); Cyberzone: future, ul. Angel Kûnchev 22; or the Telefonska palata, ul. General Gurko. Expect to pay around 1Lv/hr.

Left luggage Central train station, in the basement (daily 6am–midnight).

Libraries British Council, ul. Krakra 7 (Mon–Fri 9am–noon & 2–5pm); American Centre, ul. Kûrnigradska 18 (daily 1–5pm); French Cultural Institute, ul. Dyakon Ignatii 2 (Mon–Fri 9am–4pm)..

Newspapers Foreign newspapers can be bought from the newsstand in the basement of the *Balkan Sheraton* hotel; the newspaper stall in the Tzum shopping mall; and a few stalls on bul. Vitosha.

Opticians bul. Knyaginya Mariya Luiza 54.

Pharmacies 24hr service at Apteka Sveta Nedelya, corner of pl. Sveta Nedelya and bul. Stamboliiski.

Photographic supplies just west of bul. Vitosha at ul. Pozitano 24A.

Post office ul. General Gurko 6 (Mon–Sat 7am–8.30pm, Sun 8am–1pm).

Radio BBC World Service (91.0 VHF) broadcasts the usual English-language programmes, punctuated by news in Bulgarian every couple of hours; while Radio France Internationale (103.0 VHF) has the widest range of (Bulgarian and international) popular music.

Swimming Banya Mariya Luiza outdoor pool in the middle of Borisova gradina is the place to head for in summer, and is the nearest thing to a beach you'll find this far inland. Otherwise, try the Spartak indoor and outdoor pools, next to the *Harmony Sofia* hotel, bul. Arsenalski 4 (tram #6 from pl. Vûzrazhdane to the end).

Taxis OK Supertrans Ⓣ02/973 2121; Yes Taxi Ⓣ02/91119.

Telephones Telefonska palata, ul. General Gurko 4 (open 24hr).

Train information Ⓣ02/931 1111, Ⓣ932 3333.

Travel agents Try Zig-Zag, bul. Stamboliiski 20 (Ⓣ02/980 5102, Ⓦwww.zigzag.dir.bg), for hotel reservations and hiking tours in Bulgaria. Jamadvice, ul. Asen Zlatarov 10 (Ⓣ02/944 1429, Ⓦwww.btibulgaria.com) is a friendly, English-speaking agency that handles air tickets, while Lyuba Tours, ul. Tsanko Tserkovski 22 (Ⓣ02/963 3343, Ⓦwww.lyubatours.com), arranges tailor-made itineraries and weekend trips to Bulgarian towns and villages.

Visa extensions Available at the Interior Ministry (MVR) building at bul. Knyaginya Mariya Luiza 44 (Mon–Fri 9am–12.30pm & 1.30–5.30pm).

Travel details

Trains

Sofia to: Burgas (3 daily; 6hr 30min); Kazanlûk (3 daily; 3–4hr); Koprivshtitsa (5 daily; 1hr 40min); Pleven (hourly; 3hr); Plovdiv (20 daily; 2hr–3hr 30min); Ruse (4 daily; 7hr); Sandanski (4 daily; 3hr); Varna (5 daily; 8hr 30min); Vidin (3 daily; 5hr); Vratsa (4 daily; 2hr).

Buses

Tsentralna Avtogara to: Ahtopol (summer only 1 daily; 8hr 30min); Blagoevgrad (hourly; 2hr); Burgas (8 daily; 7hr); Dobrich (4 daily; 7hr); Gabrovo (2 daily; 3hr 30min); Haskovo (3 daily; 4hr); Kûrdzhali (3 daily; 5hr); Kazanlûk (5–7 daily; 5–6hr); Kiten (summer only 1 daily; 8hr); Lovech (1 daily; 3hr); Nesebûr (summer only 1 daily; 7hr 30min); Plovdiv (hourly; 2hr); Razgrad (2 daily; 6hr); Ruse (12 daily; 5hr); Sandanski (8 daily; 3hr); Shumen (6 daily; 6hr); Silistra (1 daily; 7hr); Sozopol (summer only 1 daily; 7hr 30min); Stara Zagora (4 daily; 4hr); Svilengrad (1 daily; 5hr); Svishtov (1 daily; 4hr 30min); Varna (5 daily; 7hr); Veliko Tûrnovo (8 daily; 4hr); Vidin (hourly; 4hr).

Trafik-Market to: Koprivshtitsa (2 daily; 2hr).

Avtogara Ovcha Kupel to: Bansko (12 daily; 3hr); Dupnitsa (hourly; 1hr 30min); Gotse Delchev (12 daily; 4hr); Kyustendil (6 daily; 2hr); Pernik (hourly; 40min); Rila Village (2 daily; 2hr); Rila Monastery (1 daily; 2hr 30min).
Avtogara Poduyane to: Botevgrad (10 daily; 1hr); Etropole (Mon–Sat 6 daily; Sun 4 daily; 1hr 30min); Koprivshtitsa (2 daily; 2hr); Pravets (4 daily; 1hr); Teteven (3 daily; 2hr 20min); Troyan (1 daily; 3hr).
Avtogara Yug to: Panagyurishte (4 daily; 2hr); Samokov (every 30min; 1hr 15min); Velingrad (4 daily; 3hr).

Flights

Sofia to: Burgas (summer only: 1 daily; 1hr); Varna (1 daily; 1hr).

International trains

Sofia to: Belgrade (1 daily; 8hr); Budapest (1 daily; 16hr); Bucharest (2 daily; 11hr); Istanbul (1 daily; 15hr); Kiev (1 daily; 38hr); Moscow (1 daily; 45hr); Thessaloniki (1 daily; 10hr).

International buses

Tsentralna Avtogara to: Athens (2 daily; 15hr); Belgrade (1 daily; 10hr); Istanbul (4 daily; 10hr); Skopje (1 daily; 5hr); Thessaloniki (4 daily; 7hr).
Trafik-Market to: Istanbul (2 daily; 10hr); Skopje (1 daily; 5hr).

2

The southwest

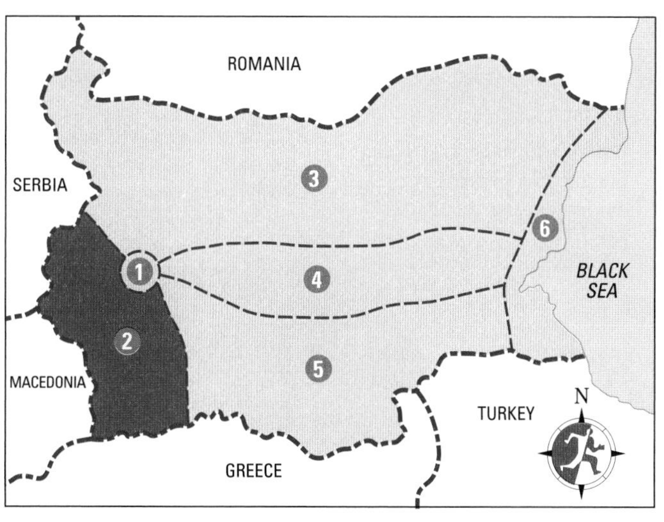

CHAPTER 2

Highlights

- **Rila Monastery** Bulgaria's most visited pilgrimage site, boasting a beautifully decorated church. **See p.136**
- **Melnik** A medieval mercantile town now the size of a village, in a captivating setting among weird pyramidal sandstone formations. **See p.165**
- **Kukeri** Nowhere in Bulgaria is the tradition of Shrovetide masked revels as well preserved as it is in the southwest: Pernik, Petrich, Razlog and especially Eleshnitsa are the best places to catch them. **See p.158**
- **Bansko** An engaging mixture of mountain village and modern holiday resort. **See p.150**
- **The train ride from Septemvri to Bansko** It may be painfully slow, but this narrow-gauge railway provides access to some of the most wonderful mountain scenery in the Balkans. **See p.159**
- **Hiking in the Rila and Pirin mountains** An area of imperious peaks and forest-shrouded lakes that offers some of the most rewarding hikes in Europe. **See p.141 & p.156**
- **Highland villages** Time seems to have stood still in the archaic, tobacco-growing regions of the far south: sample village life in Delchevo, Kovatchevitsa or Dolen. **See pp.161–163**

△ Train to Bansko

2

The southwest

The landscape of Bulgaria south of the capital is dominated by the River Struma, which rises on the southern slopes of Mount Vitosha before sweeping west then south through a series of arid gorges and fertile flood plains. Both the main southbound train route and the E79 highway to Greece follow the Struma Valley for much of its length, skirting some of the country's most grandiose scenery on the way. Although the major towns along the route are pleasant enough, most of the area's real attractions lie in the mountains to the east.

Formerly noted for their bandits and hermits, the **Rila and Pirin ranges** contain Bulgaria's highest, stormiest peaks: swathed in forests and dotted with alpine lakes they reward exploration by anyone prepared to hike or risk their car's suspension on the back roads. In the Rila range, the modern resort of **Borovets** is a major **winter sports** centre, while the much smaller **Malyovitsa**, nearby, is the starting point for some classic summer hikes. On the way you pass through the historic crafts town of **Samokov**, whose artists adorned **Rila Monastery**, the most revered of Bulgarian holy places. The

Cyrillic place names

Bansko	БАНСКО	Kulata	КУЛАТА
Belitsa	БЕЛИЦА	Kyustendil	КЮСТЕНДИЛ
Belovo	БЕЛОВО	Leshten	ЛЕЩЕН
Bistritsa	БИСТРИЦА	Malyovitsa	МАЛЬОВИЦА
Blagoevgrad	БЛАГОЕВГРАД	Melnik	МЕЛНИК
Borovets	БОРОВЕЦ	Panichishte	ПАНИЧИЩЕ
Delchevo	ДЕЛЧЕВО	Pernik	ПЕРНИК
Dobûrsko	ДОБЪРСКО	Petrich	ПЕТРИЧ
Dobrinishte	ДОБРИНИЩЕ	Pirin	ПИРИН
Dolen	ДОЛЕН	Radomir	РАДОМИР
Dragoman	ДРАГОМАН	Rila	РИЛА
Dupnitsa	ДУПНИЦА	Rozhen	РОЖЕН
Eleshnitsa	ЕЛЕШНИЦА	Rupite	РУПИТЕ
Gotse Delchev	ГОЦЕ ДЕЛЧЕВ	Samokov	САМОКОВ
Kalotina	КАЛОТИНА	Sandanski	САНДАНСКИ
Govedartsi	ГОВЕДАРЦИ	Sapareva Banya	САПАРЕВА БАНЯ
Gyueshevo	ГЮЕШЕВО	Zemen	ЗЕМЕН
Kocherinovo	КОЧЕРИНОВО	Zlatarevo	ЗЛАТАРЕВО
Kovachevitsa	КОВАЧЕВИЦА		

Pirin range is wilder and less developed, although its highest peak, **Mount Vihren**, is accessible from **Bansko**, whose nest of old stone houses makes it easily the most attractive of the mountain towns. On the southern fringes of the Pirin range near the Greek border, the monastery of **Rozhen** lies at the end of a great hike from the village of **Melnik**, known both for its wine and its vernacular architecture.

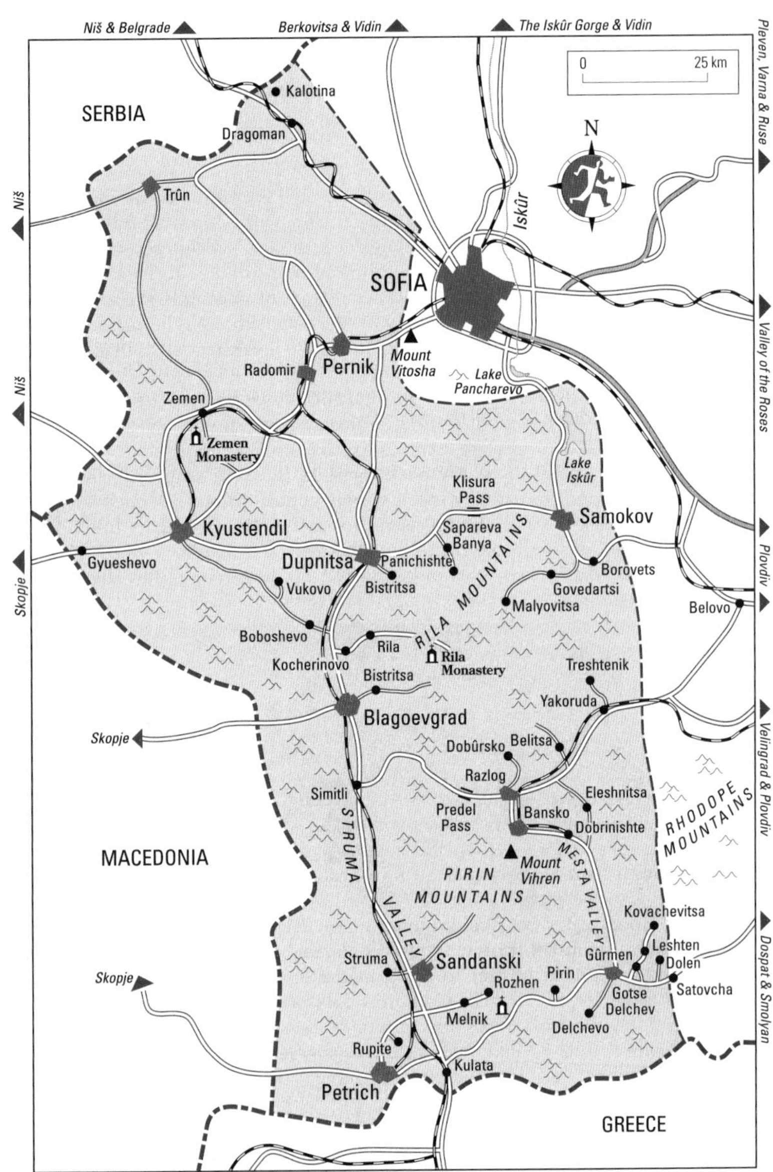

Slightly nearer to Sofia, the route leading west towards the Republic of Macedonia takes you past the ancient **monastery of Zemen** and the spa town of **Kyustendil**, which retains a smattering of Ottoman-period remains. Destinations like these – along with many others in the southwest – are possible day-trips from the capital.

Southwestern Bulgaria... and Macedonia

Once you get beyond the Rila mountains, you're entering the Bulgarian corner of a vast historical territory which, during the dying days of the Ottoman Empire, went under the name of **Macedonia**. In the decades preceding World War I, the problem of what to do with this multi-ethnic region (dubbed the "Macedonian Question" by politicians of the time) drove the diplomats of Europe to despair. Now divided between Bulgaria, Greece, and the Republic of Macedonia (formerly part of Yugoslavia), the heritage of historical Macedonia still exerts a powerful hold on the popular imaginations of all the region's inhabitants – not least because of the often heroic struggles waged by its constituent peoples to free themselves from the Ottoman yoke.

By far the greatest of the Macedonian freedom movements in the early twentieth century was the **Internal Macedonian Revolutionary Organization** or **IMRO** (VMRO in Bulgarian), members of which fought, depending on the political climate, either for the incorporation of Macedonia into Bulgaria, or for the establishment of Macedonia as a separate unit – a paradox which has turned historical discussion of the Macedonian Question into something of a minefield ever since.

To summarize a century of misunderstanding in a few words, Bulgarians (including those in the southwest) regard Macedonia and its people as a historical part of the Bulgarian nation, while citizens of the Republic of Macedonia tend to see themselves as a separate nation and the historical victims of Bulgarian arrogance and insensitivity. While disputing the latter assertion, most modern-day Bulgarians have become reconciled to the fact that the Republic of Macedonia is now an independent country with its own destiny, and are quite happy to concentrate on building good relations with their neighbours. However, arguments about history still mean a lot in these parts, so you'd be well advised to adopt a sensitive attitude when discussing the subject with locals.

Memories of Macedonian history in general, and the IMRO in particular, are strong in the southwest, with most Bulgarians – with some justification – regarding the IMRO fighters of yore as part and parcel of the Bulgarian national tradition. Since 1989 most towns in the southwest have named streets and squares after IMRO heroes, and a right-wing political party has adopted both the IMRO name and associations to become one of the most influential organizations in the region.

Despite modern-day political boundaries, the Macedonia of old still retains a certain **ethnographic unity**: the songs, dances and dialects of the Bulgarian southwest are often closer to those in the Republic of Macedonia than they are to the rest of Bulgaria. Grandiose folklore festivals like **Pirin Sings** (see p.155) are the best occasions at which to sample this unique culture, although you'll find Macedonian songs performed live or on the radio in restaurants and bars all over the region – especially in Bansko, where every tavern in town seems to offer folkloric entertainment of some sort at the weekends.

For more on Macedonia past and present, see Contexts p.465.

Southwest of the capital

Aside from its rugged yet fertile landscape and lack of tourists, the chief attractions of the region to the southwest of the capital are the small, reclusive **Zemen Monastery** and the mellow spa town of **Kyustendil**. Three or four trains a day between Sofia and Kyustendil stop at Zemen, making it possible to visit the monastery before catching a later train on to Kyustendil; unfortunately, buses between Kyustendil and Sofia take a more direct route, bypassing Zemen. Both buses and trains, though, initially pass through some of Bulgaria's most dismal urban-industrial sprawl, centred around the mining settlement of **Pernik** and neighbouring steel town Radomir.

Pernik

The remains of a fortress on Krakra Pernishki hill and the derivation of its name – from the Slav god of thunder, Perun – are the sole traces of antiquity in **PERNIK**. After 1891 this hitherto agricultural village became Bulgaria's largest centre of coal mining – an industry that, until recently, employed most of the population. Hence the city's only real attraction is the rarely open **Mining Museum** (officially Mon–Fri 8am–noon & 1–6pm), which is reached from the train and bus stations by heading down ulitsa Tûrgovska as far as the high-rise *Hotel Struma* (Ⓣ076/600545; ❷), then following the pedestrianized expanse of bulevard Krakra Pernishki to its end. During the Communist era miners received wages almost seventy percent higher than other industrial workers and enjoyed early retirement, subsidized holidays and other benefits. Today, however, the mining industry has all but collapsed, and working-class communities like Pernik have fallen on hard times. Nearby, at ul. Fizkultura 2, there's a small **History Museum** (again opening times are unpredictable, but officially Tues–Sun 9am–noon & 2–5pm), which holds a collection of ancient Thracian grave tablets found at a nearby sanctuary, as well as a few ethnographic oddments relating to the *kukeri* rites.

Pernik's New Year **Festival of the Kukeri** represents the city's only real source of excitement, re-enacting the old *survakari* and *kukeri* rites, originally intended to ward off evil spirits and promote fertility respectively. About 3500 costumed dancers dressed as yeti or nightmare apparitions and armed with wooden swords or axes participate, yelling and chanting. The festival straddles the last weekend in January every even-numbered year. The wealth of train and bus transport between Sofia and Pernik ensures that you can treat the festivities as a day-trip from the capital.

Kukeri rites – accompanied by much feasting and drinking – are also enacted in the **surrounding villages** every year on January 14. Travellers driving through the area on that date should be warned that each village exerts a symbolic "tax" on passing motorists (a small sum should suffice) before inviting them to join the revels.

Zemen Monastery and around

Forty-five kilometres southwest of Pernik, **ZEMEN MONASTERY** (*Zemenski manastir*; Mon, Wed, Fri & Sat 9am–5.30pm, Tues & Sun 11am–3pm; 10Lv) lacks the high walls and decorative facades that characterize Bulgaria's other religious foundations, and its small twelfth-century cruciform **Church of St Ivan the Theologian** appears similarly modest from the outside. Inside, however, are some of Bulgaria's finest surviving **medieval frescoes**, sensitively restored between 1970 and 1974. The frescoes – produced by anonymous artists during the 1350s for local noble Konstantin Deyan – are examples of the Macedonian School of painting, which was somewhat cruder and less formalized than the predominant style of Tûrnovo. Against a background of cool blues and greys, the saints with their golden halos and finery are depicted in hierarchies, including Deyan and his wife Doya who appear on the wall of the right-hand apse as you enter. Further along the same wall, there's an unusual rendition of Christ giving Holy Communion to the disciples, in which he's portrayed as two separate people – one giving bread, the other pouring out the wine. Elsewhere, dark blues and reds are employed to highlight the gravity of episodes like the *Treason of Judas*, the *Judgement of Pilate* and, most famously, the depiction of blacksmiths forging nails in readiness for the Crucifixion (in the second archway to the left as you enter). St John himself presides over the main doorway, his uncommonly bulbous forehead seemingly bursting with saintly thoughts. The monastery is 3km southwest of Zemen itself, overlooking the town from a secluded hillside site. It's easy to find, however: on leaving the train station, cross the car park and bear right into the village's main street (ulitsa Zemenski Manastir) and keep going.

To the southwest of Zemen, the River Struma has carved a rugged nineteen-kilometre-long defile between two massifs, known as the **Zemenski prolom**. Various **rock formations** – dubbed the Cart Rails, the Dovecote and so on by locals – are visible from the carriage window when the trains aren't plunging through a series of tunnels to escape the precipitous gorge; drivers will miss this view, however, as the road skirts round the gorge to the south. On inaccessible bone-dry crags you can also see the ruins of ancient forts, believed to have once defended the long-vanished town of Zemlen against incursions by the Byzantine Empire. The gorge ends near the village of Rûzhdavitsa, beyond which lies the broad **Kyustendil plain** – which locals proudly describe as the "largest orchard in Bulgaria". Fragrant in spring, the plain is the site of frenzied cherry-picking in June, and is richly coloured during autumn by the red apples, yellow pears and lustrous grapes that hang profusely in the **orchards** and vineyards.

Kyustendil

Bisected by the River Bansko, the town of **KYUSTENDIL**, with its fertile plain and thermal springs, has attracted conquerors since Thracian times. The Romans developed this into the "town of baths", and the Turks who settled here in large numbers after the fourteenth century constructed the *hammams* and mosques that gave Kyustendil its Oriental character. Some of this atmosphere lingers on in the old backstreets, although the centre of town has undergone considerable modernization, most of it tasteful. The town's wide, tree-shaded avenues lined with cafés are as agreeable as any in Bulgaria but specific sights are limited, so you could easily see all it has to offer in an afternoon. **Buses** to

Kyustendil leave Sofia's Ovcha Kupel terminal every couple of hours (about 2hr), and Blagoevgrad five times a day (1hr 30min). **Trains** run three or four times daily from Sofia (about 2hr 30min).

The Town

Both the bus and train stations are near the northern end of **bulevard Bûlgariya**, just beyond the high-rise landmark *Hotel Velbûzhd*. From here it's a ten-minute walk along bulevard Bûlgariya to the centre, provided you don't stop at any of the cafés en route, nor detour left onto a square featuring a modern **art gallery** (Tues–Sun 9am–noon & 2–5pm; 5Lv). The gallery is devoted to the work of local painter **Vladimir Dimitrov-Maistor** (1882-1960), who earned the honorific title of "Master" by treating uplifting themes in a vigorous, if uniform, style. Smitten by Eastern philosophy, and seeing parallels in it with the values of Bulgaria's peasantry, Dimitrov reacted against the art of the West, decrying Modernism as a destructive force innately hostile to the ideal of beauty. It's an attitude which had a profound effect on Bulgarian art throughout the twentieth century, effectively isolating it from avant-garde developments elsewhere. A recurring image in Dimitrov-Maistor's paintings is that of the idealized peasant maiden surrounded by fruit and flowers – his contemporary interpretation of the Madonnas produced by medieval Bulgarian icon painters – and there are examples aplenty on display here. A bearded, guru-like figure, Dimitrov-Maistor preferred the simplicity of village life to that of the city, and protested against the egoism of the art world by never signing his paintings. Accorded the status of a secular saint by his followers, Dimitrov-Maistor was viewed as an eccentric misanthrope by others – a rumour that he had an incestuous relationship with his sister Yordana (whose portrait hangs upstairs beside his) has recently enjoyed popular credence, although plenty of his admirers are on hand to deny it.

Further off to the left of the gallery you'll see a low red-tiled building that was once a **Dervish Bath**, with a pipe that still gushes scalding water. Directly east of here, occupying a whitewashed two-storey house at ul. Tsar Simeon I 11, the **Dimitûr Peshev House-Museum** (Tues–Sun 9am–noon & 2–5pm; 2Lv) celebrates one of Bulgaria's most unlikely heroes, the Kyustendil-born MP (1894–1973) who, contrary to the policy of the right-wing government in which he served, protested against the deportation of the Bulgarian Jews in 1943. Peshev – supported by other MPs, lawyers and local bigwigs – kicked up such a fuss over the planned deportations that the Bulgarian government resisted German demands for shipments of Jews to the death camps, opting to intern them locally instead (see box on pp.96–97 for a fuller version of the story). English-language texts, alongside pictures of Peshev and fellow protestors, tell the tale, while relics such as Peshev's backgammon board and hiking rucksack help to round out the personality of this relatively little-known politician.

A couple of blocks south of the Peshev museum is the **Chifte Bathhouse** (Mon & Thurs–Sat 5.30am–8.30pm, Wed & Sun 5.30am–12.50pm), a shabby postwar conversion of another, larger Ottoman bath, which in turn was built on top of a Roman spa centre. Divided into men's and women's sections, the warren-like, elaborately tiled interior contains a series of pools filled with 41°C, sulphate-rich water, which is also used in several local sanatoria for the treatment of gynaecological and nervous disorders. Behind the baths stands the sixteenth-century **Ahmed Bey Dzhamiya**, an impressive mosque with a tie-beamed porch, overlooking the excavated foundations of a Roman bath. There's no longer a significant Muslim population in Kyustendil, and the mosque now serves as display space for the town **history musem** (Tues–Sun 9am–noon & 1–5pm; 5Lv) – there's usually a different archeology-related exhibition here every year, but no permanent collection.

From the mosque, you can turn right to reach **ploshtad Velbûzhd**, a modernized square featuring a **memorial to Todor Aleksandrov**, the Macedonian revolutionary assassinated by a group of his own colleagues within the IMRO in 1924. Though not in Macedonia itself, Kyustendil occupied a special role in the struggles for Macedonian liberation at the turn of the twentieth century, with groups of heavily armed guerrillas regularly descending on the town before crossing the border into Ottoman territory. Beneath the chestnut trees at the southwest corner of the square, and nestling amid beautiful gardens, the **Church of Sveta Bogoroditsa** (the Holy Virgin) sports a trio of jaunty hexagonal domes and contains a rich collection of nineteenth-century icons in the porch. The church was built slightly below ground level and partially covered with earth during the Ottoman period in order to comply with restrictions governing the height and visibility of Christian places of worship. Dug out after the Liberation, the church still exudes a semi-secret, subterranean atmosphere.

Backtracking along bulevard Demokratsiya, you'll pass the tumbledown, overgrown **Fetih Mehmed Dzhamiya**, its minaret etched with hexagonal patterns, an effect achieved by inserting red tiles into the darker brown brickwork.

Hisarlûk hill

Just to the east of the mosque, traders and shoppers from the neighbouring Republic of Macedonia crowd the daily **market**, south of which pathways begin the ascent of **Hisarlûk hill**, shrouded in wooded parkland. Allow about twenty minutes to hike up the path (named the *pûtya na zdraveto* or "way of health" due to its popularity with walkers and joggers), although in summer you can take the "tourist train" which makes its way up the hill from Kyustendil's main square whenever enough people assemble. Near the summit you'll pass the *Hisarlûka* hotel, which boasts a great **view** of Kyustendil and the surrounding plain from the terrace of its café-restaurant. A little way further on, you can see the **ruins** of what was originally an extensive Roman settlement around the *Asclepion*, the sacred baths where Emperor Trajan cured his skin complaint and renamed the town Ulpia Pautalia to mark the occasion. Intermingled are the remains of a medieval fortress once occupied by the boyar Deyan. The Ottomans, who supplanted his rule over the region during the mid-fourteenth century, designated their new acquisition "Konstantin's land" – *Kostandinili* in Turkish – which eventually gave rise to the name of the town.

Practicalities

Kyustendil hasn't got a great choice of **accommodation** and you'd do best to avoid the lifeless Communist-era high-rise hotels in favour of the newer, privately run places: *Hotel Bûlgariya*, just off the central ploshtad Velbûzhd at ul. Konstantinova Banya 3 (Ⓣ078/51200 or 51202, Ⓦwww.bgglobe.net/bulgaria.html; ❹), has a variety of en-suites with fridge and TV, ranging from the bright and spacious to the cramped and gloomy; while the smaller *Lazur*, in between the stations and the centre at ul. Kiri i Metodii 15A (Ⓣ078/26368; ❸) has a handful of loudly decorated but comfortable rooms, some with shower, some with bathtub. Best option if you've got your own transport and twenty minutes' driving time to spare is the *Tri Buki*, in the hills 20km southwest of town (head out along ulitsa Tsar Osvoboditel, take the road to the village of Bogoslov and keep going; Ⓣ078/22332, Ⓦwww.tri_buki.com; ❹), a contemporary conversion of an old trade-union resort offering chic, comfy rooms with shower and TV. There's a decent restaurant, an outdoor pool in summer and a short downhill skiing piste in winter.

As far as **eating** and **drinking** in Kyustendil are concerned, the pavement cafés and pizzerias along bulevard Bûlgariya will suffice for refuelling purposes. For something more substantial, the rooftop restaurant of the *Bûlgariya* hotel is a great place to dine on traditional grills and enjoy skyline views, although the back-garden restaurant attached to the *Lazur* has marginally better standards and a longer wine list.

Moving on from Kyustendil

Bulgaria's main border crossing into Macedonia is 22km southwest of town, just above the village of **GYUESHEVO**. There are no local buses to the frontier (taxis cost about 25Lv), so if you're travelling this way it makes sense to catch one of the three daily services to Skopje (one of which continues to the lakeside resort of Ohrid), which originate in Sofia but pass through Kyustendil bus station en route. Twenty kilometres northwest of Kyustendil there's also a crossing point into **Serbia** – with no buses of any description travelling this route, you'll have to rely on taxis on both sides of the border.

If you're heading southwards, it's a toss-up between catching a bus to Blagoevgrad (5 daily; 1hr 30min), a good base for trips to the Pirin, or the nearer town of Dupnitsa (8 daily; 1hr), which offers two daily connections to Rila Monastery (see p.136) but is no place to get stranded. The only other thing in Dupnitsa's favour is that the road there passes the dreamily graceful **Kadin most**, a famous old bridge over the Struma in the middle of **NEVESTINO**, a one-horse town 15km east of Kyustendil. This five-arched seventeen-metre span was constructed after 1463 to guarantee the Ottoman lines of communication between the Danube and Salonika, although local legends advance different explanations. According to one, Vizier Isak Pasha took pity on a maiden separated from her betrothed by the river, and had it built as a wedding present – hence its original name, the Bride's Bridge. Another tale has it that the builder, Manuil, suggested to his brothers that they appease the river god by offering one of their wives as a sacrifice, the victim being whichever one arrived first with her husband's lunch. Manuil's wife turned up and was promptly immured, weeping and begging that they leave holes so that she might see daylight and continue to suckle her child.

The Rila Mountains

South of Sofia, Mount Vitosha gives way with barely a pause to the **Rila Mountains**, an area of wild highlands enclosing fertile valleys. If you're heading down the main southbound route towards Greece you'll only see the lowland town of **Dupnitsa** and the western fringes of the range, although this is the best direction from which to approach **Rila Monastery**, the finest in Bulgaria. The region's **ski resorts** and **hiking centres** are easier to reach via the town of **Samokov**, which has good transport links with Sofia.

Dupnitsa

Heading south from Sofia, the first town in the Struma Valley of any significance is **DUPNITSA**, which is still known to some locals by its Communist-era name **Stanke Dimitrov** (Stanketo for short). Its only real claim to fame is its **tobacco** industry: every year some eight million kilos of the stuff passes through Dupnitsa's warehouses and processing plants, the river is tinted a nicotine yellow, and you can see huge quantities of tobacco growing, or spread out to dry, throughout the surrounding countryside. However, the only reason for travellers to come here is to catch a bus to more appealing destinations in the Rila mountains.

If you have an hour to kill, there are a couple of monuments worth a look. Just off the modernized main square is a sixteenth-century **mosque**, whose simple domed structure has an elegance that displays Ottoman architecture's debt to Byzantine church building; it currently houses a bookshop. Behind it is the **Okoliiskata kûshta**, a house of the same period that once served as the *konak* of the Ottoman governor, and is now a small art gallery.

Dupnitsa is the jumping-off point for two **hiking routes** into the Rila Mountains. Nearest at hand is the trail beginning a few kilometres southeast of town at the village of **BISTRITSA**, from where paths lead either due east to the *Otovitsa* hut, or southeast to the *Byal Kladenets* hut. *Byal Kladenets* provides better access to long-distance hikes in the central Rila range, with a well-marked path ascending to the *Ivan Vazov* hut, which is well placed for onward assaults on the Seven Lakes (2hr 30min) or Mount Malyovitsa (6hr 30min). The other option is to take one of the three daily buses from Dupnitsa to **PANICHISHTE** just south of Sapareva Banya, then follow the asphalt road to the Lovna hut – start of a popular four-hour climb to the Seven Lakes. Remember to ask about current weather conditions before setting off, and travel properly equipped.

Practicalities

Dupnitsa's **train station** is about fifteen minutes' walk from the centre, while the **bus station** lurks a block or so off the main square. There are currently two buses a day directly to Rila Monastery and another one or two to Rila village, where you can pick up an onward service. If you need to stay in Dupnitsa, the town-centre *Rila* **hotel** (Ⓣ0701/59610 or 59630; ❷), with its bland and musty rooms, is your only option. The usual smattering of cafés adds a vivacity of sorts to the pedestrianized streets leading off the main square, and there's a nice **restaurant**, the *Panorama*, in the hilltop park overlooking the square.

Towards Rila Monastery

Roughly 20km south of Dupnitsa, a road branches east off the main highway towards **Rila Monastery**, southwestern Bulgaria's most visited tourist destination. After a couple of kilometres the road passes through the town of **KOCHERINOVO**, architecturally undistinguished but remarkable for being one of the favourite nesting grounds in these parts for storks – between May and August the rooftops are swarming with the creatures. The road then forges across the floodplain of the Struma river, passing some distinctive pyramidal sandstone formations outside the village of **Stobi** before entering **RILA**

VILLAGE, which lies at the foot of the Rila montains some 8km beyond the turn-off. Rila is a sleepy community with a few cafés, a food store and the uninspiring *Orbita* hotel (☎07054/2167; ❸), but being 27km short of the monastery that shares its name, it doesn't make a good base for sightseeing.

Beyond the village, the road enters the narrowing valley of the foaming River Rilska, fed by innumerable springs from the surrounding pine- and

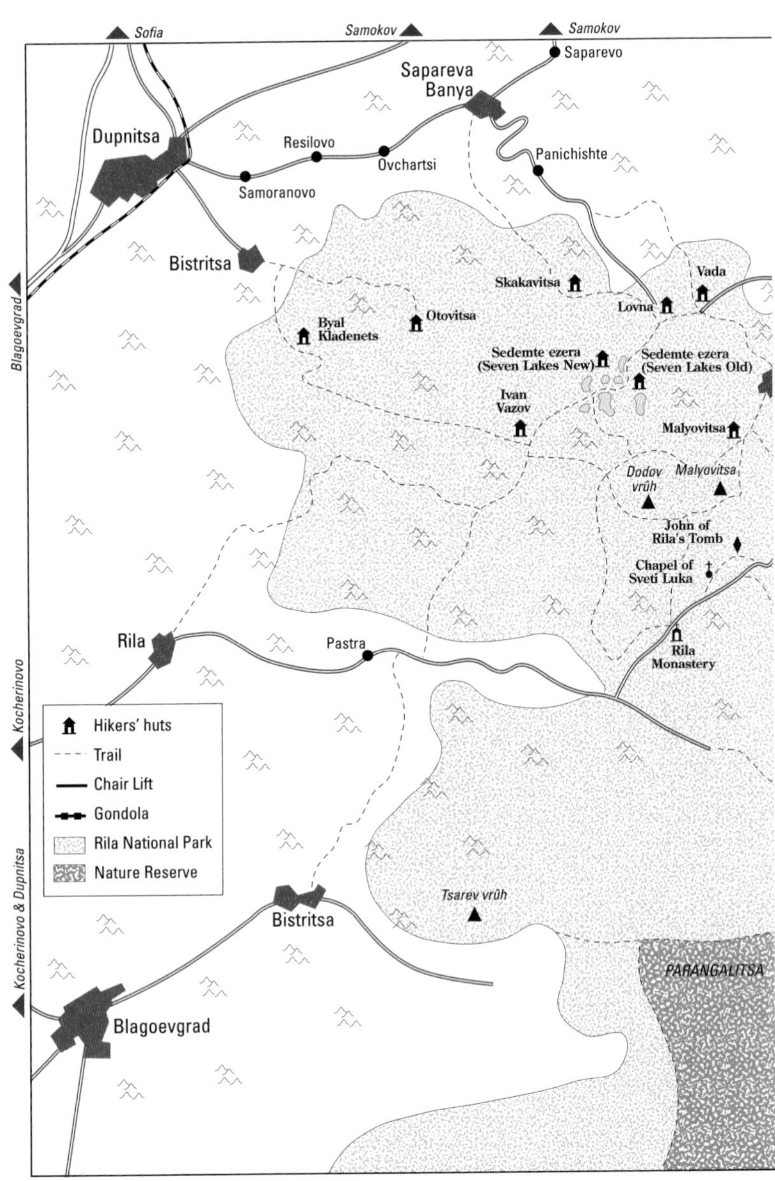

beech-covered mountains. Five kilometres out of Rila, on the left-hand side of the road, the **Monastery of Orlitsa** huddles unassumingly within a plain-looking walled enclosure. Built as a staging post for monks and pilgrims en route for the much more important foundation upstream, it's a relaxing little place, consisting of a grassy courtyard and dainty seventeenth-century church. The porch of the church, decorated by Samokov painter Nikola Obrazopisov,

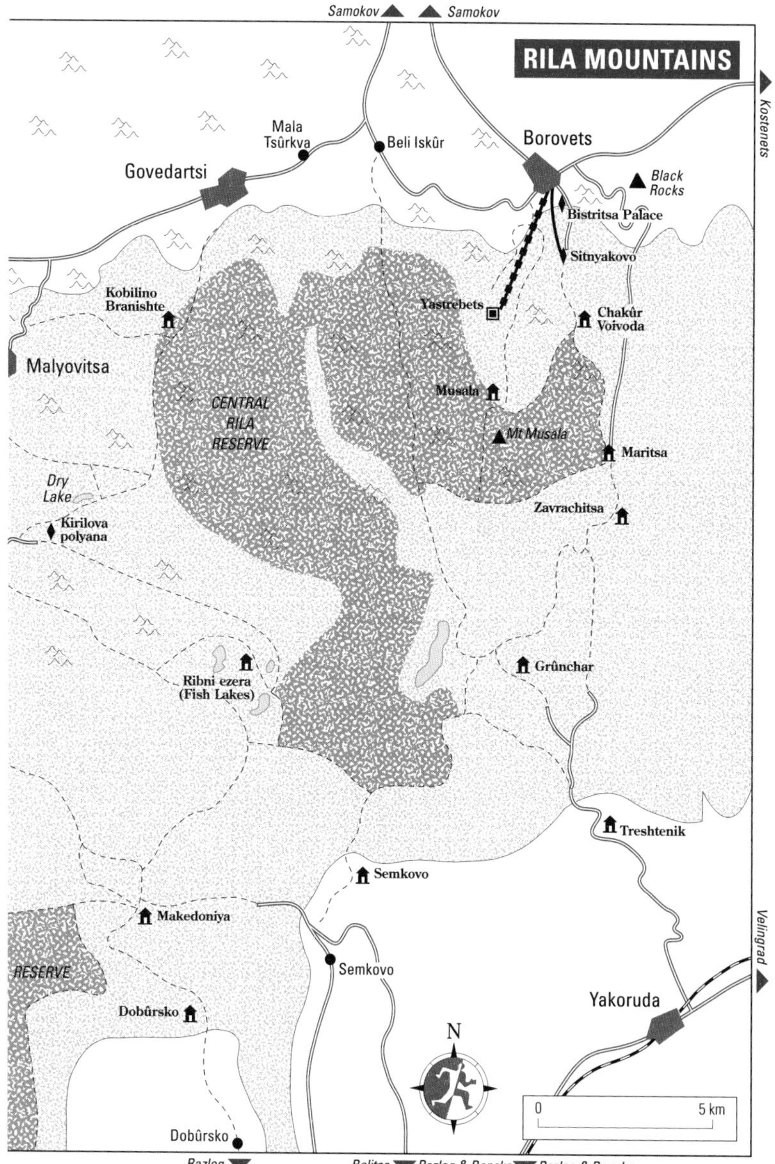

contains a lively portrayal of a procession bearing the bones of St John of Rila – which were brought back to Bulgaria for reburial in 1469 (see box opposite).

Rila Monastery

As the best known of Bulgaria's monasteries – justly famed for both its architecture and its mountainous setting – **Rila Monastery** (*Rilski manastir*) receives a stream of visitors, who now arrive by bus or car rather than on foot or by mule, as did pilgrims in the old days. Despite its popularity with tourists, the forest-girdled site still exudes the air of a wilderness, and it's easy to see why ninth-century holy man **John of Rila** (*Ivan Rilski*; see box opposite) chose this valley as his retreat. What began as a hermitage became an important spiritual centre after his death, and the monastery forged links with others in the Balkans and played a major role in Orthodox Christianity throughout the Middle Ages.

Although most visitors come on packaged day-trips, it is perfectly possible to get here independently, and the abundance of trails leading off into the densely forested hills make an extended stay more than worthwhile. Though the monastery gates are open daily to visitors from dawn till dusk, some of the sights within the complex keep more restricted hours. If you want to see (or take part in) a **service**, morning prayers start at 7 or 8am, evening prayers at 4 or 5pm. Services are preceded by monks hammering on wooden panels in the monastery courtyard, a ritual designed to remind the congregation of Christ's nailing to the cross. The start of the Saturday evening service is usually announced by a monk ringing a carillon of bells from Hrelyo's tower (see below), while the Thursday morning service is traditionally dedicated to St John himself, and features sacral chanting thought to date from the fifteenth century. Apart from Easter, the two main religious **festivals** celebrated here are the birthday (Aug 18) and feast day (Oct 19) of St John of Rila.

Getting to the monastery

Getting to Rila Monastery from Sofia comes down to how much money or time you're willing to spend. The easiest option is to take one of the **day-trips** advertised at hotel reception desks or by agents like Zig-Zag (see p.84). Usually these involve renting a car and driver with the latter doubling up as guide. Prices fall within the 160-220Lv margin – reasonable if there are three or four of you but a bit steep if you're on your own.

Travelling by public transport, it's possible to treat the monastery as a day-trip from Sofia providing you catch the morning service from the Ovcha Kupel terminal (currently departing at 10.20am) – you'll have a couple of hours to look around before catching the return service. If you're not too pressured by time there are a number of other ways of getting to the monastery: half-hourly buses leave Ovcha Kupel in Sofia for **Dupnitsa**, from where there are two daily services to the monastery (if you miss these, take one of the four daily buses from Dupnitsa to Rila village, and try to pick up a connecting service there). If you're approaching the area from the south, you might be able to save time by catching one of the hourly buses to Rila village from **Blagoevgrad** – although bear in mind that you might have a long wait in the village before a bus to the monastery shows up. Whichever direction you're travelling from, it pays to check timetables carefully at each stage of the journey in order to plan your return trip.

St John of Rila (880–946)

John of Rila, known to his compatriots as **Ivan Rilski**, was one of many ninth-century hermits and mystics who took to the wilds of Bulgaria and Macedonia in search of solitude and enlightenment. Having acquired a reputation as a wise man and healer, he finally yielded to his followers and established a monastery high in the Rila Valley, where he could combine the virtues of a religious community with ascetic solitude. It's said that he took steps to embalm himself by consuming herbs and potions, and his corpse was believed to possess curative powers. As a result, Rila became famous throughout the Balkans as a pilgrimage site.

In the Middle Ages, the bones of saints were important symbols that added legitimacy to the rule of whoever could establish control over them, so Tsar Petûr had John of Rila's **remains** moved to Sofia in the mid-900s. In 1183 they were stolen from here by the Hungarian King Béla III, who carted them off to the Catholic city of Esztergom, whose bishop reputedly went blind after denying that the bones were those of a saint and only regained his sight after publicly recanting. Their return to Sofia in 1187 was secured by the Byzantine emperor Isaac Angelus, to win support against the rebellion of the Bulgarian nobles Petûr and Asen, though this didn't prevent Asen from capturing the city and bearing the bones off to his new capital, Veliko Tûrnovo, in 1194. They finally returned to Rila in 1469 – though St John's right hand toured Russia in the sixteenth century to raise funds for the restoration of Bulgarian monasteries. The left hand is still kept in the monastery church – although it's not always on display.

Accommodation

Staying in the monastery's sparsely furnished guest "cells" (head for the lodgings office in the southeast corner of the yard; ❷) has some appeal if you don't mind the lack of hot water, or that the gates close at 8pm in summer, 5pm in winter (the porter can in theory be roused until midnight but don't bank on it). Two kilometres beyond the monastery's eastern gate and across the river, the *Rilets* **hotel** (Ⓣ07054/2106; ❹) is an uninspiring building with adequate, functional en-suites. A left turn on the access road to the *Rilets* brings you to *Bor* **camping**, a primitive but beautiful site on the riverbank. Back on the other side of the river, the *Zodiak* campsite (Ⓣ048/772657) offers bungalows (❶), a restaurant and a field for tents at the back, but can get noisy at weekends.

The monastery

Re-founded in 1335, 4km west of St John's original hermitage, Rila Monastery was plundered during the eighteenth century, and repairs had hardly begun when the whole structure burned down in 1833. Its rebuilding was presented as a religious and patriotic duty: urged on by opinion-forming educationalist Neofit Rilski (see p.153), public donations were plentiful and master craftsmen such as Aleksii Rilets and Pavel Milenkov gave their services for free. Work continued in stages throughout the nineteenth century, and the east wing was built as recently as 1961 to display the monastery's treasures, recognized by UNESCO as part of the World Cultural Heritage. The whole ensemble is ringed by mighty walls, giving it the outward appearance of a fortress.

Once you get through the west gate, however, this impression is dispelled by the harmonious beauty of the interior, which even the milling crowds don't seriously mar. Graceful arches surrounding the flagstoned courtyard support tiers of monastic cells, and stairways ascend to top-floor balconies which – viewed from below – resemble the outstretched petals of flowers. Bold red stripes and black-and-white check patterns enliven the facade, contrasting with the sombre mountains behind, and creating a visual harmony between the cloisters and the church within.

The monastery church

The **monastery church** has undulating lines, combining red and black designs with arches and a diversity of cupolas. Richly coloured **frescoes** shelter beneath the porch and within the interior – a mixture of scenes from rural life and Orthodox iconography, executed by muralists from Razlog, Bansko and Samokov, including nineteenth-century Bulgaria's greatest artist Zahari Zograf. The murals on the church's exterior include archetypal images of cataclysm: the fall of Constantinople, apocalypses and visions of hell, plagued by the bat-winged demons that seemingly loomed large in the Bulgarian imagination. On the left-hand side of the porch as you face the main entrance, the wrongdoings of sinners are portrayed with a love of grotesque detail; one picture shows rich men quaffing wine around a table, ignoring the pleas of St Lazarus, whose wounds are being licked clean by a posse of compassionate street dogs.

Inside the church, the **iconostasis** is particularly splendid: almost 10m wide and covered by a mass of intricate carvings and gold leaf, it's one of the finest achievements of the Samokov woodcarvers (see p.142). In front of the iconostasis, a wooden box hidden behind a curtain holds the holiest of the monastery's relics; a silver case containing the left **hand of St John of Rila**. The box is only opened up for the benefit of "real" pilgrims (monks are unlikely to be impressed by appeals from foreign tourists), who gaze upon the hand and cross themselves before taking away a wad of cotton wool which, by virtue of having spent time in proximity to the relic, is capable of sending those who sniff it into a heightened state of spiritual grace.

Halfway down the nave, on the left-hand side as you face the iconostasis, a wooden drawer (often closed, so ask a monk to pull it out) holds a miraculous **icon of the Virgin**, a remarkably serene example of twelfth-century Byzantine icon painting, presented to the monastery by the then Emperor Theodore Comnenus. Mounted in an elaborate frame containing other saintly relics, the icon is paraded around the monastery courtyard on the occasion of the Feast of the Assumption (*Golyama Bogoroditsa*) on August 15.

A chapel on the opposite side of the nave contains the **heart of Tsar Boris III**, buried beneath a simple wooden cross. Boris died of a mystery illness after a visit to Berlin in 1944, prompting many to speculate that he'd been poisoned by his Nazi hosts. After 1945, the Bulgarian Communists scattered his remains in the Iskûr gorge in order to prevent his grave from becoming the focus of anti-Communist sentiment, but the former monarch's principal organ survived, to be ceremonially interred here in 1993.

Beside the church rises **Hrelyo's Tower**, the sole remaining building from the fourteenth century, which you can sometimes ascend in order to visit the top-floor chapel. Its founder – a local noble – apocryphally took refuge as a monk here and was supposedly strangled in the tower; hence the inscription upon it: "Thy wife sobs and grieves, weeping bitterly, consumed by sorrow".

Other parts of the monastery

Huge cauldrons that were once used to feed pilgrims occupy the old **kitchen** (*magernitsa*) on the ground floor of the north wing, where the soot-encrusted ceiling has the shape and texture of a gigantic termites' nest. Beneath the modern east wing there's a wealth of objects in the **treasury** (daily 8am–5pm; 5Lv), including icons and medieval gospels, Rila's charter from Tsar Ivan Shishman, written on leather and sealed with gold in 1378, and the door of the original monastery church. Pride of place goes to the fourteen-inch-high wooden **cross** made by the monk Rafail during the 1790s. Composed of 140 biblical tableaux containing more than 1500 human figures (some no larger than a grain of rice), this took twelve years for Rafail to carve with a needle, and cost him his eyesight.

Whether any other parts of the monastery are open to sightseers largely depends on the whim of the current abbot, who is keen to establish the monastery as a pilgrimage site rather than a theme park. Usually, you're free to walk along the wooden galleries surrounding the courtyard, but you may not be allowed to enter any of the chambers or chapels leading off them. Most likely of the latter to be open is the **chapel of St John the Baptist**, immediately above the west gate, on the first floor: unlike the main monastery church, it's a tiny, intimate space, stacked with the towels, packets of soap and bottles of sunflower oil which pilgrims traditionally bring to the monastery as donations. The towels, once they've been sanctified through contact with the monks' hands, are sold back to the public (from a stall in the main courtyard; 2–5Lv depending on size) as mega-holy souvenirs.

Around the monastery

Just above the car park outside the monastery's western gate, beside the main hiking trail heading up into the Rila mountains (see box on p.141), a handsome slab of dark stone marks the final resting place of J. D. Bourchier (pronounced "*Bow*-cher"), the *London Times* journalist whose support for the Bulgarian cause in the years before World War I was rewarded by the granting of this grave-plot. Outside the monastery's eastern gate, a path descends towards the river and the **Church of the Presentation of the Virgin**, a decrepit late eighteenth-century structure surrounded by the graves of several generations of monks. The chapel on the church's upper storey is richly decorated with scenes from the life of the Virgin. A painting in the porch shows the Archangel Michael stomping on the body of a bearded wrongdoer. Look out for the *kostnitsa* or **ossuary** on the ground floor, housing the skulls of former monks.

Rila Monastery is the starting point for numerous short **hikes** (see box on p.141), the most agreeable of which is the short stroll to **St John of Rila's cave** (2hr return trip). The trail begins by the road about 2km beyond the east gate: a fairly obvious path bears left about 100m past the *Bachkova cheshma* restaurant, leading up through the woods to the **Chapel of Sveti Luka** after twenty minutes. The chapel, named after a nephew of St John of Rila who acted as the ageing hermit's servant, contains frescoes depicting him with the three other hermit-superstars of the Bulgarian–Macedonian borderlands: Gavril of Leshnovo, Prohor of Pchinya, and Ioakim of Osogovo. Twenty minutes further on, the **Chapel of St John of Rila** is built into the rock beside the cave or "**Miracle Hole**" where he spent his last twenty years. Having made it this far, most visitors plunge into the (admittedly rather dark) cave and work their way up through a fissure in the rock, emerging a few seconds later on the hillside just above – a reasonably unstrenuous task for the moderately fit. Traditionally, pilgrims were required to pass through this hole before proceeding to the monastery, and the conscience-smitten were regularly unable to do so. These people were judged to be sinners and forced to go home to repent for a year before coming back to Rila.

Eating, drinking and entertainment

For **snacks**, pick up delicious bread, *mekitsi* (Bulgarian doughnuts) and yoghurt from the monk-run bakery just outside the east gate. Just above here, the *Drushliavitsa* **restaurant** serves excellent local trout on an outdoor terrace beside a babbling stream. Further afield, the restaurant at the *Rilets* hotel has a terrace offering fine views of the surrounding hills, although better food is to be had at Chicho Kiro, 7km east of the monastery (and accessible via the eastbound asphalt road) at *Kirilova polyana*, where you can enjoy good home cooking and excellent sweets. **Nightlife** revolves around the subterranean bar at the *Rilets*, which hosts a **disco** if enough people turn up.

Samokov, Borovets and Malyovitsa

Access to the northern slopes of the Rila Mountains is provided by the burgeoning package resort of **Borovets**, and its smaller, less-developed neighbour **Malyovitsa**. Occasional buses run direct to both places from Sofia, although it's easier to pick up one of the half-hourly services from Sofia's Yug terminal to the provincial town of **Samokov**, from where there are numerous onward services. Samokov itself has sufficient historic interest to merit a stopoff of an hour or two, but is hardly the kind of place that you'd want to plan your holiday around. Of the numerous hiking possibilities in the region, there are a couple of classic walking routes over the mountains from Malyovitsa to Rila Monastery; those heading to the monastery by public transport from Borovets or Malyovitsa will have to head back to Samokov, catch a bus to Dupnitsa (see p.133), and change there.

The one-hour journey **from Sofia to Samokov** follows a scenic, forest-shrouded road up the narrow valley of the River Iskûr, passing the rather down-at-heel water-sports centre of **Lake Pancharevo** after about 10km. Entering the defile between the Lozhen and Plana massifs, you should be able to glimpse the ruined fortress of **Urvich**, where Tsar Shishman allegedly withstood the Turks for seven years. There's a scattering of **restaurants** along the road catering for Sofia folk out for a weekend drive: the *Zlatna Ribka*, about 10km beyond Lake Pancharevo, just before the village of **Pasarel**, is renowned for offering excellent local carp and trout. Beyond Pasarel lies the massive **Iskûr Dam** and **Lake Iskûr** – a man-made body of water 16km long, sometimes known as the "Sea of Sofia".

Samokov

Founded as a mining community in the fourteenth century, **SAMOKOV** soon became one of the busiest manufacturing centres in the Turkish empire (its name derives from the Bulgarian verb "to forge"), where all kinds of crafts guilds flourished, particularly weavers and tailors, who turned flax (still a major product) into uniforms for the Ottoman army. From the seventeenth century until the end of Turkish rule, Samokov's stature eclipsed that of Sofia and Kyustendil – and was raised even higher by the artistry of its woodworkers and painters, who decorated Bulgaria's finest monasteries. Nowadays it's a rather drab grey town, known primarily as the centre of Bulgaria's most prolific **potato-growing** area – and you'll see sacks of the things sold by roadside hawkers on your journey into town. Though foreign tourists from nearby Borovets are sometimes bussed in to wander around during the day, the place isn't really geared up for tourism, so it's best to digest what there is and move on.

The town centre

There's plenty of evidence of Samokov's past in and around the **centre**, although modern urban planning has left its monuments marooned in a sea of crumbling paving stones. The ornate **fountain** or *cheshma* on the main square is a legacy of the Turks, who considered running water an essential part of civilized living. Close by stands the only one of Samokov's once-numerous mosques to survive,

Hiking in the Rila Mountains

The **Rila National Park**, established in 1992, covers almost half the Rila mountain range (including its fourteen highest peaks), with a network of **hiking** trails and huts built in Communist times. These are slowly being refurbished with an eye to ecotourism, though most are still rudimentary, and information on vacancies or the weather remains scarce. For any of the hikes below, **food** supplies and a map of the mountains are essential, and it's prudent to pack a **tent** in case the huts are full or you need to take shelter. It's strictly forbidden to pick flowers or light fires (except at designated spots).

A noticeboard in the car park maps out the options for hikers **starting from Rila Monastery**. From here, two trails (which later converge at Dodov vrûh lead to the *Ivan Vazov* hut – about six hours' hard slog. This is a good base from which to press on to the *Sedemte ezera* or **Seven Lakes**, one of the most visually stunning areas of the Rila massif and an enormously popular target for hikers. There are two huts here: the old *Sedemte ezera* hut, on the shores of the lowest of the lakes, is pretty basic; while the new hut, 1km further west and at a slightly lower altitude, boasts almost hotel-like standards of accommodation. The lakes themselves, lying in an ascending succession of niches in the mountains, are eerily beautiful sights. It will take you a good two hours to walk from the (old) *Sedemte ezera* hut to the seventh lake and back again. From the *Sedemte ezera* huts you can descend north towards Panichishte and Sapareva Banya (passing the *Lovna* hut), or southeast towards Govedartsi (passing the *Vada* hut). Indeed the Seven Lakes can be treated as a day-trip from either the *Lovna* or the *Vada* hut – both are accessible by road and are useful as trail-heads.

The less well-trodden paths of the Rila mountains lie over on the eastern side of the range. Trails leading northeast from Kirilova polyana, 5km east of Rila Monastery, take you up towards *Suhoto ezero*, or **Dry Lake**, before wheeling northwest over the range towards Malyovitsa – although there's no hut on this route, so you'll need to camp overnight at the lake.

East of Rila Monastery, the *Ribnite ezera* (**Fish Lakes**) are another feasible destination, with a hut nearby. You can reach them by following the Kirilova polyana road to its end, and then following the Rilska up to its source in the mountains, or by a trail bearing southeast about halfway along the road, which crosses the ridge and passes some smaller lakes en route. Both walks take six to seven hours.

Southeast of Rila Monastery is another hut, *Makedoniya*, accessible by several paths originating from the minor road forking off a few kilometres west of the monastery. From the hut it's a day's hike west down to **Bistritsa** (from where buses run to Blagoevgrad), or a few hours' walk east to the *Semkovo* hut, which can also be reached from the Fish Lakes and may serve as a way-station for walkers making longer hikes (2–3 days) towards the Pirin or Rhodope mountains. Semkovo lies on the way to Belitsa and Yakoruda, two villages linked by bus or train to Razlog, Bansko and Velingrad. Hikers can also descend from here to the village of **Dobûrsko** (see p.158) via the hut of the same name. Alternatively, the *Grûnchar* hut (named "*Boris Hadzhisotirov*" on older maps), due east of the Fish Lakes, serves hikers bound for Mount Musala and Borovets, or those pursuing a more easterly path down to Yakoruda.

the **Bairakli dzhamiya** (Mon–Fri 8am–noon & 1–5pm; 3Lv), preserved as a monument to the skills of local builders rather than as a place of worship. Commissioned by the pasha in 1840, its design betrays Bulgarian influences: the roof-line mimics the shape of a *kobilitsa*, or yoke, while the interior decoration relies upon plant motifs rather than arabesques, with a magnificent sun symbol (bearing a surprising resemblance to the Star of David) beneath the dome.

Just off the square to the east, the **History Museum** (Mon–Fri 8am–noon & 1–5pm; 2Lv) traces Samokov's evolution up to the present day. The town's industrial past is remembered in a sequence of models illustrating the mining and smelting of iron ore: one shows a gargantuan, waterwheel-powered set of bellows used to force air into the furnaces. There's a disappointing lack of exhibits relating to the **Samokov school of icon painters**, who decorated churches and monasteries throughout Bulgaria in the nineteenth century, although one display cabinet does contain the personal effects of **Zahari Zograf**, the greatest of their number.

Continue east for 400m and you'll stumble upon the impressive shell of a derelict **synagogue**, built to serve Samokov's prosperous Jewish community in the nineteenth century. Next door, a walled garden filled with fruit trees wraps itself around the dazzling, blue and white **Sarafina House** (*Sarafskata kûshta*; Mon–Fri 8am–noon & 1–5pm; 3Lv), home to a rich Jewish trading family in the 1860s, and fully restored in the 1970s. Inside, chambers lead off from the main reception room, each sumptuously kitted out with traditional carpets, vivacious floral wall paintings, and intricately carved wooden ceilings.

South of the main square: woodcarving, icons and frescoes

Ulitsa Boris Hadzhisotirov leads west from the main square towards the old Bulgarian residential quarter of town, and the *metoh*, or **Convent of Sveta Bogoroditsa** at no. 77 (daily 6am–8pm). In the porch of the convent church there's a fine nineteenth-century painting of a winged Virgin Mary who extends her cloak to shelter the believers – the local priests and their flock – who herd beneath it. The church interior features colourful modern murals by local artists, imitating the folksy style of Zahari Zograf and his generation, while outside, a cobbled alley leads past a ramshackle collection of nunnery buildings and a beautifully maintained garden. A little way further on, the walled **Church of Sveti Nikolai** features cast-iron weathercocks on each of its three cupolas.

Although such skilful wrought-ironwork embodied the fusion of art and industry during the town's commercial heyday, greater fame accrued to the **Samokov school of woodcarvers**. Collectively, this refers to local artisans (some of whom studied on Mount Athos in Greece in the late eighteenth century), in particular to a group formed in the early nineteenth century, primarily to make the iconostasis for Rila Monastery. Although executed in 1793, the iconostasis of Samokov's **Metropolitan Church** on ul. Zahari Zograf, a couple of blocks west of Sveti Nikolai, is characteristic of their work. It's covered with intricate figures linked by plant-like traceries, interspersed with rosettes – which sometimes took the form of a six-petalled narcissus. The church's collection of icons presents the Samokov painting school at its best, with Hristo Dimitrov's *Enthroned Jesus* a particular highlight.

Barring the occasional angel, Samokov woodcarvers generally avoided depicting human figures, preferring to represent eagles, sparrowhawks, dragons, falcons and, above all, plants. Some of the best examples of these are to be found on the iconostasis of **Belyova church**, by the roadside 6km west of Samokov on the Sapareva Banya road.

Practicalities

There's no tourist **accommodation** in Samokov as such; the best bet is to head for nearby **Borovets**, 10km south, or Govedartsi, 12km southwest. Aside from a smattering of **cafés** on the main square, eating and drinking opportunities are scarce: the *Café Papillon*, opposite the History Museum, is probably your best bet.

Moving on from Samokov, there are buses roughly every hour to Borovets (the last one leaves at 7pm), seven daily to Govedartsi, and three minibuses to Malyovitsa. For Rila Monastery you need to take the 10am bus to Dupnitsa and change there (see p.133). Dupnitsa-bound buses go by way of **Sapareva banya**, Bulgaria's most ferocious mineral baths, whose hottest spring is fed by a superheated geyser (102°C) gushing 550 gallons of sulphurous water a minute.

Borovets

Near the turn of the century, Prince Ferdinand of Bulgaria built three villas and a hunting lodge among the aromatic pine woods covering the northern slopes of Mount Musala, a mile above sea level. The Mamrikoff family – after whom a verb meaning "to steal from an exalted position" was coined – and other wealthy folk did likewise, founding an exclusive colony, Tchamkoria, from which **BOROVETS** has developed. Effectively nationalized for the benefit of union and Party members in 1949, Borovets became a major **winter sports** resort in the 1960s, and is now largely geared towards package tourism. Lifts to a number of beginners' and intermediates' slopes are stationed right in the middle of the resort, so in terms of convenience, Borovets has got a lot going for it. It is also a popular place for Bulgarians to escape the heat during July and August, but pretty quiet during the intermediate months before and after the skiing season.

Competitively priced **package holidays** ensure that you get lodgings, skiing equipment and tuition – none of which is assured if you just turn up on spec. Also, most package operators offer lift passes and "ski packs" (including equipment rental) for a lower cost than you pay on the spot, making package holidays even more worthwhile.

Modern Borovets is a rather artificial place, with the monstrous **Hotel Rila** acting as its main point of orientation. You'd be well advised to escape to the mountains as soon as possible unless asphalt walkways lined with souvenir stalls are your cup of tea. The one worthwhile sight in the resort is the **Bistritsa Palace** (Tues–Sun 9am–noon & 12.30–4pm; 12Lv), fifteen minutes' walk northwest from the *Hotel Rila* along the Malyovitsa road. A rambling whitewashed mansion with carved wooden balconies, it was built as a hunting lodge for Tsar Ferdinand (who entertained Kaiser Wilhelm of Germany here in 1913) and used by his son, Boris, before passing into the hands of Bulgaria's Communist elite, and back again to Ferdinand's grandson, Simeon of Saxe-Coburg-Gotha. The interior is decorated in a mix of High Victoriana and Samokov woodcarvings, and bristles with animal heads and pelts, while heraldic lions crown the lampposts outside.

Skiing

The official **skiing** season lasts from mid-December to mid-April, though the snow cover is most reliable in late February and early March. Immediately in front of the *Hotel Rila*, the nursery slopes are served by ten drag lifts (daily in winter; 9.30am–4.50pm), and overlooked by a steep slope topped by the *Sitnyakovo* chalet, once one of Ferdinand's villas, that's accessible by chair lift (same hours; winter only) from behind the *Hotel Rila*. Experienced skiers favour the pistes on the western ridge of the mountain, which can be reached by a five-kilometre-long gondola (daily in winter, summer opening times depend on how full the resort is; 9am–4.30pm) running from near the *Hotel Samokov* up to *Yastrebets*, a former royal hunting lodge (now a hotel). Another chair lift serves the two ski jumps (55m & 75m long), while there are also shuttle-buses to the start of three cross-country runs at Shiroka Polyana, 2km away.

Hiking

The *Yastrebets* hotel (4hr 30min walk or 35min by gondola) is the starting point for the ascent of **Mount Musala**, the highest peak in Bulgaria (2925m). The first leg (1hr) brings you to the *Musala* hut at the foot of the mountain, whence it's an hour and forty minutes' walk to the summit. From Mount Musala it's six hours' trek southwards to the *Grûnchar* hut, where one path leads down to Yakoruda on the narrow-gauge railway line **to Bansko**; the other **to the Fish Lakes** (5hr) where, after sleeping at the *Ribnite Ezera* hut, hikers can push on to **Rila Monastery** (5–6hr).

If these sound too much effort, you could try an easy, ninety-minute walk to the **Black Rocks** (*Cheverni skali*), east of Borovets. A row of crags with sheer drops on both sides, they were used by the secret police in the late 1940s as a killing ground for "enemies of the people", who were simply pushed off to their deaths. The trail begins after the *Hotel St Ivan Rilski*, entering the woods beside a cross-braced fence. Bear right at the fork 100m later, then left downhill and left at the next fork; when you reach the farm buildings take the middle, gravelled route and turn left at the fork onto a sandy track that gets narrower and stonier en route to a picnic area near the Black Rocks.

Practicalities

Borovets has plenty of serviceable three- and four-star hotels in the centre of the resort, but finding **accommodation** from December through to early April can still be a problem if you're not on a package or haven't booked in advance. At any other time of year, there should be plenty of beds, although places may close for a while off-season.

There are innumerable places to **eat and drink** in the vicinity of the *Hotel Rila*, mostly hastily erected huts serving up pizzas, burgers, grilled chicken and beer. There are a number of places serving decent and inexpensive Bulgarian fare on the pedestrianized strip leading uphill from the *Hotel Rila* – the *Belija Kon* is a family-run place with reliable standards, while *The Blue* has funkier decor and a wider menu including plenty of fish dishes. Drinking joints come and go from one season to the next: *Bonkers* is a particularly raucous venue for (usually awful) local dance bands.

Hotels

Alpin ⓣ07128/2201, ⓦwww.alpin-hotel.bg. Centrally placed, piste-side building with mock-gothic turrets and chintzy, well-equipped en-suites. ❹

Flora ⓣ07128/2520, ⓔflora_hotel@abv.bg. Reliable mid-range choice offering functional en-suites, although the colour schemes are dowdier than elsewhere. ❸

Popangelov ⓣ07128/2666 Homely seven-room pension in the heart of the resort run by champion skier Petûr Popangelov, with skiing memorabilia cluttering the hallways. The simple doubles, triples (55Lv) and quads (70Lv) have pleasant pine furnishings and en-suite WC/shower. ❷

Rila ⓣ07128/2658, ⓦwww.balkantourist.bg. Enormous package-oriented four-star right in the middle of the resort, at the bottom of a popular ski run. ❻

Samokov ⓣ07128/2581 or 2306, ⓦwww.samokov.com. Three-hundred-room vacation hutch providing everything you need for a lazy holiday: fully equipped if dowdily decorated en-suite rooms, an indoor pool, ten-pin bowling and immediate access to the pistes. ❼

Petûr Dûnov (1864–1944) and the Dûnovisti

Every August, the Rila Mountains' Seven Lakes become a place of pilgrimage for the **Dûnovisti** (also known as the **Byaloto bratstvo** or "White Brotherhood"), members of a sect which formed around the teachings of Bulgarian mystic **Petûr Dûnov** at the start of the twentieth century.

Combining Orthodox Christianity with meditation, sun worship, vegetarianism and yoga, the sect was widely popular in Bulgaria before World War II and tolerated by both Church and state until the Communist era, when it was obliged to go underground. Having re-emerged in the 1990s, Dûnovism is now regarded as yet another authentic manifestation of Bulgaria's rich spiritual culture which also embraces Orthodoxy, paganism, faith-healing and clairvoyancey.

The son of an Orthodox priest from Varna, Dûnov studied theology in Boston, USA, returning to his homeland with a new-found enthusiasm for theosophy and spiritualism. He tried to weld the various religious and spiritual currents to which he had been exposed into a unified belief system, and after several years of solitary contemplation emerged with a book, *The Seven Conversations*, in 1900. In it he claimed that he had been appointed by God as His emissary on earth, entrusted with the task of building the "new culture of the sixth race". Precisely what Dûnov meant by the sixth race remains shrouded in verbose theorizing, but he essentially envisaged a higher level of human evolution in which man's spiritual nature would be more keenly developed – ushering in a new era of peace, love, justice and togetherness.

Dûnov immediately embarked on a speaking tour of Bulgaria, gathering followers who formed the White Brotherhood – an informal association bound together by Dûnov's personal charisma. Dûnov was already a national figure by World War I, when he was briefly interned by the Bulgarian government for his pacifist ideals. Bulgaria's defeat in the war, and the years of political instability that followed, created an urban intelligentsia disillusioned by political ideologies, and they increasingly gravitated towards Dûnov's simple message of peace, unity and nature worship. One of Dûnov's followers, Lyubomir Lalchev, was a close advisor to Tsar Boris III, leading to rumours that Dûnov himself exerted a Rasputin-like influence at court, though there's little evidence that he ever used this connection to do more than preach his message – indeed, throughout the interwar period, the only allies the Brotherhood cultivated were the Bulgarian Esperanto and Vegetarian societies.

Dûnov saw himself as a teacher rather than a leader, and thousands came to hear him deliver lectures at 10am every morning outside his house at ul. Opûlchenska 66 in central Sofia (Georgi Dimitrov, the future Communist leader, lived next door). In the 1930s he established a Dûnovist commune on the southeastern fringes of the capital, calling it *Izgrev*, or "Sunrise". He died in 1944, three months after the Communist takeover of Bulgaria, and was buried at **Izgrev** (with special permission from former neighbour Georgi Dimitrov, despite the danger that his grave might become a focus for anti-Communist pilgrimages). The Brotherhood itself was gradually harrassed into nonexistence, and the commune was demolished in the 1980s to make room for the (then) Soviet Embassy, though the suburb that now occupies the site still bears its name.

The Brotherhood re-emerged after 1989 – although typically for post-Communist Bulgaria, two competing organizations claimed the Dûnovist mantle, leading to a protracted court battle that wasn't resolved until 1995. The tradition of holding annual meetings on and around August 19 (the date chosen by Dûnov as the divine world's New Year's Day) was soon re-established, and in the week surrounding this date the Dûnovisti gather to camp by the shores of Bûbreg, the fifth of the Seven Lakes, worshipping the sun with pan-rhythmic dances accompanied by violin music composed by Dûnov himself.

Govedartsi, Malyovitsa and beyond

Thirty kilometres southwest of Samokov, Malyovitsa is everything that Borovets isn't: a tiny, secluded hiking base with limited – but rewarding – skiing in the winter, no package tourists, and a single, rather frugal, hotel. It's reached by a minor road which heads out of Samokov along the banks of the Cherni Iskûr, a burbling rivulet whose banks used to be packed with people camping wild before 1990, when the happy-go-lucky tourism of the Communist era speedily went out of fashion. A private minibus shuttles between Samokov and Malyovitsa twice daily in the summer and winter seasons: otherwise you're on your own.

You can also get to Malyovitsa via a little-frequented mountain road that leaves Borovets near the Bistritsa palace: this joins the Samokov-Malyovitsa route just short of **GOVEDARTSI**, a sleepy village worth mentioning as the location of the *Kalina* **hotel**, just off the main road (ⓣ07125/2643, ⓦwww.free.top.bg/kalina-hotel; ❷), a family-run B&B which serves as a good base for touring in the area if you've got your own transport. Continuing westwards you'll pass *Camping Bor* (ⓣ071252/304), 2km beyond Govedartsi, a secluded spot in the forest with simply furnished bungalows (❶).

A couple of kilometres west of the campsite, a branch road snakes up through the forest for 8km to **MALYOVITSA** itself, 1750m above sea level. There's not much here apart from the *Malyovitsa* **hotel** (ⓣ07125/2222; ❷), a gloomy place which will appeal to those with a taste for solitude and very few frills. There's a new slalom track and chair lift a short walk from the hotel, and plenty of huts renting out ski gear in season. However the place comes into its own as a base-camp for summer hikes, with a well-trodden trail leading south up a narrow valley overlooked by several peaks, most imperious of which is the 2729-metre **Mount Malyovitsa**.

The one-hour ascent to the *Malyovitsa* hut at the head of the valley constitutes the first leg of several hikes: from here it's seven hours' walk to the beautiful **Seven Lakes** (*Sedemte ezera*) cabin, or six hours to the *Ivan Vazov* lodge. Blasted crags surround another lake, *Strashnoto ezero*, which lies to the east of the *Malyovitsa* hut. Refuges there, and to the north of the Dry Lake (*Suhoto ezero*), serve as way-stations along the route to the hut beside the **Fish Lakes**: nine hours' hike in all. The most popular trail leads south to **Mount Malyovitsa** and **Rila Monastery**. Climbing the mountain takes about three hours, an easier ascent than by the steeper southern face. Afterwards, follow the path west along the ridge before taking the trail branching left, which leads to the monastery in the thickly wooded valley below (a further 3–4hr). For more information on hiking in the Rila range, see the map on pp.134–135 and the box on p.141.

The Pirin range and the far south

Like the Rila Mountains, the **Pirin range** can be approached from two directions. Heading down the Struma Valley towards the Greek border, the only places worth stopping at are the lively university town of **Blagoevgrad**, and **Sandanski**, jumping-off point for such destinations as the weird and wonderful **Melnik**, **Rozhen** and **Rupite**. Communications on Pirin's eastern flank tend to centre round **Bansko**, a short bus journey across the Predel pass from Blagoevgrad, and the region's best base for hiking and skiing. From Bansko there's a scenic route down the Mesta Valley to **Gotse Delchev**, another attractive town surrounded by some interesting villages. Above all, the **Pirin Mountains**, a glorious glacial landscape of peaks and lakes, offer some of the finest walking in Europe.

Heading south along the main road to Greece you're struck by the contrast between the arid highlands and the fertile bed of the **Struma Valley**, for while the region has one of the lowest rainfalls in Bulgaria, the Struma flows even in autumn. South of Blagoevgrad the E79 enters the **Kresna Gorge,** while trains forge their way through thirteen tunnels before reaching Sandanski. If you're driving along here, beware of the stream of trucks thundering along a two-lane country road designated as a European highway.

Blagoevgrad

Administrative capital of the Pirin region, **BLAGOEVGRAD**'s concrete suburbs and factories suggest a workaday town with little to tempt you away

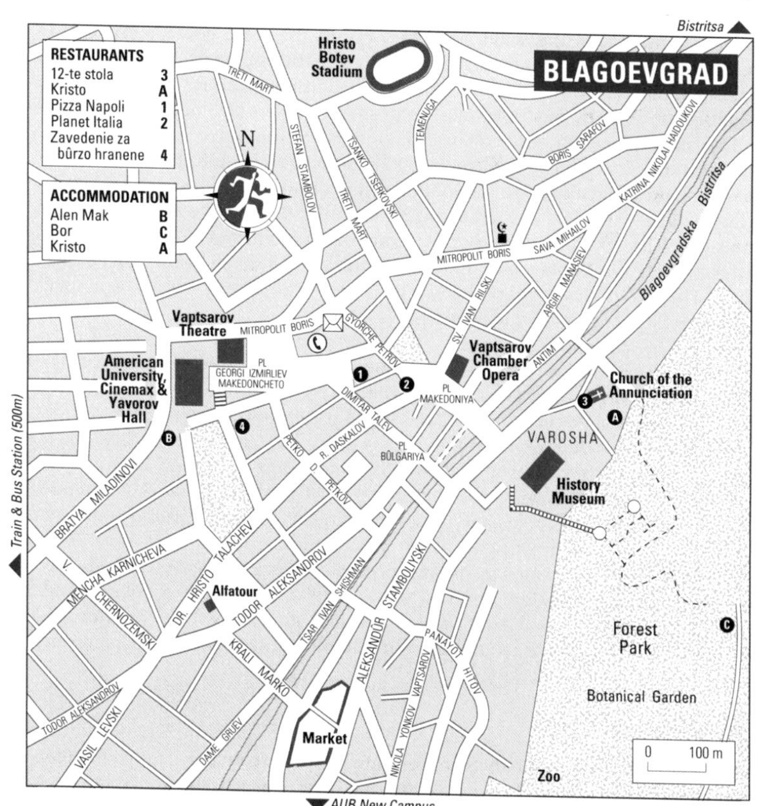

from the highway, but in reality it's the coolest place in southwest Bulgaria. While the lovingly restored old quarter and modern civic centre are the legacy of Zhivkov's decision to host an international summit here in 1988, the buzz is generated by 16,000 **university students**, the vast majority of them female (males brag of a ratio of 14:1, but six or seven to one seems likelier), making Blagoevgrad's cafés and clubs the most stylish – and flirtatious – in Bulgaria. With its lively **cultural life** and useful **transport** links to the rest of the Pirin, Blagoevgrad makes an ideal base. Hang around for a few days and you'll start to recognize (and be recognized by) the people you saw last night in a bar.

Historically Blagoevgrad was an important crafts town, predominantly inhabited by Turks from the sixteenth century until their flight in 1912, after which it was settled by local peasants and displaced Bulgarians from Macedonia and the Aegean seaboard. In 1950 it was renamed Blagoevgrad in honour of **Dimitûr Blagoev**, the founder of Bulgarian (and Russian) Marxism, and has chosen to stick with it in the post-Communist era because citizens either absolved Blagoev of any blame for Communism, or rejected restoring the former Turkish name, *Gorna Dzhumaya* – bestowed instead on a vile brand of cigarettes from one of the local **tobacco** factories.

The Town

Modern Blagoevgrad is centred around a sprawling pedestrian zone focused on the spacious flagstoned expanse of ploshtad Georgi Izmirliev Makedoncheto. Most prominent of the public buildings grouped around it is the **American University in Bulgaria** (AUB), established in Blagoevgrad in 1991 because the council offered it free use of the former Communist Party headquarters. Funded by the US and Bulgarian governments, it has 660-odd students from across the Balkans and the ex-Soviet Union, but this is set to increase as a new campus is built. East of the square, ulitsa Dimitûr Talev leads to the social hub of town, **ploshtad Bûlgariya**, surrounded by scores of **cafés** on Todor Aleksandrov, Raiko Daskalov and other sidestreets near the river, whose old houses and shops had facelifts during the Communist era. Further north on ploshtad Makedoniya, the **Vaptsarov Chamber Opera** and a statue of the Macedonian hero Gotse Delchev presage a residential area whose only "sight" is a small, abandoned sixteenth-century **mosque**.

Better to cross a footbridge and visit the Varosha, an area of preserved nineteenth-century houses around the **Church of the Annunciation of the Virgin** (*Vûvedenie Bogorodichno*), whose fluid roof-line mimics the shape of a carrying yoke, while the black, red and white pattern on its facade extends right around a three-sided arcade linking the church to a freestanding bell tower. The nearby **History Museum** (Mon–Sat 9am–noon & 1–6pm; 3Lv) exhibits some fine icons and carvings from churches in Melnik and Dobûrsko: Thracian, Roman and Greek relics jostle with stuffed Pirin wildlife, and brightly coloured folk costumes. Farther south is a large daily outdoor **market**, at its most lively on Saturdays, with sections for fresh produce, clothes and electrical goods.

Alternatively, it's only ten minutes' walk uphill to the attractive **Forest Park**, where you'll find a small **zoo** and a **botanical garden**, with a rosarium and species from both the Rila and the Pirin mountains, dotted with interesting rock forms.

Practicalities

Blagoevgrad's **train station** is about 1km southwest of the centre on ulitsa Sveti Dimitûr Solunski; bus #2 or #3 will save you a walk into town. The majority of Sofia-Blagoevgrad **buses** pick up and drop off in the car park immediately in front of the train station; most other services use the terminal 200m south along the same street.

Blagoevgrad's two downtown **hotels** cost the same, but are completely different: the allegedly three-star *Alen Mak* near the main square (Ⓣ073/23031, Ⓕ20713; ❹) is a large, soulless conference venue with notoriously bad service, while the *Kristo*, in the Varosha district, just uphill from the Church of the Annunciation (Ⓣ073/80444; ❹), is a relatively new venture offering cosy en-suites in a traditional-style galleried building. Perched on top of a hill east of town is the *Bor* (Ⓣ073/22491; rooms ❹, apartments ❼), a recently renovated hotel with small but swish en-suites, some fantastic open-plan apartments, a dinky indoor pool and a load of woodland walks on the doorstep – it's reached by a steep flight of steps behind the museum, or by road from the market.

Good places **to eat** and watch the streetlife are *Pizza Napoli*, on the eastern side of ploshtad Georgi Izmirliev Makedoncheto, and *Planet Italia*, on the nearby ploshtad Makedoniya, both of which offer tolerable thin-crust pizzas and a decent choice of big salads. For a quick, functional and good-value feed, you can't beat the cafeteria-style *Zavedenie za bûrzo hranene*, round the side of an office block diagonally opposite the American University. For something a bit more substantial, *12-te stola* in the Varosha district, has a reasonably priced range of grilled meats and a pleasant courtyard, although the restaurant of the nearby *Hotel Kristo* has a broader menu and better views from its terrace. Coolest places to **drink** are in the narrow streets between ploshtads Bûlgariya and Makedonya: current student favourites include *Swing*, *Rock House* and *Murphy's Irish Pub*, although there's a fairly rapid turnover of what's in and what's out. After midnight, **clubbers** gravitate to the numerous disco-bars off ploshtad Bûlgariya. *Underground*, recognizable by its London tube sign, is a split-level cellar with three bars (one for beer only), where you can indulge in unrestrained but trouble-free drinking and dancing to hard rock, soul or salsa.

Blagoevgrad is home to some prestigious cultural institutions and festivals: its **theatre** and **chamber opera** (both named after the poet Nikola Vaptsarov) are among the best in the provinces, and the **Pirin Folk Ensemble** (based at the Yavorov Hall, next to the American University building) is the most popular troupe in Bulgaria. Blagoevgrad's **Theatre Days** (late April to early May) are Bulgaria's equivalent of the Edinburgh Festival, with drama companies from all over Bulgaria and the Former Yugoslav Republic of Macedonia competing for prizes at the Vaptsarov Theatre.

Bansko and the mountains

Bansko, a burgeoning tourist centre that mixes traditional Bulgarian architecture with holiday-resort flair, makes a good jumping-off point for some amazing hikes in the **Pirin National Park**, and is a transport nexus, with buses to the Struma and Mesta valleys flanking the Pirin range, and trains to Velingrad in the western Rhodopes. It also gives easy access to the attractive, traditional village of **Dobûrsko** and the mountain-bottom logging town of **Dobrinishte** both of which are surrounded by stunning countryside.

The road from the Struma Valley follows the River Gradevska that separates the Rila and Pirin ranges, and crosses the **PREDEL PASS**, site of the **Pirin**

Sings folklore festival (see p.155) where amateur musicians and dancers from towns and villages throughout the region perform on a series of small stages.

The route also passes through **RAZLOG**, 6km north of Bansko, which is a less attractive town, notable only for its **kukeri rites** on January 1, when large processions of costumed revellers take over the centre.

Bansko

Winter lasts for almost half the year in **BANSKO**, a town of just under 10,000 people nestled among greenery in the shadow of ice-capped Mount Vihren, the highest peak in the Pirin range. Unlike many Bulgarian towns, its modernized centre coexists easily with the older quarters, a maze of cobbled lanes where the timber-framed stone houses hide behind thick walls with stout double doors, built to withstand siege. The money to pay for these sturdy dwellings came from a nineteenth-century upsurge in commerce, when Bansko was an important way-station on the trade routes linking the Aegean port of Kavalla with the Balkan hinterland. Home to a new mercantile elite, many of whom used their wealth to endow churches or assist in the restoration of Rila Monastery (see

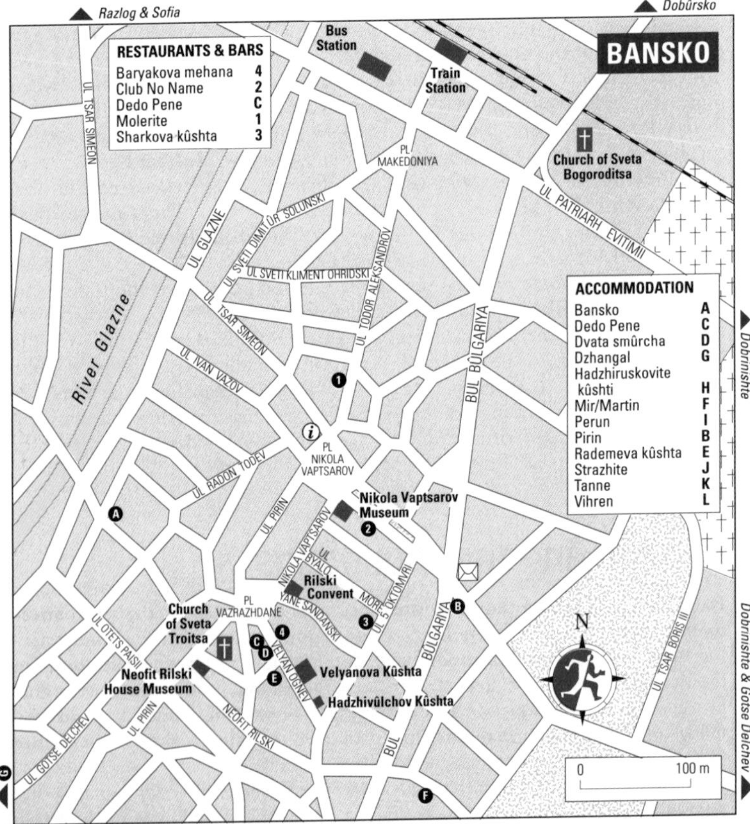

Skiing and mountain-biking around Bansko

Bansko's main **skiing** activity takes place on the slopes of **Mount Todorka**, 4km southwest of town. Access is provided by the shiny new cable car which ascends from the southwestern end of ulitsa Pirin (about thirty minutes' walk from the centre) to the 1467m peak of **Chalin valog**, starting point of some short intermediate runs. From here you can take the second stage of the cable car to the 1635m **Bunderishka polyana,** where you'll find a couple of beginners' runs, a snowboarding half-pipe, and chair lifts ferrying skiers further up the slopes of Mount Todorka. There's a big range of beginners' and intermediate descents from here, and – for advanced skiers – the punishing Alberto Tomba run. Many of the pistes converge on **Shiligarnika**, halfway down the mountain, where further chair lifts will whisk you up onto the southern shoulder of the mountain, and a further choice of blue and red runs. You can rent gear from most of the hotels, from Ulen at the chair-lift terminal or at Bunderishka polyana. Max Sport, in the same building as the *Strazhite* hotel, is the best-stocked ski shop.

Another activity that's recently caught on is **mountain-biking**, with several of the hotels renting out bikes. One popular route is to the Belizmata Reservoir, 3km southwest of town; cross the bridge near the *Bansko Hotel* and go straight until the first field track, or follow the road from the *Aneli Hotel* to the barracks and then take the track through the field. Many of the hotels rent out bikes to their guests; otherwise try Mountain Tracks on ulitsa Pirin (Ⓣ0888 788 859 or 0888 703 184), which rents out mountain bikes for 20Lv a day.

p.136), the town became an important centre for icon painters and other craftsmen. When the trade routes moved westward in the twentieth century Bankso settled back into rusticity, and despite a recent move into tourism it remains an agricultural town, with goats and donkey-drawn carts sharing road space with the latest 4WD.

Since 1990 the town has become enormously popular with Sofians as an out-of-town retreat, prompting an explosion of family-run B&Bs and cosy, traditional-style *mehanas* or restaurants. The existence of some exhilarating ski runs, newly accessible by a cable car just southwest of town, ensures that the town is increasingly popular as a winter package resort. Outside the skiing season, Bansko remains very much a weekend resort, with visitors crowding into the *mehanas* to be entertained by local folk groups singing traditional Macedonian songs about anti-Ottoman brigands. From Monday to Thursday however, many establishments shut up shop, and Bansko goes to bed early. One event worth looking out for is the **Bansko Jazz Festival**, held over a long weekend in mid-August, when top jazz musicians from Bulgaria and abroad play on an open-air stage on the main square.

Arrival and information

The **bus and train stations** are on the northern fringes of town, ten minutes' walk from the central ploshtad Vaptsarov, where Bansko's **tourist information centre** (officially Mon–Fri 9am–1pm & 2–5pm, although be prepared for unannounced closure due to staff shortages; Ⓣ07443/5048) lurks in an arcade below a concrete Cultural Centre. It can supply a useful brochure on the Bansko region and help with accommodation in town or elsewhere, and is also the place to get advice on skiing (see above) or hiking in the Pirin Mountains (p.156). Note that although many of Bansko's sights and hotels are signposted in English, the **signs** are intended for motorists and may signify a circuitous approach.

Accommodation

There's a big choice of **hotels and B&Bs** in Bansko, and as most places were constructed in the last ten to fifteen years they boast reasonably modern furnishings and fittings. **Private rooms** (➊) are available from Almatour, ul. Pirin 23 (Ⓣ07443/8395, Ⓔbansko@almatour.et). Note that the prices quoted below are summer prices; expect to pay double in winter.

Bansko ul. Glazne 37 Ⓣ 07443/8054 or 8055, Ⓔbansko@bg400.bg. Five minutes from pl. Vûzrazhdane, this hotel is one of the plushest in town, with high standards and excellent management. All rooms have satellite TV, direct-dial phone and minibar, and there's also a gym, sauna, swimming pool and bike rental. ➎

Dvata smûrcha ul. Velyan Ognev 2 Ⓣ07443/2632. Named after the two spruces that shade its garden, this pleasant family hotel serves delicious food, but can be noisy due to three *mehanas* in the vicinity. ➋

Dedo pene ul. Bujnov Ⓣ 07443/8348, Ⓦwww.dedopene.com. Four cosy low-ceilinged rooms above the galleried courtyard of Bansko's best-known restaurant. Noisy in the evening, but in the heart of things. ➌

Dzhangal ul. Gotse Delchev 24 Ⓣ 07443/2661. Modern chalet-style house in a quiet area a 10-min walk from the centre, with a garden, barbecue and sauna. The owner is an expert woodcarver and offers lessons in the art. ➋

Hadzhiruskovite kûshti ul. Pirin 33 Ⓣ07443/8422 or 8424, Ⓔengtravel@bitex.bg. Twenty-room guesthouse grouped around a grassy courtyard with dull but tolerable decor brightened up here and there by the odd Bansko rug. Rooms come with functional shower and TV. ➋

Mir (aka Martin) ul. Neofit Rilski 28 Ⓣ07443/2500, ⓌEyanka_rahova@abv.bg. Friendly, comfortable family-run place with generous breakfasts. ➋

Perun ul. Georgi Nastev Ⓣ07443/8447 or 8485, Ⓦwww.hotelperunbansko.bg. Sizeable modern complex right at the southwestern end of town near the cable car, built with Western European winter package tourists in mind. Rooms come with all the creature comforts and there's a reasonably sized pool. ➎

Pirin ul. Tsar Simeon 68 Ⓣ07443/2290 or 2295, Ⓦwww.hotelpirin.bansko.bg. Package and tour-group-oriented establishment offering modern, pale-yellow rooms with shower, TV and minibar, and a small indoor pool. ➎

Rademeva kûshta ul. Buynov Ⓣ07443/8276. Attractive old wooden building with creaky-floored en-suites overlooking a grassy backyard. No breakfast. ➋

Strazhite ul. Glazne 7 Ⓣ07443/8117 or 8118. Large modern establishment midway between the centre and the cable car, offering en-suites with TV, indoor pool and bowling alley. ➎

Tanne ul. Georgi Nastev 7 Ⓣ07443/8100 or 8101, Ⓦwww.hotel-tanne.com. Modern hotel situated, traditional-style, in a walled courtyard. Faultless rooms and service, and a gym and sauna on site. Handy for the cable car, but a 40-min walk from the town centre. ➎

Vihren ul. Pirin 55 Ⓣ07443/5622. Modern, medium-sized hotel offering smallish but neat en-suites with pine furnishings. About a 10-min walk south of the centre. ➎

Ploshtad Nikola Vaptsarov

Bansko's modern, pedestrianized zone is centred around **ploshtad Nikola Vaptsarov**, named after the revolutionary poet. On the corner of the square, near a postwar statue of Vaptsarov in a declamatory pose, is the house where he was born, now the **Nikola Vaptsarov Museum** (Mon–Fri 8am–noon & 2–6pm; 3Lv), which re-creates his childhood home and expounds on his life and poetry (in Bulgarian only). An engineer by training, he shared the Futurists' enthusiasm for the machine age and joined the wartime resistance with the courage of his Communist convictions. Vaptsarov's final poem was composed in a Sofia prison as he awaited execution in 1942:

The fight is hard and pitiless
The fight is epic, as they say:
I fell. Another takes my place –
Why single out a name!
After the firing squad – the worms.

Thus does the simple logic go.
But in the storm we'll be with you
My people, for we loved you so.

Ironically, Vaptsarov's father, Yonko, had connections at court from the days when he was an influential figure in Macedonian politics, but his demise in 1939 meant that no one was able to prevent Nikola from being shot by Boris III's lackeys. Attached to the museum is a **crafts exhibition** of textiles, woodcarvings and paintings by local artists, some of which are for sale. The carpets are simply patterned (with green and black stripes predominating) and nothing for serious collectors to get excited about, but as authentic handmade local crafts they make nice souvenirs, and cost less here than in Sofia.

Ploshtad Vûzrazhdane and the Church of Sveta Troitsa

Bansko's old town begins a short way uphill on **ploshtad Vûzrazhdane**, dominated by a large monument to Otets (Father) Paisii, also known as Paisii of Hilendar (1722–73), author of the *Slav-Bulgarian History*. Begun in 1745, when Paisii became a monk at the Bulgarian monastery on Mount Athos, but not widely distributed until over fifty years later, this seminal work exalted the nation's past glories, kick-starting the upsurge in cultural and political consciousness that became known as the "National Revival".

The growing confidence of Bulgaria's nineteenth-century elite was often expressed in the building of new churches – although the local Ottoman authorities didn't always grant permission without a bribe. The **Church of Sveta Troitsa**, on the south side of ploshtad Vûzrazhdane, got the go-ahead after Bansko merchants paid off a local official to declare that a miraculous icon had been discovered on the site (which qualified it as "holy ground" suitable for a Christian place of worship). A wall was then raised to conceal the townsfolks' enlargement of the church beyond the size set by Ottoman clerks – for which the mayor of Bansko was jailed for five years. The resulting structure is one of the largest in Bulgaria outside Sofia; a huge lump of grey-brown stone whose appearance is softened by the addition of a delicate wooden porch around the main doorway. Icons of local origin pack the spacious interior, where an intricately latticed screen partitions off the rear of the nave where women were once obliged to pray in segregation. Bansko's grannies, many of whom dress in traditional stripy aprons for the occasion, still regard attendance at the 9am Sunday service as *de rigueur*, converging on the town centre as the church's belfry rings out an impressive peal of bells.

Approaching and leaving the church through the walled enclosure you'll pass a monument remembering Peyu Yavorov (see p.103), the poet guerilla leader who celebrated Bansko's liberation from the Turks in October 1912 by proclaiming "Throw away your fezzes, brothers! From today you are free Bulgarians."

The Neofit Rilski House-Museum, The Icon Museum and the Velyanov House

Behind the church, a short distance along ul. Pirin, the **Neofit Rilski House-Museum** (daily 9am–noon & 2–5pm; 3Lv) remembers another key figure in the nineteenth-century resurgence of Bulgarian education and church life, Neofit Rilski. Born in Bansko in 1793, the son of the local priest, Rilski looked set to join one of the local icon-painting studios until a visit to Rila filled him with enthusiasm for the monastic life. He went on to become one of the great scholars of the age, translating the New Testament into Bulgarian (a work the

Orthodox Patriarchate in Constantinople tried to ban on the grounds that it had been funded by a crafty bunch of Protestant subversives – namely the Bible Society in London), and producing a mammoth Greek-Bulgarian dictionary that took a lifetime to compile. Despite his monastic vocation he pioneered the development of secular education in Bulgaria, becoming the first-ever head of the Aprilov School in Gabrovo (see p.268), before moving on to establish an equally renowned school in Koprivshtitsa (see p.295). As well as being one of the main popularizers of Otets Paisii's work (see p.153), Rilski also introduced western educational methods into Bulgaria, adopting the Bell-Lancaster system of encouraging older children to supervise the work of younger ones. The museum holds a dully didactic display of photographs and (Bulgarian-only) texts outlining Rilski's career, although the chance to pause in the lovely chestnut tree-shaded courtyard makes a visit here worthwhile.

Just off the northeast corner of ploshtad Vûzrazhdane, on ulitsa Yane Sandanski, the **Rilski Convent** (*Rilski metoh*) has now been restored to the Orthodox Church and is once again a nunnery affiliated to Rila Monastery. The convent's **Icon Museum** (Mon–Fri 9am–noon & 2–5pm; 3Lv) shows the achievements of Bansko's nineteenth-century icon painters – a school largely centred around the Vienna-educated Toma Vishanov, who, with sons Dimitûr and Simeon Molerov, travelled from village to village decorating local churches. Vishanov's exposure to Western art obviously filtered through into the style of the Bansko School, which generally features more realistic human faces than those of the highly stylized Samokov School (see p.142). There are photographic reproductions of the frescoes Vishanov and the Molerovs painted for Rila Monastery, and a good selection of icons produced by other local painters. One highlight is an anonymous *Wheel of Time*, in which everyday village scenes are encircled by portrayals of the different ages of man.

A couple of minutes' walk south of ploshtad Vûzrazhdane, the **Velyanova kûshta**, at ul. Velyan Ognev 5 (Mon–Fri 9am–noon & 2–5pm; 3Lv), is a typical stone house, packed with nineteenth-century furnishings and rugs, providing a good idea of how Bansko's better-off citizens once lived. Local lore maintains that the house was built for the craftsman Velyan Ognev of Debûr, who worked on the iconostasis in Bansko's Church of Sveta Troitsa and decided to stay on in town – falling in love with the priest's daughter was an added inducement. Highlights include a nicely restored kitchen-cum-living room, in which the entire family slept on a single mattress on the floor, and the wonderfully decorated Blue Room, covered with frescoes of fanciful cityscapes, thought to have been painted by Ognev for his wife.

Church of Sveta Bogoroditsa and the market

Across town, east of the train station, the early nineteenth-century **Church of Sveta Bogoroditsa** is an atmospheric, semi-submerged structure beside the town cemetery, though most of its treasures – including the central doors of the iconostasis, painted by Toma Vishanov – have been moved to the Icon Museum.

Last but not least, the **market** that enlivens ulitsa Tsar Simeon on Sunday mornings is worth a visit for its handwoven blankets, rugs and clothing, which are on sale alongside workaday objects such as cowbells, saddles and harnesses.

Eating, drinking and nightlife

Eating and **drinking** are practically synonymous in Bansko, with nearly forty *mehanas* offering much the same menu, and drinks served in pottery beakers. As chefs and owners change frequently, places that were good turn bad or vice

The Pirin Sings folk festival

One of the greatest of Bulgarian folklore festivals, second in importance only to that in Koprivshtitsa (see p.291), **Pirin Sings** (Pirin Pee) is a two-day celebration of the music of the Pirin region held at **Predel**, an area of meadows and woodland 15km west of Bansko on the road to Blagoevgrad. The action takes place on a series of outdoor stages, each devoted to a different part of southwestern Bulgaria, with folklore societies from every conceivable town and village strutting their stuff to appreciative crowds. Like most such events in Bulgaria, the festival combines serious ethnographical intent with the laid-back atmosphere of a mass country picnic. Many locals pay as much attention to the numerous stalls selling grilled meats and beer as they do to the official programme, and there's usually plenty of impromptu singing and dancing to get involved in. At dusk, gypsy bands gather around campfires to blast out tunes on the *zurna*, an impressively raucous wind instrument of Turkish origin.

The festival was held every odd-numbered year until 2001, after which it was decided to hold a smaller (but still highly worthwhile) festival every year, with the full-scale bash occurring at four-year intervals (the next one is in 2009).

Both the small and full-scale festivals straddle the Saturday and Sunday nearest to August 15, although it's a good idea to check precise dates with the Bansko tourist information centre (see p.151) before you travel.

versa, so you might as well choose somewhere on the basis of its music or its seating. The most atmospheric place to eat is *Dedo pene* (see "Accommodation", p.152), which offers the whole range of traditional Bulgarian food in a dining room crammed with folksy decorations – and you can sit in the galleried courtyard in summer. The *Baryakova mehana*, just off ploshtad Vûzrazhdane on ulitsa Velyan Ognev, is equal in terms of culinary excellence, and often features stirring Macedonian folk music. *Molerite*, just north of the main square on ulitsa Todor Aleksandrov, is another place with wooden benches, ethnic textiles and superb local specialities; while *Sharkova kûshta* on ulitsa 5 Oktomvri is usually pretty reliable too.

If you just want a drink or an ice cream, a dozen café-bars along ulitsa Tsar Simeon vie for custom. **Nightlife** boils down to more of the same plus whatever's cooking at *Club No Name* just east of ploshtad Nikola Vaptsarov on ulitsa Tsar Simeon.

Around Bansko

Hemmed in by the Pirin Mountains to the west, the Rila massif to the north, and the Rhodopes to the east, Bansko and its surrounding countryside can boast some great walks. Bansko itself is the most convenient starting point for hikes, although the nearby villages of **Dobûrsko** and **Dobrinishte** are also important trail-heads – the former has enough going for it to be worth a visit in its own right. The only other place worth mentioning in this neck of the woods is **Eleshnitsa**, site of a renowned folk festival on Easter Sunday.

The Pirin Mountains

Looming over Bansko to the west are the **Pirin Mountains**, Bulgaria's wildest range, consisting of 45 peaks, all more than 2590m tall. Snowcapped for much of the year, they're subject to such powerful winds and violent storms that the early Slavs were convinced that this was the abode of the Thunder God, Perun. Pure water tarns and short-lived wildflowers abound in the highland valleys, and the slopes are a botanist's delight, with clumps of Scots, Corsican, Macedonian and white pine. The **Pirin National Park** covers 40,447 hectares of this terrain including the Bayuvi dupki–Dzhindzhritsa and Yulen biosphere reserves. Its mountains are predominantly granite, with scores of glacial cirques, at the bottom of which are 186 lakes, but there is also a karst region of limestone crags and caves. The highest peaks and most of the lakes are in the northern Pirin, which is crisscrossed with hiking **trails** between *hizhi* – simple huts connected

Hiking in the Pirin

If you're considering **hiking in the Pirin**, it's essential to get a good map. The *Domino CityGuide* to the Blagoevgrad region (sporadically available in Blagoevgrad shops) includes one detailing all the trails below, and is more user-friendly than BTS maps or Kartografiya's 1:55,000 map of the Pirin, despite their greater detail. At a pinch, you could make do with the brochure from the tourist office in Bansko, which is also the place to ask about staying in *hizhi* and reserving beds. Besides this, stout boots, warm waterproof clothing, a sleeping bag and food are essential. You can camp at designated spots (not within nature reserves), but only during the summer; inexperienced hikers should avoid high peaks and snowy ground and, ideally, join a group familiar with the mountains, or hire a guide through the tourist office.

The **trails** below cover only part of the northern Pirin; determined hikers could continue farther south towards Gotse Delchev or Melnik. Staying within the region of Bansko and Dobrinishte, you can still enjoy the Pirin at its best on a two- or three-day hike around Mount Vihren and the lakes, on a circuit beginning or ending at a hut that's accessible by road from Bansko or Dobrinishte. By taking a taxi instead of walking to the hut you'll be fit to start hiking immediately. As the road from Bansko to the *Vihren* hut is more direct than the journey from Dobrinishte to the *Bezbog* hut, it's easier to start from Bansko and end at Dobrinishte, although it's feasible to complete the circuit in either direction.

From Bansko, take the minor road heading south, which forks after 6km. The right-hand, better-surfaced fork leads to the *Bunderitsa* hut 8km away, and on past the **Baikushevata mura** (Baikushev Fir) – a mighty tree 1300 years old – to the larger *Vihren* hut, 2km beyond. From here on the scenery is magnificent, whether you make the two-and-a-half hour ascent of **Mount Vihren** (2914m), Bulgaria's second highest peak – with the option of carrying on into the karst region (see below) – or trek westward past lakes and **Mount Todorin** (2746m) to the *Demyanitsa* hut (4hr). For those with more time, there's a trail (3hr) south to the **Tevno ezero** (Dark Lake) in the heart of the Pirin, and another to the *Yane Sandanski* hut, a base for weekend hikers from Sandanski. Otherwise, head eastwards to the *Bezbog* hut, on a trail (4hr 30min) that skirts the **Yulen Nature Reserve**, passing unforgettable vistas.

Starting from Dobrinishte entails reaching the *Gotse Delchev* hut by a 12km mountain road that peters out into a track. In the vicinity of the hut is the 45m-high **Visokata ela** (Tall Fir), the tallest in the Pirin Mountains, and a chair lift to the *Bezbog* (Godforsaken) hut, 700m higher up, which is also accessible by footpath (2hr 30min). Beside the lakes near the hut there are signposted trails to the **Bezbog Peak** (1hr 30min) or a larger cluster of lakes at **Popovski tsirkus** (1hr 30min), not to mention the *Demyanitsa* hut, if you're doing the circuit in the other direction.

Another possibility is to explore the **karst region** north of Mount Vihren, where the trail from Mount Vihren to the *Yavorov* hut (7hr) is the longest, hardest and most exciting in the Pirin, crossing spectacular cols, serpentines and other rock formations. The most memorable part is the **Koncheto** (Horse), a 1500-metre-long ridge less than a metre wide, above an abyss; a steel rope provides a handhold. From the *Yavorov* hut the trail continues past the **Bayuvi dupki–Dzhindzhirtsa Reserve**, a massif ringed by karstic cirques and peaks over 2800m tall, down to the Predel Pass (see p.149).

△ Shepherd

to the outside world by radio telephone. Although, by law, they are forbidden to turn anyone away, you could end up on a bed in the corridor if all the rooms are occupied.

Access to the range from Bansko is provided by the minor road which heads southwest from the town before winding tortuously up towards the *Vihren* hut, some 13km distant, which stands in the shadow of the 2914-metre **Vihren peak** – the Pirin's highest. From the hut, numerous marked paths lead across the alpine meadows or up onto the shoulder of the mountain – the box on p.156 contains more details of the routes available. During the summer there are three daily minibuses from Bansko bus station to the *Bunderitsa* hut on the eastern shoulder of Mount Vihren, continuing on to the slightly higher *Vihren* hut if there are enough passengers.

Dobûrsko

Twenty-three kilometres north of Bansko, the village of **DOBÛRSKO** perches on a forested southern spur of the Rila mountains, surrounded by a patchwork of tobacco crops, corn fields and pasture. Its greatest historical asset is the seventeenth-century **Church of SS Teodor Tiron and Teodor Stratilat** (Mon–Fri 9am–noon & 2–5pm; 4Lv), a simple stone shed of a building which lurks unassumingly behind a wall in the centre of the village. Inside are some of the most spectacular frescoes of the period, including, above the arch on the left-hand side of the nave, a much-hyped picture of the Ascension – in which Jesus is enclosed in a multicoloured rhomboid shape intended to convey the concept of the Divine Light. Elsewhere in the nave, the New Testament is related in storyboard style, while pictures of the saints to which the church is dedicated hover watchfully over the main entrance. The *Dobûrsko* hut in the hills north of Dobûrsko is the starting point for **hikes in the Rila Mountains** to the *Makedoniya* hut, the Fish Lakes and beyond (see p.141).

To **get there** from Bansko, you need to change buses in Razlog, though a taxi all the way is an affordable alternative.

Dobrinishte

Heading southeast from Bansko on the main road to Gotse Delchev, **DOBRINISHTE** (served by all Bansko–Gotse buses) is the first place of any size, a frumpy village where lumbering is the main industry. However it's a useful staging post en-route to the eastern limbs of the Pirin range, largely due to the existence of the **Gotse Delchev chair lift** (July–Aug Sat & Sun; 5Lv each way) located 12km up a side valley to the south. The lift hoists you up to the *Bezbog* mountain hut, immediately beyond which lies the Bezbog Lake – a beautifully desolate spot surrounded by grim peaks. For more on hiking routes from here, see the box on p.156.

Eleshnitsa

Nestling among hills 10km northeast of Dobrinishte, the small grey town of **ELESHNITSA** is unlikely to make much of an impression on the global tourist industry – not least because it's the site of Bulgaria's largest uranium mine. However it's also the venue for some of the most remarkable **kukeri celebrations** in the country, which here take place on Easter Sunday instead of January, the usual time for their enactment elsewhere. Each of the town's three *mahalas* or quarters organizes a team of mummers or *kukeri* who, dressed from head to toe in sheepskins, converge on the town square, accompanied by a deafening cacophany of drumbeats. They then parade around the square performing crazy, trance-like dances aimed at driving away evil spirits. In theory, the *mahala* producing the loudest, most frightening display is declared the winner, but few of the onlookers seem interested in the result, concentrating instead on the enthusiastic outbreak of mass folk-dancing which invariably follows the performance.

There are no buses to Eleshnitsa on Easter Sunday, so you'll need a car – or a taxi from Bansko – to get there (and back, as there's nowhere in town to stay).

Moving on from Bansko - the narrow-guage railway to Septemvri

From Bansko, the main roads (and most buses) either head west via the Predel Pass to Blagoevgrad (see p.147), or south through the Mesta valley to the southern Pirin town of Gotse Delchev (see below).

Alternatively, you could take advantage of the **narrow-gauge railway** from Bansko to the mainline junction of Septemvri, which passes through the spa resort ofVelingrad (see p.370). From Septemvri, you can pick up trains to either Sofia or Plovdiv. There are three Bansko-Septemvri trains a day, all of which are exceedingly slow, but it's a stupendously scenic journey, passing over a pasture- and forest-covered spur of the western Rhodope mountains. It's a route that you can follow by road, too, providing you have your own transport.

From Bansko the route heads northeast up the gradually narrowing Mesta valley, with the Rila Mountains looming up to the north, the Rhodopes to the southeast. About 20km out of Bansko a secondary road splits from the main road/rail route and heads north up a side valley towards the village of **BELITSA**. A former uranium-mining village now scarred by high unemployment, Belitsa has latterly become famous as the site of the **Belitsa Dancing Bear Park** (daily 9am–dusk; donation requested), founded in 2000 by the Austria-based Vier Pfoten/Four Paws organization (and partly funded by the Brigitte Bardot Foundation) to provide a refuge for beasts exploited as dancing bears – a practice which, despite being outlawed in 2002, still goes on in isolated cases. The sanctuary purchases bears from their (usually Gypsy) owners and lets them loose in a twenty-acre enclosure of forested hillside. Almost all of the bears were taken from their natural habitat when they were cubs, and can never be released back into the wild. The bears are reasonably sociable and you stand a good chance of seeing them lounging around in the open, unless you arrive in winter – when some of the bears are re-learning how to hibernate.

Returning to the main Mesta valley route, both road and railway pass through the logging town of **YAKORUDA** 5km beyond the Belitsa turn-off, which is a predominantly Pomak (Bulgarian Muslim) settlement – you'll see the gleaming white minarets of newly renovated mosques spearing up from the valley floor, imitating the surrounding pines. After this there's a sudden ascent into real mountain territory, where the railway and road part company: the rail route twists and turns its way east, passing through the wayside halt of **Avramovi Kolibi** – the highest "station" on the Balkan Peninsula – before descending towards Velingrad, and ultimately Septemvri. The road continues north, passing through Yundola (see p.371) before crossing a mountain pass where locals – mostly Pomaks – sell freshly picked wild berries by the roadside. The road then drops away to meet the Sofia-Plovdiv highway at **BELOVO**, a frumpy-looking town that rejoices in being the **toilet-paper capital** of the Balkans. A local factory churns out tons of the stuff, some of which is given to the workforce in part payment of wages, then sold at roadside stalls to passing motorists. If you're running a bit short, then this is definitely the place to stop off.

Gotse Delchev and around

Despite being named after Macedonia's greatest revolutionary (see box below), **GOTSE DELCHEV** is one of the Pirin's mellowest towns, set in a wide valley watered by the Mesta and suffused with a bucolic air, cows stalking the bus station and tobacco leaves drying in back gardens. Though short on sights, Gotse boasts a vivacious café society and serves as the jumping-off point for several attractive highland villages in the region, such as the beautiful **Delchevo** to the south, and **Leshten**, **Kovachevitsa** and **Dolen** to the east.

Gotse Delchev

From the bus station, ulitsa Vancharska leads past a red-brick synagogue (long since converted into apartments), to some nineteenth-century **crafts workshops** at the lower end of the main shopping street, ulitsa Tûrgovska, a cobbled boulevard lined with cherry trees and crumbling houses. On ulitsa Botev, which crosses it, the old Prokopov House contains a **History Museum** (Tues–Sat 10am–noon & 2–6pm; 2Lv) with a collection of folk costumes, and artefacts from Nicopolis ad Nestrum (see p.162), but a better set-piece is the **Rifat Bei kûshta** (same hours; 2Lv), embodying the lifestyle and crafts of the National Revival era. It's located beside the Delcheska River on the far side of the canal, near a 500-year-old, 24m-high plane tree called *Chinarbei*.

Practicalities

Gotse Delchev has two **bus stations** – the larger *dûrzhavna* (or "state") *avtogara* and the smaller *chastna* ("private") *avtogara* – both on different sides of the market at the southern end of town. As a rule, buses to and from Sofia use the *dûrzhavna*; while services to the outlying villages depart from the *chastna*. While the **tourist information centre** (ⓣ0751/22086) is too short-staffed to have regular opening hours, its brochure – with maps, details of festivals, walks and

Gotse Delchev (1872–1903)

Born in Kukush (now Kilkis in northern Greece) and inspired by Balkan revolutionaries Vasil Levski and Hristo Botev, **Gotse Delchev** dedicated himself to the cause of a free Macedonia, organizing a network of underground cells for the IMRO (see p.127 and p.467) while publicly leading the life of a teacher. An enlightened and unusually liberal revolutionary, he was similar to his idol Levski in refusing to target local Turks, declaring that they too were victims of Ottoman oppression. Whilst undoubtedly in the Bulgarian revolutionary tradition, he stood for an **autonomous Macedonia** as part of some future Balkan federation, as opposed to the right-wing, Sofia-based *Vârhovisti* or Supremists, who sought its union with Bulgaria.

Killed in a skirmish with Turkish troops three months before the long-awaited and abortive Ilinden uprising, Delchev neither witnessed nor was tarnished by the IMRO's decline into sectarian butchery, and is still honoured as a hero in both Bulgaria and the Republic of Macedonia, where his moustached portrait hangs in many a café. Initially buried in Rila Monastery, his bones were taken after World War II to the Macedonian capital Skopje, where his tomb lies in the courtyard of the Church of Sveti Spas.

The only biography of Delchev in the English language is Mercia Macdermott's *Freedom or Death* (see p.485 in Contexts). Researched in Bulgaria during the Communist period, it tends to exaggerate his role as an ardent socialist and Bulgarian nationalist, but is an inspiring account nonetheless.

local beauty spots – is very useful. Staff there can also make reservations in rooms in the highland villages, as well as at **hotels** in town. Looming above the main square, the high-rise *Nevrokop*, at ul. Mihail Antonov 1 (ⓣ0751/61244 or 61240, ⓦwww.hotelnevrokop.com; ❹), contains functional but pleasing, pastel-coloured rooms with TV, fridge and small bathroom. The *Malamovata kûshta*, just off the square at ul. Hristo Botev 25 (ⓣ0751/61231 or 61230, ⓔmaiz@goce.net; ❷), offers slightly more ramshackle en-suites with TV in a restored nineteenth-century mansion. The bright, modern *Valentino*, 3km southeast of the centre on ul. Dunav (ⓣ0751/60750 or 60751, ⓔvalentino_pgm@abv.bg; ❷), has browny-yellow rooms with TV and fridge, some with shower, others with bathtub, plus a handful of triples and roomy apartments (55Lv).

The *Malamovata kûshta* contains one of the best **restaurants** in town, with well-prepared regional specialities served up in a pleasant garden. There's no shortage of other grilled-meat eateries to choose from in the centre, with a cluster of lively establishments along ulitsa Tûrgovska.

Delchevo

You'd be foolish to visit Gotse Delchev without making the effort to visit **DELCHEVO**, a wonderfully atmospheric village perched up in the mountains just south of town. Buses are infrequent (currently Mon & Fri only at 8am & 4pm), but a taxi there and back shouldn't cost more than 30Lv. If you're driving, head out of town along ulitsa Papalezov and keep going.

Almost immediately the road begins switchbacking up a steep hillside, passing lush orchards and vineyards, with occasional gaps revealing fine views of the town sprawled across the plain below. A few kilometres out of town you'll pass the **convent of Sveta Bogoroditsa**, a minor foundation which nevertheless boasts a restful garden and a large meadow for picnics – the latter pressed into service on major Orthodox feast days like Assumption (*Golyama bogoroditsa*; August 15). After 9km of twisting and turning you arrive at Delchevo itself, its streets ranged amphitheatre-style around the curving mountainside. Most of its houses are built in the frugal Rhodope style rather than mortared and multistoreyed in the Pirin fashion – the circle of houses around the church is especially fine. There's a spectacular panorama of the Mesta valley from the village square, but nowhere to stay, or even buy food – unless the sporadically open village shop is doing business.

Highland villages east of Gotse

Although most easily reached from Gotse Delchev, the mountains on the eastern side of the Mesta valley technically represent a spur of the Rhodopes, not the Pirin. The feel of the place is different too: the land is dry and stony, with Muslim and Christian villages dotted amongst stunted oaks, acacias and wild thyme, with goats and tobacco forming the backbone of the local economy.

Village tourism is the new cottage industry and buzzword in the region, as wealthy Sofians pay to live in authentic highland hamlets, consume local food and wine and bliss out on the scenery – yet still enjoy decent bathrooms and cable TV. In fact, amenities vary from village to village – or house to house in places – from tastefully modernized stone houses to spartan lodgings with a local *Baba* (granny). Gotse's tourist office can suggest options and phone on your behalf.

Unfortunately, this rural idyll is poorly served by **buses**. The daily service to Dospat follows the main road east out of Gotse Delchev, and although it's an exhilaratingly scenic ride, the route doesn't take you near enough to any of the key villages to make it worth your while stopping off. There is one bus on alternate days to Kovachevitsa via Leshten, and one daily service to Dolen. Local **taxis** are the only other option, with prices inflated by the state of the road – the one to Kovachevitsa is awful. If you have your own transport, then visiting Dolen, Leshten and Kovatchevitsa as a day-trip makes for a great excursion – although the rustic charms of the last may well make you want to stay.

Towards Leshten

East of Gotse the main road to Dospat (see p.368), Devin (p.366) and ultimately Smolyan (p.361) dives across the Mesta valley, while a secondary road heads northeast towards the village of **Ognyanovo** on the far side of the river. On the way it passes the **ruins of Nicopolis ad Nestrum**, once a staging point on the Roman road from Constantinople to the Adriatic. There's not a lot left to see save for lines of stones in the grass, but it's an evocative site, framed by the distant mountains which stand guard on either side of the valley. From Ognyanovo an unmarked road (ask for "Kovatchevitsa" if it's not immediately apparent) winds its way eastward into the hills, passing a dirt-poor gypsy village before leaving the Mesta valley behind. It's an impressively scenic route, providing views of distant peaks to the south and west as the road heads up the scrub-covered slopes of a narrow side valley.

After 10km of potholes, however, it's a relief to reach **LESHTEN**, a pretty, picture-postcard village whose thirty-five inhabitants can be outnumbered by guests in the fifteen **apartments** here (Ⓣ07527/552 or 0751/29107, Ⓔleshten@yahoo.com; 60Lv for two people, 100Lv for three or four). Converted from traditional homes by the owner of the **restaurant** beside the church, all apartments have bare wooden floorboards, traditional textiles, simple pine furnishings and a functional WC/shower room. Some have self-catering facilities, although the quality of food and drink at the restaurant is a convincing argument for giving up cooking altogether. Four kilometres beyond Leshten, the road passes through **Gorno Dryanovo**, a Pomak (Bulgarian Muslim) village which ekes a living from nearby tobacco fields – the more enterprising locals, it is said, augment their earnings by cultivating marijuana.

Kovachevitsa

Another 4km or so uphill from Leshten, **KOVACHEVITSA** is far bigger and far less sanitized, its tumbledown stone houses leaning over narrow cobbled alleyways or mud tracks, with expansive vistas of the Pirin mountains opening up to the southwest. It has long been the favoured end-of-the-world retreat for Sofia media types – indeed numerous historical epics have used Kovatchevitsa's old houses as a backdrop – but much of the local population has moved down the valley to Gotse Delchev, leaving the elderly to tend the fields and graze the goats. Roaming the steep, crooked alleyways and admiring the sturdy, many-storeyed houses is the main activity for visitors, while there are also plenty of rural walks to enjoy – albeit along unsigned goat-tracks.

There are plenty of places **to stay**, with several old houses transformed into B&Bs. The tourist office in Gotse Delchev (if it's open) can help in making reservations; otherwise ask at the *kmetstvo* (mayor's office) at the entrance to the village or enquire at the *Sinja Vir* bar opposite. Best place is the *Kapsŭzovite kŭshti* at the downhill end of the village (Ⓣ048/969676 or 0899 403 089, Ⓔkapsazovs_houses@yahoo.com; ❺), a tastefully restored 200-year-old house with characterful rooms decorated with goat-hair rugs, iron bedsteads and quirky surrealist paintings, and a truly wondrous garden. Rooms are rented on a half- or full-board basis – and as the lady of the house is a cookery writer, it's undeniably worth it. Simpler in style but equally welcoming is the nearby home of *Maria Milcheva* (Ⓣ07527/463; B&B ❶, half-board ❷), with a French-speaking owner and three cosy rooms furnished with traditional knick-knacks and textiles, shared WC/shower in the corridor, and another fine garden; advance notice is required. The *Bayateva kûshta* in the middle of the village (Ⓣ0898 770 418; ❶) is a fine old balconied house with simply furnished rooms, a couple of which are doubles (the others sleep four or five), with shared facilities. There's a well-stocked *mehana* in the centre of the village, with a lively garden terrace, while the *Sinya Vir*, at the entrance to the village, also offers simple food.

Dolen

Back on the main eastbound Gotse Delchev-Dospat route, a fifteen-kilometre journey through the pine-covered foothills of the western Rhodopes brings you to the turn-off for **DOLEN**, a mixed Christian-Pomak village nestling between pasture-covered hills a further 3km off the main road. It's another extraordinarily time-warped place, with barnyard smells hovering over a maze of ramshackle houses and unpaved streets. To get to the oldest part of the village, take the right fork just after the ugly-looking *Valentino* hotel. It's a great place for a wander, and the locals – who you'll see sitting outside their houses in summer sorting the tobacco crop – are by and large a friendly lot.

Dolen is served by a mere three buses a week from Gotse Delchev, but more buses (including Sofia-Vûklinovo services from Ovcha Kupel) pass the Dolen turn-off. Numerous people rent out rooms on an informal basis if you ask around. Established sources of **accommodation** include *Doganovata kûshta*, the creamy-coloured house diagonally opposite the post office (Ⓣ0898 702 899; ❷), with small doubles leading off a central verandahed hall and shared WC/shower; and the *Dzhalovata kûshta* downhill near the church (Ⓣ0888 471 313 or 0888 543 440; ❷), a creaky old wooden house furnished with local rugs, where many of the rooms retain their traditional hooded fireplaces. Both of the above will offer half- or full-board arrangements – otherwise there's a quaintly uncommercialized village store-cum-café in the lower part of Dolen – just ask for the *kafene*.

Moving on from Gotse

The **Greek frontier** is just 20km south of Gotse, although a much-vaunted new border post (near the village of Ilinden) is still under construction. For the time being, Gotse is a bit cut off from the main southbound routes and **moving on** can be problematic. Barring the 7.20am bus to Petrich (daily except Tues & Thurs) and a daily bus to Dospat in the Rhodope mountains (see p.368), most head north towards Blagoevgrad, Bansko or Sofia, while the villages around Gotse receive a sparse service, often with buses only on alternate days.

There's also a spectacular **road** though the mountains **to Rozhen and Melnik**, but there are no buses and little traffic of any kind along its beaten-up eighty kilometres, with the road surface crumbling to bits in some places and covered with rock-fall debris in others. If you do attempt this route (and it is passable on rain-free days), then consider taking the detour to the village of **PIRIN** – 2km down a side road about 30km out of Gotse. Spectacularly located at the bottom of a high-mountain ravine, it's another place that seems to have been totally bypassed by the modern world, with new-fangled innovations like shops and motorcars conspicuous by their absence. Ancient stone houses perch improbably on the hillsides, while their inhabitants use four-legged transport to travel to and fro between the meagre patches of cultivable land.

Sandanski

On the other side of the Pirin Mountains from Gotse, **SANDANSKI** enjoys the warmest, sunniest climate in Bulgaria, with alpine breezes mellowing its Mediterranean aridity, and hot mineral springs whose curative effects have been appreciated since Roman times making it a **health resort** *par excellence*. You don't have to be ill to enjoy the baths and pampering at the spa centre (located in the *Hotel Sandanski*; see opposite) – great if you've just been hiking in the mountains – nor the town's festivals, restaurants and *korso*, centred around ul. Makedoniya. Moreover, Sandanski offers the best public transport access to Melnik, Rozhen and Rupite – the chief attractions in the far south – plus another way into the Pirin range, via the mountain resort of Popina Lûka and the *Yane Sandanski* hut.

Sandanski's modern appearance belies its origins as Desudava, a settlement of the Thracian Medi tribe and the likely birthplace of **Spartacus**, who led the great slave revolt against the Roman Empire in the first century BC. The revolt originated in Sicily, where Spartacus – like other Medi – had been deported to labour on the island's estates following the Roman conquest of Thrace. While a Spartacus monument is visible from the highway, vestiges of the past in the centre of town relate to the Orthodox **saints Kozma and Damyan**, local brothers whose healing skills earned them the accolade *Sveti vrach* (Blessed Doctor) – also the town's name prior to the Turkish conquest. A provincial *chiflik* under Ottoman rule, it rivalled Melnik as a market town in the nineteenth century and surpassed it after disaster befell Melnik in 1913. The town's present name, bestowed in 1949, pays tribute to the nineteenth-century Macedonian freedom fighter Yane Sandanski (see p.171).

The Town

The predominantly pedestrianized ulitsa Makedoniya runs from east to west through the centre of town, cutting through the main square, **ploshtad Bûlgariya**, on the way. It's a wonderfully leafy, café-lined boulevard, especially the section to the east of ploshtad Bûlgariya which leads towards the town's spa park. Before you reach the park, beside the ruins of an early Byzantine Episcopal Basilica, is the **Archeological Museum** (Mon–Fri 9am–12.30pm & 2.30–6pm, plus summer Sat & Sun 10am–12.30pm & 4–7.30pm; 3Lv). Built over a late Roman villa with a walk-round display of a mosaic floor found *in situ*, its upper floor is filled with funerary stoneware from the necropolis of Muletarovo, including a child's sarcophagus with bull- and ram-head reliefs. Votive tablets feature Zeus and Hera or a hunter figure presumed to be Artemis – carved in a vigorous, almost naive style suggesting that Desudava was a predominantly Thracian, rather than a Roman or Hellenic, town.

A hundred metres or so beyond the museum, on the other side of the road, lies the ziggurat-shaped *Hotel Sandanski* (see opposite), and beyond that a 192-acre **park** planted with more than two hundred exotic species including Japanese ginkos and Californian sequoias. Its large outdoor warm **pool** (May–Sept daily 9am–8pm), water-slides, boating lake and paths into the hills are all open to the public.

Practicalities

Sandanski's **train station** is 4km west of town, and although trains are met by a bus into the centre, it's not the most convenient of places for speedy arrival and departure. Far better to travel to Sandanski by **bus**: the main terminal (and the departure point for Melnik-bound services) is a few blocks downhill from ploshtad Bûlgariya, although Sofia-Sandanski buses arrive and depart from a side street immediately above the square. There's an underfunded but well-intentioned **Visitors Centre** in the municipal Palace of Culture (*Kulturen dom*) on ploshtad Bûlgariya (in theory Mon–Fri 9am–6pm, Sat 10am–5pm, but in practice too short-staffed to conform to these hours; ⓣ0746/22549), which can book private rooms (❶), supply maps and information, and arrange mountain guides.

A number of smallish, family-run **hotels** have sprung up in the town centre in recent years, all of which offer simple en-suites with a small TV: the *Andoni*, just downhill from the main ulitsa Makedoniya at ul.Voden 18 (ⓣ0746/23149; ❸), is comfortable and convenient; while the *Aneli*, just uphill from ploshtad Bûlgariya at ul. Gotse Delchev 1 (ⓣ0746/28952; ❹), offers a bit more in the way of opulence. If you're here to take the cure you should really aim for the *Sandanski* (also known as the *Hydro*) at the end of ulitsa Makedoniya (ⓣ0746/31162, ⓦwww.interhotelsandanski.com; ❻), with all mod cons, plush rooms with 1970s colour schemes, and a full range of spa treatments. If you don't mind being 4km from town, the former Politburo resort *Sveti Vrach* (ⓣ0746/28626, ⓔspartakturs@infotel.bg; ❺–❾) has equally good facilities and a wonderfully secluded hilltop setting, with a Henry Moore sculpture and a duck-filled lake in the grounds; for real opulence take the Presidential suite (350Lv) once enjoyed by Todor Zhivkov. Both the *Sandanski* and the *Sveti vrach* have large, heated indoor pools.

The *Melnik* and *Sveti vrach* **mehanas**, on ulitsa Makedoniya, serve good, cheap Bulgarian meals. Of the innumerable grill restaurants springing up all over town, *Barbeque*, just off ulitsa Makedoniya on ulitsa Voden, is probably the best. Stylish **cafés** cluster around the eastern end of ulitsa Makedoniya, near the *Sandanski* hotel, offering plenty of opportunities for alfresco evening drinking.

Melnik and Rozhen Monastery

Deservedly the most popular destination in the southern Pirin, the tiny town of **Melnik**, 20km southeast of Sandanski, is known for its robust red wine, impressive houses and natural surroundings. An ideal place to relax, favoured by Sofians and foreign diplomats at weekends, it's readily accessible on one of the three public buses daily from Sandanski. Coming by car from the Sandanski direction, head south along the main E79 highway and take the Petrich/Rupite turn-off (Melnik itself isn't signed), taking care not to head off in the Petrich/Rupite direction – double back under the highway and head east instead.

The route from Sandanski passes tobacco fields hugging the roadside above the fertile bed of the Struma, before snaking into hills that become arid and rocky, swelling into desolate mountains stretching towards Greece and the Aegean. Roads deteriorate and faded notices attest to the border zone that existed here in the Communist period, when Greece was regarded as a hostile Western state. If you're not in a hurry, stay at least one night in Melnik and walk over the hills to the Rozhen Monastery – one of Bulgaria's oldest, most picturesque foundations.

Melnik

Approaching **MELNIK** you'll catch glimpses of the wall of mountains that allowed the townsfolk to thumb their noses at the Byzantine Empire in the

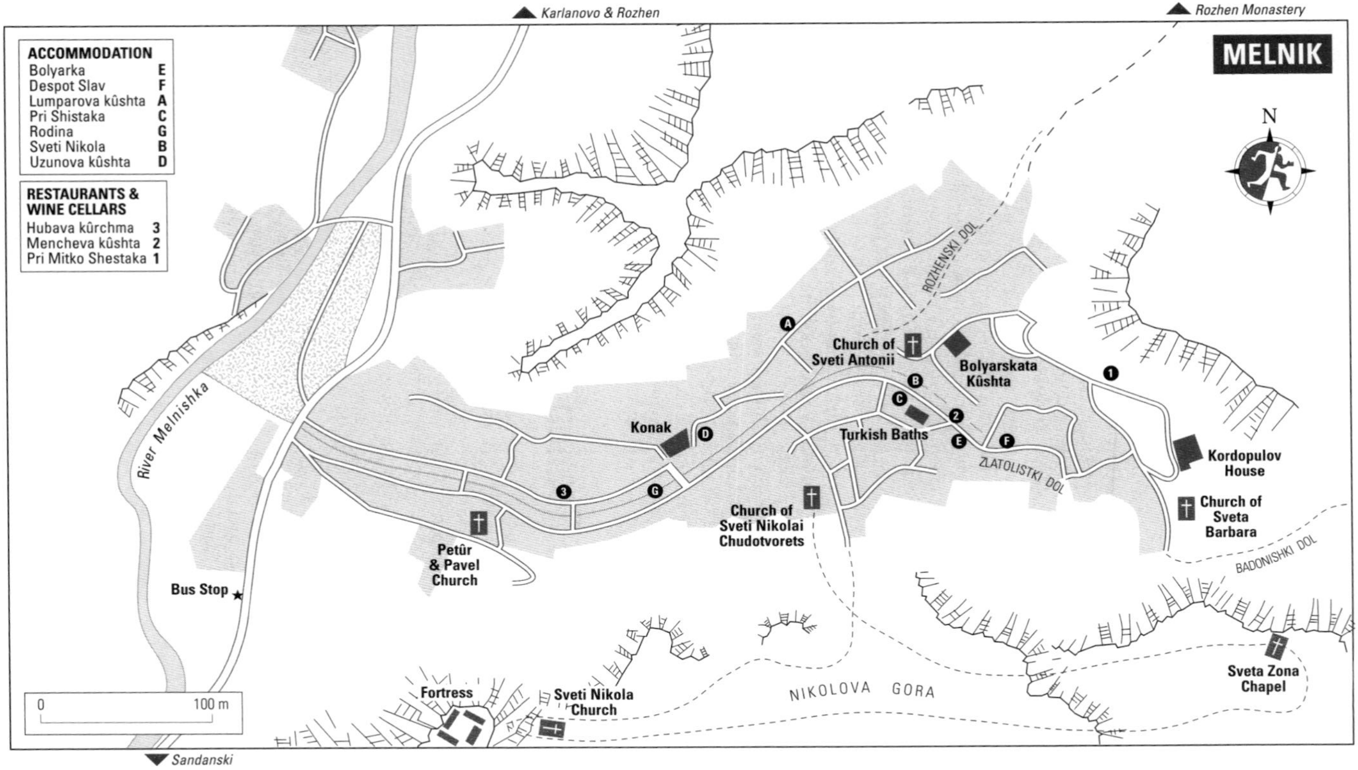

MELNIK

ACCOMMODATION
- Bolyarka E
- Despot Slav F
- Lumparova kûshta A
- Pri Shistaka C
- Rodina G
- Sveti Nikola B
- Uzunova kûshta D

RESTAURANTS & WINE CELLARS
- Hubava kûrchma 3
- Mencheva kûshta 2
- Pri Mitko Shestaka 1

Karlanovo & Rozhen
Rozhen Monastery
Sandanski
N
River Melnishka
Bus Stop
Petûr & Pavel Church
Konak
Church of Sveti Antonii
Bolyarskata Kûshta
Turkish Baths
Church of Sveti Nikolai Chudotvorets
Rozhenski Dol
Zlatolistki Dol
Badonishki Dol
Kordopulov House
Church of Sveta Barbara
Sveta Zona Chapel
Nikolova Gora
Fortress
Sveti Nikola Church
0 100 m

eleventh century. Melnik hides until the last moment, encircled by hard-edged crags, scree slopes and sandstone cones. Its straggling main street is lined with *mehanas*, whitewashed stone houses on timber props festooned with flowers, and vines overhanging cobbled alleys and narrow courtyards. Rooms for rent and wine for sale make it plain that the locals are used to tourists, while the new hotels being built attest to the sums that outsiders are now investing, yet it remains to be seen if this will reverse Melnik's extraordinary decline, from a town of 20,000 people in 1880 to a village of around 250 today. A century ago the population was largely Greek, making it a unique outpost of Hellenic civilization in a Slav sea, whence mules departed laden with wine for foreign lands. But the economy waned towards the end of the century and the Second Balkan War of 1913 destroyed the town, sundered its trade routes and provoked a bout of ethnic cleansing. Today, memories of this Greek past have faded and it's hard to imagine so many extra houses, despite the scores of ruins on the hillsides.

Melnik's **layout** is simple, with a single main street running alongside a (usually dry) riverbed spanned by rickety footbridges, then diverging into two gullies. Due to the terrain, houses are small at ground level but expand outwards further up, with the living quarters on the upper floors jutting out above the lower barred and shuttered levels that function as cellars or barns. Tiny backstreets invite aimless wandering, while the hillsides abound in tortoises and lizards.

Arrival and accommodation

Buses stop on the western edge of Melnik, just short of the gulley-side streets that serve as a town centre. The nearest **banks** and ATMs are in Sandanski, so make sure you change enough money in advance.

Private rooms (❶) do exist in Melnik, but with no information office in town you'll have to look for signs advertising *stai za noshtuvki* (rooms for rent) or ask around. Most of the family-run **B&Bs** charge 15–20Lv per head, a bit more for a room with en-suite facilities.

Bolyarka ⓣ07437/369. Plush and intimate village-centre hotel offering en-suites with laminate floors, modern furnishings and TV. There's also a small gym and sauna. ❸

Despot Slav ⓣ07437/248 or 271. Snazzy, small hotel roughly opposite the *Bolyarka*, offering contemporary-styled rooms with shower, TV and coffee- and tea-making facilities. Mostly doubles, some triples (80Lv). ❸

Lumparova kûshta ⓣ0888 804 512. At the top of a steep flight of steps on the northern side of the village, this is a typical piece of Melnik architecture: a fortress-like wine cellar with rooms above. Simple en-suites, some with great views of town. ❷

Pri Shistaka ⓣ07437/234 or 239. Three rooms (two double, one triple) above the wine cellar of the same name, featuring tiled floors, pine furnishings and reasonably sized en-suite bathrooms. Breakfast not included, though. Double ❶, triple ❷

Rodina ⓣ07437/249 or 0886 472 020. Modern building aping the style of an Ottoman-era caravanserai. Simple, functional en-suites without the folksy accoutrements you get elsewhere. ❷

Sveti Nikola ⓣ02/980 1628 or 980 3648, ⓦwww.qualityhotel-bg.com. Fancy new seven-room hotel built in outwardly traditional style, whose bright-coloured rooms boast laminate flooring, a/c and bathtubs. There's also an apartment with kitchenette. Rooms ❺, apartment ❻

Uzunova kûshta ⓣ07437/270 or 0889 450 849. Former Ottoman prison converted into agreeable ten-room B&B, with rooms arranged around a balustraded courtyard. Uninspiring grey-brown furnishings but otherwise perfectly comfortable. Mostly doubles, but some triples (60Lv) and quads (80Lv) are available too. It's popular with tour groups, so fills up quickly. ❷

The Town

Of the 72 churches active in Melnik's heyday, barely a dozen now exist, and a mere handful still function or are worth noting as ruins. Uphill to the right between the first and second bridges, the **Petûr and Pavel Church** dates from the nineteenth century and has an iconostasis painted in a bold, almost naive style, the lowest row of panels depicting the Fall, while scaly fishes flank the crucifix above the altar screen. There are turbaned Turkish gravestones in the crypt and medieval frescoes in the nave.

On the left bank of the river, shaded by 500-year-old plane trees, a cobbled square is overlooked by the derelict former **Konak** (residence) of the Turkish governor, a tall white edifice with Moorish scalloped arches. At the outset of the Balkan Wars, police chief Karim Bey had 27 eminent citizens arrested and murdered to instil fear into the population. Ironically, the erstwhile **jail** beside the Konak is now a hotel, the *Uzunova kûshta* (see p.167).

On the other side of the riverbed, the **Church of Sveti Nikolai Chudotvorets** (St Nicholas the Wonder-worker; Wed–Sun 9am–5pm) was a metropolitan church in the eighteenth century and is still the one favoured for weddings and funerals. Perched on the hillside, it is notable for its minaret-like bell tower and a long verandah overlooking the village. Inside, a wooden bishop's throne decorated with light blue floral patterns offsets a fine iconostasis where St Nicholas is portrayed seated on a throne, and St John the Baptist holds his own severed head above a narrative sequence of events in the Garden of Eden.

On a hillock near the fork in the gully, the ruined **Bolyarskata kûshta** ("Bolyar's House") was the residence of Melnik's thirteenth-century overlord, Aleksei Slav, who invited rich Greeks – then persecuted in Plovdiv – to settle here; the house was inhabited until early this century, but now little more than the outer wall of a tower remains. Nearby are the ruins of the nineteenth-century **basilica of Sveti Antonii**, a healer of the mentally ill.

The right-hand gully runs on past the overgrown remains of a **Turkish bath** towards some of Melnik's most picturesque National Revival houses. One of them, next door to the *Despot Slav* hotel, harbours a small **Town Museum** (daily 8am–2pm; 3Lv), although there's not much in it save for a few examples of the fashions worn by ladies during Melnik's nineteenth-century heyday. Far better to press on to the **Kordopulov House** (daily 8.30am–noon & 1.30–6pm; 5Lv), protruding from a rocky shoulder above the gully, its 24 windows surveying every approach. Above the ground floor, now a *mehana*, the spacious rooms are intimate, the reception room a superb fusion of Turkish and Bulgarian crafts, with painted panelling, rows of cushioned *minder* or bench-seats lining three walls, an intricate latticework ceiling and a multitude of stained-glass windows. The Kordopulov (or Kordopoulos) who built the house in 1754 was a rich merchant of Greek extraction known for his anti-Ottoman sympathies, who prudently installed a secret room as a refuge for the family in emergencies. The Kordopulovs were key figures in the town's social and political life, and Macedonian revolutionary Yane Sandanski (see p.171), who ruled over the Melnik region like a gang boss, was a frequent guest here in the years before World War I. Below ground are the wine cellars, huge wooden barrels occupying vast caverns cut from the hillside, connected to the vineyards at the rear of the house by a network of tunnels. Further up the valley yet more ruins include the shell of the medieval **Church of Sveta Barbara**.

Around Nikolova Gora

To stretch your legs before hiking to Rozhen Monastery, explore the scattered ruins atop **Nikolova Gora**, south of Melnik, where the start of the trail is signposted near the Church of Sveti Nikolai Chudotvorets. The path soon turns into a dry stream-bed then forks after ten minutes. By walking east along the ridge you can reach the **Sveta Zona Chapel**, by an isolated house overlooking Melnik, where Zona's name-day (April 1) sees an overnight vigil and the blessing of

Melnik wine and festivals

Justly famed throughout Bulgaria, full-bodied red **Melnik wine** once enjoyed an international reputation, enriching Aleksei Slav and continuing throughout the Ottoman era, when the wine trade was organized by merchants from Dubrovnik. Locals even boast that Winston Churchill ordered the wine for his son's wedding. Nowadays it provides a modest livelihood – *mehanas* slosh it around and locals are keen to flog tourists their homebrew – but the wine sold here isn't any cheaper than in a Sofia supermarket, and can even be dearer. Be especially wary of wine cellars offering what looks like a good deal on bottles of wine – they'll probably let you taste the top-quality stuff, then sell you the worst of the dregs.

The vineyards are planted with small, dark grapes of the variety known as Melnik Broad Vine, introduced from Syria in the fourteenth century. After harvesting, the grapes are allowed to cool in basements before being pressed and left to ferment in the chilly cellars that riddle the hills around Melnik.

Wine is central to two of Melnik's **festivals**. On **Trifon Zarezan** (February 14) the vineyards are ritually pruned and sprinkled with wine to ensure a bumper crop, and families sample the young wine from last year's harvest. The **harvest** can fall any time from late September to mid-October, but is always celebrated on October 18. Another festival with *horo* dancing occurs on the last Sunday in August.

children by day. From here a path turns west, passing the remains of a monastery en route to the eighteenth-century **Sveti Nikola Church**, its apses bearing traces of frescoes of Adam and Eve, and the dramatic ramparts of Aleksei Slav's **fortress**. To return to Melnik, follow the path down past a derelict modern building. The entire hike takes about an hour, with fine **views** all the way.

Eating and drinking

Half-a-dozen places to eat offer similar dishes at similar prices, and all stop serving food by 10pm. The restaurant of the *Bolyarka* (see "Accommodation", p.167) is the best in town if you want your meal to come with tablecloths and starched napkins; otherwise the *Hubava krûchma* just west of the Konak is a good place to enjoy quality local fare in a semi-folksy, semi-antique-shop interior. Similarly cosy is the *Mencheva kûshta* near the *Bolyarka* and *Despot Slav* hotels, where you can feast on grilled meats and spicy traditional stews in an engaging trio of rooms stuffed with bric-a-brac.

Venues for **drinking** include all the above, plus a dozen signposted wine cellars (*izba*) or *mehanas*, higher uphill or in the ravines. The view from the terrace of the *Pri Mitko Shestaka* cellar, up behind the *Bolyarskata kûshta*, makes the struggle uphill worthwhile.

Rozhen and the monastery

Rozhen Monastery makes a great excursion from Melnik, and although it's accessible by bus, anyone who's able would do better to walk and enjoy the scenery. The classic **trail over the hills** (6.5km; 1hr 30min) has suffered a good deal from soil erosion in recent years, and can no longer be recommended to people with heavy backpacks – or a fear of heights. It starts at the northeastern end of the village in the Rozhenski Dol ravine, just below the staircase to the *Lumparovata kûshta* hotel. About twenty minutes beyond the point where the watercourse widens, take the right-hand gully (probably marked in paint but don't bank on it) and follow it for ten minutes, before tackling a steep, stony path to the crest of the ridge, where your efforts will be rewarded by a stunning view of knife-edged crags and mushroom-like slabs of hard rock poised upon eroded columns. In Robert Littell's thriller *The October Circle*, it's here that the blind Witch of Melnik resides, foretelling the townsfolk's destiny for lumps of sugar in lieu of silver coins – a character based on the real-life oracle Baba Vanga (see p.172). The final, downhill stretch towards the monastery winds its way along stark sandy hillsides and is perilously narrow in parts.

A **longer route** (2hr 30min) with nice scenery and few gradients involves heading southeast to the village of Zlatolist and then north to Rozhen. The trail begins in Melnik in the first gully on the right, beyond the Kordopulov House; ignore subsequent paths to the right until the watercourse divides after about fifteen minutes, at which point take the right-hand gully and then a fairly obvious track over a pass and down into a broad vale. From there it's a level (but unshaded) hike to **ZLATOLIST**, which has nowhere to eat or drink but will soon be able to boast a **nunnery** built in honour of local wise woman Prepodobna Stoyna (1883–1933), a precursor of Baba Vanga. Pass through the village and take the left fork, whence a 4WD track leads to Rozhen Monastery.

If you'd rather catch a **bus** (two daily; 15min) or walk the 7km (1hr 30min) along the **road from Melnik to Rozhen**, look out for the 100m-tall sandstone pyramids on either side of the road, and the ramshackle village of **KARLANOVO**, where tumbledown houses and subsistence agriculture seem a world away from touristy Melnik. A gravel road from the centre of the village leads to the **chapel of Sveti Iliya** and the grave of **Todor Aleksandrov**, the IMRO leader after World War I who was assassinated by power-seeking colleagues in 1924. Carrying on from Karlanovo towards Rozhen, the road (unlike the walking trails) brings you to Rozhen village first instead of the monastery.

One final word of warning: heavy rain causes subsidence in the sandy area around Melnik, so none of the above itineraries should be attempted (either on foot or by car) if there's any chance of a downpour.

Rozhen Monastery

Sited on a plateau above the village, **Rozhen Monastery** (*Rozhenski manastir;* dawn to dusk) is small and outwardly austere, having survived looting and burning many times since its foundation in the twelfth century, on the site of an earlier monastery. Dedicated to the "Mother of God's Nativity", its name derives from the ancient form of the word *roden*, meaning "born". The irregular courtyard is intimate and unadorned, save for trestles supporting a canopy of vines whose root is as thick as a thigh. In the **bakery** the oven and walls consist of the same mud-and-straw bricks, giving the entire room the texture of a very coarse wholemeal loaf. Only at the far end, where cell is stacked upon cell, does the woodwork display the finesse found at Rila. The **cells** themselves are arranged to give some idea of monastic life through the ages. The accent is on asceticism, although the vivid colours of rugs and cushions counterpoint the simplicity of the furnishings, and it's clear that leading clerics led a somewhat softer life than their charges, enjoying the use of silver coffee sets and book-holders inlaid with mother of pearl.

Within the monastery, the **Church of the Birth of the Holy Virgin**'s cloister shelters a battered *Judgement Day*, which shows the righteous assisted up one side of the ladder to heaven by angels, while sinners attempting to climb the other side are tossed by demons into the mouth of a large red serpent. The torments of hell are vividly depicted on the right, where the damned meet a gory end (prodded by toasting forks and suchlike). Inside the narthex, delicately restored murals include the varied sea-beasts of a *Miraculous Draught of Fishes*, and a splendid *Dormition of the Virgin*. Inside the church itself, the endless ranks of saints covering the walls are eclipsed by a magnificent iconostasis, the work of Debûr artisans. Flowers, birds, fishes and flounces swirl about the richly coloured icons, and the whole screen – unusually wide in proportion to its height – is a triumph of the woodcarver's art.

A side chapel holds a miracle-working **Icon of the Virgin** which attracts a constant stream of pilgrims. Decked out in dark red robes, she's rather alluring, in a come-hither, early-Byzantine kind of way. To see monastic ritual at its best, attend the **Rozhenski sûbor** on the day of the Birth of the Virgin (*Malka bogoroditsa*; September 8), when the miraculous icon is paraded around the grounds and symbolic offerings are made.

Sandanski's grave

Downhill from the monastery is the nineteenth-century **Church of SS Kiril i Metodii**, behind which lies the grave of the great Macedonian freedom fighter,

Yane Sandanski (1872–1915)

Of all the Macedonian revolutionaries to have stalked the mountains of southwestern Bulgaria, **Yane Sandanski** was one of the most controversial. He was an early advocate of the creation of a Macedonia that would be separate from the influence of the Bulgarian state – and Bulgarian nationalists have viewed him as a traitor ever since. Bulgaria's post-1945 Communist rulers rather liked Sandanski because of his socialist sympathies, and went so far as to name a city after him (see p.164); in the years after 1989, however, right-wing historians have been keen to rubbish his reputation.

Born near the Struma-valley town of Kresna and recruited into the Internal Macedonian Revolutionary Organization (IMRO) by Gotse Delchev (see p.160), Sandanski first came to prominence by organizing the **kidnapping** of an American Protestant missionary, **Miss Ellen Stone**, outside Bansko in September 1901. The affair successfully catapulted the Macedonian Question into the pages of the world's press, and after a six-month period the Ottoman government agreed to pay the (then huge) ransome of US$63,000. Miss Stone was released, apparently none the worse for her ordeal, and filled with a new-found sympathy for the grievances of her captors.

Having made his reputation as a revolutionary, Sandanski became head of the IMRO in the Melnik region, which he proceeded to turn into a personal fiefdom from which rival IMRO leaders were excluded. He deliberately joined the **Ilinden Uprising** of 1903 (see p.468) six weeks too late in an attempt to save his men from annihilation and to prevent pro-Sofia elements (the "Supremists") within IMRO from establishing control over his patch. It was after the defeat of the uprising that Sandanski grew closer to the socialists, believing that their idea of a Balkan Federation would be the best framework in which a future independent Macedonia could develop. For the Supremists, who regarded Macedonia as a natural part of Bulgaria, this talk of federations had to be stamped out.

In 1905 Supremist guerillas tried to wrest control of the Melnik region from Sandanski, who retaliated by supervising the assassination of popular IMRO leader Boris Sarafov two years later. The **Balkan Wars** of 1912–13 allowed the Bulgarian state to take over the portions of Macedonia in which Sandanski operated, and he was no longer safe from Sofia's agents. Having upset everyone on the right of Bulgarian politics from Tsar Ferdinand downwards, it was only a matter of time before he himself was murdered, gunned down near Rozhen by IMRO agents (possibly with the tsar's encouragement) in 1915. After Sandanski, the IMRO increasingly passed under the control of the Bulgarian-nationalist right-wingers, although the organization's taste for internecine feuding and bloody vendettas continued, claiming the lives of numerous leading members throughout the 1920s.

Yane Sandanski (1872–1915), inscribed with one of his favourite rallying cries: "To live is to struggle: the slave struggles for freedom; the free man, for perfection!" For three days in July culminating on the last Sunday the surrounding hillside hosts a **Macedonian Sûbor** (Gathering) with music, speeches and drinking, where the police are kept busy by scuffles between supporters of the rival brands of washing powder, VMRO and OMO-Ilinden, both of which mark the anniversary of the Ilinden uprising on July 20 *and* the first Sunday in August (in deference to the Old Style date of the event).

Rozhen village

In the valley below the monastery, **ROZHEN**, a workaday village of whitewashed, vine-shrouded houses with rickety wooden balconies, is in many ways more authentic than neighbouring Melnik. You can enjoy traditional **food** and local wine on the terrace of the *Hanche Rozhen*, on the edge of the village towards Karlanovo. If you feel like staying, there are plush **apartments** at the *Complex Rozhena* (ⓣ07437/211; ❸), uphill from the road out of the village, which also has a shaded café-restaurant and an outdoor swimming pool.

The borderlands

The lower reaches of the Struma Valley are borderlands in all but name, with streams of trucks converging on the crossing **into Greece** at **KULATA**, which has a motel and all-year campsite but little else to detain you from heading straight for the 24-hour checkpoint. The other, more tenuous flow of traffic is southwest towards Petrich – the only town in the region – and the **ZLATAREVO** crossing **into the Republic of Macedonia**. However, unless you have a car, it's far easier to enter either country on a bus from Sofia or Blagoevgrad than it is to cross over from Kulata or Petrich – so there's little necessity to visit either. That said, it's hard to resist the supernatural hype of **Rupite** – a New Age pilgrimage spot as well as a Christian one – and the incongruous gangster heritage of laid-back, sleepy **Petrich** might appeal to some.

Rupite

Twelve kilometres northeast of Petrich, **RUPITE** is famed in Bulgaria as the home village and burial place of the oracle **Baba Vanga**. Legend has it that at the age of six, she witnessed an angel who offered her the choice between sight and clairvoyance, and she chose the latter. Vanga's subsequent prophecies and healing skills gained her a wide following (including Politburo members), and her vision of Varna engulfed by water was vindicated when it was discovered that the city stood upon an underground lake – from which day on, high-rise building was prohibited. In old age she had fewer VIP visitors but her predictions were still heeded – not least by people choosing their Lottery numbers.

After her death in 1996, Vanga was buried in the **Sveta Petka Church**, a postmodern fusion of Slav and Byzantine design, decorated with expressionist murals and icons by the contemporary artist Svetlin Rusev, and surrounded by an unusually well-watered and manicured park. Its location in the crater of an extinct volcano makes the place even more special for Bulgarian New Agers, who believe it's a powerful energy node – although the scruffy car park and grill-bars at the entrance to the site are unlikely to place you in a meditative frame of mind.

Getting to Rupite (and back) by **bus** from Petrich or Blagoevgrad is fraught with uncertainty, with only one or two services a day. A taxi here and back from Petrich shouldn't cost more than 20Lv.

Petrich and around

PETRICH is strictly for connoisseurs of Balkan towns that have got rich quick by shady means – sanctions-busting during the UN embargo on Yugoslavia in its case – with more dollar **millionaires** and top-of-the-range cars than anywhere in Bulgaria. It's a place that has always enjoyed raffish associations. In the 1920s and 30s, Petrich was the **murder capital** of Bulgaria, rife with so many hired killers that the price of an assassination dropped to US$6. This was largely due to the town's status as a forward base for fighters belonging to the IMRO (see p.127 and p.467), who spent most of their time selling their services to gang bosses, or squabbling with each other, rather than fighting for the liberation of Macedonia. During the Communist period, Petrich's proximity to the Greek frontier ensured a steady trickle of illicit Western goods, and Sofia folk came down here to buy much sought-after goodies like Levis jeans and Abba records from local black-market traders. In more recent years, customs officials working at the nearby Kulata border crossing (most of whom live in Petrich) have lined their pockets by demanding bribes from lorry drivers entering or leaving Bulgaria – a practice which the government elected in June 2001 launched a campaign to stop.

Other than its pavement cafés, Petrich offers few attractions to the traveller aside from the boisterous **kukeri rites** at New Year, unless you count the **museum** beneath the town hall (Mon–Fri 9am–4pm), harbouring some relics of Romano-Thracian Petra and more recent history involving the IMRO. Best thing about the place is the surrounding countryside of the fertile Strumeshnitsa Valley, whose excellent climate produces Bulgaria's earliest crops of cherries, melons and grapes, superb peaches, and even kiwi fruit.

Samuel's fortress

In a park 20km southwest of Petrich stand the ruins of **Samuilova krepost**, or "Samuel's fortress", site of a monument to perhaps the most infamous event in Bulgarian history. After being defeated in battle at Strumitsa in 1014, fourteen thousand Bulgarian prisoners were blinded on the orders of the Byzantine emperor **Basil the Bulgar-slayer**, except one man in every hundred to guide the victims back to Tsar Samuel in Ohrid (now in the Republic of Macedonia), who died of apoplexy at the ghastly sight. Two buses a day link Petrich with the fortress, but there's not much to see here save for an unkempt, little-frequented picnic site and a decaying memorial to the battle.

Practicalities

Accommodation options in central Petrich begin with the gloomy but tolerable three-star *Hotel Bŭlgariya*, directly opposite the bus station at ul. Dimo Hadzhidimov 5 (Ⓣ0745/22233, Ⓔoofice@belatour.bg; ❸). Two kilometres east of the centre, the *Agata*, next to the Tsar Samuel sports complex (Ⓣ0745/24246; ❸), offers serviceable en-suites and has a marvellous complex of outdoor swimming pools, complete with alfresco bars and cafés, right on the doorstep.

If you're heading for the Republic of Macedonia, there's a dearth of public transport to the frontier, and the lack of traffic on the road to Strumitsa (the first town on the other side of the border) makes hitching a bit risky – be prepared to pay for a taxi.

Travel details

Trains

Bansko to: Dobrinishte (4 daily; 15min); Razlog (4 daily; 20min); Septemvri (3 daily; 5hr 20min); Velingrad (3 daily; 4hr 30min).
Blagoevgrad to: Dupnitsa (4 daily; 45min); Sandanski (4 daily; 1hr–2hr 15min); Sofia (4 daily; 2hr 30min–3hr 30min).
Dupnitsa to: Blagoevgrad (4 daily; 45min); Kulata (4 daily; 2hr–3hr 45min); Sofia (5–7 daily; 2hr–2hr 45min).
Kulata to: Dupnitsa (3 daily; 2hr–3hr 45min); Sandanski (4 daily; 30–45min); Sofia (3 daily; 4hr 30min).
Kyustendil to: Pernik (6 daily; 2hr–2hr 30min); Sofia (3 daily; 2–3hr); Zemen (3 daily; 30min–1hr).
Pernik to: Kyustendil (6 daily; 2hr–2hr 30min); Sofia (hourly; 45min).
Petrich to: Sandanski (3 daily; 50min).
Razlog to: Bansko (3 daily; 15min); Dobrinishte (3 daily; 25min); Septemvri (3 daily; 4hr 45min); Velingrad (3 daily: 4hr 15min).
Sandanski to: Blagoevgrad (4 daily; 1hr–2hr 15min); Dupnitsa (4 daily; 2–3hr); Kulata (4 daily; 30–45min); Petrich (3 daily; 50min); Sofia (4 daily; 3hr).
Sofia to: Blagoevgrad (4 daily; 2hr 30min–3hr 30min); Dupnitsa (5–7 daily; 2hr–2hr 45min); Kocherinovo (4 daily; 2hr 15min–3hr 15min); Kyustendil (3 daily; 2–3hr); Pernik (hourly; 45min); Sandanski (4 daily; 3hr); Zemen (3 daily; 1hr 30min–1hr 45min).
Zemen to: Kyustendil (3 daily; 30min–1hr); Sofia (3 daily; 1hr 30min–1hr 45min).

Buses

Bansko to: Blagoevgrad (7 daily; 1hr); Gotse Delchev (8 daily; 1hr); Plovdiv (2 daily; 4hr); Razlog (3 daily; 30min); Sofia (12 daily; 3hr).
Blagoevgrad to: Bansko (7 daily; 1hr); Dupnitsa (hourly; 45min); Gotse Delchev (7 daily; 2hr); Kyustendil (6 daily; 1hr 30min); Melnik (1 daily; 1hr 30min); Petrich (7 daily; 1hr 30min); Rila village (hourly; 35min); Sandanski (10 daily; 1hr); Samokov (1 daily; 2hr); Sofia (hourly; 2hr); Velingrad (1 daily; 2hr 15min).
Dupnitsa to: Bistritsa (10 daily; 25min); Blagoevgrad (hourly; 45min); Kyustendil (8 daily; 50min); Panichishte (3 daily; 1hr); Rila Monastery (2 daily; 1hr); Rila village (5 daily; 30min); Samokov (4 daily; 1hr); Sapareva Banya (hourly; 35min); Sofia (every 30min; 1hr 30min).
Gotse Delchev *Avtogara dûrzhavna* to: Bansko (10 daily; 1hr); Blagoevgrad (8 daily; 2hr); Dolen (1 daily; 1hr); Dospat (1 daily; 2hr); Kovachevitsa (3–4 weekly; 45min); Petrich (1 daily except Tues & Thurs; 4hr); Razlog (2 daily; 1hr 15min); Sofia (8 daily; 4hr). *Avtogara chastna* to: Dolen (1 daily; 1hr); Kovachevitsa (2 daily; 45min); Leshten (2 daily; 30min).
Kyustendil to: Blagoevgrad (6 daily; 1hr 30min); Dupnitsa (8 daily; 50min); Sofia (hourly; 2hr).
Melnik to: Blagoevgrad (1 daily; 1hr 30min); Sandanski (3 daily; 30min).
Petrich to: Bansko (1 daily; 2hr 30min); Blagoevgrad (6 daily; 1hr 30min); Gotse Delchev (1 daily except Tues & Thurs; 4hr); Kulata (5 daily; 25min); Sandanski (4 daily; 30min).
Rila village to: Blagoevgrad (hourly; 35min); Dupnitsa (5 daily; 30min); Rila Monastery (2–3 daily; 30min).
Samokov to: Blagoevgrad (1 daily; 2hr); Borovets (hourly; 30min); Dupnitsa (4 daily; 1hr); Govedartsi (6 daily; 40min); Malyovitsa (minibuses; 2 daily; 1hr); Plovdiv (1 daily; 2hr 15min); Sandanski (1 daily; 3hr); Sofia (every 30min–1hr; 1hr).
Sandanski to: Blagoevgrad (7 daily; 1hr); Gotse Delchev (1 daily except Tues & Thurs; 3hr); Melnik (3 daily; 30min); Petrich (4 daily; 30min); Samokov (1 daily; 3hr); Sofia (8 daily; 3hr).
Sofia *Avtogara Yug* to: Samokov (hourly; 1hr 15min); *Avtogara Ovcha Kupel* to: Bansko (12 daily; 3hr); Dupnitsa (every 30min; 1hr 30min); Gotse Delchev (8 daily; 4hr); Kyustendil (hourly; 2hr); Pernik (every 30min; 40min); *Tsentralna Avtogara* to: Blagoevgrad (hourly; 2hr); Sandanski (8 daily; 3hr).

International trains

Blagoevgrad to: Thessaloniki (1 daily; 7hr 45min).
Dupnitsa to: Thessaloniki (1 daily; 8hr 30min).
Sandanski to: Thessaloniki (1 daily; 6hr 30min).

International buses

Blagoevgrad to: Athens (1 daily; 14–16hr); Thessaloniki (2–3 daily; 11–12hr).
Kyustendil to: Ohrid (July & Aug 1 daily; 9hr 40min); Skopje (1 daily; 3hr).

3

The Balkan Range and the Danubian Plain

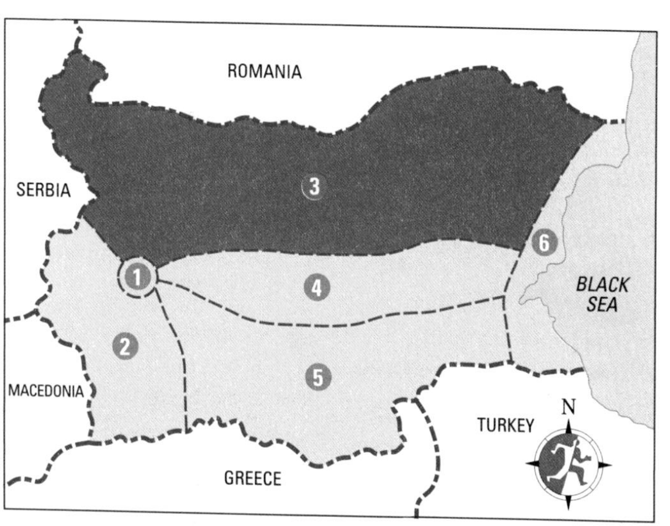

CHAPTER 3

Highlights

* **Belogradchik** An amazing landscape of time-weathered limestone pillars and cliffs. **See p.193**
* **Ruse** The most central-European of Bulgaria's urban centres, with an invigorating, big-city feel. **See p.205**
* **The Rock Churches of Ivanovo** A series of caves spectacularly decorated with fourteenth-century frescoes. **See p.215**
* **Lake Srebûrna** A reedy wonderland famous for its itinerant bird population. **See p.220**
* **Troyan Monastery** Bulgaria's third largest monastery, famed for its vivid, often macabre frescoes by Zahari Zograf. **See p.239**
* **The Tsarevets, Veliko Tûrnovo** The remains of this imposing fortress occupy a commanding spot above the River Yantra. **See p.249**
* **Church of the Nativity, Arbanasi** Though plain on the outside, this beautiful church is a riot of colour inside. **See p.255**
* **Sunflower fields** In summer you'll see field upon field of sunflowers, a valuable local crop grown for their oil-rich seeds. **See p.195**
* **Tombul Dzhamiya** Shumen's mosque serves as a major spiritual centre for the Turks of the northwest. **See p.272**
* **Thracian tombs** The "Royal tomb" in Sveshtari is just one of many providing a window into the beliefs of Bulgaria's ancient inhabitants. **See p.279**

△ Belogradchik rocks

3

The Balkan Range and the Danubian Plain

The Balkan Range cuts right across the country, a forbidding swathe of rock known to the Bulgarians as the **Stara planina** – the "Old Mountains". To the ancients they were the Haemus, lair of brigands and supposed home of the North Wind. In the seventh and eighth centuries, the Balkan Mountains were the birthplace of the Bulgarian nation-state. It was here, first at Pliska, and later at Preslav, that the Bulgar khans established and ruled over a feudal realm – known to historians as the "First Bulgarian Kingdom". Here too, after a period of Byzantine control, the Bulgarian nobility (the *bolyari*) proclaimed the "Second Kingdom" and established a new and magnificent capital at Veliko Tûrnovo. During the Ottoman occupation, the villages and monasteries of the Stara planina helped to preserve Bulgarian traditions, preparing the ground for the re-emergence of native culture during the nineteenth-century National Revival.

Given the mountainous topography and the vagaries of the road and train network, **routes** through the Balkan Range are many and complex. The main northbound route from Sofia to the Danubian citadel town of **Vidin** provides access to a range of off-the-beaten-track destinations in the rural northwest, with settlements like **Vratsa**, **Berkovitsa**, **Chiprovtsi** and **Belogradchik** giving access to the stupendous – and very varied – mountainscapes of the western Balkan Range. Attractions are by no means limited to the great outdoors: Vratsa's historical museum contains the best collection of Thracian treasures in this part of Bulgaria; while Chiprovtsi is a carpet-weaving centre of long standing. For those heading for the central and eastern Balkan Range, east–west routes between Sofia and the sea skirt the highest peaks, and tend to be much quicker than north–south routes across the backbone of the Range. Hence many people approach the area by **train** from either the Sofia–Burgas line through the Valley of the Roses (see Chapter Four), or the Sofia–Varna line which arcs round the mountains to the north. The latter gives access to three potential urban bases from which to explore the area: **Pleven**, whose numerous museums commemorate a celebrated episode from the War of Liberation, when Bulgarian independence was wrested with the aid of Russian arms; the aforementioned medieval capital of Veliko Tûrnovo, one of Bulgaria's most visually impressive cities and a convenient base for visiting a string of nearby medieval **monasteries** and a yet more brilliant ensemble of craftworking towns; and **Shumen**, close to the First Kingdom capitals of Pliska and Preslav, as well as the enigmatic cliff-face sculpture of the **Madara Horseman**. However it's in the countryside that the real rewards of travel in this region lie. There's an increasing range of accommodation both in heritage villages like **Arbanasi** and in more traditional rural settlements such as **Cherni Osûm** and **Apriltsi**, the latter two being important trail-heads for hiking routes south into the mountains. A different kind of rural environment reigns in the rolling hills of the Ludogorie north of Shumen, an enticingly undeveloped area in which the **Thracian tomb at Sveshtari** and the Muslim holy site of **Demir Baba Tekke** – both near Isperih – are the most worthwhile destinations.

The Sofia–Varna route also skirts the **Danubian Plain** (Dunavska ravnina), stretching from the northern foothills of the Balkan Range down to the banks of the river, which forms a natural boundary with Romania. Despite the name it's by no means uniformly flat, rather a rich agricultural area of rolling hills. The Central European ambience of **Ruse** and the nearby Rusenski Lom nature park – home to the **rock churches of Ivanovo** and medieval **citadel of Cherven** – are the likely highlights of any trip across the plain. Travelling from the Danube towards the Black Sea coast you'll

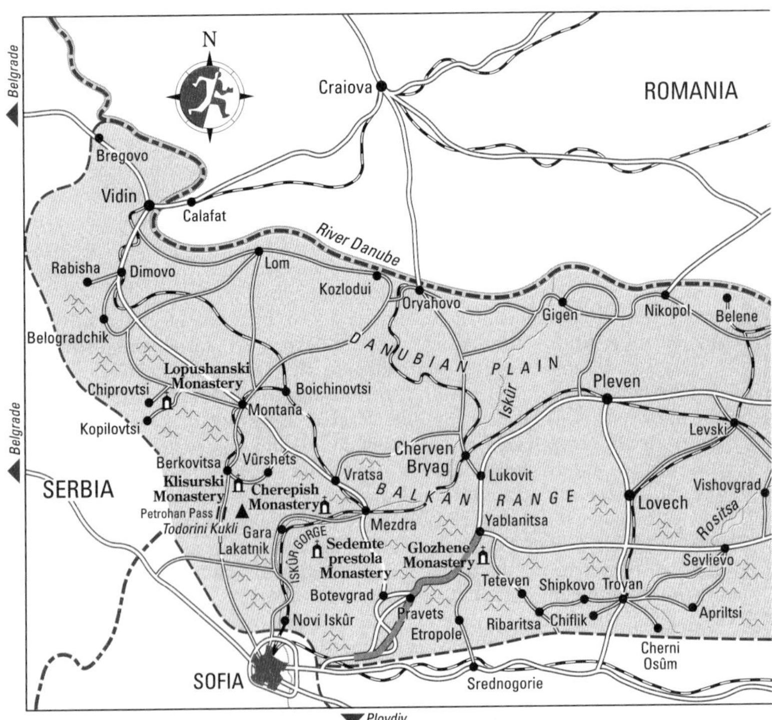

pass through the relatively unknown **Dobrudzha**, a rich, grain-producing plain which lies at the southernmost limits of the Eurasian Steppe. Although short on specific sights, its wide-open skies nevertheless exert a certain fascination.

The Western Balkan Range

Travelling between Sofia and Vidin takes you across the western spur of the **Balkan Mountains**, an area of forested highlands scattered with tortuous rock formations. Although not as high as the Rila or Pirin ranges to the south, the peaks of northwest Bulgaria present some of the country's most rewarding walking and rambling areas. Practical maps of the area are, however, thin on the ground, and serious hikers will have to pick up local knowledge from the Bulgarians staying at the region's mountain huts, or *hizhi*. The largely rural, undeveloped character of the northwest marks it out as an ideal destination for off-the-beaten-track travel, although tourist accommodation is limited to the

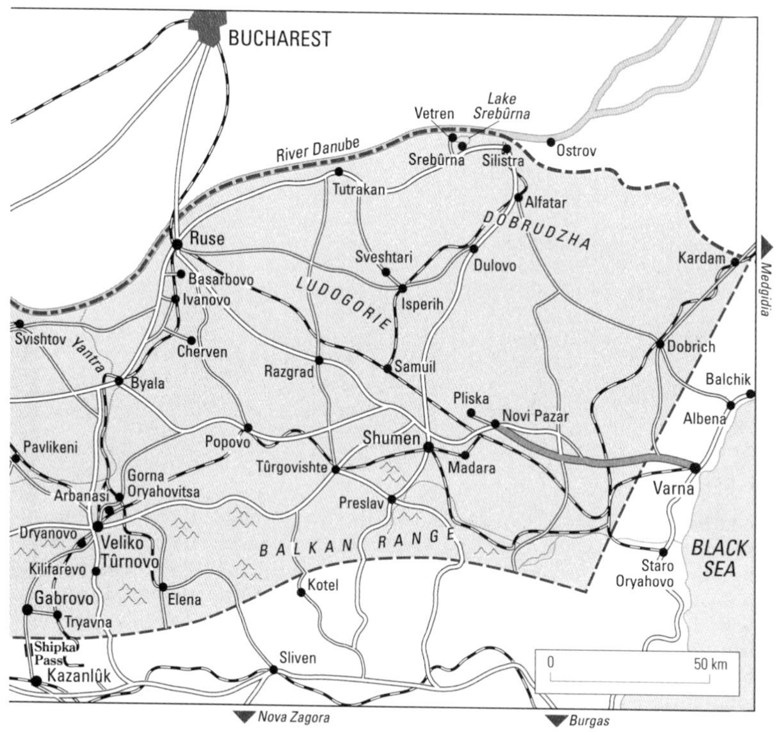

Cyrillic place names

Alfatar	АЛФАТАР
Apriltsi	АПРИЛЦИ
Arbanasi	АРБАНАСИ
Basarbovo	БАСАРБОВО
Belene	БЕЛЕНЕ
Belogradchik	БЕЛОГРАДЧИК
Berkovitsa	БЕРКОВИЦА
Botevgrad	БОТЕВГРАД
Bozhentsi	БОЖЕНЦИ
Byala	БЯЛА
Cherkovna	ЧЕРКОВНА
Cherni Osûm	ЧЕРНИ ОСЪМ
Cherven	ЧЕРВЕН
Cherven Bryag	ЧЕРВЕН БРЯГ
Chiflik	ЧИФЛИК
Chiprovtsi	ЧИПРОВЦИ
Chiren	ЧИРЕН
Dobrich	ДОБРИЧ
Dryanovo	ДРЯНОВО
Elena	ЕЛЕНА
Eliseina	ЕЛИСЕИНА
Etûra	ЕТЪРА
Etûr	ЕТЪР
Etropole	ЕТРОПОЛЕ
Gabrovo	ГАБРОВО
Gara Lakatnik	ГАРА ЛАКАТНИК
Gigen	ГИГЕН
Gintsi	ГИНЦИ
Glozhene	ГЛОЖЕНЕ
Gorna Oryahovitsa	ГОРНА ОРЯХОВИЦА
Isperih	ИСПЕРИХ
Ivanovo	ИВАНОВО
Kûpinovo	КЪПИНОВО
Kilifarevo	КИЛИФАРЕВО
Kopilovtsi	КОПИЛОВЦИ
Kopren	КОПРЕН
Kozlodui	КОЗЛОДУЙ
Lom	ЛОМ
Lovech	ЛОВЕЧ
Lyutibrod	ЛЮТИБРОД
Madara	МАДАРА
Mezdra	МЕЗДРА
Meekovtsi	МЕЕКОВЦИ
Midzhur	МИДЖУР
Montana	МОНТАНА
Nikopol	НИКОПОЛ
Novi Pazar	НОВИ ПАЗАР
Oreshak	ОРЕШАК
Osenovlag	ОСЕНОВЛАГ
Oryahovo	ОРЯХОВО
Petrohan	ПЕТРОХАН
Plakovo	ПЛАКОВО
Pleven	ПЛЕВЕН
Pliska	ПЛИСКА
Pravets	ПРАВЕЦ
Preslav	ПРЕСЛАВ
Rabisha	РАБИША
Razgrad	РАЗГРАД
Ribaritsa	РИБАРИЦА
Ruse	РУСЕ
Rusenski Lom	РУСЕНСКИ ЛОМ
Sevlievo	СЕВЛИЕВО
Shipkovo	ШИПКОВО
Shumen	ШУМЕН
Silistra	СИЛИСТРА
Srebûrna	СРЕБЪРНА
Sveshtari	СВЕЩАРИ
Svishtov	СВИЩОВ
Tûrgovishte	ТЪРГОВИЩЕ
Teteven	ТЕТЕВЕН
Troyan	ТРОЯН
Tryavna	ТРЯВНА
Tsareva Livada	ЦАРЕВА ЛИВАДА
Tutrakan	ТУТРАКАН
Veliko Tûrnovo	ВЕЛИКО ТЪРНОВО
Vetren	ВЕТРЕН
Vidin	ВИДИН
Vishovgrad	ВИШОВГРАД
Vratsa	ВРАЦА
Yablanitsa	ЯБЛАНИЦА
Yamna	ЯМНА
Zverino	ЗВЕРИНО

odd hotel, a couple of monasteries, and the aforementioned *hizhi*. There are several routes across the mountains north of the capital: travelling by train, you'll pass through the magnificent **Iskûr Gorge** before reaching the train junction at Mezdra, and then heading via **Vratsa** towards Vidin and the Danube, with the mountains to your left. Most road traffic from Sofia (including buses) bypasses the Iskûr Gorge entirely, taking the motorway northeast to Botevgrad before turning northwest towards Mezdra. It's a route which is clogged with long-distance trucks at the best of times, so you may prefer to take the minor

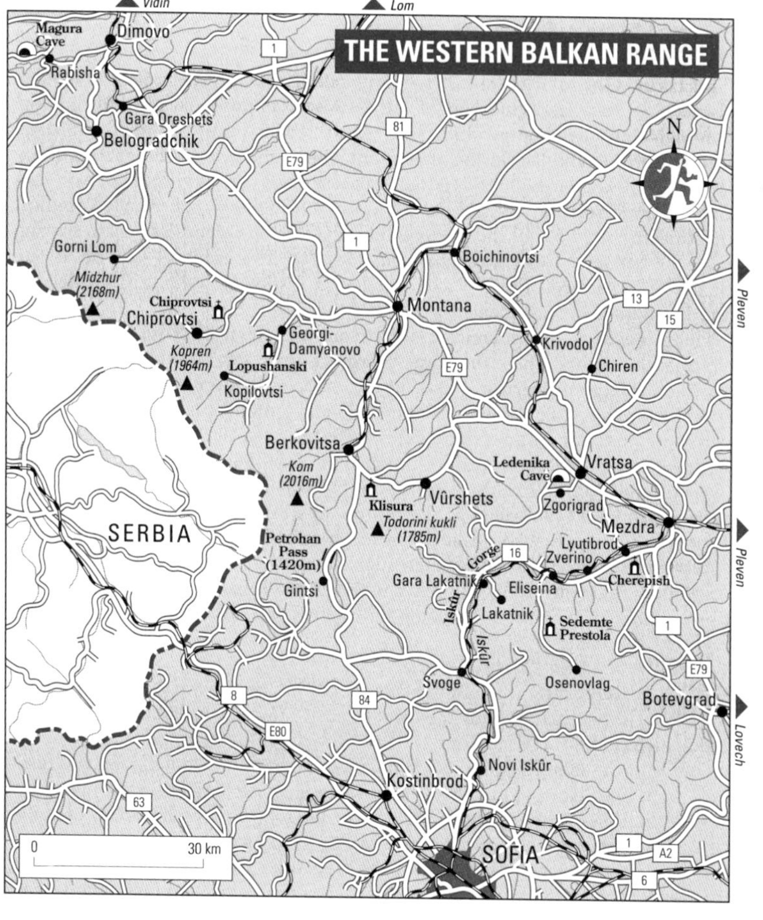

road north through the Gorge instead: a slower, but much more scenic, ride. An alternative northbound route crosses the rugged terrain of Bulgaria's western borderlands. This takes you via the **Petrohan Pass** to the mountain resort of **Berkovitsa** before rejoining the main road northwards at the region's administrative centre, **Montana**. From here it's a straightforward trip across the plains to Vidin, although minor roads head westward to **Chiprovtsi**, a historic rug-weaving centre backed by sumptuous mountain scenery, and **Belogradchik**, whose spectacular rock formations demand a detour. For those who want to explore the area **by bus**, Vratsa, Montana and Vidin are the gateway towns serving Berkovitsa, Chiprovtsi and Belogradchik respectively. You can also achieve a great deal **by train** if you're prepared to study timetables carefully, with a branch line serving Montana and Berkovitsa leaving the main Sofia–Vidin route at **Boichinovtsi**, north of Vratsa.

The Iskûr Gorge

The **Iskûr Gorge** is the most scenically impressive of the routes north. It's also within easy enough reach of Sofia to be a popular day-trip destination, although only the slow *pûtnicheski*, or "local", trains (most of which run early in the morning and late in the afternoon) stop at the smaller settlements along the gorge. Beware too that the gorge is almost totally devoid of tourist **accommodation** – Sofia and Vratsa are the most convenient places to stay. The most breathtaking stretches of the gorge, where the river is squeezed beneath soaring crags, lie between **Gara Lakatnik** and **Mezdra**; it's feasible to stop off at one of the halts between these places, indulge in a spot of walking, and pick up another train later in the day.

Things begin to get interesting just beyond the town of **Novi Iskûr**, 10km north of the capital, where the gorge burrows northwards into the Balkan massif, gradually becoming narrower and deeper, the road and railway competing for space above the river. Strewn with boulders and scored by gullies, it's archetypal partisan country. There's a monument near **Batuliya** village commemorating the 24 partisans who clashed with local police in May 1944, and a train halt called *Tompsûn* after **Major Frank Thompson** (brother of left-wing English historian and veteran CND campaigner E.P. Thompson) who fought and died with them. A member of the British mission sent to observe the effectiveness of Bulgaria's antifascist fighters (and evaluate their suitability to receive Allied aid), Thompson was fondly remembered by the postwar Bulgarian regime, and his uniform used to be exhibited in Sofia's long-defunct Museum of the Revolution.

Walks around Gara Lakatnik

GARA LAKATNIK (literally "Lakatnik Station") stands astride some promising Iskûr Gorge walking trails, the most popular of which snake their way up the **Lakatnishki skali**, a precipitous knuckle of rock just north of the station on the west side of the valley. To get there, walk downhill from the station, cross the river, turn right onto the main road and walk straight on for about 1500m. Footpaths ascend the side of the cliff from beside a small (and sporadically open) roadside café-restaurant, working their way past two *dupki* or **caves** before emerging onto the grassy uplands at the top of the *skali*. **Temnata dupka** is the larger of the two caves here, extending for nearly 3km across four levels and including several lakes fed by a subterranean river. However, it's doubtful that anyone will be on hand to offer tours to casual visitors. An alternative route into the hills is to head south along the main road from the station, turning right after about 1km onto a minor road which heads up beside the Proboinitsa stream. After about 1500m, beyond a small bridge, a path heads up the small side valley to the right, passing several waterfalls and pools before leading on to the meadowy plateau above the *skali*. Keeping to the main Proboinitsa valley road, on the other hand, will bring you after 10km to the *Proboinitsa hizha*, base camp for assaults on the 1785-metre-high **Todorini kukli**, from where paths descend to the Petrohan Pass (see p.187) on the other side. South of Gara Lakatnik, a more serviceable road heads for the pastoral highland village of **Lakatnik** itself, 8km away, and beyond that, the *Trûstena* hut, again the start of numerous walking possibilities. Bear in mind, however, that the café and food store on the station platform at Gara Lakatnik are the only reliable places in the area to pick up **food** supplies.

Monastery of Sedemte prestola

Fourteen kilometres beyond Gara Lakatnik, a minor road leaves the Iskûr valley at the village of **ELISEINA** to climb beside the Gabrovnitsa stream towards the mountain hamlet of **OSENOVLAG** 23km beyond. About two-thirds of the way along, the road passes the **Monastery of Sedemte prestola** (Seven Altars), a walled huddle of buildings surrounded by pine forests and crags. It's inside the dainty church (officially open daily 10–11am & 3–4pm, but often accessible outside these times at weekends) that the reason for the monastery's name becomes apparent, with the main altar at the head of the nave augmented by six side altars – low-ceilinged cubicles reached through arched doors on either side of the nave – each with its own small iconostasis and candle-lighting area. The wooded environs of the monastery present the perfect place for a short hike: cross the footbridge opposite the monastery gate to pick up a trail which leads up onto hay meadows and into the pines beyond. In theory the *Tûrstena hizha*, high above the village of Lakatnik to the west, is four hours' walk from here, although the path is badly marked.

Cherepish Monastery

More accessible than Sedemte prestola for those dependent on public transport, **Cherepish Monastery** lies near the halt of the same name, midway between the villages of **ZVERINO** and **LYUTIBROD**. It's also accessible from the Sofia–Mezdra road, although the turn-off is difficult to spot; the nearest landmark to look out for is the *Han Cherna* roadside café 100m to the north, which is also the only source of **food** and drink in the area. If coming by train, alight at Cherepish halt, cross the rail tracks towards a large ochre seminary building, and bear left along an asphalt track until you reach a T-junction. The monastery is down the hill to the left. Founded in the fourteenth century, Cherepish was sacked by the Turks almost as soon as it was built, and most of the current buildings date (at least in part) from the seventeenth century, when the monastery was refounded by holy man and artist Pimen Zografski. Faded fragments of Pimen's work, notably his *Tree of Jesse*, can still be seen in the monastery **church**, although much better preserved are the frescoes completed by Tryavna master Papa Vitan in 1836. His frieze of early Christian warrior saints (including George, Demetrius and other martyrdom-hungry Roman soldiers) reveal the nineteenth-century Bulgarian Orthodox Church's taste for images of steely-eyed resistance and suffering. The intricate woodcarving of the iconostasis – with gryphons and ears of corn exquisitely rendered by Debûr masters – also stands out. There's a small **museum** outside the church displaying a few monastic vestments and icons, although opening times are unpredictable. Thousands of pilgrims descend on Cherepish for the Feast of the Assumption (*Golyama Bogoroditsa*) on August 15, when the monastery grounds are full of picnicking families.

Immediately northeast of Cherepish, the Iskûr Gorge ends with a final geological flourish nicknamed *Ritlite* or the "Cart Rails": three parallel ribs of fissured rock up to 198m high which you'll see a few miles before the road and rail track enter **MEZDRA**. A useful transport hub at the junction of the Sofia–Vidin and Sofia–Pleven–Varna lines, Mezdra has little else to offer.

Vratsa

Twenty kilometres northwest of Mezdra, **VRATSA** is one of Bulgaria's most dramatically situated towns, sprawling at the base of a grizzled wall of grey mountains known as the **Vrachanski balkan**. It's this stunning rocky hinterland, starting with the **Vratsata Gorge** cutting through the mountains just west of the town centre, which constitutes the main attraction for visitors, although good **ethnographic** and **historical museums** (the latter worth visiting for the Rogozen treasure alone; see opposite) provide a respectable brace of worthwhile urban sights. Just south of Vratsa is **Mount Okolchitsa**, where **Hristo Botev**, one of the more romantic figures in Bulgaria's struggle for liberation (see p.305), met his death. An inspiring revolutionary leader as well as a poet known for his patriotic verses, Botev formed a *cheta* to lend assistance to the April Rising in 1876. Botev's men marched south into the Balkan Mountains from Kozlodui on the Danube, but were constantly harried by Ottoman forces. After days of running battles, Botev finally perished along with the remnants of his *cheta* on Okolchitsa on June 2.

The Town

Vratsa's **train and bus stations** stand together just east of the centre, from where the pedestrianized ribbon of bulevard Nikolai Voivodov curves its way northwest, passing a vast open-air market, to meet the main thoroughfare, **bulevard Hristo Botev**. Turn left here to reach a plaza built around the **Kula na meschiite**, a seventeenth-century fortified tower built by local lords as much for prestige reasons as for defensibility. Shortly afterwards ulitsa Tûrgovska breaks off to the left, a side street blessed with a picturesque collection of pastel-coloured nineteenth-century town houses. At the end of the street stands a monument to **Sofronii Vrachanski** (see box below), local church leader and key figure in Bulgaria's nineteenth-century National Revival.

The Ethnographic Museum and complex

Immediately behind the Vrachanski statue is the **Ethnographic Museum** (Tues–Sun 9am–noon & 2–5pm; 5Lv, ticket also valid for Historical Museum) housed in a National Revival-period former girls' school, a fine half-timbered structure vaguely reminiscent of Tudor architecture. Inside is one of provincial

Sofronii Vrachanski (1739–1813)

Sofronii Vrachanski was born Stoiko Vladislavov in the central Bulgarian village of Kotel in 1739. He entered the priesthood in his home town and rose gradually through the ecclesiastical ranks, becoming *igumen*, or abbot, of Kapinovo Monastery near Veliko Tûrnovo in the 1780s. During these years he was one of the most enthusiastic copiers and promoters of Otets Paisii's seminal manuscript, the *Slav-Bulgarian History*, a key text in the awakening of Bulgarian national consciousness.

In accordance with the custom of the time, Sofronii had to bribe Greek Church officials in order to be appointed bishop of Vratsa in 1794, an enterprise in which he was assisted financially by patriotic Bulgarian merchants. He was chased into exile by the local *kûrdzhali*, who were then in alliance with the wayward Ottoman ruler of Vidin, Osman Pazvantoglu, and spent the rest of his life in Wallachia where he continued to work for the Bulgarian cause. A firm believer in Russia's messianic role as the protector of Balkan Christendom, Sofronii cultivated links with the St Petersburg court, and oversaw the emigration of thousands of Bulgarian families to Russian-occupied Bessarabia in 1808. The descendants of these "Bessarabian Bulgarians" still live there, occupying a coastal strip west of the Ukrainian city of Odessa.

Sofronii is also remembered for his literary works, which include a translation of Aesop's Fables and the first autobiographical novel in Bulgarian, *The Life and Suffering of the Sinner Sofronii*, both of which assisted in the development of a standard written form of the Bulgarian language.

Bulgaria's best collections of folk costumes and crafts, strong on local marriage customs: exhibits include the enigmatic *svatbeni bardeta* or "wedding pitchers", twelve earthenware jugs hanging from a two-metre-long wooden pole. One entire floor is devoted to brass band instruments, imported from central Europe by village ensembles at the turn of the twentieth century; while, outside, a pavilion displays nineteenth-century carriages and carts (and a particularly ornate bright-blue ceremonial sled) built by the local Orazov factory, Bulgaria's leading coachmakers.

Next door to the museum is an **ethnographic complex**: a clutch of National Revival-style houses grouped around the **Vûznesenska** (Ascension) **church**, which itself contains a display of icons from the Vratsa area. A couple of the houses are open to the public (same times as museum); one displays the work of local jewellers, while the other features exhibits on Vratsa's **silk industry**. Silk was the region's major source of income a century ago, when each family would keep a tree for silkworms in the yard – a practice still continued in a few outlying villages. Examples ofVratsa-made fabrics are on show, alongside fading English-language posters offering handy hints on how to tend the worms.

The Historical Museum

Back on bulevard Hristo Botev, it's a short stroll south to another seventeenth-century tower, the **Kula na Kurt Pashovtsi**, and another modern plaza, ploshtad Hristo Botev, home to the **Historical Museum** (Tues–Sun 9am–noon & 3–7pm; 5Lv, ticket also valid for Ethnographic Museum), a gloomy concrete building which nevertheless holds an outstanding collection. Predictably, it harbours a "Botev Room" full of reminders of the warrior-poet's fateful march into Ottoman territory, but the real delights lie in the archeological section, which begins in the basement with stylish zig-zag-patterned Stone Age pots, and continues with Neolithic and Bronze Age idols, including a crowd of well-endowed fertility figures. The display of **Thracian artefacts** upstairs kicks off with finds from *Mogilanskata mogila*, a large tumulus unearthed in 1965. Three tombs were found here, dating from the fourth century BC, the largest of which contained a chieftain accompanied by two young women, both of whom appear to have suffered violent deaths at the time of the burial – possibly consorts of the deceased (one of them was sufficiently bejewelled to be a princess) who were required to accompany him into the afterlife. Three horses, two of them harnessed to a ceremonial chariot, completed the burial party. The latter were provided with decorative horse armour, their silver buckles depicting swirling animals. The more elaborately dressed of the women sported a pair of exquisitely filigreed earrings and a **golden laurel wreath** of great delicacy, featuring eighty finely sculpted leaves grouped around little berries. An adjacent cabinet displays one of the chieftain's **greaves** (metal shin-guards), engraved with the portrait of a tattooed Thracian warrior, flanked by fantastical-looking birds holding serpents in their beaks.

However, the museum's pride and joy is the **Rogozen treasure** (*Rogozenskoto sûkrovishte*), a hoard of more than a hundred silver vessels unearthed by a farmer in the village of Rogozen, near Vratsa, in 1985. This was in all probability a family treasure, accumulated by wealthy nobles of the Triballi tribe somewhere between 500 and 350 BC. Previously kept in the National History Museum in Sofia, the hoard was returned to Vratsa in 2000, and is now kept in a state-of-the-art, climate-controlled gallery on the top floor of the museum. The scenes that decorate many of the vessels portray typically Thracian concerns: hunting trips involving a variety of wild beasts, and archetypal goddess figures – one in a chariot drawn by winged horses, another riding a golden-headed lioness.

Practicalities

As with most towns in this corner of Bulgaria, the choice of **accommodation** on offer is pretty modest. The two-star, hundred-room but decidedly unpalatial *Valdi Palace*, on ploshtad Botev (Ⓣ092/624150, Ⓔvaldi@isv.net; ❷), offers habitable but dowdy en-suites, although its central-square location is a major plus. Similarly frumpy is the *Dom na Turista*, a couple of blocks west of the centre on ploshtad Cherven (Ⓣ092/661528, Ⓕ661295; ❷/❸), which has plain but acceptable en-suite doubles, or pricier renovated doubles with cable TV. A considerable step up in the comfort stakes is provided by the *Chaika*, 1km further west of the centre on the road through the Vratsata Gorge (Ⓣ092/622367, Ⓔchaika_hotel@avb.bg; ❸-❹), where you can treat yourself to deep-carpeted en-suites with modern furnishings, air conditioning and minibar – there are only five rooms so ring ahead.

The numerous pavement **cafés** that line the central bulevard Hristo Botev make Vratsa an invigorating place to be on a warm summer's day, although there's little to choose between them. The *Aleksandûr* **restaurant** on bulevard Hristo Botev is a conveniently central place in which to sample the full range of Bulgarian cooking; although it's not as picturesque a location as the *Mehana Hizha*, at the top of a steep flight of steps just beyond the History Museum, offering traditional fare in a folksy suite of rooms or on a tree-shrouded terrace. Equally pleasant for alfresco dining is the restaurant of the *Chaika* hotel, which has a big outdoor terrace on the edge of an artificial boating lake, within sight of the Vratsata Gorge.

The Vrachanski Balkan Nature Park

Much of the mountainscape west of Vratsa now comes under the aegis of the Vrachanski Balkan Nature Park (*Priroden Park Vrachanski balkan*). It's a relatively young organization and has as yet produced very little in the way of hiking maps or marked paths for independent walkers. The park maintains an information centre in the same building as the Dom na Turista in Vratsa (Mon–Fri 9am–5pm; Ⓣ092/660318, Ⓔinfocenter@city-vr.bitex.com but you might not find much there apart from a few leaflets and a non-English speaker.

The Vratsata Gorge, Ledenika Cave and Bozhiya most

The most easily accessible part of the Vrachanski balkan is the Vratsata Gorge. To get there, walk west from Vratsa's town centre past the *Dom na Turista*, to pick up the asphalt road which heads between the stupendous limestone teeth that form the **Vratsata Gorge**. You only have to venture about 2km out of town to savour the gorge at its awesome best: sheer, ragged cliffs plunging towards grassy riverbanks where locals come to sunbathe, graze their goats, or wash carpets. There are a couple of café-restaurants in the gorge bottom, one of which is attached to the *Alpiiski Dom*, a training base used by rock climbers who regard the Vratsata Gorge as the most challenging cliffscape in Bulgaria. A little way beyond the *Alpiiski Dom*, the left-hand fork of the road heads for the timelessly rustic village of **Zgorigrad**, while the right-hand fork zigzags its way uphill before emerging onto a goat- and sheep-nibbled alpine plateau, rich in wild flowers and herbs. It's an area of inestimable tranquillity and beauty, offering great views towards Mount Okolchitsa to the south. If you follow all the road's twists and turns from the valley bottom to the plateau, it's about 10km, but you're far better off opting for the various paths and short cuts which dive through fields and forests on the way up – using the pylons of a disused chair lift to guide you – and working your way back onto the road whenever the going gets too steep. However you reach the top, you'll soon pick up an asphalt track heading north across the gently undulating plateau towards the **Ledenika cave** (*Ledenichkata peshtera*; daily: summer 8am–noon & 1.30–5.45pm; winter 9am–noon & 1.30–4.30pm; 7Lv), 4km from the edge of the plateau and 16km from central Vratsa by road. The cave gets its name from the icicles that form here during the winter – *leden* means icy – and its largest chamber has been dubbed the "Great Temple". It's also a popular breeding ground for **bats**.

Another geological curiosity can be seen from the minor road heading northeast from Vratsa, just outside the village of **CHIREN**: a rock tunnel about 25m wide, 20m high and 100m long, which locals call **Bozhiya most** – "God's Bridge".

The Petrohan Pass and Berkovitsa

The road that heads northwest from Sofia, route 81, skirts round the western edges of the Balkan Range on the way to the mountain health resort of **Berkovitsa**, passing over the 1446-metre **Petrohan Pass** on the way. Most Sofia–Berkovitsa buses travel this road – Berkovitsa itself is also well served by bus from Montana (see p.189) in the northeast; and by train from Boichinovtsi, a junction on the Sofia–Vidin line.

After about 65km the road from Sofia begins to ascend the Petrohanski prohod or **PETROHAN PASS**, a wooded defile that sits between Mount Zelena Glava (literally "green-head") and the jagged **Todorini Kukli**. About 7km short of the summit you'll pass through the straggling village of **GINTSI**, where locals line the roadside to sell the best **sheeps' milk yoghurt** (*ovche mlyako*) in Bulgaria, as well as home-produced honey. The summit itself is marked by a scattering of truck-stop cafés and grill stalls, and a couple of signed trails leading east onto the slopes of Todorini Kukli. Deer, rabbits and roe deer reportedly abound here, and for the hardy souls who wish to stay, **accommodation** can be found at the *Motel Petrohan*, at the summit (Ⓣ07192/230 or 0888 325 172; ❷), with a mixture of primly decorated doubles, triples and quads, some with en-suite facilities, some without. From the pass the road zigzags down into the valley of the northward-flowing Bûrziya, from where it's a short twenty-kilometre drive to Berkovitsa.

Berkovitsa and around

Surrounded by orchards, rest homes and hills, **BERKOVITSA** itself is a drab, dozy place which nowadays betrays little of its former status as a high-altitude health resort and favoured training camp of Bulgaria's wrestlers and weightlifters. However it's an important gateway to the highland area around Mount Kom, and contains a couple of worthwhile historic sights. In addition, Klisurski monastery (not one of the major foundations, but charmingly situated nevertheless) is easily visited from here.

Berkovitsa's few remaining nineteenth-century attractions lie between the modern town square and the River Berkovska. Hidden in a lush rose garden on ulitsa Cherkovna, the sunken **Church of Sveta Bogoroditsa** (the Holy Virgin) features icons by Dimitûr and Zahari Zograf and a carved wooden iconostasis on which exquisitely wrought angels blow trumpets and dragons attack lions. Three blocks east on ulitsa Berkovska reka is the **Ivan Vazov House-Museum** (officially Mon–Fri 8am–noon & 2–5pm; enquire at the Ethnographic Museum if shut; 2Lv),

Vazov in Berkovitsa

In 1878 the infant state of Bulgaria was desperately short of trained personnel, and a reasonable level of secondary education was often enough to secure a top government job. Thus it was that the 27-year-old poet **Ivan Vazov** (see p.301) was appointed magistrate in Berkovitsa, despite his complete lack of legal experience. Faced by a local populace accustomed to the partial justice of the Ottoman courts, Vazov was soon out of his depth. On one occasion he had to sentence a dog to death for savaging a chicken – an attempt to appease townsfolk who would have otherwise taken the law into their own hands. As a result, Vazov's reputation was rubbished by a gleeful Sofia press, and the government was forced to offer him an inferior post in Vidin. Seething with humiliation, Vazov resigned and left the Principality of Bulgaria for Eastern Rumelia – where he made his name as a journalist and writer.

What's remembered most about Vazov's stay in Berkovitsa is his mildly scandalous affair with a 19-year-old Turkish girl called **Zihra**. Local legends maintain that Zihra entered Vazov's house rolled up in a carpet, or was lowered over the wall in a basket, in order to avoid the prying eyes of gossip-mongers, although the reality is more prosaic. Zihra was initially married to a local Turkish *bey* and drunkard who fell into a river and drowned during the Russo-Turkish War of 1877. The wife of Vazov's landlord and colleague, Ivan Stoyanov, took pity on Zihra, engaging her as Vazov's housekeeper, and she tended the tubercular young writer through frequent bouts of ill health. He fell for her in a big way, referring to her as his first and greatest love, but unfortunately Zihra – who clearly had a thing about men in uniform – left him for the dashing Bulgarian officer Hristo Chavov.

occupying the house where Bulgaria's "national writer" spent two years as the local magistrate. While the lower floor is taken up with the usual pictures and quotes, the upper floor features an exquisitely rendered Tryavna ceiling and the sitting rooms where Vazov and his landlord, Ivan Stoyanov, held court. Both are furnished in traditional Ottoman style, with comfy *minderi* (low bench-seats padded with cushions) surrounding a central *mangal* (lidded charcoal brazier). The **Ethnographic Museum**, just around the corner on ulitsa Poruchnik Grozhdanov (Mon–Fri 8am–noon & 2–5pm; 2Lv), harbours a display of local arts and crafts, including a room devoted to the yellow- and green-splashed pottery that used to be a Berkovitsa trademark, but is nowadays made by just a few craftspeople.

Practicalities

Berkovitsa's **train station** is fifteen minutes' walk east of town at the end of ulitsa Atanas Kyorkchiev, while the **bus station** lies on the eastern fringe of the town centre on ulitsa Brezi. The town's cosiest **accommodation** is at the *Starata kûshta*, near the museums at ul. Vladimir Zaimov 6 (Ⓣ0953/80446 or 0888 986 158, Ⓦwww.viptour-bg.com; ❸), a traditional-style house within a walled enclosure offering bright, simply furnished en-suites. If the *Starata kûshta* is full, you could try the concrete high-rise *UKK* (*Uchebno-konsultantski kompleks*), just southwest of the centre at ul. Ashiklar 16 (Ⓣ0953/88192 or 88191; ❶/❸), where the choice is between grotty but tolerable old-style en-suites or brighter, freshly furnished rooms with TV.

The best of several town-centre **cafés** is *Café Dame* just down from the main square on ul. Aleksandrovska. For **restaurants** try the *Adashite*, which offers good grilled food and plenty of outdoor seating directly opposite the church; or *Krûsteva kûshta*, an atmospheric nineteenth-century house on ulitsa Sheinovo.

There's a big Saturday-morning **market** next to the bus station, selling clothes, bric-a-brac and crafts.

The hills around Berkovitsa

You can explore the hilly terrain surrounding Berkovitsa by following any of the farm tracks leading out of town, although the most rewarding itineraries take you west towards the glowering ridge of the western Balkan Range. To get started, follow ulitsa Kiril i Metodii west from the main square, and past the sports grounds to the end of town, until it splits into right and left forks. The right fork winds its way round the near side of the *Mramor* marble factory before heading into the wooded valley of the Berkovska Reka, finishing up at the popular picnic spot of **Haidushki vodopadi** ("*haidut* waterfalls"; 1hr 30min), a series of cataracts where the young river tumbles down a boulder-strewn valley floor. The left fork zigzags steeply up towards two **mountain huts** – confusingly, both are known as *Hizha Kom* – 12km away, useful starting points for assaults on the 2016-metre summit of **Mount Kom** itself (about 2hr from either *hizha*). Attempting to walk from Berkovitsa to Kom summit and back in one day is somewhat ambitious (unless you drive as far as the *hizhi*), and most people stay at least one night in one of the *hizhi* – the northernmost one of the pair (Ⓣ0953/4024; ❷), nearest to Berkovitsa, is the newer and better equipped – where you can pick up advice on upward routes onto the mountain.

Klisurski Monastery

Ten kilometres southeast of Berkovitsa, just off the road to the dowdy (and eminently missable) spa town of Vûrshets, **Klisurski Monastery** crouches beneath the pine-laden eastern slopes of Mount Todorini Kukli. Completely renovated in the 1990s, the monastery's galleried whitewashed buildings surround a courtyard and a small church, but it's the atmosphere of rural peace – rather than any architectural or historical pedigree – that's the real attraction here. The woods outside the monastery walls are worthy of exploration, although the numerous new tracks bulldozed by forestry workers have made it difficult to pick out the hiking route to Todorini Kukli (and onwards to the *Hizha Petrohan* on the other side) that once existed here.

Three daily **buses** from Berkovitsa to Vûrshets go past the access road to the monastery, from where it's a pleasant 2.5km walk (bearing left after 200m) to the monastery itself. Catching a bus back can be more problematic: you'll have to enquire at Berkovitsa bus station about return services from Vûrshets and make your own calculations as to when you need to be back on the main road ready to flag one down. Walking back to Berkovitsa along the road (2hr) is always an option if you can avoid the summer heat.

Montana, Chiprovtsi and around

MONTANA – largely rebuilt in concrete – is a brazenly modern town with a revolutionary tradition. Originally called Kutlovitsa, the town was known as Mihailovgrad for much of the postwar period in memory of local revolutionary Hristo Mihailov, a leader of the Communist uprising of **September 1923**. Socialist historians always overestimated the importance of the revolt – a short-lived farce that never enjoyed popular support – but the way in which the right-wing Tsankov regime put the uprising down, massacring 30,000 Bulgarians within a couple of weeks, ensured that it was remembered as one of the most bloodily heroic episodes in Bulgarian history. After a local referendum in 1993 the town was renamed, ostensibly because a Roman settlement called Montana existed here in the first century AD.

Montana merits little more than a fleeting visit, to use its onward transport connections to more appealing destinations in the shadow of the mountains, such as Chiprovtsi and Lopushanski Monastery. If you've time to kill between buses – the terminal is diagonally opposite the train station – head through the fruit and veg market next to the bus station to reach a park where you'll find a small **History Museum** (Mon & Wed–Sat 8am–noon & 2–6pm), housing Chiprovtsi carpets and local costumes. Of the latter, several belong to the **Karakachani**, Greek-speaking nomadic herders common throughout the western Balkan Range until the 1950s, when a combination of settled lifestyles and intermarriage with local Bulgarians hastened their disappearance as a distinct group (although they're still very much in evidence in eastern Bulgaria; see p.320). There are plenty of **cafés** a block south of the train and bus stations on Montana's flowerbedded, fountain-splashed main square, where you'll also find a brace of **hotels**: the high-rise *Zhitomir* pl. Zheravitsa 1 (Ⓣ096/306176 or 305582; ❷), which has comfortable but characterless en-suite rooms, some with TVs; and the slightly snazzier *Ogosta*, ul. Peyu Yavorov 1 (Ⓣ096/306310 or 306309; ❹), which has the edge in terms of comfort and service.

Chiprovtsi

Regular buses make the 25-kilometre journey west from Montana to the carpet-making village of **CHIPROVTSI**, nestling beneath the highest mountains of the northeast, their jagged peaks marking the frontier between Bulgaria and Serbia. Chiprovtsi was an important gold and silver mining centre in the late Middle Ages, and Saxon miners were encouraged to settle here, bringing new technology, Catholicism and blond-haired, blue-eyed bloodlines in their wake. Despite the Ottoman conquest, the village went on to become an important centre of Catholic learning, with local children being sent to Italy for training in the priesthood. Seventeenth-century statesmen **Peter Bogdan Bakshev** (Catholic Archbishop of Sofia) and **Peter Parchevich** (Archbishop of Marcianopolis – modern-day Devnya) were born in Chiprovtsi and spent most of their lives trying to persuade the rulers of Europe to give the oppressed Balkan Slavs a helping hand. Neither lived to see the glorious failure that was the **Chiprovtsi Uprising of 1688**, when the Austrian army's successes against the Turks persuaded many in the Bulgarian northwest that the hour of their liberation was nigh. Unfortunately the advancing Austrians were slow in reaching Chiprovtsi, by which time the Ottomans had razed the village to the ground and scattered its inhabitants. It wasn't until 1737 that their descendants were allowed back. Iron-ore mining was a mainstay of the local economy right up until the late 1990s, giving the place a gruff, working-class feel, and the village's proximity to what was until 1989 a closed border zone means that tourism is still very much in its infancy. However Chiprovtsi is surrounded by some of the best scenery in the northwest, and for those prepared to rough it a bit, a short stay here has its rewards.

The Village

Chiprovtsi lacks the historic buildings that would put it firmly on the tourist route, and it's really the surrounding bowl of pastured hills that give the village its visual appeal. Buses come to rest beside a modern flagstoned square, from where a lane ascends to the right to the National Revival-era **Church of Vûsnesenie Hristovo** (the Resurrection), a sunken structure that harbours

Chiprovtsi carpets

When the Ottoman authorities finally allowed people to resettle Chiprovtsi after the 1688 Uprising, carpet-weaving quickly became a key factor in the village's regeneration. Most Chiprovtsi carpets are **kilims** – double-sided woollen carpets hand-woven on a compact vertical loom known as a *stan*. They're famous for their colour-charged, stylized geometric designs, resembling more the paintings of Paul Klee than the products of some age-old peasant craft. Most characteristic of the Chiprovtsi designs is the *karakachka* ("black-eyed bride"), a geometrical form (usually red-on-black or black-on-red) that resembles a woman carrying two buckets of water. Although of eighteenth-century origin, it clearly harks back to pagan depictions of the earth mother. Other stylized forms favoured by successive generations of Chiprovtsi weavers include *lozite* ("vines"), *piletata* ("chickens"), and *saksiite* ("flowerpots") – each serving as a symbol of nature's bounty.

The craft has changed little over the last three and a half centuries, although the quality of the wool – nowadays coloured with chemical rather than vegetable dyes – may not be what it was. Certain kilim-related **customs** still prevail: it's common, for example, for a daughter or granddaughter to be swung hammock-style in a newly completed kilim, to ensure that she, too, will grow up to be a skilled weaver.

At the time of writing, the only **retail outlet** for kilims in Chiprovtsi is the museum, where there's a wide choice of local wares, all tagged with set prices. The museum can also organize visits to the houses of individual weavers, and although they rarely have surplus kilims for sale, many will be quite happy to make a kilim to your specifications if you're staying in Bulgaria long enough (two to three months) to collect it. A good Chiprovtsi kilim will last a lifetime if used as a floor covering, longer if it's employed as a wall hanging or drape. The Chiprovtsi-style carpets on sale in Sofia (see "Shopping" p.119) tend to be twice as expensive as the ones you can pick up here.

valuable icons but is rarely open. The ruins of a Catholic basilica can be traced in the grass outside. The next-door **museum** (Mon–Fri 9am–5pm, Sat–Sun 10am–4pm; if closed, call at the museum administration office on the opposite side of the road; 2Lv) tells the story of the village in familiar words-and-pictures style. There are some delicately filigreed buckles, clasps and necklaces made by seventeenth-century silversmiths, and a whole room devoted to Chiprovtsi **carpets**, where museum staff are usually on hand to demonstrate the workings of a traditional *stan* or vertical loom.

Practicalities

State-run **buses** to Chiprovtsi depart from Montana's bus station, while privately operated services use a stop on the main road just outside the station – although it's difficult to obtain timetable information about the latter. The destination boards of most state-run Chiprovtsi-bound buses are marked either "Martinovo" (the next village up the valley from Chiprovtsi) or "MOK" (an acronym denoting the local mining company).

The friendly and helpful museum administration office (same times as the museum; ⓣ09554/2168) acts as an unofficial tourist information centre, and will organize **accommodation** in its own self-contained apartment (❷). Otherwise there are some simply furnished en-suite doubles and a handful of triples with shared facilities at the *Gostopriemnitsa Kipro*, Balkanska 46 (ⓣ09554/2974 or 2069, ⓦwww.gostopriemnitsa.netfirms.com; ❷), an attractive old-style house with wooden gallery, folksy decor and a lovely garden. There's a **restaurant** at the *Gostopriemnitsa*, numerous **cafés** round the main square, and a couple of late-opening food stores (*hranitelni stoki*). The best time to be in Chiprovtsi is during one of the Orthodox **religious holidays**, celebrated here (despite Chiprovtsi's Catholic past) with a verve and devotion that has largely disappeared from Bulgaria's main urban centres. Key dates are Ivanovden (St John's Day) on January 7, Gergyovden (St George's Day) on May 6, Petrovden (St Peter's Day) on June 29, and Ilinden (St Elijah's Day) on July 20. On each of these days, every *mahala*, or neighbourhood, cooks up a vat of *kurban-chorba* (stew made from a freshly sacrificed sheep) ready for a communal feast. On December 6 the entire population heads for the ruined **Gushovski monastery** 4km south of the village for an outdoor Mass and more communal feasting.

Chiprovski Monastery and the mountains

Having destroyed Chiprovtsi in the wake of the 1688 Uprising, the Ottomans also burned down the nearby **Chiprovski Monastery** as a token of their disapproval. About 6km east of town just off the Montana road (Montana–Chiprovtsi buses may drop you off here, but seem to have an aversion to picking passengers up), the most recent incarnation of this little-visited foundation dates mostly from the early nineteenth century, a clump of lumpy off-white outbuildings surrounding a dainty monastery church. The healing energies of the place are widely respected: prayers requesting cures for visitors' ailments are incanted daily at 10am, and the iconostasis is littered with votive offerings left by grateful believers – mostly cellophane-wrapped shirts and socks. This atmosphere of holiness extends to the accommodation policy: you can only **stay** at the monastery if the *igumen* (abbot) is convinced you have a spiritual need to do so.

West of Chiprovtsi, an imposing green-brown ridge known as the **Chiprovska planina** (Chiprovtsi mountains) marks the border with Serbia. Trails lead out of the village and up the Androvitsa and Ogosta valleys towards the fir-shrouded lower limbs of the ridge, although it's a good 6km before you hit the best of the hiking territory – so you need either a car or an early start to get the most out of the area. There's nothing to stop you exploring the mountains on your own, although bear in mind that hiking trails here are not yet properly marked or mapped, mists descend quickly, and that the summit of the ridge is a still-sensitive border. Expect to be arrested if you stray over to the wrong side. The sensible way to enjoy the region is to hire a local **guide** for about E25 a day, plus expenses, from the Chiprovtsi museum administration office: a typical one-day hike would involve 4WD transport to one of the trail heads, followed by a lateral walk along the Bulgarian side of the ridge, with stunning views of Chiprovtsi and Montana laid out below.

Lopushanski Monastery and around

Ten kilometres due east of Chiprovtsi is **Lopushanski Monastery**, situated in one of the area's prettiest valleys, the Dûlgodelska ogosta. You'll find the monastery just beyond the village of **Georgi-Damyanovo**, lurking in a grove of pine trees – a tranquil location that provided Ivan Vazov with the peace and quiet he needed to complete several chapters of *Under the Yoke*. The monastery church is particularly noted for two icons by Samokov master Stanislav Dospevski, the *Virgin and Child* and *Christ Pantokrator* – both works showing an almost photographic realism. It's an easy place to get to on public transport, with four daily Montana–Kopilovtsi **buses** passing the monastery entrance.

For a taste of the mountains, it's worth continuing west of the monastery to the village of **Kopilovtsi**, 17km upstream at the head of a northern branch of the valley. From here a badly potholed road continues a further 5km to **Kopren**, site of a few privately owned holiday villas and a (currently closed) rest home known as the Prophylactorium. Round the back of the Prophylactorium a track leads to the start of one of the nicest short walks in Bulgaria, the well-marked and well-maintained **Kopren ecotrail** (*ekopûteka "Kopren"*; 1hr 30min one way). The trail – steep and boulder-strewn in parts – works its way up a wooded ravine, passing a waterfall and several smaller cataracts, before emerging onto a highland meadow ringed by looming peaks – the imposing 1964-metre **Mount Kopren**, marking the border with Serbia, is straight ahead.

Belogradchik and around

Lying in a bowl beneath the hills just east of the Serbian border, **BELOGRAD-CHIK** literally "small white town") gives its name to Bulgaria's most spectacular rock formations, the **Belogradchishkite skali**, which cover an area of 90 square kilometres to the west. The limestone rocks greatly impressed French traveller Adolph Blanqui in 1841, who described them as an "undreamt landscape" rising to heights of 200m in shades of scarlet, buff and grey, with shapes suggestive of "animals, ships or houses, Egyptian obelisks" and "enormous stalagmites".

The towering rocks nearest the town form a natural fortress whose defensive potential has been exploited since ancient times. Begun by the Romans, continued by the Bulgars during the eighth century, and completed by the Turks a millennium later, the castle at Belogradchik used to command the eastern approaches to the Belogradchik Pass. Although no longer in use, the pass was for centuries the main trade route linking the lower Danube with the settlements of Serbia's Morava Valley. In Ottoman times the citadel and its garrison served to intimidate and control the local populace, and hundreds of Bulgarian insurgents were held here after the failed uprising of 1850. One particularly unsavoury tale relates that many of the prisoners were slaughtered when the Ottomans forced them to pass through a low doorway, only to have their heads lopped off by swordsmen lurking on the other side.

The Town and the rocks

Ruddy pinnacles of rock are immediately visible on arrival, glowering over the town from the hilltop around which Belogradchik is draped. The town's main street, lined with turn-of-the-twentieth-century houses with spindly cast-iron balconies, winds up towards the summit, passing a small **art gallery** (Mon–Fri 9am–noon & 2–5pm) with modest exhibitions of local work, a **museum** (same times; 2Lv), strong on local folklore, and the almost derelict **Huseyn Pasha mosque**, its former glory recalled in the delicate green-and-purple abstract swirls adorning the main entrance. Before long you'll reach the entrance of the **citadel** (*kaleto*; daily: June–Sept 8am–7pm; Oct–May 9am–5pm; 2Lv), three levels of fortifications representing different periods of occupation. The lowest two levels are Ottoman: solid, utilitarian blocks of stone enlivened here and there by the occasional floral-patterned relief. A steep climb between two enormous pillars of rock leads to the highest and oldest level, occupied by the medieval Bulgarian stronghold. The rocks themselves provided the perfect fortified enclosure, and apart from the tumbledown wall of a medieval reservoir there's little man-made to see. Enjoy instead the marvellous panorama of surrounding hills.

Another way of approaching the rocks begins at the other end of the main street, opposite the derelict-looking *Hotel Belogradchishkite Skali*, where concrete steps lead down into a dry valley overlooked by some of the more spectacular rock formations. A path continues along the valley floor for several kilometres, providing views of a whole series of extravagantly weathered pillars, two of which are associated with misogynistic **legends**: the *Nun*, who was supposedly turned into stone for becoming pregnant by a knight; and the *Schoolgirl*, who was likewise afflicted after she was deserted by her husband.

The number of rock eagles and other hunting birds frequenting the Belogradchik area is said to be on the increase, although the only ones you're likely to catch sight of are the stuffed versions housed in the village's small **Natural History Museum** (Mon–Fri 8am–noon & 2–5pm; ring the bell). To find it, take the road leading downhill from the *Hotel Belogradchishkite Skali* and look for a left turning into the woods.

Practicalities

Lying just off the main E79 between Montana and Vidin, Belogradchik is easily reached by **bus** from the latter. The town's **bus station** lies immediately below the main street. Trains on the Sofia–Vidin line stop at Oreshets station 10km to the east, from where there are regular buses.

Roughly opposite the bus station, the *Rai* at ul. Ivan Stratsimir 3 (Ⓣ0936/3735; ❷) is a family-run guesthouse offering six simple rooms with pine furnishings, most with en-suite WC/shower; the only minus point is that there's no breakfast. Hidden away in residential streets uphill to the south, the *Madona* at ul. Hristo Botev 26 (Ⓣ0936/5546 or 5646; ❷), is another family-run concern with minuscule but cosy en-suites in the main building, more spartan rooms with shared facilities in an adjoining annexe, and an attractive garden terrace. Also uphill from the centre in the southern part of town, the *Turisticheski Dom*, behind the sports stadium (Ⓣ0936/3382; ❷), has tatty but serviceable en-suite doubles, many with good views of the rocks. The road heading downhill from the town's central T-junction (overlooked by the uninviting high-rise *Hotel Belogradchishkite Skali*) leads after 1km to the idyllic *Madona* **campsite** (no relation to the *Madona* hotel), a friendly, partly wooded place which also has a couple of bungalows (❶), but only one WC/shower on site. The **café-restaurant** of the *Turisticheski Dom* has a terrace with spectacular views looking out towards the rocks, while that of the *Madona* has good home cooking and a vine-shaded courtyard.

The Magura Cave and Midzhur

Twenty-five kilometres northwest of Belogradchik lies the village of **RABISHA**, a couple of kilometres short of the spectacular **Magura Cave** (12Lv). As early as 2700 BC, the cave was occupied by hunters, traces of whom are now displayed in a small museum (entry included in the cave ticket) near the entrance. The cave itself is accessed by a steep (and sometimes slippery) staircase, and explorable along a 2km trail through the chambers. The most celebrated chamber is the one decorated with 4500-year-old **rock paintings** executed in bat-droppings, which depict a giraffe, hunting scenes and a fertility rite. The female figures tend to be bigger than the male figures, suggesting that women enjoyed superior status in the cave society of the time. Other chambers contain an awesome array of stalactites and stalagmites – of the latter, the so-called "Fallen Pine", 11m long and 6m in girth, is said to be the largest example ever discovered in Bulgaria. In recent years the cave's opening times have been far from predictable – best policy is to ask at the *Turisticheski Dom* or *Hotel Madona* in Belogradchik before setting out. Twenty-five kilometres due south of Belogradchik is **MIDZHUR**, at 2168m the highest of a whole series of densely wooded hills that have only recently been made accessible to hikers. For decades they were considered off limits because of the supposedly sensitive nature of the border with Yugoslavia, and there's a corresponding lack of chalets or tourist facilities in the region. If you do fancy exploring, the foothill villages of **Gorni Lom** and **Chuprene** are the starting points for footpaths into the mountains, though the nearest **accommodation** is back in Belogradchik, where you can also hire guides from the *Turisticheski Dom*.

The Danubian Plain

Stretching from the northern slopes of the Balkan Range to the Danube river, the **Danubian Plain** (*Dunavska ravnina*) is a more undulating region than its name would suggest, an agriculturally rich area crowded with maize fields, sunflowers and vineyards. The river itself forms Bulgaria's frontier with its northern neighbour, Romania, before wheeling away beyond Silistra to join the Black Sea far to the north. The shorelines possess different characters: the Bulgarian side is buttressed by steep bluffs and tabletop plateaus, while the opposite bank is low-lying and riven by shallow lakes called *baltas*, which merge first with marshes, then the Wallachian plain. Between the two lies a shoal of wooded islands that provide a haven for local birdlife, a population sustained by the river's rich stocks of fish.

In ancient times the Danube was one of Europe's most important **frontiers**, a natural barrier separating the riches of southern Europe from the barbarian tribes to the north. The Macedonian kings tried to make the Danube the northern boundary of their domains, with Alexander the Great campaigning against the Getae here in 335 BC, but their hold on the area was always superficial. The **Romans** were the first to turn the Danube into a permanent, fortified line of defence, building a series of garrison towns and administrative centres along its length. By the second century, thriving civilian towns such as Ratiaria, Oescus, Novae and Durostorum were beginning to emerge alongside the armed camps. By the fifth century, however, the frontier was being breached by raiders from the north, many of whom (including the *sklaveni*, ancestors of the Balkan Slavs) increasingly chose to settle down south of the river once their plundering days were over. Justinian attempted to stem the tide in the sixth century, refortifying the old Roman sites and establishing new garrisons along the river, but Byzantine diplomacy subsequently concentrated on paying off the barbarians to keep them sweet rather than attempting to shut them out altogether.

With the decline of the lower Danube's strategic importance the settlements along its banks began to decay, only to revive when the last of the Bulgarian kings, the **Shishmanids**, fought a delaying action against the advancing Turks from Danubian strongholds such as Nikopol and **Vidin**. The Ottomans themselves were great fortress builders, erecting the eighteenth-century citadels of

Ruse and Silistra in an attempt to strengthen the Danube frontier against the dvance of Russian power.

During the nineteenth century, increased river transport brought the goods and culture of Central Europe down the valley, turning the towns along its banks into cosmopolitan outposts of Mitteleuropa. European fashions and styles often arrived here first before being transmitted to the rest of Bulgaria, turning towns such as **Lom**, **Svishtov** and **Ruse** into unlikely centres of elegance and sophistication. With the development of the railways, however, the river trade went into decline, and nowadays most of Bulgaria's Danubian towns are quiet, provincial places, focusing their attention not on the river itself, but on the bigger cities inland. The region as a whole went into a deep economic slump after 1990, with river traffic reduced to a trickle by the war in former Yugoslavia, and killed off altogether by NATO's destruction of Yugoslavia's Danubian bridges during the Kosovo crisis of 1999. Almost all the towns along the river are visibly blighted by unemployment, poverty and economic stagnation: it's estimated that Vidin has lost almost a third of its population in the last decade, with the young in particular heading for Sofia in search of jobs. The only real exception is Ruse – an important business and cultural centre that commands the major road and train route to Bucharest and the north. Ruse is a good base from which to visit the valley of the **Rusenski Lom**, a hauntingly beautiful spot which harbours important medieval ruins, and several lesser sights along the river, such as the small port of **Svishtov** to the west. Elsewhere along the river, however, public transport is meagre, and tourist attractions few and far between. Heading along the riverbank from Vidin to Ruse for example is only practical if you have a car: most bus links connect the Danubian towns with places inland rather than with each other, and reliable accommodation is practically nonexistent.

Public transport is much better if you're travelling eastwards from Ruse into the **Dobrudzha**, a vast expanse of grain-producing flatland which extends all the way from the Danube to the Black Sea. Main attractions here are the dozy former fishing port of **Tutrakan**, and the bird-rich **Srebûrna nature reserve**, just outside the laid-back riverside town of **Silistra**. From Silistra it's a straightforward drive or bus ride across the plain towards the sea, with the Dobrudzha's main administrative centre, the former Ottoman market town of **Dobrich**, providing the only potential stopoff en route.

Vidin

"One of those marvellous cities of eastern fairytale which, secure behind their fortress walls, is decorated with spires and cupolas and minarets piled one upon another in a fantastic medley of creeds, ages and styles." So **VIDIN** was rather fancifully described by Lovett Edwards in his book *Danube Stream* in 1941. Nowadays you'll find that the truth is more prosaic: Vidin's modern skyline leaves a lot to be desired, and although the great sweep of the fortress walls still dominates much of the riverfront, the spires and minarets characteristic of Edwards' day have largely gone, to be replaced by utilitarian housing projects. Ample reason for visiting is, however, still provided by the showpiece medieval **citadel of Baba Vida**, presiding over luscious riverside parklands on the northern edge of town. Buses connect Vidin with the nearby Danubian towns of **Lom**, **Kozlodui** and **Oryahovo**, although there's little of touristic interest along this stretch of the river.

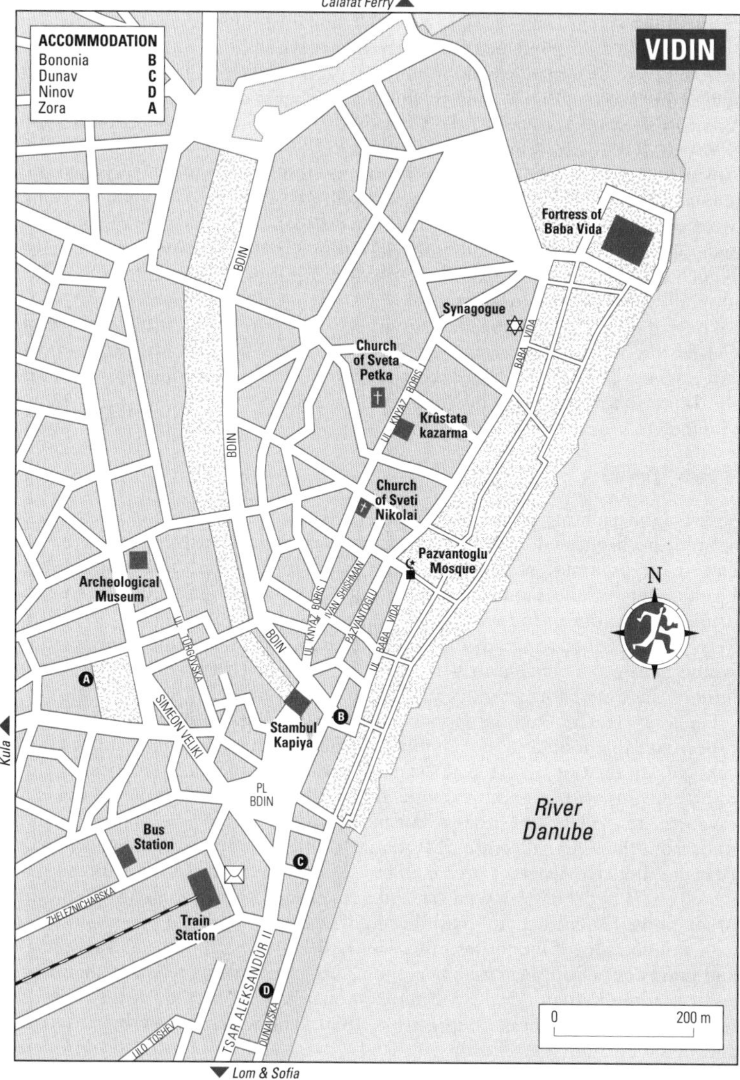

Some history

Vidin's potential as the guardhouse of the lower Danube was exploited by successive waves of Celts, Romans and Byzantines, but it was under the Bulgarian tsars and their Ottoman conquerors that the most frenzied fortress building took place. However, Vidin's relative isolation from major power centres like Tûrnovo and Constantinople made the place a breeding ground for semi-independent local kinglets, and the citadel they built was much coveted by neighbouring powers. In the fourteenth century it was the power base of **Mihail Shishman**, whom the nobles elected tsar rather than see Vidin secede from Bulgaria, and after 1371 it was the capital of an independent kingdom ruled by Mihail's grand-nephew **Ivan Stratsimir**. Vidin fought a rearguard action against Ottoman expansion in the Balkans, grudgingly accepting Turkish suzerainty in the 1390s – only to throw it off again as soon as help emerged from the West in the shape of the Crusade of 1396. The city was recaptured by Sultan Bayezid's army two years later.

In the late eighteenth century Vidin was the capital of **Osman Pazvantoglu**, a local ruler who rebelled against Sultan Selim III in 1794. Energetic, despotic and fond of inventing tortures, Pazvantoglu pillaged as far afield as Sofia in defiance of the sultan, and strengthened Vidin's fortifications with the assistance of French engineers sent by Napoleon, who envisaged him as a potential lever for toppling the Ottoman Empire.

These days Vidin is comparatively quiet, but with the Romanian town of Calafat just across the river, and the Serbian border 30km northwest, the town still retains a little of its former cosmopolitan feel. A planned road bridge over the Danube to Calafat (to be completed in 2008–9) promises to bring more vibrancy to Vidin in the future.

The Town

Vidin's modern heart stands at the southern end of the fortified old town, based around the flagstoned central square, **ploshtad Bdin**, which is dominated by customary examples of socialist urban planning: the high-rise-style former headquarters of the Communist Party vying for attention with the equally brutal modernism of the *obshtinski sûvet*, or town council building, next door. Somewhat less imposing are the structures lining the main downtown streets which radiate outwards from here – drab lumps of ochre and grey that reveal little of the town's former glory.

The only real interest in modern Vidin is the **Archeological Museum** (Tues–Sat 9am–noon & 1.30–5.30pm; 3Lv), housed in a pagoda-like nineteenth-century *konak* west of the main square at the end of ulitsa Tûrgovska. The display begins with prehistoric bone and stone tools found in the Mirizlivka cave near the village of Oreshets, but most space is devoted to Roman-period finds from the regional centre of Ratiaria, founded by Trajan in about 107 AD near the modern village of Archar, 25km southeast of Vidin. A floor mosaic on which a stag is chased by a wild cat, and a fine second-century marble sculpture of a pensive Hercules toying with his club, reveal something of the sophistication and comfort of life in this otherwise rather provincial outpost. Sarcophagi and gravestones from Ratiaria's necropolis litter the lawn outside. An adjoining section of the museum deals with the National Revival period, with particular reference to the local peasant uprising of 1850, centred on the towns of Gradets and Belogradchik.

The old town

On the northern side of the main square the borders of old Vidin are marked by the Stambul Kapiya or Istanbul Gate, a stocky portal in the Turkish style. Beyond it lies a pleasant turn-of-the-twentieth-century residential district with an extensive riverside park to the east. On the edge of the park stands the Osman Pazvantoglu mosque, the only surviving mosque in the city – most of the others were knocked down in the 1970s and 1980s. Extensively renovated in 2003, it's a graceful and alluring building, but rarely opens its doors to visitors. To one side is the squat, domed *kitabhane* or Koranic library, gradually disappearing behind a shroud of ivy and weeds. Immediately opposite stands the

Osman Pazvantoglu and the Kûrdzhali

By the early 1790s Ottoman-ruled northern Bulgaria was sliding slowly into chaos, with provincial Ottoman governors increasingly in revolt against a reforming sultan – Selim III – who they saw as a threat to their traditional powers. The provincial governors had begun to staff their private armies with a new class of disposessed freebooters, mostly former imperial soldiers, known as **Kûrdzhali**, who roamed the countryside in search of food and plunder, terrorizing Christian villages.

Foremost among the provincial power barons was **Osman Pazvantoglu**, born in Vidin in around 1758, the son of a local janissary executed in 1788 for leading a revolt. Osman himself was also sentenced to death for participating in the revolt, but managed to escape, re-emerging in the 1790s to harness the discontent whipped up by his father. Ruler of Vidin from 1794 onwards, Pazvantoglu attracted *Kûrdzhali* from all over northern Bulgaria, not least because the town was seen as a safe zone where they could store their booty and sell it – with Pazvantoglu taking a percentage of the proceeds. The Ottoman sultan laid **siege** to Vidin in 1795 and again in the winter of 1797–8, only to see the bulk of his troops melt away and join Pazvantoglu's rebels. Pazvantoglu was popular with Islamic traditionalists who saw him as a bulwark against a westernizing sultan, but he also took care to win the support of local Christians, cutting taxes and feudal impositions, and promising to treat all subjects as equals whatever their faith. For a time Pazvantoglu seemed capable of overthrowing the sultan and installing himself as ruler in Constantinople, but somehow failed to press home the advantage. Ultimately he was kept in check by the Russians, who feared that the autocratic structure of society in eastern Europe might suffer general collapse if truculent upstarts like Pazvantoglu were seen to get their way.

The **Serbian Uprising of 1804** spelled the end for Pazvantoglu. Many of his Bulgarian subjects were tempted to join their Serb neighbours, thus destroying the Muslim–Christian alliance which had thus far prevailed in Pazvantoglu's territory. January 1806 saw Pazvantoglu launch a vicious **pogrom** against Bulgarian priests and civil leaders in Vidin, fearful that they were about to launch a revolt of their own. Frequent outbreaks of plague gnawed away at the city's self-confidence, and Vidin was in steep decline by the time of Pazvantoglu's own death in February 1807. His uncharismatic successor, Idris Molla, was unable to prevent the gradual reimposition of Ottoman control.

modern **Church of Sveti Nikolai**, inside which Cyril, Methodius and other saints are rendered in colourful turn-of-the-twentieth-century realist frescoes, rather like illustrations in a children's encyclopedia. More interesting is the **Church of Sveti Panteleimon**, hidden round the back, an austere twelfth-century basilica made from heavy stone.

From Sveti Nikolai, ulitsa Baba Vida hugs the park's western flank, leading past an ensemble of sorry-looking buildings along the way: the peeling ochre plaster of the **banya** or town baths, and the shell of a derelict **synagogue**. Vidin was an important centre of Jewish culture until the late 1940s, when most local families emigrated to Israel. Parallel to Baba Vida to the west is ulitsa Knyaz Boris I, site of Pazvantoglu's **Krûstata Kazarma** (the "cross-shaped barracks"), now an ethnographic **museum** (usually Mon–Fri 9–11.30am & 2–5pm; ring the bell and hope that a curator is around; 2Lv). Across the road, stranded behind railings in a patch of wasteland between two school playgrounds, is the seventeenth-century **Church of Sveta Petka**, an unassuming, sunken structure, traces of bright blue on the exterior giving some idea of its former appearance.

From the northern end of the riverside park, stone ramparts run alongside the shoreline for over a kilometre, largely overgrown and deserted, eventually curving inland to protect the **Fortress of Baba Vida** (Mon–Fri 8.30am–5pm, Sat & Sun 10am–5pm; 3Lv). Surrounded by huge walls and a deep, dried-out moat, the fortress dates from the thirteenth century, although the brutal, blockhouse appearance of its turrets and towers owes more to the continuous improvements carried out by the Turks and the Habsburgs, who briefly occupied the town in the sixteenth century. Once inside, you can scramble around an extensive network of courtyards and ramparts, and survey the Danube from gun positions overlooking the river. Further stretches of wall extend well to the west of the citadel, and crumbling gates stand surreally amid the modern housing estates.

North of Baba Vida paths lead beside concrete flood defences and a derelict rowing centre (*grebna baza*) towards an unspoiled **riverside meadow** some 2km beyond. Intermittently shaded with trees, it's popular with local bathers, amateur fishermen and grazing flocks.

Practicalities

Most of the town's amenities lie in the modern centre a short distance from the main square: both **bus** and **train** stations are a couple of blocks to the west. The choice of places to sleep, eat and drink in Vidin is pretty limited, a reflection of both the town's declining economic fortunes and the lack of any real tourist traffic.

Top **accommodation** choice is the central *Zora*, ul. Naicho Tsanov 3A (Ⓣ094/600290 or 606330, Ⓦwww.hotelzora.hit.bg; ❹/❻), an upmarket B&B offering soothingly furnished rooms with reasonably sized bathrooms; it also has a couple of bright, tiled-floor apartments sleeping three or four. Alternatively, try the *Ninov*, ul. Dunavska 28 (Ⓣ094/600402 or 600475, Ⓦwww.nwbulinfo.com/hotel-ninov; ❹/❻), a newish, neat hotel near the riverfront with comfortable en-suite doubles with TV and air conditioning, and a handful of two- to three-person apartments with workdesk, lounge and bathtubs. If both these places are full, you're restricted to the *Dunav*, ul. Edelvais 3 (Ⓣ094/600174 or 600177, Ⓦwww.dunav-vidin.dir.bg; ❹–❺), an uninspiring downtown block offering a mixed bag of rooms, some en suite; or the *Bononia*, ploshtad Bdin (Ⓣ094/606031 or 606032, Ⓦwww.sky-vidin.com; ❹), a dilapidated two-star beside the riverside gardens, offering en-suite rooms with tired-looking furnishings and small TVs.

Daytime drinking and snacking is best in the **cafés** along ulitsa Tûrgovska, or in the riverside park, where there are several open-air establishments. The **restaurant** in the *Hotel Bononia* is the only decent place for a slap-up Bulgarian meal, although there's a tolerable pizzeria, the *Classic*, in the riverside park, with a nice outdoor terrace and a satisfying range of big salads.

Crossing into Romania

Roughly every hour a **car ferry service** (*feribot*; winter 6am–midnight; summer 24hr) shuttles between Vidin's grandiosely named International Dock, 5km north of town, and the port of Calafat on the Romanian side of the River Danube. Fares are around 7Lv for pedestrians, 25Lv per car. Bus #1 runs from outside Vidin train station to the ferry dock, but timings are irregular. A taxi from the station to the dock will set you back about 10Lv, more if coming in the opposite direction.

EU, US and Canadian citizens can enter Romania without a **visa**; other nationals should contact the Romanian embassy in their home country before setting out. Trains run from Calafat on to Craiova and Bucharest.

Down the Danube: from Vidin to Ruse

The road heading east along the Danube from Vidin passes through a string of settlements which, despite an often dramatic history, lack the kind of attractions – save for the river itself – to warrant anything more than the briefest of halts. Given the social problems of Lom and the ailing nuclear power station at Kozlodui, any description of this part of the river is bound to read more like a catalogue of places to avoid rather than a recommended tourist itinerary, unless you have a taste for ancient history or riverine wildlife. Another reason for treating this route with caution is that bus transport along this stretch of the river is notoriously meagre; even if you succeed in getting as far as Oryahovo (see below), you'll probably then have to head inland to Pleven in order to make any further eastbound progress.

Thirty or so kilometres downriver from Vidin, the village of **Archar** was once the site of Ratiaria – the capital of Upper Moesia, from where the emperor Trajan consolidated Roman rule over what's now the Romanian side of the Danube – though there's little to see beyond the relics now on show in Vidin's Archeological Museum (see p.198). A kilometre or two beyond the village of Dobri Dol, look out for signs leading to Dobrodolski Monastery, home to the curious mid-nineteenth-century **Church of Sveta Troitsa** (Holy Trinity). A buff-coloured structure topped by an unusually tall drum, the exterior is unadorned save for a series of reliefs executed in a deliberately primitivist style, harking back to medieval, almost pre-Christian, Bulgarian models. A carving above the door shows a man fighting a dog-headed snake, flanked on either side by figures of the Archangel Michael and the builder of the church himself. Beyond here the road runs behind a wooded cliff more than 100m high, which continues in an unbroken line for about 20km. The riverbank around **Orsoya**, 7km beyond Dobri Dol, is a well-known spot for watching waterfowl and wading birds.

During the last century this stretch of the Danube shore was chosen by the Turks to accommodate the *cherkezi* or **Circassians**, Muslim refugees from the Caucasus who had been expelled from their homelands by the armies of Imperial Russia. Used by the Ottomans to keep the local Bulgarians under control, many of them fled after the Liberation to escape reprisals, although a few small communities remain. Many of those who stayed were assimilated into Bulgaria's Turkish minority, with the result that surviving pockets of Circassians tend to be categorized (both by themselves and their Bulgarian neighbours) as Turks.

Lom and Kozlodui

The first major settlement east of Vidin is **LOM**, a town renowned throughout Bulgaria for the watermelons grown in the surrounding fields. Citizens of Sofia used to come up to Lom in order to stock up on the local produce – the kind of fresh fruit of which urban dwellers were often deprived – thus leading the locals to dub the train link between Lom and the capital as the *mazen vlak* – loosely translatable as the "gravy train". Slightly closer to Sofia by train than Vidin, Lom has outstripped its western neighbour as the capital's port on the Danube, and it's correspondingly uglier and more industrialized as a result. In addition, the town's large **Gypsy population** is one of the most downtrodden in Bulgaria, and gypsy demonstrations against local police harrassment have been a frequent occurrence in recent years (see p.481).

Forty kilometres east of Lom, **KOZLODUI**, the next place of any size, has a monument near the small harbour commemorating the "**landing of 1876**", when Hristo Botev (see p.305) launched his ill-fated raid on northern Bulgaria. More recently Kozlodui has become notorious as the site of Bulgaria's first and only **nuclear power station**, built with Soviet help in the 1970s. Throughout 1991 international observers became increasingly worried about the plant's safety, not least because the Soviet technicians who used to run it were being replaced by insufficiently qualified staff. Western governments successfully pressured the Bulgarians into agreeing to close down the oldest two reactors by 2003 (and the rest of the plant by 2020). Fears that the winding down of Kozlodui will leave Bulgaria bereft of electricity supplies have been partly assuaged by controversial plans to build a new, more advanced nuclear installation slightly downriver at Belene (see opposite).

Oryahovo and Gigen

Another forty kilometres downstream from Kozlodui, **ORYAHOVO** slopes up a hillside overlooking a port used for the export of grain and grapes. In 1396,

The Vlachs

One minority living along Bulgaria's riverine border are the *Vlasi* or **Vlachs**, who speak a dialect of Romanian and are found in isolated villages throughout north Bulgaria, eastern Serbia, Macedonia and northern Greece.

Precise definitions of who is a Vlach and who isn't vary from area to area. To many Balkan Slavs, a Vlach is simply a Romanian-speaker who lives outside Romania. Elsewhere (notably in Croatia, Slovenia and the Czech and Slovak republics, the term "Vlach" is used specifically to designate transhumant shepherds who speak (or used to speak) a language closely related to Romanian. The Romanians themselves are keen to promote the idea that Vlachs everywhere are far-flung members of one big Romanian family; others argue that different communities of Vlachs deserve to be treated as ethnic/linguistic groups in their own right.

The Vlachs of the Balkans are traditionally nomadic sheep farmers, pasturing their flocks on the lowlands during the winter and moving to the mountains in the summer. Nowadays, however, the attractions of urban life, and the restrictions on movement imposed by modern bureaucratic states (not least socialist ones), have meant that most Balkan Vlachs lead an increasingly sedentary lifestyle.

The origins of the Vlachs have been the cause of much inconclusive debate, but the fact that they speak a Latin tongue suggests that they are descended either from second- and third-century Roman settlers or from the native Balkan peoples – whether Dacians, Thracians, or Illyrians – who came into contact with these settlers and adopted their language. With the collapse of Roman and Byzantine power, hastened by the successive deluges of Slavs, Magyars and Turks, the Vlachs somehow ensured the survival of their tongue by retreating into highland regions and reverting to nomadism. The most enthusiastic proponents of this version of Vlach history are the Romanians, who point to the existence of the modern Romanian nation as proof that the ancient, Latinized population in the Balkans was able to retreat into the hills, only to re-emerge centuries later with its language and culture intact. Nationalist historians from other Balkan countries sometimes beg to differ, arguing that Vlachs are either ethnic Slavs or ethnic Greeks, learning Latin from their Roman or Byzantine masters, and somehow clinging on to the language due to the isolated nature of their lifestyle.

Bulgaria's Vlachs are found along the Danube and in the Dobrudzha, but during the Communist period they were encouraged to assimilate with the Slav majority, thus threatening the long-term survival of their language. The scattered nature of Vlach settlement, and the fact that many local gypsies declare themselves to be Vlach despite belonging to an altogether different ethnic group, make it difficult to ascertain exactly how many of them there are in the country.

the Bulgarians holding Oryahovo's fortress, Rachova, surrendered willingly to the Crusaders rather than fight for the Turks, but the French contingent in the crusading army pillaged and burned the town anyway, later justifying their action by claiming that they had had to take the town by force. Oryahovo is nowadays useful as a rail junction, with a couple of trains a day departing for **Cherven bryag** on the Sofia–Pleven–Varna line. There's also a ferry connecting Oryahovo to Bechet on the Romanian side of the river, although the lack of public transport links at the latter make this a bad place to enter Romania, unless you're travelling by private car.

At the confluence of the Iskûr and the Danube beyond Baikal, the **ruins of Roman Oescus** can be found about 2km north of **GIGEN** village. Excavations have uncovered ramparts, foundation walls, drains and large paving-slabs that give a fair idea of the layout of the ancient town, though the site's rich yield of statuary and mosaics is now displayed in Pleven's history museum. Like other Danubian settlements, Oescus was razed by the Huns in the fifth century, rebuilt during the reign of Justinian and destroyed again by the Avars, so it's hardly surprising that nothing remains of the great bridge over the Danube built for the emperor Constantine.

Nikopol and Belene

The road loops inland before arriving at **NIKOPOL**, 46km beyond, a sleepy backwater known primarily for the once-impregnable fortress founded in 629 by Emperor Heraclius I. Its capture by the Turks in 1393 frightened the Christian powers into organizing a crusade to retake the lower Danube. Feasting and pillaging their way south, the Crusaders treated the campaign as a sport, bringing "wines and festive provisions" instead of siege weapons. Unable to storm Nikopolis' 26 mighty towers, they instituted a blockade and began squabbling among themselves (the French, in particular, resented the fact that Sigismund of Hungary had been chosen by the pope to be supreme commander). Pigheadedness and disunity proved fatal on November 25, 1396, when Sultan Bayezid's army appeared on the neighbouring plateau. Against Sigismund's orders the French cavalry charged uphill after fleeing irregulars, only to be impaled on hidden stakes and then butchered by the Turkish cavalry. The Crusaders' defeat was shattering, and no further attempts were made to check Turkish expansion until the battle of Varna fifty years later, by which time the Ottomans were entrenched in the Balkans.

It's fairly easy to work your way up to the fortress from Nikopol's riverfront **bus station**, but there's little to see once you get there, save for earthen ramparts, and sombre views of abandoned Romanian factories on the opposite bank. Back in town, you'll find a couple of central **cafés**, and a smashed-up hotel which seems to have permanently closed its doors. Nikopol has **bus** links with the city of Pleven to the south, but not with its Danubian neighbours.

Beyond Nikopol the road cuts inland again, passing after 30km a left turn to **BELENE**, a small agricultural town standing opposite **Belene Island**, the river's largest, now notorious in Bulgaria for having been the site of one of the country's biggest Communist-era labour camps. Belene is also the intended site of a nuclear power station, long-planned by the Bulgarian authorities to provide the country with cheap electricity supplies well into the twenty-first century. The misgivings of the Romanian government – chiefly regarding the proposed installation's proximity to major population centres such as Bucharest – are unlikely to hold up the progress of the project, which is scheduled for completion in 2010. More happily, Belene is also a favoured nesting ground of **spoonbills** in May and June.

Belene labour camp

Between Nikopol and Svishtov lies a cluster of green islands whose name is now notorious in Bulgaria – **Belene**, the site of an infamous labour camp. Established in 1947, together with a smaller women's camp which was soon closed, Belene held both political prisoners and dangerous criminals. The latter were reportedly favoured by the guards, who apparently permitted them to tyrannize the "politicals" according to Stalinist practice. During the 1950s when the purges were at their height, hundreds of Bulgarians perished here through a combination of malnutrition, overwork and brutality. Prisoners directed to woodcutting on neighbouring Bûrzina Island had to chop 1120 cubic metres per day before receiving their rations, and inmates who violated camp rules (by scavenging for food, or addressing a guard as "comrade", for example) were used for target practice or marooned on rafts to freeze or suffer clouds of mosquitos.

Conditions improved somewhat during the 1960s following a limited amnesty, but Belene remained a savage place. During the 1970s many of the inmates were Pomaks, Slav Muslims from the western Rhodopes who were being pressured to drop their Islamic names and adopt Bulgarian ones instead – those who resisted ended up in Belene. Ethnic Turks who objected to the revitalized name-changing campaign of the mid-1980s were sent here too. The camp was closed down swiftly after November 1989.

Svishtov

Twenty kilometres east of Belene, **SVISHTOV** is just about the only town between Vidin and Ruse that's worth visiting as a tourist. A long-established port and crafts town that grew up just west of the former Roman city of Novae, Svishtov today preserves a smattering of nineteenth-century architecture, and a couple of worthwhile museums. The town controlled an important Danube ferry crossing point before the building of the bridge at Ruse downstream, and witnessed both the arrival of the Russian liberators in 1877 and the invasion of Romania by German and Bulgarian forces in 1916.

Easily reached by bus from Ruse, Svishtov is also at the northern end of a little-used rail line that starts in Troyan (see p.237) in the central Balkan Range, before passing through Lovech (p.235), and Levski, a junction on the main Sofia–Varna line.

The Town

Bus and **train** terminals both lie in a drab riverside area just below the bluff upon which Svishtov is built. Roads curl up into the hilltop town, converging on a main square which marks the midpoint of the principal downtown thoroughfare, ulitsa Tsar Osvoboditel. A short distance downhill from the square you'll come across a small plaza grouped around the nineteenth-century **Preobrazhenie** (Transfiguration) **Church**, which harbours a fine Tryavna iconostasis, topped with the customary bestiary of dragons and mythical birds.

Just beyond lies the attention-grabbing, pink-painted former **house of Aleko Konstantinov** (Mon–Fri 8am–noon & 1–5pm; 2Lv), a satirist remembered for creating *Bay Ganyu*, an itinerant pedlar of rose oil and rugs who remains one of the most popular characters in Bulgarian fiction. The house itself, built by Konstantinov's merchant father in 1861, was one of the first Western-style houses built in Svishtov, and is crammed with imported Viennese furniture alongside brightly coloured Bulgarian rugs. Konstantinov was killed by mistake in 1897 by assassins aiming for the lawyer with whom he was travelling, and a jar holding his heart, complete with ragged bullet hole, is the museum's most striking exhibit. The backstreets on either side of Konstantinov's house hold a couple more museum attractions, starting with the reassuringly musty **Ethnographic Museum** (same times; 2Lv) at ul. Georgi Vladiki 14, with some wonderful folk costumes and an extensive collection of *pafti*, the exquisitely wrought, metal waist buckles which form an essential part of traditional Bulgarian dress. Down a side alley from here, a half-timbered nineteenth-century house is the site of a modest **Archeological Exhibition** (same times; ask at the Aleko Konstantinov house for access; 2Lv), designed to showcase the finds excavated at nearby Novae (see below). There's not much here, to be honest, although it's worth pausing to admire the collection of clay and bone statuettes depicting human beings in a variety of erotic poses, and an impressive marble head of Caracalla – a rare portrait of a little-sculpted emperor.

Returning to the main square and heading up ulitsa Tsar Osvoboditel for about 500m brings you to the **Church of Sveta Troitsa** (Holy Trinity), arguably the crowning achievement of National Revival architect Kolyo Ficheto (see p.261). The curving lines of the roof, said to be a conscious imitation of the waves of the River Danube, were designed to offset the angular, almost neo-Gothic charms of a pinnacled octagonal bell tower – destroyed by an earthquake in 1977, the latter is currently being rebuilt.

Novae

Starting from the Church of Sveta Troitsa, it's a four-kilometre walk (or taxi ride) east along the main Ruse road to the site of **Novae**, a first-century Roman military camp which subsequently became an important civilian centre – until it was abandoned some time in the 600s. A joint Polish–Bulgarian archeological team set up camp here every spring and summer, and you're relatively free to wander around the site at all times of year providing you don't disturb areas of current excavation. The site straddles both sides of the main road, with the main legionary headquarters and barrack buildings lying over to the south side – where you can also see the remains of a fifth-century basilica. Over on the north side, where the ruins lead right down to the banks of the Danube, you can look out across the remains of the Roman legionary hospital – you can clearly make out the central courtyard, and the separate wards, each designed to hold three patients, grouped around it.

Practicalities

Should you decide **to stay**, the central *Hotel Dunav*, ul. Tsar Osvoboditel 2 (Ⓣ0631/22361; ❸), is less welcoming than the nearby *Kaleto*, on a bluff overlooking the Danube at ul. Toma Panteleev 2 (Ⓣ0631/25417 or 23247; ❸), whose en-suite rooms are generally better looked after – and the hotel's café terrace has a great view of the river. Comfiest place in town is the *Stopanska Akademija Korpus Yug*, next to the Akademik football stadium just south of the centre on the Veliko Tûrnovo road (Ⓣ0631/40082; ❹), a university-owned hotel which has neat, bright en-suites with TV. There's an attractive gaggle of **cafés** in the flagstoned pedestrian area opposite the *Hotel Dunav*, most of which serve basic snacks. Otherwise, best of the **restaurants** is the *Svishtov*, housed in the same National Revival-style building as the Archeological Exhibition (see above) and boasting an attractively shaded courtyard.

Ruse and around

"Everything I experienced later in life had already happened in **RUSE**", wrote Elias Canetti in the autobiographical *Tongue Set Free*, remembering his childhood home as an invigorating city of different races and creeds, whose cosmopolitan culture placed it firmly in the orbit of Mitteleuropa. Although the ethnic mix of Canetti's day has long since disappeared, travellers continue to be surprised by Ruse's Central European elegance. Despite being blighted by the customary concrete-and-steel overlay provided by Bulgaria's postwar urban planners, it's still a city of peaceful residential streets, where Art Nouveau-inspired ornamentation drips from delicate turn-of-the-twentieth-century houses. Ruse bears a similarity to Bulgaria's other Danubian towns in lacking a riverfront of any great beauty, but a scattering of historic sights and the relaxed feel of its downtown streets more than compensate. An important cultural centre with an animated café life, the city also plays host to one of the liveliest evening *korsos* in Bulgaria. In addition, Ruse makes a good base for exploring the nearby **Rusenski Lom** national park, home to the dramatic **Rock Churches of Ivanovo** and the ruined city of **Cherven**.

Some history

Apart from the fortress and a sprinkling of stately mosques (the former blown up by Marshal Kutuzov in the Russo-Turkish war of 1806–12, the latter demolished by post-Liberation Bulgarians), Ruse (Ruschuk to the Turks) was an unremarkable Ottoman provincial town until the enlightened governorship of **Midhat Pasha** (see box opposite), who provided the town with schools, hospitals, factories and, most importantly, the British-financed Ruse–Varna rail line – Bulgaria's first. Until the construction of the more direct Belgrade–Sofia–Istanbul line in the 1880s, travellers flooded through Ruse on their way from Central Europe to Constantinople.

Trade received a further boost after the Liberation, and for many years Ruse had more inhabitants, consulates, factories, hotels and banks than Sofia. The city's economic and cultural wealth owed a lot to the merchant families – including Germans, Greeks and Armenians – who settled here. Most numerous, however, were the **Sephardic Jews** (of whom Elias Canetti was one, born here in 1905), descendants of those Jews given refuge in the Ottoman Empire after their expulsion from Spain in 1492, and speaking Ladino, a mixture of archaic Spanish and Portuguese with numerous borrowings from the Turkish and Hebrew tongues.

Ruse lost much of its cosmopolitan character during the Communist period, but its citizens played an important part in the democratizing tide of the late 1980s, when locals began to protest against the ecological damage caused by the **chemical plant** just across the river in Romanian **Giurgiu**. Chlorine gas emissions wafting over the river from Giurgiu caused an upsurge in respiratory complaints – something that Bulgaria's Communist rulers were keen to keep quiet. The Committee for the Protection of Ruse, formed in 1988, was one of the first non-Party organizations to be created in Bulgaria, and provided the spur for reformist campaigners elsewhere. With the Giurgiu plant now closed, Ruse's air is relatively clean once more.

Ruse's post-Communist fate has mirrored that of the country as a whole, with economic decline and social decay coexisting alongside an upsurge of private enterprise, and renewed cultural contacts with the outside world. Most positively, the EU-funded renovation of many key buildings has restored to the city much of its *belle-époque* sheen.

Arrival and accommodation

Ruse's **train** and **bus** stations stand at the head of ulitsa Borisova, 2km south-west of the centre. The train station is a particularly gloomy and unwelcoming

Midhat Pasha 1822–1884

Born in the village of Zavet between Ruse and Isperih, **Midhat Pasha** enjoys an ambiguous reputation in modern-day Bulgaria. As an ethnic Turk and loyal Ottoman bureaucrat, he was on the wrong side during Bulgaria's nineteenth-century struggle for liberation, and his achievements as a statesman have been largely omitted from the history books as a result.

Educated in France, and rising rapidly through the Ottoman civil service, Midhat Pasha was a man of enlightened, westernizing tastes, who saw economic development, social reform and moderate constitutionalism as the best way to keep the empire's disparate peoples together. He put this blueprint into effect in 1864, when he was made governor of the **Tuna Vilayet** ("Danube province"), a territory which stretched over much of northern Bulgaria and eastern Serbia, and had its capital at Ruse. The region was already one of the more affluent parts of the Empire, and Midhat set about turning it into the showcase province of the Ottoman world, using state money to build roads, railways and factories. Ruse's port was modernized, and town-planning regulations stipulated that only two-storey, European-style houses were to be built in the town centre. Midhat also established cooperative banks that would extend credit to local farmers – an attempt to win the loyalty of the Christian peasantry. Midhat Pasha believed that the empire of the sultans could be saved from decay by the creation of a genuinely "Ottoman" civic identity that would transcend national and religious divisions. Few Bulgarians shared his dream, however, preferring the struggle for national self-determination to Midhat's vague promises of a democratizing multinational state.

After four years in Ruse, Midhat was recalled to Constantinople, where he occupied a series of influential posts in the imperial administration. He re-emerged as one of the key conspirators against Sultan Abdulaziz in 1876, when the crisis following the April Uprising saw the deposition of the sultan and his replacement by Murad V. Although the new ruler was speedily replaced by the authoritarian-minded Abdulhamid II, Midhat Pasha was kept on board by a regime keen to show the world a moderate, Europeanized face. Appointed to the position of Grand Vizier, Midhat drew up plans for a **democratic constitution** in December 1876 – a constitution which was quietly abandoned after Russia's declaration of war on Turkey in April 1877. Midhat left office, subsequently serving as governor in Syria, then Smyrna, before Abdulhamid felt strong enough to have him exiled to Yemen in 1881. A threat to the sultan while still alive, Midhat was murdered by Abdulhamid's agents three years later.

Modern-day Ruse folk feel rather ambivalent about Midhat Pasha. On one hand he put their city on the map, turning it into a major trade centre endowed with imposing, European-style public buildings; on the other hand he was a typical agent of Ottoman power, hunting down Bulgarian rebels (like Stefan Karadzha; see p.211) and signing their execution warrants. Hardly surprising, then, that Midhat Pasha is one local-boy-made-good who has never been honoured with a statue.

place, patrolled by crooked cab drivers and other over-friendly parasites. **Trolleybuses** #1, #11, #12 and #18 head up ulitsa Borisova to the main square, **ploshtad Svoboda**. Dunav Tours, just southwest of the main square at pl. Han Kubrat 5 (Mon–Fri 9am–12.30pm & 1–5.30pm; ⓣ082/223088), rents out **private rooms** (❷) in central locations. There's a reasonable choice of **hotel** accommodation, with enough variety to suit most tastes and budgets.

As an alternative, you could rent a bungalow (❷) or **camp** at the mosquito-prone *Lyulyaka* (mid-May to mid-Oct), which occupies a shady hillside site 6km west of town in the riverside Prista Park – take bus #6 from ulitsa Nikolaevska.

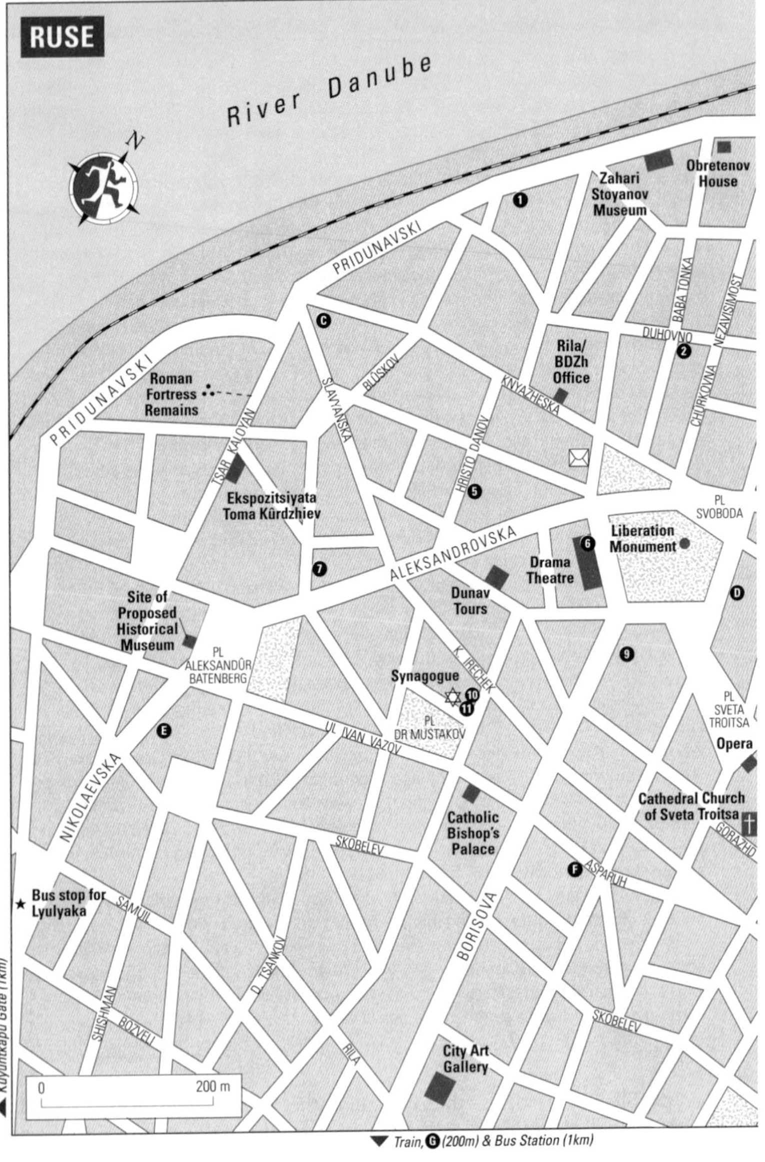

Hotels

Anna Palace ul. Knyazheska 4 ⓣ082/825005, ⓦwww.annapalace.com. Plush establishment guarded by liveried bellhops and with repro furniture packing out the lobby areas. Standard doubles have thick carpets, neutral modern furnishings and showers; apartments come with nineteenth-century ceramic ovens and full-size bathtubs. Rooms ❻, apartments ❽

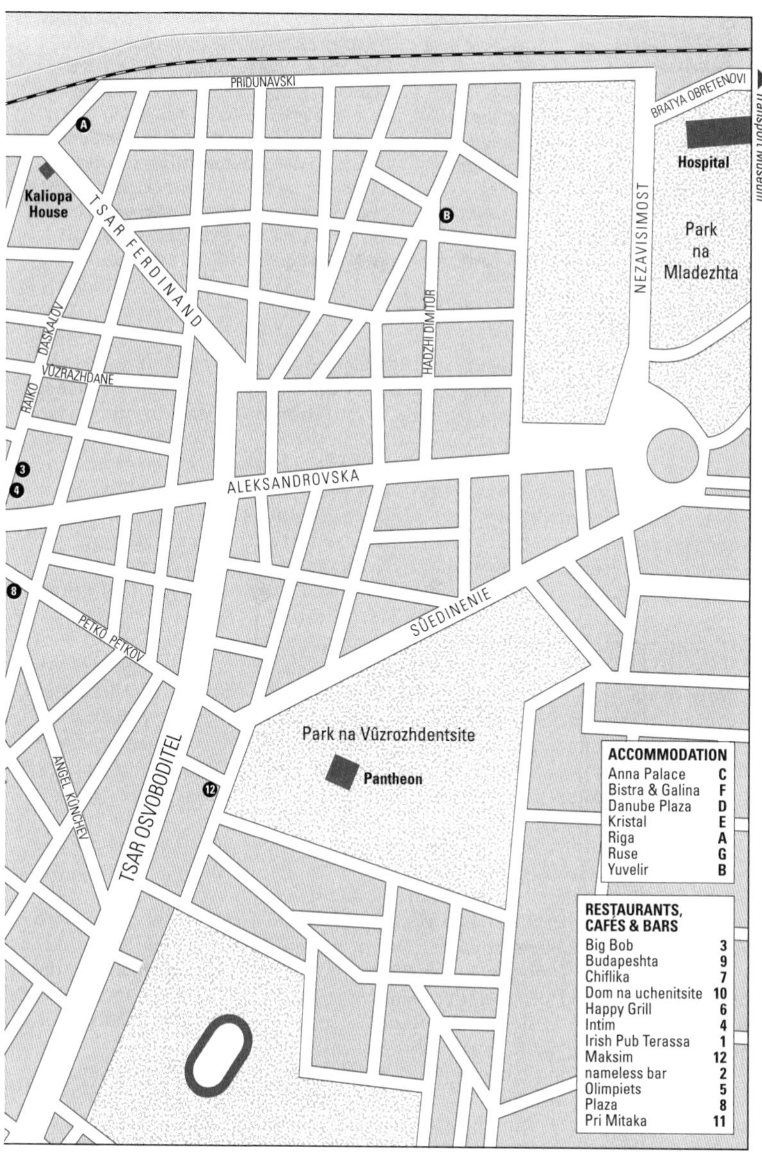

Bistra & Galina ul. Asparuh 8 ⓣ082/823344, ⓦwww.rousse.net/bghotel. Stylish modern interiors in a convenient downtown setting. Roomy en-suites with TV and minibar, all done out in pastel colours. ❻

Danube Plaza pl. Svoboda 5 ⓣ082/822929, ⓦwww.danubeplaza.com. A much-improved grey lump from the Communist era, superbly located on the main square. Comfortable en-suites with TV, and some plusher business-class rooms on each floor. ❺–❽

Kristal ul. Nikolaevska 1 ⓣ082/824333, ⓔhotel_kristal@abv.bg. Recently refurbished modern block in a reasonably central location. Rooms feature thin carpets, budget-superstore furniture and small bathrooms, but everything is clean and tidy. ❹

Riga bul. Pridunavski 22 ⓣ082/822042 or 222181, ⓕ230362. Once-swish high-rise hotel with far more rooms than potential guests, but offering improving standards of service after several years in the doldrums. Acceptable business-standard rooms, and an enviable riverside position. ❺–❽

Ruse ul. Borisova 69 ⓣ082/823255. Small place occupying one floor of an apartment block midway between the train station and the centre. Providing you can stand the rampant red, gold and blue colour scheme, you'll find the rooms neat and tidy with modern bathrooms. No breakfast. ❸

Yuvelir ul. Hadzhi Dimitûr 26 ⓣ082/823536 or 823532. Twelve odd-shaped rooms squeezed into a suburban house just east of the centre. Choose between prim, tile-floored en-suites with pine furnishings and TV, or snazzy studio apartments with bathtubs. Rooms ❹, apartments ❻

The Town

A spacious mixture of concrete and greenery bordered by flower sellers and open-air cafés, the central **ploshtad Svoboda** (Freedom Square) is watched over by one of Ruse's trademarks, the 1908 **Liberation Monument**, a classical pillar surmounted by an allegorical figure of Liberty. Occupying the southwest side of the square is Ruse's **Drama Theatre**, a once-magnificent neo-Renaissance pile that was the centre of social life in pre-Communist Ruse, when it was popularly known as the *Dohodnoto zdanie* ("cash cow" would be a very free translation) due to the profits raked in by the city council through the renting out of its floor space to shops, restaurants and a public library. Used for purely theatrical purposes after 1945, it was closed entirely in the 1980s prior to its reconstruction as a state-of-the-art drama venue. Adequate funding for the project never materialized, however, and the building still lies gutted with no completion date in sight. Next door to the theatre on the north-western corner of the square is another erstwhile social institution, the **Sladkarnitsa Teteven**, where successive generations of Ruse housewives spent their afternoons dutifully nibbling their way through a selection of fancy pastries. Sadly the café is no more, having been transformed into a garish shop, but the building still catches the eye, with a parade of rather fierce-looking caryatids holding up the facade.

Skirting the northern side of the square is the city's main commercial and social artery, **ulitsa Aleksandrovska** – venue for shopping, drinking and aimless strolling. There's a food **market** and diverse street traders along the road's eastern stretches. Aleksandrovska's western end opens out into **ploshtad Aleksandûr Batenberg**, another refined, flowerbed-filled space with more outdoor cafés, and a monument to those who fell for the motherland in the Serbo-Bulgarian War of 1885. The building at the northwestern corner of the square has been designated as the future home of the **Historical Museum**, although it's unclear when exactly this will open.

Much of the rest of central Ruse is made up of a patchwork of residential streets lined with nineteenth-century bourgeois residences, nowadays divided up into apartments. A particularly beautiful example is **ulitsa Ivan Vazov**, which runs east from ploshtad Aleksandûr Batenberg to join up with ulitsa Borisova. Among the numerous stately pieds-à-terre along its length is the **Palace of the Catholic Bishop of Ruse**, a wonderfully unrestrained architectural jumble in which Gothic, Neoclassical and Baroque elements jostle for attention. Hidden away behind a fruit-and-veg market on the adjoining ploshtad Dr Mustakov is one further reminder of Ruse's cosmopolitan past, the former **synagogue**, which spent most of the postwar period as regional headquarters of Bulgaria's equivalent of the football pools, before being returned to the Jewish community.

Along the riverfront

Ulitsa Knyazheska leads downhill from ploshtad Svoboda towards the riverfront poshtad Sveti Nikola and the former merchants' quarter of town, an area of dust-laden stuccoed buildings where Elias Canetti's family used to have a warehouse, a few steps southeast at ul. Slavyanska 12. Heading southwards from ploshtad Sveti Nikola up ulitsa Tsar Kaloyan, a pathway on the right leads to a gated archeological park marking the site of the **Sexaginta Prista Roman fortress** (*Rimska krepost "Seksaginta Prista"*; daily 9am–5pm; 2Lv), where a surviving section of third-century defensive wall runs along a bluff over-looking the Danube. A Roman garrison was established here during the reign of first-century-AD emperor Vespasian and survived for six centuries, its name (Sexaginta Prista meaning "sixty ships" in Latin) reflecting its importance as a harbour. There's a selection of richly decorated tombstones planted here and there, and a good view of the river.

Northeast of ploshtad Sveti Nikola, the cobbled bulevard Pridunavski runs along the **waterfront** – a singularly unattractive area save for a few Art-Nouveauish town houses, the odd stretch of riverside parkland, and a couple of house-museums where the bulk of Ruse's historic artefacts are kept. Slightly inland, the **Ekspozitsiyata Toma Kardzhiev** (Mon–Fri 9am–noon & 2–5pm; 3Lv), on the corner of Lyule Burgaz and Tsar Kaloyan, has changing exhibitions of historical interest.

Back on the riverfront, the **Zahari Stoyanov Museum**, bul. Pridunavski 15 (Mon–Fri 9am–noon & 2–5pm; 3Lv), commemorates the journalist, politician and author best known for his *Notes on the Bulgarian Uprisings*, a record of the author's own experiences during the 1870s. Inspired by the heroic suicide of Angel Kûnchev (see p.263), the young Stoyanov joined the revolutionary movement and toured Bulgaria helping to set up clandestine patriotic cells. By the time of the April Rising of 1876 he was attached to the rebel group commanded by Georgi Benkovski, a leader of the Rising in the Koprivshtitsa area (see p.295). Stoyanov's subsequent account served to immortalize both Benkovski and many other leading personalities of April 1876, and helped enshrine the Rising as the crucial event in the nation's liberation. Zahari Stoyanov married the youngest daughter of Baba ("Granny") Tonka Obretenova, a formidable matriarch who was at the forefront of revolutionary activity in nineteenth-century Ruse, offering her home to the patriotic underground as a safe-house and arms dump, smuggling rifles through swamps, and leading Ruse's women in an armed assault on the town prison. She raised her children as fervent patriots, her five sons taking part in the April Rising, and their portraits fill one of the rooms here (the Obretonov House-Museum, 100m away on the corner of bulevard Pridunavski and ul. Baba Tonka, is currently under reconstruction). The skull of Stefan Karadzha, preserved as a *memento mori* by Tonka after the illustrious *haidut* leader was hanged in Ruse in 1868 (he had in fact already died of wounds en route to the execution), used to be displayed here – before being banished to the museum store-cupboard on account of the unsettling effect it had on Bulgarian schoolkids.

As well as books and manuscripts recalling Stoyanov's work, the museum displays one of the suitcases Stoyanov was travelling with when he dropped dead in Paris in 1889 (you may care to note that the other suitcase is in Medven; see p.325). Much attention is also lavished on another revolutionary, Panayot Hitov, who retired to Ruse as a national hero after spending most of the 1860s and 70s leading warrior bands in the mountains. Guerrilla life is remembered with items such as Hitov's embroidered tobacco pouch, his secret money belt, and numerous antiquated pistols and shotguns.

Further along the riverbank, opposite the *Hotel Riga*, lies a museum of nineteenth-century urban life which is popularly known as the **Kaliopa House** (Mon–Fri 9am–noon & 2–5pm; 3Lv) after one of its former inhabitants, Maria Kalich – Greek wife of the Prussian consul, and rumoured mistress of Midhat Pasha – who was nicknamed Kaliopa on account of her supposed resemblance to an ancient Greek demigoddess. After Kaliopa moved out, the house was bought by filthy-rich Bulgarian merchant Stefan Kalburov, who commissioned the wonderfully opulent Neoclassical interior that visitors can see today. A wall painting of Cupid and Psyche presides over the stairs leading to the upstairs salons, where walls and ceilings decorated with Grecian urns awaited guests invited to the music recitals and literary evenings once held here.

A good ten minutes' walk further along the riverbank, the **Transport Museum**, at ul. Bratya Obretenovi 1 (officially Mon–Fri 9am–noon & 2–5pm, although in practice hardly ever open), occupies the original station building and commemorates the establishment of the Ruse–Varna railway. The lines of historic locos and rolling stock parked outside include locomotive no. 148, one of the initial set of steam engines built for the railway by a Manchester firm in 1866; and the sumptuous *Sultaniye* sleeping-carriage, used by Empress Eugénie of France in 1869 when on her way southwards to open the Suez Canal.

The Cathedral Church, the Pantheon and the City Art Gallery

A couple of blocks east of ploshtad Svoboda on ulitsa Gorazd is the **Cathedral Church of Sveta Troitsa** (Holy Trinity), dating from 1632 and twice rebuilt in successive centuries. The resulting building borrows liberally from Russian models, sporting a curious Baroque facade and a medieval Muscovite spire. Steps descend into an icon-rich subterranean nave, its stuccoed ceiling supported by trompe l'oeil marble-effect pillars crowned with Corinthian capitals.

Further east across bulevard Tsar Osvoboditel, you'll find the **Park na Vûzrozhdentsite** (Park of the Men of the Revival), where the **Ruse Pantheon** (Mon–Fri 9am–noon & 2–5pm; 3Lv), a mausoleum devoted to nineteenth-century revolutionary heroes, squats on a flagstoned plaza. It's a grossly overstated building: a kind of high-tech Maya temple surmounted by half a giant ping-pong ball covered in gold. Despite its patriotic intent, the pantheon has never been wholly popular with Ruse folk, not least because a cemetery and a church were razed in order to make way for its construction in 1975. In a symbolic attempt to re-Christianize the site, a large cross was placed on top of the pantheon in 2001. Inside lie the bones of hundreds of Bulgarians who served the national cause, the most prominent of them being honoured with marble grave slabs on either side of the chamber. Most of the Obretenov family is remembered here, alongside Stefan Karadzha, Panaiot Hitov, and many others. The central dome is flanked by four female statues – allegories, respectively, of slavery under the Ottoman yoke, the cultural awakening of the nineteenth century, the mourning of Bulgarian mothers for fallen freedom fighters, and the Liberation of 1877. The whole lacks the delicacy of the smaller, more tasteful nineteenth-century chapels – honouring, among others, Zahari Stoyanov – which lie under the trees of the surrounding park. North of here is **Park na Mladezhta**, or "Youth Park", where tree- and shrub-lined avenues provide a popular strolling area. Steps at the northern end of the park descend to the riverfront and the transport museum.

There's little incentive to stray too far south of the town centre, save for the **City Art Gallery**, at ul. Borisova 39 (Tues–Sun 8am–1pm & 2–6pm), a largely parochial collection of local artists enlivened by a couple of eulogies to peasant toil from popular postwar painter Zlatyu Boyadzhiev. The only other attraction in this part of town is the **Kyuntukapu Gate**, sole remainder of the Turkish fortress, which lies just off Alei Osvobozhdenie, 300m west of the train station.

Eating, drinking and entertainment

Most of Ruse's eating venues are found on and around **ploshtad Svoboda** and the adjoining **ulitsa Aleksandrovska**, and there's not much point in straying beyond this area unless seeking out one of the more chic restaurants. For **picnic food**, head to the fresh fruit and veg stalls at the market on ploshtad Ivan Vazov. The best places for **drinking** are the pavement cafés scattered throughout the central area, although the trendy ones go in and out of fashion very quickly.

Restaurants

Big Bob ul. Raiko Daskalov 1. Self-service restaurant doling out hearty portions of Bulgarian food. Good for a quick bowl of *bob* (bean soup) or salad.

Budapeshta ul. Borisova 13. Popular main-street restaurant currently serving mainstream Bulgarian grilled food, although it has been through several past incarnations – Middle-Eastern and Hungarian (hence the name) included.

Chiflika ul. Otets Paisii. Traditional Bulgarian food at reasonable prices, with seating on two levels and folksy decor.

Dom na Uchenite ul. Konstantin Irechek 16. Basement restaurant with a refined atmosphere, and a Bulgarian–European menu – good for fish.

Happy Grill pl. Svoboda. Bulgaria-wide franchise serving up grills and chicken-and-chips-style dishes in a central location. The large square-side terrace is always busy.

Maksim opposite the Pantheon. A limited range of traditional grill food near the park.

Olimpiets ul. Hristo Danov 4. Top-quality Bulgarian fare served up in a restaurant that mixes starched-napkin stylishness with folksy decor. Very popular on summer nights, when the big outdoor terrace is open.

Plaza ul. Petko Petkov. Popular open-air restaurant in a garden behind the *Danube Plaza* hotel, packed with locals in summer. Indifferent food, but live music and dancing most nights.

Drinking

There's a strip of flashy café-bars along the northern side of ploshtad Svoboda, and stretching eastwards to cover the first hundred metres or so of ulitsa Aleksandrovska. There's little point in giving specific recommendations here – places open up, close down, or change name with frightening regularity – but if you want cheap beer, cheery pop music, and dressed-up local youth for company, then this is the area to head for. Drinking venues with more clearly defined character include the nameless bar at the corner of ulitsas Duhovno Vûzrazhdane and Baba Tonka, which eschews techno music and attracts a discerning studenty crowd as a result; and *Pri Mitaka*, pl. Ivan Vazov 2, which squeezes a similarly bohemian clientele into a boisterous beer garden, and has a basement bar where DJs spin discs after midnight. *Intim*, on ulitsa Raiko Daskalov, is a mellow café-bar attached to a cinema and as good a place as any to start the evening. *Irish Pub Terassa*, on the riverfront at bulevard Al. Stamboliiski, is a brash modern drinking hole playing loud, mainstream music to a fun-seeking crowd.

Music venues

Ruse's **opera**, on ploshtad Sveta Troitsa, is one of the finest in Bulgaria. Other types of classical music are showcased in the annual **March Music Weeks**, which attract some of the best ensembles, soloists and conductors in Europe.

Moving on from Ruse

If you're **entering or leaving Bulgaria** via Ruse you'll first cross the three-kilometre-long *Dunav Most* or "Danube Bridge" (known as "Friendship Bridge" back in the days of socialist brotherhood), which spans the river on the outskirts of Ruse and Giurgiu. This ugly yet technically impressive structure was built by both countries (with Soviet assistance) between 1952 and 1954. Be warned that traffic on the bridge can be heavy, and waits can be unpredictably long when travelling in either direction. Citizens of the EU, USA and Canada can enter Romania without a visa; other nationals should contact the Romanian Embassy in their home country before leaving home.

Travellers **leaving Ruse by train** have a choice of services and destinations. There are direct trains to **Sofia** and **Varna**, although those travelling south into the **Balkan Range** will probably have to change at Gorna Oryahovitsa. International connections are good, with three daily trains to **Giurgiu** on the Romanian side of the bridge, and a further two daily express trains (three in summer) that continue on to **Bucharest**; one of these continues onwards to **Budapest**.

International **tickets** can be bought in advance from the Rila bureau, at ul. Knyazheska 39 (Mon–Fri 9am–noon & 12.30–5pm) or from the Rila counter at Ruse train station (opening times usually coordinated with train departures). You can also get tickets on the train itself, although prices are about fifty percent higher and payment can only be made in Bulgarian currency.

Privately run **Ruse-Sofia** buses pick up and drop off outside the train station.

Tickets for all musical events can be bought from the **concert bureau**, ul. Aleksandrovska 61 (Mon–Fri 10am–1pm & 3–6pm).

Listings

Airline ticket agent Balkan luxair, ul. Konstantin Velichkov 3 ⓣ082/821212.
Bus ticket agent Plaza Tours, ul. Petko Petkov (behind the *Danube Plaza* hotel).
Car rental Eurokontakt, bul. Gotse Delchev ⓣ082/626241.
Hospital Bratya Obretenovi on the edge of Park na Mladezhta ⓣ887.
Pharmacy Apteka Kalinovi, ul. Aleksandrovska 69 (daily 7am–11pm).
Post office pl. Svoboda (Mon–Fri 7.30am–6.30pm, Sat 7.30am–6pm).
Taxis Head for the taxi ranks at the northern end of ul. Borisova, the western end of ul. Petko Petkov (round the side of the *Danube Palace* hotel) or ring ⓣ8112, ⓣ8113 or 8141.
Telephones at the post office (daily 7am–10pm).
Train ticket agent Rila/BDZh, ul. Knyazheska 39 ⓣ082/223920.

The Rusenski Lom

Ruse is the obvious base from which to venture southwards into the **Rusenski Lom**, a steep-sided, canyon-like valley through which the River Rusenski Lom winds its way towards the Danube. The valley forms a picturesque setting for a trio of worthwhile attractions, beginning with the (still functioning) rock-hewn **monastery of the Blessed Dimitûr Basarbovski** just outside Ruse, and continuing with the much older and considerably more spectacular **rock churches of Ivanovo**, famed for their medieval frescoes. Beyond Ivanovo lies the evocatively windswept hilltop **citadel of Cherven**. Both Ivanovo and Cherven fall within the boundaries of the **Rusenski Lom Nature Park** (*Priroden park Rusenski Lom*), formed to protect the diverse flora and fauna of the valley. The riverside cliffs provide nesting grounds for hawks, eagles, griffon vultures and black storks; while on the valley floor a variety of tortoises, lizards and snakes roam among exotic ferns and orchids. There are paths in the valley floor between Ivanovo and Cherven, and although there are as yet no signs or hiking maps, you should not be discouraged from exploring.

The Rock Monastery of Dimitûr Basarbovski

Located halfway up a cliff on the banks of the Rusenski Lom, the **Rock Monastery of the Blessed Dimitûr Basarbovski** (*Skalen manastir na Prepodobni Dimitûr Basarbovski*) lies just beyond the village of **BASARBOVO**, about 7km south of Ruse. To get there, head out of Ruse on the Sofia road and take the Basarbovo exit just outside the city limits. Once you get to Basarbovo, pass right through the village and keep following the riverbank for 2km until you get to the monastery car park. A taxi shouldn't set you back much more than 10Lv each way.

Although a monastery has existed here since at least the fifteenth century, it takes its name from a seventeenth-century local monk who led a life so spiritually pure that his body miraculously failed to decompose after his death. Initially kept in a local church, his corpse was presented to the Cathedral of SS Constantine and Elena in Bucharest in 1774 in recognition of Romanian help in the Russo-Turkish wars, while the rock monastery here became an important local focus for followers of his cult. Nowadays it consists of a few uninhabited rock-hewn cells (the trio of monks still attached to the monastery reside in a pavilion down below) and a small cave-like church, reached via a cliff-hugging stairway. Inside, the main altar bears a nineteenth-century icon of Dimitûr in the company of the Virgin; while over to the left is a much older, miracle-working icon showing scenes from the holy one's life.

The Rock Churches of Ivanovo

The most famous of the ruins in the Rusenski Lom valley belong to the so-called **Rock Churches of Ivanovo** near Ivanovo village, 18km south of Ruse. Among the rocks on both banks of the river, several monasteries were hewn into the craggy gorge whose caves provided shelter for Stone Age tribes and medieval hermits alike. Monks first arrived at the gorge in the thirteenth century, a royal donation enabling one Yoakim of Tûrnovo to establish an extensive monastery complex dedicated to the Archangel Michael, its churches, cells and galleries cut from natural caves in the sheer cliff. At the time the main road linking Tûrnovo to the Danube ran through the gorge, providing the monasteries with a steady stream of pilgrims.

The churches are reached by following the village's main street northwards from Ivanovo train station for 1.5km, then turning right into a minor road which leads over the fields and down into the valley of the Rusenski Lom (4km). The road peters out at a car park-cum-picnic spot, above which lies the one church which is regularly open to tourists, the fourteenth-century **Tsûrkvata or "church" cave** (Wed–Sun 9am–noon & 2–5pm; 5Lv). Inside are two chambers, the walls and ceilings of which are covered with vivid New Testament scenes. In the first chamber, the ceiling is dominated by a depiction of Christ enveloped by a star-like form, a typical representation of the Divine Light as envisaged by the hesychast monks (see p.259) of the time. Just beyond, the *Mocking of Christ* sees the Saviour surrounded by snarling, cudgel-wielding tormentors. In the second chamber, Christ's betrayal by Judas is followed by a grisly portrayal of the latter's suicide. *The Beheading of John the Baptist* at the far end of the room betrays a similar lack of squeamishness,

Heading back to the car park you can pick up trails leading upstream along the valley floor. You can in theory walk all the way to Cherven (see overleaf) from here in four to five hours, passing the confluence of the Beli and Cherni Lom rivers (take the right fork to follow the Cherni Lom) on the way. An alternative is to head back along the road in the Ivanovo direction, turn right to find a bridge across the river, and explore the riverbank path on the other side. There's a line of rock churches in the cliffs above, and although their interiors are unlikely to be open to visitors, they provide a useful excuse to wander this far. First up, the so-called **Buried Church** (*Zatrupanata tsûrkva*) cave features a damaged mural of Tsar Asen presenting a model of the church to the Archangel, with a depiction of St Michael's miracles on the ceiling. Nearby is another, more derelict **baptismal church** (*krûshtelnata tsûrkva*) decorated with a scene of the visions of St Peter of Alexandria. Along the same bank, the **Chapel of Gospodev dol**, or "The Lord's Valley" (with portraits of its patron saints, Vlassius, Spiridon and Modestus), and the accurately named **Demolished Church** (*Sûborenata tsûrkva*), both contain murals, variously faded by time.

Practicalities

Main entry point to the region is the village of **IVANOVO** itself, 4km west of the caves and on the main Ruse–Sofia rail line – it's served by five daily *pûtnicheski* trains from Ruse. Diagonally opposite the train station, the large concrete town council building contains a small information office (*Tsentûr po ekologiya, kultura i turizûm*; Mon–Fri 8am–3pm; (T)098116/2253), where you can pick up leaflets about the nature park and book **rooms** in one of the handful of local houses that offer B&B arrangements (❶). Best of the local accommodation possibilities is the *Villa Angel*, 7km south in the village of Koshov ((T)08159/479 or 0889 899 254; ❸, ❹ full board), a six-room **guesthouse** offering simple en-suites in a delightfully rustic environment. There's a rough-and-ready **café** outside Ivanovo train station.

Cherven

Fifteen kilometres south of Ivanovo, a fork in the gorge provides a niche for the **ruined citadel of Cherven**, clinging to the rock. Formerly known as the "City of churches" or "City of bishops", Cherven was founded in the sixth or seventh century when recurrent barbarian invasions compelled the inhabitants of Ruse to seek a more defensible site inland. The citadel was devastated by the Turks, but Cherven survived as the region's administrative centre for some time, with Ottoman governors and Orthodox bishops coexisting until the seventeenth century, when they both relocated to Ruse. Nowadays Cherven resembles a desolate and brutish version of Machu Picchu (albeit at a considerably lower altitude), with its meagre remains standing high above the valley on a rocky table flanked on three sides by unscalable cliffs. There are good views of the Cherni Lom gorge, with the red-roofed houses of **Cherven village** clinging to the limestone ridges above it. You can still make out the ground plans of Cherven's many churches, although the biggest of the town's structures was the fortified complex of the local *bolyarin*, Cherven's feudal lord. A still-discernible main street runs past his palace and on towards the rude dwellings of his underlings.

It can be difficult **getting to Cherven** without a private car. Sporadic buses to the village of Cherven may be running from Ruse's bus terminal; otherwise you'll have to take a *pûtnicheski* train to the Koshov halt, walk south for 1km, turn left, then walk the remaining 7km into Cherven village. The road winds its way through the village before arriving at a car park at the base of the citadel, 1km beyond. There's a rudimentary **café** about 400m short of the citadel car park.

△ Rock Church, Ivonovo

The bridge at Byala

Running roughly parallel to the Rusenski Lom valley to the west, the main E85 road from Ruse to Veliko Tûrnovo (see p.243) forges south, through **Byala**, an eminently missable market town save for the **bridge over the River Yantra**. Lying 2km to the west of town just beside the E85, the bridge was built in 1867 by the National Revival's most prolific architect Kolyo Ficheto (see p.261), and originally rested on fourteen ornate piers – ten of which were subsequently washed away by floodwaters. The fluid, baroque forms of the remaining four are still intact, as are the reliefs of swans, nymphs and dragons that adorn the main body of the bridge.

The Dobrudzha

Beyond Ruse, routes head into an extension of the Danubian plain known as the **Dobrudzha**, Bulgaria's main grain-producing region. Numerous buses follow the main eastbound road along the Danube, calling in at the sleepy riverside town of **Tutrakan** before arriving at the much larger port of **Silistra** – site of some rewarding Roman remains and main jumping-off point for the birdwatcher's paradise of **Lake Srebûrna**. Beyond here the river swings north into Romania, leaving travellers with the choice of heading south across the Ludogorie hills towards Shumen (see p.269), or continuing across the eastern part of the Dobrudzha towards the Black Sea coast. The latter route takes you through the largely charmless regional capital **Dobrich**, which offers numerous onward bus connections to Albena (p.403) and Varna (p.386) on the coast.

Tutrakan

Fifty-five kilometres east of Ruse, the pastel-coloured houses of **TUTRAKAN** tumble down a steep hill overlooking the River Danube. Formerly an important port, it's a rather somnolent little place nowadays, but with a couple of fishing-related heritage sites, it's worth a brief stopoff before moving further east. Like much of the Dobrudzha, Tutrakan was occupied by Romania following the Balkan Wars of 1912–13, and its recapture in 1916 was one of Bulgaria's few real victories of World War I. Nowadays the town makes for a moderately diverting stopoff if you're trundling between Ruse and Silistra, but once you've had a look around, it's not worth staying.

The character of nineteenth-century Tutrakan is still preserved in the **Ribarskata mahala** (Fishermen's Quarter), an attractive huddle of whitewashed nineteenth-century houses topped off with ruddy tiles, which lies at the eastern end of an otherwise undistinguished riverfront. You can't look inside the houses though, so it's best to make tracks for the **Ethnographic Museum** (Mon–Fri 9am–noon & 3–6pm; 2Lv), a few steps back west at ul. Transmariska 5. Devoted to the history of fishing on the Danube, it's crammed full with all manner of nets, traps and harpoons – accompanied by evocative old photographs of these contraptions in use. Slightly uphill at pl. Suvorov 1, the **Historical Museum** (same times; 2Lv) offers Paleolithic bits and pieces, a few nineteenth-century icons, and more old photographs – this time showing the strange-looking **floating watermills** which once crowded the Tutrakan shoreline, using the Danube current to drive their wheels.

Practicalities

Tutrakan's **bus station** is some 2km uphill to the southeast of the town centre, although most Ruse–Silistra buses pass through the centre first, allowing you to jump off in the vicinity of the museums. If, for some reason, you do choose to **stay**, the best place to do so is the *Kompleks Royal*, an eminently comfortable family-run **hotel** 5km west of Tutrakan on the main Ruse road (☎08534/891 or 893; ❷-❸). The hotel restaurant prides itself on its fresh Danube fish dishes, and does an exemplary *ribena chorba* (spicy fish soup).

Silistra

Regular buses continue east from Tutrakan to the last town on the Bulgarian stretches of the Danube, **SILISTRA**. It's also accessible by train, lying at the end of a branch line that leaves the Ruse–Varna line at Samuil. The site of Roman Durostorum and an important garrison town in Turkish times, Silistra is nowadays a sleepy border settlement lacking the vigour and comparative sophistication of Ruse. Economic activity in the town revolves around the port, main outlet for the grain of the Dobrudzhan Plain to the southeast. For the traveller, the nearby **nature reserve at Srebûrna** provides the main reason to visit, but there's little to justify a stay of any length.

The Town

From the **train** and **bus** stations on the town's western outskirts, ulitsa Simeon Veliki winds its way eastwards through the town centre, arriving at a typically flagstoned and flowerbedded town square. A few steps beyond at ul. G. S. Rakovski 24 is the **Archeological Museum** (Tues–Sun 8am–noon & 2–6pm; 2Lv), where a rich fund of material on life in Durostorum includes the epigraph-laden tombstones of the soldiers stationed here with the XI Legion. In addition, there's a rather captivating first-century sundial, decorated with a relief of Orpheus twanging away on his lyre to an audience of attentive animals; and a hoard of Roman jewellery including some alluring golden earrings. While you're at the museum it's worth asking about the fourth-century **Roman Tomb** (*Rimska grobnitsa*) located on the south-western outskirts of town – its future as a tourist attraction is uncertain due to conservation problems, but museum staff may well open it up for individual travellers if you apply early enough in the day. Intended for a rich local family but never used, the barrel-vaulted chamber is filled with frescoes, with a scene of servants bearing funeral gifts framed by strutting peacocks and floral designs.

To the north of the Archeological Museum, nineteenth-century residential houses occupy a grid of tree-shaded streets that separate central Silistra from the river. It's among these modest turn-of-the-twentieth-century mansions, many with Art Nouveau details such as caryatids peering from upper storeys, that you get some impression of the elegance once enjoyed by the Danubian towns.

Occupying a hill 3km south of town (best reached by walking along ulitsa Izvorite from the centre) are the remains of the Turkish fortress of **Medzhitabiya**, another corner of the defensive quadrilateral built by the Ottomans, and one that was frequently attacked in the course of successive Russo-Turkish wars. The hilltop park also features a TV tower complete with revolving café, and there are expansive views of the Danube below, backed by the yellow and green hues of the Wallachian plain beyond.

Boat trips on the Danube, usually offering a grilled-fish picnic somewhere en route, are sporadically offered in the summer months – the lobby of the *Zlatna Dobrudzha* hotel (see overleaf) is the best place to make enquiries.

Practicalities

As far as **accommodation** is concerned, it's a toss-up between the gloomy *Zlatna Dobrudzha* hotel, pl. Svoboda 1 (ⓣ086/821355, ⓔturist@ccpro.com; ❸), offering frumpy but tolerable en-suite rooms; and the slightly smaller *Bartimex*, ul. Kapitan Mamarchev 20 (ⓣ086/820118, ⓔbartimex@ccpro.com; ❹), which has a more modern, brighter feel to it.

The best of the **restaurants** is the *Starata kûshta*, at ul. Lyuben Karavelov 8, in residential streets between the Archeological Museum and the river. Housed in a National Revival-style building, it has plenty of outdoor seating and a traditional Bulgarian menu. The restaurant of the *Zlatna Dobrudzha* hotel has reliable food and a large outdoor area at the back. The streets around the hotel have several **pavement cafés**, popular on summer evenings.

The **border crossing** on Silistra's eastern fringes is relatively quiet, and with public transport on the Romanian side being virtually nonexistent, is only really suitable for those with a car. The crossing is theoretically open 24 hours a day, although it may close up for a while if traffic is light.

Lake Srebûrna

Nineteenth-century Hungarian traveller Felix Kanitz called **Lake Srebûrna**, 17km west of Silistra near the Danube shore, "the Eldorado of wading birds". The lake – and the expanse of reedy marshland that spreads around it – is now a protected nature reserve, providing ninety species of wildfowl (including seventy different types of heron) with a secure habitat. The lake is also frequented by around eighty migratory species, and there's a fair likelihood of being able to see **egrets** in the summer, **pelicans** in the spring, and as many as 50,000 **geese** in the winter.

Just off the main Silistra–Ruse road, the reserve is approached from the villages of Srebûrna to the west, or Vetren to the northwest. Both are served by **bus** #222 which leaves from the main road outside Silistra bus station every two hours or so between 7am and 9pm (ask in the bus station about exact timings). You can also catch one of the frequent Silistra–Ruse buses, and ask to be set down at the Srebûrna stop on the main road – a walkable 2km away from Srebûrna village itself.

First stop should be the **Natural History Museum** (*Prirodonauchen muzei*; daily 9am–noon & 2–6pm; 3Lv), tucked away at the northeastern end of Srebûrna village but well signed. The collection of stuffed fauna inside provides a useful introduction to the wildlife of the region, and the museum's staff will be able to provide advice on paths round the lake if you can find a common language. Most people head north from the museum towards the high ground at the northwestern corner of the lake; from here you can get a decent view of what's occurring on the water.

Best place **to stay** is the *Srebûrna* on the eastern outskirts of the village (ⓣ08515/462 or 0889/441116, ⓦwww.srebarna.com; ❷), with a handful of prim, orderly en-suites in a large modern house.

Alfatar and around

Twenty-five kilometres south of Silistra on the Dulovo road, the village of **ALFATAR** has become a favourite target for coach trips operating out of Bulgaria's Black Sea resorts, thanks to the song-and-dance concerts laid on by the local folklore society. Based in a building in the centre of the village known as the **Dobrudzhanska kûshta** (Dobrudzhan House), these performances are only organized for tour groups: individual travellers will have to trawl hotel lobbies in Ruse, Silistra, or at the seaside to find out what's on offer. Those who do make it here are invited to sit in a lovely garden, where they eat freshly baked bread and sip apricot *rakiya* (very much the local speciality) while being serenaded by local grannies in traditional costume. Afterwards guests have a chance to look round the *kûshta* itself, a nicely arranged museum of Dobrudzhan ethnography which includes a re-created nineteenth-century kitchen-cum-living room – note that the dainty wooden stools were intended for the men of the family; the womenfolk knelt on cushions or busied themselves with the cooking.

The countryside around Alfatar – characterized by gently undulating hills covered with wheatfields and apricot groves – has a great deal of charm, and makes for a soothingly scenic drive if you're travelling between Silistra and the Thracian tombs at Sveshtari (see p.279). If you are heading that way, then the family-run *Hotel Kotva* (Ⓣ0855/4048 or 4049; ❷) in the largely Tatar-inhabited village of **CHERKOVNA**, 15km beyond Alfatar, is a cosy place **to stay**, and has a popular garden **restaurant**.

Dobrich

Principal town of the eastern Dobrudzha, **DOBRICH** is an obvious place to break your journey if travelling between the Danube and the coast. Between 1949 and 1990 it was named after the Soviet marshal who "liberated" the area in 1944, **Tolbuhin** (and it still appears as such on most postwar road signs and maps), but the town started life as **Hadzhioglu Bazardzhik**, supposedly named after itinerant merchant Hadzhi Oglu Bakal, who built the first house here in the sixteenth century. Circassians and Tatars formed the majority of the pre-Liberation population, and although many families fled south to avoid

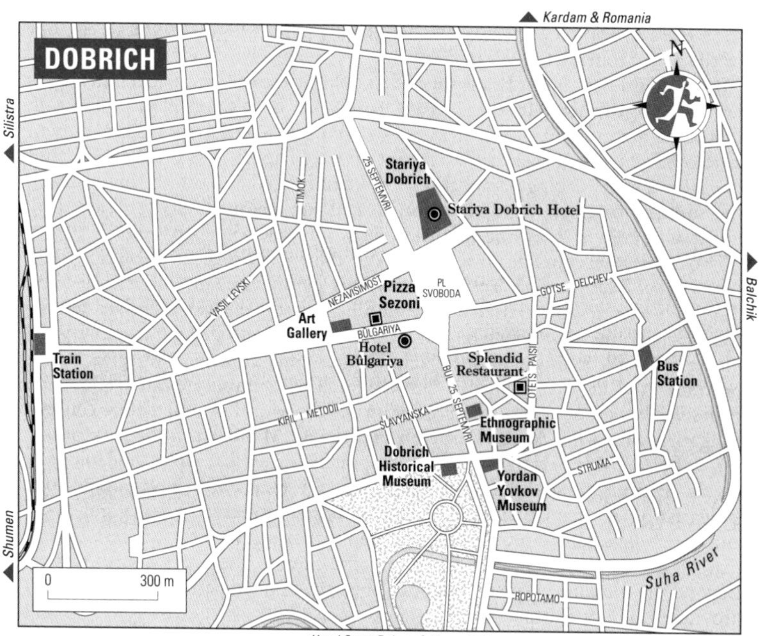

advancing Russian armies in 1877, the area retains a strong Muslim element. In the nineteenth century Dobrich was famous for its autumn horse fair, and horse-rearing remains an important part of the local economy. Several pockets of old Dobrich have been artfully preserved, and the town attracts a steady trickle of day-trippers from the package resorts of the nearby Black Sea coast.

The Town

Travelling through Dobrich in the 1870s, Felix Kanitz said that he knew of no other town in Bulgaria whose "Asiatic character … was so typical and unadulterated in appearance". Nowadays central Dobrich is resolutely modern, with stark concrete piles and plazas, although something of the nineteenth-century artisans' quarter has been rather antiseptically re-created in the **Stariya Dobrich** (Old Dobrich) quarter just off the central ploshtad Svoboda. You can watch demonstrations of traditional crafts in some twenty workshops, including pottery, blacksmithing, woodcarving, bookbinding and jewellery. The unmarked **Archeological Museum** (Mon-Fri 8am-noon & 1-5pm; 2Lv), within the courtyard of the complex, houses a small but impressive collection of 7000-year-old gold treasures and pottery discovered at Durankulak's 1200-grave necropolis, as well as Greek and Roman jewellery and artefacts including a ceramic baby's bottle, and various weaponry from both the Thracian and medieval periods. A hundred metres west of ploshtad Svoboda on bulevard Bŭlgariya is the **Regional Art Gallery** (Mon-Fri 9am–noon & 1–5pm; 2Lv), one of provincial Bulgaria's best collections. It's a good place to catch up on the leading quartet of twentieth-century Bulgarian painters – Vladimir Dimitrov-Maistor, Vasil Stoilov, Zlatyu Boyadzhiev and Dechko Uzunov – who tried to combine modernist styles of painting with indigenous Bulgarian traditions. Dimitrov-Maistor's portraits of peasant girls and Uzunov's Dobrudzha landscapes are both well represented; look out for the latter's *Dobrich in Springtime*, where ghostly peasant figures seem to rise out of the rich Dobrudzhan earth.

Bulevard 25 Septemvri heads south from ploshtad Svoboda towards an excellent **Ethnographic Museum** (daily 9am–noon & 2–6pm; 2Lv) where folk costumes, agricultural implements and weaving machines cram the rooms of a restored nineteenth-century merchant's house. The upstairs dining room and *chardak* – a south-facing verandah that the family used as a sitting room during the summer months – provide some idea of the elegant lifestyles enjoyed by those who grew rich on the Dobrudzhan wool trade a century ago.

Two more museums lie further south at the junction of 25 Septemvri and Otets Paisii. The **Yordan Yovkov Museum** (Mon–Fri 8am–noon & 1–5pm; 2Lv), a concrete-and-glass pavilion dominating the crossroads, is easiest to spot. Celebrating the Zheravna-born novelist and poet who spent many years in the Dobrudzha as a schoolteacher, the museum's collection of sepia family portraits and Bulgarian-language captions fails to communicate much about the man's work – renowned for conjuring up the lost world of nineteenth-century Bulgarian village life. At the **Dobrich Historical Museum** in the park opposite (officially Mon–Fri 8am–noon & 1-5pm; 2Lv), a similar words-and-pictures display attempts to shed light on Dobrudzhan history. The region passed from Bulgarian to Romanian rule on numerous occasions between 1913 and 1945, and the endless black-and-white photographs showing armies of different hues marching in and out of Dobrich give some idea of the area's confused past. Beyond the museum several kilometres of partly wooded parkland spread south, providing the city with a verdant recreation area.

The Dobrudzha in history

"A wintry land deficient in cultivated grains and fruit", inhabited by a people "who are barbarous and lead a bestial existence" was how the third-century BC Thracian chieftain Dromichaetes described the **Dobrudzha** to his Macedonian captive Lysimachus, berating him for bothering to invade such a barren region in the first place.

Windswept in winter and parched in summer, the Dobrudzha has always had a reputation for harshness and inhospitability. Geographically speaking, it stretches from the mouth of the Danube in the north to the Gulf of Varna in the south, marking the southwestern extremity of the great **Eurasian steppelands** that once swept uninterruptedly round the north coast of the Black Sea and eastwards towards Central Asia and Mongolia. Successive generations of horseriding invaders have used the steppe as a corridor leading to the riches of southeastern Europe, and faced by such recurring dangers, Western civilization's hold on the region was always tenuous. Successive Macedonian, Roman, Byzantine and Bulgarian empires always found the Dobrudzha to be the most difficult part of the northern frontier to defend, and by the thirteenth century, when **Tatar bands** were beginning to roam the region with impunity, the area was well on the way to becoming a lawless desert.

Arab chronicler Ibn Battuta, crossing the Dobrudzha in the fourteenth century, was struck by its desolate appearance, describing it as "eighteen days of uninhabited wasteland, for eight days of which there is no water". By the time the Ottoman Sultan Mehmet I conquered the Dobrudzha in 1416, the region was so depopulated that he had to colonize it with **Turkish settlers** in order to provide the newly won province with inhabitants capable of defending it – with the result that the local ethnic mix still includes a fair proportion of Turks. These are intermingled with the Turkish-speaking **Dobrudzha Tatars**, descendants of Crimean Tatars who were expelled from the Russian Empire in the wake of the Crimean War.

By the beginning of the twentieth century, migrant Bulgarian peasants began to outnumber the other national groups in the area, but the ethnic balance of the region was altered yet again during the interwar period, when the Dobrudzha became part of Romania. Eager to boost the Latin element among the population, the government encouraged the immigration of Romanian-speaking **Vlachs** (see p.202) from Macedonia. After regaining the territory in 1941, the Bulgarian authorities imported Slav colonists to redress the ethnic balance, but the existence of so many non-Bulgarian minorities in an area so crucial to the economy was a source of concern to the country's postwar Communist bosses. Special attention was paid to the Dobrudzha during the 1980s, when the controversial *Vûzroditelniyat protses* or Regeneration Process tried to force local Muslims to speak only the Bulgarian language in public and to adopt Bulgarian names. Nowadays you'll find inter-ethnic relations more relaxed, with the babble of Bulgarian and Turkic tongues heard on the streets of Dobrich reflecting the meeting of cultures from the Dobrudzha's turbulent past.

Practicalities

Dobrich's **train and bus** stations are on the western and eastern edges respectively of the downtown area – both involve a pretty straightforward ten-minute walk into the centre. Dobrich–Sofia buses use the car park of the *Bûlgariya* hotel (see below), where tickets can be purchased from kiosks.

Of the town's **hotels**, the eleven-room *Stariya Dobrich*, located in the old quarter at ul. Konstantin Stoylov 18 (Ⓣ058/601590; ❸), is the cosiest place to stay in town, but soon fills up. The only real competition comes from the Communist-era highrise *Bûlgariya*, right on the main ploshtad Svoboda (Ⓣ058/600226; ❺); and the newer *Sport Palace* in the city park (Ⓣ058/603622; ❹), which comes complete with swimming pool and sauna.

Best of the **restaurants** are the *Splendid*, ul. Ohrid 8, which offers grilled meats over an open fire; the *mehana* of the *Stariya Dobrich* hotel, which serves traditional Bulgarian fare in folksy surroundings; and *Pizza Sezoni* opposite the *Bûlgariya* hotel. Dobrich's pedestrianized centre is overrun with pavement **cafés** during the summer, when a certain joie-de-vivre fills the otherwise sterile flagstoned centre.

The Central Balkan Range

For more than a thousand years, the **Balkan Range** (in Bulgarian, the **Stara planina** or "Old Mountains") has been the cradle of the Bulgarian nation and the cockpit of its destiny. Sloping gently towards the Danubian Plain, the Balkan's fertile valleys supported the medieval capitals of Pliska and Preslav (mere ruins today) and Veliko Tûrnovo (still a thriving city), while steep ranges with defensible passes shielded them to the south. Much was destroyed during the Ottoman conquest, but the thread of culture was preserved by monasteries and the crafts centres that re-established themselves under the Turkish yoke.

The range's gentler slopes lie just **east of Sofia**, where small towns like **Etropole** and **Teteven** provide a measure of rural tranquillity lacking in the more touristed Balkan centres further east. First of these is **Lovech**, a well-preserved nineteenth-century town which lies within striking distance of **Troyan Monastery**, and, to the north, at the foot of the mountains, **Pleven**, site of a crucial battle in the Russo-Turkish War.

However, the best touring base in the central part of the range is **Veliko Tûrnovo**. A beautiful city in its own right, with a medieval citadel and several historic churches, Tûrnovo has good transport links with such villages rich in vernacular architecture as **Arbanasi**, **Elena**, **Tryavna** and **Etûra**. It also makes a good base for a whole cluster of monasteries: **Preobrazhenski**, **Dryanovo** and **Kilifarevo** are the big three, but numerous smaller foundations await further exploration.

The Stara Planina Tourist Association

The **Stara Planina Tourist Association** coordinates the work of six tourist offices in towns bordering on the central Balkan Range. The tourist offices share information, and can book accommodation in any of the areas covered by the association, making it possible to structure your itinerary in advance around the towns where the offices are found. It's also worth noting that they rent out **mountain bikes** (stocks permitting) for 5Lv per day, and you're allowed to return the bikes to any office within the scheme. You'll find details on addresses and opening times of the tourist offices – in **Teteven, Troyan, Apriltsi, Tryavna, Dryanovo, Sevlievo, Lovech** and **Gabrovo** – in the relevant sections of the guide.

If you want information and advice on the region before you travel, contact the Stara Planina Tourist Association, 3rd Floor, ul. Raicho Karolev 4, 5300 Gabrovo (Mon-Fri 9am-6pm) ⓣ066/809161 or 807137, ⓦwww.staraplanina.org.

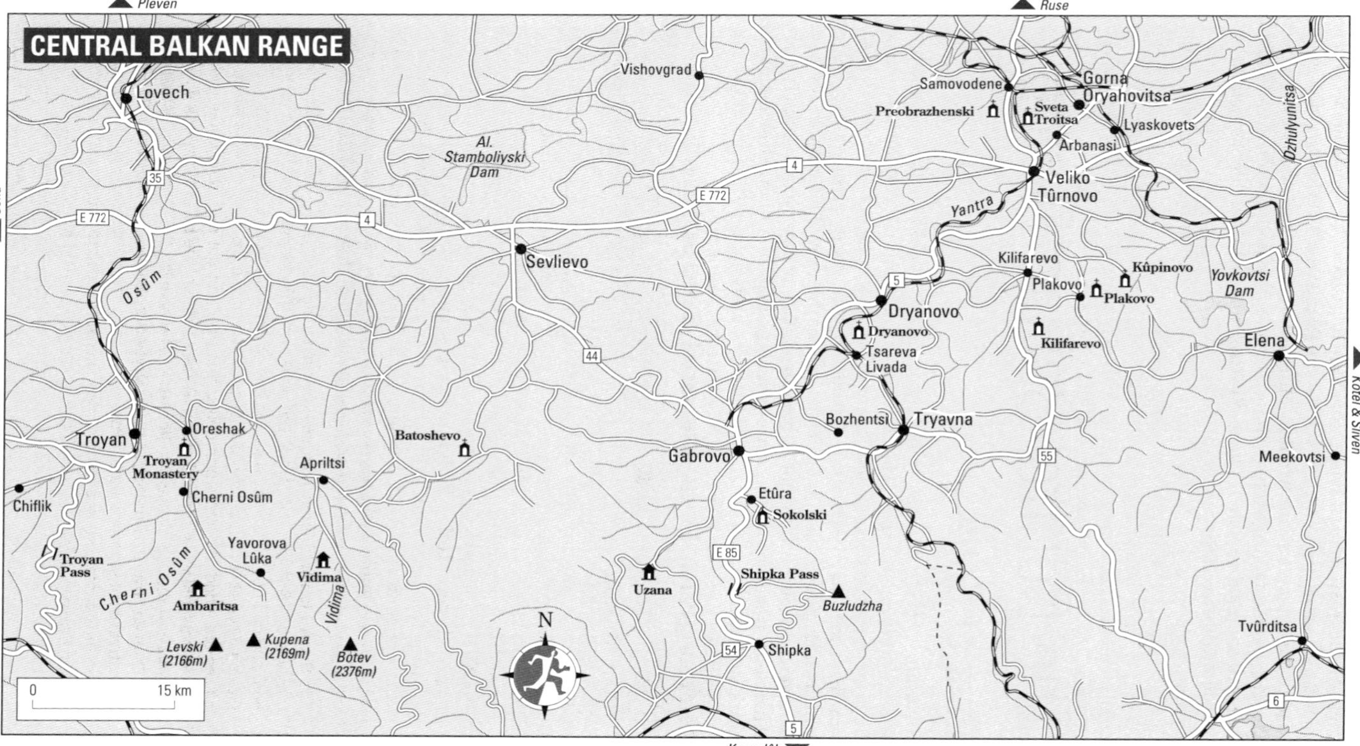
CENTRAL BALKAN RANGE
Pleven
Ruse
Sofia
Kotel & Sliven
Kazanlŭk
Lovech
Vishovgrad
Samovodene
Gorna Oryahovitsa
Preobrazhenski
Sveta Troitsa
Lyaskovets
Dzhulyunitsa
Arbanasi
Al. Stamboliyski Dam
Veliko Tŭrnovo
Yantra
Sevlievo
Osŭm
Kilifarevo
Kŭpinovo
Yovkovtsi Dam
Plakovo
Plakovo
Dryanovo
Dryanovo
Kilifarevo
Elena
Tsareva Livada
Bozhentsi
Tryavna
Troyan
Oreshak
Troyan Monastery
Batoshevo
Gabrovo
Meekovtsi
Apriltsi
Chiflik
Cherni Osŭm
Etŭra
Sokolski
Yavorova Lŭka
Vidima
Troyan Pass
Cherni Osŭm
Ambaritsa
Vidima
Uzana
Shipka Pass
Buzludzha
Tvŭrditsa
Levski (2166m)
Kupena (2169m)
Botev (2376m)
Shipka
N
0
15 km
E 772
E 85
4
5
6
35
44
54
55

The main urban centre in the east is **Shumen**, site of a fine medieval fortress and close to Bulgaria's first two capitals at **Pliska** and **Preslav**, and the enigmatic rock sculpture of the **Madara Horseman**. From here routes towards the Danube and the Dobrudzha pass through the Ludogorie hills, where the **Thracian tomb** and **Dervish Tekke** at **Sveshtari** provide the chief attractions.

Towns in the western part of the central Balkan Range can be easily reached **by bus** from Sofia. The **Sofia–Varna rail line**, skirting the mountains to the north, is the fastest way of accessing places further afield. It passes through Pleven, whence buses depart to Lovech and Troyan; Gornya Orahovitsa, with regular train and bus connections to Veliko Tûrnovo, Tryavna and Gabrovo; and Shumen, before forging onwards to the coast. Once established in any of the above places, you can explore neighbouring attractions using **local buses**.

East of Sofia

Travelling east by train, you completely bypass the foothills of the central Balkan Range northeast of Sofia. However, the main Sofia–Veliko Tûrnovo–Varna highway (a gorge-defying dual carriageway for the first 60km or so) heads straight across the westernmost shoulder of the range, passing a handful of worthwhile villages and monasteries along the way. The market town of **Teteven** and nearby village of **Ribaritsa** are the most attractive of the region's settlements if you need a base from which to explore. Otherwise, most of the area's worthwhile sights are accessible by bus from Sofia, or Lovech to the east.

Botevgrad, Pravets and Etropole

An hour's drive beyond Sofia the highway bypasses **BOTEVGRAD**, hardly worth a detour unless you're aiming for the E79 to Vratsa, Montana and Vidin, which heads north from here. Once a thriving market town, profiting from its position at the northern end of the (no longer used) Baba Konak Pass, Botevgrad is nowadays a sterile modern place whose main claim to fame is the Chavdar factory – makers of the buses that clatter their way across Bulgaria.

About 10km beyond the turn-off to Botevgrad, another minor road forks east to **PRAVETS**, a previously unremarkable village whose status as the birthplace of former dictator **Todor Zhivkov** (see box opposite) made it into one of the most prosperous communities in Bulgaria. It's in places like Pravets that nostalgia for the certainties of the Communist era is at its strongest. When Zhivkov made a much-publicized visit to his home town in May 1995 (despite being ostensibly under house arrest in Sofia at the time), he was given an emotional welcome by thousands of locals, many of whom were in tears. However, his modest childhood home is no longer open to the public, and there's little else to make a visit worthwhile.

Etropole and Yamna

Thirteen kilometres southeast of Pravets is **ETROPOLE**, a quiet agricultural town surrounded by subalpine pastures. The centre, a couple of blocks west of the bus station, harbours the usual eighteenth-century **clock tower** and a small **museum** (summer daily 8am-noon & 1-5pm, winter closed Sun; 2Lv), the latter housed in the old Turkish municipality offices and containing memorabilia of Etropole's past as a wealthy mining town that attracted Saxon immigrants in the Middle Ages. Today, most visitors come for the fresh mountain air and numerous walking possibilities, while the **monastery of Sveta Troitsa**,

Todor Zhivkov

Todor Zhivkov, Bulgaria's last and longest-serving Communist leader, was born into a peasant family in 1911 and was a minor Party functionary before emerging as mayor of Sofia after World War II. The reasons for his rise are still the subject of much conjecture: his record of wartime service with the Chavdar partisan brigade is now known to be a fiction put about by servile biographers, and none of Bulgaria's Party bosses regarded the affable and inoffensive Zhivkov as a serious political threat until it was too late. In 1954, within three years of joining the Politburo, he secured the post of First Secretary or Party Leader with the approval of Moscow, and elbowed aside the old Stalinist, Anton Yugov, to claim the premiership in 1962. He survived a coup in 1965 – a murky affair blamed on "ultra-leftists" at the time, but subsequently attributed to nationalist army officers.

Zhivkov was never a great ideologist: most of his political innovations were designed to wrongfoot opponents rather than introduce real social change. In foreign policy he slavishly followed the Soviet line, enthusiastically sending troops to help crush the Prague Spring in 1968. He tried to counterbalance this closeness to the USSR by pumping up Bulgarian nationalism at home, presenting Communist Bulgaria as the natural culmination of the national struggles of the past. Consistent with this policy were the extravagant celebrations marking 1300 years of the Bulgarian state in 1981, and persecution of Bulgaria's ethnic Turkish population in the years that ensued. It's for this abuse of Turkish human rights that the Zhivkov years will be long remembered in Turkey and the West. However Zhivkov also presided over a period of full employment and rising living standards – until the Bulgarian economy started going wrong in the early 1980s – and he's still spoken of with some affection by elderly Bulgarians bewildered by the economic changes of the last decade.

When "reform Communists" ditched Zhivkov in November 1989, it suited them to make the erstwhile dictator the scapegoat for all that was wrong in Bulgarian society. He was accordingly arrested on a charge of "embezzling state funds" and sentenced to seven years' imprisonment – although he continued to lead a comfortable, if somewhat restricted, existence under house arrest in Sofia. He remained in combative spirits, giving interviews to anyone who would listen and accusing Mikhail Gorbachev of being the one who orchestrated his downfall. According to Zhivkov, a skilful self-publicist to the end, his own form of *perestroika* was much more logical and consistent than the "anarchy" brought forth by the former Soviet leader.

When Zhivkov died on August 5, 1998, fears that his funeral would provoke a wave of pro-Communist sentiment proved unfounded. The Bulgarian Socialist (ie former Communist) Party did succeed in hijacking the event, turning it into an anti-government political meeting – rather ironic when one considers that they'd expelled Zhivkov from their ranks barely nine years before – but only 10,000 elderly mourners were there to listen.

4km to the east above the village of **Ribaritsa**, also offers an interesting diversion. Founded in 1158, the monastery complex centres around its church, with its four hexagonal towers, set in a grassy courtyard. Although the monastery was a well-known literary centre in the sixteenth and seventeenth centuries, when monks copied and distributed Bulgarian manuscripts, these days only a priest remains and its rooms are rented to tourists (Ⓣ0720/2042; ❶).

Getting to the monastery is fairly easy. About five daily buses run from Etropole to Ribaritsa, but these are usually early in the morning or late in the afternoon. Alternatively, it's an hour's **walk**: turn right out of Etropole bus station into ulitsa Partizanska, walk to the end of the street where the Ribaritsa road forks right, then after 50m bear right onto a partly asphalted track which takes you over the hills to Ribaritsa itself – where a signposted lane climbs to the monastery. Following the lane beyond the monastery takes you uphill to an area of rolling pastures traversed by local shepherds – ideal for short hikes.

For those who wish to **stay**, there's a three-star hotel, the *Etropole*, just above the bus station (ⓣ0712/3616; ❸), and a frugal but friendly establishment, the *Hotel Etropole*, on the main town square (ⓣ0712/2018; ❶). If you're interested in tranquil monastery accommodation but don't fancy hiking up to Sveta Troitsa, there are clean, simple rooms (❶) at the much smaller **monastery of Sveti Teodor Tyron**, just off the road to Etropole about 6km from Pravets, run by a hospitable elderly priest. There's more accommodation at the nearby village of Yamna (see below). As for **restaurants**, the *Oasis*, just off the market square, offers a decent range of local cuisine. Four **buses** a day make the ten-kilometre journey from Etropole to **YAMNA**, a tiny scenic village that stretches along the road into the mountains, where you'll find a couple of good accommodation options. There are plenty of picturesque walks in the region, most of them following unmarked trails, but the friendly owners of *Camping Vodenitsata* (ⓣ07106/243, ⓦwww.vodenitsata.iamna.domino.bg) can point you in the right direction. Situated at the start of the village their campsite offers a handful of small modern bungalows (❶) next to a rushing stream, and space for tents (❶). It's a rustic location complete with excellent home cooking, a hundred-year-old water mill, and an unusual natural washing machine. Further on the *Perfect Komplex* (ⓣ07106/212, ⓦwww.hotelperfect-bg.com; ❸) offers comfortable rooms with views of the valley.

Teteven and around

Back on the main highway, the next place of any importance is **YABLANITSA,** renowned for its *halva* and *lokum* (Turkish Delight), lynchpin of the local bus network and site of a turn-off for the Vit Valley, where the market town of Teteven and village of Ribaritsa provide access to some verdant pastures and craggy hills. Ten kilometres up the valley the road hits **GLOZHENE**, a drab industrialized village known chiefly for the nearby **monastery**, perched high above and practically invisible from the valley. It's a small monastery, housing a tiny nineteenth-century church enclosed by fortress-like living quarters with stone ground-floor walls and overhanging timber upper storeys. Monks will show you round a museum containing the church silver, and you can enjoy views of the surrounding countryside from the monastery's cliff-top eyrie. Most vehicles will balk at the gravelled roadway that winds up to the monastery from the village, and will opt for the longer, roundabout route, which takes you back along the Yablanitsa road for 8km before turning southwards to the village of Malûk Izvor, then eastwards on a gravel road to the monastery itself – a gorgeous rural ride by car or bike (available for rent from the tourist office in Teteven; see below). If you fancy walking, a shorter route (for which allow 50min) takes you south from Glozhene's central bus stop along the Teteven road, across a footbridge spanning the Vit, around the *Spartak* sports field, up a cobbled hillside path, then forks right up a wooded ravine.

Teteven

Surrounded by imposing mountains further up the valley, **TETEVEN** once inspired writer Ivan Vazov to declare that had he not come here, "I should regard myself as a stranger to my native land … Nowhere have I found a place so enchanting as this." An endorsement a shade too fulsome for modern Teteven, but the town is certainly appealing in a laid-back way. Teteven comes to life on Saturday mornings, when the town **market** attracts a deluge of visitors from surrounding villages – most notably the local Pomaks, easily recognizable by their *shalvari*, the brightly coloured trousers worn by the women.

Despite the undoubted prettiness of the pastel-coloured houses ranged above the **main square** (a couple of blocks south of the bus station), there's little in the way of specific sights, other than an **art gallery** (Mon–Fri 9am–noon & 2–5.30pm; 2Lv) on the square itself, displaying work by local artists, and a small town **museum** (daily 9am–noon & 2–5pm; 2Lv), also on the square, housing a colourful display of local costumes and crafts, notably the town's characteristic *chergi* – hand-woven carpets or runners. Rich in yellows, blacks and reds, the typical Teteven *cherga* features a zigzag pattern (*krivolitsa*) made up of small triangles or rhomboids. Several women still weave in Teteven, using local wool dyed with the extracts of indigenous plants, and the tourist office (see below) can arrange visits. Sadly, there's nowhere to buy *chergi* in town, although individual weavers are always happy to take orders if you're going to be staying in Bulgaria for some time.

The Teteven **tourist office**, just south of the square (Mon–Sat 9am–6pm; ⓣ & ⓕ0678/4217, ⓔvita_tur@infotel.bg), offers local advice, sells maps, rents mountain bikes for 2Lv an hour, and can book accommodation in both Teteven and Ribaritsa further up the valley. Staff here can also arrange hiking guides if you give them a couple of days' notice, and will provide information on Sûeva Dupka, a cave system 25km to the north of Teteven. Best of the town's hotels is the *Zdravets*, at ul. Petrahilya 29 (ⓣ0678/2201; ❸) up the road from the bus station, or you could try the *Olymp* hotel (ⓣ0678/2067; 40Lv double room) right next to the bus station; don't be too put off by the latter's concrete-block exterior – it has been internally refurbished to modern standards. There's an ample supply of **private rooms** (❷), although prices are little cheaper than the hotels – enquire at the tourist office. There are **cafés** aplenty around the main square, the *Zdravets* has a good **restaurant**, and the *Mehana Teteven* opposite the nineteenth-century **Church of Vsech Svyatich** (All Saints) on ulitsa Ivan Vazov serves traditional cuisine in an impressive building once inhabited by a pair of revolutionary brothers.

Ribaritsa

Twelve kilometres beyond Teteven at the end of the valley lies **RIBARITSA**, a mountain village straddling the babbling river Vit – a popular location for bathing in summer. It is served by four daily buses from Teteven, and there's ample accommodation, mostly in the form of **private rooms** (❶) bookable through the small tourist office here (Mon-Sat 9.30am-5.30pm; ⓣ06902/2400), the larger one in Teteven (see above), or directly from one of the many houses along the thoroughfare displaying signs offering *kvartiri*. **Hotels** include the *Ribaritsa* (ⓣ06902/2302, ⓦwww.hotel-ribaritsa-bg.com; ❶), up a steep track towards the end of the village and with a great view of the valley; the centrally located *Pochiven Kompleks Ribaritsa* (ⓣ06902/2301, ⓕ2381; ❷) with a fitness centre, tennis courts and comfortable rooms; and, at the very top end of the scale just beyond Ribaritsa village, the luxurious *Evergreen Palace* (ⓣ06902/2066, ⓦwww.evergreenpalace.net; ❹) with all the usual facilities. There's also a **campsite** with bungalows (ⓣ0887/41893; ❶) opposite the Shell petrol station. There are several decent **restaurants** in the village besides those in the hotels: the triangular *Alpinska Kushta* has a garden and serves tasty local dishes, while for something a little different try the *Express* – a converted railway carriage with indoor and outdoor seating offering typical Bulgarian fare.

Both the *Ribaritsa* and the *Evergreen Palace* offer **4WD safaris**; the latter also rents out bikes, and can arrange **horse riding** for 30Lv per hour. **Fishing** enthusiasts should head for the small but idyllic Varbaka lake next to the road as you enter Ribaritsa; a kiosk rents out rods and charges for what you catch. **Walks** from Ribaritsa head either southwest up the Kostina Valley (also cycleable if you rent a bike in Teteven), where, after 4km, you'll see a monument to **Georgi Benkovski**, the Koprivshtitsa-born revolutionary killed here in 1876; or south up the Zavodka Valley towards **Mount Vezhen** which, at 2198m above sea level, is the highest point in the Tetevenska planina. There's a hiker's **chalet**, *Hizha Vezhen* (also accessible by asphalt road) some two hours short of the summit. If you are hiking in the area, the 1:65,000 *Teteven Balkan* **map** (on sale at the Teteven tourist office) will prove an invaluable aid.

East of Ribaritsa, the main road climbs out of the Vit valley and crosses the hills towards Troyan (see p.237), some 40km away. It's another scenic route by car or bike (bikes rented at Teteven can be returned at the tourist office in Troyan), taking in heath-covered moorland and deep forest, although no buses pass this way.

Pleven

Sited where the foothills of the Balkan Range descend to meet the Danubian Plain, the industrial city of **PLEVEN** is an important regional centre with an unusually high quotient of worthwhile urban sights. Many of these are monuments or museums honouring the **siege of Plevna** – probably the most decisive episode of the War of Liberation. When the Russians crossed the Danube at Svishtov in 1877, their flank was threatened by the Turkish forces entrenched at Plevna (as the town was then known), which resisted three assaults costing the Russians thousands of casualties. In response to Grand Duke Nicholas's pleas, Romanian reinforcements came with King Carol I, who personally led his troops into battle (the last European sovereign to do so) crying, "This is the music that pleases me!" Russia's top generals, Skobelev and Totleben, then arrived to organize a professional siege, weakening the defenders by starvation and blasting each redoubt with artillery before the attackers made repeated bayonet charges, finally compelling the Turks to surrender on December 10. More than 40,000 Russians and Romanians and uncounted numbers of Turks and civilians died, but as a consequence of Plevna's fall northern Bulgaria was swiftly liberated. The defeat had a shattering effect on Ottoman morale, but garnered a great deal of public sympathy in the West, allowing the British and Austrian governments to adopt a much more openly anti-Russian line in the peace negotiations that followed. Pleven's other claim to fame is its extreme **climate**; Bulgaria's hottest summer temperatures are usually recorded here, and it's correspondingly cold in winter.

Easily reached from Sofia, Varna or Ruse by train, Pleven stands at the centre of an extensive local **bus network** that serves the smaller towns along the Danube to the north as well as Lovech and Troyan to the south.

Arrival, information and accommodation

Pleven's **bus** and **train** stations are at the northern end of town; to get to the centre, follow ulitsa Danail Popov (or take any bus) south until you hit ploshtad Sveti Nikolai. From here, Osvobozhdenie continues a short way south to **ploshtad Svobodata**, which in turn opens onto the main square, **ploshtad Vuzrazhdane**.

Most useful of the local **travel agencies** is Mizia, just off ploshtad Svobodata at Ivan Vazov 9 (Mon–Fri 8am–6pm; ⓣ064/801215), which organizes sightseeing

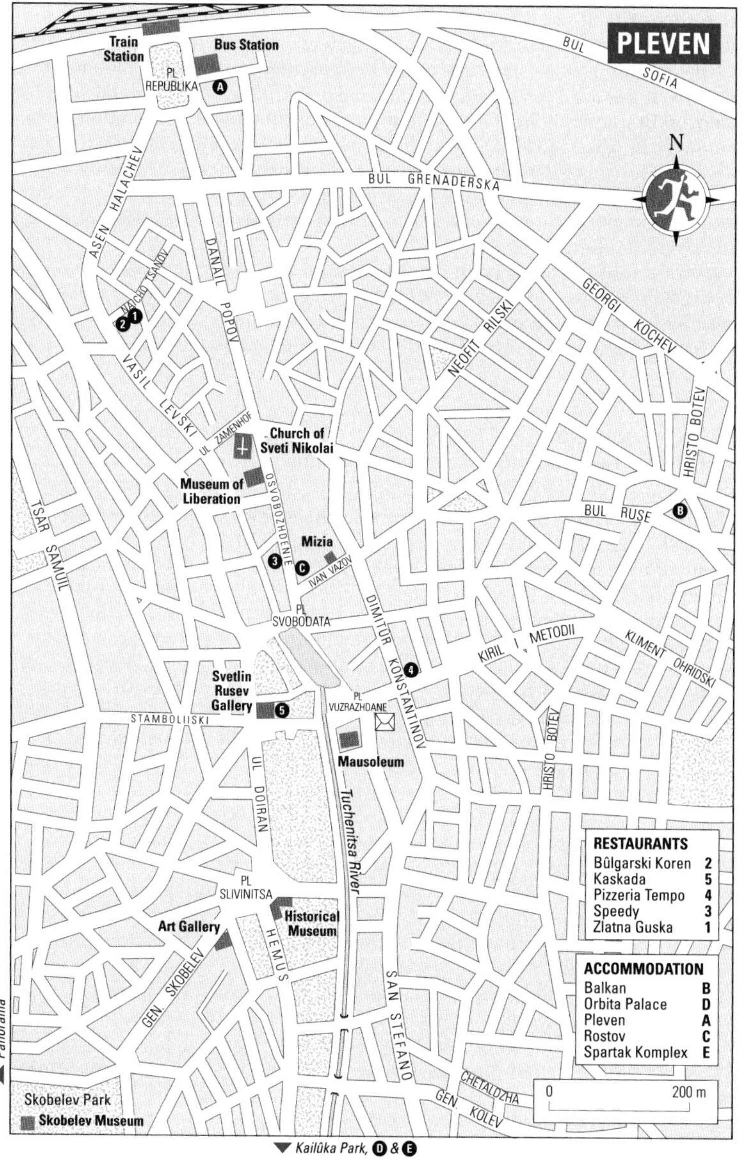

trips of the city, runs excursions to places like Etûra (see p.268) and Veliko Tûrnovo (see p.243), and can book **hotel** accommodation. The most central of the city's three high-rises is the newly refurbished *Rostov*, just off ploshtad Svobodata at Slava Aleksiev 2 (Ⓣ064/801095 or 801096; ❻), which offers a reasonable standard of comfort, including a pleasant courtyard restaurant. The slightly smarter, three-star *Balkan*, some 2km to the east of the centre at bul.

Ruse 85 (ⓣ064/822215 or ⓕ844111; ❼, but cheaper if booked in advance through Mizia), has neat and comfortable en-suite doubles with TV. The cheapest option in the centre is the rather grim *Pleven*, near the train and bus stations at ploshtad Republika 2 (ⓣ064/830181; ❸). Two hotels in Kailûka Park, 6km south of town, offer much more tranquil accommodation, but you'll need to take a taxi to reach them: surrounded by forest, *Spartak Komplex* (ⓣ064/804137; ❷) has comfortable wood-panelled rooms, while further into the park the modern *Orbita Palace* (ⓣ064/807937, ⓦwww.orbitapalace.com; ❸) offers acupuncture, mud cures and massage, and can arrange hunting trips in the Byalka hunting reserve.

If you're just passing through Pleven, there's a **left-luggage office** (*garderob*) in the train station (daily 6am–10pm, but with unpredictable lunch breaks), and another in the bus station (daily 7am–5pm). **Internet** access is available at the *Computer Club*, next door to the mausoleum on the city's main square.

The Town

At the southern end of Danail Popov, in a paved plaza, stands the sunken **Church of Sveti Nikolai**. A nineteenth-century portrait of the saint himself presides over the doorway of this simple structure, believed to date from the 1300s. Inside is a collection of icons, including works by the Samokov masters Stanislav Dospevski and Zahari Zograf, although many of the most attractive are by anonymous artists from villages in the Pleven region. An eighteenth-century *Council of All the Saints* from the village of Koinare is particularly outstanding, with a cluster of golden haloes hovering above the heads of the holy ones. Beyond the church lies **ulitsa Vasil Levski**, Pleven's busiest thoroughfare, lined with smart cafés and bars. Follow this south and you'll pass the **Museum of Liberation** in the park between Vasil Levski and bulevard Osvobozhdenie (Mon–Sat 9am–noon & 1–5pm; free), occupying the small wooden house where the Turkish commander Osman Pasha formally surrendered to Tsar Aleksandûr II. Here you'll see weaponry, mementos and plans lovingly detailing each phase of the battle.

A little further on is ploshtad Vuzrazhdane, the city's **main square**, a fountain-splashed expanse of flagstones, flowers and shrubs dominated by a Russo-Byzantine-style mausoleum (daily 9am–noon & 1–6pm; free), built to commemorate the Russian soldiers who died at Pleven, although the number of Romanian names on the lists of the fallen makes it clear who saw the worst of the fighting. Garishly modernist grey-and-brown frescoes swirl around inside, while marble tombs and plaques adorn the crypt. To the west of the square are the **old public baths**, a curious pseudo-Byzantine structure whose red-and-white striped facade could be easily mistaken for that of a church. It's now home to the **Svetlin Rusev Gallery** (daily 9am–6pm; free), honouring the Pleven-born painter and former Politburo member. His florid figurative works look strangely conservative when compared to the postwar art of the West, and are easily outshone by the other pieces in the collection – notably a striking self-portrait by Vladimir Dimitrov-Maistor.

The Historical Museum

Follow paths through the park at the southern end of the square and you reach the **Historical Museum** (officially daily 9am–noon & 1–5pm; free), housed in spacious former barracks at the foot of ulitsa Doiran. Within, a series of galleries explores successive periods of Bulgarian history through an extensive and remarkable collection of archeological artefacts. A blackened square of earth turns out to be the remains of a **Neolithic dwelling** from the fourth millennium BC, excavated near the village of Telish to the west and transferred here in the condition in which it was found. It's surrounded by a rich array of pottery from the same era, adorned with geometric designs. The collection of Bronze Age axe heads is particularly fine, though most eyes are drawn to the gold cauldron, a ritual object from the Chalcolithic period.

More pottery comes from the **Roman town of Oescus**, near modern Gigen on the Danube, an important administrative centre and home to the Fifth Macedonian Legion. On show are numerous tombstones and a fragmentary floor mosaic with various animals frolicking around a (small but discernible) scene from Menander's comedy *The Achaeans*. It's the more personal things, though, like the baby footprints impressed in a clay roof tile, and the children's toys, including a little horse on wheels, which bring these ancient people to life. The medieval period is represented by finds from another Danube town, Nikopol, whose fortress had a reputation for invincibility under both Bulgarians and Ottomans.

In the **ethnographic section** you'll see the hooded cloaks worn by shepherds of the Danubian Plain, an assortment of farm implements and a couple of blunt-ended boats carved from tree trunks used by fishermen on the river until very recently. Of particular interest are the reconstructions of sixteenth-century village huts, thatched-roofed dwellings built half above ground, half under, and surrounded by a stockade of twigs.

Upstairs are seemingly endless halls filled with weapons and uniforms from the days of the siege, including the samovars presented by Russian officers to the Bulgarian families with whom they were billeted. There's also an interesting display of theatrical costumes and other oddments.

The large and partly overgrown **courtyard** holds some of the larger Roman tombstones, votive plaques and statuary, left at the mercy of the elements, while

Bulgarian rainmaking rituals

The ethnographic section of Pleven's Historical Museum contains documentary evidence of many archaic folk practices once common throughout Bulgaria, and now on the verge of disappearing for good. Appropriately enough for a region famous for its long dry summers, pride of place goes to the **rainmaking rituals** which villagers hoped would bring an end to drought. Foremost among these was the parading of the **peperuda**, when a young girl (preferably an orphan, and always a virgin) was stripped bare by female helpers, clad in leaves and branches, and then taken round to every household in the village. The helpers would sing songs while the householder emptied a bucket of water over the *peperuda*, who responded by flapping her arms in imitation of a bird. The party then received a present of flour and beans from the householder before moving on.

Later the same day the villagers would emerge with a funeral bier bearing a **german** – a male doll endowed with an overlarge phallus (often represented by a red pepper). The *german* was then either buried near a well or thrown in the river. The doll was usually made of clay, although in the Pleven region it had to be fashioned from a broomstick stolen from the house of a pregnant woman. In some areas, the *german* could only be handled by chaste maidens, and had to spend the night prior to the ritual in the house of the girl chosen to play the *peperuda*.

The symbolic burial of the *german* seems to echo the fertility rites common to Indo-European peoples in ancient times, when, according to one branch of anthropological opinion, human sacrifices were made to mother earth in order to ensure good harvests.

in one corner you'll find the shattered remains of a more recently discarded culture, in the form of carved-up Soviet monuments, which once graced Pleven's public squares. Look out for pieces of Lenin scattered in the grass.

Skobelev Park

Just to the southwest of the barracks, a lengthy processional stairway ascends towards **Skobelev Park**, passing the city **art gallery** (Mon–Fri 10am–4pm; free) on the way. Inside are several more examples of Svetlin Rusev's work, and the inevitable idealized-peasant-girl canvas courtesy of Dimitrov-Maistor. At the top of the stairway is yet another Bulgarian-Soviet Friendship monument, followed by the gates of the park itself. The park is laid out on a hill formerly occupied by the **Isa Aga Redoubt**, the object of fierce fighting in 1877 and now restored and crowned with an obelisk commemorating the 405 troops who died capturing it. The **Skobelev Museum** (officially daily 9am–noon & 12.30–5pm; free) at the centre of the park holds a small display of photos and documents relating to the Russian general, after whom the park is named, and the siege. Numerous cannons are secreted within the greenery hereabouts, but the main focus of visitors' attention is the **Panorama** (same hours as museum; 5Lv), an enormous concrete funnel of a building housing a huge depiction of the early days of the siege, comprising three-dimensional figures set against a circular backdrop. Downstairs, a smaller diorama shows the Turkish commander Osman Pasha retreating over a bridge in the wake of the victorious Russian assault.

Kailûka Park

Leaving central Pleven by either of the main southbound boulevards, San Stefano or Vardar, it's 2km to the extensive **Kailûka Park**, laid out around the lush and rocky Tuchenitsa defile, and connected by regular buses to the town centre. Site of a Thracian settlement that the Romans took over and named Storgosia, it's here that the citizens of Pleven unwind at weekends, taking advantage of the park's swimming baths, watersports facilities, and open-air theatre. There are also a couple of restaurants, including the *Peshtera*, in a cave at the foot of a limestone cliff – and below the baths a monument to the Jews who perished here in 1944 when the camp in which they were imprisoned was destroyed by fire. (Although anti-Semitism has never been prevalent in Bulgaria, the government jailed the Salonikan Jews during the latter stages of the war to appease its Nazi allies.) Three kilometres up the River Tuchenitsa, a bronze statue of General Totleben (Russian hero of the 1877 siege) surmounts the **Totleben rampart** which separates two reservoirs: the lower reservoir is a popular bathing venue in summer. Not far from the entrance to the park on San Stefano is the castellated *Basein* sports complex (daily 9am–8pm; 2Lv), which has a small swimming pool, basketball court and snack bar. Trolleybuses #3 and #7 connect central Pleven with the northern entrance to the park.

Eating and drinking

Pleven's **eating and drinking** venues are mostly found around ploshtad Svobodata and ulitsa Vasil Levski. The best of the **restaurants** are to be found in a small complex of National Revival-era houses just off the northern end of Vasil Levski near the junction with Naicho Tsanov; *Zlatna Guska* is a traditional-style *mehana* serving the usual range of Bulgarian grills, while *Bûlgarski Koren,* just round the corner, is a step up in quality, and has a lovely courtyard built around a brace of fountains. *Kaskada*, right behind the Svetlin Rusev Gallery, is a nice outdoor restaurant serving the usual grilled snacks and sandwiches, while

Pizzeria Tempo, on ulitsa Dimitûr Konstantinov, offers decent Italian-style fare, and *Speedy*, on ploshtad Svobodata, is a popular Bulgarian fast-food restaurant. Both the *Balkan* and *Rostov* hotels have fairly good restaurants of their own.

Ulitsa Vasil Levski is the place to hang out in summertime, with a string of pavement cafés suitable for both daytime and night-time **drinking**. For late-night entertainment try *Club Utopia* on ploshtad Svobodata for mainstream techno, or *Club Faith* across the street from the Museum of Liberation for good dance music; as a last resort the *Rostov* hotel has a regular disco (10pm–5am), occasionally with live music.

South of Pleven: Lovech and Troyan

Lying just off the main road and train routes, the towns of **Lovech** and **Troyan** are often missed out by those travelling east to west. However, they do sit on one of the important trans-Balkan routes linking Pleven, on the margins of the Danubian Plain, with the Valley of the Roses to the south. In terms of scenery or sheer excitement, this can't match crossing the more famous Shipka Pass (see p.312), but there are compensations. Lusher and less craggy than the mountains further east, the landscape has its own attractions, and **Troyan Monastery** merits a visit as much as any of the other ecclesiastical treasures of the Stara Planina. The small settlements around Troyan make good bases from which to explore the mountains, and the range of accommodation now available in the villages makes them infinitely preferable to the towns for an overnight stay; the tourist office in Troyan (see p.238) can make bookings.

Plenty of **buses** ply the Pleven–Lovech–Troyan route, and Lovech is also accessible by **train**, lying at the end of a branch line which leaves the main Sofia–Varna line at the otherwise unimportant town of Levski.

Lovech

LOVECH lies an hour's drive to the south of Pleven, dunked between the rolling foothills of the Balkan Mountains. It divides precisely into two sections, the flagstoned walkways and plazas of the modern centre contrasting sharply with the grey stone roofs and protruding *chardaks* of the nineteenth-century **Varosh**, or **old town**, now an architectural preservation area. An important strategic point since Thracian times, standing guard over the northern approaches to the Troyan Pass, Lovech has become famous in more recent times for having once been the headquarters of **Vasil Levski**, whose statue and museum are now major attractions.

Nowadays Lovech is notorious for having been the site of one of Bulgaria's largest postwar concentration camps, which the inmates dubbed **Slûnchev bryag** (Sunny Beach) in a grimly ironic reference to the well-known Black Sea holiday resort. On a happier note, the town is home to the Liteks **football team**, whose rise in recent years from obscurity to the upper reaches of the league (they were national champions in 2003) is one of the more positive stories to emerge from an otherwise stagnating sport.

The Town

Lovech's bustling centre is largely modern, an area of concrete and steel grouped around the pedestrianized **ulitsa Tûrgovska**. Heading south along here, you'll soon reach the older parts of town, coming first to the **Pokritya most** or "Covered Bridge", the only one of its kind in the Balkans, and of which the locals are extremely proud. Spanning the River Osûm to link the new town with the old, it was originally designed by National Revival architect Kolyo Ficheto in 1874. The bridge burned down in 1925, and the present incarnation is the result of successive renovations – the most recent of which resulted in the arcade of boutiques, craft shops and cafés that the bridge now holds. At the eastern end of the bridge is **ploshtad Todor Kirkov**, named after the local revolutionary killed on this spot by the Turks in 1876 after taking part in the April Rising in Tryavna. Just behind the square is the town **Art Gallery** (Mon–Sat 9am–noon & 1–6pm; free), which houses a display of rustic scenes, many by local artists, and regularly rotating exhibitions. One block south, the National Revival-style facade of a kindergarten announces the boundary of the Varosh, which stretches up the flanks of the hill from here.

Most of the buildings in the Varosh are in fact modern constructions executed in traditional style, but an attempt has been made to preserve the atmosphere of the previous century in the narrow cobbled lanes that run up the hillside. One of them, ulitsa Marin Pop Lukanov, leads to a couple of buildings occupied by the **Ethnographic Museum** (daily: summer 8am–noon & 2–6pm; winter 8am–noon & 1–5pm; 3Lv). Both of the wooden houses which make up the complex were built in the first half of the nineteenth century, on seventeenth-century foundations, although they have been furnished to represent two distinct, later periods. The first house has been kitted out in the style of the late nineteenth century, when even wealthy Bulgarians seemingly spent much of their lives close to the floor, eating their food from low wooden tables and sleeping on low beds. The changing lifestyles brought about by turn-of-the-twentieth-century affluence are shown by the imported Viennese furniture that fills a couple of set-piece rooms, along with an enormous British iron bedstead. The little workroom also contains some costly imported devices of the period, including one of the earliest examples of a British-made steam iron. Below in the cellar are a wine press, vats and huge barrels, as well as a *rakiya* still and a soap-making vessel in which fats were squeezed together and blended with natural perfumes. The second house has been restored to its 1930s appearance, and has a markedly more "Western" feel, with a modern kitchen range and a cosy little study lined with books. The comfortably furnished salon is inhabited by a family of costumed mannequins, displaying the fashions of the day, all donated by the former occupants, the Rashevs. Opposite the museum, the **Kazakov Gallery** (closed for renovation at the time of writing) houses a collection of modern works by Dimitûr Kazakov.

Just up the hill from here, a modern concrete structure houses the **Vasil Levski Museum** (Mon-Fri 8am–noon & 1–5pm; 3Lv). Between 1869 and 1872, Levski was chiefly responsible for establishing a network of revolutionary cells in Bulgaria, which collected arms and recruits in preparation for a national uprising. The organization's largest base was in Lovech, where Levski usually stayed at the home of Nikola Sirkov, arriving and leaving in disguise. In 1870, the revolutionary committee in Lovech assumed leadership of the nationwide movement, becoming, in effect, the provisional government of the revolutionary underground. In 1872, however, the Turkish intelligence services managed to ensnare many local leaders, ultimately including Levski himself, who was betrayed and arrested at the neighbouring village of Kûkrina. Following interrogation and torture, he was hanged on a winter's morning in Sofia in 1873.

Despite the lack of captions in any language other than Bulgarian, several of the museum's exhibits are self-explanatory. A tunic of the First Bulgarian Legion recalls Levski's days in the 1860s fighting with fellow exiles in Serbia; there are copies of Levski's letters bearing the lion seal of the revolutionary committee; and the Lovech committee's original printing press – a wooden tray no bigger than a hand into which tiny lines of type were set – accompanied by the amazingly professional-looking documents thus produced. Levski's sabre and dagger lie downstairs, perched atop a shrine-like lump of stone.

Right next door to the museum is the **Uspenska church** (Mon-Fri 8am-5pm; free). The interior is a fresh and colourful showcase of contemporary artistry, the walls covered in a mixture of restored and completely new murals, while the ceiling and patches elsewhere are still to be attended to. It's interesting to note the continuity in the style and subject matter of the icons, and one of the most striking of the modern works shows Christ's entry into Jerusalem. Further up the hill, steps ascend to the tall and heroic **Levski statue** on Stratesh hill, where townsfolk come to admire the view. Higher again, up a badly pot-holed path, are the partly reconstructed walls of a medieval Bulgarian **fortress**, occupying a commanding position on the summit: Byzantine attempts to strangle the Second Bulgarian Kingdom at birth ended here in 1187, when they were forced to sign a peace treaty in Lovech castle recognizing Bulgarian independence.

A right fork off the main road out of the old town takes you up to Lovech's somewhat forlorn **zoo** (March-Dec daily 9am-5.30pm; 1Lv), with a collection of restless creatures in concrete enclosures.

Practicalities

Lovech's **train and bus stations** sit next door to each other on high ground west of the town centre (tickets for express buses to Sofia are sold from booths in the train station forecourt); from here a five-minute walk down ulitsa Zacho Shishkov will bring you towards the main ulitsa Tûrgovska. There's a **tourist office** next to the art gallery, which has maps and brochures, as well as details of local excursions, including to the **Devetazhkata cave**, 18km to the northeast of town, where a rich assortment of archeological artefacts have been found, indicating human occupation as far back as the Paleolithic era.

The most luxurious **hotel** in Lovech is the comfortable but dated three-star *Lovech* (Ⓣ068/685126; ❸) on ulitsa Tûrgovska in the modern town. Alternatively, there's the friendly, family-run *Tsaryana* on ploshtad Todor Kirkov, on the other side of the river (Ⓣ068/600995, Ⓔtsariana@mbox.digsys.bg; ❷); the neighbouring state-owned *Varosha* (Ⓣ068/25950; ❷) is in dire need of renovation. Next to the river on ulitsa Ivan Drasov are two comfortable hotels: the *Oasis* at no. 17 (Ⓣ068/26239; ❷) and the *Varosha 2003* at no. 23 (Ⓣ068/22277; ❷). In the old town on ulitsa Vasil Karakanovski, the *Bilyana* hotel offers clean, modern rooms in a cosy old-style house (Ⓣ068/604347; ❸).

The *Varosha mehana* on ulitsa Poplukanov has a lovely courtyard garden, surrounded by wooden balconies, and is one of the most pleasant places to **eat and drink** in old Lovech, with regular performances of traditional music in the evenings; just opposite is the *Cafene Varosha*, which offers a similar setup and standard. One of Lovech's best restaurants is the *Drakata*, on ploshtad Todor Kirkov, whose balcony affords a splendid view of the river and the covered bridge. Cafés and snack bars are in plentiful supply around ploshtad Todor Kirkov, or along ulitsa Tûrgovska in the new town. *Café Versailles*, at ul. Tûrgovska 85, is the best place in town for cocktails, again on a riverside terrace.

Troyan and around

The journey south from Lovech takes you through wooded hills to **TROYAN**, a ramshackle town ranged along the banks of the River Osûm. Though no great attraction in itself, Troyan has a relaxing, semi-rural feel, and provides transport connections to a host of places sheltering in folds of the Balkan mountains – **Troyan Monastery** and the hiker-friendly villages of **Cherni Osûm** and **Apriltsi** are the main places to aim for southeast of town, while subalpine settlements like **Shipkovo** and **Chiflik** lurk in side valleys to the west. All offer excellent walking opportunities and make good bases for exploring the Central Balkan National Park, which lies to the south, and for which the 1:65,000 *Troyan Balkan* **map** (available from Troyan tourist office; see below) is indispensable.

The Town

Troyan's **bus station** lies a couple of blocks east of the town centre, where the inevitable flagstoned main square plays host to the **Museum of Folk Crafts and Applied Arts** (daily 9am–5pm; 2Lv), a superbly organized display with English-language texts. Here you'll find comprehensive displays of local ceramics, woodcarvings, musical instruments and folk costumes, as well as reconstructions of a wood-turner's workroom and a nineteenth-century house. Also look out for the beautifully made scale-model of a street scene with busy workshops and houses, where the attention to detail is breathtaking. Troyan became a major centre of **ceramic** production in the nineteenth century, and most of the souvenir pottery you'll see for sale around Bulgaria is still made here. Troyan wares are instantly recognizable from the *Troyanska kapka* ("Troyan droplet") design, achieved by allowing successive layers of colour to drip down the side of the vessel before glazing. A few items are on sale in the museum, and visits to local ceramists, which usually involve an opportunity to purchase, can be organized through the tourist office. Next door to the Museum of Folk Crafts is the **Historical Museum** (2Lv), holding the usual patriotic exhibition chronicling the Uprising and Liberation, and occupying a building once used as a Turkish police station – you will need to ask staff at the Museum of Folk Crafts to open it.

Troyan practicalities

Ulitsa Vasil Levski, the main street, heads north from the main square passing the very helpful **municipal tourist office** at no. 133 (daily 10am–7pm; Ⓣ & Ⓕ0670/60964, Ⓔinfotroyan@yahoo.com), which sells maps, rents **bikes** (1Lv per hour), gives advice on **walking** in the Central Balkan National Park hires out English-speaking hiking guides, organizes **pony-trekking** trips (from one hour to one week), and even offers **microlite** flights over the region (2Lv per minute). It also arranges **accommodation** in small hotels and private rooms, although most of these are in the surrounding villages of Oreshak, Cherni Osûm, Chiflik and Shipkovo rather than in Troyan itself. Of the **hotels** in town, the *Nunki* (Ⓣ0670/62136; ❷) occupies an ensemble of National Revival-style buildings by the bridge, diagonally opposite the tourist office. Its simple en-suite rooms come with characterful touches, such as wood-carved ceilings or Ottoman-style *minderi* (couches). The only alternative is the *Kûpina* occupying an enviable perch on the Kûpina hill above town to the east (under renovation at the time of writing – ask at the tourist office for details). The folksy **restaurant** of the *Nunki* hotel has a typical menu of Bulgarian dishes, as does the *Fenerite mehana* on ulitsa Dimitûr Ikonomov; next door the *One* bar is a good place to down a beer or two. There are numerous **bars** and **cafés** along ulitsa Vasil Levski: *Dreams*, a swish, modern establishment right opposite the tourist office, is one of the best places for coffee and cakes. For **Internet** access, try the Internet Game Centre at ul. Vasil Levski 63. If you're in town on the last Saturday of September, you'll coincide with the annual **Rakiya Festival**, which takes place in various locations across town, with music, dancing, parades, and, of course, the opportunity to sample the local spirit from which the festival takes its name.

Shipkovo, Chiflik and the Troyan Pass

The main road heading south out of Troyan takes the high-mountain route over the Troyan Pass, but just after the end of town, two turn-offs give access to a couple of attractive side valleys. The northern turning heads up the Rûzhdavets valley, at the top of which sits the village of **SHIPKOVO**, sandwiched between steep wooded slopes with a small spa resort at its western end. Served by five buses a day from Troyan, it's an unassuming, family-oriented destination where people flock to use the open-air swimming pool in summer. The family-run *Bacchus* hotel (Ⓣ0696/385, Ⓦwww.bgglobe.net/bakhus.html; ❷) stands beside the road 1km before the centre; newly built in traditional style with wide wooden balconies and a pool, it's popular with both Bulgarian and foreign tourists. There's a cluster of trade-union rest homes and hotels on the opposite side of town, all of which can be booked through the Troyan tourist office: the *Zhiti Hotel* (Ⓣ06966/661, Ⓕ262; ❷) is a three-star place with en-suite rooms and satellite TV, while a notch lower in terms of comfort, the *Villa Borovets* (Ⓣ06966/251, Ⓕ625; ❶), is a cosy place, but with shared facilities. Beyond Shipkovo, the road winds its picturesque way over the hills towards Ribaritsa and Teteven (see p.228).

The middle turning follows the Beli Osûm river towards the village of **Beli Osûm**, an unspectacular place with a small number of **private rooms**, such as at the pricey *Haik* house (Ⓣ06965/734, Ⓔhaik@mail.bg; ❸) whose owner can arrange hiking trips in the locality. The village stretches lazily along the roadside for several kilometres before fading imperceptibly into the attractive settlement of **CHIFLIK** (five daily buses from Troyan), squeezed between narrowing valley walls. There are some very comfortable **private rooms** (❶) here; look out for roadside signs advertising the *Ilian* house (Ⓣ0670/25190), or contact the Troyan tourist office for other addresses and advance bookings. At the far end of Chiflik the road peters out beside another, much grander and more spectacularly located, open-air swimming pool, fed by mineral water which arrives ready-warmed from local springs. Overlooking the pool is the *Chiflik* hotel (Ⓣ0670/22038; ❷); set back in the forest, the *Komplex Diva* (Ⓣ0670/35035; ❹) has its own 35°C mineral pool and offers massage, sauna, and physiotherapy. From the road end, a steadily worsening asphalt track continues for 4km to the *Haidushka Pesen* **hut**, which is the starting point for the two-hour hike to the **Kozya stena ridge** and, a little way beyond, the *Kozya Stena* **chalet**.

Continuing south along the main road, you'll begin to climb slowly through dense forests towards the **Troyan Pass**, past the fledgling ski-centre of **Beklemeto** just below the summit. A wonderful panorama appears as the road crosses the 1450m-high pass, with the Stryama valley receding towards the Sredna Gora, and its highest peak Mount Bogdan (1714m), and the Plain of Thrace beyond leading to the bluish silhouette of the distant Rhodopes. At the foot of the mountains lies **Kûrnare**, a nondescript town where you can catch regular buses or trains into the neighbouring **Valley of the Roses** (see Chapter Four). The pass is accessible via a daily Troyan-Plovdiv **bus** that currently leaves Troyan at 7am, returning from Plovdiv at 1.30pm (mid-April to mid-Oct only).

Troyan Monastery

Nine daily buses head east from Troyan up the Cherni Osûm valley, through the straggling village of **ORESHAK**, to Bulgaria's third-largest monastery. Perched on the west bank of the Cherni Osûm river and shaded by trees, the **Troyan**

Monastery (*Troyanski manastir*; daily dawn–dusk; free) was founded in the early fifteenth century, though its church, Sveta Bogoroditsa, wasn't built until 400 years later. It is the church, however, that is of most interest, principally because of its interior and exterior **frescoes** by Zahari Zograf, Bulgaria's most outstanding exponent of nineteenth-century religious art. The highlight of his work is outside the church porch, a vivid series of scenes depicting the *Last Judgement*, including a suitably macabre figure of Death bundling unfortunates into the gaping mouth of hell. The theme is continued in slightly faded scenes along the west side of the church's outer wall, with St Peter admitting the virtuous to the walled garden of paradise, and a wonderfully vulgar scene revealing what the Orthodox Church really thought of rural Bulgaria's *vrachka* (wise woman), whose herbal remedies are being deposited in her hand by a demon, squatting on her head. Elsewhere, sinners of various kinds are being prodded and poked, and a group of turbaned Turks are being pulled down into the flames of hell. More of Zahari's work appears in the vestibule, where the archway leading into the nave is framed by pictures of horse-riding Russian warrior-Saints Gleb and Boris, and the artist even took the liberty of including a self-portrait (visible in a window niche on the north side of the nave), next to a picture of Hadzhi Filotei, the abbot who commissioned the work. Zahari's brother Dimitûr painted the icons which feature in the exquisite, Tryavna-produced **iconostasis**, with its intricately wrought walnut pillars topped by exotic birds of prey, each holding a snake in its beak. The only other object of note inside the church is the icon of the "**three-handed Virgin**" (who appears to be embracing the infant Jesus with more than two arms), which devoted pilgrims believe has the power to cure ailments and grant wishes.

Outside the church, on the third floor of the monastery living quarters, is a small "**hiding-place museum**" (officially daily dawn–dusk; 2Lv), set up when the ubiquitous Vasil Levski encouraged the monks to start a branch of the revolutionary underground at Troyan. The table and food bowl used by the itinerant patriot stand beside the wooden cupboard in which he supposedly hid whenever agents of the sultan came calling. An adjacent room displays icons, archiepiscopal robes and church regalia, including the surviving doors of an eighteenth-century iconostasis from the previous monastery church.

A popular side-trip from the monastery is to walk to the much smaller (and rarely manned) **Monastery of Sveti Nikolai**, 30 minutes uphill on the other side of the valley. Cross the footbridge opposite Troyan Monastery's gate and bear right, picking up a track to the left when you see a small graveyard. From here a stony path zigzags uphill, offering a challengingly steep – but well-shaded – climb. There's nothing to see at the tumbledown monastery itself, but its fragrant woodland setting makes the walk worthwhile.

Accommodation is available in the Troyan monastery from an office just inside the main gate, which offers double rooms for 40Lv – note there's a 10pm curfew. Things get busy during the days leading up to the monastery's main holy day, the Feast of the Assumption (*Golyama Bogoroditsa*) on August 15, but outside of this time you should have no problem getting a bed, though if you want to make absolutely sure, phone ahead (Ⓣ06952/2866). There's an ample supply of **private rooms** (❷) in Oreshak, the southern end of which begins just outside the monastery gates, which are best booked through the tourist office in Troyan, and a couple of **hotels** - the three-star *Sveta Gora* (Ⓣ06952/3160; ❸) in the hills above the village, and the quiet *Edelweiss* (Ⓣ0670/35452; ❶) signposted off the main street.

Food and drink is available from the stalls in the parking lot outside the monastery, or the *Manastirska Bara* restaurant opposite, which has a wooden verandah overlooking the river. Alternatively, Oreshak has a couple of restaurants on or near its main street: the *Kaiser*, roughly halfway through the village, does a good barbecue in its courtyard, and the well-known *Dobrudzhanska Sreshta*, signed off to the left if coming from the Troyan direction, offers good Bulgarian food in traditionally furnished rooms; next door is the equally popular *Oresheka mehana*. It's also worth noting that Oreshak's **Fair of Arts and Crafts** (daily 9am–5pm; craft exhibition 2Lv), just before the monastery, sells pottery, textiles and woodcarvings from all over Bulgaria of much better quality than those on sale at the touristy souvenir stalls outside the monastery itself.

Cherni Osûm

A couple of kilometres beyond the monastery, buses from Troyan come to rest in the village of **CHERNI OSÛM**, an unspoilt logging community which provides an excellent base from which to explore the upper reaches of the Cherni Osûm valley and the Central Balkan National Park, an extensive nature reserve which lies just south of the village. It's also home to a small **Natural History Museum**, located at the southern end of the village (daily 8am–noon & 1–5pm; 3Lv). Stuffed examples of the local wildlife are on show, including stags, bears and wolves, some mounted on revolving pedestals, with background tapes playing the appropriate howls and growls.

There are a few friendly, family-run **hotels** just off the main street, the most comfortable of which is the *Spomen* (Ⓣ06962/575; ❶, includes breakfast), with five comfortable en-suite rooms grouped around a central courtyard; lunch and dinner can be arranged for an extra fee. The *Otdich* hotel (Ⓣ06962/528; ❶) offers rooms with self-catering facilities; and the more basic *Sherpa* (May–Oct only; Ⓣ06962/269; ❷ with breakfast) is a traditionally furnished converted family house with a shared bathroom inside and another outside in the courtyard. The owner, Radyu Minkov, is an experienced hiker who can organize guided walks and picnics and offer guests advice on the best of the local trails, though only if they speak Bulgarian, French or German. A wonderful home-cooked dinner, with wine, is available for an extra charge. If you've got your own transport, you could consider staying in the hamlet of **Stoynovsko** (turn right over a bridge 3.5km south of Cherni Osûm) at the pricier *Rodan kûshta* (Ⓣ06962/329; ❷ with breakfast), which offers traditional-style rooms, and an Eden-like back garden with an outdoor kitchen that guests can use. Just before Stoynovsko, *Villa Ani* (Ⓣ06962/640; ❷) offers clean, comfortable accommodation. For **eating and drinking**, the *Spomen* has a small bar and restaurant, and the *Kolibito* restaurant on the square adjacent to the *Sherpa* serves good food.

The most convenient starting point for forays into the mountains is **Yavorova Lûka**, 9km south of Cherni Osûm, where a fairly obvious trail ascends southwest beside the Malka Krayovitsa stream to the *Ambaritsa* **chalet** (2hr). From here, a path climbs steadily southwards to join the ridge of the main Balkan Range (1hr), just below the 2166-metre summit of **Mount Ambaritsa**. Another option is the hike up to **Zelenikovski Monastery**: drive or walk the 5km south from Cherni Osûm to the tiny village of Vets from where a well-marked path leads first to the isolated hamlet of Glushka (50min) and then to the monastery (1hr 10min) where you can sleep for a small fee; take food and a torch as facilities are basic.

Apriltsi

Four buses a day run east from Troyan to **APRILTSI**, a large village nestling in the Vidima valley. It covers a wide area, with the suburbs of **Vidima** and

Ostrets spreading many kilometres into the side valleys which fork away from the centre of the village. Buses from Troyan terminate in Ostrets, 3km southeast of the centre, so it's best to ask the driver for "Apriltsi", ensuring that you'll be put down somewhere on the main street, ulitsa Vasil Levski, where you'll find the **tourist office** at no. 102 (summer daily 9am–5pm, winter Mon-Fri 9am-5pm; Ⓣ & Ⓕ06958/3249, Ⓔmts_apriltsi@bitex.bg). Here you can pick up hiking advice and maps, rent bicycles (1Lv per hour), and book one of a number of **pensions** or private **rooms** (❶–❷), most of which offer half- or full-board for a few extra dollars. The family-run *Tihiya Kût* **hotel** in the suburb of Ostrets (Ⓣ06958/2102 or 3363; ❷) is probably the swankiest accommodation option, featuring a stylish open-air swimming pool and stunning mountain views; the *Apriltsi* hotel (Ⓣ06958/2191; ❷) overlooking the village is a larger, dated complex with a pool, tennis court, sauna and great views, while in the centre of Apriltsi the *Dr. Tsurov* (Ⓣ06958/2436; ❶) has its own restaurant and a pleasant garden courtyard as well as an outdoor pool.

The main trail-heads for **hikers** start 5km out from the centre, at the southern end of Vidima, where a right fork in the road leads to the head of the Stûrna valley 6.5km away, while a left fork heads up the Lyava Vidima valley, passing the *Vidima* **chalet** (7Lv per person) after another 3km, then petering out 4km further on. Either spot serves as the jumping-off point for paths to the *Pleven* **chalet**, a steep one-hour climb further south. The forbidding terrain of the main Balkan Range lies immediately beyond, although you'll need a **guide** hired through the Apriltsi tourist office to make full use of it.

East towards Veliko Tûrnovo

If you have a car, it's relatively easy to cut northeast across country from the Troyan region to join the main E7772 highway towards Veliko Tûrnovo. Relying on public transport however, things are more complicated, and you may have to double back to Lovech or Pleven in order to pick up eastbound buses and trains. Most eastward road routes come together at **SEVLIEVO**, 40km from Lovech, a small rural centre whose nineteenth-century buildings have largely escaped the mania for reconstruction and renovation lavished elsewhere. Ulitsa Skobelevska, the main street, bears a decrepit-looking **Church of the Prophet Elijah** with icons by Tryavna masters; next door, the **Historical Museum** at no. 10 (Mon-Sat 10am–noon & 3.30–6.30pm; 2Lv), housed in the former village schoolhouse, details the various craft industries that characterized town life before the Liberation. One of the more important trades was leatherworking, memories of which are preserved in the **Tabahana**, Tabashka 3 (Tues–Sun 8am–noon & 2–6pm; 2Lv), a nineteenth-century tannery decked out with original tools and animal skins. There's no reason **to stay overnight** in Sevlievo, but if you have to, try either the luxurious central *Plaza Hotel*, pl. Svoboda 6 (Ⓣ0675/30743; ❻) or the smaller *Odessa Hotel* at ul. Dunov 1 (Ⓣ0675/30077; ❻).

For those with plenty of time, a car, and a pathological desire to ride the back roads of Bulgaria, a couple of interesting sights lie hidden away to the south of Sevlievo. Minor roads lead to **Gradnitsa**, 15km to the southwest, where a medieval fortress tumbles down the slopes of Prechista hill on the south side of the village. Lower layers of the remaining walls are sixth-century Byzantine, but most of the remains date from the Second Kingdom. More intrepid travellers may consider a trip to **Batoshevo Monastery**, 27km to the south on the old road to Apriltsi, situated high above the west bank of the River Rositsa, midway between the villages of Batoshevo and Stokite. Low, barn-like monastery buildings surround the Church of the Assumption, whose grey slate roof slopes down over a richly frescoed porch.

Vishovgrad

Northeast of Sevlievo lies one of the major white-wine-producing areas of Bulgaria, with low vineyard-cloaked hills feeding the wineries of towns like **Suhindol** and **Pavlikeni**. There are no real tourist centres here yet, save perhaps for the village of **VISHOVGRAD**, lying 15km north of the main Tûrnovo-bound E7772 on a minor road which cuts across country to Pavlikeni. If you're travelling by public transport, you'll have to approach the village from the north, catching a train to Pavlikeni (on the main Sofia–Varna line) and picking up a Vishovgrad bus from outside the station – most departures are timed to coincide with the arrival of trains from the Sofia direction. The village itself offers rural peace, and the chance to walk the 6km southeast to the **Emen Gorge**, where a wooden walkway leads past rushing waters to a small lake and a waterfall. Back in the village, the family-run **pension**, the *Dûlbok Zimnik* (book through Zig-Zag/Odysseia-in in Sofia; ⓣ02/980 5102; ❸) offers bed-and-breakfast and advice on local walks. The best time to be in Vishovgrad is on **St Tryphon's Day** (*Trifon Zarezan*) on February 14, when the ritual pruning of the vines is celebrated with much drinking and feasting.

Veliko Tûrnovo

The precipitously perched houses of **VELIKO TÛRNOVO** seem poised to leap into the chasms that divide the city into its separate quarters. Medieval fortifications girdling the Tsarevets massif add melodrama to the scene, yet even more transfixing are the huddles of antique houses that the writer Ivan Vazov likened to frightened sheep, bound to the rocks by wild lilac and vines, forming picturesque reefs veined by steps and narrow streets. Le Corbusier raved about Tûrnovo's "organic" architecture, and even the dour Prussian Field Marshal Helmut Von Moltke was moved to remark that he had "never seen a town of more romantic location".

But for Bulgarians the city has a deeper significance. When the National Assembly met here to draft Bulgaria's first constitution in 1879, it consciously did so in the former capital of the Second Kingdom (1185–1396) whose medieval civilization was snuffed out by the Turks. Reclaiming this heritage was an integral part of the National Revival, and since independence (especially during the socialist era) archeologists have been keenly uncovering the past of Tûrnovo "the Great" – not only the medieval citadel of **Tsarevets** but also the churches of **Sveta Gora** and **Trapezitsa**. Nor is the city an isolated case, for in the hills and valleys **around Tûrnovo** are several monasteries and small towns founded during the Second Kingdom or in the aftermath of its collapse, which make great excursions from town.

Tûrnovo's convenience as a touring base is backed up by the city's **train and bus links** with towns like Dryanovo, Tryavna and Gabrovo to the south – all easy day-trips from here. In addition, the Bucharest–Istanbul express train travels through once a day in each direction, useful if you're travelling further afield.

△ The Varosh quarter, Veliko Tûrnovo

Arrival, information and accommodation

All **trains** between Sofia and Varna stop at Gorna Oryahovitsa to the north, from where ten local trains a day cover the remaining 13km to Veliko Tûrnovo. In the middle of the day there's a large gap between services, so you can save time by hopping on the shuttle bus to Gorna Oryahovitsa's bus terminal, from where there's a connection every fifteen minutes (#10 or #14) to Veliko Tûrnovo.

Tûrnovo's **train station**, on the Stara Zagora–Ruse line, is 2km south of the centre – buses #4 and #13 (from the bus stop nearest to the station building) run to the main thoroughfare, bulevard Levski. If you don't mind a fifteen-minute uphill walk, turn left out of the station yard and keep bearing left until you reach the centre. The main **bus terminal** (*Avtogara Zapad*) is southwest of town at the end of Nikola Gabrovski: take bus #10 or trolleybuses #1 and #21 to reach the centre. Privately operated bus services from Sofia and the coast pick up and drop off outside the *Hotel Etûr*.

The **Tourist Information Centre** at ul. Hristo Botev 5 (Mon-Fri 9am-noon & 1-6pm; ⓣ062/622148, ⓦwww.velikoturnovo.info) books hotel and private rooms and can arrange car rental.

Accommodation

Hotels are plentiful enough, with a growing number of small, family-run places and modern luxury concerns competing with the larger and older establishments. More are to be found out of town in Arbanasi, which makes an appealing rural alternative to staying in the city (see p.256). There is also a **hostel** offering comfortable dorm accommodation. The **Tourist Information Centre** (see above) books rooms at most of the hotels and can arrange **private rooms** (❷).

Comfort Paneyot Tipografov 5 ⓣ062/628728. Friendly, basic but spotless pension with large en-suites and stunning views of the Tsarevets. ❸

Etûr ul. Ivailo 2 ⓣ062/621838. Imposing if slightly unkempt high-rise with good views of the old town, but slightly overpriced for what it offers. Rooms with shared facilities or en-suites. ❺

Gurko ul. General Gurko 33 ⓣ062/627838. Family-run hotel overlooking the river, offering large comfortable en-suites with TV, minibar and a/c. ❺

Hikers Hostel ul. Rezervoarska 91 ⓣ0887/098279, ⓦwww.hikers-hostel.org. Relaxed place with rustic furniture offering dorm beds, one double room, self-catering facilities and superb views of Tsarevets. ❷

Premier Hotel ul. Sava Penev 1 ⓣ062/603850. Luxurious modern place tucked away down a

Tûrnovo's uprisings

The Ottoman-ruled city of Tûrnovo played host to three proudly remembered **uprisings**. The first came in 1598, when locals aided by Dubrovnik merchant Pavel Džordžic rose up in the mistaken belief that the Austrian emperor Rudolf II had promised to send military help. The second, in 1688, came about when Polish victories against the Turks once again persuaded Tûrnovo's *charshiya* that foreign armies were preparing to ride to their aid. Local noble Rostislav Stratsimirovich, a direct descendant of Tsar Ivan Stratsimir, was declared prince of Bulgaria, then forced to flee by the Ottomans, who set fire to the town in retribution. The third, known as **Velchova Zavera** or "Velcho's plot", came in 1835, when glass merchant Velcho Atanasov Dzhamdzhiyata hatched the hair-brained scheme of laying siege to the fortress of Varna in the hope of encouraging Russian intervention. Unsurprisingly, the conspirators were captured and hanged.

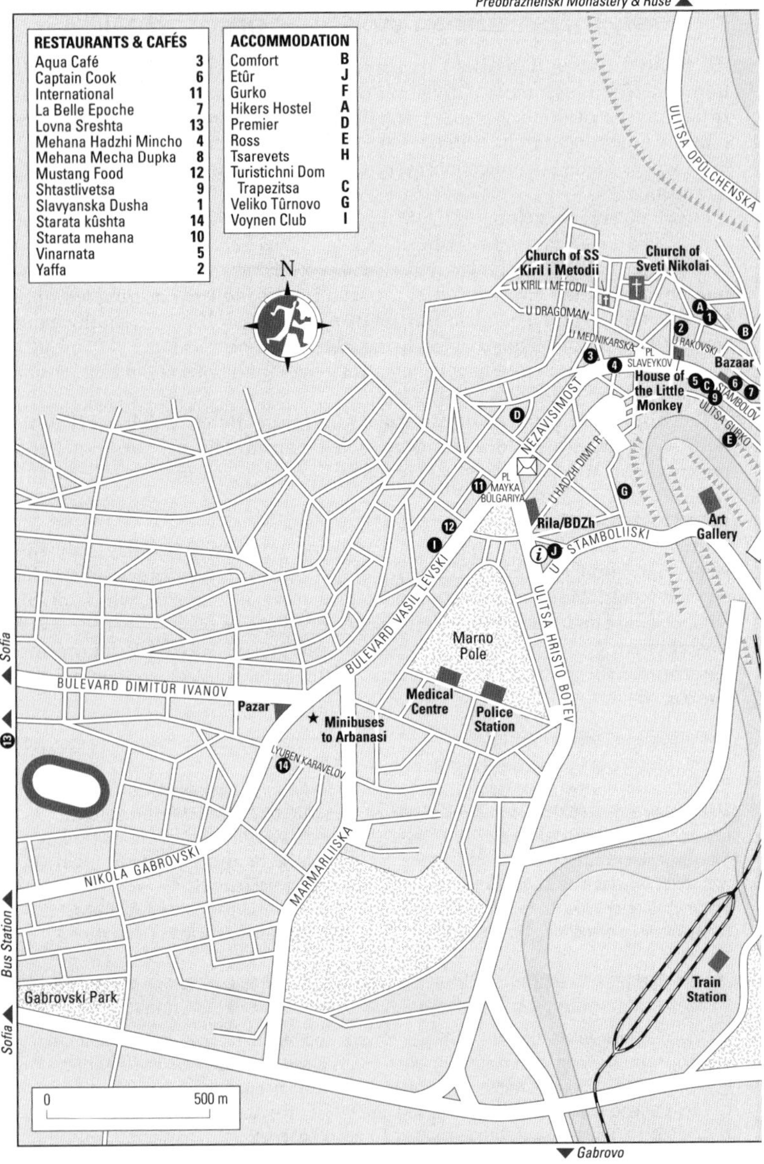

back-street. Facilities include solarium, steam room, sauna, and pool. ❻–❼

Ross Hotel ul. General Gurko 70 ☎0888/397830. Cosy and clean family-run pension overlooking the river. ❷

Tsarevets Hotel ul. Chitalistna 23 ☎062/601885. Plush sister hotel of the *Premier*. Housed in a refurbished nineteenth-century building just before Tsarevets. ❺

Turistichni Dom Trapezitsa Stambolov 79 ☎062/622061. Unassuming but friendly hotel run by the Bulgarian Tourist Union on the old town's

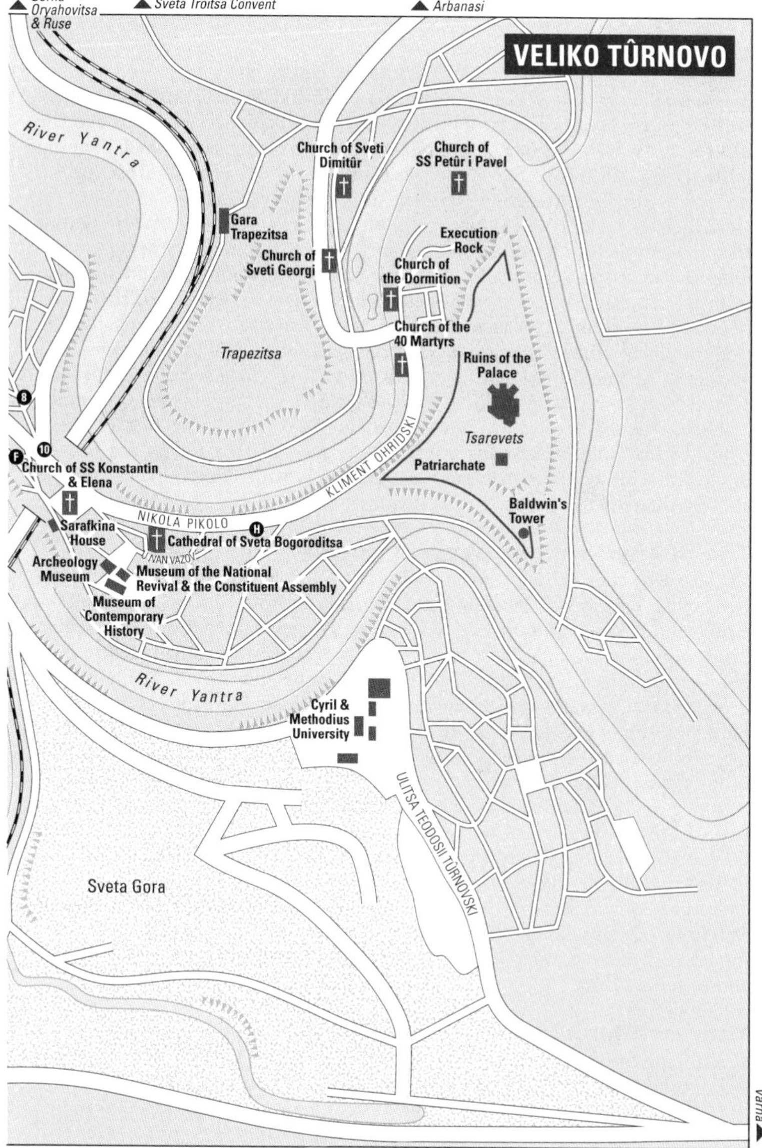

central thoroughfare. The rooms are clean with en-suite bathrooms, but fill up quickly with holidaying Bulgarians. ❷

Veliko Tûrnovo Emil Popov 2 ⓣ062/611000. Elegant four-star concrete palace aspiring to an international business standard. Rooms come with the usual comforts, satellite TV, and sweeping views of the old town. There's also an indoor pool, sauna and gym. Breakfast included. ❽

Voynen Club ul. Mayka Bûlgaria 1 ⓣ062/601521. Centrally located, clean, modern place behind Mustang Food. ❸

The Town

Lying on an incline, the city's drab **modern centre** holds most of Tûrnovo's downtown shopping area along boulevards **Levski** and **Nezavisimost**. From here you can proceed eastwards on foot and let yourself be drawn gradually into the **old town**. This is fascinating, not so much for its specific sights, of which there are relatively few, but for the feel of the place generally: there's always a fresh view of the city poised above the gorges or some new, unexpected detail.

Heading east along ulitsa Nezavisimost, you arrive at the small **ploshtad Pobornicheski** or "Combatants' Square", which has a monument to local rebel Bacho Kiro and other revolutionaries of 1876, whom the Turks hanged from gallows erected on what was then a rubbish tip. The "**House of the Little Monkey**" overlooking ploshtad Slaveikov at Vûstanicheska 14 gets its nickname from the small grimacing statuette over the balcony, although the bay windows and deeply pointed brickwork are what make it so characteristic of Tûrnovo architecture. It was designed in 1849 by Bulgaria's leading nineteenth-century architect Nikolai Fichev or "Kolyo Ficheto" (see p.261), the first of many Tûrnovo buildings to bear his imprint. Like many of the town's old houses, it sits precariously above a limited ground space, with orieled living quarters above what used to be a shop or warehouse.

The bazaar and the Varosh quarter

Various restored workshops and the facade of an old *caravanserai* make up the *Samovodska charshiya* or **bazaar** at the junction of ulitsa Rakovski and ploshtad Georgi Kirkov. Aside from one surviving coppersmith and a weaver selling handmade *chergi* or rugs, most of the craftspeople who once had ateliers here have moved out to be replaced by clothes boutiques, but it's still highly photogenic, with its wrought-iron garnished facades and cobbled slopes. Starting from the square at the end of the bazaar, you can follow ulitsa Vûstanicheska up into the narrow streets of the peaceful old **Varosh quarter**, whose two nineteenth-century churches are verging on the decrepit. The **Church of Sveti Nikolai** has a carving on the bishop's throne which shows a lion (representing Bulgaria) in the coils of a snake (the Greek Church) being devoured by a dragon (Turkey), and up the hill from here the **Church of SS Kiril i Metodii** – with its belfry and dome by Kolyo Ficheto – still serves worshippers on ulitsa Kiril i Metodii.

Heading downhill from ploshtad Kirkov, you'll come upon **ploshtad Velchova Zavera**, where Velcho the glazier, Nikola the braid maker, Ivan the furrier and other conspirators were hanged for rebelling against the Turkish authorities in 1835.

The Sarafkina House

Continuing from ploshtad Velchova Zavera along ulitsa Ivan Vazov you'll catch sight of the **Church of SS Konstantin i Elena** on the right, skulking behind foliage at the bottom of a steep flight of steps. From here you can descend to what is perhaps the most characteristic of Tûrnovo's streets, **ulitsa General Gurko**, where the houses – mainly dating from Ottoman times – look stunningly picturesque, perched along the curve of the gorge. Don't miss the *Sarafkinova kûshta* or **Sarafkina House** at no. 88 (daily except Tues 9am-6pm; 4Lv), which is so contrived that only two floors are visible from General Gurko but a further three overhang the river. The interior is notable for the splendid octagonal vestibule with wrought-iron fixtures and a panelled rosette ceiling which, like the elegantly furnished rooms upstairs, reflects the taste of the architect and owner, the moneylender Dimo Sarafkina. The emergence of bourgeois culture in nineteenth-century Tûrnovo is recalled in a gallery of sepia family photographs displayed downstairs, along with a reconstructed sitting room, furnished in fashionable "Western" style, and a small display of costumes. There's also a somewhat out-of-context collection of folkloric knick-knacks, including the ubiquitous ritual loaves, baked to celebrate such occasions as marriages, births and saints' days.

The Museum of the National Revival and the Constituent Assembly

Returning to Ivan Vazov and continuing southwards, you'll soon arrive at ploshtad Sûedinenie and a spacious blue and white building that houses the *Muzei "Vûzrazhdane i Ureditelno sûbranie"* – the **Museum of the National Revival and the Constituent Assembly** (daily except Tues 8am–6pm; 4Lv). Designed by Kolyo Ficheto in 1872 as the *konak* of the Turkish governor, Ali Bey (who mounted the trials of the rebels of 1876 here), the building subsequently hosted the first Bulgarian *sûbranie* (parliament), which spent two months in 1879 deliberating the country's first post-Liberation constitution – afterwards known as the "Tûrnovo Constitution". The union of Bulgaria and Eastern Roumelia (1885) was also signed here, and this hallowed building was exactly reconstructed (after being devastated by fire) in time to allow the proclamation of People's Power from the premises on September 9, 1944. The ground floor is occupied by a display of countless photographs and Bulgarian-only texts, paying homage to successive generations of Bulgarian patriots and their rebellions against the Turks – notably the locally based uprisings of 1598 and 1688 (see box on p.245). Unless you can read the language, though, it's all rather tedious. On the first floor, meanwhile, is the hall in which the Provisional Assembly sat, restored to its nineteenth-century appearance, with rows of benches upholstered in red velvet facing the raised daïs. Icons and ecclesiastical objects are grouped downstairs, including some fine examples from the Tryavna school; you can also look over a variety of nineteenth-century Tûrnovo metal- and woodworking tools, local pottery, weights and scales used by the money-lenders and a big still for *rakiya*-brewing.

South to Tsarevets

Steps to the right of the National Revival Museum lead down to the **Archeology Museum** (Tues-Sun 8am-6pm; 4Lv), whose collection includes various artefacts culled from the Roman city of Nicopolis ad Istrum, 17km north of Tûrnovo, founded by Emperor Trajan in 107AD to serve as an administrative centre for the Roman Empire's lower Danubian province, Moesia Inferior. Around the corner and lower down the hill, a former Turkish **prison** now holds the **Museum of Modern History** (Mon–Fri 8am–noon & 1–5pm; 4Lv), which contains a few personal effects of Tûrnovo-born politician Stefan Stambolov, an autocratic prime minister who was assassinated by disgruntled Macedonians in 1895, alongside photographs, drawings, military uniforms and firearms recalling the Balkan Wars and World War I. Above the square, the modern **Cathedral of Sveta Bogoroditsa** stands aloof on a terrace. From here, either ulitsa Ivan Vazov or Nikola Pikolo leads directly down to the entrance of Tsarevets, the medieval fortress.

Tsarevets

Approaching **Tsarevets** (daily: summer 8am–7pm, winter 9am-6pm; 4Lv) along the stone causeway that was erected after the original drawbridge collapsed beneath the *bey*'s harem, you can appreciate how the *boyars* Petûr and

Asen were emboldened enough by possession of this seemingly impregnable citadel to lead a rebellion against Byzantium in 1185. Petûr's proclamation of the Second Kingdom and his coronation occurred when Constantinople was already preoccupied by the Magyar and Seljuk Turk menace, and when a punitive Byzantine army was eventually sent in 1190 it was utterly defeated at the Tryavna Pass. Now restored, the ramparts and the Patriarchate (plus the ruins of the palace and various churches) convey something of Tsarevets's grandeur during the Second Kingdom, when travellers deemed Tûrnovo "second after Constantinople".

Gates and towers

Artisans and clerics serving the palace and the Patriarchate generally resided in the Asenova quarter below the hill, and entered Tsarevets via the **Asenova Gate** halfway along the western ramparts; foreign merchants, invited to settle here by Tsar Asen II, had their own entrance, the "Frankish" or **Frenkhisar Gate** near the southern end of the massif. Rapidly becoming a regional power, the Second Kingdom attacked and defeated the first Latin emperor of the East, Baldwin of Flanders, in 1205, the former emperor ending his days as a prisoner in the bastion overlooking the Frenkhisar Gate, thereafter known as **Baldwin's Tower**. No one knows exactly how Baldwin met his death. According to one fanciful legend, he resisted the advances of the Bulgarian queen, who promptly accused him of attempted rape and had him executed. Twenty years after Baldwin's capture, however, a hermit emerged in Flanders claiming to be the former emperor. Despite attracting a coterie of followers, the pretender was declared an imposter and put to death.

The old palace and the patriarchate

The **ruins of the palace** seem insignificant compared to the ramparts, but contemporary chronicles and modern excavations suggest that the royal complex was once splendid and opulent. Delicate columns divided the 35-metre-long throne room into aisles, which were adorned with green serpentine, Egyptian porphyry and pink marble, and mosaics and murals depicting the rulers of three dynasties. The church of the Blessed Saviour or **Patriarchate**, built early in the thirteenth century and now unconvincingly restored, was, significantly, the only structure permitted to surpass the palace in height. Ribbed with red brick and inset with green and orange ceramics, the church contains florid modern frescoes, which the visitor is invited to contemplate while curators switch on a backing tape of Orthodox choral music.

Execution Rock and the Terterid dynasty

The **Lobna skala** (Execution Rock) at the sheer northern end of Tsarevets is associated with the dynasty that followed the brief reign of the swineherd **Ivailo**

The son et lumière

Frequently on summer nights the entire Tsarevets massif is lit up by huge spotlights, and accompanied by a stirring musical soundtrack. Designed to tell the history of Tsarevets through the ages, the **son et lumière** is a stunning sight, especially when viewed from the terrace of open-air seating opposite the entrance to the fortress. Unfortunately, the shows are not guaranteed as they depend on tourist groups forking out for the electricity, but if you do hear of one taking place, don't miss it.

(1277–80). Proclaimed tsar after a popular anti-feudal revolt, Ivailo successfully organized resistance against invading Tatar hordes but neglected to guard against a coup by the *bolyari* (nobles), who had him flung off the rock. The **Terterid** dynasty which followed was chiefly concerned with its own survival and willing to suspect anyone – even the patriarch, Yoakim III, who was also executed – of collusion with the Tatars; it was only during the later, fourteenth-century reign of Todor Svetoslav that there was much progress or security.

However, Bulgarian culture – strongly influenced by that of Byzantium – revived during the Shishmanid dynasty (1323–93), and the enlightened rule of Ivan Aleksandûr and his son Ivan Shishman created the conditions whereby medieval Tûrnovo attained the zenith of its development. Trade with Genoa, Venice and Dubrovnik flourished; hospitals and hospices were maintained by the public purse; students came from Serbia, Russia and Wallachia to study at the university; and Tûrnovo became one of the Balkans' main centres of painting and literature.

Nonetheless, by the late fourteenth century the Second Kingdom had fragmented into several semi-autonomous states, and the hegemony of the kingdom had been dissipated: individually, the states were no match for the expansionist Ottoman Turks, who besieged Tûrnovo for three months before capturing, plundering and burning the city in July 1393.

The Asenova quarter

To the west of Tsarevets on both banks of the Yantra lies the **Asenova quarter**, where chickens strut and children fish beside the river. During the Middle Ages this was the artisans' quarter, which it remained until 1913, when it was struck by an earthquake which levelled most of the medieval buildings and did great damage to the (much-reconstructed) churches.

The **Church of the Forty Martyrs** (*Tsûrkva na chetirideset mûchenitsi*; closed for long-term repairs), near the bridge is a barn-like edifice founded by Tsar Ivan Asen II to commemorate his victory over the Byzantine rulers of Epirus at Klokotnitsa on Forty Martyrs' Day in 1230. Subsequently much altered, to the extent that it has, apparently, baffled restorers, the church was the burial place of St Sava, founder of the Serbian Orthodox Church, and several Bulgarian tsars; the Bulgarians saw God's hand behind the collapse of the minaret built when the Turks impiously transformed this into a mosque. Among the pillars within stands Khan Omturag's Column, filched from another site, whose Greek inscription reads in part: "Man dies, even though he lives nobly, and another is born. Let the latest born, when he examines these records, remember him who made them. The name of the Prince is Omurtag, the Sublime Khan." Not to be outdone, Asen had another column inscribed with a list of his conquests from Adrianople to Durazzo (Durrës in Albania), whose inhabitants were spared "by my benevolence".

Further north, the early twentieth-century **Church of the Dormition** isn't intrinsically interesting, but stands on the site of the monastery of the Virgin of the Prisoners, where Tsar Ivan Aleksandûr confined his wife as a nun in order to marry the Jewess Sara. The **Church of SS Petûr i Pavel** (Easter–Sept unpredictable hours; free), 200m beyond, is more remarkable: it contains several capitals in the old Bulgarian style (carved with vine leaves in openwork) and some well-preserved frescoes of which the oldest – dating back to the fourteenth century – is the *Pietà* opposite the altar. On the south wall, opposite the entrance, the church's saints' namesakes are portrayed in a lively manner. The church was the site of the massacre of the *bolyari* in 1393 (only Patriarch Evtimii's intervention dissuaded the Turks from killing the entire population)

The Bogomils

Tûrnovo was the venue for a famous synod of the Bulgarian Church in 1211, which tried (unsuccessfully) to curb the growth of a notorious medieval heresy that plagued the Second Kingdom – **Bogomilism**. The movement is thought to have emerged from the teachings of a tenth-century priest named Bogomil (literally "beloved of God"), who inherited the concept of dualism from the earlier Manichaean and Paulician heresies. This held that the entire material world was the creation of the devil, and only the human soul was the province of God. Jesus was sent to earth to defeat Satan's reign on earth, but his mission failed; the fight with Satan's power therefore continued to be a daily war of attrition for all believers. The growth of the Bogomils coincided with the fall of the First Bulgarian Kingdom to the Byzantines, and the movement was strongly critical of the Bulgarian establishment, especially the clergy. Left-wing historians have been quick to emphasize Bogomilism's social impact, especially its appeal to the poor.

Our only real knowledge of the Bogomils, however, comes from the movement's enemies – critics like the monk Cosmas, who described them as "lamblike and gentle, and pale from hypocritical fasting", but really "ravening wolves" who "sowed the tares of their preaching" among "simple and uneducated men".

Cosmas was not the only person worried by the spread of the heresy throughout the Balkan peninsula. Byzantine chronicler Anna Comnena relates how her father Emperor Alexius I had the Bogomil leader Basil publicly burned in the Constantinople hippodrome somewhere around 1100. Despite repeated efforts to stamp it out, Bogomilism remained a powerful force throughout the Balkans, although once-fashionable theories that Bogomilism became the state religion of fifteenth-century Bosnia are nowadays questioned. Byzantine propaganda accused the Bogomils of all manner of unnatural practices, most common among which was sodomy – the adoption of the word "bugger" by the English language derives from confusion over the terms "Bogomil" and "Bulgar".

and, much later, the place where the Ottoman-appointed Greek patriarch of Bulgaria was evicted by the citizenry.

On the other side of the river are two more restored churches. With its red-brick stripes and trefoil windows inlaid with orange plaques, the **Church of Sveti Dimitûr** is the best looking of the surviving medieval churches, although most of its original frescoes were painted over during the sixteenth and seventeenth centuries. It was during the consecration of the church that the *bolyari* Petûr and Asen announced their rebellion against Byzantium, and St Demetrius (who, legend has it, came from Salonika to help the oppressed Bulgarians) became the patron saint of the Second Kingdom. The **Church of Sveti Georgi**, further to the south, is smaller but has better-preserved frescoes of Orthodox saints.

Overhead rises the massif known as **Trapezitsa**, where the *bolyari* and leading clergy of the Second Kingdom built their mansions and some forty private churches, sixteen of which are currently being excavated. It's an area of great archeological importance, and although tracks onto the hilltop do exist, interlopers are discouraged.

Sveta gora

Sveta gora (Holy Hill), on the south bank of the Yantra, used to be a centre of monastic scholasticism, and nowadays provides the site for the **Cyril and Methodius University**, which can be reached via a bridge to the south of Tsarevets, or on bus #15. The rocky spur, linked by footbridge to the *Hotel*

Veliko Tûrnovo, is adorned with an obelisk commemorating the 800th anniversary of the foundation of the Asenid dynasty, but visitors are generally more interested in the contents of the large, copper-roofed **art gallery** nearby (Mon–Fri 10am–6pm; 3Lv), whose theme is "Tûrnovo through the eyes of diverse painters". A jumble of unchallenging townscapes and lionizations of medieval tsars for the most part, the collection is enlivened by a couple of naive exercises in mid-nineteenth-century portraiture by local artists Nikolai Pavlovich and Georgi Danchov.

Eating and drinking

Restaurants, cafés and **bars** line the main strip – ulitsas Nezavisimost, Stambolov and Vazov – that leads through the centre towards Tsarevets, from where the town's vibrant nightlife kicks off after dark. The main **food market** is the open-air *pazar*, on the corner of Vasil Levski and Nikola Gabrovski, and there's a 24-hour food shop with a good deli counter at ul. Vasil Levski 9.

Restaurants

Captain Cook ul. Stefan Stambolov 50A. Smart place serving a decent range of fish dishes.

International pl. Mayka Bûlgariya. Oddly kitsch basement restaurant complete with Grecian statues and a fountain. Serves dishes from around the world.

Lovna Sreshta ul. Todor Balina 16. Another place offering (seasonally available) hunting dishes as well as a wide range of Bulgarian standards, just beyond the sports stadium. Big outdoor garden, and live folk/pop music.

Mehana Hadzhi Mincho ul. Kyokotinitsa 2. Breezy, folk-style place just off ul. Stambolov. Good, cheap food in a small open courtyard.

Mehana Mecha Dupka ul. Rakovski. Cellar restaurant serving traditional Bulgarian cuisine, accompanied by nightly music and dancing.

Mustang Food pl. Mayka Bûlgariya. Neon-lit chain restaurant offering meaty dishes and salads.

Shtastlivetsa ul. Stefan Stambolov 79. Laid-back place with a wide range of pizza and pasta dishes and fantastic views over the valley.

Slavyanska Dusha ul. Nikola Zlatarski 21. Hidden away in the old town, an unpretentious *mehana* with excellent Bulgarian cuisine.

Starata kûshta ul. Ljuben Karavelov 63. One of the best restaurants in the new part of town, just off the eastern end of ul. Nikola Gabrovski, offering the usual range of Bulgarian dishes.

Starata mehana ul. Stefan Stambolov. Cosy place with good home cooking and a verandah perched above the Yantra valley.

Vinarnata ul. Stefan Stambolov 79. Traditional style *mehana* with an open fire in winter and great views.

Yaffa ul. Rakovska 1. Small and friendly with a good range of Arabic dishes and a few hookah pipes.

Cafés, bars and clubs

Aqua Cafe ul. Nezavisimost 3. Relaxed café serving alcoholic drinks and snacks with a stylish interior including a number of fish tanks. Open till 11pm.

Bacardi Club ul. Stefan Stambolov 29. Dark and loud inside, plays techno till late most nights.

City Pub ul. Hristo Botev 15. Bustling modern pub that serves food and stays open late.

Dublin Bar ul. Mayka Bûlgariya 26. Smoky, dimly lit bar serving bottled Guinness and Murphy's as well as dark Bulgarian beer.

La Belle Epoche ul. Samovodska Charshia. Smart Art Nouveau-style café and restaurant squeezed into an alley between ul. Rakovska and Stefan Stambolov.

Mosquito Bar ul. Stefan Stambolov 21. One of the coolest bars in town with a small terrace overlooking the valley and weekend DJs playing dance music till late.

Pepys Bar pl. Slaveykov 1. Sophisticated and subdued, decorated with sepia photographs and various oddments.

Scream Club ul. Nezavisimost 17. The only real disco in town playing commercial dance music all night long.

Stratilat Café ul. Rakovski 11. Popular Viennese-style café serving delicious cakes and coffee inside and outdoors.

Tequila Bar ul. Stefan Stambolov 30. Well established and fashionable, playing mainstream dance music on two floors.

Listings

Bus companies Express buses to Sofia and the coast are operated by Etap Adres (office open daily 24hr; ⓣ062/630564) just round the side of the *Hotel Etûr.*
Car rental Can be arranged by the Tourist Information Centre at ul. Hristo Botev 5 (Mon–Fri 9am–noon & 1–6pm; ⓣ062/622148).
Medical centre ul. Marno Pole 2 ⓣ062/621992.
Internet Navigator Internet, located in the dingy basement of the Evropa shopping complex at ul. Nezavisimost 3, is packed with computers and open 24hr.
Pharmacy There is a 24hr pharmacy at Vasil Levski 29.
Police ul. Bacho Kiro 7 ⓣ062/620001
Post office ul. Hristo Botev 1 (Mon–Fri 7.30am–7pm, Sat 8.30am–6pm).
Taxis Aleks OK Taxi ⓣ062/61616; Toptaxi ⓣ062/631111.
Train tickets Advance bookings and international tickets from Rila/BDZh, ul. Hristo Botev 13 (Mon–Fri 8am–4.30pm; ⓣ062/622042).

North of Veliko Tûrnovo

The terrain **north of Tûrnovo** is a wild confusion of massifs sundered by the River Yantra and its tributaries, abounding in rocky shelves rendered almost inaccessible by forests and torrents. Nearly twenty monasteries were established here during the Second Kingdom, and several survived the Turkish invasion. These formed a symbiotic relationship with the later towns and villages founded by refugees after the sack of Tûrnovo. With a car it's feasible to visit the main sites within a day, but relying on public transport (or hiking), one expedition a day seems more realistic.

Arbanasi and around

Hiding high on a plateau 4km northeast of Tûrnovo, and overlooking Tsarevets and Trapezitsa to the south, **ARBANASI** is one of Bulgaria's most picturesque villages, resembling a cross between a *kasbah* and the kind of *pueblo* that Clint Eastwood rids of bandits. People vanish into their family strongholds for the siesta, and at high noon only chickens stalk the rutted streets.

The origins of Arbanasi have presented scholars with a characteristically Balkan ethnological puzzle. The village's name led most historians to assume that it was founded by Albanian refugees fleeing Turkish reprisals after a failed fifteenth-century uprising, although this is disputed by modern Bulgarian historians eager to establish the continuity of Slav settlement in the area. What's beyond doubt is that the people who lived here in the village's eighteenth-century heyday belonged to the Greek cultural orbit, speaking Greek and giving their children Greek names. The inhabitants grew rich on the proceeds of cattle-droving, drying meat for their own consumption and selling the fat to the local Muslims, who considered it a delicacy. The leather was loaded onto caravans and taken east, where it was exchanged for Asiatic luxury goods like silk and spices.

Arbanasi's merchants invested their wealth in the big, fortress-like stone houses for which the village is famed, but they also endowed churches, chapels and public drinking fountains, turning the village into a lively urban centre for the local Christian population, hidden from the eyes of Ottoman-dominated Tûrnovo below. The town was sacked three times in the nineteenth century by the *kûrdzhali*, Turkish outlaws who menaced the townsfolk of the Balkans, and commerce became increasingly centred on Tûrnovo and other lowland towns, forcing Arbanasi's merchants to relocate their businesses. Mass emigration during the war-ravaged winter of 1877 further confirmed Arbanasi's decline. Nowadays a traditional rural population coexists with tourists and city types staying at their holiday villas.

The Village

Squatting on high ground just above Arbanasi's main square is the **Church of the Archangels Michael and Gabriel** (ask staff at the Church of the Nativity to open it) – the pair are depicted in a mural above the western portal. Dating from 1600, the church is a solid brick structure adorned with irregular lines of blind arcading, its gloomy interior illuminated by tiny, iron-grilled windows. Local schoolmaster Hristo was called on in the early eighteenth century to execute most of the frescoes, including a panoramic *Nativity* scene in the apse, but look out also for the later *Virgin Horanta* painted jointly by itinerant masters Georgi of Bucharest and Mihail of Salonika.

A cobbled path leads south of the main square towards the asymmetrical, red-tiled roof of the **Church of Sveti Dimitûr** (closed indefinitely at the time of writing). The original church perished in the earthquake of 1913, and the pale, unweathered stones of its modern reconstruction make it look more like a suburban bungalow than a place of worship. Some of the interior frescoes have been restored, and vibrant portraits of the two archangels preside over the adjoining chapel of Sveti Nestor. Richly carved Greek and Bulgarian headstones are propped up against the outer walls.

Returning to the village square and taking the main road west brings you to the finest of Arbanasi's mansions, the **Kostantsaliev House** (daily 9am-6pm; 4Lv). Like other dwellings erected after the conflagration that gutted Arbanasi in 1798, the ground floor (with servants' quarters and store-rooms) is built of stone and entered via a nail-studded gate, while the upper floor is made of wood. Many of the rooms have beautiful panelled ceilings and ornate plaster cornices bearing geometric or tulip motifs. However, the luxury didn't extend to any form of plumbing – the two toilets (his and hers) are simply holes in the wooden floor, directly above the garden. It's not hard to imagine the former owner, the Kokona Sultana (a relation of the *bey*), greeting her guests on the wooden staircase that ascends to the reception hall, from which one door leads to the "winter room" or communal bedroom. The other opens onto a corridor leading to the dining room and the office of her merchant husband, furnished with a low table or *sofra*.

Beyond the house lies the **Kokona fountain**, built in 1786 on the orders of Mehmed Said Ali, author of its Arabic inscription: "He who looks upon me and drinks my water shall possess the light of the eyes and of the soul". Turn left at the fountain to reach the village's most beautifully decorated church, the **Church of the Nativity** (*Rozhdestvo Hristovo*) (daily 9am-6pm; 4Lv). Like the others in Arbanasi it's outwardly plain, but inside you'll find richly coloured frescoes dating from the seventeenth century. The main entrance leads into a long gallery, its ceiling supported by wooden beams decorated with geometric designs and Greek-language inscriptions. At the far end of the gallery, the chapel of St John the Baptist is richly decorated with images of martyred saints, and divided into separate areas for men and women to pray. The main body of the church, to the right of the gallery, is again divided into male and female sections. The latter is the smaller of the two, notable for a frieze of Greek philosophers along one wall, while the screen dividing the male and female portions bears an extravagantly imagined rendering of the Last Judgement. At the far end of the men's chamber, the gilded iconostasis contains scenes from the Book of Genesis (in which Eden contains a dream-like menagerie of exotic animals), and a boldly colourful *pietà*.

The monasteries of Sveta Bogoroditsa and Sveti Nikola

Tracks lead downhill from here to the **Monastery of Sveta Bogoroditsa** at the northwestern end of town, whose church presides over a tranquil courtyard. The church itself (ring the bell in the porch and someone will open it for you) is unremarkable, a product of successive destructions and rebuildings, although it does contain an image of the Virgin renowned for answering the prayers of the sick. It attracts pilgrims throughout the year, with most arriving on the Feast of the Assumption (*Golyama Bogoroditsa*) on August 15, when the icon's power is at its greatest; simple accommodation is available (❸).

To the west, another asphalt road descends towards the **Monastery of Sveti Nikola**, a predominantly modern-looking complex completely refurbished in the 1890s. There's not much to see here, but its tranquil atmosphere is worth savouring and basic accommodation is also available (❶).

Petropavlovski Monastery

From Arbanasi, it's a five-kilometre walk or drive northeast to the tenth-century **Petropavlovski Monastery** (Monastery of Peter and Paul), a foundation built on the site of a Roman fort. The monastery occupies a hilltop site overlooking the town of Lyaskovets, with the gently undulating arable land of the Danubian Plain stretching out beyond. The church and outbuildings are largely unremarkable nineteenth-century affairs, with the restful courtyard garden and great views being the real attractions.

To get there, you can either walk or drive along the asphalt road heading uphill to the southeast from Arbanasi's main square, which takes you along a ridge providing views of Tsarevets; turn left after 3km, then right after another 2km, and the monastery is 200m downhill from here. Alternatively, you could catch the #14 Lyaskovets bus from opposite Veliko Tûrnovo's *Pazar*, alighting at Lyaskovets town park (recognizable by a big white Communist-era memorial on your left). An asphalt track leads uphill to the monastery from here (50min).

Arbanasi practicalities

Despite Arbanasi's proximity to Tûrnovo, both the gradient and the amount of traffic on the road make it an unappetizing, if not downright dangerous, walk – it's easier to take one of the minibuses that depart approximately every two hours from opposite Veliko Tûrnovo's *pazar*, or to take a taxi, which shouldn't cost more than 4Lv. There's a small and very helpful **tourist office**, Val Turs, in the centre just behind an antiques shop (Tues–Sun 8.30am–5.30pm; ⓣ062/602575, ⓔvalturs@vali.bg) which can provide maps and arrange private rooms (❷) and discounted **hotel** accommodation; it also offers horse riding for 24Lv per hour.

Arbanasi has plenty of **hotels** – just off the main square, the *Bolyarska kûshta* (ⓣ062/620484) has small en-suite doubles (❸), larger doubles (❸), and roomy apartments with bath (❹), all with TV and swankily furnished, and breakfast included in the price. Not far up the track opposite the Kostantsaliev House is *Faklite* (ⓣ062/604496; ❷) a renovated 270-year-old house with a small *mehana* in its old wine cellar; further on is *Kûshtata s Raloto* (ⓣ062/620370; ❸) which has simple modern rooms. The *Arbanasi kûshta* (ⓣ062/630074; ❸) is positioned a little way up the track to the left of the *Arbanasi Palace* (see next page) and offers stylish rooms with views of Veliko Tûrnovo. At the top end of the scale and just along from the main square, the comfortable but pricey *Izvora Komplex* (ⓣ062/601205; ❻) offers four-poster beds and leather furniture; most luxurious of the bunch is the *Arbanasi Palace* (☎062/630176; ❼), a former Zhivkov family residence on the southern edge of the village commanding splendid views of the Tsarevets massif immediately below. A brief visit to the timber-ceilinged hotel bar will be sufficient to give you an idea of the former dictator's taste for opulence.

There are plenty of places to **eat and drink** in the village, especially around the main square. Most of the hotels have good restaurants, while the *Piyaka* just before the square and the *Lyulaka* just down from it, are also worth trying for a traditional Bulgarian meal.

Preobrazhenski Monastery and Sveta Troitsa convent

Four kilometres north of Tûrnovo, high in the crags above the main E85 road to Ruse, sits **Preobrazhenski Monastery**, the monastery of the Transfiguration (daily dawn–dusk). Founded in 1360 by Ivan Aleksandûr's Jewish wife who converted to Christianity, the monastery was abandoned during the Ottoman period, then refounded in the 1820s by Tûrnovo guilds, who had to bribe the city's Greek bishop to get a Bulgarian abbot installed here. Dimitûr Sofyaliyata was commisssioned as architect, but after being implicated in Velcho's Plot of 1835 and hanged from the monastery gate, he was replaced by master-builder Kolyo Ficheto. Zahari Zograf was brought in to do the frescoes, until he discovered that the monks were strict vegetarians and refused to work unless he was given meat. The monks relented, issuing him a contract which euphemistically promised the artist food "suited to his delicate stomach".

Finished in the 1860s, the monastery almost looks old enough to be medieval, with a canopy of vines strung between the spartan cells. However Ficheto's elegantly proportioned, enclosed courtyard is sadly no more. Over the last decade repeated rock falls from the cliffs above have destroyed many of the monastery buildings (with more being demolished for safety reasons), although the central **Transfiguration church** still stands. Its south wall bears a remarkable painting of the *Wheel of Life* by Zograf, in which the stages of human existence correspond with allegorical representations of the four seasons. Rose- and green-hued **frescoes** predominate in the porch, with an eye in a circle (traditional symbol of the Holy Ghost) being a recurrent motif, and evil-doers being thrust across a river of fire and strangled by demons in the *Last Judgement*. The upper naos (formerly reserved for married women) contains the obligatory homage to Russia's warrior saints, Gleb and Boris, while the lower naos (where the men prayed) has saints surrounding Christ beneath the dome and submissive dragons flanking its crucifix.

Getting to the monastery is relatively easy: regular buses from Veliko Tûrnovo to Gorna Oryahovitsa pass by the turn-off, 4km north of town, from where a minor road zigzags 3km uphill through a lime forest.

Sveta Troitsa convent

More or less opposite Preobrazhenski on the other side of the valley, the **Sveta Troitsa** (Holy Trinty) **convent** (daily dawn–dusk) sits on a narrow shelf of rock, at the end of a partially asphalted road which begins in Veliko Tûrnovo's Trapezitsa quarter. The road is just about passable by car, although most people opt to walk – a journey of about ninety minutes. Founded as early as the eleventh century, Sveta Troitsa was a monastery rather than a nunnery during the Second Kingdom, when Patriarch Evtimii established a school of translators here. The convent's delicate red-brick church (also built during the nineteenth century by Kolyo Ficheto) is difficult to get access to, but the charming, flower-bedecked courtyard overlooked by sheer cliffs, and the impressive surroundings, make the trip worthwhile.

To get to the convent, leave Veliko Tûrnovo on the Arbanasi road and take a left turn soon after passing the Church of Sveti Dimitûr. Ignore roads leading left towards Trapezitsa train station, but bear left after this, and carry straight on past several decaying factories. Pay no heed to the multicoloured hiking waymarks which tempt you uphill to the right. You could also walk to Sveta Troitsa from Arbanasi, although you'll probably need local knowledge and plenty of time to spare – markings are inadequate, and paths confusing.

South of Veliko Tûrnovo

The mill town of **Gabrovo** is the main urban centre south of Tûrnovo, although it's in the smaller towns and villages, where rural architecture and crafts have been best preserved – notably **Tryavna**, **Bozhentsi** and the museum-village of **Etûra** – that the main attractions lie. Several historic **monasteries**, such as Kilifarevo, Dryanovo and Sokolski, are within easy striking distance of these places. Veliko Tûrnovo, Gabrovo and Tryavna are equally convenient as bases from which to explore the region, and even if you're reliant on **public transport** you'll find that you can reach several destinations in the space of one day-trip. Both Dryanovo and Tryavna are linked directly to Veliko Tûrnovo by train, although continuing to Gabrovo involves a change at Tsareva Livada. Buses, too, are plentiful, with hourly services linking the area's major towns. Less well served by public transport are the little-visited monasteries near the historic town of **Elena** to the southeast, although together they form an easily digestible cluster of rustic sights for those with access to a car.

Travelling onwards to the Valley of the Roses (see Chapter Four) from here involves two of Bulgaria's most scenic mountain routes. The Veliko Tûrnovo–Tryavna rail line winds its way southwards through the densely wooded **Tryavna Pass** (where Petûr and Asen defeated the Byzantine army in 1190, preserving the independence of the Second Kingdom), before joining the Sofia–Burgas line at Dûbovo. If travelling by road, the E85 heads towards the impressive **Shipka Pass** just above Gabrovo (the place to catch buses over the pass), then drops down towards Bulgaria's "rose capital", Kazanlûk.

Kilifarevo Monastery and around

Twenty kilometres south of Veliko Tûrnovo, **Kilifarevo Monastery** was a favourite retreat for the tsars of the Second Kingdom. It was also the site of the famous college established by Teodosii Tûrnovski in 1350, which translated literary works from Greek and Hebrew into Slavonic script, making them legible to scholars far beyond Bulgaria. As many as 800 monks and novices from all over the Slav world were based here at any one time, and the School of Kilifarevo might have achieved parity with the great European universities had it not been burned by the Turks in 1393. Teodosii's successor Patriarch Eftimii was imprisoned by the Ottoman conquerors, but his right-hand man, Grigorii Tsamblak, fled to Russia where he was able to carry on the Kilifarevo tradition, becoming bishop of Moscow and a saint of the Russian Orthodox Church.

Now a nunnery, Kilifarevo was rebuilt during the nineteenth century around a principal church – dedicated to St Demetrius of Salonika – designed by Kolyo

Kilifarevo and the hesychasts

In the fourteenth century, Kilifarevo was one of Balkan Christianity's most important centres, and played a crucial role in spreading one of Eastern Orthodoxy's most characteristic forms of mysticism: **hesychasm**. Taking their name from the Greek word *hesychia*, meaning "stillness", hesychasts believed that silent, solitary meditation, aided by highly ritualized forms of prayer, would eventually lead them to a revelation of the true nature of God. Central to hesychast thinking was the idea that the repetition of certain phrases (such as the mantra-like Jesus Prayer: "Lord Jesus Christ, Son of God, have mercy on me"), uttered while holding one's breath, would lead to the adept being filled with the "Divine Light"; the same light seen by the disciples of Jesus Christ when witnessing his Transfiguration on Mount Tabor. It was a popular doctrine, shrouding Christian belief in a seductive aura of mystery while at the same time holding out the possibility of true religious ecstasy to the really devout. Though the movement's critics found the possibility of seeing the Divine Light all a bit too fanciful, from the 1340s onwards hesychasm became the dominant form of monasticism in the Orthodox world. At a time when both Byzantium and Bulgaria seemed to be in decline and the threat of Ottoman Turkey was beginning to make itself felt, it seemed to offer a measure of spiritual purity and religious renewal.

The leading Bulgarian proponent of hesychasm was **St Theodosius of Tûrnovo** (Sveti Teodosii Tûrnovski), who trained at the Monastery of Paroria in the Strandzha mountains of southeastern Bulgaria before coming to Kilifarevo in 1350 to establish a monastic community of his own. One of the great ecclesiastics of the age, he cultivated links with leading churchmen throughout the Byzantine and Slav world, and played a key part in the Bulgarian state's suppression of the Bogomil heresy (see p.252). Theodosius retired to Constantinople in the 1360s, but his pupil **Euthymius** went on to become patriarch of the Bulgarian Church, where he continued Theodosius' programme of spiritual renewal. Euthymius' main contribution was in the literary sphere, translating the writings of celebrated Byzantine mystics into Old Church Slavonic (the language developed by saints Cyril and Methodius in the ninth century before embarking on the conversion of the Slavs) then distributing them among the monasteries of Eastern Europe. Euthymius' mini-Renaissance was cut short by the Turks, who subdued Bulgaria in 1393, but the fruits of his labours lived on to enrich the spiritual heritage of the Slavs. Today he is known to Bulgarians as **Patriarh Eftimii**, and streets throughout the country carry his name.

Ficheto. The main body of the church contains an iconostasis by Tryavna craftsmen, and a mesmerizing icon (on the opposite wall as you enter) of St John of Rila, painted by Ficheto's contemporary Krûstyu Zahariev. Outside, look out for a small but delicate relief of the Archangels Michael and Gabriel over the yoked south portal. Ficheto's church is tacked on to two older sixteenth-century structures which lie to the rear, the chapels of Sveti Teodosii and Sveto Rozhdestvo Bogorodichno (Birth of the Virgin). Both contain valuable frescoes from the period.

The monastery lies just off the main Veliko Tûrnovo–Stara Zagora road, about 5km south of the village of Kilifarevo. The access road to the monastery is badly signed – look out for the truck stop used by TIR drivers just opposite. Some of the six daily Veliko Tûrnovo–Kilifarevo **buses** serve isolated villages south of Kilifarevo, and may take you near the monastery; otherwise, you'll have to walk from Kilifarevo village, saving yourself a dull and potentially hazardous trudge along the main road by turning left into the village of Natsovtsi after 3km, and following the river upstream to the monastery. Basic accommodation is available (Ⓣ06114/2480; ❶).

The monasteries of Plakovo and Kûpinovo

Seven kilometres to the east of Kilifarevo, in a wooded valley near the commune of Plakovo, lies another monastery, whose superior, Father Sergius, was involved in "Velcho's plot" (see p.245) and tortured to death by the Turks after its discovery. A plaque on the stone fountain in the courtyard of **Plakovo Monastery** commemorates him and his fellow conspirators. Some of the Tûrnovo–Kilifarevo buses continue on to Plakovo; check in Kilifarevo which ones.

Tracks continue 2km beyond Plakovo Monastery to the more impressive **Kûpinovo Monastery**, where the timber verandahs of the monks' cells overlook a courtyard shaded by vines. Sofronii Vrachanski was head monk here before being elevated to the bishopric of Vratsa in 1794, putting the monastery at the forefront of the revival of Bulgarian language and scholarship. The monastery church contains an unmissable *Day of Judgement* painted by Razgrad master Yovan Popovich in 1845, with lurid scenes of the dead emerging from their graves.

Elena and around

Like nearby Kotel and Koprivshtitsa, the nineteenth-century National Revival crafts town of **ELENA**, 40km southeast of Tûrnovo and served by five daily buses, lay far enough away from the centres of Ottoman power for Bulgarian crafts and culture to flourish. The Turks used the town's population to guard the local mountain passes, giving them a measure of autonomy in return, so painters and woodcarvers of nineteenth-century Elena were able to decorate the churches of the surrounding countryside, and patriotic local merchants could finance the restoration of nearby monasteries like Kûpinovo. Although Elena has not been renovated to the same extent as other National Revival towns, the core of nineteenth-century structures grouped around the hilltop church make a visit here more than worthwhile.

Beyond Elena, roads (but no public transport) head east through lonely highland villages towards the wooded **Kotel Pass**, on the far side of which lie the historic settlements of Kotel and Zheravna (see Chapter Four).

The Town

Heading downhill from the bus station then turning left into the main street, the first building of interest you come across is the **House-museum of Ilarion Makariopolski** (officially daily 9am–noon & 1–5pm; 1Lv), located in a walled garden off to the right. Born Stoyan Mihailov in 1812, and later elevated to the Bulgarian bishopric of Constantinople (a post which brought him the honorific title *Makariopolski*), Ilarion was the leader of the Bulgarian Church's battle against Greek control, who eventually persuaded the sultan to sanction an autonomous Bulgarian exarchate in 1870. The house is a lovely timber structure from the late eighteenth century, with vast verandahs overlooking the river on the first floor, where family and guests would sleep on warm summer nights. Chunky local carpets and a child's *lyulka* (hammock-like bed hung from the ceiling) provide a sense of period domesticity.

Beyond lies a bland town square, behind which the cobbled ulitsa Stoyan Mihailovski leads uphill to the **National Revival complex** (officially daily 9am–noon & 1–5pm; 1Lv), grouped around the mid-nineteenth-century church of the Assumption. However the real star of the complex is the much smaller **Church of Sveti Nikola** slightly downhill, a sixteenth-century structure rebuilt in 1804 after being burned by marauding *Kûrdzhali*. Blindingly colourful icons and frescoes crowd a barrel-vaulted space; unremarkable in themselves perhaps, but together creating an overall impression of optimistic, ebullient spirituality. More devotional paintings are on display in the nearby **old school** (*Daskalolivnitsa*), including an 1873 *Last Judgement* displaying the hellish tortures beloved of Bulgarian artists of the period. At the bottom of the hill lies the **Ethnographic Museum**, also known as *Kûmburov han*, a former inn now taken up with displays of local trades and crafts. Characteristic of Elena are the fluffy *guberi* (fleecy rugs) in bright reds and greens, often featuring a tree-like central symbol topped by a star. In the basement loom vast wine vats and a *korab* – a long wooden trough in which the grapes were trodden.

Elena practicalities

Tourism in the town is developing slowly, and **accommodation** is limited to the modern but rather drab *Hotel Elena* on the main square (Ⓣ & Ⓕ06151/3632, Ⓔelena_hotel@abv.bg; ❶), which has simple en-suite doubles and a small restaurant; the smart new *Hotel Central* at ul. Syoyan Mihaylovski 4 (Ⓣ06151/2348, Ⓔhotel_central@elena.val.bg; ❷); or the nearby *turisticheska spalnya Dr Momchilov* at Stoyan Mihailovski 7 (Ⓣ06151/4081 & 3004; 7Lv per person), a traditional-style house offering rickety beds in spartan dorms. For food and drink try any of the cafés around the main square; the *Mehana Rai* **restaurant** just above, or the pleasant *Trukcheva Kûshta* next to the river, both with the usual range of grills and traditional dishes.

Meekovtsi

The cluster of tumbledown houses that makes up the tiny village of **MEEKOVTSI** lies 13km south of Elena, surrounded by wooded hills and barely touched by tourism. Visitors can stay at the *Kandaferi* guesthouse (Ⓣ0887 342 635 or 0887 415 079, Ⓦwww.kandaferi.com; ❶), a cosy family-run pension with its own *mehana* and unique wooden furniture carved by the owners' son. Marked paths of varying length meander through the hills and guests can use them for walking, cycling, or pony trekking. Buses only stop at the village on Fridays and Sundays, so you'll need to take a taxi or phone the *Kandaferi* to collect you from Elena.

Dryanovo and Dryanovski Monastery

Thirty kilometres southwest of Tûrnovo on the main road to Gabrovo, the drab town of **DRYANOVO** is only really of note for its proximity to Dryanovski Monastery, another 4km south. The town's only sights are down to local boy Nikolai Fichev, popularly known as **Kolyo Ficheto** (1800–1881), who is honoured with his own **Historical Museum** at ul. Shipka 82 (daily 8am–noon & 1–5pm; 3Lv) occupying a modern pavilion in the town centre. The most versatile of nineteenth-century Bulgaria's builders, he was responsible for town houses in Tûrnovo, bridges at Lovech and Byala, and numerous churches. Famous for the *Fichevska kobilitsa* (Fichev yoke), the wavy line which characterizes the roof-lines and pediments on all his best works, he often put double-headed eagles and lions on the eastern facade of his buildings, to symbolize the direction from which Bulgaria's liberation – in the shape of Russian power – was expected to come. The museum contains superb scale models of all Ficheto's key works, including the **church of Sveti Nikola**, the original of which lies 200m away on the road to Gabrovo.

Dryanovo's train and bus **stations** are both a couple of blocks east of the main thoroughfare, ulitsa Shipka, although most buses on the Tûrnovo–Dryanovo–Gabrovo route only stop on the main street.

Dryanovski Monastery

Set in a gorge beneath high crags, **Dryanovski Monastery** was chosen as the place from which to launch a local uprising in May 1876, while the fires of rebellion were still smouldering elsewhere after the suppression of the April Rising. Under the leadership of Bacho Kiro and the monk Hariton, several hundred rebels defended the monastery for almost a week against 10,000 Turkish troops rushed from Shumen, whose commander Pasha Faslû offered to spare Kiro if he publicly repented – and hanged him when he refused.

The monastery was pretty much destroyed in 1876 and rebuilt with public donations soon after the Liberation. A fine ensemble of timbered buildings was the result, although once again it's the restful ambience rather than any single architectural feature that makes the place a worthwhile visit. A small **museum** (Mon–Fri 9am–5pm, Sat & Sun 9.30am–4pm) just off the monastery courtyard, displays old photographs of Bacho Kiro and company, as well as an ossuary containing rebel skulls. The museum basement concentrates on Stone-Age pottery and arrowheads discovered in the **Bacho Kiro cave** (April–Oct daily 8.30am–6pm; Nov–March Fri, Sat & Sun 10am–4pm; 2Lv), 500m beyond the monastery at the end of an asphalt path. A small part of the cave interior is floodlit, and there are some interesting curtain-like stalactite formations to admire, but nothing that justifies a special trip.

You can **walk** from Dryanovo to the monastery in about 45 minutes, or take one of the regular Dryanovo–Gabrovo **buses** which stop beside the monastery access road (marked by a big monument to the heroes of the April Rising), from where the monastery lies 1500m downhill. You can also get to the monastery by **train**, alighting at the first stop beyond Dryanovo, the Bacho Kiro halt, and walking the remaining 100m downhill (note that only *pûtnicheski* trains stop at the halt, which amounts to little more than a shed in the middle of the forest and is very easy to miss). The **tourist office** located in an old house above a *mehana* at ul. Stefan Stambolov 7 (Mon–Fri 8am–noon & 2–6pm; ⓣ0676/2436, ⓦwww.dryanovo.com) provides maps and leaflets, and can arrange private rooms in the region. **Hotel** accommodation in the town is limited to the *Contact* (ⓣ0676/4566; ❷) with its clean, basic rooms, though more options can be found in and around the monastery: the *Vodopadi Komplex* (ⓣ0676/2314; ❸) in the monastery courtyard is comfortable enough, while the monastery itself offers double and triple rooms (ⓣ0676/2389; ❶). One kilometre down the road the *Strinava* campsite has small bungalows for ❶, and a little further on the well-positioned *Bacho Kiro turisticheska dom* (ⓣ0676/2332; 7Lv per person) has dorm beds only and a great view of the valley.

Tryavna

The old crafts centre of **TRYAVNA** may be a byword for icon painting and woodcarving, and features no fewer than 140 listed buildings, but it happily lacks the feel of a museum-town. For carless travellers, trains from Tûrnovo or regular buses from Gabrovo provide the best means of **getting there** (travelling by train from Gabrovo entails a change at Tsareva Livada, which makes it quicker to go by bus).

The town's narrow streets are evocative of the nineteenth century: although Tryavna was founded by refugees from Tûrnovo 400 years ago, the oldest buildings all post-date the establishment of an official Guild of Master Builders and Woodcarvers in 1804. Often carved with birds and flowers, the wooden houses in the **old quarter** have an asymmetrical structure that disguises the essential similarity of their interiors. Traditionally, the large room containing the hooded *kamina* (hearth) was the centre of domestic life and led directly to the *chardak* or covered terrace; guests were received in a separate room and household goods stored in the ground-floor *odaya*.

Arrival, information and accommodation

Tryavna is pretty easy to find your way around: turn right out of either the **train** or **bus station**, both north of the centre, and by walking straight on you'll pass most of the town's sights along the way. Tryavna's **tourist office**, just off the main square at ul. Angel Kûnchev 22 (Mon–Fri 9am–noon & 2–5pm; ⓣ0677/2247, ⓔtourinfo-tryavna@globcom.net), sells maps, rents out bikes and organizes accommodation in **private rooms** (❶) and local **hotels**; otherwise try *Kia-Tours* a few doors along at ul. Angel Kanchev 18 (Mon-Fri 9.30am-6pm; ⓣ0677/2303, ⓦwww.kia-tours.hit.bg) which offers much the same service. The most central hotels are the family-run *Familia*, ul. Angel Kûnchev 40 (ⓣ0677/4691; ❸), and the *Zograf* at ul. Slaveikov 1 (ⓣ0677/4970, ⓦwww.bgglobe.net/zograf.html; ❹) offering smart modern accommodation in a large old house. The *Tigûra*, just uphill at ul. Gorov 7A (ⓣ0677/2469; ❷) is a slightly cheaper option, with en-suite rooms and breakfast. Far superior but slightly further out is the *Ralitza*, a huge three-star place up a steep hill on ulitsa Kaleto, and commanding a splendid view over the town (ⓣ0677/ 2262; ❺); occupying a similar position, the *Sezoni* (ⓣ0677/2285; ❺) is a newly built luxury place with an open-air pool. On the opposite hill, facing the *Ralitsa* and *Sezoni* above the town and equally hard to reach, but much better value, is the *Trevenski kut* hotel (ⓣ0677/2033; ❷) with comfortable rooms and a garden.

The north end of town

Most of the northern end of town is modern, although the **birthplace of Angel Kûnchev** at ul. Angel Kûnchev 39 is a prime example of the nineteenth-century Tryavna housebuilder's art. Most of it was the work of Kûnchev's father, Kûncho Angelov Popnikolov, his skilled handiwork revealed in details such as the wooden panels and fitted cupboards lining many of the rooms. Disappointingly, though, only a couple of sparsely furnished upstairs rooms are on show, together with a tiny words-and-photos exhibition on the ground floor. Born in 1850, Kûnchev's patriotism led him to join Belgrade's Artillery School at the age of 17, and later spurn a lucrative job offer to work for Bulgaria's liberation. Sent to assist Levski in constructing the revolutionary underground, Kûnchev had completed two clandestine "tours" by 1872, when he was caught boarding a steamer at Ruse without a passport. Fearful of betraying secrets under torture, he shot himself, crying "Long live Bulgaria!" – in Levski's words, "the most honourable death for justice that should be considered sweetest for every proud Bulgarian of today".

Around the main square

Before long ulitsa Angel Kûnchev hits **ploshtad Kapetan Dyado Nikola**, a set-piece square which retains most of its nineteenth-century character. Dominating the scene is the **clock tower**, a solid stone pillar topped by a half-timbered octagonal structure that supports a dainty wooden bell tower. The **Church of Archangel Michael** (daily 7am–7pm; 1Lv) stands to one side, a low-lying edifice sheltering under the shallow overhang of its slate roof, from which a slender minaret-like tower emerges. Inside, the iconostasis is wonderfully rich and dark, with twelve intricate tableaux surrounding the crucifix and a carved pulpit wound around one of the columns. At the rear of the church, originally founded by the *bolyari* Petûr and Asen to commemorate their successful twelfth-century

Bulgarian house-building rituals

As late as the nineteenth century, there were a number of unusual **customs and rituals surrounding house building** in Bulgaria. It was considered unlucky to build a house near an empty well, an old watermill or a graveyard, and when doubts arose about a prospective site a bowl of water would be left there for bad omens (impurities or clouding) to appear overnight. Before the foundations were laid an animal was slaughtered on the site of the hearth or threshold, and the outlines of the walls were marked by dripping blood as an additional magical precaution. When the house was complete, blessings were shouted and the owners presented the builders with gifts before moving in themselves, preferably on a Monday, Thursday or Sunday at the time of a new moon. By custom, the eldest man would pour water over the threshold and scatter coins and wheat around the hearth in the hope of a future life "as smooth as water", prosperity and full barns. Once he had kindled the first fire with embers from the old family hearth, the woman of the family completed the occupation by breaking a loaf over the flames and hanging up a copper vessel.

rebellion against Byzantium, memorial photographs of the recently deceased are stuck into candelabras, part of the Orthodox forty-day mourning rite which Bulgarians also observe by putting up posters in the streets.

Immediately next door is the **Shkoloto** or old school, its heavy wooden doors leading to a cobbled courtyard surrounded by a timber gallery draped with ivy. On the first floor a gallery devotes itself to sentimental images of Bulgarian womanhood by contemporary Veliko Tûrnovo painter and sculptor Nikola Kazakov, as well as ceramics, sculptures and paintings by her husband, Dimitûr. Also on show is part of the personal collection of Buddhist art belonging to wealthy ex-pat Zlatko Paunov, including sixth-century bronze statues and silver jewellery from Tibet. In another gallery, there's an exhibition of the timepieces imported by middle-class Tryavna families of the nineteenth century.

Between the school and the church, an alley leads to **Raikova kûshta** at Prof. Raikov 1. Originally the home of scientist Pencho Raikov, the "father of Bulgarian chemistry", the house features exhibits on the domestic life of Tryavna's late nineteenth-century middle class, displaying the mass-produced furniture and crockery that had begun to penetrate Bulgaria from the West.

All the **museums** charge 2Lv entrance and have the same opening hours: 9am to 6pm in summer and 8am to 5pm in winter.

Along ulitsa Slaveykov

A bridge leads from the square to the cobbled **ulitsa Slaveykov**, possibly the best-preserved National Revival-period street in all Bulgaria. Unusually for a Tryavna building, the **Daskalov House** at no. 27 has a symmetrical plan with two wings joined by a curved verandah. The rooms inside are brightly carpeted, with arched windows and inbuilt *minderi*, and also contain superb panelled ceilings – sun motifs made from walnut wood, with fretted rays inlaid within a frame decorated with floral and bird shapes. The two ceilings in the first-floor bedrooms are the result of an art contest, arranged by the silk and rose-oil merchant Daskalov in 1808, pitting a master woodcarver, Dimitûr Zlatev Oshanetsa, against his apprentice, Ivan Bochukovetsa. The apprentice, who produced the ceiling known as the "Burgas sun", was reckoned by Daskalov to be the winner, although the Guild of Carvers, who oversaw the proceedings, decided in favour of Oshanetsa. However, they too were impressed with the apprentice's work, which took six months to complete, and declared him a master. Yet more woodcarvings are on show in another upstairs room, which is populated with figures of Bulgarian kings and other leading historical figures, carved by Master Gencho Marangozov during World War I. The ground floor holds a small museum of woodcarving, displaying the products of the State Woodcarving School, established in Tryavna in the 1920s to ensure the craft's survival, and including a reconstruction of a nineteenth-century woodworker's shop.

Further along ulitsa Slaveykov are a couple more exhibitions of works donated by local artists: the **Totyu Gûbenski Picture Gallery** at no. 45, and the **Ivan Kolev Exhibition House** at no. 47. The **Slaveykov Museum** at no. 50, housing the personal effects of the influential writer and teacher Petko Slaveykov, father of the poet Pencho Slaveykov, was closed for major restoration at the time of writing. By heading west from ulitsa Slaveykov, across the rail line and up ulitsa Breza, you'll reach a stairway which climbs to a church-like edifice housing the **Museum of Icon-painting and Woodcarving**. Inside are numerous sumptuous products of the nineteenth-century **Trevnenska shkola** or "Tryavna School" – a guild with a distinctive style of cutting the wood back until acanthus leaves, birds and other favourite motifs were rendered in openwork like lace covering the surface of the iconostasis.

Eating and drinking

There are numerous small **restaurants, cafés and bars** along ploshtad Kapitan Dyado Nikola and along ulitsa Angel Kûnchev. The *Stranopriemnitza*, next to the Kolev house, the *Starata Losa*, opposite the Daskalov house, and the *Zograf mehana* are worth trying for good Bulgarian food in folksy surroundings, while the well-signposted *Maestorût*, just off the main square at ul. Kaleto 7, is an excellent traditional restaurant, regarded by locals as Tryavna's best. Nightlife in town is limited to occasional live music performances in a few restaurants, while the **Slaveikov Days**, held on May 26 and 27 in odd-numbered years, bring together a range of cultural events and festivities.

Bozhentsi

Lying roughly between Gabrovo and Tryavna, **BOZHENTSI**'s cluster of two-storey houses with stone roofs and wooden verandahs gives some idea of the museum-village Tryavna could so easily have become. According to legend, Bozhentsi was founded by survivors of the fall of Tûrnovo, led by the noblewoman Bozhena and her nine sons. During the second half of the nineteenth century, Bozhentsi grew prosperous through the enterprise of its smiths, potters and weavers, and local merchants who traded as far afield as Hungary and Russia.

There are well over a hundred listed buildings in the village, but the main highlights are the **Kûshtata na Doncho Popa**, the early nineteenth-century home of a wool merchant; the **Baba Kostadinitsa House**, a much more humble dwelling which showcases the frugal lifestyle of the rural majority; and the various **workshops** used by village artisans (daily: summer 8am–7pm; winter 8am–5pm; 2Lv entrance and 4Lv for a guided tour in English).

Practicalities

Bozhentsi is an easy **day-trip** from Veliko Tûrnovo or Gabrovo. Privately owned minibuses run from Gabrovo's bus station during the summer, leaving when they have enough passengers. More regular are the Gabrovo–Tryavna buses that call at the *Torbalbuzh* stop about 2km downhill from Bozhentsi. If you're driving, you can approach Bozhentsi from the Dryanovo–Gabrovo road by turning south in the village of Kmetovtsi.

The **rooms** in Bozhentsi's old houses (❶) fill up quickly, so it's wise to book in advance through the **information centre** (Ⓣ067193/363) which sells entrance tickets at the start of the village; alternatively, there are several private hotels in renovated old houses, the largest of them the *Hadjiliev han* (Ⓣ067193/424; ❸). Five kilometres north of Bozhentsi in **Kmetovtsi**, the *Fenerite Hotel* (Ⓣ & Ⓕ 067193/267; ❷), a restored nineteenth-century inn with gallleried courtyard, offers en-suite rooms with satellite TV, and has a **restaurant** serving traditional Bulgarian fare. There are also a couple of traditional-style *mehanas* in Bozhentsi itself.

Gabrovo and around

Long known for producing leatherwork and textiles that earned the town the sobriquet of the "Manchester of Bulgaria", **GABROVO** is the focal point for trips to Bozhentsi, or south to the ethnographic complex at **Etûra** and the nearby **Sokolski Monastery**. The town itself doesn't have a great range of things to do or places to stay, but it's a charmingly laid-back provincial place, and its efficient municipal tourist office is a good place to pick up information on the surrounding region. To the Bulgarians, Gabrovo is primarily known as the home of the **Dom na Humora i Satirata**, the House of Humour and Satire, opened on April Fool's Day 1972 in recognition of the position traditionally occupied by the town in Bulgarian humour. People in every country tell jokes about the supposed miserliness of a particular community, and in Bulgaria the butt of the gags has always been Gabrovo. A **Festival of Humour and Satire** takes place each May, comprising masked carnivals, folk music, animated cartoons, prize-giving and the ritual "cutting off the Gabrovnian cat's tail" (see box below).

The Town

As usual, the more interesting parts of Gabrovo are the older quarters, lying beyond the **Igoto Bridge** on both sides of the River Yantra which carves through the long, straggling town centre. A statue of Gabrovo's legendary sixteenth-century founder, Racho the Blacksmith, stands on a rock in midstream.

Your first port of call if arriving at the nearby bus or train stations, however, will probably be **Dom na Humora i Satirata** (summer daily 9am–6pm; winter Mon-Sat 9am-6pm; 4Lv), standing on the west bank at the northern

Typical Gabrovo jokes

The tight-fisted nature of the citizens of Gabrovo has long been a subject of mirth. According to such **jokes**, *gabrovtsi* invented the one-stotinka coin, gliding, short skirts, narrow trousers, and matchboxes with only one side for striking; they stop their clocks at night and carry their shoes to reduce wear and tear; let a cat down the chimney rather than hire a sweep; and dock the tails of these luckless creatures so they can shut the door a fraction sooner, conserving warmth. One *gabrovets* says to another, "Where's your wedding ring?" "My wife's wearing it this week." Another approaches a taxi driver, asking "How much to the city centre?" to which the driver replies "Two leva – jump in." "No thanks, I just want to know how much I'm saving by walking." Two *gabrovtsi* have a wager on who can give least when the collection plate comes around; the first donates one stotinka, whereupon the other crosses himself piously and tells the sexton, "That was for both of us." And so on ...

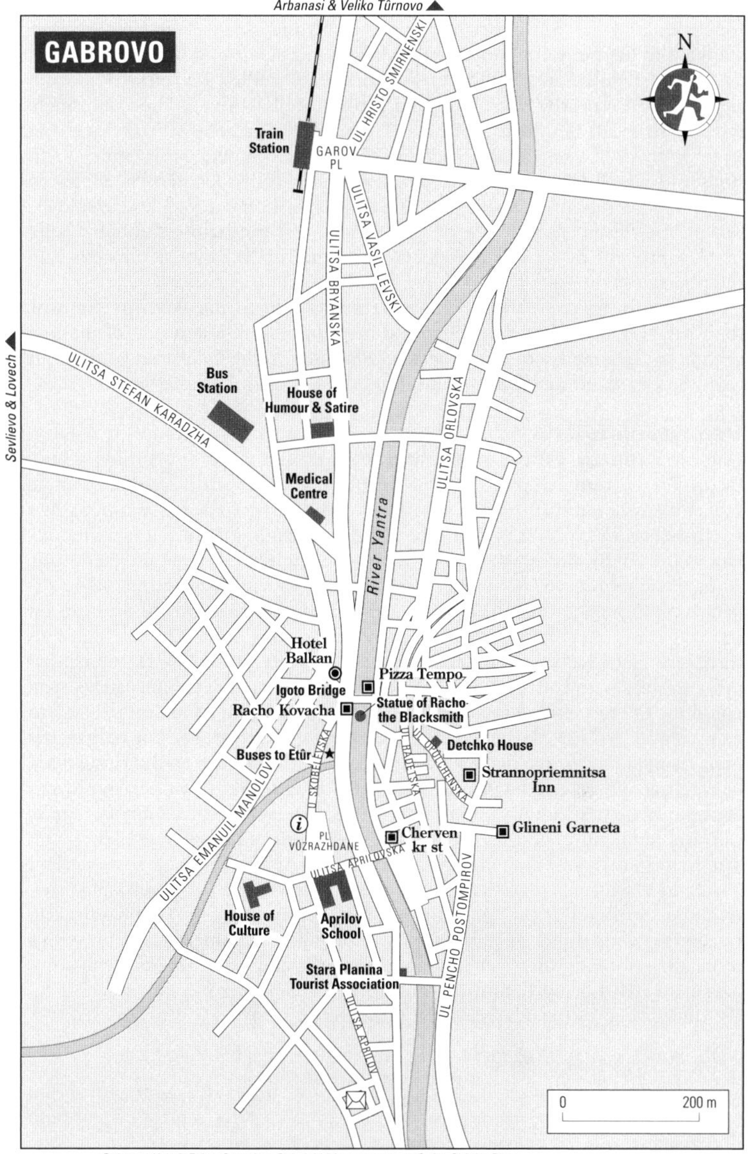

end of the centre. Inside is a massive collection of cartoons, paintings, humorous writings and photos, carnival masks and costumes drawn from scores of countries across the world. Exhibits are changed regularly, but cartoons involving ironic observations of human nature or worthy allusions to global political concerns – such as pollution – seem to be the order of the day. More intriguing, though, are the surreal paintings by Bulgarian and foreign artists – look out for

for striking images by Bulgarian artist Rosen Krustev, such as his *Hunting Scene*, showing miniature jockeys on rocking horses in pursuit of a butterfly.

Gabrovo's central area is on the east bank around ulitsa Radetska. The main sight of interest nearby is the **Detchko House**, at pl. 10 Yuli 2 (also, confusingly, referred to as the "Historical Museum"; irregular hours, but officially Tues–Sat 9am–5pm; 1Lv), a remarkable example of a restored nineteenth-century town house. Originally built for local businessman Hadzhi Detchko in 1835, the house was later used as a school and as a temporary hospital for Russian soldiers during the Russo-Turkish war of 1877. Today, you can traipse through a suite of elegantly furnished rooms which accommodate occasional concerts and temporary exhibitions.

Crossing the river by ulitsa Aprilovska brings you to the **Aprilov School**, founded by Odessa-based merchant Vasil Aprilov in 1835 and one of the first schools in the country to offer a secular education in the Bulgarian language. It also houses a small museum of education, though opening times are irregular.

Practicalities

Gabrovo's **tourist office**, on ploshtad Vûzrazhdane, near the Aprilov school (Mon–Fri 8.30am–7.30pm; Ⓣ & Ⓕ066/20914, Ⓔdid@veda.net), offers a whole range of advice on surrounding attractions and can book **rooms** and **pensions** in Bozhentsi, Etûra and other nearby villages – including Uzana, a small mountain resort 23km southwest. Staff do not speak English, however. Further south, at ul. Raicho Karolev 4, is the Stara Planina Tourist Association (Mon-Fri 9am-5.30pm; Ⓣ066/809161) which can provide information (in English) on the wider area. Accommodation in central Gabrovo is limited to the high-rise, three-star *Hotel Balkan*, ul. Emanil Manolov 14 (Ⓣ066/801054; ❺), which has prim doubles with bath and cable TV, with breakfast included. Alternatively, you could try the more modern *Gabrovo*, located around 4km south, on the way to Etûr (Ⓣ066/801715; ❹), which also has roomy apartments (❺). For **eating**, the *Stranopriemnitsa Inn*, on ulitsa Opûlchenska, serves traditional Bulgarian food in an attractive galleried courtyard, and sometimes features live folk music; not far beyond at ul. Radion Umnikov 5 is the popular, modern *Glineni Garneta* café and restaurant. The *Cherven krûst*, located behind a big white building with a red cross on it just over the bridge from the Aprilov School, has excellent food and service and a big summer garden complete with children's play area. At the eastern end of the Igoto Bridge, *Pizza Tempo* is a fairly standard Italian restaurant, while on the opposite side is *Racho Kovacha*, a small restaurant with a terrace overlooking the river serving sandwiches and other snacks. Numerous pavement **cafés** bring Gabrovo to life during the summer months, especially in the tree-shaded environs of ploshtad Vûzrazhdane.

The Etûra complex

Since Racho the Blacksmith set up his smithy beneath a large hornbeam (*gabûr*, hence the town's name), Gabrovo has been a **crafts** centre, gaining fresh impetus at the beginning of the nineteenth century when waterwheels were introduced from Transylvania. By 1870 the town had more than eight hundred workshops powered by water, making iron and wooden implements, clothing, wool and blankets sold beyond the frontiers of the Ottoman empire; today it produces textiles in quantities exceeded only by Sliven, and half the leather goods in Bulgaria. To preserve traditional skills, Gabrovo has established the museum-village of **ETÛRA** (daily: summer 9am–6pm; winter 8am–5pm; 6Lv entrance, an extra 7Lv for a guided tour), 9km from town on the banks of the Sivek, a tributary of the Yantra.

Strung out along a charming valley, with its clear bubbling stream and rich birdlife, the Etûra complex has the look and feel of a film set, and even though it's artificial, it's nonetheless convincing, and a joy to explore. Traditionally, crafts were inseparable from the *charshiya*, and a **reconstructed bazaar** of the type once common in Bulgarian towns forms the heart of the complex. Throughout much of the day artisans are at work here, hammering blades, throwing pots, carving bowls and the like, and everything they make is for sale, although note that many of the artisans leave an hour or so before the complex officially closes. Even if your interest in crafts is minimal it's difficult not to admire the interiors of the old houses, which achieve great beauty through the skilful use of simple materials. Besides dwellings and workshops, the bazaar includes a couple of places for grabbing a quick drink, including a traditional coffee house, and a bakery selling *lokum* (Turkish Delight), *halva* and other sweet treats. Another section contains a **watermill** (*karadzheyka*) and **hydro-powered workshops** for cutting timber, fulling cloth, and making braid (*gaitan*), wine flagons (*bûklitsi*) and *gavanki* (round wooden boxes).

Etûra is an easy **day-trip** from Gabrovo – or even Veliko Tûrnovo. Take trolleybus #36 from central Gabrovo to the end of the line (the Instrument engineering works), where you change to buses #7 or #8. Should you want to **stay** longer, the *Hotel Perla*, near the eastern entrance to the complex (ⓣ066/801984; ❸), has small en-suite doubles, while right opposite is the much larger *Stranopriemnitsa* hotel (ⓣ066/801831, ⓕ801834; ❹), which has some great views and includes breakfast. The *Stranopriemnitsa* **café-restaurant** is a standard *mehana*, while there's a traditional-style restaurant at the opposite end of the complex, the *Vuzrozhdeiska*, although it's only open the same times as the complex.

Sokolski Monastery

An hour or so's walk southwest of Etûra (there's no public transport, although with a car you can drive there along the track that heads east from the complex), **Sokolski Monastery** perches on a crag above the village of Voditsi. During Ottoman times the monks offered succour to Bulgarian outlaws, putting up the *cheta*, or band, of local *haidut* Dyado Nikola in the 1850s, and providing the local rebels with an assembly point during the Rising of 1876. Nowadays it's a discreet, little-visited place, with rose bushes and privet shrubs laid out in a courtyard dominated by an octagonal stone fountain. The small church, dating from the monastery's foundation in 1832, lies at the bottom of a flight of steps to the right. The dome is supported by an unusually large drum of bright blue – also the dominant colour of the frescoes inside (primitively painted by the original pastor, Pop Pavel, and his son Nikolai), which include a vivid *Dormition of the Virgin* above the main entrance. Simple accommodation is available (❶).

Shumen

Lying midway between Veliko Tûrnovo and Varna, **SHUMEN** is the obvious base from which to explore the historical sites at Madara, Pliska and Preslav. The city itself has a fair share of ancient monuments and memorial houses, not least a spectacular **medieval fortress** that once guarded the road to Preslav. As Turkish Shumla, Shumen was one of the four heavily garrisoned citadel towns that formed the defensive quadrilateral protecting the northern frontier. Although the imposing Ottoman fortifications are no more, the thriving market town that existed within is still present in the shape of one surviving mosque, the **Tombul Dzhamiya**. Modern Shumen presents a good example of what state socialism brought to urban Bulgaria. Well-built, prestigious civic buildings line a showcase main boulevard, just seconds away from neglected, potholed side streets, where single-storey shacks rub shoulders with greying high rises.

Arrival, information and accommodation

Buses #1, #10 or #12 will take you from the **train** and **bus stations** in the east of the city as far as the eastern end of the main drag, bulevard Slavyanski. A ten-minute walk along this largely traffic-free street brings you, via ploshtad Osvobozhdenie which merges into ploshtad Bûlgariya, to ploshtad Oborishte, and the Aristour bureau at ul. Ikonomov 5 (Mon–Fri 9am–5pm; ⓣ054/52509, ⓔmanager@aristour.net) where you can get **private rooms** in centrally located apartments (❶), though these disappear fast in summer. Cheapest of the city's **hotels** is the *Orbita*, 2km west of the centre in the leafy Kyoshkove park (ⓣ054/800286; ❸), with run-down but clean en-suite doubles and triples (❸) and dorm rooms for 25Lv per person. It has by far the most pleasant location making it well worth a short taxi ride from the centre. Moving up in price, the disappointing high-rise *Madara*, pl. Bûlgariya 1 (ⓣ054/57451; ❹), has en-suite rooms, cable TV and breakfast, but is surrounded by derelict buildings and ongoing construction work. More expensive, but far superior, is the *Hotel Shumen*, pl. Oborishte 1 (ⓣ054/800003; ❼), which offers a similar deal but with much higher levels of cleanliness and service, and an indoor pool and sauna.

Aristour also organizes **trips** to all the nearby historical sites, wine-tasting in Preslav, walking tours in the Shumen hills, and riding courses at the horse-breeding centre (see p.273).

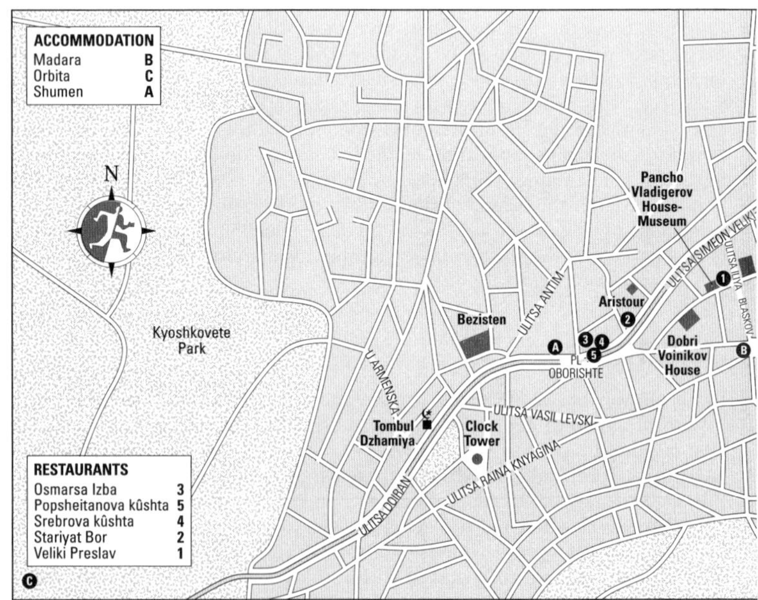

The Town

Walking down **bulevard Slavyanski**, with its blend of stately Central European and smart modern architecture, you'll see a modern red-brick building housing the **History Museum** (Mon–Fri 9am–5pm; 3Lv), and the pick of the region's archeological finds. A Bronze Age site at nearby Smyadovo yielded bone-carved idols of the fourth millennium BC, while the Thracian period is represented by silverware from two local burial sites, at Vûrbitsa and Branichevo, and a reconstructed war chariot. Also here are many of the best medieval artefacts from Pliska and Preslav, the cultural achievements of the latter revealed in the abstract floral patterns adorning the capitals of stone pillars, and in the delicacy of a tenth-century gold necklace.

Along ulitsa Tsar Osvoboditel

A hundred metres beyond the History Museum, ulitsa Layosh Koshut leads down to **ulitsa Tsar Osvoboditel**, and what's left of Shumen's old quarter. Standing at no. 115 is the rarely open **Kossuth House-Museum** (officially Mon-Fri 9am–5pm; 3Lv), a warren of panelled rooms linked by creaking corridors, where the Magyar revolutionary Lajos Kossuth stayed for three months after fleeing Hungary in 1849, before the Turks interned him in Asia Minor. Ten minutes' walk to the east, at Enyu Markovski 42, is **Panaiot Volov Memorial House** (officially Mon-Fri 9am-5pm; 3Lv), home of one of the leaders of the April Uprising who drowned while swimming across the River Yantra to escape Ottoman troops. The house preserves the humble shoemaker's quarters where Volov grew up, while an adjoining pavilion holds the obligatory words-and-pictures display detailing his revolutionary career.

A ten-minute walk west along Tsar Osvoboditel, the **Pancho Vladigerov House-Museum** (Mon–Fri 9am–5pm; 3Lv), honours the Shumen-born pianist

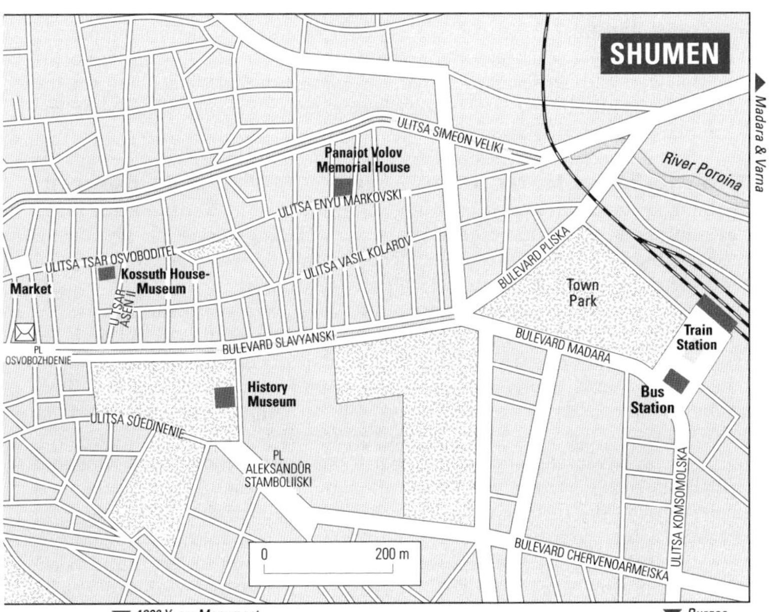

(1899–1978) who made his reputation as Bulgaria's leading composer with stirring patriotic works such as the opera *Tsar Kaloyan* (1936), and the little-performed tribute to the socialist takeover *September 9* (1949). The staff will play a tape of his music as you examine the memorabilia on show, which include Vladigerov's raffish beret and suit, and some fine Chiprovtsi carpets. Further on at no. 157, the **Dobri Voinikov House** (Mon–Fri 9am–noon & 2–6pm; 3Lv) remembers the nineteenth-century author of the plays *Princess Raina* and *Civilization Misunderstood*. There's little to see here save for a series of model stage sets, and photographs of early performers.

The Bezisten and the Tombul Dzhamiya

West of ulitsa Tsar Osvoboditel the broad asphalt sweep of ulitsa Rakovski – subsequently ulitsa Doiran – cuts past two impressive relics of Ottoman Shumla. Sheltering beneath chestnut trees is the **Bezisten**, or covered market, built to cater for the needs of Dubrovnik merchants who established a trading post here in the sixteenth century. Constructed from heavy blocks of stone retrieved from the ruins of Pliska and Preslav, it's now closed, and in need of repair. Dominating the skyline to the west are the proud minaret and bulbous domes of Shumen's main sight, the **Tombul Dzhamiya** (daily 9am–6pm; 2Lv). Built in 1744 on the initiative of Sherif Halil Pasha, a native of Shumen who rose to become deputy grand vizier in Constantinople, the complex aimed to meet both the spiritual and educational needs of the community. A *mektep*, or "primary school", occupied the east wing, while a *medrese* (Koranic school) and *kitaphane* (library) surrounded the cloistered courtyard to the east. This is dominated by the *shadirvan* or "fountain", an eclectic structure mixing Moorish arches with classical, Corinthian pillars. Inside the prayer hall, carpets cover the floor beneath a dome decorated with floral swirls and paintings of the great mosques of the Middle East. Upstairs, a balustraded balcony provides segregated accommodation for female members of the congregation. The mosque was converted into a museum during the Communist era, but has now reverted to its original role, for the benefit of Shumen's considerable Islamic community. The city is once more an important religious centre for the Muslims of north-east Bulgaria, with believers from far and wide annually descending on the Tombul Dzhamiya to celebrate *Kurban bayram*, one of the major festivals of the Islamic calendar (see Basics, p.65).

The medieval fortress and the 1300 Years monument

Shumen is surrounded to the south and west by the **Shumensko plato national park**, a tableland of dense woodland. The most accessible part of it is the **Kyoshkove Park** at the western end of town (a 15-minute walk beyond the Tombul Dzhamiya, or buses #1, #10 or #11 from the train station), where tracks lead up into the hills past the sites of World War II partisan bunkers.

Immediately above Kyoshkove (and reached by walking 2km uphill from the *Shumensko pivo* brewery at the entrance to the park) is the **Stariyat grad** or "medieval fortress" (daily: summer 8.30am-6pm; winter 8.30am–5pm; 3Lv), whose monumental, part-reconstructed walls are reminiscent of Tsarevets in Veliko Tûrnovo. The Thracians were the first to fortify the site, followed swiftly by Romans, Byzantines and Bulgars, but it was during the Second Kingdom that the fortress developed its current monumental shape. Ruins of medieval houses outside the fortress walls show that the slopes of the hill harboured a sizeable civilian population during the thirteenth and fourteenth centuries; they were subsequently driven from their homes and sent to live in the valley by the Ottomans. A small pavilion displaying finds from the fortress stands by the entrance, with an abundant collection of Thracian ceramics and brightly decorated tableware from the Second Kingdom.

Roadways lead east through the forest towards the **1300 Years of Bulgaria** monument (daily: summer 8.30am-6pm; winter 8.30am–5pm; 2Lv) – more easily accessible from a processional concrete stairway which begins just above bulevard Slavyanski, behind the History Museum. A bewildering juxtaposition of khans, monks, *haiduti* and mother heroines rendered in concrete by a sculptor with Cubist inclinations, this extraordinary hilltop structure was unveiled on the nation-state's 1300th anniversary in 1981.

Eating and drinking

At the western end of ulitsa Tsar Osvoboditel, there's a row of four **restaurants** occupying National Revival-style houses – *Popsheitanovata kûshta*, *Stariyat Bor*, *Srebrova kûshta* and *Osmarsa Izba*. The latter has the widest range of Bulgarian specialities, although all four offer good traditional cuisine and plenty of outdoor seating. A little further on is the *Veliki Preslav*, next to the Pancho Vladigerov house, also offering Bulgarian specialities. Moving up in price, the panoramic restaurant on the top floor of the *Hotel Shumen* offers good service and excellent views.

Drinking takes place in the numerous cafés that shelter under the lime and chestnut trees along bulevard Slavyanski, or in the park that runs alongside ulitsa Madara between the town centre and the train station, and the *Ulysses Irish Bar* offers bottled Murphy's and Guinness to those hankering after a pint of stout. The *Hotel Shumen* has a **nightclub** with discos and variety shows.

Around Shumen

The northeastern fringe of the Balkan Range is distinguished by three archeological sites, all easily accessible from Shumen. The ruins of **Pliska** are less interesting to look at than read about, but enough remains of **Preslav** to justify a visit if your taste inclines towards hunky masonry. As for the so-called **Madara Horseman**, the rockscapes all around make up for the eroded face of this unique and ancient bas-relief.

Fifteen kilometres northeast of the city, just beyond the village of Tsarev Brod, is the **Kabiyuk horse-breeding and riding centre**, founded by Ottoman governor Midhat Pasha in the 1860s to provide mounts for the Turkish army. Arabian, English thoroughbred and East Bulgarian (a cross-breed of domestic stock and both the former) horses are raised here, although if you want to view the stables and go on a short ride you'll have to arrange a visit through either Aristour (see p.270) or the *Hotel Shumen*.

Preslav

Founded by Khan Omurtag in 821AD, **VELIKI PRESLAV** acquired the prefix "Great" after it was made the capital of the First Kingdom, during the reign of Tsar Simeon (893–927AD) – although it began to eclipse the original capital, Pliska, at an earlier date. According to contemporary accounts, tenth-century Preslav was the most populous town in the Balkans, with extensive suburbs surrounding a walled inner town containing "large buildings of stone on both sides, decorated with wood". It also held a palace, a Royal School of Translators, the Patriarchate and other "churches ornamented with stones, wood and paintings, marble and copper, silver and gold". Preslav's downfall began when it was captured by the Kievan prince, Svetoslav, causing the Byzantine Empire to respond by razing the town in 972, and although it later revived (the palace was occupied as late as the Asenid dynasty), Preslav never regained its former size and was subsequently surpassed by Tûrnovo. Eventually it was burned down by the Turks, who used the remains to construct their own buildings, including the Tombul Mosque in Shumen.

The Archeological Museum and the ruins

The **ruins of Preslav** are scattered over farmland signposted to the south of the modern town. Head north from Preslav's main square towards the site, which lies beyond the scruffy town park. Beyond the crest of a hill lurks a modern concrete bunker holding an **Archeological Museum** (daily: summer 9am–6pm; winter 9am–5pm; 3Lv), where plans and diagrams can be consulted before venturing out into the relic-strewn fields. The museum displays numerous examples of the ceramic tiles used to decorate the medieval town's buildings showing the swirling abstract patterns which characterized decorative arts during the First Kingdom. Prime pieces from Tsar Simeon's golden age include a unique ceramic icon of St Theodore, and the exceptional gold treasure of Preslav, which is kept locked away in a strong room – a member of staff will open it up for you. Choice pieces include a necklace adorned with enamel plaques showing birds and floral designs and a gold and emerald brooch.

Approaching the ruins from here you'll pass through the northern gate, first sign of the sturdy **walls** which envelop the medieval city – reconstructed with modern stone to something approximating their original height. To the west are the bare ruins of the **palace** where the tsar held court. Further west, the traces of a vast monastery complex lie raked across the hillside. Beyond the south portal on a hillock is the **Zlatna tsûrkva** or "Golden Church", so called because the dome was said to be covered in gold leaf. Several arches, the bulk of its walls and twelve marble columns (some truncated) still remain, although you'll have to study the model in the Archeological Museum to appreciate its true grandeur.

Practicalities

Despite its venerable history, modern Preslav is a grim place, offering few inducements to spend longer than an afternoon, and regular bus services to Shumen happily mean that you don't need to. If you do choose to stay, your best bet is to arrange a **private room** through Aristour back in Shumen (see p.270); otherwise, the only available **accommodation** in the centre is at the somewhat rundown *Hotel Preslav* on the town square (☎0538/2508; ❶), which also has an **Internet** club. A far better option is to walk or take a taxi 3km out of Preslav to the comfortable *Omortagov Most* hotel and restaurant (☎0538/2112; ❶). There are several **cafés** serving light snacks clustered around the bus station and the town square, but, frustratingly, finding anything more substantial to eat isn't easy – try the small unnamed restaurant at ul. Stamboliiski 88, behind the town square.

The Madara Horseman

The most popular destination for excursions from Shumen is the village of **MADARA**, 10km to the east and served by frequent trains, where a range of cliffs show signs of human occupation dating back to the third century BC. The main road through the village leads up to Madara's most famous sight, the mysterious bas-relief known as the **Madara Horseman** (daily: summer 8am–7pm; winter 8am–5pm; 3Lv). Carved into the rockface at a height of 95m, this is so eroded that details are only apparent by the light of a setting sun, but the carving is said to represent a horseman whose mount is trampling a lion with the assistance of a greyhound, while he holds the reins in one hand and a wine cup in the other. Various Greek inscriptions next to the carving provide ambiguous clues to its age: the oldest inscription, recording a debt owed by the Byzantine emperor Justinian II to Khan Tervel, suggests that the Bulgars carved the horseman in the eighth century. However, some scholars believe it is far older than that. The figure, they argue, represents the nameless rider-god of the Thracians, and is of Thracian or Getae origin, the inscriptions merely evidencing that it was later appropriated by Bulgarian rulers.

Around the Horseman

To the right of the relief, a path winds off towards the **Large Cave** (*Golyamata peshtera*) beneath a giant overhang of rock. Beyond is a smaller cave, where flints, bones and pottery were discovered; while just above, you'll catch sight of the remnants of a fourteenth-century **rock monastery**, its crudely dug cells pitting the cliff face.

Not far away you'll find the source of the River Madara where Thracian period plaques and statues honouring the rider-god, Dionysus, Cybele and three water nymphs have been discovered; and remains of an early medieval **grain store** where enormous clay vessels were sunk into the ground to keep cool.

Early Bulgarian remains and the fortress

Most of the early Bulgarian finds are located to the left of the Horseman, where the barest outlines of eighth- and ninth-century churches and monastic complexes lie scattered at the foot of the cliff. Many of the churches were adapted from or built on top of earlier pagan structures – a sign that Madara was an important religious site from the earliest times. Paganism remained ingrained among the Bulgars long after Christianity became the official religion in 865 AD, and although the precise nature of their beliefs remains shrouded in mystery, the discovery of the eighth-century **Old Bulgarian baths** points to the existence of water-based purification rituals.

A rough-hewn pathway works its way up the cliff face to the plateau above. Roughly 500m to the west lies a **ruined fortress** of fifth-century origin, although the remaining walls mostly date from the Second Kingdom. There are also two **tumuli** left by the Getae – who buried their dead in ceramic urns – 300m north of the fortress, but the real attraction is the **view from the plateau**. Roman ruins are scattered about at the foot of the massif, while the surrounding plain is cut off by the Balkans to the south and the Ludogorie hills to the north – where sharp eyes might be able to discern the ruins of Pliska (see p.277) amid the acacia groves.

Practicalities

It's pretty easy to see the site and return to Shumen in the space of a morning or afternoon, though there is **accommodation** near the Horseman, should you wish to stay. The *Madara turisticheska dom* (Ⓣ0531/32091; ❶, dorms 11Lv per person) a few metres up the road from the Horseman is dilapidated but offers superb balcony views of the rocks and the valley; much more comfortable is the *Madarski Konik* hotel (Ⓣ0531/32063; ❷–❸) just below, which also has a restaurant. Bungalows are available for rent at the *Madara* **campsite** (May–Sept; ❶),

The Protobulgarians

Known to English-speaking historians as the **Bulgars**, and to the Bulgarians themselves as the *prabûlgari* or **"Protobulgarians"**, the rulers who founded Pliska and Preslav, and who may have been responsible for commissioning the Madara Horseman, started out as Turkic nomads from the Eurasian steppe.

Originating in western Siberia, the Bulgars coalesced into three warlike tribes in the sixth century: the **Onogurs**, **Utigurs** and **Kutrigurs**. The latter were the first to descend on the Balkans, reaching the walls of Constantinople twice in the mid-500s AD before being pushed back by the armies of Emperor Justinian. For the next half-century Byzantine diplomacy concentrated on keeping these three tribes at each other's throats, in an attempt to preserve the balance of power in the territories north and east of the Black Sea. Eventually, however, they began to cultivate the friendship of the Onogurs, who by this time ruled a swathe of steppe north of the Caucasus mountains – subsequently called **Old Great Bulgaria** by Byzantine chroniclers. The alliance was cemented in 619 with the baptism of the Onogur Khan Organa, together with his son Kubrat in Constantinople.

Nevertheless, things went awry when the Onogurs were driven from their lands by another Turkic tribe, the rapidly expanding Khazars. Kubrat's successor **Asparuh** led his people southwest to the Danube expecting hospitality from his Byzantine ally Emperor Constantine IV, who instead sent an army to prevent Asparuh from crossing the river. The Byzantine attempt failed, and by 681 Constantine was forced to recognize the existence of an **independent Bulgar state** ruled by Asparuh from his capital at Pliska.

The new kingdom was initially limited to the flatlands either side of the Danube, stretching from the Balkan Range in the south to the Carpathians in the north. However, the Bulgars began to expand beyond the Balkan Mountains and put down urban roots under Asparuh's successor, **Khan Tervel**, and the centuries-old culture of these Turkic-speaking steppe dwellers began to die out. An aristocratic elite ruling over a population of Thracians and Slavs (the latter, valued by the Bulgars as frontier settlers, became increasingly numerous), the Bulgars gradually lost their separate ethnic identity and became assimilated by their subjects. The process was confirmed by Tsar Boris's conversion to Christianity in 865 and the suppression of paganism that followed – many of the old Bulgar families, unwilling to break with the old faith, were simply wiped out.

Little is known about the beliefs and customs of the Bulgars. Byzantine chroniclers have provided us with a few scraps, telling us that they worshipped their ancestors, practised shamanism, sacrificed steppe wolves in times of trouble, and probably indulged in polygamy. Some Turkic-speaking Bulgars still exist, the so-called **Volga Bulgars** who survive in isolated pockets south of Kazan in Russia. They converted to Islam in the tenth century and enjoyed independent statehood until the thirteenth, when they were submerged beneath the advance of their fellow Muslims, the Tatars.

about 200m to the south, where you can also pitch tents for the same price. As for **eating** and **drinking,** light snacks are offered in Madara village at the *Mundaga* bar on the right before the railway crossing, as well as at the café and restaurant just outside the complex.

Pliska

Ten kilometres north of Madara, the ruins of **Pliska** are less well preserved than those in Preslav, but in its heyday during the First Bulgarian Kingdom (681–1018AD), Pliska was a sophisticated and important settlement, covering

23 square kilometres and protected by citadels on neighbouring hills. It was sacked by the Byzantine emperor Nicephorus in the early 800s, but retained its status as the capital, and it was to Pliska that the disciples of Cyril and Methodius, Naum and Kliment, came in 885 to help spread the Slav alphabet. Pliska's days of glory were over by 900, after Tsar Boris I had come out of monastic retirement to stamp out a return to paganism sponsored by his son Vladimir – one of Boris's acts was to move the capital to Preslav in order to make a fresh start.

The ruins

The ruins (entered by a minor road which runs 3km eastwards from the village of Pliska) still occupy a considerable area, although most of the buildings have been reduced to low walls. As you can see from the reconstruction in the **museum** (daily 9am–5pm), Pliska originally had three lines of defences: a ditch, behind which was the outer town (with workshops and basic dwellings), a stone wall with four gates, surrounding the inner town, and finally a brick rampart around the so-called Little Palace. What remains of the former Royal Basilica (a few reconstructed walls and column fragments) lies a further 2km beyond the entrance to the ruins at the end of an asphalt track, an impressive but poignant sight stranded among corn fields.

Practicalities

Unless you have a car, **getting to Pliska** from Shumen is time-consuming, and only really worth the effort if you have a strong enthusiasm for First-Kingdom remains. Regular buses travel from Shumen to the industrial town of Novi Pazar, 8km southeast of Pliska, from where four daily buses make their way to the village itself; from here it's still a thirty- or forty-minute walk. *Nadezhda Business Club*, clean and friendly though less upmarket than its name suggests, is just off Pliska's main square and serves food and drink till 1am.

The Ludogorie

North of Shumen, the low-lying **Ludogorie hills** separate the Balkan Range proper from the flatter terrain of the Danubian Plain and the Dobrudzha beyond. The region harbours a large Muslim population of Turkish and Tatar descent, although it's a predominantly rural area with few worthwhile urban centres. The main town, **Razgrad**, is of limited appeal, although quieter **Isperih**, further northeast, is the gateway to one of Bulgaria's most compelling off-the-beaten-track destinations, **Sveshtari** – famous for its **Thracian tombs** and the Muslim holy site of **Demir Baba Tekke**.

Razgrad is served by plenty of intercity **buses** from Shumen and Ruse, as well as Ruse–Varna **trains**. Isperih is more tricky to get to, with less frequent buses departing from Ruse, Razgrad, Shumen, Dobrich and Varna. It also lies on a branch line which leaves the Ruse–Varna rail route at Samuil. Services along this route are sparse, but there is at least one through train from Sofia to Isperih a day.

Razgrad

Situated midway between Shumen and Ruse, **RAZGRAD** sprawls messily around the banks of the Beli Lom. Since the Liberation in March 1878, the narrow lanes and artisans' stalls that characterized the town during Ottoman times have gradually succumbed to modern urban planning. Apart from a restored *Varosh* quarter north of the river, where a succession of whitewashed National Revival-style houses provide homes for various artists' and writers' unions, Razgrad remains fairly lacklustre, largely because its one great attraction – the seventeenth-century **Ibrahim Pasha mosque** – looks set to remain closed for renovation for many years to come. An imposing block of heavy masonry topped by a graceful dome and tapering minaret, it's a lasting tribute to the skills of its Albanian and Bulgarian builders – and to the Turkish governor Ibrahim, who commissioned it in 1614.

Razgrad's only other sight, lying east of town on the Shumen road, just beyond a large pharmaceutical factory, is the remains of **Abritus**, the fortified Roman town that guarded the road between the Danube and Odessos (now Varna) on the Black Sea. Part of the walls that once surrounded the town (originally standing 12–15m high) can be seen by the roadside, while near the site of the town's eastern gate stand the foundations of the so-called **Peristyle building**, a 23-room complex grouped around a columned courtyard, once used by shopkeepers and artisans. Signs in English describe the outdoor artefacts and a small, irregularly open **museum** at the site displays pottery fragments and grave inscriptions, plus a collection of bronze tablets depicting the variety of deities – ranging from familiar Greco-Roman figures such as Zeus and Hera to more exotic rider-gods and mother goddesses from the Middle East – worshipped by the cosmopolitan bunch of troops used to garrison the area. The museum's most valuable treasure – a gold drinking cup in the form of a winged horse – is too valuable to be on open display, and remains locked in a strongroom.

Practicalities

Razgrad's **train station** lies 5km north of town: although all trains are met by buses into the centre, it's not the most convenient point of arrival. The **bus terminal** is on the eastern edge of town, within walking distance of both the Ibrahim Pasha mosque (about 15min west) and the ruins of Abritus (about 15min east). Razgrad has a couple of acceptable **hotels** if you get stranded: the basic two-star *Central*, ul. Beli Lom 40 (Ⓣ084/660919; ❸), and the towering, ziggurat-like, three-star *Razgrad* on ulitsa Zheravna, above the main square (Ⓣ084/660801; ❹). The hotel has a 24-hour **Internet club,** a restaurant, and a sixteenth-floor bar and nightclub (daily 6pm-4am) that's well worth a visit for the stunning panoramic views from its terrace. Plenty of **cafés** and a couple more clubs cluster around Razgrad's main square.

Isperih

Forty kilometres northeast of Razgrad, **ISPERIH** is a sleepy market town lying between gently undulating pastures. It has a pleasant town centre splashed with the usual pavement cafés, and an animated Friday-morning **market** which attracts villagers from all over the Ludogorie. However, the town's importance to travellers is really as a jumping-off point for the historical sites around Sveshtari, 7km northwest (see opposite).

Head downhill from Isperih's **bus station** to reach the town centre, where you turn left then bear left past a small park to find the administrative building of the **town museum** (Mon–Fri 9am–5pm; Ⓣ08331/5619; 2Lv) which houses an exhibition covering the region's history (in Bulgarian). Staff can book **private rooms** in nearby village houses (❶), most of which are in Malûk

Porovets (served by infrequent buses), a rustic spot 8km northwest of town on the Ruse road. Clean and basic **accommodation** can be found at the *Isperih turisticheska dom* on ul. Valentina Tereshkova 6 (☎08331/2261; ❷), while somewhat more upmarket and at the other end of town is the *Alen Mak* hotel on ul. Vucha 1 (☎08331/2359; ❹).

Sveshtari

One kilometre beyond **SVESHTARI** lies what is arguably the finest **Thracian tomb** yet discovered in Bulgaria. Found in 1982 in a mound of earth known locally as **Ginina Mogila**, it is the largest of a group of 26 *mogili* (tumuli) lying about 2km beyond the western fringes of the village. The "Royal tomb", as it's known, dates from the third century BC, and is composed of an antechamber and two mortuary chambers, intended for a local chieftain and his wife, while the decoration indicates a melding of Thracian and Hellenistic religious elements. Above the doorway is a wonderful frieze, adorned with a bull's head motif, and a series of caryatids runs along the walls, their arms upraised in a gesture of worship. The whole is encased in a protective shell and is open to visitors. Two more tombs, for the time being known simply as **tomb #12** and **tomb #13**, have been discovered near Ginina Mogila, and a much larger mound (named **Omurtag** after the Bulgar khan who was once thought to be buried here) is currently being excavated nearer to the village and was not open to the public at the time of writing. The **Sveshtari Mogili information centre** at the site (Wed–Sun 9.30am-5pm, closed Dec–Feb; ☎08332/2579) runs regular tours of the three main tombs in Bulgarian, English or German for 10Lv per person.

Archeologists believe that as many as five necropolises were in use around Sveshtari, comprising more than 100 *mogili* in total. Some theories suggest that the configuration of the tombs either mirrors the constellations, or symbolizes the holy trinity of the Thracians, while ruins elsewhere in the vicinity have led many scholars to identify the Sveshtari neighbourhood with **Hellis**, capital of the **Getae** (see overleaf). Cracks in some of the tombs suggest that an earthquake hit the area sometime in the second century BC, probably causing the abandonment of the city.

Getting to Sveshtari

It's too far to walk from Isperih to Sveshtari, so you'll have to either arrive by car (on leaving Isperih, follow signs to Tutrakan), or take the Isperih–Sveshtari bus that runs every couple of hours. To **get to the tombs** and the information centre, take a left turn out of Isperih, past the Omurtag Mogila on your left, and into a grove of trees – Ginina Mogila is over to the right. Continuing along the road brings you **to Demir Baba Tekke** (see below) after about 2km, then rejoins the Isperih–Ruse road just north of the village of Malûk Porovets.

The Thracian Tomb

The most striking aspect of the **Thracian tomb** is its small size – visiting it is a low-key, almost intimate, experience, and how much you get out of it will depend on your enthusiam for ancient remains. The tomb itself, thought to have been built in the late fourth or early third century BC, is entered via a corridor lined with well-cut slabs leading to three chambers united by a semi-cylindrical vault; the central one is occupied by two stone couches on which lie a Thracian king and his wife (five horses were buried in the antechamber

The Getae

It's hoped that examination of the remains found in the Sveshtari tomb will shed new light on the civilization of **the Getae**, an important Thracian tribe who inhabited both banks of the lower Danube in classical times. Ancient authors disagreed on whether to classify the Getae as Thracians or as Dacians (who lived north of the Danube in what is now Romania), although it's safe to assume that all these groups came from the same ethnic roots.

Thucydides alluded to their skill as horsemen, and they proved more than a handful for successive invaders – from Darius' Persians in the fifth century BC to the Romans in the first. In 335 BC **Alexander the Great** chased the Getae north of the Danube and destroyed some of their settlements, but failed to subdue them. His successor, Lysimachus, was captured by Getae ruler Dromichaetes in 292 BC, only to be lectured on the value of peace and sent home. However, their period of greatest glory came in the first century BC, when King **Burebista** presided over a short-lived Danubian empire which exercised control of the whole western seaboard of the Black Sea – from what is now the Ukraine in the north to Apollonia (present-day Sozopol) in the south.

Evidence suggests that the Getae honoured a trinity of deities comprising mother earth, sun and moon, and, indeed, items of treasure recovered from the Sveshtari tombs were often found positioned in symbolic groups of three. A sceptical Herodotus relates how the Getae believed they were immortal, and worshipped a certain **Zalmoxis** (thought to be a north Balkan version of Orpheus; see p.369), who hid himself in an underground chamber for several years before re-emerging, much to the surprise of his contemporaries, to proclaim that he had died and come back to life again. Herodotus also tells of how the Getae sent "messengers" to Zalmoxis every five years by choosing a suitable courier, then tossing him onto a forest of upturned spear-points.

to ensure them a mount in the afterlife). The ten stone caryatids and Doric semi-columns that line the tomb's walls show obvious Hellenistic influences, though their sturdy upraised arms and full skirts suggest aspects of the Thracian mother goddess. At one end of the chamber, you can discern faint traces of a wall painting depicting a mounted horseman – presumably the deceased – being offered a wreath by a female deity, another possible representation of the mother goddess.

Demir Baba Tekke and Hellis

Beyond the tomb, the road continues through a wooded valley, past an (unsigned) parking and picnic area, where a path leads downhill towards **Demir Baba Tekke**, a sixteenth-century Muslim shrine built on the grave of semi-legendary holy man Demir Baba. The *tekke* itself is a simple structure, a seven-sided tomb-cum-temple topped by a dome, but is accorded an other-worldly grandeur by the limestone cliffs which rear up immediately behind. A Neolithic settlement has been discovered by the **Pette Pûrsta spring** at the foot of the cliffs, and the site was subsequently home to a Thracian sanctuary, so the place's importance as a spiritual centre predates the arrival of Islam in the fourteenth century.

The *tekke* is sacred to the **Aliani** (see box opposite), a Muslim group whose rituals are open to the influence of the neighbouring Christian community, and both Aliani and Christian families visit the *tekke* on key holy days to picnic and dance to impromptu folk music. The most important dates are March 22 (*Chetirideset mûchenitsi* or Forty Martyrs' Day), May 6 (*Gergyovden* or St George's Day to the Christians; the spring festival of *Hidrelez* to the Aliani), August 2 (*Ilinden* or St Elijah's Day, adopted by the Aliani as a midsummer festival), and a hastily improvised autumnal date to mark the end of the harvest. People come here all year round to perform certain **rituals**: strips of cloth are tied to trees or the bars of the *tekke* windows to ward off evil, and items of female underwear are passed through a hole in a stone in the courtyard to ensure fertility. Inside the *tekke*, pilgrims lay presents (socks, handkerchiefs or small pieces of embroidery) on the tomb of Demir Baba, chant prayers and light candles.

Behind the *tekke*, a path leads up the side of the cliff to emerge on the plateau above, where the scant remains of Thracian stone circles and walled sanctuaries present further evidence that the territory around Sveshtari was of great religious significance to the ancient people.

Shortly after Demir Baba Tekke on the road to Sveshtari village, and currently under excavation, the remains of the ancient walled city of **HELLIS** (fourth–third century BC), destroyed by an earthquake around 250 BC, emerge from the roadside. The estimated 3000 occupants of this once thriving city are thought to have been the Getae who were responsible for the neighbouring tombs at Sveshtari. A small but informative exhibition (in English) is housed next to the site.

Practicalities

The nearest **accommodation** to the tombs is in private rooms in the village of Malûk Porovets (booked through the museum in Isperih; see p.278), or at the basic *Ahinora* chalet, just up the road from the picnic area near Demir Baba (Ⓣ08331/4750), with dorm beds for 10Lv a night. There are a couple of **food stores** (*hranitelni stoki*) in Sveshtari village as well as a small **hotel** above the *Dani* café with two comfortable double rooms (Ⓣ0888/205249; ❷), but the only **restaurant** in the vicinity is the *Ahinora*'s ground-floor *mehana*.

The Aliani

Many of the Muslim communities of the Ludogorie are **Aliani** (known to the Turks as *Kizilbazi* or "red-heads"), a heterodox group who, like the Shiites, claim spiritual descent from Ali, the Prophet's son-in-law. Originally from Iran and Azerbaijan, the Aliani were distrusted by orthodox Sunni sultans, who had them forcibly resettled in the Balkans in order to serve the Ottoman empire as frontier troops. Mixing traditional Islamic beliefs with elements of Sufi mysticism and pre-Islamic Iranian sun worship, the Aliani exerted a strong influence over dervish orders, notably the powerful Bektashi, a connection which helped protect the Aliani from outright persecution. The Aliani of northeastern Bulgaria shunned links with Sunni Muslims, but entered into a symbiotic relationship with their Christian Bulgarian neighbours, sharing customs, superstitions and rites. In the early fifteenth century, an Aliani leader from Silistra, Sheikh Bedredin Simavi, began preaching the equality of all the sultan's subjects, and led a combined Muslim-Christian revolt against the Ottoman feudal order. It took four years before the rebellion was stamped out.

Today the Aliani live in Sveshtari and several other villages between Isperih and the Danube. They don't have mosques in the traditional sense, preferring to meet for prayers in the house of a leading community member, and Aliani women don't wear the veil. They also have relaxed attitudes towards alcohol, and *rakiya* plays an important part in the rites conducted at Demir Baba.

Travel details

Trains

Berkovitsa to: Boichinovtsi (4 daily; 1hr); Montana (4 daily; 45min).
Boichinovtsi to: Berkovitsa (4 daily; 1hr); Vidin (4 daily; 2hr 30min).
Dimovo to: Boichinovtsi (5 daily; 2hr).
Dobrich to: Kardam (4 daily; 1hr 15min); Sofia (3 daily; 9hr); Varna (2 daily; 2hr).
Gabrovo to: Tsareva Livada (7 daily; 30min).
Gorna Oryahovitsa to: Pleven (12 daily; 1hr 30min); Ruse (10 daily; 2hr 30min); Shumen (9 daily; 1hr 30min); Sofia (8 daily; 4hr 30min); Tûrgovishte (1 daily; 2hr); Veliko Tûrnovo (10 daily; 30min).
Isperih to: Samuil (3 daily; 45min); Silistra (3 daily; 1hr 30min); Sofia (1 daily; 12hr).
Kardam to: Dobrich (3 daily; 1hr 15min).
Levski to: Lovech (6 daily; 1hr 30min); Pleven (7 daily; 30min).
Lovech to: Levski (6 daily; 1hr 30min); Troyan (2 daily; 1hr 10min).
Montana to: Berkovitsa (4 daily; 45min).
Pleven to: Gorna Oryahovitsa (14 daily; 1hr 30min); Levski (hourly; 30min); Ruse (4 daily; 3hr 30min); Shumen (hourly; 4hr 30min); Sofia (10 daily; 3hr); Varna (5 daily; 5–6hr).
Ruse to: Gorna Oryahovitsa (6 daily; 2hr 30min); Ivanovo (5 daily; 30min); Pleven (4 daily; 3hr 30min); Ruse (1 daily; 3hr); Samuil (5 daily; 1hr 30min); Sofia (4 daily; 7hr); Varna (3 daily; 3hr 30min).
Samuil to: Isperih (3 daily; 45min); Ruse (5 daily; 1hr 30min); Silistra (3 daily; 2hr 30min).
Shumen to: Gorna Oryahovitsa (9 daily; 2hr); Kaspichan (8 daily; 40min); Pleven (5 daily; 3hr 30min); Plovdiv (1 daily; 4hr 30min); Sofia (4 daily; 7hr); Varna (9 daily; 1hr 30min).
Silistra to: Isperih (3 daily; 1hr 30min); Samuil (3 daily; 2hr 30min).
Sofia to: Cherepish (6 daily; 2hr); Eliseina (6 daily; 1hr 30min); Gorna Oryahovitsa (6 daily; 4hr 30min); Lakatnik (7 daily; 1hr); Lyutibrod (6 daily; 2hr); Pleven (hourly; 3hr); Ruse (4 daily; 7hr); Vidin (4 daily; 5–7hr); Zverino (7 daily; 1hr 30min).
Svishtov to: Levski (4 daily; 1hr 30min); Troyan (3 daily; 5hr).
Tûrgovishte to: Gorna Oryahovitsa (5 daily; 2hr).
Tryavna to: Tsareva Livada (11 daily; 15min).
Tsareva Livada to: Gabrovo (6 daily; 30min); Gorna Oryahovitsa (3 daily; 1hr); Plovdiv (1 daily; 3hr); Ruse (5 daily; 1hr); Stara Zagora (3 daily; 2hr); Tryavna (6 daily; 15min); Tulovo (6 daily; 1hr 30min); Veliko Tûrnovo (9 daily; 50min).
Veliko Tûrnovo to: Dryanovo (6 daily; 30min); Gorna Oryahovitsa (6 daily; 30min); Tsareva Livada (8 daily; 50min).
Vidin to: Boichinovtsi (4 daily; 2hr 30min); Sofia (4 daily; 5–7hr).

Buses

Belogradchik to: Lom (4 daily; 1hr 30min); Montana (1 daily; 1hr 15min); Oreshets (4 daily; 30min); Rabisha (2 daily; 30min); Vidin (4 daily; 1hr 45min).
Berkovitsa to: Montana (13 daily; 30min); Vûrshets (3 daily; 40min); Vratsa (1 daily; 1hr 30min); Sofia (10 daily; 2hr 20min).
Botevgrad to: Pleven (1 daily; 2hr); Sofia (hourly; 1hr).
Dobrich to: Albena (every 20min; 40min); Balchik (every 30min; 1hr); Durankulak (3 daily; 2hr 30min); Isperih (2 daily; 2hr); Kavarna (hourly; 1hr 30min); Ruse (2 daily; 4hr); Shumen (2 daily; 2hr 15min); Silistra (8 daily; 2hr 15min); Sofia (4 daily; 7hr); Varna (every 30 min; 50min).
Elena to: Veliko Tûrnovo (4 daily; 1hr 15min).
Gabrovo to: Bozhentsi (3-4 daily; 20min); Burgas (4 daily; 5hr); Dryanovo (hourly; 50min); Lovech (7 daily; 1hr 30min); Kazanlûk (9 daily; 2hr); Pleven (7 daily; 2hr); Plovdiv (2 daily; 3–4hr); Sevlievo (hourly; 30min); Sofia (9 daily; 4hr); Stara Zagora (6 daily; 2hr 40min); Troyan (1 daily; 2hr); Tryavna (hourly; 50min); Varna (2 daily; 4hr); Veliko Tûrnovo (hourly; 1hr).
Isperih to: Dobrich (2 daily; 2hr); Gorna Oryahovitsa (1 daily; 2hr 30min); Ruse (2 daily; 2hr); Shumen (2 daily; 1hr 30min).
Kozlodui to: Lom (2 daily; 1hr); Lovech (2 daily; 3hr); Pleven (2 daily; 3hr); Sofia (1 daily; 3hr); Vratsa (4 daily; 2hr 30min).
Lom to: Belogradchik (4 daily; 1hr 30min); Kozlodui (2 daily; 1hr); Oryahovo (2 daily; 2hr); Vidin (5 daily; 45min).
Lovech to: Kazanlûk (1 daily, 3hr); Pleven (hourly; 40min); Sevlievo (5 daily; 30min); Sofia (7 daily; 3hr); Teteven (4 daily; 2hr); Troyan (hourly; 1hr); Veliko Tûrnovo (1 daily; 2hr); Vratsa (1 daily; 2hr 30min).
Montana to: Belogradchik (1 daily; 1hr 15min); Berkovitsa (13 daily; 30min); Chiprovtsi (7 daily; 50min); Kopilovtsi (4 daily; 1hr 15min); Lopushanski Monastery (4 daily; 45min); Vûrshets (1 daily; 1hr); Vidin (1 daily; 3hr); Vratsa (6 daily; 40min).
Novi Pazar to: Shumen (7 daily; 1hr).
Oryahovo to: Lom (2 daily; 2hr); Sofia (2 daily; 3hr); Vratsa (10 daily; 2hr 15min).

Pleven to: Belene (4 daily; 1hr 30min); Gabrovo (6 daily; 3hr); Lovech (hourly; 40min); Oryahovo (3 daily; 2hr 30min); Nikopol (4 daily; 1hr 15min); Svishtov (hourly; 1hr 15min); Teteven (2 daily; 2hr 30min); Troyan (1 daily; 1hr 30min); Veliko Tûrnovo (Mon–Fri only, 1 daily; 3hr 30min); Vidin (1 daily; 4hr); Vratsa (1 daily; 2hr 15min).
Rabisha to: Belogradchik (2 daily; 30min).
Ruse to: Byala (2 daily; 1hr); Dobrich (2 daily; 4hr); Isperih (2 daily; 2hr); Pleven (1 daily; 2hr 30min); Razgrad (4 daily; 1hr 15min); Shumen (2 daily; 2hr 15min); Silistra (10 daily; 2hr 45min); Sofia (12 daily; 5hr); Svishtov (hourly; 1hr 30min); Tutrakan (12 daily; 1hr 20min); Varna (2 daily; 3hr 45min).
Sevlievo to: Lovech (5 daily; 30min).
Shumen to: Burgas (5 daily; 3hr); Dobrich (2 daily; 2hr 15min); Novi Pazar (6 daily; 1hr); Preslav (8 daily; 30min); Razgrad (5 daily; 1hr); Ruse (6 daily; 2hr 15min); Sofia (2 daily; 5hr 30min); Silistra (3 daily; 3hr); Varna (hourly; 2hr).
Silistra to: Alfatar (hourly; 45min); Dobrich (8 daily; 2hr 15min); Ruse (10 daily; 2hr 45min); Shumen (3 daily; 3hr); Sofia (4 daily; 7hr); Tutrakan (12 daily; 1hr 20min); Varna (6 daily; 3hr 30min).
Sofia *Avtogara Poduyane* to: Botevgrad (hourly; 1hr); Etropole (Mon–Sat 7 daily; Sun 4 daily; 1hr 30min); Pravets (4 daily; 1hr); Teteven (3 daily; 2hr 20min); Troyan (Mon–Sat 2 daily; Sun 3 daily; 3hr). *Avtogara Sofia* to: Dobrich (4 daily; 7hr); Gabrovo (2 daily; 3hr 30min); Lovech (1 daily; 3hr); Ruse (12 daily; 5hr); Shumen (6 daily; 6hr); Silistra (4 daily; 7hr); Svishtov (1 daily; 4hr 30min); Veliko Tûrnovo (8 daily; 4hr); Vidin (7 daily; 4hr); Vratsa (hourly; 2hr).
Svishtov to: Ruse (hourly; 1hr 30min); Veliko Tûrnovo (3 daily; 2hr 45min).
Teteven to: Lovech (3 daily; 2hr); Pleven (1 daily; 2hr 30min); Ribaritsa (hourly; 30min); Sofia (4 daily; 2hr).
Troyan to: Apriltsi (4 daily; 1hr); Cherni Osûm (hourly; 40min); Chiflik (5 daily; 45min); Lovech (hourly; 1hr); Shipkovo (5 daily; 45min); Sofia (4 daily; 3hr).
Tryavna to: Gabrovo (every 30min; 50min).
Veliko Tûrnovo to: Burgas (5 daily; 4hr 30min); Elena (4 daily; 1hr 15min); Gabrovo (11 daily; 1hr); Kazanlûk (1 daily; 2hr 30min); Kilifarevo (6 daily; 50min); Lovech (4 daily; 2hr); Plovdiv (2 daily; 4hr 30 min); Ruse (7 daily; 1hr 30min); Sevlievo (4 daily; 1hr); Sofia (hourly; 4hr); Svishtov (7 daily; 2hr 45min); Varna (hourly; 5hr).
Vidin to: Belogradchik (2 daily; 1hr 45min); Kula (hourly; 45min); Lom (8 daily; 45min); Montana (1 daily; 3hr); Pleven (1 daily; 4hr); Sofia (7 daily; 4hr 30min).
Vratsa to: Berkovitsa (1 daily; 1hr 30min); Kozlodui (4 daily; 2hr 30min); Mezdra (every 40min; 20min); Montana (6 daily; 40min); Oryahovo (10 daily; 2hr 15min); Pleven (2 daily; 2hr 15min); Sofia (hourly; 2hr); Zgorigrad (Mon–Sat 12 daily; Sun 7 daily; 20min).

International trains

Gorna Oryahovitsa to: Bucharest (3 daily; 5–6hr); Budapest (1 daily; 18hr); Istanbul (1 daily; 13hr); Kiev (1 daily; 36hr); Moscow (1 daily; 48hr); Thessaloniki (1 daily; 13hr).

The Sredna Gora and the Valley of the Roses

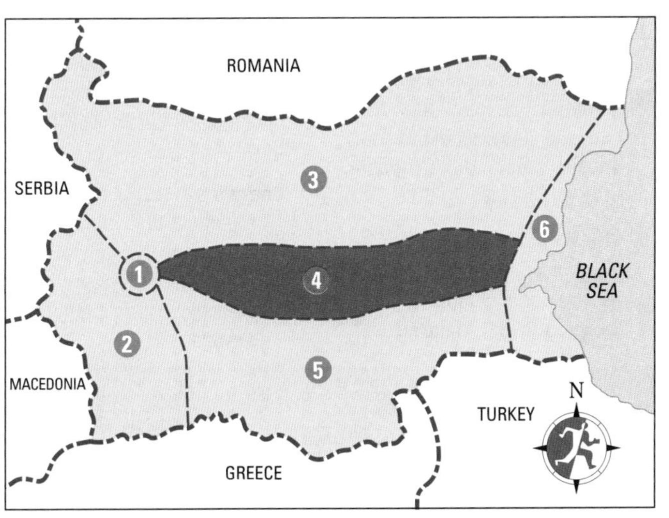

CHAPTER 4

Highlights

* **Koprivshtitsa** A beautifully preserved museum town, famous as the site of the April Rising of 1876, and home to the finest National Revival architecture in Bulgaria. **See p.289**
* **Starosel** Enigmatic burial mounds from the fifth century BC, excavated in 2000 and now one of the most visited archeological sites in the country. **See p.298**
* **Vasil Levski's Birthplace, Karlovo** This modest dwelling was once home to Bulgaria's great national hero – don't miss the little chapel outside, a virtual shrine to the "Apostle of Freedom". **See p.302**
* **The Thracian Tomb, Kazanlûk** A reproduction of the nearby burial chamber, with its colourful and detailed murals illustrating a Thracian funeral feast. **See p.310**
* **The Shipka Pass** Famous as the scene of truly heroic resistance by Bulgarian and Russian forces against a much larger Turkish army in 1877. **See p.312**
* **The Neolithic Dwellings, Stara Zagora** Dating from 5500 BC, these domestic remains are among the most important archeolgical treasures in Bulgaria. **See p.314**
* **Kotel** Take a leisurely stroll around the cobbled lanes of this quiet and unspoilt village. **See p.321**
* **Zheravna** A restful highland village of cobbled alleys and wooden houses, many of which preserve their original nineteenth-century interiors. **See p.324**

△ Gypsy family on the road

The Sredna Gora and the Valley of the Roses

The most direct route between Sofia and the Black Sea coast cuts straight across central Bulgaria, between the mountains of the Balkan Range to the north, and the **Sredna Gora** to the south. Lining the valleys of the latter are some of Bulgaria's most historic villages, renowned for their folkloric and revolutionary traditions – above all, **Koprivshtitsa**, the starting point of the ill-fated April Rising of 1876, and the site of some of Bulgaria's finest nineteenth-century architecture. Nearby are the museums and memorials of **Panagyurishte**, another centre of the Rising, and the ancient Roman spa town of **Hisar**. The eastern stretches of the Sredna Gora are gentler and less dramatic, but the city of **Stara Zagora**, site of one of Bulgaria's greatest archeological treasures, the 7500-year-old Neolithic dwellings, provides an excuse to break your eastward journey.

Between the Sredna Gora and Balkan ranges lies the **Valley of the Roses** (really two valleys: the upper reaches of the Stryama and the upper reaches of the Tundzha), named after the rose plantations to which the area owes its wealth. Though the valley is at its best when the rose crop is harvested in May, interest is provided throughout the year by the historic settlements lining the valley floor. Those most deserving of attention are **Karlovo**, the birthplace of the freedom fighter Vasil Levski and the best preserved of the valley's market towns, and the region's most convenient touring base **Kazanlûk**. Known for the Rose Festival, a folkloric bash which attracts visitors in early June, Kazanlûk is also home to a unique collection of Thracian tombs, earning this part of the valley the title of Bulgaria's "Valley of the Kings". To the north of Kazanlûk lies the **Shipka Pass**, amidst some of the highest peaks of the Balkan Range, the site of a crucial battle during the Russo-Turkish War of 1877–78.

Midway between the valley and the Black Sea, **Sliven** is the starting point for excursions to the highland craft towns of **Kotel**, a carpet-weaving centre, and **Zheravna**, with its unique nineteenth-century rural architecture. Strictly speaking, both these places belong to the Balkan Range, but are included in this chapter because they're more easily visited by those travelling the Sofia–Black Sea route.

Cyrillic place names

Blue Rocks	СИНИТЕ КАМЪНИ	Panagyurishte	ПАНАГЮРИЩЕ
Gradets	ГРАДЕЦ	Shipka Pass	ШИПЧЕНСКИЯ ПРОХОД
Hisar	ХИСАР	Sinite Kamûni	СИНИТЕ КАМЪНИ
Kalofer	КАЛОФЕР	Sliven	СЛИВЕН
Karandila	КАРАНДИЛА	Sopot	СОПОТ
Karlovo	КАРЛОВО	Srednogorie	СРЕДНОГОРИЕ
Katunishte	КАТУНИЩЕ	Stara Zagora	СТАРА ЗАГОРА
Kazanlûk	КАЗАНЛЪК	Starosel	СТАРОСЕЛ
Klisura	КЛИСУРА	Strelcha	СТРЕЛЧА
Koprivshtitsa	КОПРИВЩИЦА	Yambol	ЯМБОЛ
Kotel	КОТЕЛ	Zheravna	ЖЕРАВНА
Kûrnare	КЪРНАРЕ	Zlatitsa	ЗЛАТИЦА
Medven	МЕДВЕН		

The Sredna Gora

… So, proudly you may gaze
Unto the Sredna Gora, the forest's single queen,
And hear the ring of swords, and all this song can mean …

Pencho Slaveykov, *The Song of the Blood*

The **Sredna Gora** or "Central Highlands" stretch from the Pancharevo defile outside Sofia almost as far as Yambol on the Thracian plain. With its forests of oak and beech and numerous caves and hot springs, the region was inhabited by humans as early as the fifth millennium BC. The Thracians subsequently left a hoard of gold treasure at **Panagyurishte** (since moved to the National History Museum in Sofia, see p.108), and a brace of burial mounds outside the village of **Starosel**; while their Roman conquerors built a walled spa-city at **Hisar.** For many Bulgarians, however, the Sredna Gora is equally famous as the "land of the

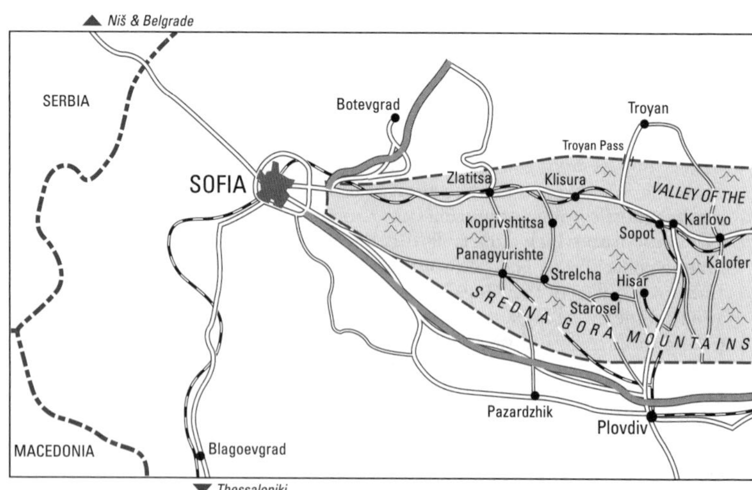

April Rising", the nineteenth-century rebellion against Ottoman rule that started in **Koprivshtitsa**. For tourists, too, this town is the region's highlight, its peerless National Revival architecture and pastoral beauty making it a must-see.

Lying roughly midway between Sofia and Plovdiv, the Sredna Gora is a popular excursion from both towns. Koprivshtitsa is served by minibus from Sofia, and by trains travelling the Sofia–Burgas route, although be aware that Koprivshtitsa's train station is over 12km north of the village itself (a connecting bus meets services). Panagyurishte is served by buses from Sofia and trains from Plovdiv, while Hisar can be reached by bus from either Karlovo, in the Valley of the Roses, or Plovdiv. However, **buses** running across the Sredna Gora range are few and far between, making travelling from Koprivshtitsa to Panagyurishte hugely inconvenient.

Koprivshtitsa

The small town of **KOPRIVSHTITSA** (pronounced "Kop*ri*shtitsa"), in the upper reaches of the Topolnitsa valley, is a lovely ensemble of half-timbered houses nestling amid wooded hills which, thanks to its elevated position 1060m above sea level, escapes the soaring summer heat experienced by much of lowland Bulgaria. It would be an oasis of pastoral calm were it not for the annual influx of summer visitors, drawn by the superb vernacular architecture and the desire to pay homage to a landmark in the nation's history. From the Place of the Scimitar Charge to the Street of the Counter Attack, there's hardly a part of town that isn't named after an episode or participant in the **April Rising of 1876**, when Bulgaria's yearnings for freedom from the Ottoman yoke finally boiled over (see p.292). It was Koprivshtitsa's role as a centre of commerce that provided the material basis for such an upsurge in national consciousness. Sheep and goat farming formed the backbone of the village's wealth, and the resulting wool and dairy products (including carpets, socks and cheese) were traded throughout the Levant. By the time of the Rising, Koprivshtitsa had a population of 12,000. After the Liberation, however, commercial life began to shift to the lowland towns, and places like Koprivshtitsa stagnated – leaving it as a kind of fossil. These days, its much reduced population of around 2600

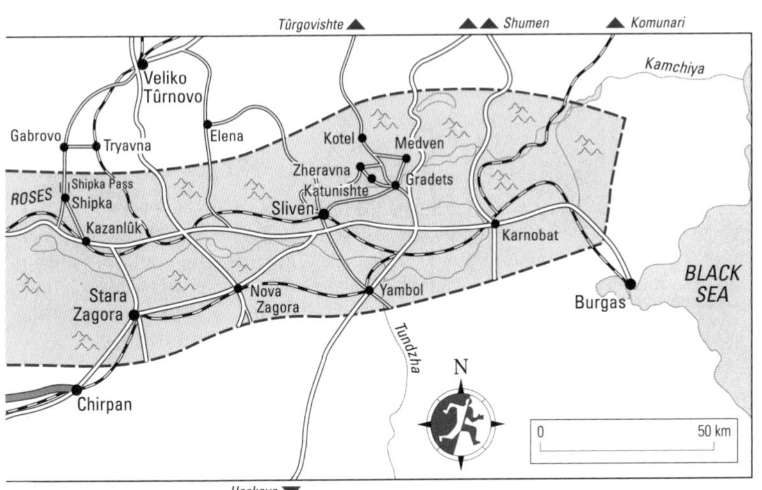

relies heavily on tourism, yet, despite its museum-town status, it also remains a working agricultural community, with horsepower still a vital and visible part of everyday life. Horse-drawn carts loaded with hay, farm workers or shop goods trundle along the cobbled lanes, and if you're in town on a Friday morning, you can take a wander round the market on the main square, where horseshoes, harnesses, farm tools and other rustic neccessities are put out for sale.

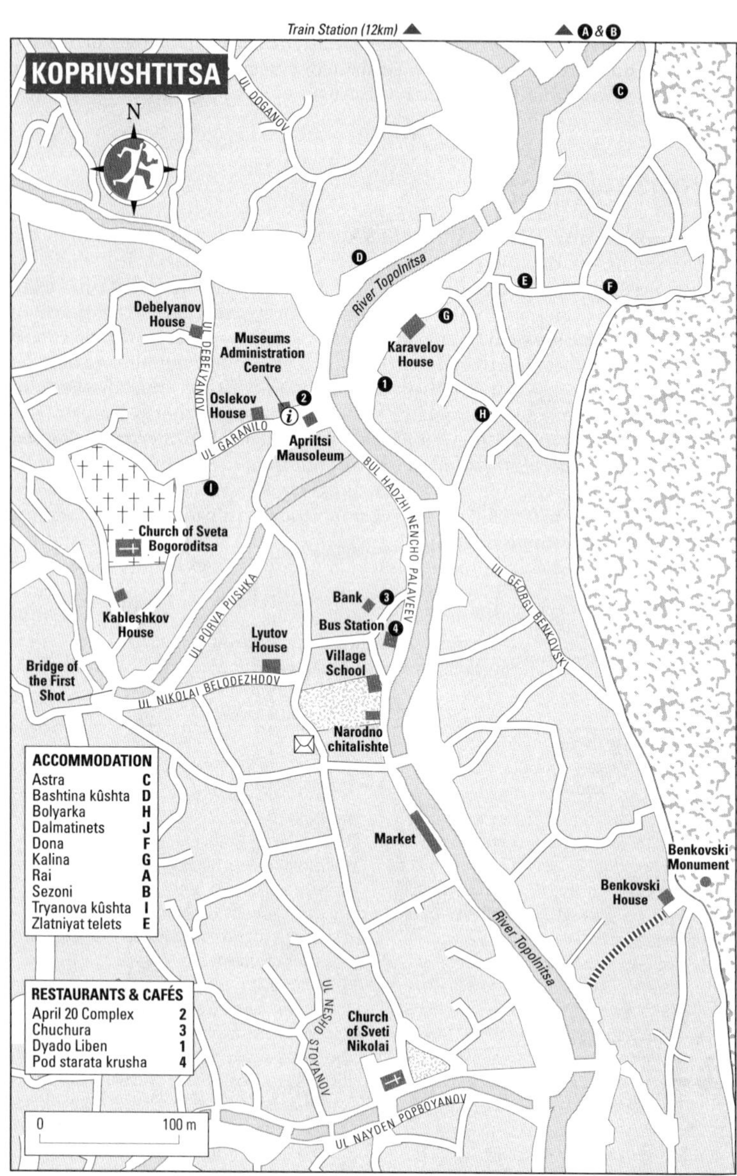

Koprivshtitsa also occupies an important place in the Bulgarian folk music calendar. The **Koprivshtitsa national music festival**, a huge gathering of musicians from all over the country, takes place on a hill outside the town every five years (the next one is due in August 2010). A smaller **regional festival** involving local folk groups is held annually (except when the big event takes place), usually on the weekend nearest to the Feast of the Assumption (*Sveta Bogoroditsa*), on August 15. Other traditional celebrations to look out for are **Iordanovden** (6 Jan), when the priest throws a wooden cross in the river and local lads dive in to retrieve it, and the feast of **Todorovden** (St Theodore's day, the first Saturday of Lent), which is celebrated with horse races on the meadow at the northern end of the village.

Arrival and information

Train services stopping at the Koprivshtitsa halt are met by a bus (1Lv) that ferries you the 12km south to the town itself. The times of buses back to the train halt are posted in the rarely staffed **bus station**, 200m south of the main square. There are four daily Sofia–Koprivshtitsa minibuses: at the time of writing, two depart from the Trafik-Market bus park just outside Sofia's central train station, while the other two start out from Avtogara Poduyane. The **tourist information centre**, tucked away in the northwestern corner of the main square (Ⓣ07184/2191), has unpredictable opening times; when it's shut, try the next-door **museums administration office** (daily 10am-6pm; Ⓣ07184/2180 or 2114) which can provide some general information. You can cash travellers' cheques at the DSK **bank**, midway between the main square and the bus station (Mon–Fri 9am–3pm).

Accommodation

Finding somewhere **to stay** in Koprivshtitsa is only likely to be difficult during the big five-yearly festival, when it's wise to reserve weeks ahead. At other times, **private rooms** (❶) can be arranged by the **tourist information centre** (see above), when it's open – be prepared to ask around for rooms if it's closed. You may have more luck with the museums administration office (see above), whose staff sometimes know of a few places offering accommodation. There are plenty of small **hotels** and pensions scattered throughout the village, most of them welcoming, family-run affairs.

Astra ul. Hadzhi Nencho Palaveev 11 Ⓣ07184/2364, Ⓔhotel_astra@hotmail.com. Out in the northeastern quarter of town, this small family-run pension has comfy rooms and shared facilities. ❷

Bashtina kûshta ul. Hadzhi Nencho Palaveev 32 Ⓣ07184/3303, Ⓦwww.fhhotel.info. Modern building offering en-suites with TV and contemporary furnishings – in contrast to the folksy decor on offer elsewhere. The top-floor rooms with attic roofs are the cosiest. ❸

Bolyarka ul. Petûr Zhilkov 7 Ⓣ0887 757 915. Four-room B&B just uphill from the centre, offering bright, pine-furnished rooms, a couple with little balconies, and a lovely garden. French-speaking hosts. ❷

Dalmatinets ul. Benkovski 62 Ⓣ07184/2904. Hidden away in the backstreets at the south end of town, this modern hotel offers balconied rooms with en-suite facilities – and a cosy café-restaurant serving breakfast and evening meals. ❷

Dona ul. Hadzhi Gencho 13 Ⓣ07184/2440, Ⓦwww.cometodona.hit.bg. Family-run B&B with prim, unassumingly furnished en-suites. The main attraction is the garden, which is transformed into a barbecue restaurant whenever enough guests assemble. ❷

Kalina ul. Hadzhi Nencho Palaveev 35 Ⓣ07184/2032. Large, gated complex immediately opposite the main square. Rooms are on the small side but the nineteenth-century-style furnishings and carved wooden ceilings are appealing. ❸

Rai ul. Dyado Liben 8 Ⓣ07184/2637. In the north-east of town, the *Rai* offers a couple of large rooms with balconies and a smart apartment, all with great views. ❸

Sezoni ul. Doncho Vatah Voyvoda 12 ⓣ07184/3032, ⓦwww.sezonihotel.com. Family-run B&B at the north end of town, offering laminate-floored rooms with a few olde-worlde knick-knacks to provide character, each with small but super-modern bathroom. Nice garden. English spoken. ❷
Tryanova kûshta ul. Gereniloto 5 ⓣ07184/3057. Old house just up from the main square, with delightful low-ceilinged en-suites in the National Revival style (although the TVs look somewhat more contemporary), and a communal *chardak* (porch) overlooking a grassy courtyard. ❷–❸
Zlatniyat telets ul. Hadzhi Gencho 1 ⓣ07184/2825. Reasonably central guesthouse offering four en-suite doubles, and four quirky split-level apartments. ❷–❸

The April Rising of 1876

The **1870s** were troubled times in the Balkans, as a tired and corrupt **Ottoman empire** tried to stem the tide of protest from subject nationalities longing for independence. In Bulgaria, the rise in education and literacy brought about by the National Revival had engendered an upsurge of national consciousness, and a generation of idealistic revolutionaries, such as Vasil Levski, Angel Kûnchev, Lyuben Karavelov and Hristo Botev, succeeded in placing the idea of liberation in the forefront of Bulgarian minds.

Revolutionary strategy

In order to coordinate the struggle, various nationalist groups came together to form the Bucharest-based **Bulgarian Revolutionary Central Committee**, or **BRCK**. The network already established by Levski – who had travelled the country setting up revolutionary cells – was put at the BRCK's disposal. The death of Levski in 1873, and the failure of an uprising in Stara Zagora in 1875, persuaded many in the BRCK that the policy of fomenting armed insurrection had been a mistake. However several of the participants in the Stara Zagora uprising (future prime minister Stefan Stambolov among them) were determined to have another go. Encouraged by the Ottoman failure to put down a major revolt in Bosnia, and believing that Serbia and Russia were simply waiting for an excuse to declare war on Turkey, the veterans of Stara Zagora assumed control of the national movement and started planning another uprising.

Their **strategy** was based on the time-honoured guerrilla methods of the *haiduti*, Balkan outlaws who could survive for months in the mountains, harrying Turkish outposts and relying on the goodwill of the local populace for food and shelter. A series of *cheti*, or mobile armed groups, were formed to move through the countryside, avoiding heavily defended Ottoman positions, and gathering support where they could – eventually, it was hoped, snowballing into a popular revolt that would provoke foreign intervention. Bulgaria was divided into four regions (centred on Sliven, Vratsa, Plovdiv and Veliko Tûrnovo), each responsible for organizing its own military action. The organizers placed their emphasis on the mountain regions of Bulgaria, firstly because the ethnic makeup of the highlands was solidly Bulgarian, and secondly because they calculated (wrongly, as it turned out) that it would be difficult and time-consuming for the Ottoman authorities to send in reinforcements. The idea of the Rising caught the popular imagination, and preparations were impressive: village tailors secretly made uniforms for the insurgents, lead was melted down to make bullets, and rudimentary cannons were made from cherry trees, one of which can still be seen in the Benkovski House (see p.295).

The Rising begins

The Rising was scheduled for May 1, and on April 14 insurgent leaders were summoned to the Oborishte clearing, 25km southwest of Koprivshtitsa, to receive their final instructions. Unfortunately one of those present at the meeting, Nenko Terziiski, was a spy for the Ottoman authorities, who responded by sending a small unit to Koprivshtitsa to arrest local rebel leader **Todor Kableshkov**. Kableshkov

The Town

Koprivshtitsa straggles along either side of the River Topolnitsa, whose tributaries divide the town into five quarters (*mahala*) where stone bridges and the burble of water enhance the beauty of the **architecture**. More than 380 of the town's houses date from the National Revival era, the most elaborate from 1842 to 1870, when the symmetrical Plovdiv style took hold. Many have large wooden gates with separate doors for people and wagons; carved stone

had no choice but to launch the Rising ahead of schedule on April 20, capturing the Ottoman *konak* and dispatching the famous **Bloody Letter**, written in the blood of the first dead Turk, informing the Panagyurishte leaders that fighting had already broken out.

A Bulgarian **provisional government** was declared in Panagyurishte, but the authorities reacted swiftly, and the Ottoman governor of Plovdiv dispatched irregular troops to suppress the Rising. These were made up of Pomaks, Bulgarian Muslims eager to settle private scores with their Christian neighbours, and *bashibazouks*, rapacious freebooters drawn from the Tatar and Circassian populations, only recently expelled from Russia and therefore hostile to Slavs in general. As the *bashibazouks* burned the neighbouring towns of Panagyurishte and Klisura, refugees flooded into Koprivshtitsa spreading panic, and the local *chorbadzhii* (rural middle class) attempted to disarm the insurgents. The rebels took to the hills, where rain played havoc with their homemade gunpowder, and eventually they were hunted down. Koprivshtitsa's *chorbadzhii* bribed the *bashibazouks* not to burn the village, which survived unscathed to be admired by subsequent generations as a symbol of heroism.

Elsewhere in Bulgaria, the premature launching of the Rising took most insurgents by surprise. The **Batak** area rose up on April 21, but was soon mercilessly crushed (see p.368). By the time the central Tûrnovo region began its action on April 28 it was already too late, and most of the leaders were arrested before any serious fighting took place. In a bizarre coda to the Rising, poet and revolutionary **Hristo Botev** (see p.305) collected emigrés living in Serbia and Romania, crossed the Danube in a hijacked Austrian steamboat on May 17, and tried to lend support to his (already defeated) countrymen by marching on Vratsa. They were wiped out on nearby Mount Okolchitsa.

The aftermath

Despite many individual acts of bravery the Rising failed to win mass support, largely because local civilians were too afraid of Turkish reprisals. The expected intervention of Serbia and Russia took too long to materialize: although the Serbs later fought a short war with Turkey in the summer of 1876 (in which many Bulgarian exiles participated), they were quickly routed. However, the savagery of **Ottoman reprisals** against civilians (see p.368) in the aftermath of the Rising convinced the great powers of Europe that the Ottoman Empire could no longer be allowed a free hand to discipline its Balkan subjects. As news of the so-called "Bulgarian atrocities" spread, traditional allies like France and Britain lost the political will to shore up the empire against its critics. This suited Russia, which was angling for the creation of a Bulgarian state to serve its own interests in the region.

Ordinary Russians were in any case outraged by the treatment of their fellow Slavs by the Ottomans, and pressed for war. The government of Sultan Abdulhamid spoke vaguely of introducing reforms, then drew back from real action, giving Russia the excuse it needed to attack. Tsar Aleksandr II finally declared war on April 12, 1877, almost a year after the outbreak of the Rising. By the following January, the Ottomans were suing for peace, and Bulgarian independence was at last on the agenda.

fountains and troughs adorn the cobbled lanes that wend between them. The total effect is both delicate and rugged, as red, blue and ochre-painted stucco counterpoints the natural tones of wood and stone.

The six house-museums open to the public can be visited in any order, but the most obvious starting point is from the **main square**, dominated by the stone **Apriltsi Mausoleum**, inscribed "Let us guard the national liberty for which the heroes of the rising of 1876 fell." A combined **ticket** valid for all the houses (10Lv) is available at the museum administration office on the main square, or at the Oslekov or Kableshkov houses. Tickets for individual houses are priced at 5Lv each.

The Oslekov House

One of the finest houses in Koprivshtitsa stands just uphill from the main square, on ulitsa Garanilo. The **Oslekov House** (Mon 9.30am–noon & Tues–Sun 9.30am–5.30pm) was built in 1856 for local tax collector and much-travelled merchant, Nincho Oslekov. Its facade is upheld by pillars of cedarwood imported from Lebanon, and adorned with views of Padua, Rome and Venice - just some of the foreign cities visited by its proud owner - painted by the Samokov craftsman Kosta Zograf (brother of the icon painter, Zahari Zograf). The upstairs rooms have lovely fretted wooden ceilings and panelled walls, especially in the Summer Guest Room, where one of the murals shows the original, symmetrical plan of the house, never realized since Oslekov's neighbours refused to sell him the necessary land. It was here that the uniforms for the revolutionaries of 1876 were made, and a spinning wheel and some of the shears, thimbles and suchlike employed in that furtive endeavour are on display.

The Debelyanov House and the Church of Sveta Bogoroditsa

On a sidestreet leading north from ulitsa Garanilo stands the small **Debelyanov House** (Tues–Sun 9.30am–5.30pm), where the symbolist poet Dimcho Debelyanov was born in 1887. Painted royal blue with a white trim, its timbered upper floor contains a humdrum exposition of his tragically short career, with such personal items as his childhood cradle, and the suitcase of books that accompanied him to war. Amongst the many sepia photographs are portraits of two of his lovers, Ivanka, to whom he dedicated his poems, and the doomed Elena, whose father disapproved of the relationship so strongly that he finally killed both her and himself. There's also an intimate oil portrait of Debelyanov, executed by his friend, Georgi Mashev. In the garden is a poignant statue of Dimcho's mother, vainly awaiting his return from the battlefields of Greece, where he was killed in 1916.

An identical statue broods over his **grave** in the local cemetery, at the top of ulitsa Garanilo, whose inscription is from one of his own poems: "Delaying in a gentle dream she becomes her own child." Also in the cemetery stands the **Church of Sveta Bogoroditsa**, whose tolling bell proclaimed the beginning of the 1876 Rising. Built in 1817 on the site of an older church burnt down by the Turks, it is partly sunken into the ground to comply with the Ottoman edict that no Christian building should be taller than the local mosque. The interior is rustic in its simplicity, aside from an elaborate iconostasis by Teteven craftsmen, containing several icons by Zahari Zograf.

The Kableshkov House

Leaving the churchyard by a gate on the far side and turning left, you'll come to the **Kableshkov House** (Tues–Sun 9.30am–5.30pm). Built by a local master-craftsman in 1845, its square plan and the combination of one curved and two square oriels on each side reflect the influence of the Plovdiv style. The ground floor preserves the simple living quarters of a reasonably prosperous *chorbadzhii* family, including a "women's work room" with a spinning wheel, and the room where Todor Kableshkov was born in 1851. Weapons used in the Rising are displayed on the top floor, whose circular vestibule has a wonderful ceiling with an abstract pattern based on the reflection of sunlight on rippling water. Kableshkov's decision to start the Rising ahead of schedule, after Turkish soldiers came to arrest him, was made at the "House of the Conspiracy" on a nearby street.

Kableshkov was later captured near Troyan, but managed to kill himself with a police revolver in Gabrovo, and is commemorated by a statue close to the **Bridge of the First Shot**, where the Rising began.

The Lyutov House and beyond

Cross the bridge and head up ulitsa Nikola Belodezhdov and you'll come to the white **Lyutov House** (Tues–Sun 9.30am–5.30pm), distinguished by its double staircase and yoke-shaped porch, which is decorated on one side with a small lion breaking free of its chains, signifying Bulgarian aspirations of freedom. Built for a prosperous yoghurt merchant by Plovdiv craftsmen in 1854, the house, boasting one of Koprivshtitsa's most sumptuous interiors, is famed for its wealth of murals: palaces, temples and world cities splashed across the walls and *alafranga*; wreaths, blossoms and nosegays in the Blue Room; and oval medallions adorning the ceilings. The house also holds a fine collection of Viennese furniture, while a splendid rosewater fountain forms the centrepiece of the extravagant parlour. The basement houses an exhibition of *plûsti*, the locally made felt rugs which traditionally feature bold, sun-symbol designs.

Nearer the river stands a handsome pair of civic buildings, financed by local patriots. The former **Village School**, built in 1837 – the school where the great educational reformer Neofit Rilski (see p.153) taught and to which rich merchant families from all over Bulgaria sent their children – is now a conference and exhibition centre, while the nearby **Narodno chitalishte**, founded in 1869 as public reading rooms, played a big part in the National Revival, spreading literacy and nurturing a sense of national identity in towns and villages.

From Sredna mahala to Byalo Kamûne

To see more of life in Koprivshtitsa, take a ramble through the **Sredna mahala** (Central) and **Byalo kamûne** (White Rocks) quarters. Sredna withdraws from an outdoor **market** into a *kasbah*-like maze of reclusive houses and lanes where elders gossip and goats forage. With luck, you'll emerge at the **Church of Sveti Nikolai**, behind a high wall with a bell tower above the gateway. Despite the church's dedication, its iconostasis dwells on St Spiridion, whose life is told in ten medallions surrounding a figure of the saint. On the corner of the lane is a **fountain** donated by the Moravenovs, a leading family in the early eighteenth century.

Walk downstream and cross the river to reach Byalo kamûne, a *mahala* of stolid timber buildings on a steep slope, where the **Benkovski House** (Mon & Wed–Sun 9.30am–5.30pm) recalls another revolutionary. Georgi Benkovski (1844–76) helped to rebuild the clandestine networks set up by Levski, after the latter's execution. A tailor by profession, he made the rebels' white uniforms and silk banner – embroidered with the Bulgarian Lion and the words *svoboda ili smûrt* (Liberty or Death!). During the Rising his *cheta* wheeled south via Panagyurishte, trying to rally the locals, but was chased northwards and wiped out near Teteven. His career is covered in usual didactic style; among the texts is a quote from the Rising's chronicler, Stoyanov: "Koprivshtitsa was a republic for centuries, without senators, ministers or presidents; ten times more liberal than France, and a hundred times more democratic than America".

On the hillside above the house looms a striking **monument to Benkovski**, in the form of a socialist superhero astride a leaping horse.

The Karavelov House

Returning towards the main square along the east bank of the Topolnitsa, you'll find, near the Freedom Bridge, the **Karavelov House** (Mon & Wed–Sun 9.30am–5.30pm), where Lyuben Karavelov was born in 1834. The son of a sausage merchant, his itinerant career was typical of the many patriots who spent years in exile trying to win support for the Bulgarian cause. Educated in Moscow, he was a strong believer in the need to attract Russian and Serbian help, and based himself in Belgrade, where he met Vasil Levski. His enthusiasm for the idea of a Balkan Federation proved too radical for his hosts, who forced him to flee into Habsburg territory, where he was promptly jailed. Karavelov later found refuge in Bucharest, where he organized the BRCK and for ten years advocated armed struggle in the columns of the émigré newspapers *Svoboda* and *Nezavisimost*. After Levski's execution, however, he repudiated direct action in favour of change through reform and education, and was ousted from the leadership of the committee by Hristo Botev.

The house itself contains the usual items of nineteenth-century domestic life, while in the little courtyard stands the rough wooden bench where Karavelov Senior made his sausages. Also on show is the printing press on which Karavelov's newspapers were produced, brought to Bulgaria after the Liberation. An adjacent summer house contains the personal effects of his younger brother, Petko, a prominent liberal politician after the Liberation, and twice premier.

Eating and drinking

There's no shortage of places to **eat and drink** in Koprivshtitsa, with little to choose between the numerous establishments offering good, traditional Bulgarian food. Try *Pod Starata Krusha*, next to the bus station, or the nearby *Chuchura*, a small, traditional-style *mehana*. The *Dyado Liben Inn*, across the river from the main square, occupies a lovely old house, with a restaurant upstairs and tables outside in the courtyard. The *April 20 Complex* on the main square harbours a café, restaurant, and the occasional lacklustre disco. For picnics, there's a fair range of fresh produce on sale at the **market** south of the bus station (daily except Sun).

Panagyurishte

After Koprivshtitsa, other towns in the Sredna Gora are an anticlimax, particularly **PANAGYURISHTE**, 39km southwest, whose memorials to the Rising hardly compare with Koprivshtitsa's magnificent houses. With a car, you could consider driving south across the mountains simply for the pleasure of the scenery en route – relying on meagre public transport however (a few **buses** a day from Sofia's Avtogara Yug and three **trains** daily from Plovdiv), it hardly seems worth it.

The Town

Despite its antiquity as a settlement, the existing town is predominantly modern, as Panagyurishte was set ablaze by the Turks for its participation in the

April Rising – the town was the base for Georgi Benkovski's cavalry division. The most obvious starting point is the austerely laid-out main square, **ploshtad Pavel Bobekov** – named after a local insurgent and overlooked from a hillside to the east by the **Memorial to the April Rising**, a towering structure typical of the part modernist, part Socialist Realist style that characterized Bulgaria's public monuments in the 1970s and 1980s. The memorial is reached by a processional stairway that runs past the **Church of Sveta Bogoroditsa**, partially burnt in the aftermath of the Rising. Patches of charred murals (immediately on the left as you enter) have been left *in situ* as a reminder of the conflagration. The rest of the interior was colourfully decorated by Samokov painters in the 1890s, covering the walls with a pictorial history of the life of the Virgin consisting of more than a hundred individual scenes – each inscribed with the name of the local benefactor who paid for it.

West of the main square, ulitsa Raina Knyaginya heads uphill into what remains of the old town. The two towers of the colonnaded, turquoise-coloured **Church of Sveti Georgi** precede the **Shtûrbanova House** at no. 26, home to a prominent member of the local rebel government during the Rising. The house forms one part of a complex of buildings holding the town **museum** (Tues–Sun 9am–noon & 2–5.30pm; 2Lv), that bristles with antique militaria, including a cherry-tree cannon. Opposite the church, across a small square, ulitsa Oborishte leads to the **Raina Knyaginya House-Museum** at no. 5 (Tues–Sun 9am–noon & 2–5pm; 2Lv). As a girl, Knyaginya was the rebels' flag-bearer, mockingly nicknamed *knyaginya* (princess) by her Turkish captors. Tortured in Plovdiv, and then exiled to Russia, she returned to Bulgaria after the Liberation to become a schoolteacher in Veliko Tûrnovo. The house contains sepia family portraits alongside a "Liberty or Death" flag woven by Knyaginya herself in 1901, in memory of the one she had carried during the Rising. She is buried in the garden with her mother and father – the latter a casualty of the Rising.

Practicalities

Arriving in town by **bus**, head up the road beside the stream past a hospital to find the main square, on the right. The **train station** is a bit further southeast of the centre down ulitsa Shiskov. Accommodation is provided by the *Kamengrad* **hotel**, an unmissable four-storey structure centrally located at ul. Bobekov 2 (ⓣ0357/6113; ④). It boasts tidy twin rooms with shower, TV and air conditioning, and a good **restaurant**.

Hisar

Situated in the verdant foothills of the Sredna Gora, **HISAR** (sometimes written as "Hisarya"), 55km east of Panagyurishte, was one of the great watering-holes of antiquity, and the local bottled mineral water is still sold across the country. It was the **Romans** who founded the spa, building marble baths, aqueducts, temples and – after raids by the Goths in 251 – fortifications to protect the town, which they called Augusta. Subsequently an episcopal seat, it was devastated by Crusaders despite their appreciation of this "fair town", 150 years before its conquest by the Turks, who restored the baths in the sixteenth century and renamed the place Hisar ("the fortress"). Developed as a health resort for factory workers in Communist times, Hisar has fallen on hard times since the democratic changes of the early 1990s, and the elegant tranquillity once offered by its (now overgrown) parks and flowerbeds is long gone. Proximity to the recently discovered Thracian tombs at Starosel (see below), 20km to the southwest, may help to speed Hisar's return to Bulgarian tourism's premier league.

The Town

A couple of blocks south of the bus and train stations, a sizeable chunk of Hisar's history confronts visitors in the form of the damaged but still imposing **fortress walls**, originally 2–3m thick and defended by 43 towers. The Roman builders employed the technique of *opus mixtum*, bonding stone and brick with red mortar – hence the sobriquet Kizil Kale (red fortress) which the Turks coined when they besieged the town in 1364.

The northern wall that runs along bulevard Botev is bisected by a promenade, leading towards the massive **Kamilite Gate** in the south wall of the fortress, so called after the camels that once passed through it. En route to this you'll see a pseudo-Grecian colonnade and **fountain**, where visitors fill bottles with mineral water and have their portraits taken against a backdrop of crumbling *fin-de-siècle* buildings. A right turn at the Kamilite Gate, followed by a left turn up a flight of steps at the bottom of a hill, will bring you to a fourth-century **Roman tomb** (opening times vary) with frescoed walls and a mosaic floor. Stonework, coins and other finds are displayed in a small **History Museum**, at ul. Stamboliiski 8 (Mon-Fri 9am–noon & 1–5pm; 2Lv), one block east of the main drag.

Practicalities

Hisar is best reached by bus from Karlovo or Plovdiv, although there are occasional trains from the latter too: the stations are on the northern side of the centre, just outside the town walls. Hisar's only habitable **hotels** are about 1km east of here: the *Hisar* (Ⓣ0337/62781, Ⓕ63815; ❸) is just about acceptable, with simple if slightly shabby en-suite rooms, while the *Augusta* (Ⓣ0337/63821, Ⓦwww.augustaspa.com; ❺) is in a different league altogether – rooms have TV and en-suite bathrooms fed by mineral water, and there are both indoor and outdoor pools and a range of spa treatments on site. The *Augusta* rents bikes for 2.50Lv an hour, and organizes trips to Starosel for about 25–40Lv per person depending on numbers. Daytime **eating and drinking** centres around the numerous cafés on the main square, although there's not much going on at night. At the southern end of town, the *Kamilite* restaurant, just beyond the Kamilite gate, serves a wide range of Bulgarian meat-based standards in a large open-air courtyard with frequent live music.

Starosel

Twenty kilometres southwest of Hisar (take the Plovdiv road then turn onto the westbound Strelcha road after 8km), **STAROSEL** is a dusty village typical of the southern Sredna Gora, its one-storey houses sheltering secretively behind mud-brick walls. The place shot to prominence in 2000 with the discovery of two grave barrows dating from the fifth century BC, leading to speculation that the capital of the once-powerful Thracian Odrysae tribe may well have been in the valley below. Starosel is served by five daily buses from Karlovo via Hisar, although the tombs are quite a walk from the village, and it's much more convenient to come by car.

The **tombs** (both daily: May–Sept 9am–6pm; Oct–April 10am–4pm; 3Lv) are reached by following a minor road north out of the village – signs reading "*Trakiiskite hramove*" ("Thracian Temples") guide the way. After 3km the first of the tombs, covered in a protective wooden shell, hoves into view on the left. Consisting of a simple quadrangular chamber fronted by an impressive six-pillar colonnade, it probably had a combined role as aristocratic mausoleum and ancestor-worshipping temple.

A similar purpose was served by the larger of the two tombs, a conical mound nestling amid low hills some 3km further on. The biggest tumulus yet discovered in Bulgaria, it's thought to be the last resting place of a powerful Odrysae king. The stepped entrance to the tomb, made from huge blocks of tufa brought from Zlatitsa 40km to the north, leads through to a circular inner chamber, where a conical ceiling – intricately fashioned from overlapping stone plates – is just about visible behind modern protective scaffolding. Round the back of the mound, look out for a huge stone trough presumably used for preparing ritual wine.

The Valley of the Roses

Lying midway between Sofia and the coast, the **Valley of the Roses** (*Rozovata dolina*) is perhaps the most over-hyped region of Bulgaria. A sunbaked and dusty place for most of the summer, from mid-May to early June it's partially

Roses: Bulgaria's gold

The **rose-growing area** between Klisura and Kazanlûk produces seventy percent of the world's attar – or extract – of roses. Considering that perfumiers pay more than US$45 million a year for this, it's not surprising that roses are known as "Bulgaria's gold". Rose-growing began as a small cottage industry during the 1830s (supposedly started by a Turkish merchant impressed by the fragrance of the wild Shipka rose), and initially involved small domestic stills comprising a copper cauldron from which water-cooled pipes dripped the greenish-yellow rose oil. It became big business early in the twentieth century, but virtually ceased during World War II when Nazi Germany discouraged the industry in order to sell its own ersatz scents – since then Bulgaria's rose-growers have vastly expanded their operations.

Each acre planted with red *rosa damascena* or white *rosa alba* yields up to 1400 kilograms of blossom, or roughly three million rosebuds; between 3000 and 6000 kilos are required to make one litre of attar, leaving a residue of rosewater and pulp used to make medicaments, flavourings, *sladko* jam and *rosaliika* liqueur. The rose bushes (covering over 14,000 acres) are allowed to grow to head height, and are harvested during May between 3am and 8am before the sun rises and evaporates up to half of the oil. Nimble-fingered women and girls do most of the picking, while donkeys are employed to carry the petals away to the modern distilleries around Rozino, Kûrnare and Kazanlûk. Kazanlûk also has a research institute where pesticides are tested and different breeds of rose developed; according to the director, its gardens contain every variety in the world.

transformed by the blooms that give it its name. Even then, however, much of the rose-growing activity takes place around the villages on the margins of the valley, and if you're speeding through the region by road or rail you won't see a thing. Whatever the time of year its towns can seem unexciting – "ramshackle collections of unplastered cottages which might have dropped off a lorry," thought Leslie Gardiner, and he wasn't far wrong. One compensation of travelling through the valley is bewitching views of the imposing ridge of mountains to the north, which forms the backbone of the Balkan Range, or Stara planina ("old mountain"). Access to the mountains is via the towns of **Klisura**, **Sopot**, **Karlovo** and **Kalofer**, all occupying honoured niches in Bulgarian history as the scene of heroic events or the birthplace of writers or national heroes, but have little that's worth seeing beyond memorial museums to local sons, captioned in Bulgarian only. The region's main town **Kazanlûk** is similarly bland, although it does feature some remarkable **Thracian tombs**, and hosts the Festival of Roses in early June. Within easy reach of the town to the north is the rugged **Shipka Pass**, heroically defended by Russian and Bulgarian troops during the 1878 War of Liberation.

Regular **trains** from Sofia to Karlovo or Burgas make it easy enough to travel through the valley (although express services don't stop at the smaller places en route, and there are few trains of any description between late morning and early evening). Coming down from the Balkan Range via the Troyan or Shipka pass, you can pick up the valley route at Kûrnare or Kazanlûk; Srednogorie and Karlovo are linked by buses or branch-rail lines to both the Sredna Gora and Plovdiv.

Towards Kazanlûk

Immediately beyond the halt for Koprivshtitsa, trains enter a long tunnel beneath the Koznitsa spur, emerging into the Stryama Valley, the upper part of the Valley of the Roses. Bleached and arid from the end of the rose harvest until the autumn, the valley looks surprisingly lush the rest of the year, when groves of fruit trees give way to pastures dotted with wild flowers, and the surrounding hills are covered by deep forests.

Despite its dramatic situation at the head of the valley, there's little reason to stop at **KLISURA**, although this small town "of tiles and flowers" is lauded for having been burned down during the April Rising, as described in Vazov's epic *Under the Yoke*. From here onwards it's roses all the way – at least during May. The next small town, **Kûrnare**, is the point of departure for Bulgaria's highest road, which winds north across the scenic Troyan Pass (see p.239).

Sopot

Further east along the valley, the sleepy little town of **SOPOT** hardly justifies breaking your journey, but might be worth a brief excursion from neighbouring Karlovo. Sopot's claim to fame is as the **birthplace of Ivan Vazov**, Bulgaria's "national" writer, a bronze statue of whom stands on the main square. Immediately to the west lies Vazov's birthplace, now preserved as a **museum** (Tues–Sun 8am–noon & 1–5.30pm; 2Lv). The buildings, grouped around a peaceful vine-shaded courtyard, suggest the comfortable home of a middle-class merchant, with some choice pieces of furniture in the guest room, and good-quality imported porcelain. One room, which once served as a study is today populated by a glassy-eyed company of costumed dummies, dressed in period

Ivan Vazov (1850–1922)

Born into a Sopot merchant family, **Ivan Vazov**'s youthful patriotism took him into exile in Romania as a teenager, where he met other Bulgarian revolutionaries (Hristo Botev and Stefan Stambolov among them), and began writing for émigré journals. On returning to Sopot he threw himself into revolutionary politics, but was forced to flee on the eve of the April Rising because of the threat of imminent arrest. Perhaps because he was unable to participate himself, the events of April 1876 inspired Vazov to write his best poetry.

After the Liberation the new state was desperately short of trained administrators, and Vazov, despite having no experience in the law, was appointed magistrate in **Berkovitsa** (see p.187). Unsurprisingly, this wasn't a great success and, threatened with demotion, a chastened Vazov withdrew to Sopot to lick his wounds. He soon relocated to Plovdiv, then the capital of Eastern Roumelia, where he became active in local politics and journalism. After the reunification of Eastern Rumelia and Bulgaria in 1886, Vazov fled to Odessa in order to escape the clutches of the anti-Russian prime minister, Stefan Stambolov, who distrusted Vazov's solidly Russophile sympathies. It was in Odessa that Vazov began work on **Under the Yoke** (*Pod Igoto*), his classic tale of small-town life before and during the April Rising.

Vazov returned to Bulgaria in 1889, and settled in Sofia, where episodes of *Under the Yoke* were published in the journal of the Ministry of Education. An immediate success, it made Vazov a national institution. After serving as Minister of Education (1897–99), he continued to write a stream of novels, articles and poems until his death in Sofia in 1922.

Under the Yoke remains the most admired of his works. Set in the imaginary town of Byala Cherkva (a thinly disguised version of Sopot), the novel follows the experiences of local patriots involved in the preparations for the April Rising, and culminates with their grisly deaths at the hands of the avenging Turks. Very much Bulgaria's "national novel", it was translated into English in 1893, and Sofia Press in Bulgaria published a new English translation in 1960. Both editions are exceedingly difficult to track down.

clothing and grasping musical instruments of various kinds, illustrating the kind of gatherings that once took place in the Vazov household. A separate, building houses an exhibition of photographs, documents and copies of Vazov's works in various languages.

Sopot's other main attraction is the boulder-strewn **pine forest** that stretches up the lower slopes of the Balkan Range immediately north of town. Criss-crossed by paths, it's an excellent place for tranquil woodland walks, and a welcome escape from the often heat-hazed valley below. To get there, head uphill from the Vazov museum as far as the church tower, behind which a flight of steps leads to the edge of the woods.

Finally, the mountain ridge above Sopot is one of the most popular **paragliding** venues in Bulgaria. Local outfit Skynomad (ul. Vasil Levski 15, ⓣ03134/4251 or 0888 370 937, ⓦwww.skynomad.com) organizes everything from one-off tandem flights (from €60/120Lv to week-long courses (from €300/600Lv) from March through to November, and will arrange accommodation locally for its customers.

Practicalities

Sopot is easily reached from Karlovo, just 5km down the road. **Bus** #4 from Karlovo's main street (every 20–30min) drops you on the main square. The comfiest place **to stay** is the *Motel Shterev* (aka *Hacienda*; ⓣ03134/6161; ❸), just west of Sopot in the village of Anevo; its ten tile-floored en-suites have TV and air conditioning, and there's a restaurant, gym, sauna and a tiny pool in the grounds. The same outfit runs the *Hotel Shterev* on Sopot's main square (Ⓣ03134/2233; ❷) which is better on the inside than it looks from the outside – expect en-suite rooms with reasonably new furnishings and soothing colour schemes. Places to **eat and drink** are limited to the mundane cafés round the main square. *Rodeo*, at the back of the square, is the best of the bunch, serving the usual grilled snacks.

Karlovo and around

Set against a backdrop of lofty, arid crags and hollows descending to slopes partly covered with cypresses and fig trees, **KARLOVO** is one of the most attractive towns in the Valley of the Roses, despite its dreary suburbs and the presence of a large army garrison. Hidden uphill, the charming old quarter, birthplace of the great revolutionary, Vasil Levski, is a pleasant place to wander.

Halfway between the train station and the centre of town, ulitsa Vasil Levski meets **ploshtad Vasil Levski**, an ensemble of nineteenth-century houses

Vasil Levski (1837–73)

Born **Vasil Ivanov Kunchov** and raised by a widowed mother, who supported them both by working as a dyer, Karlovo's most famous son briefly considered the priesthood and medicine before dedicating himself to the cause of Bulgaria's liberation. Like many patriots of the time, he chose exile, joining Rakovski's Bulgarian Legion in Belgrade, and after its disbandment sought refuge in Romania, where he and Hristo Botev spent one winter nearly starving to death in an abandoned windmill. He took part in Panaiot Hitov's notorious cross-border guerilla raid of 1867, and was given the name Levski (from the word *lûv*; lion) because of the courage with which he went into battle.

However the failure of such raids – infuriating the Turks but winning little sympathy from the local population – convinced Levski that Ottoman rule could only be overthrown by a revolutionary organization based within Bulgaria itself. He developed the idea that an elite group of committed activists, or "apostles", should travel the length and breadth of the country establishing a secret revolutionary network. Armed with funds from Bulgarian merchants in Bucharest, Levski set out on the first of his clandestine trips around Bulgaria in 1868, and over the next few years succeeded in establishing a virtual state-within-a-state dedicated to armed insurrection. In 1872, he was effectively appointed leader of the coming revolution by the newly formed Bulgarian Revolutionary Central Committe (BRCK) in Bucharest.

Towards the end of 1872, the revolutionary leader Dimitûr Obshti led an ill-advised attack on a postal wagon to raise funds for arms purchases. Ambushed by gendarmes, Obshti told the Ottoman authorities everything, in the hope that it would save him from the death sentence, but also because Levski distrusted him and had tried to freeze him out of the movement. Mass arrests followed, and Levski hurried to his headquarters in Lovech to try and destroy the organization's archives. Arrested at a nearby inn, Levski was executed the following February in Sofia, on the spot now marked by the Levski monument. The traitor Obshti preceded him to the gallows.

Although he became a national hero to subsequent generations, Levski may well have felt uncomfortable in the Bulgaria which came into being after his death. He was a convinced republican (hence the exploitation of his legacy by the equally anti-royalist Communists), and also a believer in racial harmony – he made it clear more than once that he was fighting against Ottoman power on behalf of all Bulgarians, and not just the Slavs.

around a statue of Levski, brandishing a pistol and with a small lion, representing Bulgaria, at his side. Off to the south is the colonnaded basilica of the **Church of Sveti Nikola**, with its separate and once-elegant bell tower, both, sadly, in a state of disrepair. Just uphill from here, cobbled alleys lead into a quarter full of nineteenth-century houses and spruced-up mansions. The bright blue bell-tower of the **Church of Sveta Bogoroditsa**, on ulitsa Vasil Levski, is the most eye-catching feature of this part of town; the church itself is also worthy of closer attention, not least for the colourful modern fresco on the porch, showing a particularly saintly-looking Vasil Levski, clad in ecclesiastical vestments and accompanied by a gathering of venerable churchmen. The dark interior is rather sombre in comparison, though it's enlivened by a splendid, and very high, wooden pulpit, and an ornate iconostasis adorned with double-headed eagles. A little further up and on the opposite side of the street, the **Centre for Crafts and Cultural Traditions** at no. 31A (*Tsentûr za zanayati i kultirni traditsii*; Mon–Fri 9am–5pm; free) occupies an attractively restored nineteenth-century house, and displays local woodcarving, embroidery and carpet weaving inside. At the top of the street is the disused **Kurshum Dzhamiya** (Lead-roofed Mosque), dating from 1485, which has a spacious porch with cedarwood pillars, and a minaret shorn off just above roof level.

Further uphill lies **ploshtad 20 Yuli**, a split-level mix of *fin-de-siècle* and concrete postwar edifices that forms the rather soulless centre of the new town. Heading west from here, you'll find the **Vasil Levski House-Museum** (daily 8.30am–1pm & 2-5.30pm; 2Lv), behind a low wall at ul. Gen. Kartsov 57. A simple quadrangle with a verandah, its living quarters are austere, furnished with the usual low wooden table and stools, while a single shelf arranged with pewter dishes provides the nearest thing to ornamentation. Levski's mother worked at the *boyadzhiinitsa* (dyeing shed), which is today filled with earthenware pots. Behind the house, a gallery holds a collection of paintings of Levski, in a variety of Christ-like attitudes, as well as photographs of his comrades in the First and Second Bulgarian Legions, and a few documents and weapons. The semi-divine treatment continues just outside the enclosure, in a tiny chapel where you can view a clump of Levski's hair, reverently housed in a glass reliquary beside the altar, while a tape recording of solemn chanting plays in the background.

Practicalities

From Karlovo's **train station** it's about 1km uphill to the centre; head straight across the park outside and up ulitsa Vasil Levski to reach the sights, or through the park and bear left to find the **bus station** – although some bus services, notably those to and from Plovdiv, stop outside the train station itself. There's a small **tourist information centre** at the end of ulitsa Vodopad, (summer officially daily 9am-7pm, winter times unpredictable; ⓣ0335/5373, ⓔinfokarlovo@rozabg.com). You should be able to see all of Karlovo's sights (and make a short trip to Sopot into the bargain) in the space of a day, but if you wish **to stay** the night, your choices are limited to the rather basic family-run *Hemus Hotel*, two blocks north of the station at ul. Levski 87 (ⓣ0335/4597; ❷), with drab decor and shared facilities, or the more comfortable two-star *Hotel Shterev*, on the main square in the upper part of town (ⓣ0335/93380; ❹–❻), which has a mixture of unrenovated, brown-furnished rooms with old-style bathrooms, and pristine modern en-suites with minibar and TV.

A few **cafés** are clustered around the main square, with the terrace of the *Hotel Shterev* providing the best venue for people-watching. *Edno Vreme*, east of the square at ul. Rakovska 9, is the best of the **restaurants**, offering everything from trout to roast beef in a nineteenth-century house surrounded by a well-kept garden. **Internet** access is available at *Europeonline*, ul. Levski 35, and at *Cyber Warrior*, opposite the mosque.

The Stara reka and the Balkan Range

Karlovo makes an excellent base from which to explore the imperious peaks of the **Balkan Range** to the north. The main route to the uplands, along the gorge of the **Stara reka** ("old river"), begins immediately north of Karlovo town centre. The dramatic, steep-sided limestone defile has been declared a nature reserve, which means that the usual restrictions (don't pick plants and don't stray from marked paths) apply. The area features on the excellent 1:65,000 *Troyan Balkan* hiking map, which may be available at Karlovo's tourist information centre (see previous page), though to be on the safe side try and pick it up from Zig-Zag/Odysseia-In in Sofia (see p.84).

To get to the gorge, follow ulitsa Vodopad north from Karlovo's main square, passing an area of riverside parkland where locals set up their barbecues and splash around on hot summer days. At the top of ulitsa Vodopad you'll find a hydroelectric plant overlooked by a small waterfall; just before the plant, a waymarked path heads left up the hillside. It's a steep, winding track, but after about an hour a marvellous panorama of the gorge rewards your effort. From here, the path charts a course along the rocky walls of the gorge before arriving at the *Hizha Hubavets* hut after another hour or so. Here the gorge splits from the main path; following the right fork, you'll ascend to the *Hizha Balkanski Rozi* hut (1hr 30min) then the *Hizha Vasil Levski* hut (1hr more), which lies just beneath the main ridge of the Balkan mountains. With a good map, walking experience and plenty of time to spare, you can ascend the ridge: dog-legging your way up to the 2035m **Kostenurkata** ("the tortoise") just above *Hizha Levski* takes around 1hr 30min; otherwise the main routes lead to the 2376m **Vrûh Botev** to the east (3hr), and the 2166m **Ambaritsa** to the west (2hr 30min). All these peaks provide access to lateral hikes along the ridge of the Balkan Range, or lengthy descents to the trailhead villages on the northern side of the Range, notably Apriltsi (see p.241) from the Vrûh Botev direction, or Cherni Osûm (see p.241) from Ambaritsa. Vrûh Botev is also accessible by car from Kalofer (see below).

Kalofer

Whether travellers heading east from Karlovo see vineyards, tobacco plants or roses depends on the season, but whatever the time of year you'll pass some of the grandest peaks in the Balkans. Crossing the Staga ridge, which joins the Sredna Gora to the Balkan Range, the road enters the small town of **KALOFER**, nestled in a lovely valley, and cut through by the River Tundzha. Like Karlovo, it has an attractive old quarter, and is indelibly associated with another revolutionary, **Hristo Botev**, whose ubiquitous portrait has become an icon.

A heroic-modernist **statue** of Botev overlooks the main square from the foothills of the highest peak in the Balkan range (2376m), which now bears his name, while Botev's exploits are detailed in a large modern **museum**, off to the right of the main square among the trees (Tues–Sun 8am–5.30pm; 2Lv). Inside is a didactic, Bulgarian-only words-and-pictures chronicle of Botev's life, centred around the printing press on which he published the nationalist newspaper *Zname*. Outside is the tiny cottage where Botev was born, an even simpler dwelling than Levski's childhood home. If asked, the curator will open up the school museum (same times) on the opposite side of the square, where you can peer at a couple of re-created nineteenth-century schoolrooms and ponder the conditions in which Botev and his father once taught.

Hristo Botev (1848–1876)

Professional revolutionary, poet and idealist, **Hristo Botev** is perhaps the most romantic figure in Bulgaria's pantheon of heroes. After imbibing patriotism from his Kalofer schoolteacher father he became immersed in radical politics while a high-school student in Odessa. Devouring the texts of Russian revolutionaries like Herzen and Bakunin, Botev developed an enduring faith in republicanism, socialism, and the revolutionary potential of the masses. Thrown out of school for being a weak student, Botev returned home to serve as his father's assistant in Kalofer school, but had to leave town in 1867 after delivering a provocative speech on the Feast Day of Saints Cyril and Methodius. Ten years of exile in Romania followed, during which time he hung out with Vazov and other penniless Bulgarian outlaws in Braila, shared an abandoned windmill with Levski, and began writing for émigré newspapers. Landing a job as a schoolteacher in Izmail (a town on the northern bank of the Danube with a predominantly Bulgarian population), he renewed contacts with the Russian underground, but soon had to leave town under a cloud. According to fellow revolutionary and writer Zahari Stoyanov, Botev asked for voluntary contributions from his pupils' parents (again in order to finance a celebration of SS Cyril and Methodius' Day), then ran off with the money. Apologists maintain that he hadn't been paid for three months, and this was his only way of getting even.

A trail-blazing career in émigré journalism followed: Botev launched his first paper in Braila in 1871, before moving to Bucharest to work on Lyuben Karavelov's titles *Svoboda* ("Freedom") and *Nezavisimost* ("Independence"). Another self-published periodical, *Budilnik* ("The Alarm"), came along in 1873, and in 1875 he became editor of the Bulgarian Revolutionary Central Committee (BRCK)'s official organ, *Zname* ("The Banner"). As an editor Botev combined caustic revolutionary prose with his own poems: eulogies to liberty, Levski and the legendary *haidut* Hadzhi Dimitûr among them. However Botev's firebrand rhetoric caused rifts within the BRCK. Attacking erstwhile mentor and BRCK president Lyuben Karavelov for not being revolutionary enough, Botev took virtual control of the movement. After presiding over the failed Stara Zagora uprising of 1875, however, he retired to lick his wounds.

Plans to launch another new paper, *Nova Bûlgariya*, were cut short by the April Rising of 1876, when Botev – a man with no military experience whatsoever – agreed to lead a *cheta* or armed group across the Danube in support of the rebels. The plan was to march to the town of Vratsa in northwestern Bulgaria (see p.183), where weapons – purchased with money already sent to Bucharest by Vratsa community leaders – would be delivered to the locals and the banner of rebellion raised. Older, wiser revolutionaries disowned the project.

Biographers still disagree as to whether Botev's decision to take up arms was a coolly thought-out act of martyrdom or merely the emotional response of a man out of touch with reality. The idea of sacrificing blood for the motherland is a constant theme of Botev's poetry, so it's possible that he was reconciled from the outset to the idea of a glorious death. Whatever the motives, the expedition soon degenerated into farce. Launched several weeks after the Rising itself had been put down, it was doomed before it even started. Having hijacked the Austrian steamship *Radetsky* in order to cross the Danube on May 17 (see p.293) and landed at Kozlodui with two hundred men disguised as market gardeners, Botev's first speech on liberated "Bulgarian" soil had to be delivered in Romanian – the local inhabitants were all Vlachs. Botev's stirring oratory succeeded in recruiting a grand total of two people to the cause. Undeterred, and now the owner of a white horse confiscated from a local merchant, Botev led his men inland through an area where hostile Tatar and Circassian villages outnumbered those inhabited by Bulgarians. Even the latter were nonplussed by Botev's arrival: the insurrectionary network he expected to find here simply didn't exist. The Ottoman authorities, who had followed Botev's progress all the way from the Danube, had no trouble in neutralizing the *cheta*, killing most of its members and scattering the rest. Botev himself was cut down on Mount Okolchitsa near Vratsa on May 20.

If you have a car, you can also use Kalofer as a jumping-off point for excursions to **Vrûh Botev**, the Balkan Range's highest peak, which looms over the town from the northwest. An asphalt road (May–Oct) winds tortuously to the summit; it's a signed left turn as you enter Kalofer from the west.

Practicalities

As Kalofer's station is several kilometres outside town, all **trains** are met by a bus. There's also a direct **bus** service to Kalofer from central Karlovo every hour or so. The **tourist office**, occupying a white house on the western side of the main square (daily 9am–12.30pm & 1–6pm; ⓣ03133/2988, ⓦwww.kalofer.com & ⓦwww.centralbalkan.bg), offers advice on the whole of the central Balkan region, sells local crafts, and can book you into **B&B accommodation** in the village for 10–12Lv per person. Best of the B&Bs is *Tsutsova kûshta*, a pleasant National Revival-era house at ul. Blûskova 7 (ⓣ03133/2483, ⓦwww.cucovata.hit.bg; ❶), where ethnic trinkets adorn the comfortable double rooms, though bathrooms are shared. Three kilometres northwest of Kalofer (take the left fork on entering town from the south and keep going), the small *Raiski kût* hotel (ⓣ048/860715; ❷) looks like an overly ornate Legoland palace, but the rooms are simply furnished and boast shower and TV, and there's a relaxing stream-side garden. Back in central Kalofer, the *Rivedo*, on the eastern side of the square, does good grilled **food** and is also the handiest place for a drink.

Kazanlûk

Forty kilometres beyond Kalofer, **KAZANLÛK** is the capital of the rose-growing region, although you wouldn't necessarily realize that unless you pass through town during the first weekend of June, when the long-standing but fairly lacklustre **Festival of Roses** (*Praznik na rozata*) takes place. Involving folk music, dancing, and the appointment of a carnival queen, this is basically a tourist event – the rose harvest itself takes place in villages far from town at unsociably early hours of the morning. Nowadays Kazanlûk is enjoying a new lease of life as the centre of the *Dolinata na trakiiskite tsare* – the **Valley of the Thracian Kings**. Once an important area of Thracian settlement, the vicinity of Kazanlûk is dotted with countless burial mounds, many of which are still to be excavated. Enough of them have been opened to the public, however, to make the town an essential stopoff for anyone remotely interested in the Bulgarians' ancient antecedents. The most famous of the tombs lies just outside the town centre and contains unique paintings, although only a replica of the tomb is accessible to the public. Further groups of tombs lie in the surrounding countryside, and can be visited by arrangement with the local history museum providing you give a few hours' notice (see below for details).

While there's a reasonable selection of accommodation in Kazanlûk, the town's location at the centre of both north-south and east-west routes makes it a feasible day-trip destination from Plovdiv, Gabrovo, Veliko Tûrnovo, or – at a pinch – Sofia. It also lies at the southern end of the **Shipka Pass** road, one of Bulgaria's most spectacular cross-mountain routes.

Some history

The area around Kazanlûk has attracted successive waves of settlers and invaders, not least because of its strategic importance in controlling approaches

△ Kazanlûk shoe shop

to the Shipka Pass. In ancient times, the Tundzha Valley was the domain of the Thracian **Odrysae**, who exploited the vacuum left by the retreat of the Persians in the fifth century BC to forge a powerful tribal state on the southern slopes of the Balkan Range. Their power was temporarily broken by Philip II of Macedon in 342 BC, but they re-emerged a generation later under **King Seuthes III**, an unruly vassal of Alexander the Great's successor Lysimachus, who built a new capital, Seuthopolis, 7km west of present-day Kazanlûk – now submerged beneath a reservoir. The River Tundzha is thought to have been navigable as far as Seuthopolis in ancient times, bringing trade, profits and Hellenistic culture to the Odrysae – who expressed their wealth in the solid, but exquisitely decorated **tombs** which abound in the region. Seuthopolis soon fell into decline however, and a deluge of **Celts** occurred around 280 BC, many of whom settled in the plain just east of Kazanlûk. There was a fortified medieval Bulgarian settlement at Krûn, just to the northwest (where a village of the same name still exists), but the town of Kazanlûk itself is relatively modern, dating from the Ottoman occupation. Its name loosely translates as the "place of the copper cauldrons", a likely reference to the giant stills in which rose oil was prepared. By the turn of the twentieth century Kazanlûk's streets were filled with the shops and store-houses of the rose merchants – a breed of Balkan trader that has long since disappeared, squeezed out by social ownership and state control.

Arrival and accommodation

Kazanlûk's **train** and **bus stations** are just south of the centre on the scruffy ulitsa Sofronii Vrachanski, from where a five-minute walk up bulevard Rozova Dolina will bring you to the town's main square, ploshtad Sevtopolis. There's a reasonable choice of **accommodation** in the centre, and a couple of out-of-town places which are easily accessible if you have your own transport. Campers can pitch tents in the grounds of the *Krûnsko hanche* motel (see below).

Hotels

Hadzhieminova kûshta ul. Nikola Petkov 22 ⓣ0431/62595, ⓕ63063. Four-room hotel in the Ethnographic Complex offering traditionally furnished rooms with carved wooden ceilings and sheepskin bedspreads. Apartments have bathtubs, regular rooms have basic showers. Apartments ❸, rooms ❶

Kazanlûk pl. Sevtopolis ⓣ0431/63210 or 63666, ⓔhotelkazanlak@abv.bg. Standard high-rise three-star on the main square offering neat pastel-hued rooms – although you'll have to shell out a bit extra if you want a proper bathtub. There's an indoor swimming pool on site. ❹–❺

Krûnsko hanche 4km north of town on the Shipka road ⓣ0431/63123. Roadside motel with a couple of nondescript accommodation blocks and a grassy camping ground out the back. Doubles come with dated brownish colour schemes, simple showers, TV and sagging beds. There are also some very basic four-person bungalows (20Lv), and a restaurant on site. Buses #5 or #6 pass by. ❷

Palas ul. Petko Staynov 9 ⓣ0431/62311 or 64411, ⓦwww.hotel-palas.com. Medium-sized hotel on a quiet central side street boasting rooms with reproduction nineteenth-century furniture, fancy drapes, cable TV and proper bathtubs. There's also a sauna, solarium and swimming pool. ❺

Sveti Georgi in the village of Enina 6km north of town ⓣ04326/2045. Modern building in the style of a rich nineteenth-century merchant's house, with comfortable, balconied en-suites, a walled garden and an excellent restaurant with tables grouped around a tiny outdoor pool. To get there, take the Shipka road and turn right after 2km. ❸

Vesta ul. Chavdar Voyvoda 3 ⓣ0431/20350 or 40039, ⓔcomplexvesta@abv.bg. Family-run place offering neat, tiled-floor rooms with TV and fridge, 5min north of the centre. Breakfast is served in a shady courtyard. ❸

Zornitsa Tyulbeto Park ⓣ0431/63939, ⓦwww.zornica.bg.com. Modern building on the brow of the hill behind the Thracian tomb, with spacious, creamy-coloured rooms with modern toilet/shower and TV, an outdoor pool that's popular with the locals in summer, and great views across town from the terrace. ❺

The Town

The hotel and civic buildings on Kazanlûk's main square – **ploshtad Sevtopolis** – present an uncompromisingly modern contrast to the remnants of the prewar town that straggle untidily westwards. The nineteenth-century **Church of the Assumption**, just off the square to the east, contains an exquisite iconostasis carved by Debûr craftsmen, while a host of finds from ancient Seuthopolis are displayed in the basement of the **Iskra Museum**, to the north of the square (Mon-Fri 9am–noon & 2-5.30pm; 2Lv). Weapons, pottery, and coins minted by Seuthes III help to illustrate life in his capital, while the reconstructed floor plans of domestic houses reveal the bowl-like depressions that served as cult hearths, for appeals to tribal deities. Upstairs is a display devoted to nineteenth-century life, with huge copper stills impressively illustrating the rose-oil business, and a picture gallery with a reasonable cross-section of twentieth-century Bulgarian art and a smattering of saintly icons.

Ten minutes' walk northeast of the museum, on the far bank of the Starata Reka, ulitsa Knyaz Mirski runs off beside an **Ethnographic Complex**. Along here, several nineteenth-century houses have been restored to their former splendour, one of which serves as a **museum** (mid-May to mid-Oct Mon-Fri 9am–5pm; for winter hours enquire at the Iskra Museum; 2Lv), where period furnishings and an elegant walled garden recall the lifestyles of Kazanlûk's rose merchants. If the rose industry fires your imagination, you might want to trek out to the **Museum of the Rose Industry** (*Muzei na rozite*; mid-May to mid-Oct: daily 9am–5pm; 2Lv), 2km from the centre along the Shipka road – buses #5 or #6 pass by. Though there's relatively little information given in English, the museum successfully conveys an idea of how rose jam, toothpaste, eau-de-cologne, jelly and, of course, attar of roses are produced. The plantation out the back will be of interest to those who have a working knowledge of rose cultivation but is not laid out as an attractive garden.

Tyulbeto Park and the Kazanlûk Tomb

On a hillside immediately north of the Ethnographic Complex, **Tyulbeto Park** is the site of two renowned funerary monuments. A stairway beyond the park gates ascends to the skeletal remains of the **Turbe of Lala Shahin Pasha**, conqueror of much of Bulgaria and first Ottoman governor of Rumelia. He fell in battle here, and it's thought that his entrails were interred on the spot before the rest of him was carried back to Bursa (probably embalmed in honey) to be buried in a much finer *turbe* closer to home.

Immediately behind the *turbe* is a protective structure built over the so-called **Kazanlûk Tomb** (*Kazanlûshkata grobnitsa*), first of the many **Thracian tombs** in the area to be excavated. Originating in the late fourth- or early third-century BC, the burial chamber was unearthed by chance in 1944 during the construction of an air-raid post, and is now a listed UNESCO monument. Its frescoes are so delicate that only scholars with authorization from the Ministry of Culture may enter (and only then with a good reason), but the replica (April–Oct daily 9am–5pm; for Nov–March hours, enquire at the Iskra Museum; 5Lv), built 50m east along the path, is an atmospheric enough re-creation. Once inside, the domed burial chamber is approached through a low-roofed, narrow antechamber decorated by two bands of murals – one ornamented with plant and architectural motifs, the other displaying battle scenes. The floor and walls are stained a deep red, while in the cupola are the **paintings** for which the tomb is famed. They depict a procession of horses and servants approaching the chieftain for whom the tomb was built, who sits behind a low table laden with food. His wife, face downcast in mourning, reposes on an elaborate throne beside him, and the couple touch hands in a tender gesture of farewell. A bowl of pomegranates – a fruit associated with immortality - is offered to the deceased by a female figure to the right, who has been linked with both the Great Mother Goddess common to Thracian tribes, and the queen of the Underworld in the Greek pantheon, Persephone. Racing chariots wheel around the apex of the dome, a possible reference to the games that often accompanied a Thracian funeral (see below). With its graceful composition and naturalistic details, the painting is a masterpiece of Hellenistic art, although opinions differ as to whether the frescoes are the work of an itinerant Greek master or an inspired local.

The Valley of the Thracian Kings

The area northwest of Kazanlûk was a sacred place for the inhabitants of Seuthopolis, and they left a string of necropoli on either side of the road that runs along the Shipka Pass. Not all the 1500 **burial mounds** (*mogili*) in the vicinity contain the stone-built tombs of the wealthy, and it's not known which classes of Thracian society actually qualified for one: kings, priests, or noble families in general. It is clear, however, that the prevalence of tombs reflects the growing wealth and self-confidence of Odrysian society from the fifth century

BC onwards. After years of intense archeological activity, a group of four tombs has now been opened to the public. However the Ministry of Culture looks set to limit further excavations, as the number of open tombs is outstripping the ability of the authorities to look after them adequately. **Visits to the tombs** must be arranged through the Iskra Museum – arrive early in the morning or try ringing ⓣ0431/63762. The cost of 6–10Lv per person per tomb (most people visit three or four to make the trip worthwhile) includes an English-speaking guide, but you'll need to pay extra for a driver if you don't have your own transport.

The nearest of the tombs to Kazanlûk on the south side of Shipka village is the fifth-century-BC **Mogila Ostrusha**, which contains a remarkable granite burial chamber in the form of a miniature Greek temple – indeed it may have served as a place of worship before being used as a tomb. The ceiling of the

The Thracian way of death

The Bulgarian countryside is dotted with **Thracian burial mounds**, or *mogili*, the majority of which remain unexcavated. They were erected by a society which set great emphasis on the role of the tomb, both in providing the deceased with a lasting memorial and in creating a focus for the ancestor-worship cult which flourished in this culture. Some tombs served as family mausoleums, containing the bones of several generations. Principal tombs that are open to the public can be found near Kazanlûk and Sveshtari (see opposite and p.279); otherwise, most Bulgarian museums house Thracian burial finds of one sort or another.

According to **Herodotus**, deceased Thracian nobles were laid out for three days, during which time a short period of mourning was held, followed by a great communal feast. The body was then either buried or cremated, with a tumulus raised over it, and a series of athletic games and contests were begun, the biggest prizes being awarded for single combat. Herodotus also notes that amongst those tribes where polygamy was practised, the wives of a dead warrior would compete vigorously for the honour of being declared his favourite, and so be slaughtered and buried alongside him. This assertion is partly borne out by the evidence of some of the excavated tumili, where the bones of young females have been found lying next to those of the chieftain. In many cases, however, the deceased made do with the company of his favourite horse.

Modern archeological evidence points to a rich **funerary culture**, full of symbolic actions whose meanings can only be guessed at. Many tombs were regularly reopened so that sacrifices and other rituals could be carried out, suggesting that burial places served as cultic centres for the surrounding settlement. In some areas, the body was disinterred and moved to another location, either within the tomb or elsewhere, pointing to ritual reburial as an important part of funerary practice. Each season of excavation reveals yet stranger rites: one of the Sveshtari tombs was found to contain half the skeleton of a large dog – the other half had been buried outside, possibly a ritual means whereby the spirit dog would guard the approaches to his master's tomb, as well as keeping by his side.

Indeed, hunting dogs may well have accompanied tribal chieftains into the afterlife, the existence of which the Thracians took for granted, although it's unclear as to whether life beyond the grave was enjoyed by all, or merely the elite group of nobles and priest-kings. However, Herodotus relates how certain tribes mourned the birth of children, thinking of the sufferings they would endure through life, and would celebrate "with merriment and rejoicing" the death of one of their number, who could no longer by touched by pain or sorrow. Thracian beliefs about the immortality of the soul undoubtedly spread southwards to Greece, where they contributed to the development of mystery cults such as *Orphism* (see p.369).

chamber was painted with a grid of small scenes, of which only one survives in recognizable form – a faded and tiny portrait of a red-haired girl, unique for the period.

The remaining tombs date from at least a century later than Ostrusha and, like the Kazanlûk tomb, are built in the form of a domed burial chamber approached through a narrow, corridor-like antechamber. Two are in the Shushmanets complex, an ensemble of six mounds on the eastern fringes of Shipka village. The burial chamber of the **Mogila Shushmanets** itself is characterized by a single Doric column which supports the ceiling, while the nearby **Mogila Helvetsia**, named in honour of Switzerland, whose government paid for its excavation, boasts an elegant pointed-arch entrance. Finally, out beyond Shipka village on the Gabrovo road, the **Mogila Arsenalka** (so named because of its proximity to the Arsenal Kalashnikov factory) features an outer facade fashioned from blocks of porphyry granite quarried on the south side of the valley. Inside, the chamber is simple and undecorated but exudes harmony, with a stone bed for the deceased and a circular hearth on the floor for lighting sacrificial fires.

Eating and drinking

Central Kazanlûk doesn't have a great deal going for it as far as dining is concerned, although the *Hotel Kazanlûk* has a good-quality if rather staid restaurant with a no-nonsense meat-and-two-veg culinary repertoire. There's also a café-pizzeria on the ground floor with a long square-side terrace. Next to the Ethnographic Complex, the restaurant of the *Hadzhieminova kûshta* (see "Hotels"; p.309) runs the full gamut of Bulgarian cuisine and has a decent range of freshwater fish, all served up in a courtyard shaded by figs and other trees. *Kûshtata*, midway between the town centre and the Museum of the Rose Industry by the side of the Shipka-bound road, is another good place in which to enjoy quality Bulgarian dishes in a pleasant garden setting. The streets to the west of the main square are lined with **cafés** and **bars**.

The Shipka Pass

For drama and majestic vistas, few routes in Bulgaria match crossing the **SHIPKA PASS**. Particularly at sunset, when the mountains darken and a chill wind disperses the tourists, you can feel something of the pass's potent historical significance. Ever since Alexander the Great drove back a force of Triballi here in 335 BC, control of Shipka has been an important strategic imperative.

When present-day Bulgarians think of Shipka, however, they recall the Russo-Turkish War, when 6000 Russians and Bulgarians resisted a 27,000-strong Ottoman force that had been dispatched northwards to break the siege of Plevna (modern-day Pleven) in August 1877. Snow exacerbated the hardships of Radetsky's ill-equipped Bulgarian volunteers (many of whom had been civilians in Gabrovo just days before), and despite the local women who brought supplies, the defenders' ammunition was exhausted by the third day of the **battle** and they resorted to throwing rocks, tree trunks and finally corpses at the Turks. The pass held, however, and in due time Plevna surrendered, whereupon the Russians reinforced Radetsky's army and ordered it to fight its way down the snowy mountainside to defeat the remaining 22,000 Ottoman troops outside Kazanlûk – which it did.

The **journey** across the mountains between Kazanlûk and Gabrovo takes about ninety minutes **by bus**, and it's wise to book seats when leaving either town – even if you're planning to stop halfway and then continue on or return by a later service (there are usually some empty seats by the time buses reach the pass). Most visitors head for three major destinations around Shipka: the scenery and war memorials of the **summit** itself; the neighbouring **Mount Buzludzha**, where renowned *haidut* Hadzhi Dimitûr bit the dust; and the **Shipka Memorial Church**, just 12km north of Kazanlûk.

The Shipka Memorial Church

From a stop near the corner of Sofronii Vrachanski and Rozova Dolina in Kazanlûk, you can catch bus #6 out to **Shipka** village, a rustic huddle of buildings a little way off the main road to the pass. From the wooded hillside rise the gold onion domes of the **Shipka Memorial Church** (daily 8.30am–4.30pm), built by the Czech architect Tomisko after the Liberation as a monument to both Russian and Bulgarian dead, and finally consecrated in 1902. Conceived by philanthropic Russian aristocrats and financed by public donations, the edifice was modelled on Muscovite churches of the seventeenth century.

The church is a vibrantly coloured confection of pinks and greens, topped off with a fifty-metre-high spire on the bell tower. Its **interior**, the work of Bulgarian artists under the direction of the Russian painter Pomerantsev, is perhaps the best example of the academic realist style that flourished in Bulgaria around the turn of the twentieth century. Folk-influenced floral and geometric patterns rich in primary colours weave their way around naturalistic depictions of Bulgarian saints and tsars. Many of them are dressed in Byzantine costume, a reminder of the pre-World War I days when Bulgaria's desire to extend its frontiers towards the former imperial capital was reflected in a passion for all things Byzantine.

At the western end of the church, murals portray great figures from Russian history, including the fourteenth-century ruler Dmitri Donskoi being blessed before going off to smite the Tatars, and an allegorical scene of Cyril and Methodius bringing literacy to the Slavs.

The pass

Though the car park at the summit of the **pass** itself has degenerated into a truck-stop, it's impossible not to be awed – and exhausted – by the final ascent of the nearby **Mount Stoletov**, whose summit the Bulgarians held during the battle, and which overlooks the pass. Visitors struggle up five hundred steps, past heroic bas-reliefs, to reach the towering stone **Freedom Monument**, erected in the 1890s, which commands a glorious panorama of the Sredna Gora and the Valley of the Roses (the monument itself can be seen from Kazanlûk). The tower contains a symbolic sarcophagus and a **museum** of weapons and paintings detailing each phase of the battle, but the real lure is the observation platform on the roof, affording superb views of the mountains. From here you can see the **Russian cemetery**, 300m to the northwest, which is the largest of the many concentrations of cannon and gravestones planted on the slopes of surrounding hills.

Accommodation at the Shipka Pass is pretty limited but does at least offer a wonderful sense of isolation. Right by the summit, the humdrum *Hotel Shipka* (Ⓣ04324/2730; ❶) is a large gloomy building offering humbly furnished rooms and shared facilities; while the *Opûlchenets*, on the opposite side of the road (Ⓣ0888 213 507; ❶–❷), has slightly comfier rooms with 1970s decor and simple showers. There's also a rather forlorn **campsite** (mid-May to Sept) with chalets, 1km down the road towards Gabrovo. Don't miss sampling the buffalo-milk yoghurt, a local speciality sold at the pass.

Mount Buzludzha

From the pass a side road runs 12km east to **Mount Buzludzha**, topped by a bizarre structure resembling a spaceship come to earth, that counterpoints the monument at Shipka. It was on Mount Buzludzha that Hadzhi Dimitûr and his rebels died fighting the Turks on August 2, 1868, while the Bulgarian Socialist Party was founded on the same day in 1891, following a clandestine congress, also on the mountain. The "spaceship" was built to house a museum covering both events, although it's now in a semi-derelict state. This gem of Communist kitsch can in any case only be reached by car, as there are no longer any buses from Kazanlûk.

Beyond the Valley of the Roses

East of Kazanlûk the Tundzha Valley broadens out, although it continues to be flanked by the wall of the Balkan Range and the lower, wooded hills of the Sredna Gora. Lurking on the far side of the latter is **Stara Zagora**, Bulgaria's sixth-largest city, with a population of 150,000. Home to one of the most important Neolithic sites in Europe, Stara Zagora warrants at least a brief detour, especially for those travelling southwards from the Valley of the Roses towards Plovdiv, Haskovo, Kûrdzhali or Turkey – all are easily accessible by train or bus from here.

Another obvious stopoff on the way to the coast is **Sliven**, the most important town between the Valley of the Roses and the sea. Lying snug beneath the craggy Balkan Range, it is a good base from which to explore the **Blue Rocks** nearby or the historic craft villages in the mountains to the north, **Kotel**, with its array of intriguing museums, and **Zheravna**, a captivating huddle of rustic architecture which is worth the effort required to get there.

Stara Zagora and around

STARA ZAGORA means "Old Town Behind the Mountain", an apt name for this settlement on the far flanks of the eastern Sredna Gora, with a history of occupation stretching back some 7000 years. Neolithic farmers were the first on the scene (see p.317), while it was the Thracians, in the fifth century BC, who established the first significant town, which they called Beroe. Reconstructed and refounded by the Romans as Augusta Traiana in the second century AD, it stood at the crossroads of two important trade routes, and commanded a fertile area still noted for its wheat and fruit orchards. This attractive location had its downside, though; the town was repeatedly attacked, destroyed and rebuilt by a succession of native and foreign conquerors throughout the Middle Ages, each time acquiring a new name. Under Ottoman rule, Stara Zagora was one of the centres of the Bulgarian renaissance, and its school attracted such pupils as Levski, Botev and Raina Knyaginya. Burned down by the Turks in 1877 for welcoming the Russian army of General Gurko, and subsequently rebuilt on a strict grid plan, today the city has an urbane, modern appearance, centring on leafy boulevards and lively cafés.

Arrival, information and accommodation

Stara Zagora's **train station** lies about five blocks south of the central City Garden, near the bottom of bulevard Ruski; the **bus station** is further east on bulevard Slavyanski – both are just ten minutes' walk from the centre. There's no tourist office in Stara Zagora although the website of the Regional Economic Developmernt Agency (Ⓦwww.szeda.bg) has plenty of visitor-related information. There's a good choice of smart, modern, mid-price **accommodation** in Stara Zagora, although budget places are thinner on the ground and advance booking is recommended whatever the season.

Hotels

Dedov ul. Tsar Simeon Veliki 162 Ⓣ042/602667, Ⓦwww.dedov.bg. Friendly, family-run place offering some exceedingly comfortable rooms, each with TV, a/c, fridge, and repro furniture – except the exquisite top-floor mansard rooms, which are resolutely contemporary in style. Most rooms come with bathtub. Breakfast served in a lovely garden. ❻

Ezeroto ul. Bratya Zhekovi 60 Ⓣ042/600103 or 600104, Ⓔezeroto@mail.bg. Modern comforts can be taken for granted at this four-star hotel, overlooking the lake in the park between the train station and the centre. Rooms come in some odd colours but they're reasonably spacious and the furnishings are new. Ask for a south-facing, park-side room. ❻

Hizhata Ayazmo Park Ⓣ042/643128. Slightly further afield, in the pleasant surroundings of Ayazmo Park, the newly renovated *Hizhata* is a relatively economical option and fills up quickly as a result. Rooms are simple but have shower and TV, while the on-site restaurant boasts wonderful views of town from its hillside terrace. ❸

Tangra ul. Lyuben Karavelov 80 Ⓣ042/600901 or 600902, Ⓕ600903. A pleasant modern hotel about six blocks east of the centre, offering clean, tiled en-suite rooms with TV and minibar, some with frumpy blue decor, others bright and cream-coloured. Breakfast is included in the price. ❺

Vereya ul. Tsar Simeon Veliki 100 Ⓣ042/618600. The largest and most central of Stara Zagora's hotels is the comfortable and recently refurbished *Vereya*, though the string of late-night cafés and bars on its doorstep means it's also in one of the noisier locations. ❺

Zheleznik ul. Parchevich 1 Ⓣ042/622158. High-rise opposite the bus station with a large stock of recently renovated, pastel-coloured en-suites with modern bathroom fittings, although not all come with TV. Standards of customer service are still in the Communist era. ❹

The Town

The heart of town is the elegant **City Garden**, near the intersection of the main east–west and north–south thoroughfares, bulevards Tsar Simeon Veliki and Ruski. Pensioners gather on the benches to gossip and couples stroll along the shady paths between the flowerbeds, while a row of booksellers runs off towards the **Eski dzhamiya** (Old Mosque). Built in 1409, this squat edifice has a seventeen-metre-wide dome that was considered a great architectural feat at the time. Sadly, the building is now derelict and no longer open to visitors.

Diagonally across the Garden loom the old and new **Opera Houses**, home to the oldest and most prestigious provincial opera company in Bulgaria – it was here that the famous singer Boris Christoff first made his name. Across the way to the west, a sizeable restored section of a **Roman theatre** is visible behind the town council building. To the east of here, on ulitsa Dimitûr Naumov, you can get a good idea of bourgeois life during the National Revival, at the **Museum**

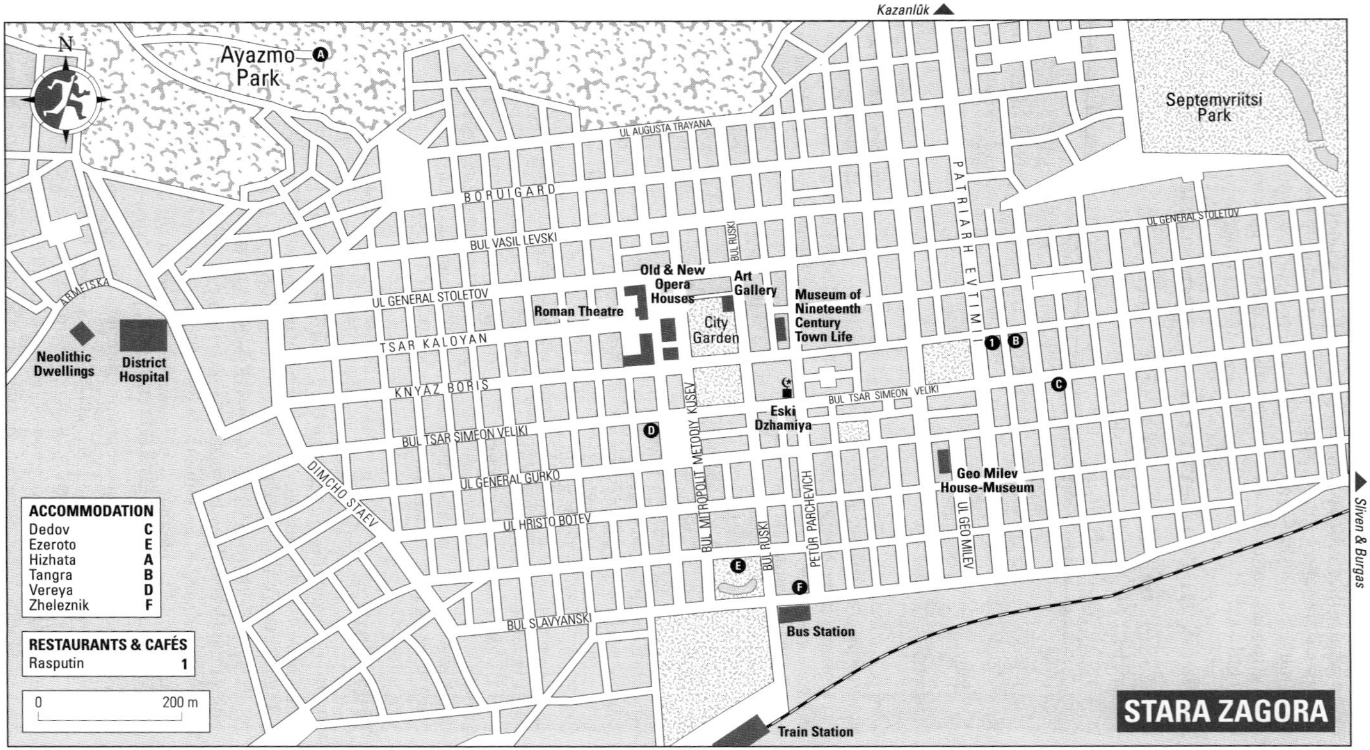

STARA ZAGORA

Sliven & Burgas
Kazanlŭk
Septemvriitsi Park
Ayazmo Park
Train Station
Bus Station
Geo Milev House-Museum
Museum of Nineteenth Century Town Life
Art Gallery
City Garden
Old & New Opera Houses
Roman Theatre
Eski Dzhamiya
District Hospital
Neolithic Dwellings
PATRIARH EVTIMII
UL GEO MILEV
PETŬR PARCHEVICH
BUL RUSKI
BUL MITROPOLIT METODIY KUSEV
BUL TSAR SIMEON VELIKI
UL GENERAL STOLETOV
TSAR KALOYAN
KNYAZ BORIS
UL GENERAL GURKO
UL HRISTO BOTEV
BUL SLAVYANSKI
BUL VASIL LEVSKI
BORUIGARD
UL AUGUSTA TRAYANA
DIMCHO STAEV
ARMEISKA
N

ACCOMMODATION

Dedov	C
Ezeroto	E
Hizhata	A
Tangra	B
Vereya	D
Zheleznik	F

RESTAURANTS & CAFÉS

Rasputin	1

0 200 m

of Nineteenth-Century Town Life (*Kûshta-muzei Gradski bit*; Tues–Sun 9am–noon & 2–5pm; 2Lv), housed in a distinctive ochre-painted mansion. Back on bulevard Tsar Simeon Veliki, opposite the mosque, the **Art Gallery** (Tues–Sat 9am–noon & 2–5pm; 2Lv) displays work by local artists, and is worth a quick look on your way to the **Geo Milev House-Museum** (Mon-Fri 8.30am–noon & 1-4.30pm; 2Lv), the home of the poet whose verses on the subject of the 1923 Uprising caused his untimely death. The museum contains several rooms re-creating his abode, a section on other local poets such as Ivan Hadzhihristov, and a nice café.

The Neolithic dwellings

Stara Zagora's chief attraction, the **Neolithic dwellings** (*Neolitni zhilishta*) were unearthed in 1969 during the construction of a hospital. Of the several dwellings excavated – the remains of a settlement destroyed by fire c. 5500 BC – two houses were preserved in the state in which the archeologists found them and covered by a custom-built pavilion, which is now a **museum** (July–Aug Tues–Sun 9am–noon & 2–5pm; Sept–June Tues–Sat only; 5Lv; guided tour in English or French depending on which members of staff are on duty 5Lv). Inside, first impressions are of a moonscape of crumbling walls and pottery, but familiar domestic details become recognizable on closer inspection.

Each family occupied a single-roomed dwelling, usually detached – although the two preserved here were built back-to-back, possibly the sign of an extended family. In one corner of the house stood a basic stove, in which bread was baked from flour ground on a nearby millstone. Amazingly, the floor is still scattered, in places, with burnt grains. Another corner of the room was a cult area, used to keep idols of the household gods. A **gallery** in the basement holds the artefacts unearthed by the excavation, covering several millennia – the earliest ones include household implements such as sickles and spoons made out of bone – although most objects belong roughly between the sixth and fourth millennia BC. Some of the day-to-day pottery used by the Neolithic inhabitants of the houses preserved upstairs shows a surprising degree of sophistication, decorated with geometric patterns and chequerboard designs, while pots adorned with human stick figures, classic maze patterns and primitive animals have been identified as cultic vessels. One of the more intriguing pot fragments shows a shaman performing a rain-dance. The collection of marble and clay female fertility goddesses also gives a fascinating insight into the religious beliefs of these ancient people; the strictly symbolic older figures, with their outsized hips and posteriors, being replaced in later periods by more naturalistic forms. Pottery animals, including a headless hedgehog, may have had some ritual significance, while the poignant models of tiny houses, furniture and sheep appear to have been used as children's toys. A delicate child's bracelet from the fifth millennium BC is one of the oldest pieces of gold jewellery ever found.

To **get there**, walk west along ulitsa General Stoletov for fifteen minutes until you reach the district hospital (*okrûzhna bolnitsa*), then bear left into Armeiska, where steps between the residential blocks on the left descend towards the museum, in a drab, squat building behind the basketball court.

Eating and entertainment

For **eating**, the *Tangra*, *Dedov* and *Ezeroto* (see "Accommodation", p.315) all have good restaurants, while *Rasputin*, not far from the *Tangra*, at ul. Kiril i Metodi 64, serves good-quality Bulgarian standards in an intimate little courtyard, and is regarded as the best in town. Cafés and *sladkarnitsi* on Mitropolit

Kusev and Tsar Simeon are the best places in which to linger over a **drink** or an ice cream.

Folkloric events worth catching include the **Trakia Pee** ("Thrace Sings") festival involving folk groups from throughout Thrace performing in outdoor venues in late May or early June, and the national **festival of Gypsy music** which takes place in Ayazmo Park, north of the centre, in late June or July. Other civic events worth catching include the **festival of the Opera and Ballet** in May and the **beer festival**, held every August - a good opportunity to sample the famous local brew, Zagorka.

Sliven and the Blue Rocks

SLIVEN lies at the feet of craggy mountains that once sheltered so many bands of *haiduti* that Bulgarians called it the "town of the hundred *voivods*" after the number of their chieftains. The heyday of famous *haiduti* such as Hadzhi Dimitûr and Panayot Hitov coincided with the industrialization of Sliven, where Bulgaria's first textile factory was established in 1834 – its founder, Dobri Zhelyazkov (known as *Fabrikadzhiyata*, "the gaffer"), acquired parts and plans of looms by smuggling them back from Russia in bags of wool. The industry grew rapidly, and Sliven was soon likened to a "Bulgarian Manchester". Nowadays, Sliven makes a convenient stopoff between Sofia and Burgas on the coast – not so much for the town itself as for the nearby **Blue Rocks** (*Sinite kamûni*), an alluring outcrop of grey-purple stone which lies on the eastern outskirts of town. The cable-car ride to the summit of the rocks, site of the mountain resort of **Karandila**, is a popular local outing.

Arrival and accommodation

Sliven's **train station** is about 3.5km southeast of the centre, at the end of Sliven's main artery, bulevard Hadzhi Dimitûr: trolleybus #13 will take you as far as the market on ulitsa Tsar Simeon, a few steps west of the main square. The **bus station**, also on bulevard Hadzhi Dimitûr, is roughly halfway between the city centre and the train station. There's a reasonable choice of **hotel** accommodation in Sliven, although some of the better options occupy out-of-town locations in the Blue Rocks and Karandila area.

Hotels

Byala Mechka Karandila ⓣ044/667150. Small family-run hotel on top of the Blue Rocks, about 1km southeast of the chair-lift terminus. A brace of simple but tidy en-suite doubles and a couple of lounge-style apartments with TV. Great away-from-it-all location with mountain walks on the doorstep. ❷

Imperia pûtya za Karandila ⓣ044/667599 or 667573, ⓦwww.hotelimperia.net. Businesslike four-star 4km northeast of town owned by former footballer and mayor of Sliven Yordan Lechkov (which, for anyone who remembers the quarter final of the 1994 World Cup, is reason enough to stay). Standard doubles are soothingly decorated and have TV, desk space and bathtubs. There are also some roomy, stylish apartments (240Lv). There's a gym and a kidney-shaped pool on site, and a chair lift to the Blue Rocks a short walk away. ❼

Natsional ul. Konstantin Irechek ⓣ044/662929, ⓦwww.nationalsl.com. Small city-centre hotel attached to the well-known restaurant of the same name (see p.321), offering plush-carpeted, pastel-hued rooms with a/c, TV and fridge. The top-floor attic rooms are the cosiest. ❻

Sliven pl. Hadzhi Dimitûr 2 ⓣ044/627056 or 624056. Standard Communist-era high-rise with functional "standard" doubles featuring shower and TV, and slightly smarter "lux" rooms. The main selling point is the ultra-central location. ❸–❹

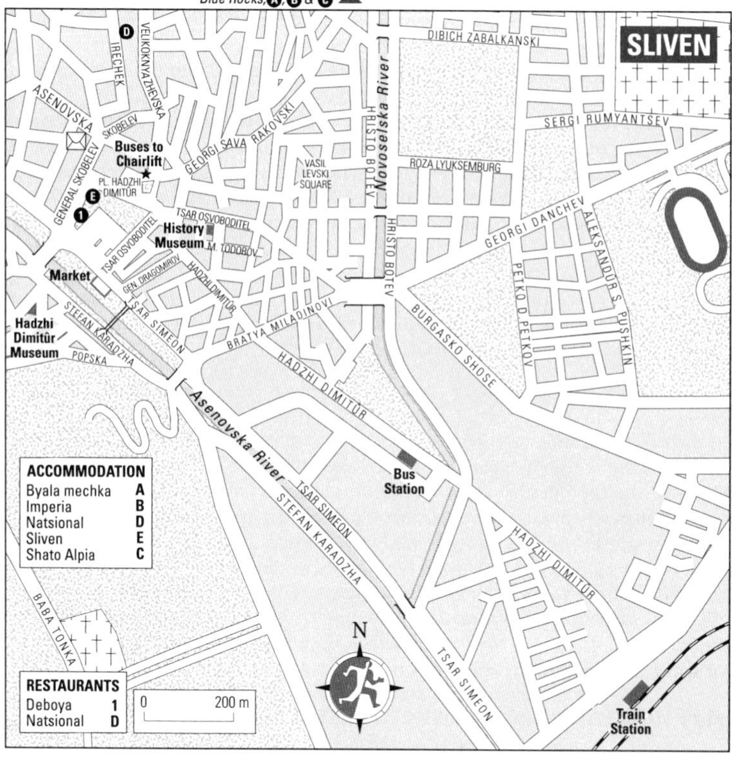

Shato Alpia ul. Velikoknyazhevska 13, 4km northeast of town next to the Karandila chair lift ⓣ044/622432, ⓦwww.alpia-tur.hit.bg. Boldly imaginative building that looks like a cross between a mountain chalet and a Romanesque cathedral, Rooms (some with shower, some with bathtub) are decked out in weird browns and greys, but are still eminently comfortable. ❹

The Town

A sprawl of crumbling apartments and red-roofed houses, Sliven converges on a leafy plaza where the high-rise *Hotel Sliven* and an ugly concrete theatre complex fail to provide the focal point that the planners have evidently been groping for. The square is named **ploshtad Hadzhi Dimitûr** after Sliven's most famous son (1840–68), a statue of whom stands to the northeast of the hotel. To learn more about Dimitûr, head off past the **Deboya** or "Depot" – once an arsenal and then a *caravanserai* – through the covered **market** beside the River Asenovska.

Down a side road, at the corner of ulitsa Asenova, the **Hadzhi Dimitûr House-Museum** (Mon 2–5pm, Tues–Sat 9am–noon & 2–5pm; 2Lv) honours the man who became Panaiot Hitov's standard-bearer by the age of 20, later teaming up with Stefan Karadzha in Romania to form a *cheta* that made guerrilla raids into Bulgaria. Eventually Turkish troops caught up with them at Mount Buzludzha, where Dimitûr fell in battle, and Karadzha was clapped in irons and taken to be hanged in Ruse. The building itself used to be an inn, run by Dimitûr's father; today you can see everything set up as it was when he lived here. Frugal bedding on the floor denotes the guests' sleeping quarters: the family lived in the more comfortable rooms to the rear, dining on a balcony carpeted with rush mats.

Sliven's other sights can be found along two streets running eastwards from the main square. **Bulevard Tsar Osvoboditel** is an attractive pedestrian zone of shops and cafés, ending in a very busy crossroads, though you'll need to keep your wits about you to dodge the speeding skateboarders and cyclists. Note the impressive **thousand-year-old oak tree** that survived the burning of medieval Sliven by the Turks. Among the best of the collection at the **History Museum** at no. 18 (Mon–Sat 9am–noon & 2–5pm; 2Lv) are funerary relics from Kaloyanovo – where a Thracian chieftain was buried with his favourite horse and Greek pottery – and a collection of superbly intricate *shishane* rifles, showing the artistry of nineteenth-century local gunsmiths.

The Blue Rocks

In the early morning and late afternoon, the porphyry massif to the northeast of Sliven assumes a smoky blue hue in the translucent light. A welcome respite from the town, the appropriately named **Blue Rocks** (*Sinite kamûni*) feature scree slopes swathed in wiry trees and shrubs, with a profusion of streams and butterflies; the crags above are eyries for birds of prey, while animals such as boar, foxes and deer roam this rocky terrain. Just beyond the summit of the rocks lies the area known as **Karandila**, a plateau of pastureland and forest crisscrossed by hiking trails.

You can drive to the Karandila area by a circuitous but scenic route, following the Kotel road from Sliven and taking a signed left turn 15km out of town. However a more popular excursion is to ascend the rocks by the **chair lift** 4km northeast of central Sliven (near the end of bus route #12 from the corner of ploshtad Hadzhi Dimitûr and ulitsa Rakovski), a clearly visible left-turn off the Kotel road. Located just beyond the *Shato Alpin* hotel (see p.319), the **chair lift** (*lifta*; 6Lv one-way; 10Lv return) in theory operates between 8.30am and 6.30pm (except on Mondays when it doesn't start up until 12.30pm), with shorter hours in winter and breaks for maintenance in spring and autumn. However there are often long breaks for lunch, and staff may wait for enough customers to turn up before switching it on.

The best-known feature of the Blue Rocks can actually be reached on foot, by slogging uphill to the fifth pylon of the chair lift and then bearing left. A jagged arch nearly 8m tall, the **Ring** (*Halkata*) is associated with several legends. Ancient mariners supposedly moored their boats here during the Flood, while fairy tales have it that a girl passing through will turn into a boy (or vice versa), and a couple doing so will fall in love forever.

The chair lift gets you to the summit in twenty minutes, giving wonderful views only slightly marred by the TV tower on **Mount Tyulbeto** (if you miss

The Karakachani festival

The Karandila area becomes especially animated on the third weekend of August, when there's a festival celebrating the music and culture of the **Karakachani**, a minority community who live scattered throughout the Sliven and Kotel area. Although today's Karakachani no longer lead the nomadic pastoral lives of their forefathers, they retain a distinct identity, speaking a dialect of Greek and bringing out their dazzling white-smocked costumes on feast days.

the chair lift back down, it takes an hour to scramble down the mountainside, following a path below the lift). Once at the top, head right up the steps from the terminal and across the road into the woods, where a trail soon emerges at the *Pobeda* **hut**, which has dorm beds and a café. One kilometre east of the chair lift, the *Karandila* hotel, though a concrete eyesore and eclipsed by the nearby *Byala Mechka* (see p.318) and other privately run places along the same road, is a popular food-and-drink stopoff for day-trippers.

Eating and drinking

There are plenty of snack bars, pizzerias and simple grills along bulevard Tsar Osvoboditel, though for a more leisurely dining experience try the *Deboya*, diagonally opposite the *Hotel Sliven*, where you can feast on meat and fish in an atmospherically arched, low-ceilinged interior or a glass pavilion at the front; or the *Natsional* restaurant (see "Hotels"; p.318), where just about every dish in the traditional Bulgarian repertoire is served up in a huge garden with running water and flowerbeds.

Café-hopping along bulevard Tsar Osvoboditel on warm summer evenings is about the limit of Sliven's **nightlife**, although there's the occasional disco held in the modern theatre opposite the *Hotel Sliven*.

Around Sliven

Like Koprivshtitsa in the Sredna Gora or Elena in the Balkan Range, **Kotel** and **Zheravna** were important centres of Bulgarian culture during the nineteenth century, whose contribution to the National Revival was way out of proportion to their small size. Located in the hilly sheep-rearing terrain northeast of Sliven, they're both picturesque highland settlements with their fair share of traditional wooden architecture. Nearby, the villages of **Katunishte** and **Medven** are well known for retaining considerable numbers of nineteenth-century houses, although tourism in both places is minimal. Indeed, given the region's undoubted charms it's surprising how stagnant tourism has become here, though accommodation (albeit limited) does exist, and if an off-beat village holiday is what you're after, Zheravna, in particular, is as good as they get.

It's worth making the effort for the scenery alone, with the road from Sliven zigzagging over the Blue Rocks massif and down into pine-clad valleys where gypsies camp among the wildflowers and herds of sheep block the roads. It's an enchanting, almost time-warped corner of Europe which still follows a pastoral way of life, with many of the villages along the route preserving rickety examples of nineteenth-century village architecture, although rural poverty and depopulation has given the whole region a careworn feel.

Getting around the region by **public transport** isn't difficult providing you start from Sliven, from where there are around eight daily buses to Kotel, three to Zheravna. You can treat either place as a day-trip from Sliven, but not both: despite their proximity to each other, Kotel and Zheravna are connected by just one bus a day, currently leaving Kotel at 3.30pm.

Kotel

Founded by sixteenth-century migrants from the Ottoman-dominated plains, **KOTEL** was one of those remote towns where Bulgarian customs and crafts survived centuries of Turkish rule, to re-emerge with new vigour during the

Kotel carpets

Alongside Chiprovtsi (see p.191), Kotel is Bulgaria's major carpet-weaving centre. Manufactured here since the seventeenth century on vertical looms, Kotel carpets come in the form of either **kilims** (carpets with a complex design and a distinct border round the edges) or **chergi** (carpets with simpler designs, often just stripes of different colours). *Chergi* are often long, thin affairs used as runners, although they may be stitched together to form a larger floor covering. They're invariably made from sheep's wool nowadays, although rough goat's wool carpets were popular in the past. Also made here are the tufted woollen **rugs** known variously as *guberi*, *kitenitsi* or *postelki* and traditionally used as blankets.

Kotel **designs** are very distinctive, and always feature four colours; black, red, blue and green. Kilims usually have lozenge- or diamond-shaped geometric patterns, many of which symbolize the stars, sun, moon, or more abstract ideas like the struggle between good and evil – shown by juxtaposing triangles of different colours. Kilims featuring the design known as *tablite* (literally "the trays") were traditionally made for the weaver's first-born granddaughter; those featuring *krûsti* ("crosses") were made for a grandchild's christening.

There's very little in the way of a retail **market** for carpets in Kotel itself. The Carpet Exhibition (see opposite) has a small range of pieces for sale, and can arrange visits to see weavers at work. If you're staying in Bulgaria for more than a month or two, you can order a rug from a weaver, pay a deposit, and pick it up later. When buying from individuals, however, all prices are subject to negotiation, so it pays to check prices at the Carpet Exhibition first to get an idea of the going rate per square metre. As a general rule, anything bought in Kotel is about half the price of carpets bought in Sofia or the Black Sea coast.

National Revival. This was in part due to the special privileges awarded the town by the Ottoman authorities, who employed *Kotlentsi* to defend the nearby mountain passes against brigands and allowed them to carry arms in return. Uniquely in Ottoman-occupied Bulgaria, the locals were allowed to build fortifications around the town in 1800 to deter attacks by the *kûrdzhali*, outlaws who sacked nearby Zheravna instead. Such was the extent of Kotel's autonomy that not only were Turks forbidden from settling here, they weren't even allowed to enter the town on horseback. Kotel's main source of income was from **sheep- and goat-breeding**, with local herdsmen crisscrossing the eastern Balkan Range seeking pastures. Herders often spent up to three years away from home at a stretch, and were engaged to local girls *in absentia* to prevent them from settling down elsewhere.

Though much of old Kotel was destroyed by fire in 1894, one quarter, containing around a hundred houses from the National Revival period, survived to become the subject of modern-day preservation orders. The local industry is **carpetmaking**, with weavers still producing handmade kilims and *chergi*, either at home or in the factory just outside town. Kotel is also the site of Bulgaria's foremost **folk music school** (*muzikalno uchilishte*), where talented youngsters from all over the country come to study traditional instruments – you may get to see a performance if you visit the town as part of a tour group.

The Town

From Kotel's bus station, flights of steps ascend to a plaza dominated by the **Pantheon of Georgi Sava Rakovski** (Mon–Fri 8am–5pm, Sat & Sun 9am–5pm; 3Lv). A gigantic stone cube with glass panels, it supposedly holds the bones of Rakovski, a Kotel-born revolutionary, and there is a **museum** devoted to him and other local patriots – notably church leaders Sofronii Vrachanski and Neofit Bozveli – as well as educationalist Petûr Beron, who wrote the first Bulgarian-language school primer in 1824. Arranged in a series of gloomy subterranean halls, the museum is more like the sepulchral vault of an ancestor-worshipping cult than a tourist attraction, with the shrivelled, embalmed heart of Petûr Beron on display, along with some of Rakovski's letters and personal effects, and an extensive collection of weaponry. The alleged tomb of Rakovski lies in a sombre marble hall down a further flight of stairs, where suitably solemn taped music is played when visitors enter.

Follow ulitsa Izvorska from the plaza down past the **Church of the Trinity**, and you'll enter the Galata quarter of squat, vine-covered wooden houses and steep, cobbled alleys, where the **Carpet Exhibition** (*Izlozhba na kotlenski tûkani*; officially Mon–Fri 8am–noon & 1–5pm; 3Lv), housed in a old schoolhouse, displays a colourful collection of antique and modern kilims, alongside some rather ill-advised contemporary tapestries based on medieval frescoes. From the fountain opposite, ulitsa Shipka runs uphill to an **Ethnographic Museum** (July–Sept daily 9am–6pm; Oct–June Mon–Fri 8am–5pm; 3Lv), which occupies the house of a nineteenth-century seed merchant. Although well off by Kotel standards, the family of eight all slept in the same room (on a floor softened with layered carpets), as was the custom, with the baby slung from the ceiling in a hammock-like cot. The kitchen was housed in a small,

Georgi Sava Rakovski (1821–67)

Of all the patriots produced by nineteenth-century Kotel, **Georgi Sava Rakovski** is the most fondly remembered. In many ways he was the father of the national liberation movement, taking the Bulgarian tradition of *haidutstvo*, or banditry, and turning it into revolutionary doctrine. Born into a leading Kotel family and educated in Odessa, Rakovski first appeared on the political stage in 1841, when the Bucharest authorities sentenced him to death for trying to invade Ottoman territory with a guerilla band. He escaped to resume his career as an underground agitator, heading for Belgrade in 1860 where he formed the Bulgarian Legion, enabling young exiles to gain battle experience by fighting alongside Serbia in the latter's struggle against the Turks. He was also an indefatigable publicist, launching émigré newspapers and penning the epic poem *Gorski pûtnik* ("Woodland wanderer"), a paean to the idealized Balkan outlaw of popular legend.

Increasingly influential in émigré circles, Rakovski's big idea was to send compact groups of armed men into Ottoman territory to gather support from the local populace, and instigate a mass uprising. The bigger the uprising, the better the chance of winning sympathy from the great powers. In 1867 a trial run of Rakovski's theory took place, with *cheti* led by Panaiot Hitov and Filip Totyu heading into occupied Bulgarian territory. The action achieved little, however, and Rakovski died a broken man in October of the same year. Rakovski's successors continued to use his insurrectionary blueprint to tragic effect, with guerilla leaders like Stefan Karadzha, Hadzhi Dimitûr and Hristo Botev marching off to instant martyrdom. Only Ottoman over-reaction to the April Rising of 1876 saw the fulfilment of the final part of Rakovski's plan – intervention by brother Russia and defeat for the Turks.

The return of Rakovski's bones from Bucharest in 1897 was the occasion of national rejoicing, although rumour has it that the whole thing was funded by Macedonian insurgents who smuggled gold ingots across the border inside Rakovski's coffin. Initially Rakovski's remains were kept in the Church of Sveta Nedelya in Sofia (see p.90), but were scattered by a bomb explosion in 1925, and no one knows who the bones purporting to be his in Kotel really belong to.

separate building in the courtyard, now restored to its original appearance and stocked with the usual array of period culinary implements. The opening times of both these museums tend to be regulated by the arrival of coach parties, so you may have to knock to gain access. Carrying straight on along ulitsa Izvorska from the Carpet Exhibition, you'll come to the bosky **Izvorite Park**, named after nearby springs. There are so many that settlers likened them to a bubbling cauldron (*kotel*) – hence the name of the town. These days the park is looking a little overgrown and neglected, though it's still a wonderful place for woodland walks.

At the far, western end of Izvorite Park, the **Natural History Museum** (daily 9am–6pm; 3Lv) is popular with Bulgarian school parties, housing as it does the biggest and best-presented collection of stuffed fauna in the country. Although labelled exclusively in Bulgarian, it's an enjoyable display, and may constitute your only real chance of getting up close to the local wolves and bears.

Practicalities

There's a shortage of decent **accommodation** in Kotel, and it pays to ring in advance if you want to secure a bed. The only reliable town-centre place is the *Starata Vodenitsa*, west of the bus station at ul. Luda Kamchiya 1 (Ⓣ0453/2360; ❷), a modern building incorporating traditional touches such as wooden panelling and Kotel carpets – rooms share toilets/showers in the hallway. Two kilometres south of town on a partly wooded hillside, the *Chukarite* (Ⓣ0453/2475; ❷) is a small hotel boasting neat and tidy en-suite rooms with TV – it's accessible by a signed road which winds past a couple of derelict campsites.

Best places **to eat** are the restaurant of the *Starata Vodenitsa*, where meat-heavy Bulgarian standards are served by costumed waiting staff in an attractive courtyard; and just uphill from here the small *Bistro Elpida*, a functional but friendly place beside Izvorite Park and on the way to the Natural History Museum.

Zheravna

ZHERAVNA huddles on a ridge 6km off the main road between Sliven and Kotel, surrounded by steep pastures and maize fields. Its spacious and elegant wooden houses date from as early as the seventeenth century, when the village earned its living from sheep-breeding and diverse crafts, and the cobbled alleys still reverberate to the tinkle of goat bells and the rumble of donkey-drawn carts. With an array of **house-museums** open to visitors (all Tues–Sun 9am–noon & 2–5pm; 3Lv), and a population of less than seven hundred, it offers a good mix of day-tripper-oriented tourism and rural peace.

The main road into Zheravna terminates at a car park at the bottom of the village where there's a bus stop and a small market. Heading uphill from here you'll soon come upon the village's main street, which ascends gently past the best of the houses. Built by itinerant Tryavna craftsmen in the mid-1700s, the **Sava Filaretov House**, home of a local educationalist, is a triumph of the woodcarver's art, squatting beneath a vast overhanging roof supported by spindly pillars decorated with zigzags and sun symbols. Inside, the main living and sleeping room is a picture of domestic harmony with ornate fitted cupboards stuffed with rugs, while the *minsofa*, or guest room, has the strangest of domed ceilings. The first-floor verandah boasts a *guber*-carpeted platform where the family would have slept on warm summer nights. A little further up the road is the **Rusi Chorbadzhii House**, a typical example of a nineteenth-century merchant's home, with more kilim-rich wooden interiors. There's a dazzling display of local carpets in the basement. Signposted high up on the northwestern side of the village is the **Yovkov House**, where writer Yordan Yovkov (1880–1937) spent the first years of his life before moving to the Dobrudzha, with his parents and their flocks of sheep. Yovkov remained a regular visitor to his native village, and tales of nineteenth-century Zheravna life form the core of his best-known short story collection, *Legends of the Stara Planina*. Also in the upper part of the village, you'll find the **church of Sveti Nikolai**, whose frivolous birthday-cake interior features a painted icon screen and leafy-capitalled columns. Lining the porch outside are stacks of eighteenth-century gravestones, carved with crosses, sun symbols and vividly depicted dragons.

An accommodation bureau (*byuro na nastanyavane*; irregular hours) opposite the bus stop offers traditionally furnished **private rooms** in village houses from around 16Lv per person. There are also several reliable **B&Bs**, including *Ekohotel Zheravna*, just uphill from the bus stop (Ⓣ04585/359, Ⓦwww.ekohotel-jeravna.hit.bg; ❸), a wonderfully olde-worlde balconied wooden house with an assortment of en-suite doubles and triples sporting traditional textiles. *Filyovata kûshta*, just uphill from the main street in the northern part of the village (Ⓣ04585/389 or 0898 698 566; ❸) also has a handful of comfy doubles and triples, all en-suite – a couple come in true Zheravna style with wood-panelled interiors and traditional textiles, while the others have tiled floors and modern fittings. *Hadzhigergevata kûshta*, at the western end of the village (Ⓣ0887 719 964 or 0887 718 709; ❸), is a 250-year-old house with carved wooden ceilings and a few other restored period touches. Rooms are simply furnished and facilities are shared, but you do get to sleep under traditional goat-hair rugs instead of a duvet.

As far as **eating and drinking** goes, both the *Ekotel Zheravna* and the *Filyovata kûshta* have their own restaurants, each offering a range of traditional dishes in a pleasant outdoor setting.

Katunishte and Medven

Six kilometres southeast of Zheravna, and accessible by an asphalt road which arcs towards Gradets on the main Sliven to Kotel road, **KATUNISHTE** is another village which harbours a rich ensemble of century-old wooden houses. It's an evocative spot, stretched along a babbling stream amidst woodland and wheatfields, but is immeasurably poorer than its neighbour, in a worse state of preservation, and has no museum-houses to visit.

In a similar state, **MEDVEN** lies slightly further afield in a lovely hill-encircled bowl, some 8km northeast of Gradets. Central Medven looks like a typically depressed post-Communist village, but the outer *mahali* (quarters or suburbs), where geese and turkeys stalk the cobbled alleys, seem to have come straight out of the nineteenth century. It's reached by turning off the Sliven-Kotel road just north of Gradets – although it might not be very well signed. Unfortunately only two buses a week make the trip from Sliven; one alternative is to catch a Sliven–Kotel bus, ask to be set down at the Medven turn-off, and walk across the hills.

A left turn in the centre of the village brings you to the most atmospheric of the old quarters, where there's a small **museum-house** honouring local boy-made-good **Zahari Stoyanov** (Wed–Sun 8am–noon & 1–5pm; 2Lv), whose eyewitness account of the 1876 insurrection, *Notes on the Bulgarian Uprisings*, became a classic piece of reportage. There's not much to see save for the author's coat, favourite ashtray (a curious affair in the form of a partridge), and the suitcase he was using when he suddenly dropped dead in a Paris hotel in 1889.

On no account leave Medven before embarking on the forty-minute walk to **Siniya Vir** ("Blue Whirlpool"), a popular local beauty spot which is reached by following the asphalt road beyond the Stoyanov House down to the river, crossing the bridge and following the path along the opposite bank. After crossing a weir you arrive at the pool, a wonderful cliff-enclosed stretch of turquoise fed by a slender waterfall issuing from a cleft in the rocks.

Should you wish to **stay**, the small family-run *Hotel Medven*, ul.Vasil Lolov 10 (Ⓣ04582/2458, Ⓦwww.infotour.org/tarnovo/medven.html; ❷), to the right of the village's main crossroads as you enter from the Sliven direction, offers cosy low-ceilinged rooms (a couple of doubles plus a triple and a quad) decked out with striped rugs. The lovely garden restaurant here is also the best place in the village **to eat**.

Travel details

Trains

Hisar to: Plovdiv (2 daily; 1hr).
Karlovo to: Burgas (5 daily; 4–6hr); Kalofer (5 daily; 20min); Kazanlûk (5 daily; 45min–1hr 15min); Koprivshtitsa (5 daily; 1hr); Plovdiv (Mon–Fri 6 daily; Sat & Sun 4 daily; 1hr 45min); Sliven (4 daily; 2–3hr); Sofia (6 daily; 2–3hr).
Kazanlûk to: Burgas (5 daily; 3hr); Karlovo (6 daily; 1hr); Sliven (5 daily; 1hr 30min); Sofia (3 daily; 3–4hr).
Koprivshtitsa to: Burgas (3 daily; 5hr); Karlovo (5 daily; 1hr); Sofia (5 daily; 1hr 30min–2hr 30min).
Panagyurishte to: Plovdiv (3 daily; 2hr).
Sliven to: Burgas (5 daily; 1hr 45min).
Sofia to: Karlovo (5 daily; 2hr 30min–3hr 30min); Kazanlûk (3 daily; 3hr 30min); Koprivshtitsa (5 daily; 1hr 30min–2hr 30min).
Stara Zagora to: Burgas (3 daily; 2hr 30min–3hr 30min); Plovdiv (4 daily; 1hr 30min–2hr); Tulovo (5 daily; 30min); Varna (1 daily; 4hr).

Buses

Hisar to: Karlovo (10 daily; 35min); Panagyurishte (2 daily; 1hr 30min); Pazardzhik (1 daily; 2hr); Plovdiv (hourly; 1hr); Starosel (5 daily; 40min).
Karlovo to: Hisar (10 daily; 35min); Kalofer (hourly; 30min); Klisura (7 daily; 50min); Plovdiv (hourly; 1hr 15min); Sopot (every 15–30min; 15min); Starosel (5 daily; 1hr 25min); Troyan (April–Oct 1 daily; 2hr 30min).
Kazanlûk to: Burgas (4 daily; 4hr); Gabrovo (10 daily; 2hr 15min); Lovech (5 daily; 2hr 30min); Sofia (4 daily; 3hr 30min); Stara Zagora (8 daily; 45min); Veliko Tûrnovo (4 daily; 3hr).
Koprivshtitsa to: Sofia (4 daily, 2hr).
Kotel to: Burgas (2 daily; 4hr); Plovdiv (2 daily; 3hr); Sliven (8 daily; 1hr 30min); Zheravna (1 daily; 30min).
Panagyurishte to: Hisar (2 daily; 1hr 30min); Pazardzhik (12 daily; 45min); Plovdiv (3 daily; 2hr); Sofia (3 daily; 2hr).
Sliven to: Burgas (15 daily; 3hr); Haskovo (3 daily; 4hr); Katunishte (3 daily; 1hr 15min); Kotel (8 daily; 1hr 30min); Medven (every Tues & Sat; 1hr 30min); Shumen (2 daily; 3hr); Stara Zagora (9 daily; 1hr 45min); Veliko Tûrnovo (6 daily; 4hr); Zheravna (3 daily; 1hr 15min).
Sofia *Avtogara Poduyane* to: Koprivshtitsa (2 daily; 2hr). *Avtogara Yug* to: Panagyurishte (3 daily; 2hr). *Tsentralna Avtogara* to: Kazanlûk (4 daily; 3hr 30min); Stara Zagora (hourly; 5hr). *Trafik-Market* to: Koprivshtitsa (2 daily; 2hr).
Stara Zagora to: Gabrovo (5 daily; 3hr); Harmanli (4 daily; 2hr); Haskovo (9 daily; 1hr 15min); Kûrdzhali (7 daily; 2 hr); Kazanlûk (8 daily; 45min); Plovdiv (14 daily; 2hr); Sliven (14 daily; 1hr); Sofia (hourly; 5hr); Varna (4 daily; 4hr); Veliko Tûrnovo (4 daily; 4hr).
Zheravna to: Kotel (1 daily; 30min); Sliven (3 daily; 1hr 45min).

5

The Rhodopes and the Plain of Thrace

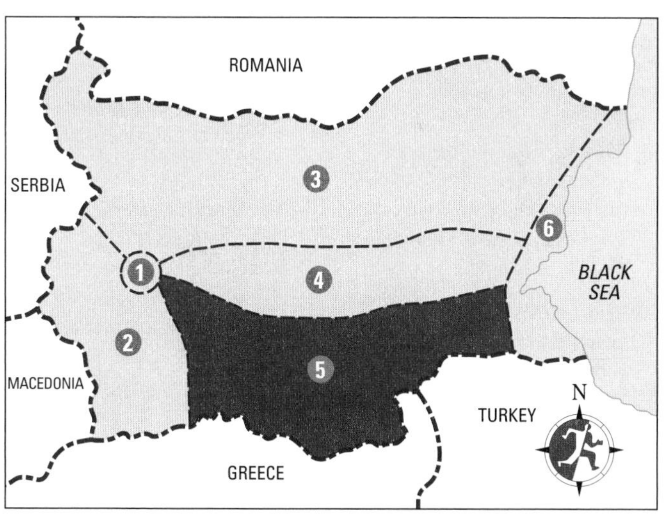

CHAPTER 5

Highlights

* **The Old Quarter, Plovdiv** A superb assemblage of National Revival architecture with several beautiful houses open to the public. See p.341
* **The Roman Theatre, Plovdiv** One of the best preserved Roman monuments in Bulgaria, still used for concerts and plays today. See p.345
* **Bachkovo Monastery** Bulgaria's second largest monastery, stunningly located in the Rhodope mountains, is famed for its frescoes. See p.354
* **Shiroka Lûka** An unspoilt village nestling in the Shirokalûshka valley, renowned for its bridges and colourful Kukeri festival. See p.364
* **Trigrad Gorge** A stunning gorge deep in the Rhodope mountains, home to the Devil's Throat cave. See p.366
* **The Historical Museum, Kûrdzhali** One of the best collections of its kind, showcasing local trades, crafts and folklore, and an impressive display of archeological finds. See p.373
* **Perperikon** A spectacular hilltop temple and fortress hewn from rock and linked to the worship of Dionysus and the cult of Orpheus. See p.374
* **The Rock Formations, Kûrdzhali** A large expanse of weird and wonderful rock formations, raised in volcanic eruptions 40 million years ago and rich in folk legend. See p.375
* **The Madzharovo Nature Reserve** A spectacular managed nature reserve, where you can spot some of Bulgaria's – and Europe's – rarest birds, as well as a host of other scarce and endangered animals. See p.376

△ *The Last Judgement* fresco at Bachkovo Monastery

5

The Rhodopes and the Plain of Thrace

Few parts of Bulgaria are as closely associated with antiquity as **the Rhodopes and the Plain of Thrace**. If the Balkan Range was the cradle of the Bulgar state, then the fertile plain between the Sredna Gora and the Rhodope Mountains was the heartland of the Thracians and the magnet that drew conquerors like Philip of Macedon and the Romans, whose legacy still remains in the graceful ruins of **Plovdiv**. Bulgaria's second city, and a fair rival to the capital in most respects, Plovdiv never fails to charm with its old quarter – a wonderful melange of Renaissance mansions, mosques and classical remains, spread over three hills. The whole region is full of memories of the Turks, whose descendants still inhabit the area around **Kûrdzhali**, while the mosques and bridges built by their forebears constitute the chief sights of **Pazardzhik**, **Haskovo**, **Harmanli** and **Svilengrad**, strung out along the route between Sofia and Istanbul, nowadays busy with convoys of Turkish *gastarbeiter* bound for Germany.

The Rhodope Mountains to the south of the plain harbour **Bachkovo Monastery** and small towns such as **Shiroka Lûka** and **Batak**, whose fortified houses testify to the insecurity of life in the old days, when bandits and Muslim zealots marauded through the hills. While **Pamporovo**, Bulgaria's premier ski resort, attracts thousands of winter tourists, the Rhodopes have become a key summer destination for hikers and those in search of rural tranquillity. The scenery in Bulgaria's southern margins can be truly stupendous, ranging from rugged gorges to dense pine forests and alpine pasturelands, with the stunning caves around the **Trigrad Gorge**, and the wonderful hikes around the pilgrimage site of **Krûstova Gora** being two of the highlights.

The **website** Ⓦwww.rodopi-bg.com is a useful source of information about the region.

Cyrillic place names

Ardino	АРДИНО	Madzharovo	МАДЖАРОВО
Ahridos	АХРИДОС	Manastir	МАНАСТИР
Asenovgrad	АСЕНОВГРАД	Mezek	МЕЗЕК
Bachkovo	БАЧКОВО	Mogilitsa	МОГИИЛИЦА
Batak	БАТАК	Momchilgrad	МОМЧИЛГРАД
Belintazh	БЕЛИНТАЖ	Momchilovtsi	МОМЧИЛОВЦИ
Belite Brezi	БЕЛИТЕ БРЕЗИ	Mostovo	МОСТОВО
Belovo	БЕЛОВО	Narechenski Bani	НАРЕЧЕНСКИ БАНИ
Borovo	БОРОВО	Orehovo	ОРЕХОВО
Chepelare	ЧЕПЕЛАРЕ	Pamporovo	ПАМПОРОВО
Devin	ДЕВИН	Pazardzhik	ПАЗАРДЖИК
Dolen	ДОЛЕН	Perperikon	ПЕРПЕРИКОН
Dorkovo	ДОРКОВО	Plovdiv	ПЛОВДИВ
Dospat	ДОСПАТ	Rudozem	РУДОЗЕМ
Gela	ГЕЛА	Septemvrl	СЕПТЕМВРИ
Harmanli	ХАРМАНЛИ	Shiroka Lûka	ШИРОКА ЛЪКА
Haskovo	ХАСКОВО	Smolyan	СМОЛЯН
Ihtiman	ИХТИМАН	Stoikite	СТОИКИТЕ
Ivailovgrad	ИВАЙЛОВГРАД	Svilengrad	СВИЛЕНГРАД
Kapitan Andreevo	КАПИТАН АНДРЕЕВО	Tatoul	ТАТУЛ
Kûrdzhali	КЪРДЖАЛИ	Trigrad	ТРИГРАД
Kostenets	КОСТЕНЕЦ	Velingrad	ВЕЛИНГРАД
Krûstova Gora	КРЪСТОВА ГОРА	Yagodina	ЯГОДИНА
Krumovgrad	КРУМОВГРАД	Yundola	ЮНДОЛА
Lûki	ЛЪКИ	Zabûrdo	ЗАБЪРДО
Madan	МАДАН	Zlatograd	ЗЛАТОГРАД

The Plain of Thrace

Watered by the Maritsa and numerous tributaries descending from the Balkans and the Rhodopes, the **Plain of Thrace** (*Trakiiskata nizina*) has been a fertile, productive land since antiquity. The ancient Greeks called it Upper or Northern Thrace, to distinguish it from the lush plains on the far side of the Rhodopes in Greece and Turkey, collectively known as Thrace after the tribes who lived there. A Bulgarian legend has it that God, dividing the world among different peoples, forgot them until a delegation of Bulgars mentioned the oversight. God replied, "There is nothing left, but since you are hard-working folk I will give you a portion of Paradise." And so the Bulgars received part of Thrace.

The E80, which now links Istanbul and Sofia, essentially follows the course of the Roman Serdica–Constantinople road, past towns ruled by the Ottomans for so long that foreigners used to call this "European Turkey". The most important town, of course, is **Plovdiv**, which quite simply overshadows all the others. The provincial centres of **Pazardzhik**, **Haskovo**, **Harmanli** and **Svilengrad** have their points of interest, but hardly warrant extensive investigation.

Communications along this route are all fairly straightforward. Roughly every hour, trains depart **from Sofia** bound for Plovdiv – a journey of two and a half hours by express (*bûrz*) or intercity services. If you'd rather travel by road, take one of the hourly buses from opposite the train station, which do the journey in around the same time. **From other parts of Bulgaria**, there is at least one direct train a day from both Burgas and Varna on the coast; while travellers coming from Ruse and Veliko Tûrnovo will probably need to change trains at Stara Zagora. Numerous buses and at least two trains a day link Plovdiv with **Istanbul**: travelling by road you'll cross the border at Kapitan Andreevo (see p.351), by train at Svilengrad (p.350).

Sofia to Plovdiv

Travelling west to east along the E80, the first town you come across after leaving Sofia is **IHTIMAN**, set amid beautiful subalpine scenery, with a central **hotel**, *Air Sofia* (Ⓣ0724/2015, Ⓦwww.airsofia.com; ❺), and the smart 18-hole *Air Sofia Golf Club* and horse riding centre (Ⓣ0724/3530; 50Lv per game) on the outskirts. If you're on a direct bus, you'll follow the dual carriageway almost as far as Plovdiv, bypassing the towns below, but if you're taking the Sofia–Plovdiv rail line, or driving along the old Sofia-Plovdiv road, you'll wind your way in a leisurely fashion through the hills that precede the Maritsa Valley, before entering **KOSTENETS**, a small town encroaching on **Momin prohod**, or the "Maiden's Pass". This gets its name from the daughter of a rich merchant of Philippopolis, whose long-standing paralysis vanished when she bathed here in the **mineral springs**, whose mildly radioactive waters are still used today to treat diabetes, ulcers, rheumatism and skin diseases. **BELOVO**, the next town, is a stop for most express trains, and has a mineral swimming pool 5km to the east beside the highway. From the next proper town, **SEPTEMVRI**, you can catch a **narrow-gauge train** to Velingrad in the western Rhodopes (see p.370) and Bansko in the Pirin Mountains (see p.150).

Pazardzhik

A market town founded by Crimean Tatars during the reign of Sultan Bayezid II, **PAZARDZHIK** was the site of the third-largest fair in the Ottoman Empire, capable of stabling 3000 horses and 2000 camels in its *caravanserai*, and until the late nineteenth century commercially more important than Sofia. Many of the Bulgarian artisans who began settling here towards the end of the sixteenth century adopted Islam, and Pazardzhik remained a predominantly Turkish and Muslim town until the 1960s, when large numbers of Gypsies were settled here to dilute their influence. Bulgarians from elsewhere stigmatize Pazardzhik as full of criminals, and its motorists as the worst drivers in the country. Though the truth of this is disputable, **pickpockets** are a definite hazard here, and with few sights of much interest and a relatively poor choice of hotels and restaurants there is little reason for visitors to linger in Pazardzhik.

The Town

Although the town has long since lost the appearance of an Ottoman bazaar, Pazardzhik's mercantile traditions live on in one of Bulgaria's liveliest daily street markets, lining the alleys of the pedestrianized downtown area just east of the main square, **ploshtad Cherven**. Directly behind the square, at Georgi Kirkov 34, is the **City Historical Museum** (Mon–Fri 9am–noon & 2–5pm;

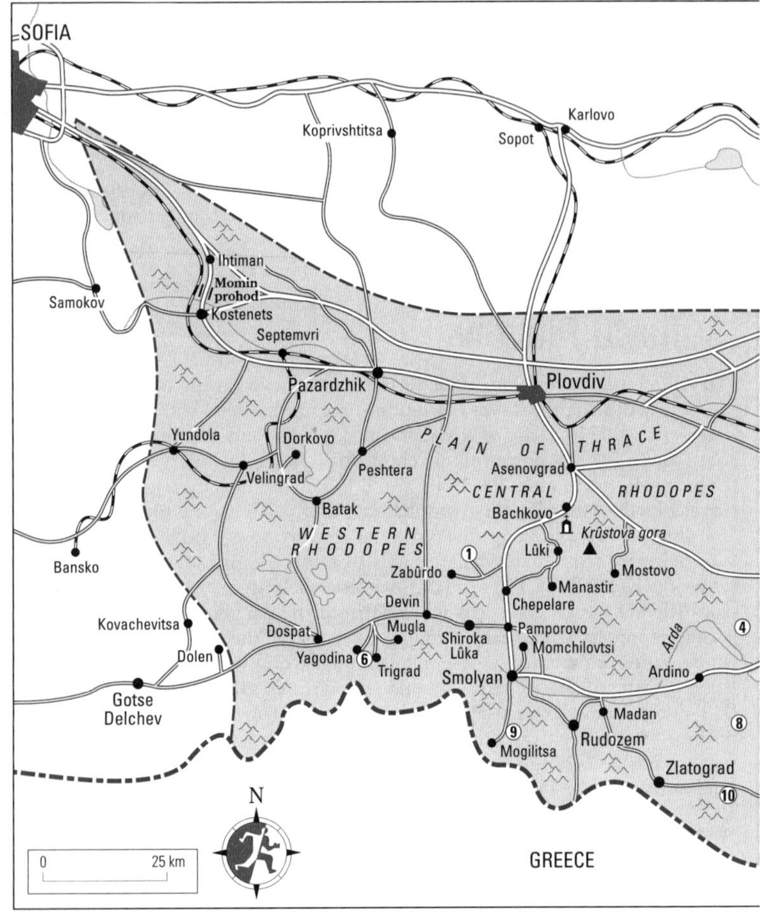

3Lv), an uninspiring collection largely concentrating on Thracian and Roman oddments.

A short distance south of the square, the pink stone **Cathedral of Sveta Bogoroditsa** is an example of the National Revival style applied to church architecture, partly sunk beneath street level to comply with the Ottoman restrictions on Christian places of worship. Its walnut iconostasis is perhaps the finest product of the nineteenth-century School of Debûr (in western Macedonia), whose craftsmen endeavoured to show the psychological relationships between human figures rather than fill the icon screen with plant and zoomorphic motifs in the manner of the Samokov woodcarvers.

Zahari Zograf aside, Bulgaria's most famous nineteenth-century painter was probably **Stanislav Dospevski** (1826–76), whose former house and studio opposite the cathedral is now a **museum** (officially Mon–Fri 9am–noon & 2–4pm; 2Lv). Born in Pazardzhik and educated at the Academy of Fine Art in St Petersburg, Dospevski drew extensively during visits to Odessa and Constantinople, but

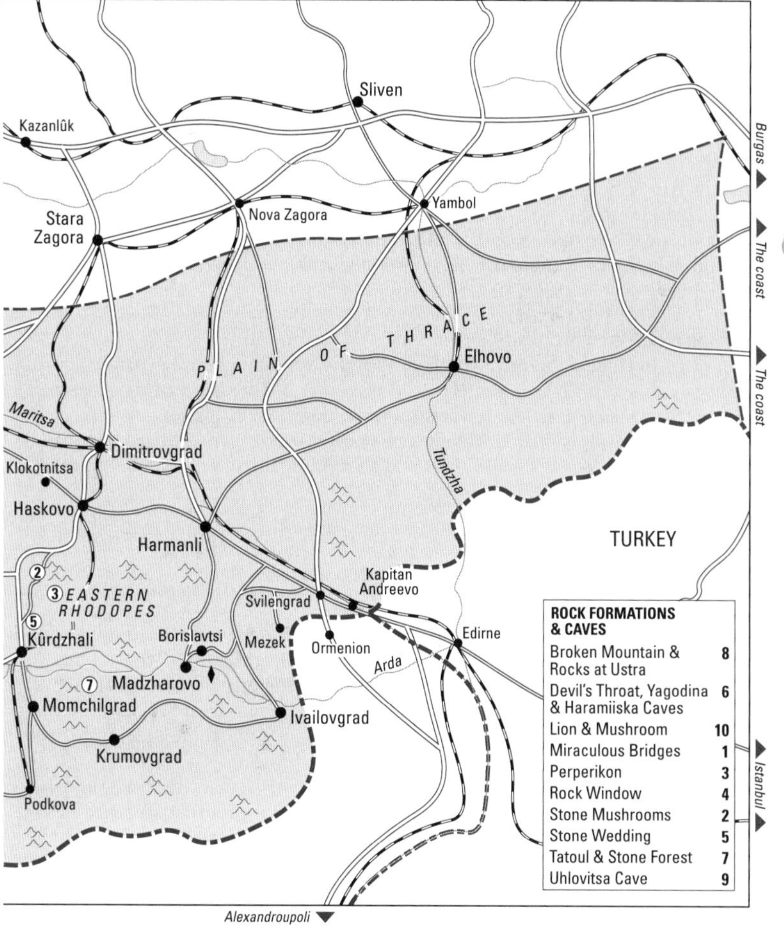

is best remembered for his icons, portraits and murals, several of which decorate the walls of the house. A participant in the April Rising, he was flung into the dungeons of Constantinople and died before Bulgaria's Liberation.

Most of Pazardzhik's surviving nineteenth-century houses lie near the Dospevski museum, where squat pastel-coloured structures huddle along either side of a stream, or among the tree-lined residential streets just west of the cathedral. Here, at Kiril i Metodii 4, is an **Ethnographic Museum** (Mon-Fri 9am–noon & 1.30-4.30pm; 2Lv), which has the usual selection of costumes and crafts from the National Revival period. Another block west is the rather dilapidated walled **Church of SS Konstantin i Elena**, with faded murals of the saints above the portal.

Finally, on the far side of the park north of the centre, is the **Kurshum dzhamiya**, or "Bullet Mosque", so-called because of its pointed dome. Built in 1667, it is larger and grander than the mosques in Plovdiv and Haskovo, but sadly derelict.

Practicalities

Pazardzhik's **train station** lies about 5km south of the centre, and all arrivals are met by buses into town. The **bus terminal**, a couple of blocks north of the town centre, is a more convenient point of entry.

With regular buses to **Plovdiv**, **Batak** in the Rhodopes and **Panagyurishte** in the Sredna Gora, Pazardzhik is the kind of place to spend an afternoon before moving on. If you do wish **to stay**, however, your best bet is the small, family-run *Riva*, ul. Tsar Asen 23 (Ⓣ034/444734; ❶), a quiet pension in the backstreets near the bus station. Otherwise, options are limited to the basic, socialist-era *Hotel Trakiya*, on the main square (Ⓣ034/446008; ❹), or the over-priced *Elbrus*, pl. Olimpiiski 2 (Ⓣ034/445530; ❻), which features a late-night **bar** and **disco**.

Beyond Pazardzhik

The road **between Pazardzhik and Plovdiv** runs straight as an arrow across the widening plain beside the River Maritsa, flanked by acres of trees bearing apples, plums and pears. Bulgarians say that, traditionally, passers-by may pick fruit from roadside orchards providing they eat it on the spot, but removing any constitutes theft in the eyes of the law. The road finally enters Plovdiv through the city's northern suburbs.

Plovdiv

Lucian the Greek called **PLOVDIV** "the biggest and most beautiful of all towns" in Thrace; he might have added "and Bulgaria", for the country's second-largest city (with a population of 360,000) is one of its most attractive and vibrant centres, with arguably more to recommend it than Sofia, which the proud locals tend to regard with some disdain. Certainly, there's plenty to see: the old town embodies Plovdiv's long and varied history – Thracian fortifications utilized by Macedonian masons, overlaid with Byzantine walls, and by great timber-framed mansions erected during the Bulgarian renaissance, looking down on the Ottoman mosques and artisans' dwellings of the lower town. But Plovdiv isn't merely a parade of antiquities: the city's arts festivals and trade fairs rival Sofia's in number, and its restaurants and promenade compare very favourably with those of the capital.

Some history

An ancient Thracian site, rebuilt and renamed by Philip II of Macedon in 342 BC, classical **Philippopolis** was initially little more than a military outpost designed to keep a watchful eye over the troublesome natives. It was a rough frontier town that the Macedonians deliberately colonized with criminals and outcasts; the Roman writer Pliny later identified it with Poneropolis, the semi-legendary "City of Thieves". Under Roman rule urban culture developed apace, with the town's position on the Belgrade–Constantinople highway bringing both economic wealth and a strategic role in the defence of Thrace.

Plovdiv was sacked by the Huns in 447, and by the seventh century, with the Danube frontier increasingly breached by barbarians, the city was in decline. With the arrival of the Bulgars, Byzantine control over the area became increasingly tenuous. "Once upon a time", lamented Byzantine chronicler Anna Comnena in the twelfth century, "Philippopolis must have been a large and beautiful city, but after the Tauri and Scyths [Slavs] enslaved the inhabitants …

The Plovdiv fair

A trade centre of long standing, **Plovdiv** became Bulgaria's principal marketplace during the 1870s, when the railway between Europe and Istanbul was completed and the great annual fair held at Uzundzhovo since the sixteenth century was moved here. Plovdiv's first international trade fair (1892) was a rather homespun affair – a man from Aitos proposed to show his hunting dogs, while Bohemia exhibited beehives – but since 1933 the event has gone from strength to strength, and nowadays claims to be the largest of its kind in the Balkans. There are actually two annual **fairs**: the spring event, devoted to consumer goods, in early May, and the larger autumn industrial fair, during the second half of September. Both are held at the complex on the north bank of the river. Members of the public are free to come along, and there's a special bus service laid on between the train station and the fairground.

it was reduced to the condition in which we saw it." In Comnena's time Philippopolis was a notorious hotbed of heretics, a situation usually blamed on local Armenians, who migrated to Thrace en masse in the eighth and tenth centuries, bringing with them the dualistic doctrines of Manichaeanism and Paulicianism. Although these heresies eventually fizzled out, Plovdiv's Armenian population has endured to this day.

The Byzantine town was further damaged by the Bulgarian Tsar Kaloyan in 1206, and it was a rather run-down place that the Turks inherited in the fourteenth century, renaming it Filibe. It soon recovered as a commercial centre, with a thriving Muslim quarter, complete with bazaars and mosques, growing up at the base of the hill where Plovdiv's Christian communities continued to live. Many of the latter were rising members of a rich mercantile class by the mid-nineteenth century, and they expressed their affluence in the construction of opulent town houses that showcased the very best of native arts and crafts. Plovdiv's urban elite also patronized Bulgarian culture, and had the Great Powers of Europe not broken up the infant state of Bulgaria at the Congress of Berlin in 1878, Plovdiv would probably have been designated as its capital. In the event, it became instead the main city of **Eastern Rumelia**, an Ottoman province administered by a Christian governor-general. Much of the Christian population naturally wanted union with the rest of Bulgaria, which was finally attained in 1885.

Plovdiv has continued to rival Sofia as a cultural and business centre ever since, not least because of the **international trade fairs** held here in May and September (see box above). With its longstanding liberal-bourgeois tradition, Plovdiv is politically the "bluest" city in Bulgaria, a stronghold of the conservative SDS since the demise of Communism, whose proximity to Turkey and Greece has ensured that private enterprise has flourished here more than anywhere else in the country.

Arrival, orientation and information

Trains arrive at the central train station (*Tsentralna gara*) to the south of central Plovdiv, near two of the city's three **bus terminals**: Rodopi, serving the mountain resorts of the south, is just on the other side of the train tracks (accessible via the underground walkway from the station), while Yug bus station, serving the southeast, is one block east of the train station. Sever bus station, which runs services to northern towns such as Panagyurishte, Ruse, Pleven and Koprivshtitsa, is several kilometres north of the river – reached by bus #12 from the train

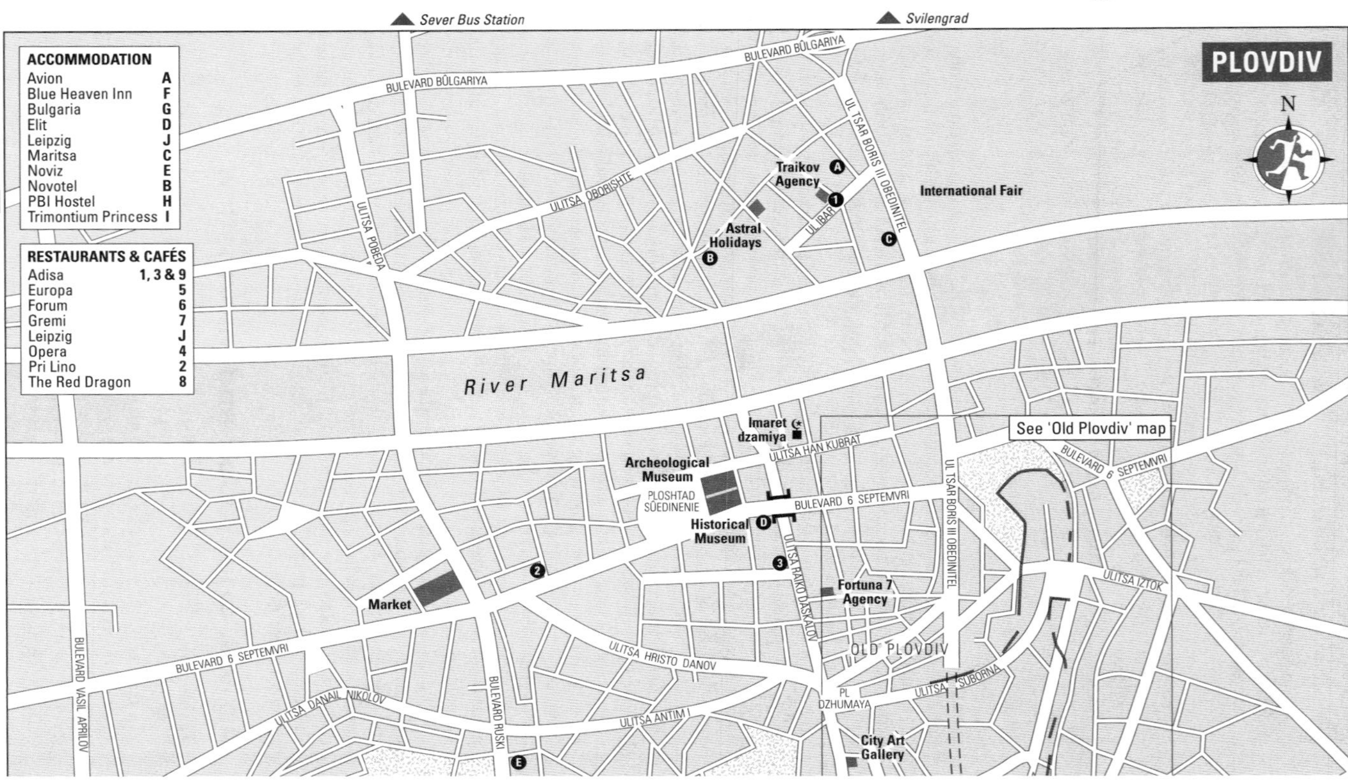
PLOVDIV
N
Sever Bus Station
Svilengrad
Sofia
ACCOMMODATION
Avion A
Blue Heaven Inn F
Bulgaria G
Elit D
Leipzig J
Maritsa C
Noviz E
Novotel B
PBI Hostel H
Trimontium Princess I
RESTAURANTS & CAFÉS
Adisa 1, 3 & 9
Europa 5
Forum 6
Gremi 7
Leipzig J
Opera 4
Pri Lino 2
The Red Dragon 8
BULEVARD BÛLGARIYA
ULITSA OBORISHTE
ULITSA POBEDA
UL TSAR BORIS III OBEDINITEL
UL IBAR
Traikov Agency
Astral Holidays
International Fair
River Maritsa
Imaret dzamiya
ULITSA HAN KUBRAT
See 'Old Plovdiv' map
Archeological Museum
PLOSHTAD SÛEDINENIE
Historical Museum
BULEVARD 6 SEPTEMVRI
ULITSA RAIKO DASKALOV
Fortuna 7 Agency
ULITSA IZTOK
Market
ULITSA HRISTO DANOV
OLD PLOVDIV
PL DZHUMAYA
ULITSA SUBORNA
ULITSA DANAIL NIKOLOV
ULITSA ANTIM I
BULEVARD RUSKI
BULEVARD VASIL APRILOV
City Art Gallery

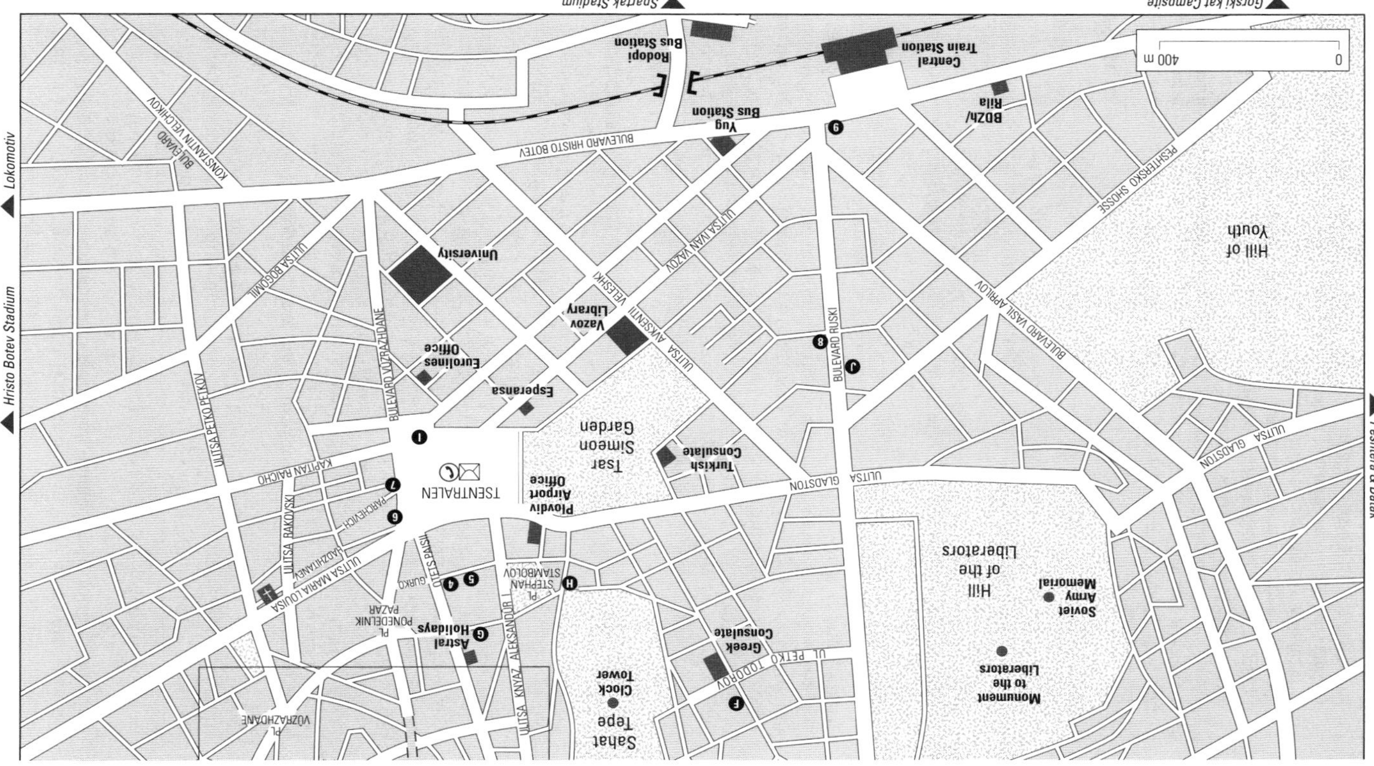
Hristo Botev Stadium
Lokomotiv
Spartak Stadium
Gorski kat Campsite
Peshtera & Batak
ULITSA PETKO PETKOV
BULEVARD KONSTANTIN VELCHIKOV
ULITSA BOGOMIL
PL VŬZRAZHDANE
ULITSA RAKOVSKI
ULITSA MARIA LOUISA
HADZHIYANEV
KAPITAN RAICHO
PARCHEVICH
PL PONEDELNIK PAZAR
GURKO
OTETS PAISII
Astral Holidays
ULITSA KNYAZ ALEKSANDŬR I
PL STEPHAN STAMBOLOV
Plovdiv Airport Office
TSENTRALEN
BULEVARD VŬZRAZHDANE
Eurolines Office
University
Esperansa
Vazov Library
Tsar Simeon Garden
Sahat Tepe
Clock Tower
BULEVARD HRISTO BOTEV
Rodopi Bus Station
Yug Bus Station
ULITSA AVKSENTII VELESHKI
ULITSA IVAN VAZOV
Turkish Consulate
Greek Consulate
UL PETKO TODOROV
ULITSA GLADSTON
BULEVARD RUSKI
Central Train Station
BDZh/ Rila
Hill of the Liberators
Monument to the Liberators
Soviet Army Memorial
BULEVARD VASIL APRILOV
PESHTERSKO SHOSSE
Hill of Youth
0
400 m

station, or minibuses #4, #17 and #19 from the centre. A brisk ten-minute walk north of Yug bus station, along ulitsa Ivan Vazov – or three stops on buses #2 or #102 – brings you to **ploshtad Tsentralen**, immediately north of which is the modern town centre.

Though most of Plovdiv's sights are near enough to be explored on foot, the city is divided into two distinct parts, quite different from each other in atmosphere: the nineteenth-century **Stariyat grad** or "Old town", covering the easternmost of Plovdiv's three hills; and the **lower town** – predominantly modern with a scattering of Turkish and Roman relics – which spreads across the plain below.

In the absence of a tourist office you'll have to get **information** from hotel receptionists (try the *Trimontium Princess*, *Novotel*, *Leipzig* or *Bulgaria* first) or private agencies such as Astral Holidays, which has two offices, one in the centre at ul. Otets Paisi 24 (Mon-Fri 9am-7pm & Sat 10am-3pm; ⓣ032/626608, ⓦwww.astralholidays.bg), the other near the Plovdiv Fair at ul. Belgrad 18 (Mon-Fri 9am–7pm; ⓣ032/962515) – take bus #2 or #102 from the station and alight once you've crossed the river. The Esperansa agency (see below) also gives out information. While all the agencies dispense free brochures, for up-to-date **maps** such as the *Plovdiv City Guide* you'll have to search the bookstalls around ploshtad Tsentralen and the southern end of ulitsa Knyaz Aleksandûr I. Look out for the free weekly cultural guides *Navigator* and *Programata* and the monthly *Plovdiv Visitor's Guide*, distributed at hotels, bars and restaurants.

Accommodation

The only time you might have trouble finding somewhere to stay is during the trade fairs, when all the better hotels and private rooms are taken; if you're particular about where you stay, reserve a month ahead. The most convenient source of **private rooms** is Esperansa, at ul. Ivan Vazov 14 (daily ⓣ10am–8pm; ⓣ032/265127), which charges 20Lv for a single and 30Lv for a double room in the centre. For motorists coming from Sofia or Turkey it's easier to use the Traikov Agency, on the north side of the river at ul. Ibar 31 (Mon–Fri 9am–5pm; ⓣ032/963014, ⓔet_traykov@yahoo.com), which charges similar rates and also rents apartments with kitchens (40Lv a night). Plovdiv's **hotels** are almost as expensive as Sofia's and hike their **prices** by up to 100 percent during the fairs; they're also a highly variable bunch so it pays to be choosy. The influx of backpackers has generated a surge of decent new **hostels** offering sociable dorm accommodation in line with the prices of private rooms. Unless otherwise stated, all the hotels below are marked on the Plovdiv map on pp.336–337. The city's three **campsites** are some way from town along the Sofia–Plovdiv–Istanbul E80 highway – too far away for those who want to be at the centre of things.

Hotels

Avion ul. Han Presian 15 ⓣ & ⓕ032/967451. Small, modern establishment in a quiet location north of the river, offering apartments for up to four people with TV and a/c. ❺

Bulgaria ul. Patriarh Evtimii 13 ⓣ032/633599, ⓦwww.hotelbulgaria.net. Smart and very comfortable three-star place right in the heart of the city, just off ul. Knyaz Aleksandûr I, which makes the street-facing rooms rather noisy. ❻

Elit ul. Daskalov 53 ⓣ 032/624537. Basic, though spotless little hotel in a fairly central location, on the corner of bul. Septemvri 6. ❹

Hebros ul. Konstantin Stoilov 51 ⓣ032/260180, ⓦwww.hebros-hotel.com (see map on p.342). A lovely National Revival-style house in the heart of the old town. Its atmospheric en-suite rooms come with original nineteenth-century furnishings, and there are also a couple of apartments with cosy sitting rooms, and one with a kitchen, for up to four people. In 2003 its restaurant was voted best in Bulgaria by *Bacchus*, a well-respected wine magazine. ❼

Leipzig bul. Ruski 70 ⓣ032/632250 or 632251, ⓕ451096. Unexceptional though above-average old-style high-rise, handy for the station, and serving a very good breakfast, but almost 1km west of the centre. ❷

Maritsa ul. Tsar Boris III Obedinitel 42 ⓣ032/952735 or 952727. Modern, unexciting high-rise opposite the international fair on the north bank of the Maritsa (bus #2 or #102 from the station), though it's quite a distance from the town centre. ❼

Noviz bul. Ruski 55 ⓣ032/631281, ⓦwww.noviz.com. Small, comfortable hotel, with a/c, cable TV, minibar and fridge in all rooms; there's also a sauna, massage room and solarium. A little overpriced for this backstreet location, though. A 15-min walk from pl. Dzhumaya. ❻

Novotel ul. Zlatyu Boyadzhiev 2 ⓣ032/934444, ⓔreservation@novotelpdv.bg. Plovdiv's plushest hotel, on the north bank of the Maritsa, with a/c, indoor and outdoor pools, sauna and tennis courts. ❽

Residence – The Old Town ul. Knyaz Tseretelev 11 ⓣ032/620789, ⓦwww.plovdivresidence.com. Sumptuously furnished place with fantastic views from its terrace. ❺

SN ul. Hristo Dyukmedzhiev 28 ⓣ032/260135, ⓕ262591. Tiny, three-roomed hotel tucked down a side street 5 min from pl. Dzhumaya. ❸

Trimontium Princess ul. Kapitan Raicho 2 ⓣ032/605000, ⓦwww.trimontium-princess.com. Centrally located high-class hotel with lavishly furnished large, comfortable rooms. Reduced rates available at weekends. ❽

Hostels

Blue Heaven Inn ul. Petiofi 15A ⓣ032/635123, ⓦwww.blueheaveninn.5u.com. Friendly backpacker hostel offering spacious triple rooms, free Internet, tea and coffee, laundry and pick-up service. ❷

International Hostel ul. Petko Slaveykov 5 ⓣ032/635115 (see map on p.342). Simply furnished but clean, this is a cut-price version of the *Hebros*, in an atmospheric National Revival house in Old Plovdiv. The helpful staff can arrange trips throughout the region. Dorm beds 24Lv, double rooms ❷

PBI Hostel ul. Naiden Gerov 13 ⓣ032/638467, ⓦwww.pbihostel.com. Centrally located hostel with dorm beds and one double room. Offers free laundry, tea and coffee, Internet access and a discount for stays longer than two nights. Dorm beds 16Lv per person, doubles ❷

Raiski kût Hostel ul. P.R. Slaveykov 6 ⓣ032/268849 (see map on p.342). Family-run place in the old town offering clean, simple double rooms. ❷

Campsites

Chaya 11km east of Plovdiv just off the old E80 to Haskovo, on the banks of the River Chepelarska ⓣ032/263763. A pleasant site let down by its proximity to a truck stop and a busy road. Open all year. 15Lv per tent, bungalows ❶

Gorski kût 4km west of town on the old E80 to Sofia ⓣ032/951360. Most convenient of the sites; take bus #4, or minibus #3 from opposite the Trimontium Princess hotel. Open all year. Tents 3Lv per person, bungalows ❷

9th Kilometer 9km west of town, well signed off the old E80 to Sofia ⓣ032/632992. A modern place with a smart restaurant and the choice of double bungalows in neat grounds or motel rooms. Open all year. ❷

Modern Plovdiv

Modern Plovdiv revolves around **ploshtad Tsentralen**, an arid concrete plaza dominated by the post and telephone office and the monolithic **Hotel Trimontium Princess**. Remnants of a **Roman forum** were discovered during the development of the area – you can explore a section of this marble-paved, once-colonnaded square by descending into a sunken area in front of the hotel. Further remains can be seen on the other side of the post office. Just east of here is ulitsa Kapitan Raicho, a leafy residential street enlivened by a daily open-air clothes market.

To the west of ploshtad Tsentralen, the **Tsar Simeon Garden** – a lovely patch of greenery with an unusual musical fountain at its heart – marks the tail end of the evening *korso*, an animated **promenade** in which hundreds of people stroll down Plovdiv's main street, **ulitsa Knyaz Aleksandûr I**. Pedestrianized and lined with shops and café-bars with outdoor tables, the street was named after the ideologue Vasil Kolarov in Communist times, but now rejoices in its prewar title once more. The **City Art Gallery** at no.15 (Mon-Sat 9am-5.30pm; 2Lv, free on Thurs) houses a fine collection of nineteenth-century portraits, including one deeply reverent, almost iconic *Portrait of Bishop Sofronii of Vratsa*, painted in 1812 by an unknown artist. Also look out for Tsanko Lavrenov's pictures of nineteenth-century Plovdiv, painted in the 1930s and 1940s and suffused with a dreamlike nostalgia. The ground floor is given over to regularly changing exhibitions of modern works, including many by local artists.

Ploshtad Dzhumaya and beyond

Further north, ulitsa Knyaz Aleksandûr I leads onto **ploshtad Dzhumaya**, where Plovdiv's history and social life coexist in an amiable confusion of monuments, cafés and stalls, around a concrete pit exposing the **ruins of a Roman stadium**. This is but a meagre section of the original, horseshoe-shaped arena where the Alexandrine Games were held during the second and third centuries: as many as 30,000 spectators watched chariot races, wrestling, athletics and other events from the marble stands that once lined the slopes of the neighbouring heights.

A more impressive structure is the **Dzhumaya dzhamiya** or "Friday mosque", with its diamond-patterned minaret and lead-sheathed domes. Its thick walls – badly cracked in places - and the configuration of the prayer hall (divided by four columns into nine squares) are typical of the so-called "popular mosques" of the fourteenth and fifteenth centuries, although it's believed that the Dzhumaya might actually date back to the reign of Sultan Murad I (1362–89). It is open most days, and visitors are welcome to inspect the pale blue interior, with its fountain and floral-pattened walls.

Northeast of the mosque lies the old *charshiya*, or **bazaar quarter**, where narrow streets still bear the names of the trades that used to operate from here: ulitsa Zhelezarska was the preserve of the ironmongers, and Abadzhiiska, that of the weavers and cloth merchants. The name *abadzhiya* derives from *abas*, the coarse woollen cloth that the Plovdiv merchants bought from Rhodopi shepherds before exporting it throughout the Levant. In Ottoman times Plovdiv's commercial district stretched from here northwards to the River Maritsa, and in the sixteenth century the Arab traveller Chelebi counted 880 shops raised "storey above storey". There is little trace of the old crafts and trades today, but the modern ulitsa Raiko Daskalov is nevertheless lined with shops, banks and cafés, with stalls selling books as far north as the pedestrian subway beneath bulevard 6 Septemvri, and clothes stalls right across the **footbridge** to the north bank of the Maritsa, making it almost as lively as it must have been in Chelebi's day.

Imaret dzhamiya and the Historical and Archeological museums

Just south of the river stand two further relics of Turkish rule. The Turkish baths near ploshtad Hebros were allowed to rot for decades but have recently been restored and now host exhibitions and performances, while Plovdiv's Muslim community has repaired and reopened the **Imaret dzhamiya**, on ulitsa Han Krubat (daily from noon for prayers), whose prayer hall contains honeycomb squinches, traces of Arabesque frescoes, and the tomb of Gazi Shahabedin Pasha. The mosque was built on Sultan Bajazet's orders in 1444, and got its name from the pilgrims' hostel (*imaret*) that once stood nearby. Zigzag brickwork gives the minaret a corkscrew twist, jazzing up the ponderous, red-brick bulk of the building, which a frieze of "sawtoothed" bricks and a row of keel arches with tie beams fails to do.

Further west, on ploshtad Sûedinenie, the **Historical Museum** (summer Mon-Sat 9am-5pm, winter Mon-Fri 8am-4pm; 3Lv) houses photographs and documents chronicling the unification of north and south Bulgaria in 1885, and occupies half of a crumbling building shared by the **Archeological Museum** (Mon-Fri 9am–12.30pm & 1–5.30pm; 2Lv), much of whose collection remains in storage while it awaits renovation or relocation. Only the entrance hall is open at present, containing an assemblage of Thracian and Roman finds, including a replica of the gold Panagyurishte treasure contained in the National History Museum in Sofia (see p.108).

Old Plovdiv

With its cobbled, hilly streets and orieled mansions, Plovdiv's old quarter (most of which is designated an "Architectural-Historical Reserve") is a painter's dream and a cartographer's nightmare. Attempting to follow – let alone describe – an itinerary is impractical given the topography and the numerous **approaches**, each leading to a different point in the quarter. Glimpses of ornate facades or interiors tempt visitors to stray down the occasional alleyway or into a courtyard – and generally speaking, that's by far the best way to see the area.

Along ulitsa Sûborna

Most people approach the old town from ploshtad Dzhumaya, from which ulitsa Sûborna gently draws you upward into Old Plovdiv. A flight of steps to the right leads to the **Danov House** (Mon–Fri 9am–12.30pm & 1.30–5pm; 3Lv), the former domicile of Bulgaria's first large-scale publisher and now home to a museum of printing. Danov was one of those who regarded distribution of the printed word as a patriotic duty, a crucial step in the people's struggle against five centuries of Ottoman rule. Besides printing books he opened Bulgaria's first bookshops in Plovdiv and Ruse, made globes, thermometers and weighing scales for schools, and founded Plovdiv's first daily newspaper, *Maritsa*, in 1878 – a title resurrected after the changes of November 1989.

Old Plovdiv's National Revival architecture

Blackened **fortress walls** dating from Byzantine times can be seen lurking beyond several streets, sometimes incorporated into the dozens of **National Revival-style houses** that are Plovdiv's speciality. Typically, these rest upon an incline and expand with each storey by means of timber-framed oriels – cleverly resolving the problem posed by the scarcity of ground space and the nineteenth-century merchants who demanded roomy interiors. The most prominent oriel on the facade usually denotes the grand reception room inside, while the sides of the upper storeys sometimes feature blind oriels containing kitchen niches or cupboards. Outside and inside, the walls are frequently decorated with niches and *trompe l'oeil* floral motifs and columns painted in the style known as *alafranga*, executed by itinerant artists. The rich merchants who lived here also sponsored many of the artistic developments that made up the Bulgarian National Revival, and much of Plovdiv's cultural role is reflected in the numerous small art galleries and concert venues that crowd into the houses.

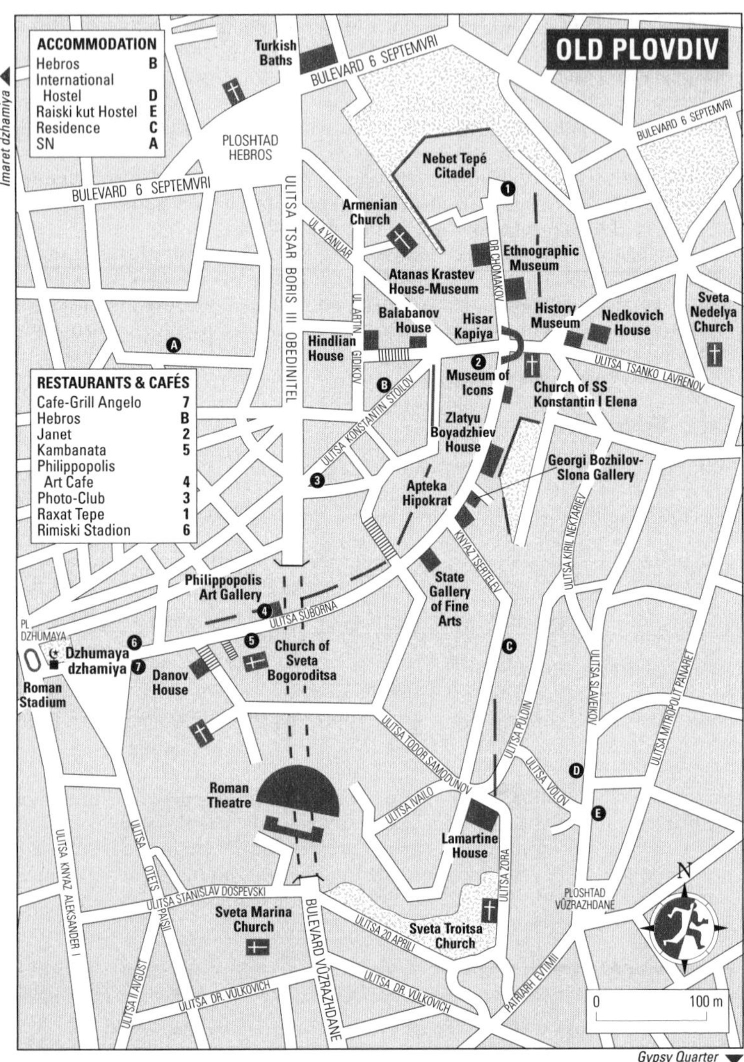

Perched on a bluff just beyond, the imposing **Church of Sveta Bogoroditsa**, with its pink and blue bell-tower, is decorated with frescoes of Orthodox saints, and one traumatic scene of chained peasants being threatened by a sword-wielding Turk. It also contains some icons by the Samokov master Stanislav Dospevski. Opposite, in a smartly renovated old trader's house, is the **Philippopolis Art Gallery** (Tues-Sun 10am-6pm; 2Lv) whose impressive domestic collection includes seascapes by Alexander Mutafov, landscapes by Georgi Kovachev and Tsanko Lavrenov, and works by Svetlin Rusev. Also worth seeing are the furnishings and medallions in the nineteenth-century **Apteka Hipokrat** (Mon-Fri 9am–5pm; free) which has been preserved as a pharmacy museum. It's uphill just past a branch of the **State Gallery of Fine Arts** (Mon-Sat 9am-12.30pm & 1-5.30pm; 2Lv, free on Thurs). The absorbing collection of nineteenth- and twentieth-century Bulgarian paintings includes several portraits by Dospevski and some garish examples of Vladimir Dimitrov-Maistor's work. Ivan Angelov's studies of peasant women and Georgi Mashev's nightmarish, fable-like visions are among the other highlights.

Up some steps to the right after Apteka Hipokrat is the private **Georgi Bozhilov-Slona Gallery** on ulitsa Knyaz Seretelev, which houses a permanent exhibition of Bulgarian modernists. Further along ulitsa Sûborna, the spacious **Zlatyu Boyadzhiev House** (summer daily 9am–noon & 1–6pm, winter Mon-Fri 8.30am-noon & 1-5pm; 3Lv) is now a gallery devoted to one of postwar Bulgaria's best-loved painters. Works like *Pernik Miners*, and numerous others romanticizing rural peasant life, show a genuine sympathy for the struggles of working people and won Boyadzhiev the favour of the Party. After a stroke paralysed his right hand, he turned to painting with his left and produced earthier, more mystical pictures like *Dve svadbi* (Two Weddings) and *Orfei* (Orpheus).

Just beyond here, at no. 22, the **Museum of Icons** (Mon-Sat 9am-12.30pm & 1-5.30pm; 2Lv) is rich in fifteenth- and sixteenth-century specimens rescued from the region's churches, while next door is the walled **Church of SS Konstantin i Elena** (daily 9am–5pm). The frivolous floral patterns adorning its porch give way to a riotously colourful interior, with the brightly painted geometric designs of the ceiling held aloft by pillars topped with Corinthian capitals. Scenes from the Gospels cover the surrounding walls, and there's a fine gilt iconostasis by Debûr master Ivan Pashkula, partly decorated by Zahari Zograf.

Upon leaving the church you can turn left at the **crossroads** to reach the Balabanov and Hindlian houses; go straight uphill past the Ethnographic Museum towards the Nebet Tepe Citadel; or turn right and pass under the Hisar Kapiya – as described in the following sections.

Around Nebet Tepe

Turn left at the crossroads then head downhill and you'll come to the maroon-coloured **Balabanov House**, on the corner of Konstantin Stoilov and 4 Yanuari (daily 9am–5.30pm; 3Lv). Once the home of merchant Luka Balabanov, it's now a venue for modern art shows and contains some fine ceilings and a large scale-model of Old Plovdiv. More impressive, however, is the pale blue **Hindlian House** (Mon-Fri 9am–5pm; 3Lv), further downhill at ul. Artin Gidikov 4. The Hindlians were Armenian merchants who travelled as far as Alexandria, St Petersburg and Venice, hence the cityscapes painted in niches upstairs, where the salon contains a wall fountain that once gushed rosewater. An eclectic collection of furniture from other homes fills much of the house, including two Biedermeier-period sitting rooms packed with trinkets from Vienna. Downstairs, the family bathroom resembles a miniature *hammam*, with a marble floor and fountain. Many of Plovdiv's surviving Armenian families still live nearby, sustaining their identity through an **Armenian church** (Mon-Fri 10am-5.30pm & Sat-Sun 10am-1pm), school and cultural centre, with a monument in the yard recalling the Plovdiv Armenians who died for "Mother Bulgaria" in the Balkan Wars and World War I.

Back at the crossroads, take ulitsa Dr Chomakov northwards to the summit of the hill on which the old town is built, and you'll pass Plovdiv's most photographed building, the **Kuyumdzhioglu House**, named after the Greek merchant who commissioned it in 1847. It was built by Hadzhi Georgi of Constantinople, who combined Baroque and native folk motifs in the richly decorated facade, painted black with a yellow trim, its undulating pediment copying the line of the *kobilitsa* or carrying yoke. Now an **Ethnographic Museum** (Tues–Sun 9am–noon & 2–5pm; 4Lv), the mansion's lower rooms display fine paste jewellery and traditional Rhodopi folk costumes and crafts, a rose-still and a splendid oil painting of Plovdiv streetlife during the nineteenth century. Upstairs is a grand reception hall with a rosette-and-sunburst ceiling, and two rooms furnished with objects reflecting the *chorbadzhii's* taste for Viennese and French Baroque. During the summer, the building plays host to regular **concerts**, of classical and traditional folk music.

Further up the street and signposted to the left, the private **Atanas Krastev House-Museum** (daily except Wed 10am-1pm & 2-6pm; 2Lv) contains modern paintings and sculpture collected by Atanas Krastenev (1910-2003), a popular intellectual nicknamed the "mayor of Old Plovdiv", who initiated the renovation of 130 buildings in the old town between 1954 and 1986. Old Plovdiv received UNESCO's gold medal for exceptional services to protect European culture in 1974, and Krastev was given the title of Honoured Cultural Worker, and Honorary Citizen of Plovdiv. On show here are portraits of Krastev by Bulgarian modernists including Zlatyu Boyadzhiev, Dimitûr Kirov, Ivan Kirkov, and Georgi Bodzhilov-Slona.

At the top of ulitsa Dr. Chomakov, beyond some derelict nineteenth-century houses, lie the overgrown ruins of the **Nebet Tepe Citadel**, marred by graffiti and rubbish. Although it's difficult to discern precise features among the pits and rubble, the site is archeologically rich. Fortified by the Thracian Odrysae tribe as early as the fifth century BC, the hilltop and the settlement of Eumolpios, below, were the beginnings of modern Plovdiv, captured by Philip II of Macedon in 342 BC. Philip ordered the former to be rebuilt in tandem with the new town – modestly named Philippopolis – which his son, Alexander the Great, abandoned in search of new conquests in Asia. Over the following centuries, the inhabitants must have often resorted to the secret **tunnel** linking Nebet Tepe with the riverbank, as the town and citadel were sacked by Romans, Slavs, Bulgars, Byzantium and the Ottoman empire, to name but a few.

From Hisar Kapiya to the Roman theatre

Turn east at the crossroads, around the corner from the Church of Sveti Konstantin i Elena, and you'll pass under the gloomy-looking **Hisar Kapiya** or "fortress gate", which has been rebuilt countless times since Philip II of Macedon had it raised to form the citadel's eastern portal. Beyond the gate, it's the structure rather than ornamentation that makes the the **Georgiadi House** on ulitsa Tsanko Lavrenov, home to the **Museum of History** (Mon–Fri 9am–noon & 1–5pm; 3Lv), so remarkable: the architect has combined "box" oriels with bay windows on a monumental scale. Built for a rich Turk in 1846–48, the mansion contains a gallery where musicians once played, plus various salons dedicated to Bulgaria's liberation from the Turks. Pride of place is given to replicas of the bell that tolled and a cannon that fired during the April Rising, when the *bashibazouks* (see p.293) hung Plovdiv's streets with corpses that the population were forbidden to bury. For her relief work, Britain's Lady Strangford has a street named after her and her picture in the museum; Disraeli, on the other hand, is execrated for condoning the atrocities and ensuring that one-third of newly liberated Bulgaria was returned to the Turks in the form of Eastern Rumelia. The next-door **Nedkovich House** (Mon–Fri 9am–noon & 1–5pm; 3Lv) contains an impressive collection of nineteenth-century furnishings.

The alleys running downhill behind the Georgiadi and Nedkovich houses lead to several **craft workshops** and many humbler dwellings that have yet to be renovated despite their obvious architectural merits. The only exception is the recently restored **Church of Sveta Nedelya** on the left, a three-aisled basilica that contains a delicately carved wooden iconostasis and bishop's throne. Walk further down Lavrenov and at the end of the road you'll come across yet more sadly neglected and rubbish-strewn **Roman remains**. It's difficult to make out much, although the recumbent columns, Corinthinan capitals and large, ornate fragments of shattered entablature indicate a civic building of some size and importance. Just beyond, the dusty roads and shabby houses mark the beginning of Plovdiv's Gypsy quarter. Most visitors, however, head south from here along ulitsa Kiril Nektariev, one of old Plovdiv's best roads: few facades can match that of the house at no. 15, embellished with swags, medallions and intricate tracery in a vivid shade of blue. Follow Nektariev to the end (the far end of the road is known as ulitsa Pûldin), and you'll arrive at the Mavrudi House at the corner of Knyaz Tseretelov and Todor Samodumov, a large buff-coloured mansion with dozens of windows and sturdy ribs supporting the oriels. Popularly referred to as the **Lamartine House** after the French poet who stayed in July 1833, writing *Voyage en l'Orient* and recovering from the cholera that killed his daughter in Constantinople, it now contains a small **museum** (daily 9am-5pm; free). There's little to see save for a few pictures of the poet and the places he visited on his travels, accompanied by a few lines of appropriate text, but it's worth peeping inside merely to admire the unusual circular lobby of the house itself.

Ulitsa Tsar Ivailo continues south from here to the **Roman theatre** (daily 9am–5pm; 3Lv), whose stands provide a wonderful view of the distant Rhodopes, and a splendid venue for **concerts and plays**. These imposing ruins are practically the only remains of an acropolis which the Romans built when they raised Trimontium from the position of a vassal town to that of provincial capital during the second century. The acropolis, like the residential districts below, was devastated by Kiva's Goths in 251, and later used as building material when the town revived. From here, paths descend to bulevard Vûzrazhdane, at the point where it enters the tunnel beneath the hill, beside which stands the walled **Church of Sveta Marina** (entered from ulitsas Dospevski or Dr Vûlkovich), with boldly coloured murals beneath its porch and beguiling devils, storks and other creatures peeping out from the wooden foliage of its intricate iconostasis.

Southwest of Old Plovdiv

As well as the three hills covered by the old town, there are three more heights ranged across the southwestern quarter of Plovdiv. The one nearest to the centre, **Sahat Tepe**, provides a great view of the city, and the site for what some believe is the oldest **clock tower** in Eastern Europe, restored by the Turks in 1809, with an inscription enjoining visitors to "look upon" it "and admire!" From here one can gaze levelly across to the giant **Soviet Army Memorial** nicknamed "Alyosha" (which Plovdiv's SDS Mayor wanted to remove but couldn't afford to) on the **Hill of the Liberators**, which also has a pyramidal monument to the liberators of 1878 on a lower peak, where a Thracian temple dedicated to Apollo once stood. Further to the southwest lies the **Hill of Youth**, the largest and most park-like of the three.

Eating

Plovdiv is full of kiosks and cafés selling coffee, *hamburgeri*, sandwiches and other **snack food**, especially along Otets Paisii and Knyaz Aleksandûr I, where you'll also find a *McDonald's* (the first to open in Bulgaria) at no. 42. For fresh fruit and veg, there's an outdoor **market**, known as the Polnedelnik pazar, on ploshtad Vûzrazhdane, to the east of Otets Paisii, and a larger one near the junction of bulevards Ruski and 6 Septemvri west of ploshtad Sûedinenie.

The choice for evening **meals** is equally wide. Some of the most stylish places are in the National Revival-style houses of Old Plovdiv. They are expensive by native standards, but still affordable to most visitors, if you don't mind splashing out 20–40Lv for a first-class meal.

Modern Plovdiv

Adisa A popular, three-outlet chain serving an excellent selection of cheap, ready-prepared Bulgarian dishes at ul. Opalchenska 4 in the centre, ul. Ivan Vazov 98 opposite the train station, and at ul. Ibar 31 opposite the Plovdiv Fair.

Café-Grill Angelo ul. Konstantin Irechek 5. Pleasant patio restaurant, serving inexpensive grilled meat dishes and pizzas, hidden behind the Dzumaya Mosque beneath a shady canopy of chestnut trees.

Europa General Gurko 17. Quiet garden restaurant with moderately priced dishes, off ul. Knyaz Aleksandûr I.

Forum bul. Vûzrazhdane, off pl. Tsentralen. A flashy but reasonably priced place with a kids' playground and naff music, serving regular Bulgarian food and catering to families. Daily 24hr.

Gremi bul. Vûzrazhdane. Next door to the *Forum*, this lively restaurant, on several levels of a turn-of-the-century house with a palm-filled garden, serves good mixed grills and fish at moderate prices. Daily 24hr.

Leipzig bul. Ruski 70. The patio restaurant of the hotel of the same name, serving reasonably priced Bulgarian standards.

Opera General Gurko 19. An inexpensive garden restaurant next door to the *Europa*, serving a wide range of pizzas and the usual Balkan grills. Daily noon–midnight.

Pri Lino bul. 6 Septembri 135. A lavishly decorated place situated in a converted mosque with a good standard of Bulgarian and international cuisine.

The Red Dragon ul. Philip Makedonski 27a. Authentic Chinese restaurant with great food and attentive staff, diagonally opposite the *Leipzig* hotel.

Rimski Stadion pl. Dzhumaya. Traditional Bulgarian fare is on offer in this attractively situated restaurant with average prices, just below ground level alongside the Roman stadium.

Old Plovdiv

Hebros ul. Konstantin Stoilov 51. This hotel restaurant was voted Bulgaria's best by the authoritative *Bacchus* wine magazine in 2003. The above-average prices charged on the limited menu of Bulgarian dishes are justified by the high standards of cuisine and service.

Janet ul. 4 Yanuari. Located in an atmospheric old house with indoor and outdoor seating and a good range of slightly pricey Bulgarian and international dishes.

Kambanata ul. Sûborna. Modern a/c restaurant built into a cellar beneath the Church of Sveta Bogoroditsa. The affordable menu features snails and other oddities, besides all the usual native dishes. Daily noon–midnight.

Philppopolis Art Cafe ul. Sûborna 29. Smart outdoor café next to the art gallery overlooking the town and offering a menu of light dishes.

Photo-Club ul. Konstantin Stoilov 36. Reasonably priced terrace restaurant serving Bulgarian and international food. Daily noon–midnight.

Raxat Tepe ul. Dr. Chomakov. Open courtyard right by the Nebet Tepe citadel, serving grilled snacks and other light meals. Summer only.

Drinking

As elsewhere in Bulgaria, you can snatch a quick **coffee** or **fruit juice** almost anywhere in the downtown area from breakfast time till after midnight – and the same goes for drinking alcohol, whether you're talking beer, vodka or cocktails.

Arena Pleasant outdoor café in Old Plovdiv next to the Music Academy and overlooking the amphitheatre.

Balaban In Old Plovdiv on a street behind and above the *International Hostel*. A cosy, old-fashioned café-bar with low wooden ceilings.

Big Ben Knyaz Aleksandûr I 29. A place to lounge in wicker chairs under a canopy, and watch the *korso*. Does good ice creams and coffee.

Blues etc ul. Preslav 29. A smoky basement bar just around the corner from the *Blue Heaven Inn*. Stays open late and has an English-language snack menu.

Caligula Knyaz Aleksandûr I 30. Great central spot for an alfresco beer and a traditionally baked pizza. It's also a nightclub, though the sleazy unisex pole-dancing show which kicks off after 1am might not be to all tastes.

Dreams Knyaz Aleksandûr I 42. Trendy and continually busy place serving up coffee, cakes and ice cream, with extensive outdoor seating on the edge of pl. Stephan Stambolov.

Dzumayata ground floor of the Dzumaya mosque. Excellent modern café serving traditional Turkish coffee and sweets right by the mosque entrance.

Jeeves Club ul. Benkovski. Modern bar decked out in polished aluminium with an upstairs techno club.

Maria Louisa bul. Maria Louisa 15. Stylish arty bar on two floors, with basement DJ at weekends.

Nylon ul. Benkovski next to the *Jeeves Club*. The most underground of Plovdiv's bars, its rock music and murky interior attract a lively crowd.

Simfoniya Tsar Simeon Garden. Very popular 24-hour terrace restaurant and bar beside the "musical fountain", offering light meals and extensive drinks menu. Also has a children's play area.

Sinyata kûshta ul. Slaveikov 25. Cosy bar housed in a National Revival mansion. Good place to drink or enjoy a quiet evening meal.

Entertainment and nightlife

Plovdiv takes its culture seriously, and hosts a comprehensive programme of music all year round. Unfortunately, there's no centralized office where you can find out what's on and events are simply publicized by banners or posters – invariably in Bulgarian only. **Classical concerts** take place at the Plovdiv Philharmonic Orchestra's concert hall on the south side of ploshtad Tsentralen, while the *Mesalitinov Theatre* at Aleksandrovska 36 is the best venue for **drama**.

There's a busy schedule of festivals too. During the first half of January, the **Winter Festival of Symphony Music** allows the Philharmonic Orchestra to flex its muscles; international virtuosi participate in the prestigious **Festival of Chamber Music**, held in the courtyard of the Ethnographic Museum in June every odd-numbered year (native ensembles play on until September, and during even-numbered years); and **Trakiisko lyato** (Thracian Summer) in August features pop and classical music, as well as **folk dancing** ensembles from as far away as Egypt, performing in the spectacular surroundings of the Roman theatre – which is also used for staging **opera** and **drama** in May and September (coinciding with the fairs).

Most of the city's nightlife revolves around well-advertised *chalga* or commercial folk music clubs such as *Maritsa*, *Incognito* and *Gladiatori*; check in one of the weekly cultural guides (see p.338) for the latest alternatives. Otherwise try *Petnoto na Rorshach* at ul. Yoachim Gruev 36, which has reasonable DJs most nights and puts on bands from time to time; *Plazma*, at bul. Hristo Botev 82, for commercial house and techno; *Marmalad* at ul. Bramya Puliyevi 3, a cool club-cum-café; and *No Sense* at ul. Evlogi Georgiev 5, which plays a mix of rock and dance music. Over the summer there are also three discos in a building near the rowing lake (*grebnata baza*) in Loven Park, 5km west of the centre, which is a popular hangout. You can get there on bus #5 or #15 but will need to take a taxi back.

Listings

Airlines Tickets for all airlines serving Bulgaria are available at the Plovdiv Airport office, ul. Gladstone 4 (Ⓣ032/633081), Fortuna 7 at ul. Benkovski 1 (Mon–Fri 9am–6pm; Ⓣ032/622595 or 628929, Ⓦwww.fortuna7.visa.bg), and Astral Holidays' offices at ul. Otets Paisi 24 (Ⓣ032/626608, Ⓦwww.astralholidays.com) and ul. Belgrad 18 (Ⓣ032/652515).

Books and newspapers There are two foreign-language bookshops: at ul. Tsaribrod 1 opposite the mosque, and at ul. Alexander Batenburg 53 close to the post office. A stall on the pl. Tsentralen sells foreign newspapers.
Buses Eurolines has an office immediately behind the *Hotel Trimontium Princess* at ul. Krali Marko 4 (Mon–Sat 9am–6pm; ⓣ032/269652). At the Yug bus station Hebros Bus (daily 7.30am–7.30pm; ⓣ032/626916) is an agent for Eurolines, and sells tickets for western European destinations as well as Greece and Turkey; Metro (daily 8am–10.30pm; ⓣ032/267879) books seats on daily services from Yug bus station to various Turkish cities.
Car rental Rent-a-car, ul. Vasil Levski 14 ⓣ032/969666; Drenikov, bul. Maritsa 98 ⓣ032/650042.
Car repairs Opel, north of the river at bul. Vasil Aprilov 158 ⓣ032/940898.
Consulates Greece, Preslav 10 ⓣ032/632003 or 632330, ⓔgrconsplov@mbox.digsys.bg; Turkey, Filip Makedonski 10 ⓣ032/632309, ⓔtcbk_filibe@plovdiv.ttm.bg.
Dentist Odesay Dentist bul. Ruski 102 ⓣ032/643543.
Hospital Sonel Farma Medical Centre, bul. Hristo Botev 47A ⓣ032/632094.
Football Plovdiv has two first-division teams: Botev and Lokomotiv. Botev, currently the city's premier outfit, play at the Hristo Botev stadium east of the centre on bul. Iztochen (trolleybus #3 from the station), and have a hard core of supporters, known as the "Canaries Ultras", with a reputation for violence, some of them linked to far-right groups. The Lokomotiv stadium is farther south off bul. Sankt Peterburg, and best reached by taxi.
Internet Implosion at ul. Emil Delavel 11 (24hr; 1Lv/hr), and a cluster of several clubs next to the university.
Pharmacies Kamea, next to Union Bank at bul. 6 Septemvri 76, is open 24 hours a day.
Police ul. Knyaz Bogoridi 7 ⓣ032/932239.
Post office pl. Tsentralen 1 (Mon–Sat 7am–7pm & Sun 7–11am).
Telephones At the post office on pl. Tsentralen 1 (daily 7am–10pm)
Train tickets Domestic and international bookings from BDZh/Rila, opposite the train station at bul. Hristo Botev 31A (Mon–Fri 8am–6pm, Sat 8am–2pm; ⓣ032/643120).
Websites ⓦwww.plovdivcityguide.com and ⓦwww.plovdiv.org are two of the more useful sites.

Plovdiv to the Turkish border

There are good reasons why so many visitors travel between Plovdiv and Turkey nonstop. The settlements along the way are mainly workaday places lacking in specific attractions, and there are more facilities for travellers along the E80 than there are off the highway.

Travelling **by road** you'll pass **Klokotnitsa** village, just west of Dimitrovgrad, the site of Ivan Asen's victory (1230) over Theodor Comnenus, the usurper of Byzantium, that forced the empire to recognize Ivan as "Tsar of the Bulgarians

Moving on from Plovdiv

From Plovdiv there are frequent trains to **Sofia** plus two daily expresses to **Burgas** and one to **Varna**. Reaching **central or northern Bulgaria** often entails a change of trains at Stara Zagora, but direct services run to Karlovo, Asenovgrad and Hisar. Travelling to **Turkey** from Plovdiv, the Balkan Express runs daily trains to Istanbul throughout the year (8hr 30min), while an additional service, the Istanbul Express, operates between May and September. If travelling to **Greece**, there's a connecting service to Thessaloniki at Svilengrad (12hr). You can buy tickets at the railway bookings office on bulevard Hristo Botev (see "Listings", above).

Hebros Bus (see "Listings", above) offers daily **buses** to Thessaloniki (14hr), and Athens (23–26hr), and daily services to Istanbul (6hr). Metro (see "Listings", above) also runs daily services to Istanbul as well as less frequent services to Izmir (8–10hr), Bursa (7–8hr) and other destinations in Turkey.

and Greeks" and accept the betrothal of his daughter to Baldwin, the teenage emperor of Byzantium. Approaching the border **by train** means a brief encounter with Dimitrovgrad – full of power stations and reeking chemical factories – before speeding on to Svilengrad and the Turkish border or catching a bus or train south to Haskovo and Kûrdzhali.

Haskovo

Little visited by tourists except as a stopover en route to Turkey, **HASKOVO**, 78km southeast of Plovdiv, has the dubious honour of being home to the country's largest cigarette factory, although the place has slightly more to offer than first meets the eye, hosting festivals throughout the year and serving as a springboard for visiting the nature reserve at Madzharovo (see p.376). Aside from that, its appeal lies in the faintly raffish mixture of Turkish and Bulgarian culture, symbolized by the oldest mosque in the Balkans and a smattering of National Revival buildings. The town was founded in around 1395 and named Haskoy by the Turks, who predominated here for the next five hundred years until the development of the tobacco industry and the Balkan War of 1912 swelled the number of Bulgarians, who now form the majority. Relations between the two are good, however, with both communities represented in local politics.

The Town

Civic and social life revolves around **ploshtad Svoboda**, a T-shaped junction of flagstones and flowerbeds centred on a memorial to the dead of successive wars. The **History Museum**, on the junction's southern arm (Mon–Fri 8.30am–5pm), contains a fine collection of pre-Ottoman artefacts – especially Roman, Byzantine and medieval **coins** – but passes over five centuries of Turkish rule in relative silence; the tobacco workers' strike of 1927 gets more attention.

A block or so south towards the river, a graceful minaret rises above the **Eski dzhamiya** (Old Mosque), whose facade has been replastered so that it's hard to believe that this was the first mosque erected on the Balkan peninsula, immediately after the Ottoman conquest. Even during the 1980s, when mosques elsewhere in Bulgaria were locked and derelict, Haskovo's remained in use, its prayer hall covered in carpets and its imam unfazed by foreign visitors, who are nowadays more welcome than ever.

Follow bulevard Bûlgariya beside the River Haskovska (or take bus #1, #12 or #101) to find the **Church of Sveta Bogoroditsa**, a simple basilica of heavy brick filled with fussy woodcarving. By crossing over the road bridge and heading back towards the centre just off Tsar Osvoboditel you can also visit the **art gallery** housed in the **Paskalevata kûshta**, at ul. Episkop Sofroni 3 (Mon-Fri 9am-noon & 2–5pm; free). This period-furnished house was the birthplace of Aleksandûr Paskaliev, a pioneer of Bulgarian publishing.

The wooded **Park Kenana** to the north of town is a favourite place for recreation, with tennis courts, restaurants and cafés; catch bus #2 or #102 from ploshtad Spartak, on the north bank of the bend in the river. On the last weekend in May special buses are laid on to take people to the **Gathering of Beautiful Trakiya**, a festival of folk groups from the southeastern Rhodopes and Aegean Thrace. Two other events for music lovers are the three-day **Jazz Festival** in late September or early October, and the festival of **Symphonic Music** named after the violinist Nedyalka Simeonova, at the end of October. While the festival of **Young Poets** (late March/early April) celebrates new poetic talent, the **Haskovo Fair** (around Sept 8) is a trade fair with some sports events to enliven things.

Practicalities

From the **bus station** on bulevard Sûedinenie, ten minutes east of the centre along ulitsa San Stefano, there are hourly buses to Kûrdzhali, Svilengrad, Harmanli, Plovdiv and Sofia, but the most useful are the three daily buses to Madzharovo – enabling one to reach the nature reserve there (see p.376). There are also six daily buses to Istanbul. The **train station**, 1.5km further out along bulevard Sûedinenie (bus #5, #12 or #13), is of less use.

The *Aida* on ploshtad Svoboda (ⓣ038/665164; ❷) is the cheapest, though least attractive, of Haskovo's **hotels**; far better value is the smart *Rodopi* at bul. Bûlgariya 39 (ⓣ038/609660; ❷), while the four-star *Haskovo* at ul.Vasil Drutenel 20, just along from the *Aida* (ⓣ038/602525; ❻) offers the highest standards. If you've got your own transport, the modern *Bulgaria* (ⓣ03722/2404; ❷) in the small spa resort of Haskovski Mineralni Bani, 20km from town (also accessible by bus), has comfortable accommodation, hot pools, a sauna and fitness facilities; it's just by the crossroads as you enter the resort.

There's no shortage of places **to eat and drink** around ploshtad Svoboda. One that's highly rated is the *Gurkovata kûshta*, in an old house in the Bulgarian quarter with a garden and private rooms, which can be reached from the Church of Sveta Bogoroditsa by heading up ulitsa Berkovski and turning right into General Gurko. It charges around 20Lv for a three-course meal, and stays open until midnight. In the centre at ul. Otors Paisi 23, the *Orient* serves decent Turkish cuisine on the second floor.

Harmanli

Founded by the Turks in the sixteenth century, **HARMANLI**, 33km east of Haskovo, gets its name from the threshing mills (*harman*) that once abounded on the surrounding plain, nowadays given over to growing cotton, mulberries (for silkworms) and tobacco. It's a tiny, sleepy place that seems to ignore the E80 and the outside world, where dry fountains and riverbeds speak of a desolation measured out over coffee and worry-beads. The shell of the *Hotel Hebros* guides strangers from the bus station to the central square, near Harmanli's only "sights", both of which date from the 1500s. To one side of the hotel stands the chunky ruined wall of an Ottoman **caravanserai**, while behind the supermarket is the hump-backed **Gurbav Bridge**, with its flowery dedication in Arabic:

> **As a token of his gratitude to God the Grand Vizier ordered an arch like a rainbow to be built over the River Harmanli ... and alleviated rich and poor alike from their sorrows. The world is a bridge which is crossed by both king and pauper. When I saw the completion of this bridge, in praying to God, I spoke this inscription.**

Practicalities

Harmanli's centrally located **bus terminal** is preferable as a point of arrival to the **train station**, some way out to the southeast and connected to town by bus. The towering **hotel** block opposite the bus station, the most convenient place to stay, is actually made up of three private hotels – the *Bulgaria* (ⓣ0373/2158; ❶), the *Hebros* (ⓣ0373/8427; ❶), and the *Prince* (ⓣ0373/8981; ❷) – you'll be greeted by three receptionists bizarrely vying for business, though there's little to distinguish the rooms other than price.

Svilengrad and the borders

Despite its proximity to two busy border crossings, **SVILENGRAD** seems almost as dozy as Harmanli. There's little specific to see save the sixteenth-century

Mustafa Pasha Bridge – known to the locals as *Stariya Most* – which links the town with village-like suburbs on the far bank of the River Maritsa. This 295-metre-long structure of Karabag stone supported by thirteen arches is an even finer achievement than Harmanli's similar Gurbav Bridge. There's a surprising range of **accommodation** in the town, of which the best are the comfortable *Central* on the main square (Ⓣ0379/70320; ❸), which boasts an English-themed pub, and the Greco-Roman-style *George*, just off the square at ul. Septembritsi 2 (Ⓣ0379/71797; ❷).

Worth a visit if you have a car are a couple of antiquities near the village of **MEZEK**, 10km southwest of town, reached by turning off near the truck park for the Greek border crossing. Just before the village, a road to the left leads past an army base to a **Thracian tomb**, 21m long and corbel-roofed, like the stairway in the Great Pyramid, with a circular funerary chamber (where bronze artefacts were found, from the fourth century BC). If you find the tomb locked, ask staff at the municipality office in Mezek (Mon-Fri 8.30am-noon & 1-5.30pm) to open it. About 1km beyond Mezek, the ruined **Neutzikon fortress** (or *Kaleto*) is the best preserved of the many fortresses raised to guard against Byzantine incursions during the eleventh and twelfth centuries. Both languish in a so-called *granichna zona*, or **border zone**, which used to be strictly off-limits in Communist times and is still patrolled by border police, nowadays engaged in keeping refugees out rather than Bulgarians in. You'll be expected to produce your passport and a valid reason for being here if you're stopped.

Crossing into Greece or Turkey

Svilengrad's **train station** is 5km west of town, with irregular buses to and from the centre, so travellers heading for Turkey should either stay aboard the train from Plovdiv and skip Svilengrad entirely, or be sure to leave plenty of time to get to the station to catch a train to Istanbul around midnight. Trains to Alexandroupoli in Greece run daily, while the 24-hour **road crossing into Greece**, 2km nearer town than the station, is used almost exclusively by truckers.

Far more traffic crosses the **Turkish border** at **KAPITAN ANDREEVO**, 15km beyond Svilengrad (three buses daily), where vehicles entering Bulgaria are liable to rigorous examinations. Inside Turkey (where motorists and train passengers undergo customs at Kapikule), it's pretty easy to catch a *dolmus* (shared taxi) to **Edirne**, 19km east, which should drop you in the centre near the town's splendid mosque; the bus station is 3km to the southeast and the train station 2km further out.

The Rhodopes

According to Thracian mythology, the mortal lovers Hem and Rhodopis dared call themselves after the divine Zeus and Hera, who duly punished the couple by turning them into mountains separated by the River Maritsa – him the Balkans and she **the Rhodopes**. Straddling Greece and Bulgaria, the Rhodopes are the land where panpipes, Orpheus and the Orphic Cult originated, a region rich in gems and ores, but otherwise not fit for much beyond raising sheep and growing tobacco. Unlike the rest of Bulgaria, whole communities converted to Islam after the conquest, and of the numerous Turks who settled here many outstayed the empire's collapse – their descendants now constitute Bulgaria's largest ethnic minority. While hydroelectric schemes and tourism have pushed the Rhodopes into the twenty-first century, the region is still, as Leslie Gardiner noted in the 1960s, a weird mixture of opposites: "donkeys and turbo-generators, Alpine flowers and tropical foliage, bikinis in winter and thick Turkish woollens in summer".

While the ski resort of **Pamporovo** and the **Bachkovo Monastery** are well known to foreigners, the region's scenic highlands and picturesque villages have only been "discovered" quite recently. Of all Bulgaria's mountain ranges, this is the best for **walking** (the central and western Rhodopes especially), **caving** (around **Trigrad**), **birdwatching** (near **Madzharovo**) and other special interests. The Rhodopes are also the home of some fantastic folk music and **festivals** (mostly in August) at **Shiroka Lûka, Rozhen**, **Dorkovo** and **Madzharovo**. The first is deservedly renowned for its traditional architecture though it is far from the only village in the range with stone houses and bridges, nor even the finest example of the genre, an accolade which belongs to the Agushev Konak at **Mogilitsa**, near the regional capital, **Smolyan**. In the eastern Rhodopes, **Kûrdzhali** can serve as a base for exploring the recently discovered 4000-year-old temple and fortress at **Perperikon**, the lesser but equally fascinating ruins at **Tatoul**, and the weird rock formations of the region, and its museum has a fine collection of folk costumes, gemstones and historical artefacts.

The legacy of its history is far from abstract here, as Bulgarians recall five centuries of oppression epitomized by the massacre at **Batak** in 1876, while the Pomak (Slav Muslim) and ethnic Turkish inhabitants of the Rhodopes have living memories of the "name-changing campaign" and "Great Excursion" of the late 1980s, when more than 200,000 of them fled to Turkey (most later returned). Though it's partly due to the state's efforts to hide what was happening in the region that the Rhodopes remained *terra incognita* for so long, even in olden times road-builders were sometimes attacked by villagers, who preferred to be as remote as possible – as the Turks living between **Krumovgrad** and **Ivailovgrad** still do.

Tourist facilities and public transport vary from good to nonexistent, though the recent growth in **private hotels** is gradually reaching most areas. While a car provides greater flexibility, there's enough transport and accommodation for you to be able to visit almost all of the region's attractions, given sufficient time. **Buses** from Plovdiv run to Bachkovo, Pamporovo and Smolyan in the central Rhodopes, Velingrad to the west, and Kûrdzhali to the east; while Madzharovo can be reached from Haskovo. With the exception of the scenic narrow-gauge line linking Septemvri on the plain with Bansko in the Pirin Mountains, the limited **train** service in the Rhodopes is of little use.

Organized tours

Should you wish to join an **organized hiking tour** in the region, contact the Sofia-based adventure tourism agency ZigZag Odysseia-In (see p.84), whose Rhodopes itinerary includes Mostovo, Krûstova Gora, Manastir, Rozhen, Progled and Trigrad, and can be extended into the Pirin and Rila mountains if desired. Tours booked abroad through a foreign operator are likely to be handled by **SunShine Tours**, also based in Sofia.

The central Rhodopes

The northernmost spurs of the Rhodopes rear up from the plain barely 10km south of Plovdiv, with numerous minor roads running up the narrow valleys of the streams that gush down to feed the Maritsa. The main route south, however, into the **central Rhodopes** starts beyond the town of **Asenovgrad**, and follows the ruggedly beautiful valley of the River Chepelarska past the historic **Bachkovo Monastery** up to the ski resorts of **Chepelare** and **Pamporovo**, before descending to **Smolyan**. This road is well served by bus, unlike those in other parts of the highlands, where you need a car to get around or enough time to go walking. The scenery in this region is magnificent and there are enough villages offering accommodation to support all kinds of hikes around **Mostovo**, **Manastir** and **Progled**.

Asenovgrad

Half-hourly buses speed across the dusty plain between Plovdiv and **ASENOVGRAD** 20km south, a light and breezy town built around a large park. Train and bus terminals lie on the northern outskirts, from where it's a short walk through a park and across the river to a modern town square. Two church spires are visible on the hill immediately above: the resplendently ochre-coloured Sveti Dimitûr on the left and the smaller Sveta Troitsa on the right. More interesting, however, is the town's main shopping thoroughfare running south from the square, where a small **Historical Museum** (under renovation at the time of writing) holds local Neolithic and Thracian finds – including a fine bronze helmet and the iron wheel rims of a Thracian chariot.

It was the Thracians who first fortified a crag overlooking the entrance to the Chepelarska gorge, which can be reached by a side road 2.5km south of town. If it seems a hard slog, remember that the thirteenth-century **Church of Sveta Bogoroditsa** just below the summit was rebuilt by a disabled man who walked every day to work on his self-appointed task. Higher uphill are the **remains of a medieval fortess** founded during the eleventh century and enlarged after Asen II's victory over the Byzantine Empire in 1230, half of which slid down the hill some years ago. From this derived Asenovgrad's medieval name, Stanimaka – "protector of the mountain pass".

If you want **to stay**, you could try either the two-star *Hotel Asenovets* on the main square (Ⓣ0331/62127; ❸), or the comfortable *Cosmos* at ul. Sûedinenie 18 (Ⓣ0331/22004; ❹), though you'd do better to take one of the regular buses up the valley towards Bachkovo, Chepelare or Smolyan.

Towards Bachkovo

Just beyond Asenovgrad the road enters the impressive **Chepelarska gorge**, its river nowadays harnessed to produce electricity. Heavy trucks bound for the mines around Ardino are another sign that modernization has come to the Rhodopes, though goatherds with their flocks and mule trains bearing packs are still a common sight. The area immediately south of Asenovgrad is a popular weekend picnic spot, with pebble-strewn riverside beaches, trails into the forested hills, and numerous roadside cafés.

Throughout the centuries of Ottoman rule, the Rhodopes were the region most consistently infested with outlaws: *haiduks*, whom the Bulgars now romantically view as precursors of the patriotic *cheti*, but also bandits of Turkish origin known as *kûrdzhali*, who spread terror among the villages. The last wave of armed resistance to authority occurred in 1947–49, when anti-Communist partisans operated in the hills around Asenovgrad.

Bachkovo Monastery and around

Nine kilometres south of Asenovgrad, the village of **Bachkovo**, with its stone houses overgrown with flowers, gives no indication of what to expect 1.5km further up the road at **BACHKOVO MONASTERY** (*Bachkovski manastir*; daily 6.30am–9pm; free). Gardiner's description of it as "a mixed bag of buildings – chapels, ossuaries, cloisters, cells – daubed with frescoes more naive than artistic" doesn't do justice to Bulgaria's second largest monastery, which, like Rila, has been declared a world monument by UNESCO. It was founded in 1083 by two Georgians in the service of the Byzantine Empire, one of whom, Grigoriy Pakuryani, renounced the governorship of Smolyan and Adrianople to devote the remainder of his life to meditation.

You enter the monastery through a small iron-plated door which opens onto a cobbled courtyard surrounded by wooden galleries. There are also a couple of fountains, where locals and pilgrims alike fill up their plastic bottles. The wall of the refectory on the left is covered with **frescoes** providing a narrative of the monastery's history: they show Bachkovo roughly as it appears today, but watched by God's eye and a celestial Madonna and Child, with pilgrims proceeding to a hill in the vicinity to place icons. Other frescoes depict the slaying of the dragon: a powerful archetype in ancient European mythology, repeated in the image of the Thracian Rider, and later incorporated into Christian iconography, in which St George and St Demetrius perform similar symbolic acts. It can also be read as an allusion to the Turks who laid waste to Bachkovo in the early sixteenth century, and the patient restoration of the monastery by the Bulgarians.

Though it's not immediately apparent, the monastery consists of two separate courtyards connected via the wing containing the seventeeth-century **refectory** (*trapeznitsa*; 4Lv entrance, guided tour 5Lv extra), whose vaulted hall is decorated with a *Tree of Isaiah* and a *Procession of the Miraculous Icon* executed by pupils of Zahari Zograf. If the gate into the second courtyard is open, you can view one of Bachkovo's churches, **Sveti Nikolai**, whose porch features a fine *Last Judgement*, which includes portraits of the artist Zograf and two colleagues in the upper left-hand corner.

The oldest building in the monastery is its principal church, **Sveta Bogoroditsa**, built in 1604. Frescoes in the porch of its bell tower depict the horrors in store for sinners: among the scenes of retribution, a *boyar* (a medieval nobleman) is tormented on his deathbed by a demon dangling a doll-like figure over him (presumably representing the man's ailing soul), while women watch in horror. The entrance is more cheerful, with the Holy Trinity painted on strips set at angles in a frame, so that one sees God or Christ flanking a dove, depending on which side you approach from, like a medieval hologram. On the right of the nave as you enter is a fourteenth-century Georgian **icon of the Virgin** which legend claims to be an authentic portrait of Mary, painted by the Apostle Luke. The icon plays a central role in celebrations of the name-day of the Assumption of the Virgin (August 15), and a ritual procession to a chapel in the nearby hills 25 days after the Orthodox Easter (see below).

Walks around the monastery

If you want to make more of your visit, there's a pleasant thirty-minute walk to a shrine near the spot where Bachkovo's treasures were once hidden from the Turks – a deed commemorated by an annual procession of believers bearing an icon. The path begins opposite the monastery gates and passes by the **church of Sveta Troitsa**, which contains early medieval frescoes and life-size portraits of Tsar Ivan Aleksandûr (1331–71) and his family who endowed the monastery, but is kept locked to protect them from looters. Don't be led astray by the red arrows near the picnic-meadow, fifteen minutes or so further on. Instead take the path straight ahead across the meadow, which leads shortly to a sign marking the **Chervenata Stena nature reserve** of Balkan plant species, and a chapel built beside a stream, on the far side of which rock-cut steps lead to a cave chapel and a stone-built one – the three are collectively known as **Ayazmoto**.

The **trail** continues upwards via dramatic waterfall basins (traversable only in summer on ladders made of branches) and punishing switchbacks (known as the "Forty Legs"), to the *Martsiganitsa* chalet (☎048/760036) with dorm beds for 12Lv per person – a strenuous but exhilarating three- to four-hour trek. From the chalet, an easier path leads back down to the road a few kilometres past the monastery in the direction of **Narechenski Bani**. This small resort with open-air mineral baths makes a good base for exploring some more delightful trails into the foothills, which abound in butterflies, insects, fungi and rare herbs; if you're lucky, you might even see a spotted eagle.

Practicalities

An easy day-trip from Plovdiv, the monastery can be reached by any of the thirteen daily **buses** to Chepelare or Smolyan, as well as on hourly services from Asenovgrad to Bachkovo, which run past the monastery drive. It's hard to find out the exact times of buses returning (there's usually one every hour until about 5pm), so you may be in for a wait, though minibuses between Smolyan and Plovdiv sometimes pick up passengers here.

In the vicinity of the monastery are three **restaurants**, the best of which is *Vodopada*, whose patio is centred on a little waterfall gushing out of the hillside. There are also a number of snack stalls selling drinks and ice cream. You can stay in the monastery's guest "cells" (☎03327/277) for 15Lv per person per night without hot water, 22Lv with. Across the river the *Eco* **hotel** (☎0889/715685; ❷) has clean doubles, while further on, the *Dzhambura* (☎03327/320; ❸) offers more comfortable and attractive rooms as well as a good restaurant. The next available **accommodation** is 14km farther on in **Narechenski Bani**, which also has two decent hiking chalets, plenty of private rooms (❶; ask around at the bus station), the friendly *Lyubina* hotel and restaurant (☎0334/2240; ❸) and two local tavernas serving delicious traditional food.

Hikes around Manastir

About 40km south of Bachkovo, **MANASTIR**, 1500m above sea level, is the highest village in Bulgaria and (they say) the Balkan peninsula. With its steeply terraced houses, potato and tobacco plots, stacks of firewood and scampering goats, Manastir makes a good base for hiking and gives a feel for rural life in the Rhodopes. The easiest way to get there is on the daily **bus** (at 5pm) from **Lûki**, 20km north.

One of the best hikes from Manastir is to **Progled**, a trip which can be done in three to four hours, but is far nicer stretched out with an overnight stay at a hiking chalet; you'll need map #4 in the *BTS* Rhodopi series. The trail begins behind Manastir, blue and white markers starting at a fountain five minutes' walk uphill, whence it's fifteen minutes to a flat, stony track where you bear

△ Roman stadium, Plovdiv

Hiking around Krûstova Gora and Mostovo

South of Bachkovo, there are some superb **hikes** amidst stunning mountain scenery, which can be tackled by arranging for a driver to drop you at one location and pick you up elsewhere – a strategy which can also be applied to longer hikes involving an overnight stay at the *Svoboda* chalet or Manastir (see below). Such **buses** as exist in the region centre on the ugly mining village of **Lûki**, 24km south of Bachkovo, with one a day from Plovdiv and four from Asenovgrad, plus local services to Belitsa (two daily) and Borovo (one daily). All the walks described below are covered by the two BTS **maps** of the Rhodopes, #3 and #5.

One of the most rewarding walks in the area is to the summit of **KRÛSTOVA GORA** (Hill of the Cross), a place of pilgrimage for centuries until the Communists suppressed it, but now revived. Its holiness derives from a fragment of the True Cross which was sent for safekeeping to Bachkovo after the fall of Constantinople, and transferred to a monastery here after Bulgaria was invaded by the Turks. Although the relic was lost when the monastery was ravaged, people came to pray and claimed to have seen a gleaming cross in the sky. The spring below the peak was also said to have medicinal properties. After the Ottoman yoke was lifted a cross was erected on the summit weighing 99 kilos (three times the age of Christ when he was crucified) and the **Sveta troitsa** church was built with stones from the original monastery. Legend has it that if a pregnant woman enters the church she can choose the sex of her child. The other church and the chapels lining the way to the summit were only built a few years ago. Traditionally, pilgrims spend the eve of *Krûstovden* (September 14) camped out on the mountain, before greeting the sunrise with a special liturgy devoted to health; in 1998, 20,000 people attended. People also come at Easter, Christmas and New Year (despite the snow), and you'll encounter a few souls on any day of the year. Spartan dorm beds are available for 5Lv per person (ⓣ048/929329).

Krûstova Gora is accessible from the village of **BOROVO** off the road to Lûki, where you can stay at either the *Eco Spalnya* (ⓣ048/868630; ❷), which has sweeping views of the valley, or the *Borikite* (ⓣ0889 534 649, ⓦwww.borokite.bol.bg; ❷), with a pleasant garden and excellent home-cooked food. A nicer approach is to walk there from **MOSTOVO**, on the other side of the hills. The village's name derives from a natural rock bridge (*most*) in the gorge below, where the river vanishes underground – you can see it before entering Mostovo, then pick up **the trail to Krûstova Gora** near the top of the village, on ulitsa Hristo Smirnenski. Initially a steep goat track that divides after 45 minutes, the path to Krûstova Gora is clearly signposted and walkable in just over an hour – providing you turn right upon emerging from the woods. By turning left instead you'll be on the trail to Velichki Vrûh, passing an ex-Party hunting lodge en route to the **Karadzhov Kûmak** (1hr 30min) – colossal rocks dimpled with giant "fingerprints" and topped with the ruins of what's thought to be a Thracian temple. A further hour brings you to a clearing where the trail starts descending; an hour and forty minutes later you face a brief, taxing ascent of a ridge called the **Rodopskoto konche** (Rhodope Horse), before reaching a forestry road down to Perleza, a good place to be met if you're not up to carrying on to the *Svoboda* chalet (a further two hours). Also well worth a visit are the face-shaped rocks and Thracian remains above the tiny hamlet of **BELINTAZH** which lies 10km along the dirt track to Tri Mogili after Mostovo and is served by a daily bus from Asenovgrad. The hospitable owners of *Kûshta Chotrovi* in Belintazh (ⓣ0888/013226 or 0889 375 418) offer dorm accommodation for 5Lv per person, good food, and useful local information.

right into the woods after 500m to find an old Roman road. Another twenty minutes brings you to a junction of trails, a blue one to the *Svoboda* and a red one to the *Prepsa* chalet. The latter passes a beautiful clearing of fallen pines and purple thistles and is easy-going all the way, so that you arrive at *Prepsa* two and a half hours after setting out, in the mood to press on to *Svoboda* (2hr) or westwards to Haidushki polyani (35min) and the *Momchil Yunak* chalet (1hr more).

Haidushki polyani (Outlaws' Meadows) is a trade union resort where you can sink a beer before examining an obelisk in the woods, on the spot where leaders of the Macedonian revolutionary movement decided to launch the 1903 Ilinden uprising. The partisan figures on the obverse side typify the Communist Party's efforts to identify itself with past liberation movements. Sporadic red and white markers indicate the trail from here to *Momchil Yunak* (ⓣ03021/8371), with dorm beds for 15Lv per person, a basic chalet near an ex-Party villa that's now the *Elitsa* hotel (ⓣ03021/8765; ❹). From here it's twenty minutes' walk to the main road; if you're heading to **Progled**, simply stay on the main road, and follow it downhill for 11km.

Practicalities

There's no shortage of places **to stay** in any of the villages mentioned above. In **Manastir**, your best bet is with the Angelovi family (ⓣ030528/289; ❶) or the Petrovi family (ⓣ030528/292; ❶), both of whom provide breakfast, and serve delicious home-cooked Rhodopean dishes. The bar-grill on the square can rustle up surprisingly good **meals** and sometimes has music and dancing.

OREHOVO, a quiet village of ageing stone-roofed houses lies 7km off the main road, midway between Bachkovo and Chepelare, and is famed for its male folk ensemble. The tourist information centre (Mon-Fri 8.30am-12.30pm & 1.30-5.30pm; ⓣ03053/3490) arranges rooms in the village, and *Kûshta Rai* (ⓣ03053/2737; ❷), an eco-house constructed from traditional building materials, offers cosy wood-panelled rooms. The village hosts a folk music festival on the last weekend of July, and the bagpipe-playing owner of *Kûshta Rai* can arrange impromptu performances for those interested.

Six kilometres after Chepelare is **PROGLED**, a village perched on the side of a steep hill with pricier accommodation reflecting its proximity to Pamporovo. Of the small chalet-style family hotels (whose prices tend to halve in summer) try the *Priroda* (ⓣ03021/8879, eprogreso@infotour.org; ❸), the equally comfortable and very friendly *Sarievi* (ⓣ03021/8588; ❷), or *Kushta Milushevi* (ⓣ0321/8809; ❸). All have satellite TV and rent ski equipment. The village also boasts a surprisingly classy restaurant, the *Progledski Hanche*, which is open 24 hours.

Chepelare, Progled and Zabûrdo

The small mountain town of **CHEPELARE**, 6km north of Progled, is popular with Bulgarians who want somewhere quiet to relax and enjoy the fresh air and scenery, and are unfazed by such blots on the landscape as a timber mill or the Orion ski factory – the only one in Bulgaria. Aside from its **ski run** – at over 5km, the longest in the Rhodopes – the only specific attraction is the well signposted **Speleological Museum** (officially Tues–Sat 9am–5.30pm, but hours variable) that whets your appetite to visit the local caves; some "cave pearls" from the Yagodina Cave (see p.367) are its most prized exhibit.

Chepelare has many new family **hotels** that compare favourably with the older complexes at Pamporovo (see below). The smart new *Agarta* at ul. Bor 2 (ⓣ03051/4408; ❸) is the best value, offering doubles, triples and maisonettes with luxury furnishings; the *Belona* at ul. Shina Andreeva 39A (ⓣ03051/4433, ⓔh_belona@hotmail.com; ❸) is a less fancy option, while *Ivan*, ul. Progres 6 (ⓣ03051/3113; ❶), *Martin*, ul. Kiril Madzharov 23 (ⓣ03051/2194 or 2164; ❷), and *Savov*, ul. Devech 7 (ⓣ03051/2036; ❷) are of a decent standard for the price, with satellite TV and en-suite bathrooms; all rent out ski equipment and can arrange bus transfers to Pamporovo. There's an ample supply of **private rooms** (❶) too; the **tourist information centre** at ul. Belomorska 44 (Mon–Fri 9am–5pm; ⓣ&ⓕ03051/2110) will be able to point you in the right direction. The best **restaurants** in which to enjoy Rhodope specialities, and a roaring log fire, are the *Gergana* and *Gorski Kût*, both moderately priced; for pizza and cakes try the *Vienska Salon* on the main square. **Nightlife** revolves around the *Zdravets* disco, also on the main square, which plays a mix of commercial dance and folk music all night long.

In a valley off the main road, 28km northwest of Chepelare, **ZABÛRDO** is the best-known **weaving** village in the Rhodopes, and home to the colourful rugs and blankets that abound in the region. Here, you can buy a *kozek* (the local word for a rug) from individual weavers, and watch them at their work. Unusually for what is a predominantly Pomak (Slav Muslim) village, Zabûrdo has a **folk music festival** on the Day of the Assumption (August 15). With a car, you can also visit from here the so-called **Miraculous Bridges** (*Chudnite mostove*), rock formations which form a natural bridge over a narrow stream, created when an earthquake destroyed a cave. Near the second bridge is the entrance to the Icy Cave, which remains below freezing even in summer, while nearby is the Big Cave, where pottery fragments dating from the sixth century BC have been discovered. The bridges are sited in another side valley, accessible by a fork in the road to Zabûrdo. Simple **accommodation** is available at the *Chudnite Mostove* chalet (ⓣ03059/3261; ❶) which also has a small restaurant.

Pamporovo

PAMPOROVO, the "Gem of the Rhodopes", currently looks rather tarnished, with some of its hotels showing their age, while others are undergoing renovation as establishments change hands. It's also become known as the "Sunny Beach" of winter tourism, overrun with groups of English and Irish tourists on cheap package tours who party rowdily most nights. That said, it's a stunning location, and is still a user-friendly ski resort where mild weather and good snow-cover make skiing conditions near perfect from mid-December to mid-April, with a range of classes and pistes to suit everyone from absolute beginners to the pros. Over summer it is marketed as a mountains-and-lakes resort, with a number of organized walking and cycling tours on offer – though hikers would do better elsewhere – but in May and from September until the start of the skiing season Pamporovo is pretty folorn, with only a few hotels and facilities open.

Buses drop you at the junction of the Plovdiv to Smolyan road and the slip road to the main complex of hotels. The beginners' slopes are just below the outlying *Malina* chalet complex, reached by bus or a thirty-minute walk from the centre of the resort. **Equipment** can be rented there, at the bus depot, or at the Studenets way-station (accessible by chair lift from *Malina* or the bus station). Chair lifts also run from Ardashlar (just below *Malina*) and from Studenets to the 1926-metre-high summit of Mount Snezhanka, starting-point of many of the **ski runs**. Advanced skiers can take a drag lift from Studenets up the side of "The Wall", the most difficult and demanding run at Pamporovo.

The **TV Tower** on Mount Snezhanka (daily 9am–4.30pm) has a café and an observation gallery giving a marvellous view of the Rhodope Mountains and, on clear days, parts of the Pirin and Rila, too – and makes a useful landmark for hikers. Twenty minutes' walk from here, the **Orpheus Rocks** (*Orfeevi Skali*) overlook a superb panorama of the mountains surrounding the Smolyan Valley.

Practicalities

As independent travellers are charged considerably more for rooms, tuition and equipment than people on **package holidays** (and might find that everything's booked up anyway), would-be skiers are strongly advised to take one of the cheap deals offered by foreign tour operators (see p.30), plus the optional "ski pack" which covers all rentals and lift rides. If you do just turn up on spec, the *Finlandia* (ⓣ & ⓕ03021/8374; ❼), *Sveti Georgi* (ⓣ03021/8478, ⓕ8575; ❻) and *Snezhanka* (ⓣ03021/8316, ⓕ8273; ❻) are the least expensive hotels and include breakfast and use of swimming pool and fitness facilities, while the *Malina Village's* chalets with underfloor heating and satellite TV (ⓣ03021/8388, ⓔmalina.villages@mail.bol.bg; 130Lv, with 4 people sharing) work out to be the cheapest beds at the resort. For a touch more luxury, you could try the *Perelik* (ⓣ03021/8405, ⓕ8418; ❼), which has a swimming pool, disco, tennis courts and a bowling hall, or to really splash out head for the pristine *Grand Hotel Murgavets* (ⓣ & ⓕ03021/8366, ⓦwww.murgavets-bg.com; ❽). You could also stay in Chepelare (see p.358) or down the valley in Smolyan (see opposite), from where there are regular buses up to the pistes of Pamporovo during the winter season. If you have your own transport, the tiny village of **STOIKITE**, 5km to the west, has its fair share of **private rooms** available from its tourist office on the main square (Tues–Sat 9.30am-12.30pm & 2-7pm; ⓣ03021/8241) or try *Jana* (ⓣ03021/751; summer ❶, winter ❷). The *Sveta Elena* hotel (ⓣ03021/8570; ❸) 3km above the village has more comfortable accommodation.

Traditional Rhodope dishes like spit-roasted lamb (*cheverme*), stuffed vine leaves (*sarmi*), white bean stew (*Smolenski bob*) and a local variation on the cheese-filled *banitsa* are on offer at "folk-style" **restaurants** such as the *Chevermeto* and *Malina* – and at the restaurant of the *Rhodopa Tourist* hotel in the village of Stoikite – all of which feature music and dancing. Otherwise **entertainment** consists of the usual après-ski parties and bar crawls, and discos in the *Prepsa* and *Perelik* till the small hours.

Around 6km to the east lies **MOMCHILOVTSI,** though it's best reached by bus from Smolyan, a further 8km south. Set on a steep slope with gorgeous views in all directions, it's certainly a very peaceful place: on a hazy summer afternoon the silence is interrupted only by the occasional cock-crow and the intermittent buzzing from the couple of saw mills, which still form an important part of the village economy. Though Momchilovtsi may, at first glance, seem little more than a rustic backwater, it's also a popular retreat for wealthy Bulgarians, and in recent years there's been a spate of building work, with modern apartments and villas arising amongst the chicken-coops and wood sheds. There are a few family-run hotels scattered around, including the *Shipkata*, ul. Stamboliiski 22 (ⓣ03023/2204; ❸) and the *Rodopchanska*, ul. Byalo More 40 (ⓣ03023/2863; ❸), both of which have cosy, traditionally furnished rooms. The eponymous *Momchilovtsi*, just down the road from the bus station (ⓣ & ⓕ03023/2311; ❷), is a smart modern place offering large, comfortable apartments sleeping either three or four people, and has its own restaurant. You can also rent bikes and book private rooms (❶) and hotel accommodation through the local **tourist office** (Mon-Fri 9am-5pm; ⓣ03023/2803, at weekends call ⓣ0887/256407). There's a small local history **museum** just below the main square, as well as an **art gallery**, both of which can be opened by staff at the tourist office.

Nine kilometres away, next to the *Momchil Yunak* chalet (see p.358), is a recently opened **snowboard park** with jumps and slopes where you can rent equipment for 20Lv per day.

Smolyan

A conglomerate of three villages (Smolyan, Raikovo and Ustovo) that straggles for 15km along the banks of the River Cherna, **SMOLYAN**, the administrative and cultural capital of the central and western Rhodopes, embodies Communism's attempt to mould the mixed Christian–Pomak agrarian population of Bulgaria's southern margins into the urbanized citizens of a modern socialist state. Situated 1000m above sea level, it's one of the highest towns in Bulgaria, which means that the climate in summer is a lot fresher and more bearable than much of the rest of the country. Attractively squeezed between pine-clad peaks, the modern housing estates perched above the centre have maintained something of the region's traditional highland architecture, giving the whole place a rural feel, underscored by the goats and piles of logs in the backstreets.

Arrival and information

Smolyan has two bus stations, at opposite ends of town. Coming from Sofia, Plovdiv or anywhere north or west you'll probably **arrive** at Avtogara Smolyan on ulitsa Minyorska, just downhill from the upper end of bulevard Bûlgariya, which runs down into the centre. You can walk it in ten minutes or wait for buses #1, #2 or #3, which run from one end of Smolyan to the other via the modern centre, terminating at Avtogara Ustovo, the station that serves Kûrdzhali and other points east. However, some buses from Plovdiv that bypass Pamporovo and come via the Rozhen Pass arrive at Ustovo, while private buses from Plovdiv drop passengers outside the *Hotel Smolyan*, smack in the centre every hour.

Beside the hotel, the helpful **tourist information centre** (Mon–Fri 9am–5pm; ⓣ & ⓕ0301/62530, ⓔsmoltic@yahoo.com) can advise on trips and activities in the Smolyan region and books **private rooms** (❶).

There are two **post offices** (both Mon–Fri 7.30am–6pm, Sat 8am–11pm), one on bulevard Bûlgariya, next to the *Olimp* café, and another in the administrative complex, just around the corner from the **telephone office** (daily 7am–10pm). **Internet** access is available at the museum (see p.362).

Accommodation

Just a couple of minutes' walk from Avtogara Smolyan is *The Three Fir Trees*, approached down a flight of steps from bulevard Bûlgariya at ul. Srednogorets

The Rozhen Observatory and festival

Visible for miles around, the lofty white dome of **Rozhen Observatory** contains a mammoth optical telescope manufactured at the Zeiss works in East Germany, which has scanned the cosmos since the 1970s. The site was chosen because of the clear skies and absence of background light; besides the main telescope, there are three smaller ones on other hilltops. As they only work at night, people who take the trouble to fix a **visit** (book in advance on ⓣ03021/8357) are denied the thrill of stargazing but may still enjoy the telescope and its vintage early 1960s computer hardware, which are mainly used for checking astronomical maps.

The Rozhen peak near the observatory is the setting for the largest folklore festival in the Rhodopes – the **Rozhenski sûbor** – where almost every village is represented by dancers, singers or musicians. It's usually held on the last weekend in August, but check with the tourist office in Smolyan to be sure (see above). One or two buses a day from Plovdiv cross the Rozhen Pass en route to Smolyan (and vice versa), running past the slip road to the observatory, or you can walk here from Progled in an hour cross-country (or a couple of hours along the road).

1 (Ⓣ0301/38228, Ⓔdreitannen@mbox.digsys.bg; ❶), a small, modern place with a friendly English-speaking owner who's a mine of local information and also runs guided coach tours around the region. The *Babylon*, located uphill at ul. Han Presian 27 (Ⓣ0301/32668; ❷), is a larger establishment with its own restaurant. The large three-star *Hotel Smolyan* is a little out of the way of things at the bottom of bulevard Bûlgariya (Ⓣ0301/62053; ❷) and is beginning to show its age, although it has perfectly good, comfy rooms with TV and bath. It also has its own restaurant and bar, both overpriced. Further to the east, in the Raikovo district, is the modern *Kiparis*, ul. Sokolitsa 31 (Ⓣ0301/64040, Ⓔhotelkiparis@dir.bg; ❹), which has simply furnished en-suite rooms, with a Jacuzzi, sauna and fitness centre on site. Alternatively, you could base yourself in the picturesque mountainside suburb of **Smolyanski Ezera**, where several small lakes surrounded by crags and forests provide a setting for the *Smolyanski Ezera* mountain chalet (Ⓣ0301/63458) with dorm beds for 6Lv per person, and the all-year *Panorama* **campsite** – accessible by bus #4 from Avtogara Smolyan – which enjoys a truly spectacular view. Accessed by a rough track is the cosy family-run *Villa Chapov* (Ⓣ0301/34286; ❸) which rents out bikes and snow shoes and provides transport to the ski lifts. You could also stay in the charming, laid-back little town of **SMILYAN**, halfway between Smolyan and Mogilitsa. The number of private rooms and small hotels in Smilyan is increasing each season, and the best of these is the *Dairy Inn* (Ⓣ03026/2241; ❸), which, as its name suggests, is attached to a working dairy, where guests can sample some of the milk and cheese made there, or even try their hand at working some of the machinery themselves. You could also try the spotless *Dangulevi* (Ⓣ03026/2356; ❶) just along the road. The only time when rooms may be scarce is during the annual **Milk Festival**, on the last weekend of August, when local cattle breeders parade their finest beasts, dressed in flowers, beads and bells, to compete for the coveted title of "Miss Cow".

The Town

A four-lane boulevard carrying so little traffic that its overhead walkway is practically redundant runs through the **civic centre**, passing a lead-domed **planetarium** whose shows (Mon–Sat; 5Lv) are available in foreign languages once a day at 2pm and include footage from Rozhen Observatory (see p.361). The post office, the town hall, the Rhodope Drama Theatre and other public buildings are all massed on the hillside, in a sprawling concrete complex which also houses a couple of cafés and a supermarket.

Several flights of steps behind the post office lead up to Smolyan's **Ethnographic Museum** and **Art Gallery** (both officially Tues–Sun 9am–noon & 1–6pm; 5Lv). Though not labelled in English, the museum has a superb collection of artefacts from the Bronze Age onwards, including a restored Thracian helmet with elaborate cheek-guards, and "secret" Christian gravestones resembling Muslim ones but carved with crosses underneath. There's also a large

Moving on from Smolyan

Chances are you'll be catching a **bus** out of Avtogara Smolyan, which not only serves Plovdiv but Lûki (see p.355), Mogilitsa (see opposite), and Devin in the western Rhodopes. Except for the 5.30am service via the Rozhen Pass, all buses to Plovdiv pass through Pamporovo and Chepelare. If you're heading towards Kûrdzhali, you can take a state bus from Avtogara Ustovo. There are also **minibuses** from *Hotel Smolyan* to Plovdiv and Ustovo to Kûrdzhali.

collection of traditional local instruments, such as bagpipes (*gaidi*) and lutes (*tamburi*), and colourful carpets (*chergi*) and tufted goat's-hair rugs (*halishta*) – still manufactured around Smolyan. Best of all are the grotesque *Kukeri* costumes, worn by celebrants at New Year in the Rhodope and Pirin regions. Another room on the top floor is devoted to photos and models of traditional architecture in villages such as Shiroka Lûka and Mogilitsa – especially the Agushev konak (see below). The **art gallery** across the way is likewise worth a visit, with Rhodope landscapes by Dechko Uzunov and Vasil Barakov, Nensko Balanski's iconic *Woman with a Cup of Coffee*, and temporary exhibitions of graphics or photography. Perhaps because of their elevated position, neither place appears to receive many visitors and you may have to knock to gain access.

The older quarters of town contain a few more sights such as a sixteenth-century **mosque** that's visible on the way in from Pamporovo; the National Revival-style **Pangalov House** on ulitsa Veliko Tûrnovo (not open to visitors); the churches of **Sveta Nedelya** and **Sveti Todor Stratilat** in Raikovo; and **Ustovo**, which, in parts, still resembles the village it once was, sited higgledy-piggledy on the hillsides around the confluence of the Cherna (Black) and Byala (White) rivers.

Eating and drinking

Bulevard Bûlgariya is lined with **restaurants** and pavement **cafés**, such as *Pizza Lucia* at no. 57 and the excellent *Otmora* at no. 35, which serves a good range of national and international dishes and offers some splendid mountain views from its terrace. Perched high above the town at ul. Snezhanka 16 is the *Riben Dar*, a fish restaurant with over a hundred different dishes. There are numerous places to **drink**, including *Café Cinema* at no. 51, which does a good range of cakes and cocktails, and *Starata Kûshta*, a National Revival-style house dating from 1840, with outdoor seating, reached by steps up from the main drag at ul. Studenska 2 (evenings only). A limited menu of grilled snacks is also available. Nightlife in Smolyan consists of commercial pop and folk at *Topstars*, and slightly better dance music at *Buksy* – both on bulevard Bûlgariya.

Mogilitsa and the Agushev Konak

Having seen the model of the Agushev konak in Smolyan's museum, you may want to check out the original in the otherwise unremarkable village of **MOGILITSA**, 26km south of town. You can do this in a day by taking the bus from Avtogara Smolyan terminal to Arda (the next village up the valley), which stops in Mogilitsa en route, then catching the bus back to Smolyan. Alternatively, you could catch the evening Arda bus, and stay at the *Babachev Guest House* (ⓣ03036/466 ❶) in Mogilitsa or at the *Milchovata kûshta* in the tiny hamlet of Bukata immediately to the east (ⓣ03036/297; ❷) and visit the konak next day. The *Milchovata* arranges horse riding, bike rental, and fishing excursions, as does Mogilitsa's tourist information centre (daily 9am-5.30pm; ⓣ03036/331 or 315).

The **Agushev konak** (Wed–Sun 9am–noon & 1–5.30pm) is a splendid example of the fortified manor houses built by rich Rhodope merchants in Ottoman times, when villages like Mogilitsa owned vast herds of sheep and were far wealthier than today. As the largest sheep-owners in the region, the Agushevs could afford to build a winter residence in Mogilitsa (1812–42) and a summer one in the hills (which hasn't survived). Divided into three walled compounds (for Agushev's household and the families of his eldest sons), the complex is visually unified by its thick slate tiles and pinnacled chimneys, with latticed screens designed to preserve the privacy of the women's quarters while allowing air to circulate (it has 86 doors and 221 windows altogether). The interior is comfortably furnished, with many large, panelled rooms, and some remarkable features, such as an enormous hall with high *minderi* for seating guests and some intricately carved ceilings with sunburst and diamond patterns. Aromatic box-shrubs were planted outside the sliding screens of the summer rooms to deter flies, while built-in wardrobes, painted red, green and blue, in the bedrooms, acted as insulators against the cold. Wool-dyeing took place in upstairs workrooms, containing looms and bales of brightly coloured yarn, and family members slept in cosy panelled rooms furnished with couches covered in goat-hides.

Just 3km east of the village, at **Sinite virove** (the Blue Pools), is the stunning **Uhlovitza Cave** (Wed-Sun 9am-5pm), just one of twenty or so in the Mogilitsa region, and best known for its series of waterfalls and curious rock formations. The bus from Smolyan to Arda will stop nearby.

The western Rhodopes

Despite an average altitude of only 1000m, the **western Rhodopes** offer some of the finest **walking** in Bulgaria. Their perfectly proportioned gorges and crags are covered by aromatic pines and spruces, with lizards and bluebirds flashing among the rocks, as hawks and eagles soar overhead. Around **Trigrad** there are some fabulous caves such as the Devil's Throat, as well as the annual bagpipe festival at the picturesque villages of **Shiroka Lûka** and **Gela**.

Shiroka Lûka makes a popular excursion from Pamporovo or a pleasant stopover en route to the sleepy hill towns of **Devin** and **Dospat**. From Dospat you can head north to the historic town of **Batak** and on to the spa resorts of **Velingrad** and **Yundola** – which can also be reached by bus from Plovdiv, or on the narrow-gauge railway running between Septemvri and the Pirin mountain town of Bansko. Unfortunately, public transport in the region is particularly poor, with infrequent and unreliable bus connections. Unless you have plenty of time – and patience – you would do better to rent your own transport; if you do get stuck somewhere, though, **hitchhiking** is a common and acceptable option, for tourists and locals alike.

Travelling through the region you're struck by the degrees of separation between its Christian and **Pomak** (Slav Muslim) inhabitants, with some villages exclusively one, others a mixture of both. Broadly speaking the area is Christian as far west as Devin but the majority of villages thereon are Pomak. While a mosque or a church is an obvious sign, many Pomak villages weren't allowed to build mosques during Communist times and have only begun to do so recently. Most feature a boxy prayer hall and a white pencil-minaret in the Ottoman style. Although Pomak women cover their heads and bodies, this stipulation is variously interpreted in different villages: some wear a headscarf (*zabradka*) and a long dress or pantaloons (*shalvari*), with others sporting a white wimple and a dun-coloured smock, or even a half-veil (*feredzhe*).

Shiroka Lûka and around

SHIROKA LÛKA, nestling in the deep and narrow valley of the Shirokolûshka river, is a popular destination for coach parties from Pamporovo, wanting to see a genuine Rhodope village. Its name means "broad meadow", and with its humpbacked bridges and asymmetrical half-timbered houses topped by their distinctive flagstone tile roofs, this remarkably unspoilt settlement of 2000 people could have been lifted off a picture-postcard. The advantage of coming on a tour is that you get to see a performance by local musicians at the **National School of Folklore Arts** – something you would miss should you turn up on spec – and also stand a chance of visiting the **Sgurov konak** (containing the local Ethnographic Museum), which tends to remain shut until a tour bus arrives. You may have more luck with the walled **Church of the Assumption** at the western end of the village, dating from 1834, where worshippers are greeted by a sobering fresco of a funeral procession surrounded by prancing demons. Inside, the church walls are adorned with more wonderfully naive frescoes, including one of Elijah ascending to Heaven in a smoking chariot, a trail of black smoke billowing in its wake. Note also the iconostasis, with its series of panels, painted in the same "rustic" style, relating the story of Adam and Eve and the Fall. Essentially, however, Shiroka Lûka is a place to stroll around the cobbled lanes and enjoy picnics in the surrounding meadows – unless you happen to be around for the first weekend of March, when there's a *kukeri* **carnival** of dancers and musicians in weird costumes, playing out an ancient fertility rite. It also hosts the **International Bagpipe Festival** (Ⓦwww.gaidaland.com) in August, Bulgaria's largest such gathering and a rare chance to hear the awesome sound of *Sto kaba gaidi* – sixty to one hundred bagpipers playing together. The festival kicks off with a procession of dancers and musicians on the Saturday morning, followed by performances at the National School of Folklore Arts, with more playing and festivities at nearby Gela (see below) on Sunday.

There's little in Shiroka Lûka to detain you for more than a day, but if you do wish to stay, there's a choice of several attractive **hotels**. The newly renovated *Zgorovska kûshta* (Ⓣ03030/531; ❷), on the main road at the Pamporovo end of the village, has comfortable rooms and a good restaurant, while the *James kûshta* on ulitsa Churshishka (Ⓣ0887/136207; ❸), is slightly more upmarket, a spruced-up old house with several comfortably furnished rooms and an affable South African host offering excellent home-cooked cuisine. There's also the centrally located *Gaida Inn* (Ⓣ03030/758 or 227, Ⓦwww.gaidaland.com; ❷) again in a characterful old house, and with a cosy *mehana* downstairs. Alternatively, you could try the larger *Shiroka Lûka*, on the hill above the music school (Ⓣ03030/341; ❷), which also has its own restaurant. Both the hotel restaurants mentioned here are much preferable to the village's stand-alone **restaurant**, also, inventively, called the *Shiroka Lûka*, a folksy tourist-trap geared up for coach parties, and which is otherwise deserted.

The helpful **Rhodopi tourist centre** (daily 8.30am-noon & 1-6.30pm; Ⓣ03030/233, Ⓦwww.shiroka-luka.com), located just off the main square, can provide maps, brochures, timetables and details of accommodation throughout the region, including **private rooms** in the town (❶). If you're looking for an even quieter spot to rest up, the nearby villages of **STOIKITE** and **GELA** - legendary birthplace of **Orpheus** – have their fair share of private rooms to rent, generally in cosy, modern chalet-style accommodation. One bus a day serves each village, leaving Shiroka Lûka in the morning and returning in the evening. The new *Gela hotel* (Ⓣ03030/308; ❷) has great views, or try the cosy two-star *Gerust* hotel (Ⓣ03030/760 or 0887/835311; ❷). Otherwise Kalinka Draganova (Ⓣ03030/560 or 0889 206 378) can arrange **private rooms** (❶) in Gela. With only a few dozen inhabitants, it's a lovely, peaceful place, whose origins go back over 3300 years, and where the calm is broken only by Shiroka Lûka's international bagpipe festival which moves up to Gela on the first Sunday of August (see above). Look out for the *silivriak*, otherwise known as the

Orpheus Flower, an endemic Balkan species whose small pink bells are said to have been formed from the blood of the mythical musician after the Bacchantes threw his butchered body into the river.

Thirty-four kilometres west of Shiroka Lûka, **DEVIN** is a pleasant enough town in a bowl between rugged mountain ranges, famous for its bottled water, but there's little to do other than enjoy the warm pool and baths (closed for renovation at the time of writing) at the **spa** to the left of the bridge beyond the bus station. There's a big military garrison here, and the presence of a firing range in the surrounding hills ensures that hiking possibilities are limited. Aside from a mosque and a church, the only official "sight" is a display of Rhodope folklore in the **museum** on the main square (officially Tues–Sat 10.30am–12.30pm & 1.30–5.30pm; 2Lv). Beyond the square, at ul. Osvobozhdenie 50, is the *Manolov* (Ⓣ03041/4832; ❷), the cheapest of Devin's **hotels** and comfortable enough. The *Ismena* at ul. Guritsa 41 (Ⓣ03041/4872; ❸) has a great position overlooking the town, offers various spa therapies, and was voted "Best Family Hotel 2001" by the Bulgarian Restaurant and Hotel Association for its consistently high standards. It's preferable to the smart but somewhat sterile and pricey *Spa Hotel* at ul. Druzhba 2A in the centre (Ⓣ03041/2577, Ⓕ2513; ❻), which offers hot pool, sauna and fitness centre.

Three **buses** a day leave Avtogara Smolyan for Devin, passing through Shiroka Lûka en route, from where up to seven local services a day also go to Devin. From Devin, two or three daily buses head westwards to Dospat (see p.368).

Trigrad and around

The star attraction in the southwestern Rhodopes is the locality of **Trigrad**, with its awesome **gorge** and **caves**. Getting there without a car can be a challenge, as it's reached by only one bus a day from Devin (Mon–Fri). Hitching is an option: quite a lot of traffic runs the 9km along the main Devin to Dospat road to Teshel, from where you could walk to Trigrad (10km) or **Yagodina** (8km), along minor roads, both of which run through gorges noted for their caves. Once there, you could easily **hike** round all the sites in the area within two to three days. The region is covered by **map** #2 in the BTS Rhodopes series.

Trigrad

The **TRIGRAD GORGE** (*Trigradsko zhdrelo*) is one of the most spectacular vistas in Bulgaria, its sheer walls overhanging the foaming River Trigradska, which disappears into a stupendous cave called the **Devil's Throat** (*Dyavolsko gûrlo*), accessible via a 150-metre-long tunnel at ground level (Wed–Sun 9am–5pm; hourly tours). The thunder of water is audible long before you sight a huge waterfall that vanishes into the bowels of the earth; objects swept into the cave are never seen again. As big as two cathedrals, the cave is traversed by stairways, and bats flit around the shaft of light entering through a mossy fissure overhead. On leaving, you can walk uphill to a viewing platform above the void where the Trigradska goes underground – in legend, the entrance to the underworld used by Orpheus (see box on p.369) – or scramble down beside the mouth of the road tunnel to find a placid pool at the bottom of the gorge, where the river reappears.

Fifteen minutes' walk beyond the Devil's Throat lies the sprawling village of **TRIGRAD**, whose mosque and tiny church reflect the relative size of its Muslim and Christian communities – and their closeness. The village was wealthy during Turkish times (when one landowner alone had 12,000 sheep), but is nowadays something of a sleepy backwater, disturbed only once a year by the **Orphic Mysteries Folk Music Festival**, the second weekend in August, which attracts hundreds of visitors from miles around. One of the best places **to stay** in the village is at the *Silivriak Hotel*, on the highest street to the right above the main square (Ⓣ03040/220; ❸). It's run by the custodian of the Devil's Throat cave, Kostadin ("Kotse") Hadzhesky, one of Bulgaria's foremost cavers and the person to ask about serious speleology. There are a few more small, family-run hotels in the village such as the *Zdravets* (Ⓣ03040/391; ❷), which also runs organized excursions, and the *Izgrev* (Ⓣ03040/545; ❷). Alternatively, you could stay at the *Chairite* cottage (Ⓣ03040/220; 98Lv per night for up to 6 people), located in the protected lake district of the same name, 19km east of the village, a superb place to study the local flora and fauna. For **horse riding** and **motorbike tours** in the region contact Arkan Tours (Ⓣ03040/363, Ⓦwww.arkantours.com).

Yagodina

The road to Yagodina runs through the longer but less precipitous **Buzhnov Gorge**, past the mouth of a side canyon that's great for hiking and caving. Only 2km long and 2–4m wide, the **Haidushki dol** (Outlaws' Ravine) ascends in cascades to its watershed between two peaks connected by a natural rock bridge called the **Devil's Bridge**, after a legend that only he can cross it. This wild karst terrain abounds in caves – 102 have been found so far – which are mostly only accessible to cavers. However, Kotse (see above) can arrange a trip to the **Haramiiska Cave** (around 30Lv per person) that needs more nerve than skill, where you crawl into one chamber before being lowered 42m in a harness into another cavern – an awesome but safe experience, as the guides take every precaution.

The **Yagodina Cave** (*Yagodinska peshtera*), 2km up the road, is an established attraction, with 45-minute tours (Tues–Sun 9am–4.15pm; 15Lv) covering 1km of the 10km labyrinth, the largest cave-system in Bulgaria. You'll need warm, waterproof clothing, as the temperature is 6°C and water drips constantly, enlarging the stalactites at a rate of one centimetre every fifty to a hundred years. Don't miss the **cave pearls** formed by drops falling on tiny pebbles, gradually coating them with a lustrous shell; and the **Devil's Face** on the wall, which bears an uncanny resemblance to Old Nick. Look out also for the **Newly-weds** formation, where 21 weddings have taken place between Bulgarian caving enthusiasts, who also host an annual Speleologists' Party in the cave on January 1.

While the lowest of the cave's three levels was flooded 300,000 years ago, the uppermost later served as a **Prehistoric cave-dwelling**, where excavations have unearthed Stone and Bronze Age kilns, potsherds and grindstones that can be seen *in situ* after finishing the tour of the lower cave. It's thought that groups of 20–30 people lived here, using several hearths as the direction of the draught varied with the seasons, blowing in the mouth of the cave or out of a hole at the back. Head down the road past the entrance to the lower cave, cross a wooden bridge and then a concrete one to regain the road to Yagodina, which is all uphill but has a path that cuts the walk to under an hour. Hikers refresh themselves at a *cheshma* inscribed with a paean to water by Saint-Exupéry, before entering **YAGODINA**, a purely Pomak village with a smart new mosque. Visitors can stay at a number of small hotels: the *Yagodina* (Ⓣ030419/310; ❷) is the most central and has its own restaurant; further along is the *Snezhana* (Ⓣ030419/263; ❷), which can organize fishing and riding trips, as well as some live folk music, or you could try the small *Iglika* chalet (Ⓣ030419/263; ❶) in the hills. Both the *Snezhana* and *Iglika* have cooking facilities, though meals can be arranged on request. Alternatively, you could hike to Trigrad (1hr 45min) and sleep there. To get to Trigrad, continue straight ahead on entering the village, past the post office, till you see a barn. The path beside it joins a track that soon reaches the junction of many paths; the one to the right that disappears behind a rock leads to a wide highland meadow, where you pick up a trail near the left-hand scarecrow, which, after an uphill slog, levels out in the woods. Turn left when you come to a broad path and you'll start descending the heights above Trigrad, to enter the village near the *Silivriak Hotel*.

Dospat

Three daily buses connect Devin with **DOSPAT**, 40km west. You'll pass through lots of Pomak villages en route before descending into this small town once noted for its folk costumes and festivities but now known for its reservoir and clean mountain air. Downhill from the bus station is a small square with a mosque, where a right turn takes you towards the jade-green **reservoir**, distantly overlooked by a nice **hotel**, the *Tihiyat kût* (☎03045/2082; ❷). To reach it, head uphill from the bus station and fork left – it's at the far end. Fork right and you'll find the *Panorama* (☎03045/2183; ❸), which has a pool, sauna, and excellent views.

Dospat is a turning point, where you can either head north along the desolate route to Batak (see below), or **continue westwards** past the turn-offs for Dolen and Kovachevitsa, towards Gotse Delchev in the Mesta Valley and the Pirin Mountains beyond (see p.146). This route passes through some of the loveliest countryside in Bulgaria, with an ever-changing panorama of gorges, forests and meadows dotted with a succession of highland villages, where tobacco farming is the main source of income. Be warned, though, that there's only one daily **bus** from Dospat to Gotse Delchev, and one to Batak, and these can be erratic; check times in advance. The Batak bus is signposted for Pazardzhik, as it terminates there.

Batak

The highlands to the north of Dospat are as thickly wooded and thinly populated as any in the Rhodopes, with not a single village on the road to Batak, only hunting lodges and the socialist-era *Rai* hotel (☎03553/2004; ❶) beside the Golyam Beglik Reservoir. In such a lonely, peaceful setting, it's hard to imagine that **BATAK** was once a byword for infamy that reverberated across Europe. During the April Rising of 1876 the Turks unleashed *bashibazouks* and Pomaks from other settlements to rape, pillage and slaughter the populace. Five thousand people – nearly the entire population – were hacked to death or burnt alive, an act for which the Pomak commander responsible was decorated. Britain's prime minister Disraeli cynically dismissed the **atrocities** to justify the continuing alliance with Turkey, until the weight of reports by foreign diplomats and J. A. MacGahan of *The Daily News* became impossible to ignore. Yet only a sustained campaign by trade unions, Gladstone and public figures like Victor Hugo and Oscar Wilde prevented Britain's support of Turkey in the Russo-Turkish War of 1877–78. Although the defeated Turks were obliged to concede an independent Bulgaria under the Treaty of San Stefano, Disraeli ensured at the Congress of Berlin that Macedonia and Thrace were returned to the Ottomans, and the half of Bulgaria south of the Balkan range became the Turkish protectorate of Eastern Rumelia – in return for which Turkey rewarded Britain with Cyprus.

The Town

As a bloody milestone on the road to liberation the massacre is still commemorated in April, and the town echoes with memories of the dead. One wall of the **museum** on the main square (daily 8.30am–12.30pm & 1.30–5.30pm; 3Lv for both this and the Ethnographic Museum) is inscribed with a seemingly endless roll-call of those who died, and sepia photographs show old women who survived sitting beside piles of skulls and bones – some set out on a table to form the words *Ustanak ot 1876*: (Rising of 1876). Display cabinets are filled with press reports and denunciations of the Turks and those who seemed to lend them support – including Turgenev's attack on Disraeli and Queen Victoria, *Croquet at Windsor*. A burnt tree trunk commemorates local rebel leader Trendafil Kerelov, who was lashed to it before it was set alight. Exhibits upstairs relate to Batak's contribution to the Balkan and World wars, including documents from the nearby partisan camp of Tehran – so-named in honour of the Allies' summit in 1943 – and a gruesome photograph of heads left on a wall in the village.

Immediately opposite the museum lies the low, roughly hewn **Church of Sveta Nedelya** (enquire at the museum if it's closed), where MacGahan found naked corpses piled one metre deep. Its bare interior contains stark reminders of the violence: the bloodstains on the walls have never been expunged; signs point to bullet holes in the walls; a glass case holds one of the heavy woodsmen's axes used to bludgeon the *Batachani* into submission; while in a sunken chamber at the end of the church lie the bones of the massacred.

After all this you may not have much stomach for further sightseeing, though there's a small **Ethnographic Museum** (opened on request; ask at the

The Orphic mysteries

The **legend of Orpheus** originated in ancient Thrace, where he was supposedly born in the vicinity of Gela, of a Muse (perhaps Calliope, patron of epic poetry) and King Oeagrus of the Odrysae tribe (Apollo in other versions of the story). His mastery of the lyre moved animals and trees to dance, and with his songs – which had previously enabled the Argonauts to resist the Sirens' lure – Orpheus tried to regain his dead wife, Eurydice, from the underworld. His music charmed Charon, the ferryman, and Cerebus, the guardian of the River Styx, and finally Hades himself, who agreed to return Eurydice on the condition that neither of them looked back as they departed – but emerging into the sunlight of the overworld, Orpheus turned to smile at Eurydice and so lost her forever. Thereafter, Orpheus roamed the Rhodopes singing mournfully until he was torn apart by "the women of Thrace" (whom Aeschylus identifies as followers of Dionysus – the "Bacchantes"). His head continued singing as it floated down the River Mesta to Lesbos, where it began to prophesy until its fame eclipsed that of the Oracle at Delphi.

Despite having its origins in Thracian religion, the myth of Orpheus had a bigger effect in Greece, where an **Orphic cult** rich in mysticism was well established by the fifth century BC. Itinerant priests offering initiation into the Orphic mysteries traversed the Greek world, and Orphic communities arose in southern Italy and Sicily. Original texts codifying Orphism's basic tenets have been lost, although later Hellenistic writers held that initiates were vegetarians and that they regarded the material world as evil (describing the body as a "prison", according to Plato), and the spiritual world as divine. Little is known about the cult's practices, but it's thought that the ritual involved the mimed – or actual – dismemberment of a person representing Dionysus, who was then "reborn" as a free soul after death. Another theory has it that the cult's true, secret purpose was to bestow upon its adherents longevity, or even physical immortality.

museum) one block north of the church; and an **art gallery** (Mon-Fri 8.30am-12.30pm & 1.30-5.30pm) occupying a National Revival-style house east of the main square on ulitsa Apriltsi.

Practicalities

Batak's **bus station** is at the eastern end of the main street, **ulitsa Apriltsi**. The only **accommodation** possibilities exist around the Batak Reservoir (*Yazovir Batak*), about 6km from town, whose power station is the only blot on this beauty spot. Here you'll find the *Panorama Hotel* (ⓣ03553/2064; ❷), which is open year-round and offers hovercraft and boat rides on the lake as well as off-road 4WD trips and bike rental. *Villa Yuk* (ⓣ0889/873289; ❶) has small bungalows in the forest, and numerous signs advertise **private rooms**. Try *Yoana mehana* just off the main road for traditional Bulgarian fare, or continue towards the lake to *Ostrava mehana* which offers similar dishes and has a lakeside cocktail bar. Velingrad buses pass by.

Velingrad and around

With its diverse springs, excellent climate and leafy parks, **VELINGRAD** is one of Bulgaria's most popular spa towns, although those not intent on taking a cure will find little else to do here. It consists of three villages originally named Kamenitsa, Lûdzhene and Chepino – lumped together in 1948 and renamed after local partisan heroine Vela Peeva. Both the train and bus stations are a few minutes' walk east of the modern centre, which in turn lies just to the east of **Lûdzhene**, where Velingrad's oldest baths, the **Velyova banya** (founded in the sixteenth century, although the buildings are modern), stand in a park beside the Yundola road. Just to the north of the centre is **Kamenitsa**, fringed by wooded parks that harbour the town's open-air baths, most of the modern spa facilities, and a small Ottoman-period *hammam*, the **Kremûchna banya** or "Flint Baths".

Velingrad's third cluster of baths lies 2km south of the centre in the **Chepino** quarter (bus #1 from the centre), where mineral water flows free from taps in the streets. Above Chepino to the south lies the Kleptuza spring, waters from which flow down to the **Kleptuza lake**, just east of Chepino: with pedalos, rowing boats and lakeside walkways, this is the most popular of Velingrad's resort areas.

Practicalities

The helpful **tourist information centre** at ul. Vasil Aprilov 5 (Mon-Fri 8am-7pm, Sat & Sun 10am-6pm; ⓣ0359/51667) can organize various local excursions including one to a nearby factory producing handmade rugs, and arrange accommodation in **private rooms** (❶–❸) and **hotels**. Two huge luxury spa hotels occupy the top end of the market: the *Dvoretsa* (ⓣ0359/56200, ⓦwww.dvoretsa.com; ❹) is a five-star affair in the woods just outside the centre, boasting indoor and outdoor hot pools and over a hundred therapies; the equally comfortable *Olymp* (ⓣ0359/56100, ⓦwww.olymp.velingrad.com; ❸) dominates the hillside towards Lûdzhene and offers a less comprehensive list of treatments. In central Velingrad the *Kamena*, ul. Edelvais 4 (ⓣ0359/58538 or 23142, ⓔkamena@velingrad.com; ❸), has indoor and outdoor pools, tennis courts, a nightclub, and spa therapies, while the much smaller *Markita* at ul. Tsar Ivan Asen II (ⓣ0359/58994 or 58974, ⓦwww.markita.com; ❸) has an outdoor pool and a bar. All the hotels have very good restaurants, while Velingrad's main square has no shortage of places to **eat** and **drink**. The *Omar* at bul. Sûedinenie

500, centred on a pleasant terrace and large swimming pool, is regarded as the town's best, and puts on a nightly floorshow.

There are three buses a day running between Velingrad and Plovdiv and regular services between Yundola and Batak. Moving on, however, many travellers opt for the three daily trains to Bansko in the Pirin range (see p.150). The narrow-gauge line switchbacks through glorious pine forests and subalpine meadows, calling at Avramovi Kolibi, the highest station on the Balkan peninsula, before descending to the logging town of Yakoruda and skirting the southern flanks of the Rila Mountains en route to Razlog (see p.150) and Bansko.

Yundola and Dorkovo

A 16km bus ride to the northwest of Velingrad, **YUNDOLA** is another small health resort 1390m above sea level, set amid rounded hills and copses of trees. It used to be a popular rest-home for trade unionists and Young Pioneers, but is chiefly remarkable for its inhabitants' longevity. The prevalence of **centenarians** in Bulgaria is ascribed to features of life in the highlands, where "Nature takes years off the weak and adds them to the strong" – as Leslie Gardiner was told. Human longevity is supposedly extended by pure air, climatic extremes, a lack of stress, and a spartan diet with little meat and plenty of yoghurt.

The village of **DORKOVO**, 14km northeast of Velingrad, is notable only for its annual **folklore festival**, on the first Sunday in August, which aims to represent the blend of three cultures – Christian, Pomak and Vlach – that characterizes the Chepino Valley. There's a strong Macedonian element, as most of the villagers are descended from Macedonians who came here as refugees after the Congress of Berlin. Before then Dorkovo was a Pomak village, but many of the inhabitants fled after 1877, fearing reprisals for their participation in the slaughter at Batak. Buses to Batak can take you as far as the turn-off for Kostandovo, halfway there – you'll have to walk or hitch the remaining 7km.

The only **accommodation** hereabouts is at Yundola's vastly overpriced *University Complex* (☎037/5928436; ❹).

The eastern Rhodopes

The **eastern Rhodopes** were the Ottomans' first conquest and their last foothold in Bulgaria before the Balkan Wars of 1912–13, and to this day many of the inhabitants are of ethnic Turkish origin. Geographically it is distinguished by 2500 hamlets and villages (far more than in either the central or the western Rhodopes) and comparatively low highlands (the average altitude is 329m). Traditionally, this was the poorest, least developed region of Bulgaria – a condition that only began

Goats in the Rhodopes

Goats are still the basis for life in many Rhodope communities. Every family owns several, which are entrusted to the village goatherd, or *manzardzhiya*. Their milk is drunk or turned into yoghurt and cheese, which together with salted goat's meat (*pastûrma*) forms the villagers' wintertime staple; goats' hair is woven into rugs which can last for eighty years; and their skin can be made into everything from wine-sacks and sandals to bagpipes (*gaidi*). During the Ottoman occupation, when Bulgarians were forbidden to carry arms, goats' horns served as daggers, and many of the country's most famous *haiduks* (including the female outlaw Rumena Voivoda) started their careers as goatherds.

to be remedied after dams and nonferrous metal plants were established in the 1950s, and which seems likely to relapse as these industries collapse today.

From a tourist's viewpoint the chief attractions are birdwatching at the nature reserve on the River Arda near Madzharovo, the rock-hewn hilltop temple and fortress at Perperikon, and the variety of strange rock formations in the Kûrdzhali region. However, as the reserve is only accessible by bus from Haskovo and the widely scattered rocks can only be reached by car, anyone coming from Smolyan and reliant on buses is limited to hiking around Belite Brezi or a visit to Kûrdzhali, a town whose past is more intriguing than its present.

Heading east from Smolyan to Kûrdzhali

Fairly regular buses run from Smolyan to Kûrdzhali, passing Pomak and Turkish villages and the entrance to the **Arda Gorge** (a lovely spot for walking and picnicking if you have your own transport), en route to the mainly Turkish mining town of **ARDINO**. A few kilometres further on, the *Belite Brezi* hotel (Ⓣ03561/2982 or 0889/676981; ❶) and campsite is the starting-point for many fine **hikes**, including a seven-hour trail to the 90m-high **Ardino waterfall** on the River Arda. From there, it's only another hour or so's walk to the **Devil's Bridge** (*Dyavolskiyat most*), one of the humpbacked bridges built by the Turks on the Arda's tributaries along the route from Plovdiv to the Aegean. Though you wouldn't think so from its meagre source near Mogilitsa, the Arda is vital to the region, flowing through serpentine gorges to feed the reservoirs and power stations near Kûrdzhali, Madzharovo and Ivailovgrad.

Another road from Smolyan approaches Kûrdzhali by way of Momchilgrad, running closer to the Greek border, through the mining centres of **MADAN** (from the Arabic word for "ore") and **ZLATOGRAD** (Gold Town). Like **RUDOZEM**, nearer Smolyan, they did well under Communism, but the 1990s saw the mining industry crippled by spiralling energy costs and the collapse of the lev and the price of nonferrous metals on the world market. The last mines closed in 1999, while plans to kick-start trade with Greece by opening a new border crossing near Rudozem have been in the pipeline for years, but have so far come to nothing.

Zlatograd's fortunes have been recently revived, however, by the opening of the **Ethnographic Museum complex** (daily 9am-noon & 1-6pm; 2Lv), a marvellous collection of beautifully renovated nineteenth-century buildings 1km west of the bus station. Within the main complex are two guesthouses, a *mehana*, the traditional workshops of a cutler, a goldsmith, a tailor and a woodcarver, and the **Ethnographic Museum** itself, which displays local costumes, tools and functioning vertical and horizontal looms. A traditional café serves coffee made from rye and boiled on a bed of hot sand, while a little beyond is the **Education Museum** with a mocked-up classroom and a collection of faded photographs and dog-eared books. Across the river is the *Vodenitsata* or **Water Mill Museum**, a stone millhouse containing an intriguing water-powered contraption (*tepavitsa*) made of four massive wooden hammers that full rough woollen material with deafening regularity.

The complex's useful **tourist information centre** (Ⓣ03071/2169) sells a ticket covering all the sites, and can arrange accommodation in the region as well as excursions to Thracian remains. You can stay within the complex at either the lavishly furnished 130-year-old *Pachilovska kûshta* (Ⓣ03071/4166; ❸), or at the less luxurious, but equally atmospheric *Krucheva kûshta* (book through the *Pachilovska kûshta*; ❶). In a concrete block the other side of the river is a budget alternative, the *Grebentsi* at ul. Evgenya Pachilova 4 (Ⓣ03071/2158), which has simple but very clean dorm rooms (7Lv per person) downstairs, or more comfortable doubles with cable TV upstairs (❶).

Kûrdzhali and around

Founded by the seventeenth-century Turkish general Kûrdzhi Ali on the site of a much older settlement, **KÛRDZHALI** was one of the last towns to remain in Ottoman hands – old photos and paintings of the town depict a maze of lanes thronged with hawkers in fezzes, veils and pantaloons, mingling with Bulgarian peasants, brigands and Turkish officers. When it finally fell to the Bulgarian army in 1912, however, it had fewer than 3000 inhabitants, and only a trace of its erstwhile exoticism lingers in the bazaar quarter today. Other than to visit the excellent Historical Museum, there are few reasons to spend more than an afternoon before moving on. However, for those with a car, it can serve as a base for trips to the ruins of **Perperikon** as well as numerous **rock formations** – the nearest is 4km from town – or a stopover en route to the nature reserve at Madzharovo.

The Town

The train and bus stations are at the eastern end of town, from where you can catch any bus along the broad sweep of bulevard Bûlgariya into the centre, where the **municipal garden** (*Gradska gradina*) with its elegant floral arrangements, makes a useful focal point. North of here is the commercial quarter, where butchers, fruit sellers and artisans ply their trades in shacks beside a **mosque** whose Ottoman minaret is all that distinguishes it from dwellings in the area. The nearby riverside offers a view of the suburbs on the far bank of the Arda, connected by a bridge to bulevard Availo, which cuts across town from east to west.

The town's most interesting sight by far is the **Historical Museum**, the largest in the Rhodopes, and one of the best collections in Bulgaria, on a nameless street some four blocks east of bulevard Republikanska (Tues–Sun 9am–4.30pm; 4Lv) and housed in a vast Moorish edifice built in the 1930s as a Muslim college, though never used as such. The ground-floor history section includes a reconstruction of a locally excavated 6000-year-old dwelling-workshop, a curious jasper pendant in the form of a zoomorphic swastika and delicate gold jewellery discovered in a Thracian necropolis. Other artefacts on show here include fragments of tenth-century church murals and a fearsome-looking medieval catapult, covered in plate armour. The first floor is given over to displays of minerals, crystals and the natural history of the eastern Rhodopes, including photos of some of the nearby strange rock formations (see p.375). Above this, on the top floor, is a truly absorbing exhibition illustrating traditional local crafts, industries and folk rituals, including reconstructions of a leather workshop, smithy and dairy, as well as the more usual domestic set-ups. There's also a fine collection of ritual costumes, with the monstrous *kukeri* again stealing the show. Note also the *survakar* costume, worn by a young boy who would go from house to house at New Year, striking people with a stick, for good luck. The local tobacco industry is represented by stacks of the dried leaves, cut into several different shapes, and a collection of sepia photographs showing nineteenth-century peasants working on the crop, in scenes which you will see along roadsides, virtually unchanged, today. The museum is also the best place to find leaflets and information about the nearby sites of **Perperikon** and **Tatoul**.

The **art gallery** at ul. Republiska 53 (closed for renovation at the time of writing) contains an exhibition of icons, and works by Bulgarian artists including

Vladimir Dimitrov-Maistor, Ivan Mrkvichka, and Yaroslav Veshin. In the southern suburbs is the **Assumption of the Virgin Mary Monastery**, built between 2000 and 2003 as a jubilee monastery

The sturdy exterior walls and hefty wooden gate emphasize the incongruity of such a building in a predominantly Muslim town, though within is a peaceful sanctuary of neat lawns, flowerbeds and colourful murals, where visitors can stay in comfortable en-suite rooms. The complex surrounds a mid-twentieth-century church which houses a casket containing what are thought to be fragments of the holy cross discovered at Ahridos below Perperikon in 2002.

Practicalities

When it's open, the **tourist information centre** in the park next to the stadium (awaiting completion at the time of writing) will be able to provide maps, brochures and general information on the area, and arrange trips to Perperikon and the nearby rock formations. Until then, try the Kûrdzhali Regional Economic Development Agency in the municipal offices at bul. Bûlgariya 41 (Ⓣ0361/66966).

Accommodation options in and around Kûrdzhali include the comfortable, three-star, high-rise *Hotel Arpezos* (Ⓣ0361/60200 or 60234, Ⓕ60220; ❸) not far from the riverside at bul. Republikanska 46, which has an indoor swimming pool and top-floor bar, and the perfectly decent *Ustra* (Ⓣ0361/64722; ❹), further to the east at ul. Gen. Delov 1. On a hilltop overlooking the town from the north is the recently refurbished *Residentia* (Ⓣ0361/65557; ❷), while, for an unusual place to stay, try one of the comfortable en-suite rooms at the Assumption of the Virgin Mary Monastery (Ⓣ0361/62494; ❸). Further from the town just after the village of **ENCHES** and reachable only by taxi or car, there's floating accommodation on the lake at Kûrdzhali dam (*yazovir Kûrdzhali*). Small wooden bungalows (Ⓣ0361/63191; ❶) with a common bathroom are crammed onto a pontoon shared by the *Pristan* restaurant. Next door is a similar structure supporting the *Moby Dick*, a restaurant that blares out noisy commercial folk music most nights, while on the other side the *Emona* restaurant is housed on a small ship.

There are several **bars** and **cafés** behind Kûrdzhali's municipal offices on ul. Exarch Yosef, while you can sample good local **food** at the restaurant in the *Hotel Arpezos*, noted for regional specialities such as mutton, sausages (*suzdurma*), *baklava* and figs, along with Armira wine from the Ivailovgrad district. You could also try the well-regarded *Smokinite*, a traditional-style *mehana* serving good-quality Bulgarian cuisine, though it's a little out of the way at ul. Dimitûr Madzharov 9, on the edge of the industrial zone south of the river.

Kûrdzhali is a good point from which to head on to **Turkey**, with around five daily buses to Istanbul and Bursa, as well as daily services to Izmir and Odrin.

Perperikon and Ahridos

Mistakenly listed as a medieval stronghold in the 1930s, the spectacular rock-hewn ruins of **PERPERIKON** failed to attract world interest until 2001 when an excavation team lead by Professor Nikolai Ovcharov began collecting evidence that proved the hilltop site dates back to between 6000 and 5000 BC. Professor Ovcharov put forward the hypothesis that here was the long-lost Rhodopean temple to Dionysus, closely linked to the ancient cult of Orpheus and referred to by Greek and Roman historians. The site was conquered, abandoned, and rebuilt by successive civilizations resulting in the current gradual unearthing of a kaleidoscope of remains that have yet to be fully excavated and conclusively pieced together. The complex's main features are a 4m-wide **stone passage** cut 8m into the rock at places and leading steeply up to a **stone throne** within the once towering **great palace.** At either end of the palace's vast hall are the eastern and western **crypts** – the latter containing fifteen sarcophagi covered by stone slabs. Just above is the circular **altar** positioned in the centre of what is thought to have been an open-roofed oval temple dedicated to Dionysus, where high priests predicted the future by reading the flames from wine poured onto the altar fire. Beyond the temple, a steep path leads up to the hilltop where a series of stone foundations surrounds the **acropolis**, a once powerful colonnaded fortress with walls three metres thick. To the west lie the foundations of the **small palace** and a deep **reservoir** cut into the rock, the largest to have been found in the Rhodopes. At the edge of the site at its highest point are the remains of a **medieval tower**.

In a field below Perperikon lie the freshly excavated foundations of **AHRIDOS**, thought to have been the wealthy administrative capital of the eastern Rhodopes between 900 and 1200 AD, with earlier Thracian finds at the site dating back to 500 BC. The major building of the complex is a ninth-century church, which was elegantly decorated and entered by crossing a partially surviving mosaic made of square and triangular marble blocks depicting a cross. In 2002 archelogists discovered what are thought to be fragments of the holy cross at the site, which are now stored in the church at Kûrdzhali's Assumption of the Virgin Mary Monastery.

At the time of writing there was no information available at the ruins of either Perperikon or Ahridos and visitors had to buy a map of the site and a guide book (available in English) from Kûrdzhali's Historical Museum before setting off. All this is due to change in the near future, with plans for a car park and on-site information centre close to fruition; in the meantime check the excellent website (Ⓦwww.perperikon.bg) for the latest discoveries and updates. Buses run three times a day from Kûrdzhali to the village of Gorna Krepost, 1km from Perperikon.

Rock formations in the Kûrdzhali region

Most of the odd **rock formations** in the Kûrdzhali region originated in the volcanic eruptions that raised the land from the sea forty million years ago, and whose ashes solidified into the porous golden-coloured rock known as tufa, which is easily eroded – the same process that created the "fairy chimneys" of Cappadocia in Turkey. Kûrdzhali's formations are far smaller, but diverse enough to appeal to geologists or anyone with more than a passing interest in such things. As all except one are near out-of-the-way villages, you'll need a **car** and **map** #6 in the *BTS* Rhodopi series (which doesn't show all of the sites, but identifies the localities).

The nearest rock formation to Kûrdzhali is marked on maps as the *Piramidite* (Pyramids) but known to locals as the **Stone Wedding** (*Vkamenenata svatba*), after a legend that a wedding party was turned to stone by the gods to punish the bridegroom's mother for envying his bride's beauty. The clusters of pink and red-tinged tufa do indeed resemble a procession frozen in mid-motion, but the villagers of Zimzelen, just uphill, have no qualms about using clefts in the rock as goat pens. This is the only formation within walking distance of Kûrdzhali (about 1hr) – take the road uphill past the Bulgarian and Turkish cemeteries, then follow the surfaced fork and the rocks are visible at a distance – though it's easier to take a taxi than risk getting lost.

Further afield, the **Stone Mushrooms** (*Kamenite gûbi*) stand about 2.5m high, their brown-spotted stalks and pink caps with green undersides coloured by traces of manganese and other minerals. Legend has it that they represent the heads of four sisters decapitated by Turkish brigands for stabbing their chief when he tried to rape them. A large dark rock nearby is known as the Murderer. The Mushrooms are located near Beli Plast, 20km north of Kûrdzhali, along the minor road to Haskovo (not the E85).

Spectacularly suspended in the air by two green tufa columns (a third has been destroyed) and a limestone "bridge", the **Rock Window** (*Skalen prozorets*) stands 10m high, 15m long, 7m wide and 1.5m thick. It's situated between the hamlets of Zrûnche and Krushka just beyond Kostino, about 15km northwest of Kûrdzhali.

Just outside the village of Tatul, roughly 20km northeast of Momchilgrad, the **Stone Forest** (*Vkamenenata gora*) consists of a dozen charred-looking stumps up to 1.5m high and 4m in diameter, which are marked with rings and may actually be prehistoric trees, covered in lava.

The ridge of the **Broken Mountain** (*Yanuk tepe*) looks like someone has taken a cleaver to it, terminating midway in a precipitous drop with rilolite columns strewn around – the result of a landslide late in the nineteenth century, near Vodenicharsko. Nearby, the fantastic **Rocks at Ustra** (*Skalite na Ustra*), huge purple pillars in the form of prisms, cones or stairways, perch on the hillside above Ustren. Both formations are in the vicinity of the small town of Dzhebel, 21km southwest of Kûrdzhali.

The **Mushroom** (*Gûbata*) and the **Lion** (*Lûvût*) are examples of two kinds of tufa formation in the vicinity of Benkovski, on the road to Zlatograd. Shaped like a giant puffball mushroom, with a stalk that narrows at the bottom and a brown, flattened cap 3m in diameter, the Mushroom lies 1.5km southwest of Benkovski. The Lion – which resembles a lion's head and gets its texture and colour from particles of gritstone – is in the same area, but closer to the village of Kitna (or Kitka).

The Madzharovo nature reserve

For birdwatchers, the chief attraction of the eastern Rhodopes is the **nature reserve** on the River Arda, established in 1994 under the Bulgarian-Swiss Biodiversity Conservation Programme. The gorges of the Arda are one of the few breeding grounds in Europe for three different **vultures** (the Egyptian, Griffon, and Black), and the habitat of eight kinds of **falcons**, and nine kinds of **woodpecker**, as well as black storks, bee-eaters and other species. Falcons catch mice, lizards, suslik, snakes, large insects and birds, while the vultures feed only on carrion, cleansing the environment of pathogenic micro-organisms. You may also catch sight of the now scarce **karakachan sheep**, an endemic Bulgarian strain, once herded in large numbers by the nomadic Karakachan people, who would drive them to winter pasture in northern Greece. Stricter border controls and collectivization under the Communist regime led to their decline, but they are now being successfully bred on the reserve, along with the traditional breed of sheepdog, to protect them from prowling wolves.

Guided tours are arranged through the **Nature Information Centre** (daily Mon–Fri 9am–5pm; ⓣ03720/345 or 0889/453908, ⓦwww.niccerbg.com) off the road by the bridge across the River Arda, near Madzharovo. Besides photos

> For information on other birdwatching sites, contact the Bulgarian Society for the Protection of Birds (BDZP), 1111 Sofia, PO Box 50 ⓣ & ⓕ02/9715855, ⓦwww.bspb.org. There's also a regional centre in Plovdiv (ⓣ & ⓕ032/626212).

Madzharovo's Thracian Festival

The inhabitants of the small dreary town of Madzharovo are known as "Thracians" by the Bulgarians, due to their being descended from refugees from Aegean Thrace who fled during the Greek civil war of 1945. The town's **Thracian Festival**, which takes place in the last week of September, is a lively affair involving two days of dancing, music, wrestling and fireworks.

of the birds, mammals and flowers within the nature reserve (named in Bulgarian and Latin), there are three cosy double bedrooms (❷) for the use of visitors, which should be reserved well in advance through the information centre. Breakfast or full board can be provided, at extra cost. If the birdwatchers' chalet is full, try the pleasant, three-star *Rai* (Ⓣ03720/230; ❸) at ul. Dimur Madjarov 48 in nearby **MADZHAROVO**, which has its own restaurant and café.

Buses from Haskovo (see p.350) are the only means of reaching the reserve without a car. There are three services daily to Madzharovo. While there are no buses from Krumovgrad to Madzharovo, there are two from Krumovgrad to Studen Kladenets, a village set in a lunar landscape 30km upriver from Madzharovo, where the ravines of the Vûlchi Dol are home to another **vulture colony**. Though there is no visitor centre nor anywhere to stay here, staff at Madzharovo nature reserve can arrange access to two birdwatching hides.

From Momchilgrad to Ivailovgrad

The only reason for travelling this far east is to experience the most **Turkish region** of Bulgaria. In Momchilgrad and Krumovgrad you'll hear more Turkish spoken than Bulgarian (which isn't even *understood* by some people), and satellite dishes, trade and transport are oriented towards Turkey. People have redder skins, broader faces and stockier physiques than the inhabitants of the western Rhodopes – as sure a sign of their Turkish ancestory as their names (written in Turkish, rather than Cyrillic on the tombstones). While being able to speak Turkish will help, people are generally reserved towards outsiders due to the region's long history as an embattled borderland and the vicissitudes of ethnic–state relations (see "Bulgaria's Muslim Minorities" in Contexts) having inculcated habits of clannishness and isolation.

The landscape is characterized by eroded, deforested expanses which, seen by moonlight, resemble deserts or lunar surfaces. With its dry sandy soil and Mediterranean climate, it has always needed irrigation to produce crops, and the minerals in the mountains – zinc, lead, gold and silver – made mining more profitable than agriculture until the Turks introduced the cultivation of tobacco, which is still the main crop. They chiefly grow an aromatic strain called *dzhebel basma*, a name deriving from *djebel*, the Arabic word for hill, and you will often see little old women selling bunches of the dried leaves by the roadside.

MOMCHILGRAD, 10km south of Kûrdzhali, marks the start of the highlands, encrusted with **ruined fortresses** built by both Bulgaria and Byzantium, when the area was contested by the two empires. A stunning example lies 8km from Momchilgrad on the edge of the tiny village of **TATOUL**, served by six daily buses that stop on the way to Nanovitsa from Momchilgrad. Thought to have originally been a Thracian hilltop temple dating back to 2000 BC, fortifying walls suggesting a change of use were added around 600-500 BC. A circular stone altar similar to that at Perperikon (see p.375) lies atop the hill close to a massive grain store. Most striking is the single tomb carved into the flat surface of the highest rock, reached by a series of steps, and accompanied by a similar tomb slightly below – both with drainage channels hinting at the possibility of human sacrifice rather than burial, or perhaps the production of sacred wine. Very little is known of the site despite recent excavation work, but a popular theory suggests that the rocky grave could be that of Orpheus, who allegedly once expressed a desire to be buried somewhere between the earth and the sky.

More recently, it was in Momchilgrad that the worst violence of the "name-changing campaign" occurred, when about forty people died in clashes between protestors and the militia in the winter of 1984–85. These days, relations between the two communities are good, with Christians and Muslims working together in local politics and business. Should you wish to **stay**, your best bet is the *MG* hotel (ⓣ03631/3034; ❷), which occupies a fine hilltop site on the eastern side of the village, has an outdoor swimming pool, and an excellent terrace restaurant with panoramic views of the eastern Rhodopes, and can provide information about Tatoul and other local attractions. The succession of Muslim villages over the next 30km culminates in an elegant, isolated **mosque** before the road descends to **KRUMOVGRAD**, a smaller town with some cafés for a pit stop and the *Ahriga Hotel* (ⓣ03641/2383; ❷) should you need to spend the night before catching a bus to Istanbul (ask at the Avar Tourism office next to the *Ahriga*; ⓣ03641/4054), Haskovo or Plovdiv.

Beyond Krumovgrad lies splendid open rolling countryside, planted with wheat and dotted with copses where livestock graze around waterholes, but eerily devoid of human settlements so far as you can see. There are, in fact, dozens of Turkish hamlets in the hills that are so small and isolated that none of the children go to school, which explains why the Ivailovgrad region has the highest illiteracy rate in Bulgaria (60 percent). Fifty-nine kilometres east of Krumovgrad, **IVAILOVGRAD** marks a return to the Slav, Christian areas of settlement, and boasts the impressive remains of the **Armira Roman Villa**, a 22-room complex built around 130 AD for the Roman noblemen and army officers who used the region for rest and recreation. Invading Goths destroyed it some 240 years later, but several mosaic floors have survived including a depiction of the owner and his two children. Motorists can also visit the Thracian tomb at **Mezek** as a detour off the road to Svilengrad (see p.351), though be sure that all your documents are in order, as there's a **checkpoint** at the hydro-electric dam on the Arda Reservoir. Ivailovgrad's **tourist information centre** (Mon-Fri 8.30am-5.30pm; ⓣ03661/2039, ⓔtic_ivaylovgrad@abv) can arrange trips to both sites and open up the **Historical Museum**, which has an exhibition about the town's now defunct silk industry. **Accommodation** is available at either the *Bor-Hasienda* (ⓣ03661/296; ❶), or the *Ahrida* (ⓣ0898/628653; ❶). Despite its proximity to Greece and Turkey, there's nowhere to cross the **frontier** until you reach Svilengrad.

Travel details

Trains

Asenovgrad to: Plovdiv (14 daily; 25min).
Dimitrovgrad to: Harmanli (4 daily; 1hr); Haskovo (4 daily; 30min); Kûrdzhali (4 daily; 2hr); Momchilgrad (3 daily; 2hr 15min–2hr 45min); Plovdiv (7 daily; 1hr 30min); Svilengrad (4 daily; 1hr).
Harmanli to: Dimitrovgrad (3 daily; 1hr); Plovdiv (5 daily; 2hr–3hr 30min); Simeonovgrad (6 daily; 15min); Svilengrad (6 daily; 30min).

Haskovo to: Dimitrovgrad (4 daily; 30min); Kûrdzhali (3 daily; 1hr–1hr 45min); Momchilgrad (6 daily; 2hr–3hr 15min); Stara Zagora (3 daily; 1hr 30min–2hr 30min).
Kûrdzhali to: Dimitrovgrad (4 daily; 2hr); Haskovo (3 daily; 1hr–1hr 45min); Momchilgrad (4 daily; 30min); Podkova (4 daily; 50min); Stara Zagora (3 daily; 3–4hr).
Momchilgrad to: Dimitrovgrad (4 daily; 2hr 15min–2hr 45min); Haskovo (4 daily; 2hr–3hr 15min); Kûrdzhali (4 daily; 30min); Plovdiv (1 daily; 5hr); Podkova (4 daily; 20min); Stara Zagora (2 daily; 2hr 15min–4hr 30min).
Pazardzhik to: Plovdiv (15 daily; 30–45min).
Plovdiv to: Asenovgrad (15 daily; 25min); Burgas (6 daily; 3hr 45min); Dimitrovgrad (7 daily; 1hr–1hr 30min); Hisar (3 daily; 1hr); Karlovo (5 daily; 1hr 45min); Momchilgrad (1 daily; 5hr); Pazardzhik (20 daily; 30–45min); Septemvri (8 daily; 45min–1hr); Sofia (14 daily; 2hr–3hr 30min); Stara Zagora (13 daily; 1hr 30min-2hr); Svilengrad (3 daily; 2hr); Varna (3 daily; 6hr); Yambol (9 daily; 1hr).
Podkova to: Dimitrovgrad (4 daily; 3hr 30min); Kûrdzhali (4 daily; 50min); Momchilgrad (4 daily; 20min).
Septemvri to: Bansko (3 daily; 5hr); Plovdiv (6 daily; 45min–1hr); Sofia (8 daily; 1hr 30min–2hr 15min); Velingrad (5 daily; 1hr 30min).
Svilengrad to: Harmanli (6 daily; 30min).

Buses

Asenovgrad to: Bachkovo (7 daily; 30min); Lûki (4 daily; 45min); Plovdiv (hourly; 30min).
Bachkovo to: Asenovgrad (7 daily; 30min).
Batak to: Pazardzhik (6 daily; 1hr 20min); Velingrad (5 daily; 1hr).
Devin to: Dospat (2–3 daily; 1hr); Plovdiv (4 daily; 2hr 15min); Nastan (9 daily; 15min); Smolyan (2–4 daily; 2hr 30min); Trigrad (1 daily Mon–Fri; 30min).
Dimitrovgrad to: Haskovo (every 30min; 25min).
Dospat to: Batak (1 daily; 1hr 30min); Gotse Delchev (1 daily; 1hr); Pazardzhik (1 daily; 3hr); Plovdiv (2 daily; 3hr 15min); Smolyan (1 daily; 3hr).
Harmanli to: Haskovo (every 30min; 40min); Ivailovgrad (3 daily; 2–3hr); Sofia (3 daily; 5hr); Stara Zagora (5 daily; 1hr); Svilengrad (7 daily; 45min).
Haskovo to: Dimitrovgrad (every 15min; 25min); Harmanli (14 daily; 40min); Ivailovgrad (3 daily; 3hr); Kûrdzhali (12 daily; 50min); Krumovgrad (3 daily; 4hr); Madzharovo (3 daily; 2hr) Plovdiv (14 daily; 1hr 30min); Sofia (14 daily; 4–5hr); Svilengrad (hourly; 1hr 20min).
Ivailovgrad to: Haskovo (3 daily; 3hr); Kûrdzhali (2 daily; 3hr).
Kûrdzhali to: Gorna Krepost (Perperikon) (3 daily; 20min); Haskovo (hourly; 50min); Ivailovgrad (2 daily; 3hr); Krumovgrad (hourly; 30min); Momchilgrad (every 30min; 30min); Plovdiv (hourly; 2hr 30min); Sofia (7 daily; 5–6hr); Smolyan (2 daily; 3hr); Varna (2 daily; 5hr); Zlatograd (6 daily; 1hr).
Krumovgrad to: Kûrdzhali (6 daily; 30min); Plovdiv (1 daily; 3hr); Sofia (1 daily; 8hr); Stara Zagora (1 daily; 4–5hr); Studen Kladenets (2 daily; 2hr).
Lûki to: Asenovgrad (4 daily; 45min); Belitsa (2 daily; 15min); Manastir (1 daily; 30min); Plovdiv (1 daily; 1hr 15min); Smolyan (1 daily; 1hr 15min).
Madzharovo to: Haskovo (3 daily; 1hr 15min); Plovdiv (1 daily; 2hr 30min).
Manastir to Lûki (1 daily; 30min).
Pamporovo to: Plovdiv (6 daily; 2hr 30min); Smolyan (hourly; 30min).
Pazardzhik to: Batak (2 daily; 1hr 20min); Dospat (3 weekly; 3hr); Gotse Delchev (1 daily; 4hr); Panagyurishte (hourly; 1hr 30min); Plovdiv (18 daily; 40min); Septemvri (3 daily; 30min).
Plovdiv *Avtogara Yug* to: Asenovgrad (every 30min; 30min); Blagoevgrad (1 daily; 4hr); Burgas (2 daily; 4hr); Dupnitsa (1 daily; 5hr); Hisar (hourly; 1hr); Karlovo (hourly; 1hr 15min); Kyustendil (2 weekly on Mon & Fri; 4–5hr); Pazardzhik (18 daily; 40min); Sliven (6 daily; 3hr 15min); Sofia (hourly; 2hr); Varna (2 daily; 5hr); Velingrad (1 daily; 1hr 15min). *Avtogara Rodopi* to: Devin (2 daily; 2hr 15min); Dospat (2 daily; 3hr 15min); Gotse Delchev (1 daily; 6hr 30min) Haskovo (13 daily; 1hr 30min); Kûrdzhali (hourly; 2hr 30min); Krumovrad (1 daily; 3hr); Madan (3 daily; 3hr 30min); Pamporovo (8 daily; 2hr 30min); Rudozem (3 daily; 2hr); Smolyan (5 daily; 3hr); Zlatograd (3 daily; 4hr). *Avtogara Sever* to: Gabrovo (3 daily; 3hr); Kazanluk (3 daily; 2hr); Koprivshtitsa (1 daily; 2hr 30min); Panagyurishte (2 daily; 2hr); Pleven (1 daily; 4hr 30min); Ruse (1 daily; 7hr); Sevlievo (1 daily; 4hr); Troyan (3 daily; 3hr 30min); Veliko Tûrnovo (3 daily; 4hr).
Shiroka Lûka to: Devin (5–7 daily; 2hr); Smolyan (3 daily; 1hr 20min).
Septemvri to: Pazardzhik (5 daily; 30min).
Smolyan *Avtogara Ustovo* to: Kûrdzhali (2 daily; 3hr); Madan (9 daily; 30min); Momchilovtsi (10 daily; 40min); Rudozem (hourly; 20min); Zlatograd (6 daily; 1hr) *Avtogara Smolyan* to: Devin (6 daily; 2hr 30min); Gela (1 daily Mon–Fri; 1hr 40min); Mogilitsa (2 daily; 1hr); Pamporovo (hourly; 30min); Plovdiv (hourly; 3hr), via Rozhen Pass (1 daily; 4hr); Shiroka Lûka (6 daily; 1hr 20min).
Svilengrad to: Dimitrovgrad (1 on Sat & Sun; 2hr); Harmanli (hourly; 45min); Haskovo (hourly; 1hr 30min); Kapitan Andreevo (9 daily; 20min); Plovdiv

(3 daily Mon–Fri; 2hr); Sofia (4 daily Mon–Fri; 4hr).
Velingrad to: Batak (2 daily; 1hr); Blagoevgrad (1–2 daily; 3hr); Plovdiv (3 daily; 1hr 15min); Yundola (3–4 daily; 30min).
Zlatograd to: Kûrdzhali (1 daily; 1hr); Plovdiv (3 daily; 3hr 30min); Podkova (2 daily; 40min); Smolyan (2 daily; 1hr 15min); Sofia (3 daily; 5hr 30min).

International trains

Plovdiv to: Istanbul (1 daily; 8hr 30min).
Svilengrad to: Alexandropolis (1 daily; 6hr); Istanbul (1 daily; 7hr); Thessaloniki (1 daily; 13hr).

International buses

Haskovo to: Istanbul (6 daily; 5hr).
Kûrdzhali to: Bursa (7 daily; 10hr); Ismir (4–5 daily; 12–15hr); Istanbul (7 daily; 7hr); Odrin (7 daily; 3–4hr).
Krumovgrad to: Istanbul (1 daily; 6–8hr).
Plovdiv to: Amsterdam (1 weekly on Thurs; 26hr); Athens (1 daily; 23–26hr); Berlin (4 weekly on Mon, Wed, Fri & Sat; 21hr); Istanbul (4 daily; 6hr); Paris (3 weekly on Mon, Wed & Fri; 27hr); Thessaloniki (4 daily; 14hr); Xanti (3 weekly on Mon, Wed & Sat; 12–14hr).

The Black Sea Coast

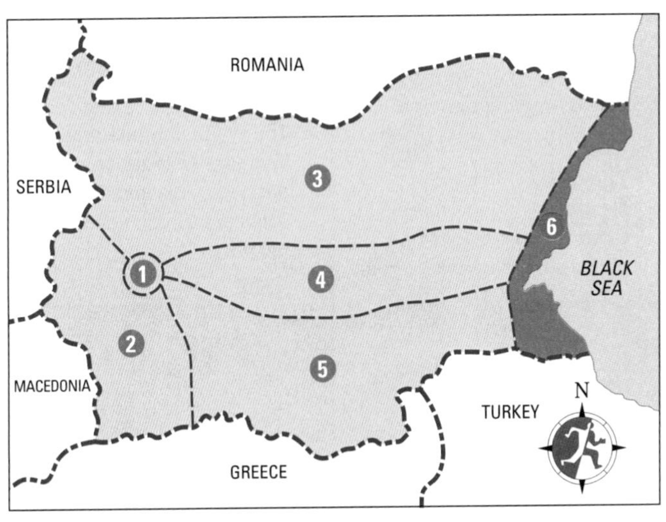

CHAPTER 6

Highlights

* **Varna Archeological Museum** One of Europe's finest collections of Thracian artefacts, and Bulgaria's largest array of Roman-era funerary sculpture. **See p.390**

* **The Roman Thermae, Varna** Extensive remains of a bath complex which once stood at the very heart of social and cultural life in the wealthy Roman colony of Odyssos. **See p.393**

* **The Quiet Nest, Balchik** Queen Marie of Romania's former summer residence overlooking the bay. **See p.405**

* **The medieval churches of Nesebûr** A unique assemblage of Byzantine-era churches, influenced by both the Greek and Slavic cultures. **See p.418**

* **Sozopol** The old town features charming cobbled streets, a wealth of wooden houses and tiny chapels. **See p.425**

* **Istanbul** Inexpensive organized coach tours run to this ancient city, straddling two continents. **See p.401**

* **The Sea Gardens, Burgas** Extensive and immaculate, punctuated with fountains, flowerbeds and statues. **See p.424**

* **The Black Sea beaches** Beautiful white sands – most dazzling at Sinemorets – and some great beach bars. **See p.434**

△ Old town and harbour, Nesebûr

6

The Black Sea Coast

The Bulgarian **Black Sea coast** has quietened down a bit since its heyday in the 1970s and 1980s, when it served as the playground for the entire Eastern Bloc, but it is still a magnet for hundreds of thousands of Bulgarians and foreign visitors. The vast tourist complexes built to attract West European package tourists still do good business, Bulgarians are taking more holidays here than ever before, and the Russians, Poles, Germans and Czechs who descended on Bulgaria's seaside towns in the Communist era

Cyrillic place names

Aheloi	АХЕЛОЙ	Kosti	КОСТИ
Ahtopol	АХТОПОЛ	Kranevo	КРАНЕВО
Aladzha Monastery	АЛАДЖА МАНАСТИР	Krapets	КРАПЕЦ
Albena	АЛБЕНА	Lozenets	ЛОЗЕНЕЦ
Arkutino	АРКУТИНО	Malko Tûrnovo	МАЛКО ТЪРНОВО
Asparuhovo	АСПАРУХОВО	Nesebûr	НЕСЕБЪР
Balchik	БАЛЧИК	Obrochishte	ОБРОЧИЩЕ
Bûlgarevo	БЪЛГАРЕВО	Obzor	ОБЗОР
Bûlgari	БЪЛГАРИ	Pomorie	ПОМОРИЕ
Banya	БАНЯ	Primorsko	ПРИМОРСКО
Brûshlyan	БРЪШЛЯН	Rusalka	РУСАЛКА
Burgas	БУРГАС	Shabla	ШАБЛА
Byala	БЯЛА	Shkorpilovtsi	ШКОРПИЛОВЦИ
Cape Kaliakra	НОС КАЛИАКРА	Sinemorets	СИНЕМОРЕЦ
Chernomorets	ЧЕРНОМОРЕЦ	Sozopol	СОЗОПОЛ
Devnya	ДЕВНЯ	Stone Forest	ПОБИТИ КАМЪНИ
Druzhba	ДРУЖБА	Strandzha Nature Park	СТРАНДЖА
Durankulak	ДУРАНКУЛАК	Sunny Beach	СЛЪНЧЕВ БРЯГ
Dyuni	ДЮНИ	Sveti Konstantin	СВЕТИ КОНСТАНТИН
Elenite	ЕЛЕНИТЕ	Sveti Nikola	СВЕТИ НИКОЛА
Emona	ЕМОНА	Sveti Vlas	СВЕТИ ВЛАС
Evksinograd	ЕВКСИНОГРАД	Tsarevo	ЦАРЕВО
Golden Sands	ЗЛАТНИ ПЯСЪЦИ	Tyulenovo	ТЮЛЕНОВО
Gramatikovo	ГРАМАТИКОВО	Varna	ВАРНА
Kamchiya	КАМЧИЯ	Varvara	ВАРВАРА
Kavarna	КАВАРНА	Vinitsa	ВИНИЦА
Kavatsite	КАВАЦИТЕ	Zvezdets	ЗВЕЗДЕЦ
Kiten	КИТЕН		

are returning in large numbers. Private enterprise has taken off here quicker than anywhere else in Bulgaria, and the wealth of bars, restaurants and seaside landladies offering rooms lends the area a vibrant quality that much of inland Bulgaria lacks.

Many continue to think of the Bulgarian coast in terms of its big package-oriented complexes, the largest of which have discouragingly ersatz names like **Sunny Beach** and **Golden Sands** and are correspondingly characterless once you arrive. Newer resorts like **Albena** have a more varied range of hotels and activities, and the most recent "holiday villages" such as **Elenite** compare favourably with villa settlements in the Mediterranean. Holidays in such places are cheap and beaches are clean, but none of these purpose-built resorts reveals much of what the Black Sea is really about – and they are sited sufficiently far away from centres of population to prevent you from finding out for yourself. Independent travellers should stick to the main seaside towns, where **private rooms** are plentiful, family-run **guesthouses** are on the increase, and out-of-town **beaches** are easy to reach on foot or by bus. The ideal base for exploring the northern coast is the riviera town of **Varna**, which, after Sofia and Plovdiv, is Bulgaria's most animated metropolis. North of Varna crumbling rock formations and imposing cliffs characterize the coast around **Balchik** and **Kaliakra**, while to the south lie quieter seaside backwaters and the **Longoza**, a dense riverine forest that lines the lower banks of the **River Kamchiya**.

Controlling access to the southern half of the Black Sea coast is the rough-edged trawler port of **Burgas**, far outshone by the historic peninsula towns immediately north and south – old Greek fishing villages like **Sozopol** and **Nesebûr**, the latter noted for its ruined Byzantine churches, and swarming with visitors in the summer. The coast beyond Sozopol and the Turkish border offers a succession of glorious white sand **beaches** and a wide variety of flora and fauna, ranging from the near-tropical forest around the **River Ropotamo** to marshes rich in birdlife. Numerous local museums recall the Greek settlers who colonized the area six centuries before the birth of Christ.

The Black Sea coast is governed by the **seasons**. The tourist season runs from late May to late September, and is at its height in August, when transport and accommodation are overburdened. It's difficult to find private rooms at this time, but you shouldn't find yourself stranded without a bed for the night if you persistently ask around; solo travellers, however, may be asked to pay double rates or share with a stranger, as owners are loath to lose money. From October to April the coast can be freezing cold, and a number of hotels close down entirely. Outside Varna and Burgas, many museums and tourist attractions open only during the summer, and hours become erratic as tourist numbers begin to slacken off in September.

However you travel, your likely **point of arrival** on the coast will be either Varna or Burgas, from where **buses** can take you to the smaller towns and resorts. It's also possible to travel **on from Bulgaria** to destinations elsewhere in the Black Sea regions, with regular buses to Istanbul, and seasonal bus services to Odessa and Kiev.

The **website** Ⓦ www.beachbulgaria.com is a good source of information on resorts and hotels all along the coast.

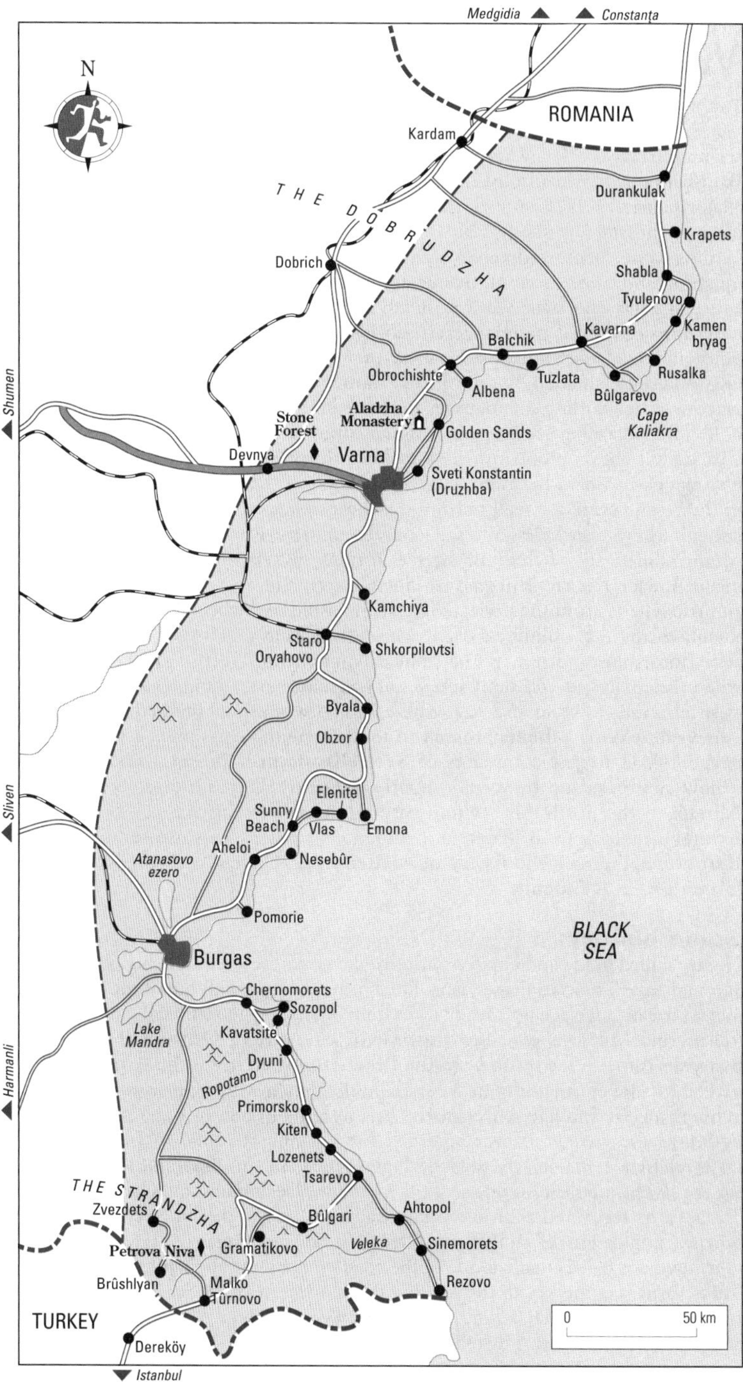
N
Medgidia
Constanța
ROMANIA
Kardam
THE DOBRUDZHA
Durankulak
Krapets
Dobrich
Shabla
Tyulenovo
Kamen bryag
Kavarna
Balchik
Rusalka
Obrochishte
Tuzlata
Albena
Bûlgarevo
Cape Kaliakra
Shumen
Stone Forest
Aladzha Monastery
Golden Sands
Devnya
Varna
Sveti Konstantin (Druzhba)
Kamchiya
Staro Oryahovo
Shkorpilovtsi
Byala
Obzor
Elenite
Sliven
Sunny Beach
Vlas
Emona
Aheloi
Nesebûr
Atanasovo ezero
Pomorie
BLACK SEA
Burgas
Chernomorets
Sozopol
Kavatsite
Lake Mandra
Dyuni
Harmanli
Ropotamo
Primorsko
Kiten
Lozenets
Tsarevo
THE STRANDZHA
Ahtopol
Zvezdets
Bûlgari
Veleka
Sinemorets
Petrova Niva
Gramatikovo
Brûshlyan
Malko Tûrnovo
Rezovo
TURKEY
0
50 km
Dereköy
Istanbul

Varna and around

Back in the days when **VARNA** was a cholera-ravaged Ottoman garrison town, British troops passed through on their way to the Crimean War; one of them, Major General J. R. Hume, described the town as "no paradise … a wretched place with very few shops". Not so long ago many foreign visitors may have said the same, but in recent years Bulgaria's third city has struggled more than most to westernize. Signs of change are everywhere, from the giant advertising hoardings splashed with Western brand names to the numerous street traders, hawking all kinds of touristry knick-knacks. The streets are lined with fashion boutiques, exchange bureaux, Japanese car showrooms, video-rental stores and fast-food outlets staffed by miniskirted waitresses, while baseball-capped youths practise skateboarding manoeuvres in the main square, or stroll along the main boulevards in a range of pseudo-designer summer threads.

Varna still has its problems – loss-making **shipyards** southwest of the centre give the place a hard industrial edge – and most of the consumer goods on sale in the town centre are well beyond the means of those who inhabit the high-rise suburbs. Nevertheless, the self-confident riviera-town swagger of the place comes as a breath of fresh air after the more austere appearance of much of inland Bulgaria. It rivals Sofia and Plovdiv in providing a wide range of sights and **museums**, from the outstanding treasures in the Archeological Museum to the off-the-wall ghoulishness of the Museum of Medical History. Of its cultural attractions, most notable is the annual **Varnensko lyato** (Varna Summer), which celebrates its eightieth anniversary in 2006 – a summer-long festival of classical music, folklore and jazz, which attracts world-class performers.

As well as being a **beach resort** in its own right, Varna offers access to the purpose-built tourist complexes of **Sveti Konstantin** (formerly "Druzhba") – now swallowed up by Varna's suburbs – **Sunny Day**, **Golden Sands** and **Albena** to the north. Also within easy reach are bustling seaside villages like **Kranevo**, and popular day-trip destinations such as the nature reserve at **Kamchiya**, the rock monastery of **Aladzha**, and Queen Marie of Romania's former palace at **Balchik**.

Some history

Highly skilled gold- and coppersmiths lived around the Gulf of Varna 6000 years ago, and their Thracian descendants littered the interior with burial mounds, but Varna's importance as a port really dates from 585 BC, when a mixed bag of Apollonians and Milesians established the Greek city-state of **Odyssos**. The town's best years came in the second and third centuries when it was the Roman province of Moesia's main outlet to the sea, a bustling place where Greek and Thracian cultures met and mingled. Devastated by the Avars in 586 AD, and repopulated by Slavs (who were probably responsible for renaming it *Varna*, or "Black One"), it nevertheless remained the region's biggest port and an important staging-post for the Byzantine fleet on its way to the Danube. Declining somewhat under the Turks, Varna recovered as an important trading centre in the nineteenth century, when a population of Bulgarians, Greeks, Turks and Gagauz (Turkic-speaking Christians, see p.402) made it one of the coast's more cosmopolitan centres. To the Turks, Varna was the key to the security of the western Black Sea, and the town's military role is still reflected in the students of Varna's Naval Academy, who stride around town in uniforms belted with ceremonial daggers.

Arrival, information and city transport

Varna's **train station** is just south of the centre, a ten-minute walk up ulitsa Tsar Simeon into town. The main **bus terminal** is 2km northwest on bulevard Vl. Varnenchik (if you miss your bus try the Mladost private bus station across the road); take bus #22 or #41 from here to reach the streets surrounding the central **Cathedral of the Assumption** (an area known as *Tsentar* or "centre" on bus destination boards), a few paces north of the main downtown area. Varna **airport**, on the city's western outskirts, is served by bus #409, which passes through central Varna before continuing on past Sveti Konstantin to Golden Sands.

Central Varna is easy to explore on foot, although **local buses and trolley-buses** come in handy if you're heading for the suburbs or the seaside resorts to the north – most stop either in front of or behind the cathedral. **Tickets** are bought from the conductor, with a flat fare of 50st covering most central city destinations. Up-to-date **maps** which include bus routes are available from Isak bureau and Astra Tour in the train station (see below) as well as from bookshops and, sporadically, from street stalls. Buses run from around 6.30am to 11.30pm, although services to the northern beach resorts stop at around 10pm.

Taxis leave from in front of the train station, and can also be found around the junction of bulevards Knyaz Boris I and Slivnitsa. However, the meters on these vehicles are rarely working, so unless you can negotiate a reasonable price in advance, it's worth looking beyond these prime rip-off spots for your cab ride.

Accommodation

There's an ample stock of accommodation in Varna throughout the year, and several accommodation bureaux around town. If you arrive by rail, you can make enquiries at the Isak bureau (ⓣ052/602318) or Astra Tour (daily 7am-9.30pm; ⓣ052/605861), side by side on the platform and open daily from 7am to 9.30pm. Both offices can arrange hotel accommodation and have plenty of **private rooms** (❶), many of which are reasonably central, though the cheapest tend to be very grotty. At the bus station the Beni accommodation bureau (daily 8.30am–6.30pm; ⓣ052/505795) offers a similar service with matching prices, while in town try Alfatour at bul. Mariya Luiza 26 (Mon-Fri 9.30am-6.30pm, Sat 10am-2pm; ⓣ052/616080, ⓦwww.alfatour.bg), which also arranges air ticket reservations, car rental, and boat trips.

Hotels

You'll find no shortage of **hotel rooms** to choose from in Varna, largely due to the increasing number of small pensions and family-run hotels. Where you stay will depend on what you want to do: the central hotels are within walking distance of downtown sights, while those places northeast of the centre are more suburban in atmosphere and offer easy access to the beaches.

Central Varna

Akropolis ul. Tsar Ivan Shishman 13 ⓣ052/603108, ⓕ603107. Spotless new motel-style place behind a residential block just east of the train station, offering roomy en-suite doubles which will sleep three if necessary. Breakfast is available in the hotel café for an extra charge. ❹

Cherno More bul. Slivnitsa 33 ⓣ052/612236, ⓕ612220. Very central but ageing high-rise,

with four restaurants and several bars. The comfy en-suite doubles all come with TV, and it offers better value than the nearby *Odesos*. Self-service breakfast. ❺

Odesos bul. Primorski 4 ⓣ052/640300, ⓕ630403. Unremarkable and somewhat overpriced three-star place, but it's in a great location, next to the Sea Gardens, offering en-suite doubles with balconies and cable TV. Breakfast included. ❻

Palitra Konstantin Doganov 11 ⓣ052/610055, ⓕ610055. Small, friendly pension with smart en-suites, though a little out of the way, located 1km west of the cathedral. ❹

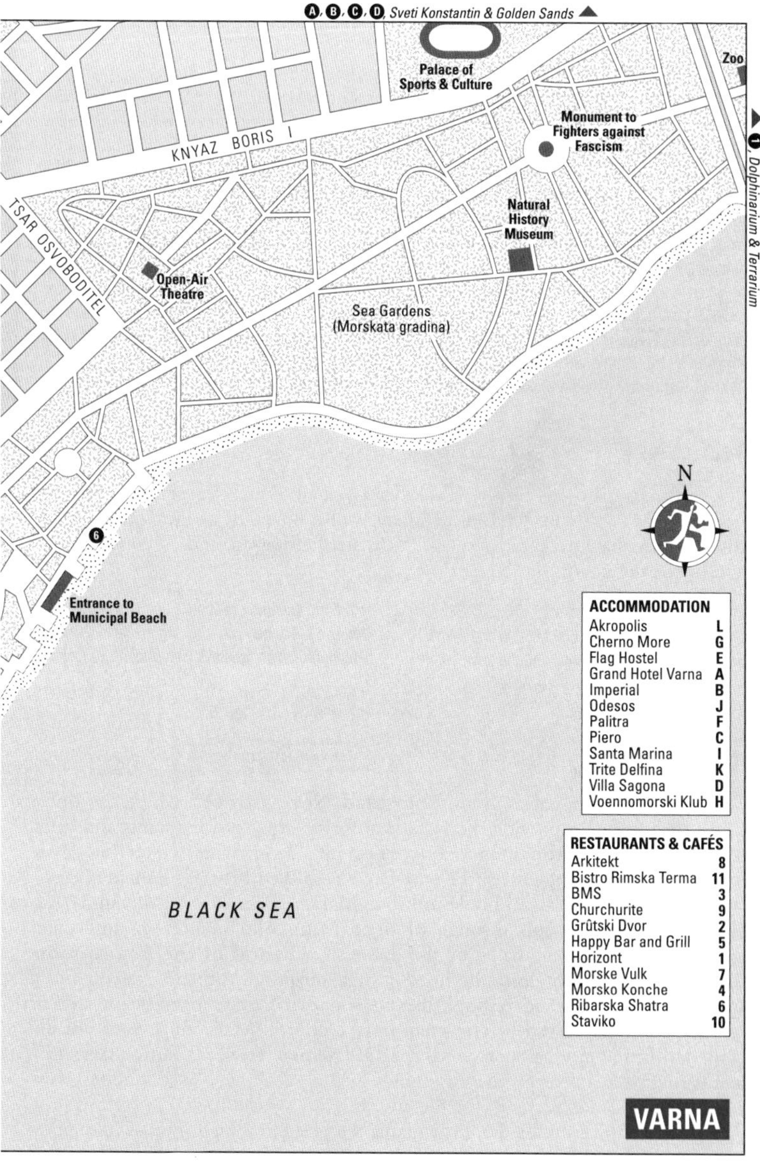

Santa Marina ul. Baba Rada 28 ⓣ052/603826 or 603827, ⓕ603825. Bright, modern, clean downtown hotel hidden away in residential streets behind hotels *Cherno More* and *Odesos*. All rooms have satellite TV and telephone, and breakfast is included. ❺

Trite Delfina ul. Gabrovo 27 ⓣ052/600917. Small pension in the backstreets near the train station. Friendly, with clean en-suite rooms, but fills up quickly. ❸

Voennomorski Klub bul. Varnenchik 2 ⓣ052/617965. Hotel on the top two floors of the Naval Club, with slightly decrepit but perfectly clean en-suite rooms. Very reasonably priced for central Varna. ❷

Northeast of the centre

Grand Hotel Varna Sveti Konstantin ⓣ052/361491 or 361498; ⓦwww.gh-varna.com. Large five-star hotel in the middle of the Sveti Konstantin resort, but not as good as the *Imperial* (see below). It boasts saunas, indoor sports facilities, a casino and swanky nightclub on site. ❾
Imperial ⓣ052/355211, ⓦwww.rivierabulgaria.com. Bastion of luxury in the *Riviera* holiday complex on the southern fringes of Golden Sands, once reserved for top Party functionaries. It's the region's best hotel, although you'll have a 20km taxi ride into town. ❼
Piero Sveti Konstantin ⓣ052/362424 or 361445. Very cosy pension tucked away on the southwest fringe of Sveti Konstantin. Three en-suite doubles with TV and telephone (❹), and three two- to four-person apartments (❻) with nice big bathrooms. Breakfast included. Take bus #8 from in front of the cathedral to the Sveti Konstantin resort.
Villa Sagona Sveti Nikola 8 ⓣ052/303783. Snug little pension in a villa 5km out of town in the suburb of Sveti Nikola (still known to many locals by its Communist-era name, Pochivka). All rooms come with TV and fridge, and guests have use of a tennis court and swimming pool. Take bus #8 or #9 from in front of the cathedral to the Sveti Nikola/Pochivka stop. ❺

Hostels

There were no hostels on the Black Sea coast until an enterprising Australian opened Varna's first in 2004; others may well follow suit as locals catch on to the lucrative backpacker market so it's worth asking around as you travel up and down the coast.

Flag Hostel ul. Opalchenska 25 ⓣ052/648877, ⓦwww.flaghostels.com. Comfortable and friendly new place close to the beach and the town centre with dorm accommodation for up to 18 people. Free use of kitchen and washing machine. 20Lv per person; reduction for stays longer than two nights.

The Town

Varna's social life revolves around **ploshtad Nezavisimost**, where the opera house and fountain provide the backdrop for an array of restaurants and cafés. The square is the starting point of Varna's evening promenade, which flows eastwards from here along bulevard Knyaz Boris I. To the north of ploshtad Nezavisimost, Varna's main lateral boulevard (bul. Mariya Luiza to the east; bul. Hristo Botev to the west) cuts through ploshtad Mitropolit Simeon, an important traffic intersection dominated by the domed **Cathedral of the Assumption**. Constructed in 1886 along the lines of St Petersburg's cathedral, it contains a splendid iconostasis and bishop's throne, supported by a magnificent pair of winged panthers, carved by craftsmen from Debûr in Macedonia. South of the cathedral in the city gardens stands the **Old Clock Tower**, a fairly unremarkable structure paid for by the city guilds in the 1880s, whose silhouette serves as something of a trademark for the city.

In general, however, the downtown area is a place in which to stroll and enjoy the vigour of emergent enterprise culture rather than visit specific sights. Most of the latter are to the south and east, among the residential streets between the centre and the port, although the very busy but otherwise undistinguished bulevard Mariya Luiza is home to the biggest of the city's museums.

The Archeological Museum

The **Archeological Museum** (Tues–Sun 10am–5pm; 4Lv) occupies Varna's former girls' high school on the corner of Mariya Luiza and Slivnitsa. There's a display of nineteenth-century icons upstairs, but it's the archeological collection on the same floor, scattered throughout innumerable halls, which commands most attention.

The Chalcolithic necropolis

Bulgaria's claim to be one of the cradles of European culture was bolstered by the discovery of a **Chalcolithic** (the era when Neolithic man began to smelt copper) necropolis on the outskirts of town in 1972. Dating from the fourth millennium BC, the necropolis was unusual in that it contained many graves in which effigies, rather than human dead, were buried – probably to ensure the continuing health of the living. The gold trinkets with which these symbolic corpses were adorned are displayed extensively in the museum: baubles, bracelets, and pendants in the shape of animals. Many pieces are simply executed; others display an incredible degree of skill considering that they were made 6000 years ago. They're possibly the oldest examples of gold jewellery ever discovered, and have led many to assume that metalworking techniques were developed in Bulgaria independently of the other loci of civilization in the Near East. There's also an intriguing collection of pottery from the Neolithic period on show, including a small clay human head, presumably a ritual object, recovered from the settlement of Arsenala, which is now submerged beneath Varna Lake.

Thracian, Roman and Bulgarian artefacts

No less impressive than the Chalcolithic collection is the Hellenistic-era jewellery from Odyssos. On one gold earring, found in the grave of a Thracian lady from the fourth century BC, a superbly detailed figure of a winged Victory, clothed in wispy, billowing drapery, can be viewed through a magnifying lens. The assemblage of artefacts from the Roman period, meanwhile, provides vivid evidence

The Thracian horseman

Even the smallest of Bulgaria's historical museums devotes at least some space to a display of stone tablets portraying the principal deity of Thrace during the Roman era, the **Thracian horseman** (*Trakiiski konnik*; sometimes also translated as the "Thracian rider" or the "Thracian hero").

In ancient times, in the lands bordering the Black Sea, the **cult of horse and rider** was common among the Thracians and the plain-dwelling Scythian nomads to the north, as well as Asiatic peoples across the Bosphorus to the east. The horse was regarded as an animal capable of reaching the underworld and communicating with the dead, while the rider was deemed a protector of both nature and the souls of the departed. An early manifestation of the rider cult is included in Homer's *Iliad*, in which an archetypal horseman figure, the Thracian King **Rhesus**, has his prized herd of horses stolen by wily Greeks Odysseus and Diomedes.

Stone tablets bearing reliefs of a spear-wielding horseman, often accompanied by a hunting dog, began appearing in Thrace in the third century BC, and soon became universal throughout the eastern Balkans. Tablets were placed in sanctuaries and sacred caves, often those linked with deities associated with health or the protection of nature like Asclepius and Apollo; and they were increasingly used as **funerary monuments**, implying that bereaved families were eager to identify the deceased with the person of the rider god himself. The stylized iconography of the Thracian horseman probably found its way into the subsequent Christian art of the Balkans, with the familiar, spear-wielding, mounted hero re-emerging in medieval icons of **St Demetrius** and **St George**.

of the city's high status and Romanized culture: strigils used by citizens to scrape themselves clean in the public baths, lamps decorated with gurning theatrical masks, fine surgical equipment and a fragment of a marble plaque carrying a public announcement of upcoming gladiatorial bouts, dated to AD 221. As well as documenting their comfortable lives, the museum's collections also record the deaths of the well-to-do in Roman Odyssos, with the finest display of Roman-period **funerary sculpture** in Bulgaria. Prominent Greek and Roman citizens were honoured with a tombstone depicting scenes of funeral feasts, usually showing the deceased reclining on a couch attended by a spouse, children and servants. Townsfolk of Thracian origin preferred a grave plaque decorated with a relief of the so-called **Thracian horseman** (see box, p.391), the rider god whose worship became universal among the natives from the Hellenistic era onwards.

Bulgarian gold and silver from the fourteenth century introduces a collection of **medieval weaponry**, **jewellery**, and fine **pottery**, including some later examples of colourful faïence ware, imported from Venice and Asia Minor. The extensive collection of **icons** on the top floor includes some high quality examples of the Tryavna school, and is complemented by a display of ecclesiastical plate and vestments.

The City Art Gallery

A couple of hundred metres to the east of the Archeological Museum, on Lyuben Karavelov, is the **City Art Gallery** (Tues–Sun 10am–5pm; 2Lv), whose ground floor hosts high-profile temporary exhibitions. Visitors to the permanent collection on the first floor are greeted by a row of seventeenth-century diplomats painted by Flemish portraitist Anselmus von Hulme; beyond these are several rooms of contemporary art. Beside a few lionizations of the Bulgarian peasantry courtesy of Vladimir Dimitrov-Maistor (see p.130) and Stoyan Venev, most room is taken up with works by previous winners of the Varna Graphics Biennale, held in the summer during odd-numbered years.

From bulevard Knyaz Boris I to the sea

Many of Varna's attractions are to be found amid the crumbling turn-of-the-twentieth-century buildings which lie between **bulevard Knyaz Boris I** and the **port**, where the commercial bustle of the city centre gives way to quiet residential streets lined with chestnut trees. Huddled among the town houses are several excellent museums, a couple of churches, and the best of Varna's Roman remains. Careful map-reading is often required to find them, but it's worth the effort.

The Armenian church and the Church of Sveta Bogoroditsa

From the Archeological Museum, bulevard 27 Yuli leads south to ploshtad Ekzarh Iosif, where elderly *Varnentsi* gather for an evening chat, and locals bring jerry cans and flagons to collect the hot mineral water gushing from a public fountain. Just beyond, at the junction of Koloni and Kliment, is a small nineteenth-century **Armenian church**, squeezed into the corner of a schoolyard. Serving a local population of about 3000, the church contains naive icons covered in Armenian script. Outside, a small tablet commemorates the genocide of 1915, when up to one and a half million Armenians lost their lives at the hands of the Ottomans – suggesting a shared history of suffering in which both Armenians and Bulgarians find common cause.

Of more historical value, however, are the intricately carved iconostasis and bishop's throne of the seventeenth-century **Church of Sveta Bogoroditsa** at

Han Krum 19, a partly sunken church whose tower was added later once Ottoman restrictions had been removed.

The Roman thermae and the Church of Sveti Atanas

Across the road from the Church of Sveta Bogoroditsa stands a vast tower of crumbling red brick, once the western wall of the **Roman thermae** (Tues-Sun 10am–5pm & Sat 10am-5pm; 3Lv), a sizeable complex thought to have been built in the late second or early third century – coins found on the site bear the image of the emperor Septimus Severus (AD 193-211). Scrambling among the ruins, it's possible to imagine the ritualized progress of the bathers from the *apodyterium*, or changing room, through the rising temperatures of the *frigidarium*, *tepidarium* and *caldarium*; and then back again. The daily visit to the baths was an important part of social life, and bathers would circulate and exchange gossip in a large central hall, or *palaestra*, which also served as a venue for athletic contests and daily workouts.

The adjacent **Church of Sveti Atanas** (daily 9am-5.30pm) is a classic example of National Revival architecture. An arcaded porch precedes a sumptuous interior, with a rich, gilt iconostasis, carved wooden ceiling, and painted marble-effect pillars. The icons on display here contain many of their original Greek inscriptions, which is unusual in that in most churches they were scratched off once the Bulgarians took control.

The Ethnographic Museum

A ten-minute walk west from here brings you to the **Ethnographic Museum** (daily 10am–5pm; 4Lv) occupying a National Revival house on ulitsa Panagyurishte. It's an interesting and attractively arranged collection, but one that concentrates exclusively on Bulgarian ethnography, despite the fact that Varna was a predominantly Greek, Turkish and Gagauz town until the Liberation.

Downstairs lie reminders of the region's traditional trades and occupations: among them a variety of fishing nets, wine barrels, wattle-and-daub beehives and a nineteenth-century *yamurluk* or hooded cloak, as worn by the shepherds who roamed the hills of the interior. On the first floor, there's a display of **regional costumes**, showing great diversity of styles, largely because the area inland of Varna was a crossroads of migrating peoples. One distinct local group were the *chenge*, represented here by a wedding scene from the village of Asparuhovo, 50km west of Varna. Faceless costumed dummies are grouped around a ceremonial wooden wedding sledge, with the bride surrounded by men in black hats wreathed with flowers. Items relating to regional folk beliefs include the embroidered **masks** worn during *Kukeri* (spring) and *Survakari* (New Year) rites, and a couple of the **New Year camels** paraded through the streets in some areas – approximations of the humped beast made from sheepskin and mounted on skis. Also on display are a variety of **ritual loaves** baked to mark specific occasions: the *Kravai* for New Year or St John's Day; the "Pony" (*Konche*) for Todorovden (the feast day of St Theodore, patron of horse-breeding); or the *Proshtupalnik* – shaped like a baby's foot – to celebrate a child's first steps. On the topmost floor are the inevitable restored living rooms, comprising an elegantly furnished salon, drawing room and bedroom, offering an insight into the lives of the new urban middle classes of *fin-de-siècle* Varna, some of whose fashionable costumes are also on show.

The City Historical Museum

Bearing southeast from the Ethnographic Museum along Han Omurtag will bring you to ulitsa 8 Noemvri and the **City Historical Museum**, at no. 5

(Tues–Sat 10am–5pm; 3Lv). A pretty dull collection of black-and-white photos, documents and brochures traces the development of Varna from nineteenth-century Balkan backwater to the comfortable bourgeois European town and seaside resort it had become by the early twentieth century. Among the street scenes and portraits of prominent citizens are pictures of the annual **beauty contests** – a competition which *Varnentsi* claim the dubious honour of inventing. Initially contestants were dubbed "Sea Hyenas" (perhaps because of their long, stripy bathing suits), and as costumes got skimpier during the 1920s they were renamed "Sea Nymphs". In the basement there's a reconstructed tailor's workshop of the 1940s, and a few period magazines and more photos. Just outside is the rusted hulk of a nineteenth-century British-made steam engine, and immediately to the south are the overgrown remains of more **Roman baths**, this time dating from the late fourth century, and far less extensive than the better-preserved *thermae* on Han Krum.

The Museum of Medical History

Considerably more interesting is the **Museum of Medical History**, ul. Paraskeva Nikolau 7 (Mon–Fri 10am–4pm; free), sheltered within the sandy-coloured nineteenth-century building that once housed Varna's first public hospital. Inside, a words-and-pictures display adopts a patriotic tone, attempting to show how the medieval Bulgarian state inherited the medical wisdom of the ancients and transmitted it to the rest of Europe – only to have their standards of public hygiene ruined by the Turks, who made everybody live in smelly, unsanitary cities. However, the early Bulgarians were not without their forays into perversity. An array of tenth-century **skulls** on the ground floor reveals that one in three of the local population had been subjected to a symbolic form of trepanation (the practice of drilling holes in the skull) – in which the bone had been scratched and dented but not actually pierced. Archeologists presume that this had some kind of ritual purpose – but quite what, no one knows.

Less macabre but equally disconcerting are the ferocious-looking early twentieth-century surgical instruments on display upstairs, along with a reconstructed turn-of-the-twentieth-century dentist's consulting room and antiquated x-ray machines.

The Sea Gardens

The massed flowerbeds of Varna's extensive *Morskata Gradina,* or **Sea Gardens**, were laid out at the end of the nineteenth century by Czech horticulturalist Anton Novak (invited here by those other Bohemian Bulgarophiles, the Skorpil brothers), who supposedly modelled them on the Baroque palace gardens of Belvedere and Schönbrunn in Vienna. The park's tree-lined pathways are patrolled from dawn to dusk by young families, courting couples and skate-boarding teens, and there's the usual scattering of street vendors, offering the ubiquitous corn on the cob and packets of sunflower seeds. During the summer a road train leisurely shuttles passengers back and forth through the park from the Dolphinarium to just below the *Odesos* hotel for 50st.

The Navy Museum and the Aquarium

At the western end of the park, the gunboat responsible for the Bulgarian navy's only victory lies honourably embedded outside the **Navy Museum** (Tues-Sat 10am-6pm; 4Lv). The boat in question, the *Drûzhki* (Intrepid), sank the Turkish cruiser *Hamidie* off Cape Kaliakra during the First Balkan War of 1912. Since Bulgaria's navy was reduced to a rump by the Neuilly Treaty of 1919, and later collaborated with Hitler's *Kriegsmarine*, there's little else for it to take pride in, and the museum itself houses a musty collection of naval relics, mostly from the nineteenth and twentieth centuries, including model ships, uniforms and various ship fixtures, all, as usual, labelled in Bulgarian only. Just beyond is the **Aquarium** (daily 9am–7pm; 2Lv), a small collection of fresh- and seawater creatures, whose habits are explained in Russian and German translations only. Most interesting specimens are the sea-needles, who reproduce when the female of the species deposits her eggs in a pouch on the male, who is expected to do the brooding; the Black Sea turbot, a denizen of the sea bed which assumes the colour of rocks to disguise itself against predators; the translucent ghost shrimps; and the freshwater sturgeon, which can grow to a length of 9m in the wild, although those confined here are rather smaller. There's also a small collection of poorly stuffed and pickled specimens in an adjoining room.

A little way to the east, pathways descend to Varna's *Morski bani* or municipal **beach**, where bathers can look out at the shoals of tankers and cargo vessels anchored in the bay. The beach stretches northwards for a couple of kilometres, lined with a succession of outdoor bars, clubs and restaurants which, in summer, remain buzzing well into the early hours. At the far end of the beach, steaming mineral water spews out of the hillside, collecting in a pool often used by elderly bathers well into winter.

The Natural History Museum, the Zoo, the Terrarium and the Dolphinarium

Back in the park, tree-lined avenues stretch eastwards towards the Socialist-Realist **Monument to Fighters against Fascism**, to the south of which lurks an unassuming **Natural History Museum** (Tues–Sun 10am–5pm; 3Lv), providing a useful introduction to the coast's flora and fauna, if you can make out the Bulgarian captions. Live specimens prowl their spartan quarters with apparent contentment in the small **Zoo** just beyond (daily 8am–8pm; 1.50Lv) featuring camels, lions, wolves, ostriches, and pelicans among others. A little further on is the **Dolphinarium** (shows at 11am, 2pm & 3.30pm Tues–Sun; 16Lv). The **Terrarium** (daily 9am-9pm; 1.80Lv) lies just beyond, an unassuming building that hosts a fascinating collection of live creatures including black widow and tarantula spiders, several rare chameleons, various deadly snakes, and a crocodile. On the other side of Knyaz Boris I looms the ultra-modern **Palace of Sports and Culture**, venue for concerts and indoor sports such as wrestling and basketball.

The Park of Fighting Friendship

Among the housing estates that mark the city's northwestern margins lies the bizarrely named **Park of Fighting Friendship** (bus #22 from the cathedral), where a granite monument tops a Thracian tumulus marking the site of the **Battle of Varna**. An army of 30,000 Crusaders made their way here in November 1444, intending to meet a fleet of Venetian and Genoese ships before sailing on to Constantinople. Unfortunately, the fleet had already set off, in a vain attempt to stop Sultan Murad II and his forces from crossing the Bosphorus. Murad rapidly made his way up the coast and during the subsequent clash, King Ladislas III of Poland and Hungary (known to the Bulgarians as Vladislav Varnenchik) recklessly led a charge to capture Sultan Murad in his tent, but was cut down in the attempt. His army wavered, forcing János Hunyadi to order an inglorious retreat, marking the end of Christendom's last attempt to check the Ottoman advance.

A small **museum** (officially daily 9am–5pm; 3Lv) built into the mound displays medieval armour and tributes to the various East European races that made up Ladislas' army.

The northern suburbs and Evksinograd

Varna's northeastern suburbs have always been favoured by city folk as a place to relax; the villas and holiday cottages of the more affluent cling to vine-covered hillsides overlooking the sea, or nestle in small gardens rich in fruit trees. The one specific sight in the region is **Evksinograd Palace**, a former residence of monarchs Aleksandûr and Ferdinand, built in the style of a French chateau. Less interesting to visit but worthy of mention is the village of **VINITSA** 10km northeast of town (bus #31 from opposite the cathedral), still inhabited by one of the Black Sea's more elusive and mysterious minorities, the **Gagauz** (see p.402). Three kilometres up the hill from the beaches of Sveti Konstantin, Vinitsa is a relatively unspoilt village with plenty of private rooms, although there is no *kvartirno byuro* so you'll have to ask around.

Evksinograd Palace

Built under the name of "Sandrovo" by Prince Alexander Batenberg in 1882, and renamed (combining the Greek word *euxine* – "hospitable" – with the Slavonic *grad* – "town" or "fortress") by his successor Ferdinand, **Evksinograd Palace** is nowadays notorious for being the former holiday home of the Bulgarian Politburo. It still belongs to the state, and members of the government spend their holidays here, ensuring that it's usually fully booked during July and August. The only way for independent travellers to stay is to reserve well in advance through the government website Ⓦhttp://travel.government.bg/en/evksinograd which should procure you a room in the *Tunela* hotel (Ⓣ052/393140 or 361247; ❹–❽) or one of the smaller villas within the grounds. The large, comfortable en-suites come with all the mod cons you would expect, and make for a relaxing retreat.

You can't visit the palace itself, but there are sometimes guided tours of the grounds on offer to tourists staying at the *Tunela*, Sveti Konstantin or Golden Sands (independent travellers can enquire about tour availability from the reception desk of the *Tunela*). These lead past the vineyards where Bulgaria's most sought-after wines and brandies are produced, and descend towards the seafront through the botanical gardens laid out for Ferdinand by French horticulturalists at the turn of the twentieth century. The Communist Party hierarchy built themselves a deluxe beach complex in the woods overlooking the shore, complete with state-of-the-art health clinic and sports hall – the latter including a bowling alley. Each member of the Politburo had his own beach house, linked by secret tunnel to a central command bunker – in the unlikely event of being taken unawares by the apocalypse while bathing. Party Secretary Todor Zhivkov's beach house was, of course, bigger than the rest, isolated from those of his comrades on the other side of the headland.

The entrance to the palace lies on the main coast road running north out of Varna (bus #7 or #8 from in front of the Cathedral).

Sveti Konstantin (Druzhba)

Immediately beyond Evksinograd, suburban Varna fades imperceptibly into the first of the great tourist complexes built in the postwar drive to develop the coast. Originally named "Druzhba" ("friendship"), **SVETI KONSTANTIN** (bus #8 from in front of the cathedral) first admitted Western tourists in 1955, and has since served as a prototype for others. The elite trade union rest-homes which used to grace the northern end of Sveti Konstantin are now hotels operating under the banner of the **Sunny Day** (*Slûnchev den*) resort, which has its own beach, but to all intents and purposes is still part of Sveti Konstantin. Taken together, Sveti Konstantin and Sunny Day are still quite small compared with the mega-resorts of Golden Sands and Albena further north, so there's less in the way of things to do – although the centre of Varna is only 12km away.

The resort has a park-like cosiness, with an abundance of oaks and cypresses, a number of small beaches and coves, and hot mineral pools on the seafront. On the downside, it's not the best managed of places, being poorly lit at night and frequented by stray dogs. The Swedish-built *Grand Hotel Varna* in the centre of Sveti Konstantin is still one of the city's better business hotels (see p.390) and the emergence of several small family-run hotels on the western fringes of the resort has meant that there's more scope for independent travellers here than previously. The Hit Tourism accommodation bureau (daily 10am–7pm; ⓣ052/363335) in the centre of the resort arranges private rooms and bungalows (❶). Food and drink in the resort's numerous café-restaurants is generally more expensive than in central Varna.

The Stone Forest

Roughly 18km due west of Varna on either side of the Devnya road, the desolate scrubland is interrupted by scores of curious stone columns standing as high as 7m, known as *pobiti kamûni* or "standing stones", usually translated as the **Stone Forest**. These strange, snake-haunted formations were created around fifty million years ago when fragments of two chalk strata gradually bonded together in the intervening sand layer, by a process analogous to stalactite formation. Nowadays the area is a popular spot for picnics and leisurely hikes. **Getting there** is difficult unless you have your own transport: the region is best accessed by travelling west out of Varna along the old main road to Devnya, ignoring the Devnya-bound A2 motorway to the north which runs parallel.

Eating and drinking

The majority of Varna's places to eat and drink are along the route of the evening *korso*, which stretches **east from ploshtad Nezavisimost** along bulevard Knyaz Boris I, before turning down Slivnitsa towards the Sea Gardens. There are plenty of **cafés** and **restaurants** lining the route, although the Varna restaurant scene changes so rapidly that it's sometimes difficult to provide precise recommendations. In general the places along this main strip are more expensive than elsewhere in Bulgaria, but not prohibitively so. On the whole, restaurants in Varna tend to open daily from noon until 11pm or midnight, unless otherwise stated below.

The **snack bars** around ploshtad Nezavisimost and along bulevard Knyaz Boris I are the best places to grab **breakfast**; while a succession of *sladkarnitsi* along bulevard Knyaz Boris I sell pastries, *banitsa* (small savoury pastries, filled with sheep's cheese), small pizzas and other snacks throughout the day. If the local fast food doesn't appeal, there's a *Pizza Hut* at bul. Knyaz Boris I 62, a *KFC* just opposite the cathedral and a *McDonald's* on ploshtad Nezavisimost.

For **evening drinking**, most of central Varna's cafés serve alcohol well into the night, and, in summer, a string of seemingly numberless outdoor **bars** and fish restaurants lines the municipal beach, accessible via pathways that lead down from the Sea Gardens. Most of these are temporary, seasonal affairs, and few have regular names, and it's best simply to wander along until you see a place that takes your fancy.

Restaurants

Arkitekt ul. Musala 10. Excellent traditional restaurant in the courtyard of a National Revival-style wooden house. The best place in town for grilled sausages and beer in frosty mugs.

Bistro Rimska Terma ul. 8 Noemvri. Modern, chic place just downhill from the *thermae*, with excellent Bulgarian cuisine and friendly service; the prices are high but deservedly so.

BMS bul. Knyaz Boris I 42 on the corner of ul. 27 Yuli. Tasty ready-made Bulgarian dishes – Bulgaria's answer to *McDonald's*.

Chuchurite ul. Panagyurishte. Traditional-style *mehana* serving the usual range of grilled meats, situated in an attractive old wooden house opposite the Ethnographic Museum. Next door is a tiny, atmospheric little coffee bar with flagstone floors and outdoor seating in summer.

Happy Bar and Grill pl. Nezavisimost. Varna's home-grown restaurant chain, with a variety of chicken-and-chips-style dishes as well as a few Bulgarian regulars. Reliable food, breezy service and modest prices.

Hashove bul. Primorski 4. The terrace restaurant of the *Odesos* hotel is relatively expensive – you're really paying for the location – but the food is varied and decent enough, with a wide range of fish dishes.

Horizont in the Sea Gardens opposite the zoo. Stylish restaurant with a range of moderately priced international dishes and live piano music nightly.

Morske vulk ul. Odrin. Popular hangout of the local alternative crowd, serving generous portions of mostly Bulgarian dishes.

Paraklissa corner of Paraskeva Nikolau and bul. Primorski. Some of the best and most imaginative traditional Bulgarian food in Varna, served up in the courtyard of the Museum of Medical History. It's more expensive than most, but worth the extra cost.

Panorama top floor of the *Cherno More* hotel. Excellent food in elegant surroundings, with live chamber music or jazz most nights.

Ribarska shatra on the beachfront below the Sea Gardens. One of the few fish restaurants along here which remains open year-round. It's also a nice spot for a drink, with its great sea view.

Staviko ul. 8 Noemvri 11. Good-quality Bulgarian standards in a convenient location behind the Roman baths, near the entrance to the church of Sveti Atanas. There's a roof terrace, and occasional live music in the basement dining hall.

Cafés and bars

Café-Club 2001 bul. Knyaz Boris I 46. Trendy spot for coffee and cocktails, with indoor and outdoor wicker seating.

Davidoff Slivinitsa, opposite the *Cherno More* hotel. Elegant, regularly packed coffee bar, with outdoor seating and serving the best cocktails in Varna.

Grûtski dvor bul. Knyaz Boris I 57. Smart outdoor garden café serving luxuriant, creamy coffees and good ice cream.

Morsko konche pl. Nezavisimost. Offering a wide choice of pizzas, including one topped with banana, this small establishment near the Opera House is also a popular drinking spot for Varna's student population.

Piano Club Musala corner of pl. Nezavisimost and Musala. There's no piano, and it isn't a club, just a small conservatory-style bar, but it's a nice-enough place for an evening drink.

Planet ul. Tsar Simeon I 26. Café and nightclub open 24hr, opposite the train station – useful when catching late or early trains.

Tonga on the beachfront below the Sea Gardens. One of the more reliable of the seaside bars, right on the sand. It's a nice place for a drink and a snack during the day, and is regularly crowded in the evenings.

Nightlife and entertainment

Those looking for a taste of seaside hedonism should head for the numerous nightclubs and bars which line the beach below the Sea Gardens. Unfortunately, most are only open for the summer season, but a few remain in business at other times of year. Frequent name changes make individual recommendations difficult, but the outdoor *Club Momo* opposite the Natural History Museum is well established and *Club Extravagance* on the beachfront hosts nightly parties with local DJs. Other dance parties and occasional gigs take place, but the venues change with alarming frequency, so you'll need to rely on local knowledge, or have a go at deciphering the fly-posters.

The **Opera House**, on ploshtad Nezavisimost (box office: Mon–Fri 10.30am–1pm & 2–7.30pm; ⓣ052/223039, ⓦwww.operavarna.bg) is Varna's main cultural institution, with operatic and other musical performances put on year-round. Many other major events, including orchestral concerts, take place in the open-air theatre (*Leten teatûr*) in the Sea Gardens; the modern Festival

Vampires and vampire hunters

The ugly, industrial town of Devnya, 30km west of Varna, is now known only for its highly noxious chemical industry, but during the nineteenth century its reputation was widespread as Bulgaria's **vampire** capital. Reports brought back from the Black Sea region by contemporaneous travellers reveal that belief in vampires was widespread among the Bulgarian peasantry of the time. Travelling in the 1880s, the Czech Balkanologist Konstantin Jireiek found a wealth of vampire lore in the isolated rural communities west of Varna, with inexplicable illnesses among humans, and particularly sheep – the region's main source of income – being attributed to a visitation by some bloodthirsty demon, and local wise men (known as *vampirdzhiya* or *dzhadzhiya*) being paid handsomely by villagers to drive the fiends away. According to Jireiek, the vampire hunters of Devnya were considered the best in eastern Bulgaria.

The belief was that people became vampires if proper burial customs were not observed or if certain portentous events happened before their death: for example, a shadow passing across their body, or a dog or cat jumping across their path. After burial, an invisible spirit would rise up from the grave each night, feeding off local flocks and bringing listlessness and ill health to the human population. Vampires could also assume solid form, often living among humans for many years, getting married and having children before being detected. To chase the vampires away, a *dzhadzhiya* would be summoned to walk among the flocks, holding an icon aloft. The icon also came in handy when trying to identify the resting place of the vampire. If it began to tremble when held above a particular grave, it meant that the culprit had been found. The best way to deal with a vampire was to exhume the body, stab it through the heart with a hawthorn branch, then burn it with kindling taken from the same shrub. If the vampire was in spirit form, it could be driven into a bottle which was then thrown onto a fire.

The beliefs noted by Jireiek were by no means isolated cases. The British travellers St Clair and Brophy, who lived in a village south of Varna in the 1860s, wrote of a boy forbidden from marrying his sweetheart because locals earnestly believed that he was of vampire descent. They also relate how peasants in a neighbouring village burned a man alive for vampirism, because he was fond of nocturnal walks and was "found to have only one nostril".

According to Jireiek, the best vampire hunters were thought to be descended from *vûlkodlatsi*, literally werewolves, who resulted from the sexual union of a vampire and a young maiden, and were the only living beings who could see vampire spirits. The *vûlkodlatsi's* vampire-hunting descendants were also thought to have another supernatural power: the ability to detect buried treasure. In an area full of ancient Thracian, Roman and Byzantine remains, it's not difficult to see why the idea of hidden hordes of goblets and coins – all waiting to be unearthed by the lucky peasant – exerted such a hold on the popular imagination.

Another associated piece of local lore concerns the Lake of Varna (a fjord-like inlet stretching west from the city), which used to be known as Vampire Lake. According to popular belief, the lake required an annual human sacrifice, the last recorded instance of which was in 1933, when one Ana Konstantinova went swimming there despite warnings, and was duly sucked underwater.

Hall (*Festivalen kompleks*) on Slivnitsa 2; or, on occasion, the Palace of Sport and Culture out on bulevard Knyaz Boris I. All the above are pressed into service during the annual **Varnensko lyato**, or "Varna Summer", featuring symphonic, operatic and chamber music (mid-June to September), which attracts some of the world's finest orchestras and companies. The Varna Summer also comprises the Varna **jazz festival**, and an international **film festival** (both usually in August). A complete schedule and advance tickets are available from the ground floor of the Festival Hall itself. Throughout the summer months, the area around the entrance to the Sea Gardens is given over to a variety of fairground rides and stalls, completing the seaside holiday atmosphere; the colourful **market** held daily opposite the Cathedral of the Assumption offers an alternative mood and is the best place to pick up locally made souvenirs.

The **cinema** in the Festival Hall shows the best range of first-run and cult films, most of which are shown in their original language, with Bulgarian subtitles. The smaller Mustang Cinema, next to the restaurant of the same name on bulevard Varnenchik, shows less recent Hollywood blockbusters, again with Bulgarian subtitles. For children, there's a **puppet theatre** at ul. Dragoman 6, although it takes a summer break in July and August.

Listings

Airlines Tickets for all airlines are available at Alfatour, bul. Mariya Luiza 26 (Ⓣ052/616080, Ⓦwww.alfatour.bg), and from Vectra Travel, bul. Osmi Primorski Polk 54 (Ⓣ052/600225 or 601760, Ⓦwww.vectratravel.com).
Airport information Ⓣ052/500840, Ⓦwww.varna-airport.bg.
Car rental Avis, at the airport Ⓣ052/500832; Hertz, at the airport Ⓣ052/510250. In addition, several travel agencies in town deal with car rentals – try City-Rent through Vectra Travel (see above).
Car repairs Try the big city-centre depots at bul. Vl. Varnenchik 262 (Ⓣ052/449885), and bul. Vl. Varnenchik 184 (Ⓣ052/441252).
Dentist Dental polyclinic at bul. Sûborni 24.
Hospital bul. Sûborni 40. In emergencies call Ⓣ150.
Internet Doom has several clubs: ul. 27 Yuli 13; bul. Osmi Primorski Polk 81; ul. Roza 36.
Pharmacies Sanita, bul. Vladislav Varnenchik 12, is open 24hr.
Police ul. Panagyurishte 1. Ⓣ052/611516.
Post office The main post office is at bul. Sûborni 36 (Mon–Sat 7.30am–7pm, Sun 8am–noon).
Telephones At the main post office (above).

North of Varna

When people think of the coastline north of Varna they normally think of sprawling tourist complexes like **Golden Sands** (Zlatni pyasûtsi) and **Albena**, and, indeed, the first 50km of the E87's northward progress can seem like an endless procession of high-rise hotels and dusty building sites. Once you get away from the main road, however, even the biggest of the resorts can be quite peaceful and relaxing, making good use of the sandy beaches lining the shore and the forests which form their immediate hinterland. Golden Sands is near enough to Varna to be on the urban bus network, while Albena is served by regular minibuses from a stop 200m west of Varna's cathedral.

Beyond Albena the atmosphere changes, with the less crowded towns and villages of the Dobrudzhan littoral perched above an increasingly rocky coast, which culminates in the dramatic cliffs of **Cape Kaliakra**. Although all the settlements along this stretch of the water make good **day-trips by bus** from

Moving on from Varna

A large number of **international buses** leave Varna: the ticket offices at the main bus station provide information and tickets on daily services to Istanbul, seasonal departures (weekly in summer) to Odessa and Kiev, as well as regular departures to France, Italy, Greece and many other European destinations. Domestic and international **train bookings** can be made from BDZh/Rila, ul. Preslav 13 (Mon–Fri 8am–5pm, Sat 8am–noon; ⓣ052/632348).

For international **airline tickets** try Alfatour or Vectra Travel (see "Listings" opposite).

The only international **boat trips** currently running from Varna port are to Odessa in Ukraine from where you can sail on to Sevastopol and Yalta. Tickets (80Lv one way) can be purchased from Korabna Agency (Mon–Sat 10.30am-5.30pm; ⓣ052/601330 or 633433) which has a small kiosk at the port. The Ukrainian Embassy in Varna at ul. General Kolev 92, fifth floor (ⓣ052/321800; Mon–Fri 9am–noon) arranges visas with a week's notice for 80Lv or charges 160Lv for its 24-hour express service.

Varna, the picturesque town of **Balchik** is the most likely base to appeal to the non-package tour crowd.

Golden Sands (Zlatni pyasûtsi)

Tourists generally balk at pronouncing Zlatni pyasûtsi, so most Bulgarians along the coast will understand if you say "Goldstrand" or **GOLDEN SANDS** instead. It's a polyglot place: of all the nationalities here, Germans predominate, and two members of the 2nd of June terrorist group were actually arrested here in 1978 after being recognized by a West German prison warder who, like them, was on holiday. The resort's myriad hotels occupy a wooded, landscaped strip behind Zlatni pyasûtsi's greatest asset, its **beach**: a soft, pale golden expanse 4km long, sloping gently into an undertow-less sea.

Golden Sands also offers a wide range of bars, restaurants and discos; and **activities** such as scuba diving, waterskiing and paraskiing are offered by kiosks along the beach. The strolling areas behind the beach feature well-tended gardens, outdoor pools, and plenty of sports facilities for children. A group of hotels at the southern end of the resort operates separately under the name of the Riviera Holiday Club, site of the *Imperial* hotel (see p.390).

Practicalities

Independent travellers are charged much more for hotel rooms than those who have booked a package holiday, but if you do fancy the idea of spending the odd night here then your first port of call should be the accommodation bureau (*byuro za nastanyavane*) in the administration building on the main E87 highway, which runs along the upper, western fringe of the resort (ⓣ052/355683 or 355694, ⓦwww.goldensands.bg), where staff can fix you up with hotel rooms (❹–❺). Avoid the resort's much neglected *Panorama* campsite at all costs.

There are several ways of getting here by bus from Varna: #9 from in front of the cathedral to the Riviera Holiday Club; #109 from the train station or in front of the cathedral to the administration building; or #409 from the airport to the administration building.

Aladzha Monastery

In the Hanchuka Forest, 7km southwest of Golden Sands, dozens of cells and chambers hewn into a cliff comprise what remains of **Aladzha Monastery**

The Gagauz

Bulgaria's Black Sea shore hosts several communities of **Gagauz**, a Turkish-speaking Christian people whose origins remain the subject of much controversy. Turkish sources maintain that they are descended from the **Seljuk Turks** of Sultan Izzedin Kaykaus, who came to the area in 1261 and soon converted to Christianity under pressure from their Bulgarian neighbours. This is disputed by Bulgarian ethnologists, who suggest that they are descended from the original **Bulgars**, the Turkic nomads who descended on the Balkans in the eighth century. Perhaps the most likely theory is that they are descended from the **Cumans**, another Turkic tribe who started moving into eastern Bulgaria in the twelfth century, and formed the backbone of the short-lived fourteenth-century coastal empire of Balik and Dobrotitsa, which was centred on the towns of Balchik (see p.404) and Kavarna (see p.406).

Although many Gagauz were Islamicized and assimilated by their Turkish conquerors during the Ottoman era, enough of them remained Christian to ensure their continued existence as a distinct community. Many of them **emigrated to Bessarabia**, where they could practise their Christian faith more freely than they could under the Ottomans. They still retain a strong presence in the former Soviet republic of Moldova, where the Gagauz lands around the provincial town of Komrat enjoy autonomous status. Those Gagauz who remained in Bulgaria found themselves increasingly torn by the **national struggles** of the nineteenth century, when many identified themselves with Varna's Greek population in order to distinguish themselves both from their Turk overlords and from the Bulgarian peasants who were increasingly moving into the city. Most Gagauz joined the Greeks in opposing the opening of Bulgarian-language schools and churches, and therefore received little sympathy from the Bulgarians after the Liberation. Unlike the Greeks, however, the Gagauz had no other national homeland to emigrate to, and despite their small numbers, they still retain a distinctive presence in Vinitsa, Kichevo, and a succession of villages strung out over the hills north of Varna. Older Gagauz still speak a dialect of Turkish among themselves, but a literary version of the Gagauz tongue never developed in Bulgaria, and knowledge of the language is slowly dying out among the young.

(daily 9am–6pm; 3Lv). The caves to the west were occupied during the Stone Age by people whom Strabo called "pygmies", and served as a place of refuge during the Dark Ages. A Christian church may have existed here as early as the fifth century, though the monastery itself was probably established during the thirteenth century, in the same way as the Ivanovo rock monasteries.

Aladzha's monks were *hesychasts*, striving to attain union with God by maintaining physical immobility and total silence. However, they did get round to painting several exquisite murals in the chapels, which can be seen at the end of the first and second galleries. Nowadays they're scrappy and faded, although in olden times they were sufficiently impressive to earn the monastery its name – *Aladzha* means "multicoloured" in Turkish.

A **museum** at the entrance displays models of how the monastery used to look when occupied, alongside ornaments, weapons and other artefacts dating from around 5000 BC, discovered in a Chalcolithic necropolis on the western outskirts of Varna in 1972. You might enjoy poking around the various catacombs and surrounding woods – the latter a place of many **legends**. Its mythical guardian, Rim Papa, is said to awake from a cotton-lined burrow every year to ask whether the trees still grow and women and cows still give birth, and go back to sleep upon being answered in the affirmative.

The best way **to get to the monastery** is to walk from Golden Sands: it's about 6km uphill from the resort (signed from the crossroads near the main administration building), along an asphalt road – not too unpleasant providing you avoid the midday heat.

Kranevo

Just beyond the northern end of Golden Sands, **KRANEVO** is a rapidly expanding village sitting at the southern tip of a glorious curve of beach which extends onwards towards the mega-resort of Albena, some 4km distant. Kranevo's growing number of private rooms and family-run hotels make it a useful budget alternative to its more package-oriented neighbour, although there is little here in the way of sights or entertainment: you can walk along the sands to Albena if you fancy using the facilities there. The main E87 coastal road forges through the eastern fringes of Kranevo, and it's here that Varna–Albena and Varna–Balchik buses pick up and drop off. A 1km walk downhill brings you to what passes for the village centre, a parade of hastily constructed cafés and restaurants leading down towards the beach.

Rooms (❶) are available from the tourist information bureau in the centre (May-Sept daily 8am-8pm; ⓣ0579/66810; be prepared to ask around outside these times), with prices around 10Lv per person depending on proximity to the shore. One of the best hotels is the *Apolon*, on the main road near the southern entrance to the village (ⓣ0579/66646; ❸), which offers comfy, characterful en-suite rooms with TV and telephone. A cheaper option is the two-star *Mage* (ⓣ0579/66412; ❶), close to the beach. Both have good restaurants, although there are plenty of places offering grilled fish in the village centre. Food and drink in Kranevo is significantly cheaper than in neighbouring Albena up the road.

Albena and around

The step-pyramid architecture of **ALBENA**'s hotels marks it out as one of the more architecturally inventive of Bulgaria's purpose-built resorts; it's also the most efficiently run, the cleanest, and by far the most expensive. It's an attractive, if a little sterile-looking place, with well-tended flowerbeds and lawns lying behind an extensive and usually crowded beach, lined with bars and kebab stalls, while the range of activities on offer here is second to none. Bordering the resort to the south is an area of swamp-like semi-submerged forest known as the **Balta**; access to this alluring landscape is via the asphalted track to the *Gorski kût* restaurant.

Albena is bypassed by the main road, but well served by minibuses from Varna (departing from a stop 200m west of the cathedral) and buses from Balchik (see p.406). Arriving at the terminal at the eastern end of the resort, you'll find a small **tourist bureau** (daily 8am–midnight; ⓣ0579/62920). Here you can get rooms in any of the resort's forty **hotels** (❹–❽), with prices ranging from 70Lv per person in the two-star places, to 120Lv per person in the best of the beachside establishments, most of which are patronized by German tour groups, with standards of comfort and service to match. Albena also has a good **campsite** (off the entrance road to the left) with well-shaded areas for tents, and en-suite four-person bungalows (❸), some of which have self-catering facilities. If you're keen to stay in Albena, it's worth contacting the resort's marketing department (ⓣ0579/62090, ⓦwww.albena.bg) in advance – independent travellers will be given a significant reduction on the walk-in rates quoted above.

Food and drink in Albena are among the most expensive in Bulgaria and, unless you periodically escape to neighbouring Kranevo or Balchik (see overleaf), this may not prove the inexpensive holiday destination you anticipated. There are plenty of alfresco restaurants, bars and cafés along the resort's main thoroughfares and beside the beach, most catering to the German package tourists: individual recommendations are impossible, though, as things change from one season to the next.

Albena boasts at least five **sailing and windsurfing** schools strung out along the beach, offering boat and board rental from about 10Lv per hour, as well as week-long courses (around 180Lv for fourteen hours' tuition). There's also a **scuba-diving** centre, with prices starting at 55Lv for an introductory session, and 490Lv for a week-long course. The resort's **riding** centre is currently the best in Bulgaria, with twelve hours of tuition costing around 200Lv, and a variety of rides (ranging from one-hour "gallops" to day-long picnics) laid on for all abilities.

The Tekke at Obrochishte

Beyond the vast roundabout marking the western fringe of Albena, the E87 heads eastwards along the coast, although most traffic takes the inland route through the village of **Obrochishte**, overlooked from a hillside by the partially ruined Dervish monastery of **Ak Yazula Baba Tekke**. This sixteenth-century foundation consists of two seven-sided structures roughly 50m apart, with the smaller of the two, on the right, containing the still-intact *turbei,* or **tomb**, of Ak Yazula Baba himself. A fourteenth-century holy man who subsequently became an object of veneration for local Muslims, Yazula Baba attracted Dervish communities to the area and, although the latter have long since departed, the Tekke is still a powerful draw for both Muslims and Christians alike. Bulgarians believe it to be the last resting place both of St Athanasius (patron saint of lost sheep), and of the country's first Christian ruler, Knyaz Boris I, and pious shepherds used to sacrifice hundreds of sheep here on St George's Day – hence the name Obrochishte, which means "place of sacrifice". Even today local Muslims and Christians observe common holidays and join in each other's rites, assembling here to eat a sacrificial meal (followed inevitably by drinking and dancing) on four important dates of the year: Atanasovden (St Athanasius's Day, 19 Jan), Gergyovden (St George's Day, 6 May), Kurban bayram and Sheker bayram (both moveable Muslim feasts, see p.65 for details). The *turbe* is open daily between 9.30am and 4pm (2Lv entrance), and pilgrims can always thrust their hands through a special opening in the building to acquire good fortune from the head of the saint buried within. Visitors also hang clothes or strips of cloth on neighbouring trees to ensure good health and protection from evil. The roofless ruin to the left of the *turbe* is the old Dervish *imaret*, or refectory, where people gather on the four main holy days to cook vast cauldrons of meat.

Only 3km from the Albena roundabout, Obrochishte is an easy walk from the resort itself: an asphalt path runs parallel to the road on the lefthand side. Otherwise, hourly Albena–Dobrich buses pass through the village.

Balchik

Occupying a succession of sandy cliffs and crumbling sugar-loaf hills, **BALCHIK**'s whitewashed cottages hover precipitously above a series of ravines running down to the sea. It's the kind of scene beloved of artists, and Balchik-inspired seascapes are a regular sight in provincial galleries throughout Bulgaria. Founded by the Milesians in the sixth century BC and named Krounoi ("The Springs"), the town was a valued haven for Greek merchants attempting to pass the treacherous waters around Cape Kaliakra, as well as an important centre for viniculture – hence its later name, Dionysopolis, honouring the god of the vine. By the sixth century AD, the harbour had silted up, and the Turks were subsequently to dub the town Balchik, or "Town of Clay".

Despite being popular with Bulgarians who take advantage of the numerous private rooms and inexpensive hotels, Balchik doesn't see many foreign tourists, largely because it lacks a really good beach. Package tourists from Albena (see p.403) are, however, bussed into town during the day to stroll around the streets and visit Balchik's main attraction: the **summer palace of Queen Marie of Romania**, a reminder of the interwar years when Balchik was ruled from Bucharest.

The Town

Assuming that you arrive at the **bus station**, any exploration of Balchik should begin with the **National Revival Complex** at Hristo Botev 4 (officially Mon–Fri 9am–noon & 2–5pm; 2Lv): head uphill from the bus station and take a left when you see the whitewashed church bell-tower. The complex consists of a reconstructed nineteenth-century schoolhouse (note the cage for unruly pupils) which shares a pleasant garden with the Church of Sveti Nikolov, built in 1845 by local National Revival architect Koyu Raichov. The iconostasis is decorated with pictures by itinerant artists from Galichnik in western Macedonia, and there's a splendid gold-suffused portrait of the saint himself, patron of seafarers, on the left side of the nave as you enter. There is no entry fee for the church but its opening hours are erratic; you may need to ask staff at the History Museum (see below) to open it.

Heading downhill from the bus station you'll soon come across the **History Museum** on ploshtad Nezavisimost (Mon–Fri 8am–noon & 2–5.30pm; 2Lv), which contains marble and bronze statuary from Dionysopolis, including a torso of the deity himself. Opposite is a small **Ethnographic Museum** (same times; 2Lv) displaying traditional local costumes and reconstructed nineteenth-century peasant interiors. From here the main thoroughfare, ulitsa Cherno More, winds down to the port, passing on the way a flight of steps leading up to an **art gallery**, at ul. Otets Paisii 4 (officially Mon–Fri 9am–noon & 1–5pm; 2Lv), which features icons from local churches. At the bottom of the hill, a small whitewashed mosque stands inland from the port, where looming grain silos blight a lively seafront square.

From here an esplanade stretches westwards past the misshapen concrete lumps that form Balchik's sea defences. There are a few areas of sand (shipped in every spring to create an artificial beach), although most sunbathers prefer to position themselves on the various piers and jetties protruding into the bay.

The palace of Queen Marie

Two kilometres west of town, ranged on a hillside overlooking the sea, is the **Quiet Nest** (summer daily 8am-9pm; winter hours unpredictable; 10Lv for both the palace and the gardens), summer residence of Queen Marie of Romania. Kent-born Marie, a granddaughter of Queen Victoria, ordered the construction of a series of follies here in 1936, presided over by a whimsical-looking villa topped by a minaret (the reconciliation of her Christian and Muslim subjects was one of Marie's pet projects, inspired either by her adherence to the Baha'i faith or by her Turkish lover). The villa is a relatively modest affair as far as royal residences go: the ground floor is taken up with an art gallery and souvenir shop while the first floor shows Marie's hammam-like bathroom, boudoir, bedroom and salon as well as a two-room museum; behind the palace is an intriguing labyrinth of steeply ascending narrow terraces. Immediately below there's a popular artificial beach, as well as a number of bars. The surrounding **botanical gardens** (summer daily 8am–9pm; winter hours unpredictable), home to more than six hundred varieties of trees, shrubs and cacti, are dotted with enchanting pavilions where visitors can stay (Ⓣ0579/74452; ❹). Descending towards the sea just behind the villa are six terraces – one for each of Marie's children, the sixth one (truncated by the cliff) symbolizing Mircea, who died of typhus at the age of two. To the east of the villa are several set-piece follies, including a water mill, a rose garden, a Roman bath, and a small chapel, where naively executed frescoes include a picture of Marie herself in Byzantine garb. The queen left instructions for her heart to be buried within the chapel in a jewelled casket – the latter was hurriedly removed from Balchik in 1940, when Bulgaria regained the southern Dobrudzha.

You can see the Quiet Nest's minaret clearly from Balchik's seafront esplanade: unfortunately, the gardens are not accessible from here, its lower gates locked to discourage bathers from picnicking in the grounds. Head instead for the northern entrance, just off the Balchik–Albena road – best reached by following ulitsa Primorski westwards from the port, or taking the Balchik–Albena bus (every 30min from Balchik's port area; ask to be put down at *dvoretsa*, "the palace").

Practicalities

Balchik's bus station (where minibuses for Varna line up waiting for passengers) is on the high ground above the town centre, just over 1km from the seafront. From here ulitsa Cherno More winds down the hill to the town centre and the port, to the east of which lies the main beach. Albena–Balchik buses pick up and drop off at ploshtad Ribarski, by the port, where you'll find the Chaika tourist office, (daily 8am–8pm; Ⓣ & Ⓕ0579/72053, Ⓔchaika@mail.bg), which can arrange private rooms (❷) graded according to their distance from the sea; expect to pay 15Lv per person for something 1km away, slightly more for something central. Otherwise, the best hotels are the *Jupiter*, just above the beach at ulitsa Timok 1 (Ⓣ0579/76470; ❹), offering clean, modern en-suite rooms, and the *Byala Kûshta*, five minutes west of the port at Geo Milev 18 (Ⓣ0579/73822 or 73951; ❹), which has lovely pine-floored rooms with sea views, satellite TV and breakfast included. The nearby *Two Cocks* (Ⓣ0579/76455 or 76460) offers a similar standard, with comfortable en-suite doubles (❹), sea-facing apartments (❺) and a swimming pool.

Opportunities for eating and drinking in Balchik tend to be concentrated on the seafront path west of the port, where several outdoor restaurants and cafés serve grilled fish, coffee and spirits until late: *Lotos* is one of the best of these. *Morsko Oko* is a traditional-style *mehana* right behind the tourist office on Primorska, while just off ploshtad Ribarski, facing the sea, is *Roma Club*, a flashy pizza and pasta joint.

Kavarna and Cape Kaliakra

Eighteen kilometres along the coast from Balchik, **KAVARNA** was probably founded by the Mesembrians in order to challenge the importance of the harbour at nearby Krounoi. A predominantly Greek and Gagauz town in the nineteenth century, Kavarna was burned to the ground by marauding Circassians (Turkic Muslims from the Caucasus) in July 1877, and at least 1000 of its townsfolk murdered. Nowadays it's a quiet place, lying a couple of kilometres inland from the seafront, where there's a small beach resort, the **Morska zvezda**, and a port used for the export of Dobrudzhan grain. It's a good spot from which to explore the coastal cliffs just to the east which culminate in the dramatic **Cape Kaliakra**.

Kavarna

Ulitsa Dobrotitsa heads from the bus station into the town centre, where steps behind the *Julie* hotel descend to a fourteenth-century Turkish *hammam* containing the **Marine Museum** on ulitsa Chirakman (summer Tues–Sun 8am–noon & 2–6pm; winter hours unpredictable; 3Lv) where visitors can see a 3000-year-old anchor as well as a collection of other treasures from the sea. Nearby at ul. Chernomorska 1B the **Historical Museum** (Tues–Sun 8am-noon & 2-6pm; 3Lv) houses an exhibition telling of the local noble Balik, who set up an independent principality based on Kavarna in the 1340s, extending his power southwards as far as the River Kamchiya. His son Dobrotitsa wrested independence from his nominal suzerains the Bulgarian tsars, and severed links with the Tûrnovo patriarchate, accepting the writ of Constantinople instead.

A couple of blocks west of here lies an **Ethnographic Museum** (Mon–Fri 8am–noon & 1–5pm; 3Lv), housed in a former schoolhouse, its classrooms now decorated in the style of a typical small-town family home of the nineteenth century. Among the oddities on display is a mirror framed by fine lacy curtains: the curtains were drawn for forty days in the event of a death in the family.

As for **accommodation** the *Julie* hotel at ul. Dobrotitsa 6 (ⓣ0570/85889; ❷) is modern and comfortable with a bar and restaurant, while a little further from the centre, several hillside hotels overlook the newly built Chirakmana area on the seafront, among them the *Kavarna* (ⓣ0570/85101; ❷), which is clean though a little sterile and often overrun with tourist groups, and the *Venera* (ⓣ0570/82254; ❷), which has a much cosier atmosphere and an excellent restaurant. The beachfront shops and cafes that make up the Chirakmana area are reached by regular buses from town; there's also a Chinese **restaurant** and a cluster of places serving seafood and Bulgarian dishes. Finally, there are a couple of very tranquil alternatives 4km before Kavarna on the road from Balchik. The *Saint George* (ⓣ0570/86174, ⓕ82097) is a slightly run-down complex of two hotels (❷), a restaurant and a tree-shaded campsite (5Lv per person) with a great view of the bay. Nearby, the single track road after the turning to the *Saint George* leads to the luxury hotel complex of *Byala Laguna* (ⓣ0579/76917; ❼) which occupies an idyllic and isolated spot on the coast with outdoor restaurants, a swimming pool and fitness facilities.

Cape Kaliakra and Bûlgarevo

Bulgarians make much of the "Beautiful Headland" – as **CAPE KALIAKRA** (3Lv admission if the kiosk on the road to the cape is manned), a reddish crag rearing 70m above the sea, was dubbed during the Middle Ages. Along the shore are ruined fortifications raised as early as the fourth century BC (according to Strabo) and subsequently enlarged by the Roman and Byzantine empires, which reached their zenith during the fourth century when the *bolyari* Balik and Dobrotitsa ordered shafts dug through the rock so that the garrison could be supplied by sea. Legend has it that during the Ottoman conquest forty women tied their hair together and jumped from the rocks rather than be raped by the Turks. The headland is covered in evocative ruins, mostly dating from the Middle Ages, and a **museum** in one of the caves (mid-May to mid-Oct daily 10am–7pm) commemorates Russian Admiral Ushkov's defeat of the Turkish fleet in 1791 and the sinking of the Ottoman gunboat *Hamidie* by the Bulgarian navy in 1912. There's also some delicately wrought medieval jewellery on display, and gaming dice used by thirteenth-century soldiers. The cave is said by Muslims to contain the grave of **Sari Saltuk**, a mythical Turkish hero who, in the style of St George, came here to kill a seven-headed dragon and thereby free two of the sultan's daughters. Christians claim that it is the last resting place of St Nicholas, who saves seafarers from shipwreck and guides fishermen towards their prey.

Four **buses** a day travel to the cape from Kavarna, via the Gaugauz village of **Bûlgarevo.** Alternatively, it's a straightforward one-hour walk across a coastal heath, covered in prickly shrubs and wild flowers. However, the asphalted track is unshaded, and the going can be tough at the height of summer. Luckily there's a **café-restaurant** in a cave next to Kaliakra's museum, but no **accommodation**.

BÛLGAREVO itself has a couple of **restaurants** and boasts an Internet connection in its tiny **Ethnographic Museum** (Mon-Fri 9am-noon & 2-6pm; free). It also has the very helpful **Kaliakra Nature Information Centre** (daily 9am-6pm; ⓣ05744/424) opposite the main square, which has films and photographs of the region, arranges **private rooms** in the village (❶), and rents out bicycles (1Lv per hour). For those willing to go a little further to eat, 1km out of Bûlgareyo on the way to Kavarna is an unmarked road to the left. Five hundred metres further on, a rutted dirt track bears right towards the coast and a steep concrete road down to a mussel farm that doubles as an idyllic and incredibly popular seafront restaurant, *Dalboka* (ⓣ048/911377), with mussels as its speciality.

Rusalka and the coastal steppe

From Bûlgarevo, a minor road runs northeast to the one-horse settlement of **Sveti Nikola**, where the Vodasport centre (ⓣ05744/601 or 0888 397 160, ⓦwww.vodasport.net) offers various **underwater** experiences in the Bulgarian Black Sea's most impressive diving waters, ranging from a two-hour "try-a-dive" (40Lv) to a full PADI Open Water Diver Course (480Lv), all of which are best booked in advance. The road out of Sveti Nikola towards the coast leads sharply downhill to Taouk Liman, the Bay of Birds, better known as the **Rusalka Holiday Village**. A villa complex accompanied by the usual bars and restaurants, Rusalka is a quieter alternative to the bigger resorts to the south, a temptingly isolated place whose brace of shingle beaches is framed by moody, crumbling cliffs. Rusalka is a small enough resort to have an intimate, family feel, with plenty of supervised activities to keep young children busy, while older holidaymakers can enjoy scuba diving, windsurfing, tennis or horseriding. There's also an imaginatively conceived **Underwater Museum**; really a collection of ancient anchors positioned a few metres offshore, which can be visited in the company of a guide from the resort's scuba-diving school. Accommodation in Rusalka's villas (ⓣ02/9624215) is relatively expensive (❺) but all food and most activities are included in the price. Buses to Rusalka leave Kavarna every thirty minutes.

Rusalka stands in the middle of one of the last surviving stretches of uncultivated **steppe** in Europe, a thin coastal ribbon rich in wild grasses, herbs, insects and bird life. Carpeted by wild flowers in May, the steppe is taken over by hardier, though no less alluring, thistles as the summer progresses. Group walks and 4WD safaris, led by expert guides in the local flora and fauna, are sometimes on offer from Rusalka; otherwise it's a question of just heading north or south out of the resort and seeing where you end up. Resist the temptation to pick any plants; most are protected by law. The steppe can also be accessed from the village of **KAMEN BRYAG**, 5km up the coast from Sveti Nikola and reachable by one early **bus** a day from Kavarna (Mon-Fri only). Two **restaurants** and a barely stocked shop service the village, which has long been a popular summer hangout for adventurous young Bulgarians. **Accommodation** can be found by asking the village's elderly residents if they have rooms available (❶); the *Trita Kestena* restaurant (ⓣ05744/759) also has **private**

rooms and **bungalows** (❶). **Camping** on the clifftop is free though there are no toilets or washing facilities other than those provided by the restaurants. Climbers are attracted by the region's limestone cliffs and a centre in the village is currently being set up to offer guided deep-water climbs (Ⓣ02/8622589 or 0888 847 776). A track leads east out of the village onto a heath-covered clifftop, where you're bound to come across one of the many family graves hewn out of the rock here, remnants of a second-to-fifth-century **necropolis** thought to be the work of Sarmatians – a northern Black Sea tribe who travelled down from the Crimea before intermarrying with local stock and disappearing for ever. Work your way south from here to find a path leading down to the ruins of a late-Roman fortress and a grass-tufted clifftop meadow known as **Yailata**, a sublime spot from which to survey the northern coastline.

The potholed road north of Kamen Bryag passes a landscape littered with rusting metal tanks that once stored oil pumped from the ground; now mostly derelict, they spew out a constant stream of hot sulphurous water that locals and tourists alike use as showers. In the next village north, **TYULENOVO**, a small **restaurant** nestles on rocks overlooking a tiny natural harbour, and just up the road the *Orbita* **hotel** (Ⓣ & Ⓕ05743/3261; ❷) has a restaurant and clean modern rooms looking out to sea.

Around Shabla, and the Durankulak border crossing

The majority of buses heading north from Kavarna take the main E87 road further inland and aim for **SHABLA**, a small farming town made up of the neat, whitewashed one-storey houses so typical of the Dobrudzha. A couple of **restaurants** serve decent food and drink in the centre and the refurbished *Shabla* **hotel** (❷) has simple, clean rooms. In summer local minibuses offer a shuttle service from here to the seafront, 5km northeast of town, where the *Dobrudzha* **campsite** offers comfortable bungalows for rent (❷) and accepts campers for 5Lv per person. There are a couple of beach bars and a restaurant serving grilled fish, but this relatively little-visited part of the coast seems a world away from the packed beaches of Varna, Golden Sands and Albena. Immediately north of the campsite are two lakes shrouded in bullrushes, the **Shablensko ezero** and the **Ezerechko ezero**, frequented by many varieties of birds, principally ibises, herons and grebes. Beyond here an enticing landscape of deserted beaches and crumbling ochre cliffs carries on for kilometres. Incidentally, a couple of kilometres before Shabla is another village, confusingly named **Shabla**, which has a lighthouse to differentiate it. A rutted track leads to the left of the lighthouse, past a cluttered mix of ramshackle fishing huts and newly built villas, to the signposted *Bai Pesho* fish **restaurant**, poised on rocky cliffs above the sea and offering several **private rooms** (Ⓣ0888/221771; ❷) as well as its legendary *ribena churba* (fish soup).

Served by a single daily bus from Shabla, the seaside village of **KRAPETS**, 10km north, is a sleepy place known for its dunes and bird life. Locked in rural solitude, it's an ideal place to get away from it all, but the beachside **campsite**, the *Krapets*, with bungalows (Ⓣ05749/215; ❶), just outside the village, is in a sorry state though improvements are expected. The nearby three-star **hotel**, the *Yanitsa* (Ⓣ05749/324 or 325; ❸), is a pricier and far superior alternative which also has an excellent restaurant.

Further up the coast is **DURANKULAK**, another rural community famous for being the epicentre of the 1900 peasant rebellion against the *desyatŭk*, a crippling tax imposed on agricultural produce by the Radoslavov regime. Six kilometres east of town is the Durankaluk lake **nature reserve**, where the entire population of the globally threatened red-breasted goose winters; white pelican, pygmy cormorant and the bittern, among many other bird species, can also be spotted there. The lake's largest island, reachable by road, is home to the Durankulak **Archeological Park** where remains of some of Europe's first stone-built architecture dating back to 7000 BC can be found alongside a 1200-grave prehistoric necropolis, a temple to the goddess Kibella, and a proto-Bulgarian village from 900-1000 AD. On the lake's northern shore, accessed by a marked track from the road northeast of Durankulak is the popular *Zlatna Ribka* **restaurant**, serving fresh fish from the lake. Three kilometres further north are two neighbouring beachfront **campsites**, *Kosmos Camping* (Ⓣ05748/263; bungalows ❶, camping 5Lv per person) with adequate facilities and a well-positioned restaurant; and the brand-new *Dell Camping*, a centre for "professional education and recreation" offering deluxe bungalows and facilities intended for clients of Dell and Microsoft in Bulgaria, but also available to individuals (❸). Needless to say, it has the only Internet facilities for miles around.

Crossing **the border** to Romania 6km north involves catching one of the three daily buses from Shabla to Durankulak before completing the remaining 6km of the journey on foot or by taxi. The 24-hour border post is relatively quiet, but you should still allow an hour if crossing by car, less if you're on foot. Taxi drivers on the other side will take you to the resort town of **Mangalia**, 10km away, where you can link up with the Romanian public transport system.

South of Varna

Although there's no direct rail link along the coast it is possible to travel from Varna to Burgas by train: a time-consuming inland journey, usually involving at least one change. It's far better, however, to take one of the regular buses running **south of Varna** along the E87 highway, a road that winds its way across the coastal hills, occasionally offering glimpses of the sea. Ultimately you hit the mega-resort of Sunny Beach some 100km to the south, but the towns you pass along the way are among the quietest of the Black Sea coast. They're seldom visited by anybody but Bulgarians, and some are visibly suffering from the decline in the cheap-and-cheerful Eastern European tourism of the Communist era. You'll find a scattering of campsites, and plenty of families offering **rooms**, but the *kvartirno byuros* that used to handle them are thin on the ground – be prepared to ask around.

Kamchiya

South of Lake Varna the highway swings inland to climb the Momino plateau, and you won't catch sight of the sea again for another 55km unless you take one of the minor roads which branch off towards the coast. The first of these, approximately 25km out from Varna just beyond the village of Bliznatsi, descends to the mouth of the **Kamchiya**, a slow-moving silt-laden soup of a river where you'll find a small resort beside the wooded estuary. The main attraction is the **Kamchiya nature reserve** slightly upstream, an area of marshy forest and luxuriant vegetation known as the Longoza, which covers about thirty square kilometres. The waters are rich in pike and carp, and wild pigs run free in the woods. In high season **boat trips** commence from the river's mouth, although the Longoza's elusive pelicans, kingfishers and waterfowl tend to make themselves scarce when they hear the tourists coming.

Only two buses a day run from Varna to Kamchiya, making it just about feasible as a day-trip. There's a lovely **beach** just north of the estuary, with a few food-and-drink shacks, and the *Kamchiya* hotel (☎05144/320 or 329; ❸), which boasts its own swimming pool, restaurant and nightclub. Most of the campsites signposted off Kamchiya's maze of narrow roads don't actually cater for campers, but offer Communist-era bungalows of varying standards: *Camping Rai* (☎05144/262) has comfortable bungalows with en-suite bathrooms (❷) and allows camping for 7Lv per person, while *Camping Mechta* (☎05144/223) has basic bungalows with communal facilities (❶).

Shkorpilovtsi

Further south a minor road leaves the E87 at Staro Oryahovo for **SHKORPILOVTSI**, 11km away on the coast. Currently a modest resort with a dune beach, much of the seafront – including the last remaining campsites in the region – has been bought up by ambitious developers, so don't be surprised if the place resembles a construction site when you arrive. In the meantime *Hotel Jordash* (☎05140/235, ⓔjordash@abv.bg) has air-conditioned rooms (❷) and bungalows (❶), and you can pitch a tent in its grounds for 10Lv. Just beyond is the *Hotel Alexander* (☎05140/373) which has a small restaurant on the beachfront and offers comfortable apartments (❷). The town itself was named after the Czech Skorpil brothers who "founded" Bulgarian archeology in the late nineteenth century. Karel and Herman Skorpil came to Varna in 1882 and immediately began sorting out and cataloguing the region's antiquities, a collection that formed the basis of the Varna Historical Museum (see p.393). They were pioneers in the field of medieval Bulgarian archeology too, and Karel was honoured by being buried among the ruins of the medieval capital Pliska (see p.276).

Byala, Obzor and beyond

Seven kilometres beyond Staro Oryahovo, the highway veers eastwards, passing vineyards whose grapes are made into Dimyat **wine** at **BYALA**, a small town facing Cape Atanas. There are plenty of private rooms here, and a sprinkling of largely Bulgarian tourists, though despite the town's increasing popularity it has yet to be overrun with the trinket stalls and accompanying paraphernalia that blight the streets of similar places such as Obzor. The **tourist information centre** (Mon-Sat 8am-8pm; ☎05143/2406) on the main street can arrange private rooms (❶); on the edge of town and with great views of the coast is the *Hotel Laguna* (☎0888 310 012; ❷); nearby is *Byala Vista* (☎0898 517 444, ⓦwww.byalavista.com) with self-catering apartments (❷). A couple of kilometres south, the excellent *Chayka* fish restaurant overlooks the bay and Byala's harbour.

The small resort of **OBZOR** is 5km south of Byala. Known to the Greeks as Heliopolis, or City of the Sun, the town's heyday came in the Roman period, when, under the name of Navlohos, it became a fortified trading settlement. The broken columns of the Temple of Jupiter can still be seen in the large park to the left of Obzor's main square, but its principal asset nowadays is the aforementioned beach to the north. Much more animated than Byala, its bustling streets jammed with traders selling plastic souvenirs, Obzor is popular with Bulgarians and East Europeans, and is well served with family-run cafés and restaurants. **Private rooms** are available from the Soti-Sis tourist office (daily 9am-8pm; ☎0554/32887 or 32888) at the bus station for (❶), and incoming buses during the summer are met by a cluster of locals eager to rent rooms (❶). *Gergana Camping* (☎0888 620 515) at the southern end of town has bungalows

(❶) and charges 5Lv per person for campers. Those seeking a higher standard of accommodation can try the *Paraiso Beach* hotel on the seafront at ul. Chernomorska 16 (Ⓣ0554/33290 or 33291, Ⓕ33295; ❸); further up the scale and a little further along the same road is the *Helios Beach* hotel (Ⓣ0554/32115; ❽) with pool, sauna and fitness centre.

Heading south, 4km out of Obzor, a left turn leads to *Chayka Camping* (open July & Aug only) one of the few remaining seaside **campsites** in the region with bungalows (❶) and camping for 4Lv per person. The road then turns inland once more, ascending the ridge of a mountain that slopes down to Nos Emine, Bulgaria's stormiest cape, where a signpost for **Irakli** points left off the main road and leads you to a small beach bar and **campsite** (Ⓣ0554/37267) offering basic bungalows (❶). The as yet unspoiled beach beyond the bar is popular with Bulgarian naturists who pitch tents there for free and use the campsite's facilities. A rough track from Irakli winds its way several kilometres to the tiny hillside village of **EMONA** which has fantastic views of the cape, and where the only disturbances are goat bells and the occasional howl of a jackal. Most of the clean modern rooms at *Hotel Emona* (Ⓣ054/37093; ❶) have sea views and its **restaurant** serves decent Bulgarian cuisine; the only alternative is the characterful *Zayek* restaurant a few streets below, again with good Bulgarian cuisine as well as great home-made *(domashen) rakia*.

Back on the road from Obzor you'll pass through **Banya**, a pleasant highland village presiding over a carpet of vineyards. From here there is a slow climb through dense forest after which the main road descends for a magnificent view of Nesebûr, the southern coastline and the distant Strandzha massif.

Sunny Beach and around

Slûnchev bryag – called Sonnenstrand by the Germans and **SUNNY BEACH** by the Brits – is Bulgaria's largest, and least atmospheric, coastal resort. It's a vast, only partly shaded expanse of hotels interspersed with restaurants, snack bars and other places to spend money, and on (rare) rainy days its soullessness quickly becomes apparent. Its main drawback is sheer size: it's impossible to explore the resort's facilities without shuttling up and down the main strip by bus, and the anonymous gridiron-style layout of the place can be disorientating. While many of the resort's individual hotels (especially those favoured by Western package groups) have been tastefully refurbished, the general infrastructure – the roads, pavements and stretches of park – remain poorly cared for. Independent travellers would be better off staying in nearby Nesebûr, a perfectly handy base from which to make use of Sunny Beach's admittedly excellent eight-kilometre-long stretch of sand – which has received the coveted international Blue Flag award – and for taking advantage of some of the liveliest nightlife to be found on the Black Sea coast.

Though Varna–Burgas buses pass through Sunny Beach, most people approach the resort from Burgas, from where there are bus services every twenty minutes. You'll be hard pushed to find accommodation in high season if you just turn up on spec, and it's best to make enquiries in advance: the Kometa 2 **tourist office** in the centre of Sunny Beach (daily 9am-9pm; Ⓣ0554/22176, Ⓦwww.kometa2.com) arranges accommodation in hotels (❸–❹) and self-catering apartments (❺–❼). Otherwise, tourist offices in Burgas or Nesebûr should be able to help. The website Ⓦwww.nesebar.com is also a useful source of information.

Sveti Vlas and Elenite

Hourly buses head from Sunny Beach to **SVETI VLAS**, 6km away on the northern shoulder of the bay. Increasingly popular as an elite vacation venue for Bulgarians, the village is currently groaning under the weight of over-hasty development. New hotels abound, and there are the makings of a good beach, 1km away from the village across untidy scrubland. Kometa 2 tourist bureau has another office here (daily 9am–9pm; ⓣ0554/68294; ⓕ68112) and can arrange private rooms (❷) as well as hotel accommodation. One of the best of the new **hotels** is the four-star *Sineva*, (ⓣ0554/68934, ⓕ68308; ❺), which offers very comfortable air-conditioned rooms as well as fitness facilities and a swimming pool overlooking the sea. A slightly cheaper option is the *Santorini* (ⓣ0554/68894; ❹), which has a decent restaurant and is close to the beach.

Buses continue northwards to the **ELENITE HOLIDAY VILLAGE**, 6km further up the coast, a predominantly package destination divided into two villa colonies sharing restaurants, bars and discos. It's a well-run resort with pristine two- and three-storey villas, a good beach, good sporting facilities, and childcare provision in a central kindergarten, although it can seem rather isolated if you're after more than just a beach holiday. A central reception desk ⓣ0554/68960, ⓔelenite@nesebar.com) allocates all-inclusive room packages (❼).

Nesebûr

Three kilometres south of Sunny Beach, a slender isthmus connects the old town of **NESEBÛR** (ancient Mesembria) with the mainland, ensuring a constant stream of visitors to what was once undoubtedly a beautiful spot. Harbouring the best of the coast's nineteenth-century **wooden architecture**, as well as a unique collection of medieval **churches**, it's easy to see why Nesebûr has become the most publicized (and commercialized) of Bulgaria's Black Sea attractions. At the height of summer the town can be more than a little oppressive, its narrow cobbled streets crammed with packs of tourists, countless tacky souvenir stalls, and persistent restaurant touts, but a willingness to put up with the crowds is rewarded by Nesebûr's many fine sights.

A thriving port in **Greek and Roman** times, Nesebûr really came into its own with the onset of the **Byzantine** era, when it became the obvious stopover for ships sailing between Constantinople and the Danube. The Byzantines used Nesebûr as a base from which to assail the **First Bulgarian Kingdom** during the eighth century, provoking Khan Krum to seize it in 812. The bellicose Bulgar captured tons of booty in the process, including the formula for "Greek Fire", an explosive mixture which the Byzantines relied on for their military superiority over the "barbarians".

Nesebûr passed from Byzantine to Bulgarian ownership several times throughout the Middle Ages, and was one of the last outposts remaining in the hands of the beleaguered Byzantine Empire in its dying days, but it continued to thrive regardless. Under the Ottomans, it remained the seat of a Greek bishopric and an important centre of Greek culture, which is why so many medieval churches have survived here. In the long run, however, Varna and Burgas were to grow at Nesebûr's expense, hastening its decline into a humble fishing port. After the Russo-Turkish War of 1828, when the bulk of the population sided with the Russians, most of Nesebûr's leading families emigrated to Odessa, leaving a much diminished population earning a living by building caïques. Nowadays Nesebûr depends on **tourism**, its fishing fleet unable to employ enough of the 7000 inhabitants, of whom about 3000 live on the peninsula, the remainder on the mainland.

Arrival, information and accommodation

Getting to Nesebûr is easy: buses run every twenty minutes from Sunny Beach, and every forty minutes from Burgas, 35km down the coast. There are

The Black Sea Greeks I: Ancient Colonists

Why, or precisely when, the ancient Greeks first ventured north into the Black Sea remains the subject of much conjecture. The vast, mysterious body of water, which they initially called the *Axeinos*, or "inhospitable", sea, lay on the very fringes of the known world, and was regarded as a treacherous and forbidding place even for experienced mariners, who were more used to island-hopping in the Aegean; Herodotus tells us that from one end to the other was a voyage of nine days, while the lands around were home to "the most uncivilized nations in the world". Heroic legends such as the tales of the **Argonauts**, the intrepid band of Golden-Fleece-seeking adventurers who sailed to Colchis (modern Georgia) on the far coast, and the **Amazons**, the wild tribeswomen whose domain lay beyond the northern shores, emphasize the awe in which the sea was held in antiquity. By the seventh century BC, however, Greeks from Asia Minor were beginning to establish a string of colonies in the region, first along the coast of northern Turkey, subsequently moving on to the shores of what is now Bulgaria, Romania and Ukraine.

Overpopulation and political upheaval at home obviously helped to precipitate this sudden burst of outward migration, but opportunities for trade played a part too – the lands around the sea had an almost mythical reputation for wealth, and a wide variety of goods was traded. Pioneers in colonizing the Black Sea were the Greeks of **Miletus** (a city-state on the Aegean coast of Turkey), although some Bulgarian historians argue that they merely followed in the footsteps of their neighbours the Carians: a race from Asia Minor (closely related to Bulgaria's Thracians) who had developed mercantile contacts in the Black Sea several generations earlier.

Apollonia (now Sozopol) was Miletus' first colony on the Bulgarian coast, soon followed by **Odyssos** (Varna), **Anchialos** (Pomorie) and **Krounoi** (Balchik). In many cases the colonists settled on or near an existing Thracian port: this was certainly so with **Mesembria** (Nesebûr), where the natives were ejected by newcomers from the Greek mainland city of Megara and its colony of Byzantium. Having settled down and established a network of maritime trade, the Greeks optimistically renamed the sea *Euxinos*, or "hospitable" – which remained its name throughout the Classical era.

These colonies couldn't have survived without friendly contacts with the Thracians, and a mutually beneficial system of **trade** developed. The Thracians obtained wine and salt (salt-pans are still a feature of the regional economy, especially around Pomorie) in return for grain and livestock – which the Greeks then re-exported at a tidy profit. **Intermarriage** must have been common from the earliest days, and cities such as Odyssos developed a thriving hybrid culture where colonists and natives lived cheek-by-jowl, observing each other's customs and paying homage to each other's gods.

also regular minibuses from Burgas, and infrequent "water taxis" from Sunny Beach, as well as an express bus service, running four or five times a day in summer, from Varna. The website Ⓦwww.nesebar.com contains some useful **information** on accommodation in the town. Internet access is available in the new town opposite the post office.

There is a wide choice of **accommodation** available, largely consisting of a growing number of small, family-run hotels; however, these tend to fill up quickly during summer, and you'd be well advised to book in advance. It's also worth noting that the larger hotels in the new part of town, towards Sunny Beach, are often fully booked by package tour groups at this time of year. **Private rooms** (❷), many of them in atmospheric old houses, are available through Messemvria Holidays, located in an alleyway on the corner of ul. Ribarska and ul. Mesembriya (daily 9am–8pm; Ⓣ0554/45880, Ⓦwww.messemvria.com), which can

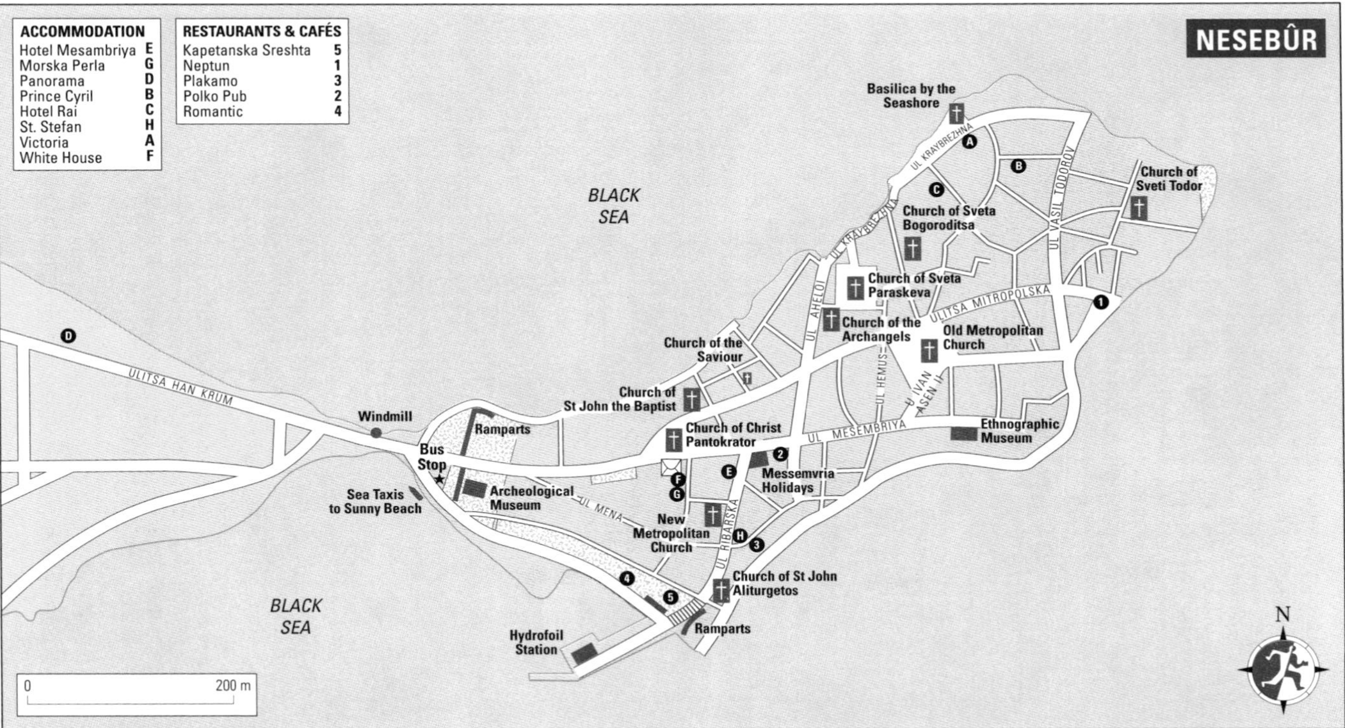
NESEBÛR
ACCOMMODATION
Hotel Mesambriya E
Morska Perla G
Panorama D
Prince Cyril B
Hotel Rai C
St. Stefan H
Victoria A
White House F
RESTAURANTS & CAFÉS
Kapetanska Sreshta 5
Neptun 1
Plakamo 3
Polko Pub 2
Romantic 4
Basilica by the Seashore
UL KRAYBREZHNA
Church of Sveti Todor
UL VASIL TODOROV
Church of Sveta Bogoroditsa
Church of Sveta Paraskeva
ULITSA MITROPOLSKA
Church of the Archangels
Old Metropolitan Church
UL AHELOI
UL HEMUS
U IVAN ASEN II
Church of the Saviour
Church of St John the Baptist
Church of Christ Pantokrator
UL MESEMBRIYA
Ethnographic Museum
Messemvria Holidays
New Metropolitan Church
UL RIBARSKA
Church of St John Aliturgetos
Ramparts
BLACK SEA
Sunny Beach & Burgas
ULITSA HAN KRUM
Windmill
Bus Stop
Sea Taxis to Sunny Beach
Archeological Museum
UL MENA
Hydrofoil Station
0
200 m
N

△ Docked boats at sunset, Nesebûr

also book hotel rooms (❸–❺) or self-catering apartments (❸–❼) and arranges a variety of excursions. Ecotour (daily 9am-7pm; Ⓣ0554/43200) is based in the post office of the new town and can arrange private rooms (❶).

Hotels

Hotel Mesambriya ul. Ribarska Ⓣ0554/43255. Rather drab and old-fashioned hotel, but as the old town's cheapest it's often booked up by tour groups in high season. ❸

Morska Perla ul. Tsar Simeon 4 Ⓣ0554/45606. Modern three-storey block, behind the post office. Most of the neat en-suite rooms have balconies, and there's one ground-floor apartment. ❺

Panorama corner of ul. Vasil Levski and ul. Han Krum Ⓣ0554/44236. Modern high-rise in the new part of town, across the causeway, which offers small balconied rooms with a/c and a top-floor restaurant. Tends to be block-booked by tour groups in summer. ❹

Prince Cyril ul. Slavyanska 9 Ⓣ0554/42220, Ⓔprincecyril_hotel@abv.bg. Nicely decorated hotel, whose pine-furnished en-suite rooms come with TV and fridge, and there's also a couple of four-person apartments. ❺

Hotel Rai ul. Sadala 7 Ⓣ0554/46094. Small, cosy hotel with comfortable, a/c en-suites, down a side street off ul. Kraybrezhna. ❸

St. Stefan ul. Ribarska Ⓣ0554/43603. One of Nesebûr's newest, and priciest hotels, in a very central location, just opposite the church of the same name. Most of the plainly furnished rooms come with balconies, and there's also a gym, sauna and Jacuzzi on site. ❹

Sveti Georgi ul. Sadala 10 Ⓣ0554/44045. Unremarkable modern place a few doors down from the *Victoria*, with clean en-suites and a communal TV lounge. Usually fully booked by tour operators. ❹

Victoria ul. Kraybrezhna 22 Ⓣ0554/46000. Stylish modern hotel in a typical old wooden house, offering smart rooms with balconies, some with splendid sea views. ❺

White House ul. Tsar Simeon 2 Ⓣ0554/42488. Modern block next door to the *Morska Perla*, with clean en-suites and a couple of roomy apartments sleeping up to four people. ❹–❼

The Town

Approaching the peninsula you'll pass a wooden **windmill** of the type once found by the dozen in every coastal town. Ahead loom the massive **ramparts** that protected Nesebûr in antiquity; blocks from the Greek fortifications of the fourth century BC serve as foundations for the masonry and brick walls of Roman and Byzantine times. Just inside the gateway, an **Archeological Museum** (Mon–Fri 9am–1pm & 2–7pm, Sat 9am–1pm, Sun 2–6pm; 2.50Lv) houses an interesting collection of votive plaques, tombstones, coins and other evidence of Nesebûr's classical past (captioned in English). One of the more intriguing artefacts on show is a small statue showing three separate images of Hecate, goddess of witches and fertility, dating from the second century BC. There's also a votive relief dedicated to the goddess by the *strategoi* or military rulers of Mesembria, from the same era. Other items include pottery imported from Greece, and gold jewellery such as some finely crafted earrings decorated with lions' heads, from the Hellenistic period. The basement, meanwhile, holds a small display of icons, dating back to the sixteenth and seventeenth centuries, as well as an eighteenth-century bishop's throne; the sixteenth-century icon of *Christ and the Pharisees* is particularly well preserved.

A rash of shops and outdoor cafés along ulitsa Mesembriya masks the transition into the **old town**, a maze of cobbled lanes and wooden houses juxtaposed with many of Nesebûr's antique churches. The Muskoyanin House, at ul. Mesembriya 34, contains an **Ethnographic Museum** (daily 9am–1pm & 2–7pm; 2.50Lv), with a disappointing lack of information on the fate of Black Sea Greeks (see boxes, p.414 and p.429). However, it's worth visiting to see the cunningly asymmetrical interior of the house, whose cosy wooden living-quarters overhang a sturdy ground floor of undressed masonry.

Nesebûr's churches

Though usually termed "Byzantine" by foreign art historians, Nesebûr's **churches** are understandably regarded by the locals as masterpieces of Bulgarian culture. Most of them are the result of three waves of building that corresponded to the era of Byzantine rule and the First and Second Bulgarian Kingdoms (which naturally drew upon Byzantine traditions). As they date from a period when control of the town changed hands frequently, and the ethnicity of the people who built them is hard to discern, it's probably fairest to regard them as products of a great Orthodox civilization – both Slav and Greek – which flourished in the Balkans during the late Middle Ages.

You first encounter an example from the reign of Tsar Ivan Aleksandûr (1331–71), who was responsible for several of Nesebûr's churches. A chunky, ruddy-hued structure of stone and brick, the **Church of Christ Pantokrator**, on ulitsa Mesembriya, is notable for its exterior decoration, with blind niches, turquoise ceramic inlays and red-brick motifs – all redolent of late Byzantine architecture. An unusual feature is the frieze of swastikas (an ancient symbol of the sun and continual change) on the apses. Currently used as an "art gallery" – basically a small shop selling mediocre works by local artists – the church is usually accessible during the daytime.

Just downhill from here, on ulitsa Mitropolska, lies the **Church of St John the Baptist**, whose plain, undressed stone exterior dates it to the eleventh century. Also converted into an art gallery, only one of its frescoes now survives: dating from the seventeenth century, it depicts St Marina pulling a devil from the sea before braining it with a hammer – possibly representing local merchants' hopes that their patron saint would deal with the Cossack pirates who raided Nesebûr in those days.

Better-preserved frescoes can be seen in the early seventeenth-century **Church of the Saviour** (*Sveti Spas*; Mon–Fri 10am–5.30pm, Sat & Sun 10am–1.30pm; 1.50Lv), whose dull exterior conceals colourful frescoes commissioned by local merchants of the time – evidence that a thriving and wealthy culture existed in Nesebûr even at the height of the Ottoman occupation. Scenes from the

Fishing in the Black Sea

The harbours of old peninsula towns like Nesebûr, Pomorie and Sozopol remain clogged with the small boats that traditionally provided most local families with a livelihood – **fishing**. Although the numbers of full-time fishermen are in decline, most families still have access to a boat and augment their income by fishing in the coastal waters.

The working year is dictated by the seasonal migrations of fish. Most activity takes place in the spring and autumn, when shoals of *skumrii* (mackerel) and *palamudi* (brown-striped tunny fish) pass along the Black Sea coast on their way between the waters of the Crimea and their wintering grounds in the Sea of Marmara and the Aegean. The *hamsiya*, or Black Sea anchovy, also makes fleeting appearances off the Bulgarian coast during its extensive circuits of the Black Sea, but the rest of the time people hunt *barbun* (mullet), *safrid* (scad), *kalkan* (turbot) and *tsatsa* (sprat) – piles of the latter, deep-fried and crispy, are a staple of coastal snack bars.

In recent decades it's become increasingly difficult to make a living from fishing, due to the **depletion** of the Black Sea's stocks. Those with small fishing operations feel particularly threatened by the big state-owned fleets operating out of Burgas, and are agitating for a complete ban on trawling in coastal waters. Such a ban would help preserve the small-town economy of places like Pomorie and Sozopol, but may not be enough to save the Black Sea's fish.

lives of Christ and the Virgin predominate, defaced by centuries-old graffiti of sailing vessels – an art form common to Nesebûr's churches, and executed by those praying for safety on the seas. One of the prettiest parts of town lies beyond, its cobbled alleys overhung by half-timbered houses carved with sun-signs, fish and other symbols. Here you'll find the **Church of the Archangels Michael and Gabriel**, featuring a chequered pattern of brick and stone on its blind niches, and the recently restored **Church of Sveta Paraskeva**, studded with green ceramics, which now houses an art gallery. Both date from the same period as the Christ Pantokrator church. Further northeast is the comparatively plain, nineteenth-century **Church of Sveta Bogoroditsa**, whose unremarkable facade hides an interesting collection of icons, some dating back to the seventeenth century. Also worth a look is the bishop's throne, with its armrests carved in the form of smiling fish.

The historic centre of town is now a small plaza occupied by picture-sellers, surrounding a pit containing the ruined **Old Metropolitan Church** (*Starata Mitropoliya*), built in the fifth or sixth century. It was here that bishops officiated during Nesebûr's heyday as a city-state, when Byzantine nobles demonstrated their wealth and piety by endowing more than forty ecclesiastical edifices. Several were concentrated at the northern tip of the peninsula, where the **Basilica by the Seashore** proved to be so vulnerable to raids by pirates that a fortified keep was added. Both are now in ruins, as is the old windmill in the vicinity, while the thirteenth-century **Church of Sveti Todor** nearby has become a gallery.

To wrap up Nesebûr's churches in some kind of chronological order, head back along ulitsa Mesembriya, then turn left down ulitsa Ribarska to find the **New Metropolitan Church**, known as Sveti Stefan (daily 9am–6pm; 1.50Lv). Founded in the tenth or eleventh century during the First Kingdom, the church was enlarged under the Second Kingdom, then supplanted the Old Metropolitan Church in the fifteenth century. Most of the frescoes that you see today were added in the sixteenth and seventeenth centuries. So alike are the faces of the seven handmaidens who accompany the Virgin to the Temple (on the southwest pillar) that legend has it that the unknown artist was infatuated with his model. The patron who financed the church's enlargement is given pride of place among the *Forty Martyrs* on the west wall. Also note the bases of the marble columns, which originally formed the capitals of pillars in a pagan temple, and the opulently carved eighteenth-century bishop's throne, one of the best of its kind in Bulgaria.

It's fitting to end with the ruined **Church of St John Aliturgetos**, in splendid isolation by the shore, at the bottom of ulitsa Ribarska. Though never consecrated, St John's represents the zenith of Bulgarian–Byzantine church architecture, achieved during the Second Kingdom. Its exterior decoration is strikingly varied, employing limestone, red bricks, crosses, mussel shells and ceramic plaques, with a representation of a human figure in limestone blocks embedded in the north wall.

Eating and drinking

There's a surfeit of **places to eat** on the peninsula, from summertime harbour-side kiosks selling mackerel, mussels and other snacks, to dozens of restaurants trying to attract foreign tourists with pizzas, *bratwurst* and roast-beef lunches. As you might expect, many of these establishments are pretty ropey, and over-priced, tourist traps, though it's still possible to get a decent meal in town; as a general rule, it's best to avoid those places which employ touts to hassle passers-by. If it's seafood you're after, the *Kapetanska Sreshta* fish restaurant is a nice enough, though expensive, place overlooking the harbour, while the *Romantic*, a few doors down, has a particularly nice terrace. You can also try any of the restaurants with sea-facing terraces along the southern side of the peninsula: *Neptun*, towards the far end of town, is a reliable option, while *Plakamo*, just down from the New Metropolitan Church at Ivan Aleksandûr 8, is family-run and relatively sheltered. In the centre, opposite Messemvria Holidays, *Polko Pub* serves an extensive range of pizzas, while over on the mainland, the *Panorama* hotel has a top-floor restaurant with good views of the coast.

Pomorie

Continuing south from Nesebûr, beyond **Aheloi**, the road passes the salt-pans surrounding Lake Pomorie, one of Bulgaria's main sources of salt, and renowned for its therapeutic **mud baths**. Sited upon a peninsula beside the lake, **POMORIE** (pronounced "Pah-mor-ye") would probably resemble Nesebûr if it hadn't been gutted by fire in 1906 and rebuilt in concrete during the 1950s. Pomorie's ancient precursor, Anchialos, was founded by the Apollonians, became rich through the export of salt and wine, and found favour in the Roman era as an exclusive health resort. The lakeside sanatorium remains important to the local economy, as does another speciality of long standing, the locally produced aromatic dry *Pomoriiski dimyat* **wine**. Apart from an abundance of private rooms and an underused stretch of beach, however, there's little in modern Pomorie to justify a stopover.

The Town

Pomorie's **bus station** is separated from the centre by a three-kilometre stretch of grotty industrial suburbs, best avoided by catching bus #1 (every 20–30min). This runs past the **Monastery of St George**, whose domed belfry is visible to the right. A medieval foundation re-established by the Ottoman governor Selim Bey (who reputedly converted to Christianity after being cured of illness

The Burgas lakes

Midway between Pomorie and Burgas the road passes **Atanasovsko ezero**, the largest and most ecologically important wetland reserve in Bulgaria. This ten-kilometre-long stretch of shallow inland water is frequented by more than 300 species of birds – representing nearly three-quarters of the country's total – including such rare visitors as the Dalmatian pelican, corncrake and pygmy cormorant, as well as thousands of more common birds such as the sandwich tern. The lake serves as the midway point on the "Via Pontica" – the route used by birds migrating between Scandinavia and Africa – and tens of thousands of white storks have been recorded circling the area on their way south. Plant life is equally varied and abundant, while Europe's smallest mammal, the Etruscan shrew, also makes its home here. Immediately west of Burgas is **Burgasko ezero**, which has been transformed over recent years from an almost hopelessly polluted body of water into an important nature reserve, and a protected breeding site for night herons, squacco herons and little egrets. Just south of here is the final major reserve, **Poda Lagoon**, where you'll find the only colony of spoonbills on the Black Sea coast, which nest here between May and June.

The **Poda Information and Visitors Centre** (Ⓣ056/850540, Ⓦwww.bspb-poda.de), at the edge of the lagoon, is open daily, and arranges tours of the site. For further information on all the lakes, contact the Bulgarian–Swiss Biodiversity Conservation Programme (Ⓣ056/49255, Ⓔbw@bsbcp.org) or try the **website** Ⓦwww.pomonet.bg/bourgaslakes.

by a miraculous spring), the monastery now occupies a rather functional array of nineteenth-century buildings, brought to life by the shrubs and pot-plants that fill the courtyard. The seaside town proper centres on a lively pedestrianized zone, with a fishing port one block to the south, and the small eighteenth-century **Church of the Transfiguration** lying at the eastern end of the peninsula. Pomorie's **beach** occupies a four-kilometre-long sand bar which stretches north from the tip of the peninsula, and separates the town's famous salt-pans from the open sea. This is a prime spot for **bird-watching**, with a number of rare species, such as the pygmy cormorant and the corncrake, frequenting the long strip of salty water, where artificial breeding platforms have been set up to encourage the large numbers of avocets and other wetland birds which come here. You won't find much else here apart from a few huts selling drinks and snacks, although the underdeveloped nature of the place may come as something of a tonic after Sunny Beach.

Practicalities

Private rooms (❶) can be rented from Pomerie's numerous accommodation bureaux: Palikastro Tour (daily 10am–8pm; ⓣ0596/22070, ⓦwww.palikastro.hit.bg) and Lilit Tourist Agency (daily noon–9pm; ⓣ0596/24905), both on the main road into town, Knyaz Boris I, are worth trying. *Interhotel Pomorie* on ulitsa Javorov 3 (ⓣ0596/22440, ⓕ22280; ❹) is the town's best hotel, designed to resemble a ship jutting into the sea; only slightly cheaper is the modern *Manz II* in the centre (ⓣ0596/24819; ❹). The nearest **campsites** are the *Evropa*, 2km along the Burgas road, where there's another popular stretch of sandy beach; and *Kûmping Aheloi*, occupying an isolated coastal spot just south of the town of Aheloi on the road to Nesebûr (Burgas–Nesebûr buses drop off by the entrance). There's no shortage of **restaurants and bars** in the pedestrianized zone in the centre of town.

Burgas and around

Overlooked by most tourists and often dismissed as a polluted industrial dump, to be passed through quickly on the way to more desirable locations along the coast, **BURGAS** is a surprisingly attractive city, which makes a welcome break from the crowds and commercialism of the nearby seaside resorts. Though the city's suburbs are certainly dreary, the centre is pleasantly urbane and tourist-friendly, due to recent efforts to improve its seedy image. As the site of an oil refinery and associated chemical plants, Burgas is far more industrial than any of its neighbours on the coast, and its deep harbour is home to Bulgaria's oceanic fishing fleet. The presence of visiting ships and passing tourists gives the town a certain cosmopolitanism – especially in late August, during the **folk festival** – but nothing to compare with the cultural life of Varna.

Road traffic southwards is borne by a thin finger of land that separates the gulf itself from the land-locked Burgasko ezero to the west (see box opposite), while further down lie the picturesque freshwater resevoir of **Mandrensko ezero** (Lake Mandra) and the **Poda Lagoon** (see box opposite), lying beside the main E87 road 10km south of Burgas.

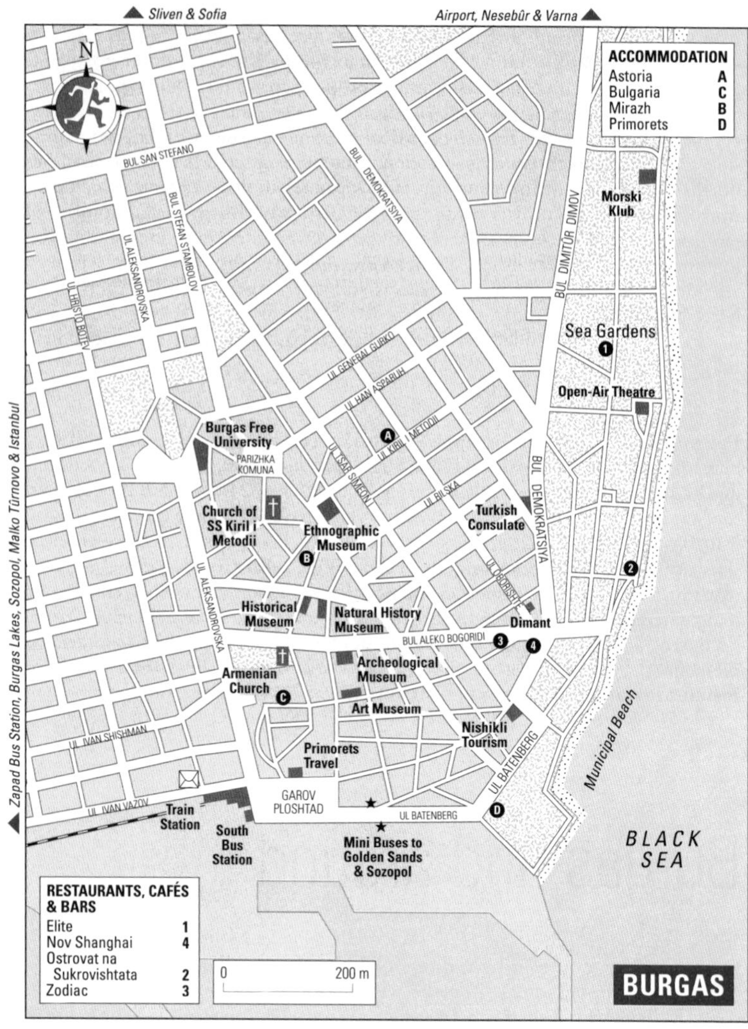

Arrival and accommodation

Both the **train** station and the main **bus** station (Avtogara Yug) are just south of the centre on Garov Ploshtad. The half-hourly bus #15 from the airport ends up here too, and it's the best place to pick up a taxi. There's a left-luggage office behind the bus station. An addtional bus station, Avtogara Zapad, lies 3km northwest of the centre (bus #4 from the centre), although you're only likely to use it if you're travelling to or from Malko Tûrnovo.

Private rooms in downtown apartment blocks are available from Dimant, bul. Tsar Simeon 15 (summer daily 8am–10pm, winter Mon–Fri 9am–6.30pm; Ⓣ056/840779, Ⓔdimant91.abv.bg), for 9Lv per head; Primorets Travel

Pollution in the Gulf of Burgas

Arriving at Burgas you'll see both the best and the worst of what the coast has to offer: while glorious beaches and rich wetland reserves lie a few kilometres away both north and south, the city itself is one of the **most polluted** in Bulgaria.

The **Black Sea** as a whole is in a sorry state. Rivers such as the Don, Dniestr, Dniepr and Danube carry the waste products of a vast industrial hinterland into a sea which is largely closed – only the Bosphorus to the south provides an outlet for the accumulated gunk. The depths of the Black Sea have always been low on oxygen, leaving only a thin upper layer of water capable of sustaining life. Twentieth-century pollution is rendering this layer thinner than ever, and intensive fishing threatens to reduce even further the stock of marine animals this once-rich body of water contained. **Dolphins**, previously a common sight off the Bulgarian shore, are increasingly rare: the fish they used to feed off are gone.

Burgas' problems are compounded by the presence of a vast chemicals plant, **Lukoil Neftohim**, on the western outskirts of town (you're sure to pass it if entering or leaving the city by train). Neftohim's waste products used to be diluted in a series of water tanks before being released into the gulf, but during the Communist period few paid attention to the kind of toxins which were allowed to seep into the sea this way. Nowadays emissions of this kind are more closely monitored – funds permitting – and stiff fines imposed on transgressors, but the Gulf of Burgas remains pretty ugly. The tankers and cargo ships frequenting the port here all shed a little oil from time to time, and the currents in the gulf tend to circulate within the bay itself instead of diluting these concentrations of waste in the open sea. Nevertheless, locals continue to patronize Burgas' municipal **beaches** in large numbers, either to sunbathe or indulge in a variety of water sports; the long concrete pier is a magnet for teenagers, who use it as a diving platform. However, neighbouring resorts don't seem to have been affected by the city's environmental problems. Coastal waters around Nesebûr to the north or Sozopol to the south are remarkably pure, and you shouldn't have any qualms about bathing there.

opposite the bus station at Garov Ploshtad 3 (daily 7am–7pm; ⓣ056/842727) also arranges rooms (❶). The town's **hotels** tend to be overpriced for what they are; the cheapest is the *Mirazh*, ul. Lermontov 48 (ⓣ056/845647; ❷), which offers basic rooms in a downtown block, while the other downtown options are the *Primorets*, at the bottom end of the Sea Gardens at pl. Aleksandûr Batenberg 2 (ⓣ056/841417, ⓕ842934; ❻), and the imposing but slightly dated *Bulgaria* on ulitsa Aleksandrovska (ⓣ056/842820 or 842610, ⓕ841291; ❺). The *Astoria*, at ul. Kyril i Metodi 38 (ⓣ056/820670; ❹), is a rather more modern option, offering comfortably furnished en-suites with TV and minibar. The nearest **campsite** is *Kraimorie*, 14km south of town and 2km off the coastal road: any bus heading south can drop you at the turn-off.

The Town

Social and commercial life in Burgas centres on **ulitsa Aleksandrovska**, the long boulevard that scythes north–south through town. The upper part is sedate, shaded by trees and largely residential, while the lower end of the avenue is brash and colourful, lined with cafés and thronged with people. Everyone comes here to stroll in the evening, walk their dogs or just sit and drink a coffee or two. Midway along is a spacious plaza whose surprisingly spruce, marble Soviet war memorial has been outclassed by the gleaming white stone and bronzed glass of **Burgas Free University**, Bulgaria's first privately funded fee-paying college, offering courses in marketing.

The other axis of social life in Burgas is **bulevard Aleko Bogoridi**, which turns off by the towering *Hotel Bulgaria*, in the direction of the Sea Gardens to the east. Narrower than ulitsa Aleksandrovska, but likewise full of shops and cafés, it runs past the small **Armenian Church** of St Hach, a modern structure with an elaborate bell-tower, ministering to the needs of the town's few hundred Armenian residents. A third of the way along bulevard Bogoridi is an **Archeological Museum** (summer Mon–Sat 9am–1pm & 2–6pm; winter hours unpredictable; 2Lv) housing a display of Roman-period votive tablets, Thracian jewelley and Neolithic pots. One block south of the museum at ul. Vodenicharov 22, a Moorish-style former synagogue contains an **Art Museum** (Mon-Fri 9am–1pm & 2-6pm; 2Lv), with a fine display of eighteenth- and nineteenth-century icons on the top floor.

North of bulevard Bogoridi, residential streets huddle around the **Church of SS Kiril i Metodii**, built between 1894 and 1905. The saints are depicted in peeling murals above the entrance, framed by Art Nouveau stained glass. A couple of minutes' walk east, the **Ethnographic Museum**, at ul. Slavyanska 19 (Mon-Sat 9am–1pm & 2-6pm; 2Lv), exhibits fishing paraphernalia, regional textiles and fearsome *kukeri* costumes. Just south of here, the **Natural History Museum**, at ul. Konstantin Fotinov 30 (Mon-Sat 9am–1pm & 2-6pm; 2Lv), has the usual collection of stuffed animals, while the **Historical Museum** round the corner, at Lermontov 31 (Mon-Sat 9am–1pm & 2-6pm; 2Lv), houses an unimaginative display of sepia pictures of old Burgas and Bulgarian-only texts detailing the region's history.

Bulevard Bogoridi ends near the attractive and well-kept **Sea Gardens**, laid out with flowerbeds, statues and fountains, and dotted with cafés. There are some splendid views of the sea from the terraces, while the shady avenues provide a refreshing respite from the oppressive summer heat. Steps from here descend to the city's long sandy **beach**, patrolled by lifeguards and fringed by more restaurants and bars. Strong winds along this coast make **windsurfing** a popular activity, and boards may be hired from the *Morski Klub* – the poor water quality failing to dampen the spirits of the locals, who appear perfectly happy to share the bay with oil tankers and cargo vessels. Two **websites**, Ⓦwww.bourgas.net and Ⓦwww.bourgas.com, have some general information on the city, the former providing up-to-date details on the battle against pollution.

Eating, drinking and entertainment

Restaurants and **cafés** vie for custom along ulitsa Aleksandrovska and bulevard Bogoridi, where you can eat seafood in one place, cakes in another, and enjoy a post-prandial drink somewhere else, all the while sitting outdoors, observing the *korso*. Most promenaders are dressed to the hilt, be they out for the night, window-shopping, or simply walking the dog. *Nov Shanghai* is a decent and very popular Chinese restaurant on the corner of bulevards Bogoridi and Demokratsiya, while the nearby *Zodiac* at bul. Bogoridi 49 serves up the usual grilled meats and salads. The beachfront also has its share of eating places, such as *Ostrovat na Sukrovishtata*, a traditional-style *mehana* near the steps leading down from the Sea Gardens, and there are several beach-hut **bars** to choose from. The *Bulgaria* has a rather stylish and comfortable ground-floor bar, with

Moving on from Burgas

Burgas is the transport hub for the whole coastline from Nesebûr down to Ahtopol. If you miss one of the **buses** to Sozopol, Nesebûr or Sunny Beach, private buses depart in-between times from the eastern side of Garov Ploshtad. Nishikli Tourism runs four buses a day to **Istanbul** from its office at ul. Bulair 39 (Ⓣ056/841261) and numerous centrally located travel agents – try Dimant at Tsar Simeon 15 – also handle reservations for Istanbul-bound buses. Eurolines has an office at the bus station (Ⓣ056/845722) and several other agencies clustered nearby offer tickets to destinations all over Bulgaria and Europe. International air tickets can be booked through Blue Sky travel agency on ul. Bogoridi 42 (Ⓣ056/840809, Ⓕ842256) which also arranges accommodation and car rental. Travellers heading for Turkey should be able to get a visa at the border crossing; in case of any difficulty, there's a **Turkish Consulate**, north of the Sea Gardens at bul. Demokratsiya 38 (Mon–Fri 9am–1pm & 2.30–5pm; Ⓣ056/42718 or 47010).

plush seating and decorative fountains, the perfect setting for an iced tea or a cocktail on a hot day.

The town's biggest **nightclub** is the *Tequila Club* in the Sea Gardens just off bul. Dimitûr Dimov; further into the gardens is *Elite*, a stylish outdoor bar that stays open late. Some of the best music can be heard at the annual **International Folk Festival** in the last week of August, held in the open-air theatre in the Sea Gardens.

Sozopol

There are only two settlements of any size on the south side of Burgas bay: **Kraimorie**, a naval town serving a big base on the nearby peninsula of Aitia, and **Chernomorets**, a small beach resort with a neatly manicured park. The latter has numerous **private rooms** (❶) that can be booked through Dank93 Tourist Service (daily 8am-11pm; Ⓣ0550/72307) at ul. Sveti Nikola 34 opposite the bus station and a **campsite**, the *Gradina* (Ⓣ0550/22524; double bungalows (❶–❸), camping 8-20Lv per person), located on the beach to the south. The Siroko Surf School (Ⓣ0888 835 561) below the campsite offers windsurfing lessons for 25Lv per hour, kitesurfing lessons for 40Lv per hour and runs two-day catamaran courses for 180Lv; it also has schools on the beaches at *Zlatna ribka* campsite (see p.427) and *Kavatsite* campsite (see p.431).

Both towns are served by hourly buses on the Burgas–Sozopol route, but it's better to press on to the small fishing port of **SOZOPOL**, the favoured resort of Bulgaria's literary and artistic set since the beginning of the last century, and popular with German and Eastern European package tourists since the 1970s.

An engaging huddle of nineteenth-century houses on a rocky headland, backed up by two fine beaches, scores of bars and restaurants, and a lively promenade, Sozopol is fast overtaking Nesebûr as the coast's prime attraction. Slightly incongruously, its harbour also serves as one of Bulgaria's chief naval bases, with ranks of gunboats anchored off the neighbouring island of Sveti Kirik.

For the first ten days of September, Sozopol hosts the Apollonia Arts Festival, comprising classical music, jazz, theatre and poetry, and frequent open-air pop concerts take place throughout the summer. Be warned that finding accommodation can be difficult in July and August, when the tourist season is at its height.

Some history

Stone anchors in the local Archeological Museum suggest that traders from the Aegean visited Sozopol harbour as early as the twelfth century BC, although the identity of these early seafarers remains the subject of much conjecture. More certain is the town's status as the first of the Greek colonies along the coast, founded around 610 BC by a party of adventurers from Miletus, who included

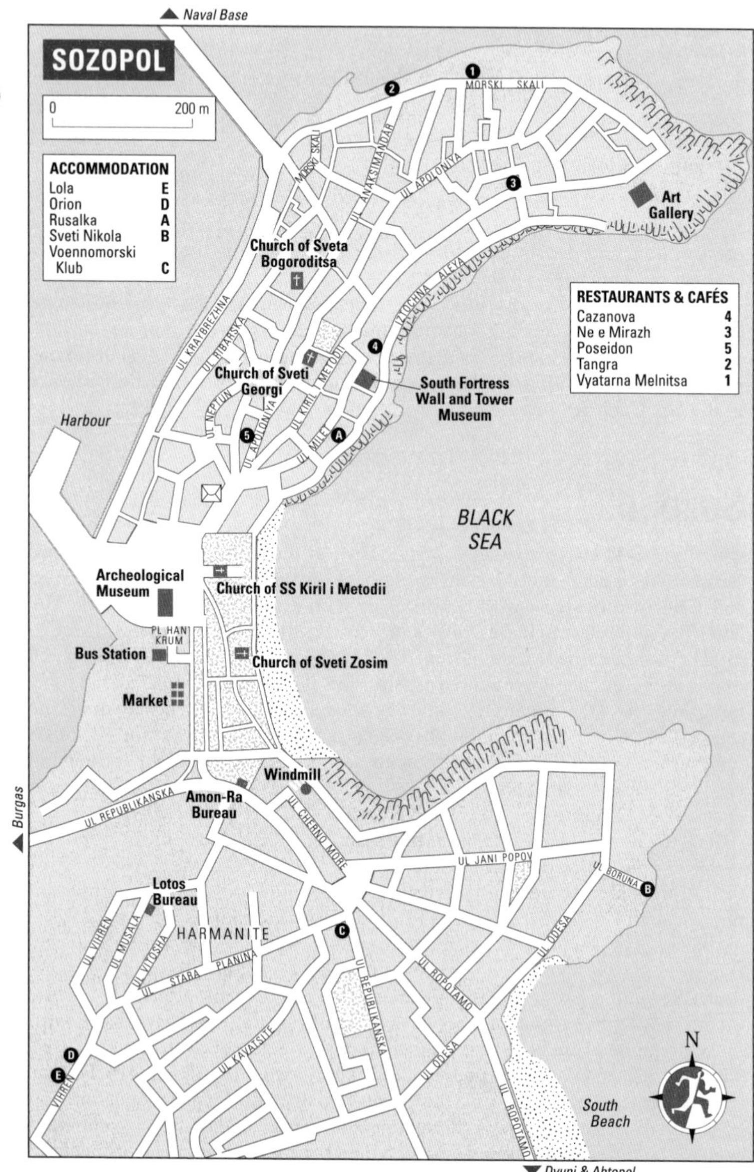

in their number the philosopher Anaximander, who is credited with making the first world map (now lost) and being the first theoretical astronomer – his speculations on the nature of the universe, including the then revolutionary notion that the earth floats free and unsupported in space, formed the basis of modern cosmology. The Greeks named the town Apollonia Pontica after Apollo, the patron of seafarers and colonizers, and prospered by trading Greek textiles and wine for Thracian honey, grain and copper. Apollonia's major customer was Athens, and the decline of the latter in the fourth century BC ended the town's brief reign as a minor maritime power.

Having spent several centuries existing quite happily on the fringes of more powerful Thracian and Macedonian states, the Apollonians flirted with various anti-Roman alliances in the first century BC in order to try and stave off the inevitable advance of Latin power. In 72 BC, their attachment to the Black Sea empire-builder Mithridates of Pontus was punished by the Roman general Marcus Lucullus, who sacked the town and carried off the treasured statue of Apollo that had graced its harbour.

Apollonia disappeared from the records of chroniclers during the latter stages of the Roman Empire, re-emerging in 431 as **Sozopolis**, the "City of Salvation". Under the Byzantines the town soon developed a reputation for the good life, and rebellious nobles and troublesome bishops were "retired" here by emperors unwilling to see their peers too harshly punished. However, marauding armies returned during the fourteenth and fifteenth centuries, and following the Turkish invasion Sozopol sank into anonymity, replaced by Burgas as the area's major port.

Arrival and accommodation

Just 35km south of Burgas, Sozopol is easily accessible by **bus**. Arriving at the bus station on ploshtad Han Krum, you may be approached by locals offering **private rooms**, although these could well be overpriced, especially in high season, when you'll find it near impossible to get accommodation of any kind unless you book in advance. There are several local agents which are worth trying: Lotos (Ⓣ0550/23925) at ul. Musala 7, and Amon-Ra (Ⓣ0550/22208, Ⓦwww.amonra.domino.bg), in the new town at ul. Republikanska 1, both offer rooms ranging from old houses on the peninsula, to the more spacious chalet-style buildings of the Harmanite district (❷). Agents' opening hours tend to be erratic, though, and, as usual along the coast, staff tend to speak German rather than English. Note also that many places will insist on a minimum stay of at least three or four days, or even a week, at busy times of year.

The new part of town also has some good small **hotels**, among them *Sveti Nikola*, at ul. Boruna 1 (Ⓣ0550/23333; ❸), a friendly place perched on the rocky seafront. The *Orion*, Vihren 28 (Ⓣ0550/23193; ❸), offers better value, with small but comfortable en-suite rooms with TV and balconies – some with quite spectacular views – as well as several four-person apartments for 90-100Lv. Nearby, at no. 32, the modern *Lola* (Ⓣ0550/22412; ❹) has simple, clean rooms, with air conditioning. Most, if not all of these may well close out of season, in which case the *Voennomorski Klub*, or Navy Club, ul. Republikanska 17 (Ⓣ0550/24362; ❷), is a reliable, year-round source of cheap if unexciting en-suite rooms. In the old town, *Rusalka* at ul. Milet 36 (Ⓣ0550/23047; 60Lv double room) has rooms overlooking the bay. The *Zlatna Ribka* **campsite** (Ⓣ0550/22427; 7Lv per person camping, double bungalows (❶–❸), 3km north of town, is one of the south coast's best, situated on a part-sandy, part-rocky coastline – the bus from Burgas passes the site on its way into town.

The Town

Sozopol divides into two parts: the **old town** on the peninsula, and the modern, **Harmanite** district on the mainland (whose name means "The Windmills"). There are two **beaches** with a small admission charge: one nestling within the curve of a sheltered bay where the peninsula joins Harmanite; the other further south, beyond a headland. Walking between the two entails a foray into the backstreets of Harmanite, uphill from a solitary wooden **windmill** which now serves as a bar.

The touristic hub of Sozopol is a cobbled **concourse** between the peninsula and Harmanite, flanked by souvenir stalls and portrait artists, always thronged with strollers and bombarded by a cacophony of rock and pop. Alongside runs a shady municipal **park**, carpeted with cottony wads of blossom during early summer; east of this is the beach. Sheltering among the trees is the pale sandstone **Chapel of Sveti Zosim**, honouring the patron saint of seafarers, the Orthodox Church's answer to Apollo. The **Church of SS Kiril i Metodii**, further north, is currently closed.

The Archeological Museum and South Fortress Wall and Tower Museum

On the other side of the concourse from the church, Sozopol's municipal library forms the backdrop for a temporary **amphitheatre**, erected for use during the Apollonia Festival and serving as a concert venue throughout the summer. Hidden around the side of the library, the **Archeological Museum** (summer daily 8am–6pm; winter closed Sat & Sun; 2Lv) displays an extensive collection of ancient amphoras and barnacle-encrusted anchors, dredged from the sea off Sozopol. There's also some colourful imported Greek tableware, dating to the sixth century BC, as well as examples of rough Bronze Age pottery from a range of sites along the coast, including Kiten and Varna Lake. One of the more interesting exhibits, though, is a tiny wooden figure, tentatively identified as a representation of Apollo, dating to the fifth century BC and discovered in Sozopol harbour. Positioned on the east of the peninsula above the sea, the **South Fortress Wall and Tower Museum** (daily 9.30am-7.30pm; 2Lv, or 4Lv with lecture) is the largest building to have been excavated in Sozopol. A well from 300 BC and an ancient corn storage room are the highlights of this somewhat limited museum.

The old town

The **old town** begins beyond the post office, where three cobbled roads thrust into a labyrinth of alleys and vine-shaded houses, and tourists are ambushed by old ladies brandishing lace tablecloths for sale. The best examples of traditional architecture lie towards the head of the peninsula along ulitsas Apoloniya and Kiril i Metodii. In winter, boats and fishing tackle are kept inside the stone lower storeys; families occupy the creaking wooden rooms upstairs, which extend so far out that they threaten to touch the houses on the other side of the street. Some of their eaves are carved with suns or fish, for good luck.

Several shed-like *paraklisi* or **chapels** can be found scattered throughout the old town, usually bare inside save for a picture of the saint to whom they're dedicated. Despite its central location, it can be difficult to find the **Church of Sveta Bogoroditsa** hidden within a walled courtyard on ulitsa Anaksimandûr and currently closed to the public. Surrounded by noisy bars and cafés just south of here, the **Church of Sveti Georgi**, on ulitsa Apoloniya, offers at least some respite from the general hubbub and holiday crowds, and is open year-round. It

The Black Sea Greeks II: the modern era

Occasionally you still come across elderly residents of Sozopol speaking **Greek** among themselves – a reminder that the Greek population of the coast remained an important feature of local life well into the last century. The Greeks of the coastal towns had maintained some degree of wealth and influence under Turkish rule, and thus seemed poised to take advantage of the upsurge in commerce that occurred in Ottoman lands in the wake of the Crimean War. However, the decline of Turkish power and the rise of **modern national movements** had a detrimental effect on the cosmopolitan culture of the Black Sea towns, whose ethnic groups squabbled among themselves rather than unite to challenge the moribund Ottoman Empire. The Greeks, inspired by the existence of an independent Greek state from 1830 on, came under the influence of the **Megáli Idhéa** (Great Idea) of liberating all the Hellenes within Turkish territory and forging a new Byzantine empire.

The idea that the Black Sea towns formed an integral part of the Hellenic world was anathema to the **Bulgarians**. Increasingly numerous in the coastal towns due to migration from the countryside, they saw the Greeks – who controlled the Church, education, and most local trade – as agents of the ruling Ottoman elite. The Ottomans played one group off against the other, eventually acquiescing to Bulgarian demands for the establishment of a Bulgarian Orthodox Church independent of Greek control – a move that infuriated the Greeks.

With the foundation of a Bulgarian state after 1878, mistrust between the two groups faded into the background, only to re-emerge in 1906 when the Greek patriarchate in Constantinople tried to appoint a new bishop of Varna without the prior agreement of the Bulgarian government. The new bishop, Neophytos, was prevented from disembarking at Varna's harbour by a hostile crowd, and a donkey in priest's robes was paraded through the streets. Things took an uglier turn in Pomorie, where the local Greeks were rumoured to be arming themselves to prevent a Bulgarian takeover of their churches. Greek-owned shops and houses were put to the torch, and many Hellenic families fled to Greece.

After World War I both governments agreed to settle their differences with an exchange of populations. According to the **Mollov-Kafandaris Agreement** of 1924, Black Sea Greeks would quit the coastal towns to be replaced by ethnic Bulgarians from Aegean Macedonia and southern Thrace. Greeks in Sozopol, Pomorie, Nesebûr and elsewhere had to choose between declaring themselves to be Bulgarians and adopting Slav names, or leaving. The poorer Greek families stayed behind because they lacked the resources to contemplate uprooting themselves and starting afresh, and their descendants were largely assimilated by the Bulgarian majority over the next seventy years. Despite the population exchange, the atmosphere of the coastal towns didn't change that much – most of the new arrivals tended to be vine-growers and fisherfolk, very much like those who moved out, and locals still joke that the incoming Bulgarians from southern Thrace usually spoke better Greek than the Hellenes they were replacing.

The bitterness that used to characterize relations between Greeks and Bulgarians on the coast has these days largely disappeared, especially now that the straitjacket of Communist educational policy – which trumpeted Bulgarian achievements at the expense of everyone else's – has been cast aside. Many Bulgarian families on the coast can dredge up a Greek ancestor or two – nowadays the subject of fond reminiscences rather than ethnic angst.

houses a colourful nineteenth-century iconostasis, including an arresting image of the Archangel Michael trampling a sinner.

Sozopol's former high school at the far end of ulitsa Kiril i Metodii now contains an **Art Gallery** (Tues–Sun 9am–7pm; 1Lv), although most of the works on the ground floor look like the daubs dashed off by holidaying artists between drinking bouts at the local *mehana*. Things are more interesting upstairs, where works by local marine artists Aleksandûr Mutafov and Yani Chrisoupolus document pre-World War II Sozopol and the working lives of its fisherfolk.

Eating, drinking and nightlife

There are dozens of **cafés** and snack stalls along the concourse leading to the old town, and beside both beaches, while most of the residents of Harmanite seem to be converting their garages and front gardens into *café-apéritif* **bars**. As for **restaurants**, places come and go and standards are variable, so some trial and error is inevitable. Sozopol offers the widest and freshest selection of fish on the coast, although you can't always tell whether your fillet has been recently grilled, or merely heated up in a microwave, and sea views can be enjoyed at the numerous places along Morski Skali or Istochna Aleya, the path along the eastern side of the peninsula. The *Poseidon*, at ul. Apoloniya 7, and the *Vyatarna Melnitsa*, at Morski Skali 27, are both touristy folk-style places with outdoor seating and easy-listening live music, while the *Tangra*, at Morski Skali 25, is as good a place as any to enjoy standard Bulgarian fare. *Ne e Mirazh* (It's Not a Mirage) on ul. Gani Radev 5 combines nightly live music sessions with excellent food and is hugely popular despite having only a handful of tables. For something slightly more upmarket, the *Cazanova*, on Istochna Aleya, is an Italian-influenced joint built into an overhanging portion of coastal cliff. In the uphill part of Harmanite, the restaurant of the *Hotel Orion* has an inviting east-facing terrace.

Aside from promenading in the old town or attending a **concert** in the amphitheatre, nightlife consists of a couple of **discos** full of teenage Bulgarians, open from 10pm till dawn: venues tend to change, although they're usually to be found in Harmanite near the south beach.

South of Sozopol

South of Sozopol, the coast offers some of Bulgaria's most glorious stretches of **sandy beaches**. A whole string of semi-deserted beaches are punctuated by areas of coastal wetland, notably the lush woodlands around the estuary of the **River Ropotamo**, while the sandy soil of the coastal hills provides a tenuous base for prickly conifers. Hugging the Turkish border just west of the coast are the mountains of the **Strandzha**, covered by Bulgaria's deepest and least-explored **forests**.

The resorts along this stretch of the Black Sea were largely frequented by Eastern Bloc tourists in the past, and now depend on Bulgarians for custom. If you don't mind the absence of other foreigners or the lack of nightlife, quiet seaside towns like **Primorsko**, **Kiten** and **Ahtopol** offer inexpensive lodgings and proximity to a beach (the size and quality of which vary). Beyond Ahtopol a lonely coast road continues to **Sinemorets**, a middle-of-nowhere village whose stunning beaches have been sadly blighted by a grotesque seven-storey hotel and now face the very real threat of rampant resort development.

Those with private **transport** can cruise the area and pick their ideal bathing spot; travellers reliant on local buses will have to time things carefully. There are hourly buses from Sozopol to Kavatsite, Dyuni, Ropotamo, Primorsko and Kiten, and six buses a day between Sozopol and Tsarevo; five of them continue on to Ahtopol. In high season, services fill up quickly and drivers won't stop to pick up travellers at roadside halts if the vehicle is already packed. In addition, frequent private buses service the coastal stops between Burgas and Ahtopol.

Kavatsite and Dyuni

Four kilometres down the coast from Sozopol, the highway descends towards a long sandy bay backed by two campsites. At the northern end of the bay on the right-hand side of the road is the *Smokinite* **hotel** (Ⓣ0550/22408 or 22471; ❸), a slightly down-at-heel concrete holiday complex offering fairly standard en-suite rooms, a few alfresco restaurants and an outdoor swimming pool. Immediately beyond lies **KAVATSITE**, a vast wooded campsite with an abundance of bungalows with varying standards (❶–❺), the odd restaurant, and direct access to a huge sweep of sandy beach. The southern reaches of Kavatsite run straight into the shaded *Smokinya* site close to the sea (Ⓣ0550/24356; ❶, camping 6Lv per person) where makeshift beach bars fuel a wild outdoor party scene during July and August. At the southern end of the bay is a dune-punctuated stretch of beach, popular with naturists, where Bulgarians often pitch tents for free. Coastal bus services will drop off at the entrance to Kavatsite on request, as will the hourly open-sided tourist buses that run between Sozopol and Dyuni in season.

The luxurious **Royal Dyuni Resort**, 4km beyond Kavatsite, was one of the last tourist complexes built on the coast. The somewhat sterile resort is divided into a seaside marina and two hillside colonies and offers all-inclusive packages (Ⓣ0550/22356, Ⓦwww.duni.bg; ❽). Dyuni's chief attraction is the marvellous sandy **beach** that extends southwards for 3km, protecting an inland plain of marsh and reed and **Lake Alepu**, a lagoon surrounded by dunes and sand lilies. The area is vastly popular with beach-hoppers, although it has a tendency to become increasingly litter-strewn as the season progresses – unfortunately, only those portions of the beach within the orbit of Dyuni are regularly cleaned.

Arkutino and the River Ropotamo

Four kilometres south of Dyuni, **ARKUTINO** (the name refers to an area rather than a precise settlement) is the site of a pleasant motel, the *Arkutino* (Ⓣ0550/33194; ❷), and an inviting moonscape of shifting, scrub-covered coastal **dunes**. From here several unmarked walking trails run south along the coast, picking their way over shrub-carpeted clifftops before emerging at the estuary of the Ropotamo River, where there's an attractive stretch of near-deserted sand which can only be reached on foot. On the opposite side of the main road from the motel, there's a small area of coastal swamp accessed by wooden walkways (daily 8.30am-6.30pm; 2Lv), allowing glimpses of **giant waterlilies** that bloom in late summer.

The River Ropotamo

A few kilometres south of Arkutino, the highway crosses the **River Ropotamo**, whose estuary has been designated a **nature reserve**. Local tourist agencies imbue the Ropotamo with the mystique of the Florida Everglades, especially its **waterlilies**, although the reality can be something of a letdown. Boat trips (departures depend on the volume of custom; 8Lv) usually cover the stretch from the highway to the estuary, missing the best of the flora and fauna. This lies beyond the waterlily lake along the banks upriver, which are lined with oaks, beech, willows and creeping lianas. The river attracts fishermen with its abundance of whitefish, barbel, grey mullet and carp; dragonflies, small black turtles and (non-poisonous) watersnakes are also found here. To the south of the river mouth rises **Cape Maslen**, where the sea has hollowed out caves that are sometimes frequented by **seals**.

The easiest way to see the river is to book an **excursion** with one of the many travel agents in Sozopol (15-25Lv per person). Otherwise, Sozopol–Tsarevo **buses** stop at the bridge from where boats take off, but drivers seem reluctant to pick up passengers here – so be prepared to hitch back.

Primorsko, Kiten and Tsarevo

On the other side of the cape, the peninsula village of **PRIMORSKO** commands the northern approaches to another glorious curve of a **beach**, running along the bay to the south. It's a dusty place blighted by uncontrolled holiday-house construction, but its popularity as an inexpensive resort for Bulgarians and Czechs gives the place an appealing vigour. Most of the accommodation is in **private rooms** (❶–❷) available from a *kvartirno byuro* on the main square where Sozopol–Tsarevo buses stop), although there are a couple of smallish **hotels** in the grid of streets that form the village centre. The *Flamingo*, ul. Mart 8 (Ⓣ0550/33031 or 3225, Ⓕ32272; ❸), at the eastern end of the peninsula, is small but modern and comfortable, while the *Metropol* (Ⓣ0550/33166; ❸) is a stylish, modern villa containing smart rooms with TV. Paths lead downhill from the square to the beach, where you'll find a small cluster of bars and grilled-fish **restaurants**.

Two kilometres south of Primorsko lies the **Primorsko Holiday Village**, known until recently as the International Youth Centre and originally intended as a holiday camp for Eastern Bloc students. With the demise of fellow socialist regimes, the centre lost its *raison d'être*, and fell into stagnation for a few years before being absorbed by the Albena group (Ⓦwww.albena.bg), which renamed it but has yet to modernize the uninspiring facilities. It commands direct access to the southern end of Primorsko beach and currently has a couple of **hotels** (Ⓣ0550/30105; ❸) and a neighbouring **bungalow** settlement (❷–❻).

Kiten and Lozenets

Barely a kilometre beyond the Primorsko Holiday Village, the coast road runs into **KITEN**, another peninsula village girdled with beaches, the attractive and sheltered **Atliman bay** to the north garnering more bathers than the slightly scruffier, wind-whipped expanse of sand to the south. It's a low-key, family-oriented (and almost exclusively Bulgarian) resort, full of trade union-owned rest homes. Although hotels in all but name, many of these establishments still cater for those employed by a particular factory or company, and only open their doors to outsiders if occupancy is low. However most private houses in the village offer **rooms**, though the tourist service kiosk, located next to the first *mehana* after the bus station, only seems to open at peak times, so you may have to ask around. In addition, there's a growing number of small family-run **hotels**: the *Elit*, not far from the beachfront (Ⓣ0550/36897; ❹), has simple en-suite doubles with TV and fridge. Of the two **campsites**, the *Atliman* at the northern entrance to the village is preferable to the unkempt *Kiten* to the south. With virtually every garage and garden in Kiten transformed into a rudimentary café or restaurant, you're unlikely to have any problem finding somewhere to **eat** or **drink**.

LOZENETS, the next town down the coast, offers a calmer alternative to the crowded streets of Kiten. It attracts fewer tourists and the wide main boulevard is refreshingly free of stalls flogging the ubiquitous plastic trinkets and inflatable animals. A laid-back crowd of water-sports enthusiasts have begun to frequent the town, taking advantage of its tranquillity and the windy beaches beyond. At the north end of the beach the Oxo Surf School offers **windsurfing** lessons for 30Lv per hour (June-Sept daily 8.30am-7pm; ⓣ0887 601 694 or 0888 308 630). During the summer season locals meet incoming buses to offer **private rooms** (❶). Of the many newly built **hotels** the *Phoenix* (ⓣ0550/57332, ⓔhotel_feniks@mail.bg; ❷) on the edge of town has modern doubles with fridge and minibar, while the central *Lozenets* at ul. Veleka 8 (ⓣ0550/57546, ⓕ57545; ❹), with a pool and air-conditioned rooms, is larger and a little less cosy. *Villa Alba* on the outskirts of town arranges tailor-made activity holidays through its website (ⓦhttp://villaalba.clubextreme.org) including horse riding, diving, windsurfing and mountain biking. The coolest **bar** in town is *By the Way* on ulitsa Ribarska, where windsurfers gather to sample its vast array of cocktails, while *Starata Kushta* (ⓣ0550/57257; ❹) at the other end of the same street is one of the best places to eat, with traditional Bulgarian decor and cuisine; it also offers clean double rooms.

Tsarevo (Michurin)

A century ago, tsars Ferdinand and Boris used to enjoy bathing near the Greek-populated village of Vasiliko, now known as **TSAREVO**. In 1948 the Communists renamed it "Michurin" (in honour of the Soviet plant-breeder), by which name it is still known to many of the locals, despite having officially reverted to its prewar title. The old town is calm and quiet with a Holy Trinity National Revival-style church overlooking the sea that houses a small **History Museum** (daily except Sat 9am-noon & 3-9pm; free). The main street of the new town runs downhill to a park, with the harbour to the south and a small beach on the other side of the rocky promontory. **Private rooms** (❶) are available from the Tsarevo tourist bureau (ⓣ0550/52460) at ul. Michael Gerjikov 18 down the road from the bus station; of the **hotels** available *Skritiya Muzhe* (ⓣ0889/239198; ❷) is small and snug in the old town and has a decent restaurant. **Campers** can head either for the *Arapya* site, 3km north of town, an appealingly isolated spot with a good beach, or for the *Nestinarka* site 2km south on the beach. Both offer old and new bungalows (❶) as well as camping facilities.

The far south

Beyond Tsarevo the E87 swings inland towards the Strandzha and the frontier crossing at Malko Tûrnovo (see p.436), while a well-surfaced minor road continues along an increasingly rocky coastline before reaching the next town of any size, **Ahtopol**. Occasionally forced inland, the road dives between coastal hills, where herders watch over grazing sheep and pigs. Eight kilometres beyond Tsarevo the road passes through **VARVARA**, a sleepy village built around a small shingle cove. There's little here save for a couple of central snack bars, but the village's **private rooms** (there's no *kvartirno byuro*, so you'll have to ask around) are increasingly popular with urban Bulgarians eager for a taste of seaside rusticity; overlooking the village square is *Pri Dimo* - a popular outdoor **restaurant** that also offers rooms (❷). The beach at Ahtopol is just about walkable from here, and there are plenty of grassy clifftops to explore in the vicinity.

Ahtopol

Surrounded by a girdle of trade-union rest homes, **AHTOPOL** is a tranquil, sea-battered little place whose peninsular position echoes that of Sozopol and

Nesebûr. From the bus station, situated at the western end of town, the main street leads down towards a small fishing harbour. Just above is a **museum** (Tues–Sun, irregular hours; 1Lv) which recalls the original Greek settlement of Agathopolis, and a flight of steps leading into the rather bland town centre. At the head of the peninsula, surrounded by well-tended flowers, stands the **Hram Vûsnesenie Gospodne** (Chapel of the Ascension), a low, unadorned structure with vivid nineteenth-century frescoes behind its icon screen.

The peninsula has several tiny shingle **beaches** separated by rocky headlands, with a much larger sandy one to the north, beyond the rest-home colony. A bureau next to the bus station rents out plentiful **rooms** (❶), while *Boruna* hotel at ul. Briz 8 (Ⓣ0550/62255; ❶) has similarly priced rooms with magnificent sea views and an outdoor restaurant. *Hotel Valdi* (Ⓣ0550/62320; ❸) on ulitsa Cherno More has air-conditioned rooms, Internet access, and offers a free daily boat trip to Sinemorets (9.30am, returns from Sinemorets at 5.30pm; non-guests 5Lv). You'll find **cafés** and a **market** on the street across the park from the bus station. Crowded on the edge of the village are numerous Communist-era bungalow sites offering accommodation (❶), but if you don't mind the walk, *Camping Delfin*, 2km north, is far more picturesque with a couple of rows of basic bungalows (❶) perched on a hilltop facing Ahtopol across the bay.

Sinemorets

From Ahtopol the coast road heads south through a forest thick with Strandzha oak, before dropping down to cross the reed-shrouded **River Veleka**. On the opposite bank stands the windswept hilltop settlement of **SINEMORETS**, a village that until 1989 was out of bounds to outsiders due to its proximity to the Turkish border. Since then it's been discovered by beach-hoppers, and wealthy city-dwellers building seaside villas and second homes. It's a strange mixture of bucolic village and building site, the kind of place where expensive cars trundle down the dirt tracks that serve as streets, and shepherds wander by with flocks of sheep. Sinemorets's new-found fame rests on its two **beaches**: the south beach, accessible by a track which leads eastwards through the village towards the headland before veering south, is a dazzling expanse of fine white sand bordered by rocky promontories that have been hacked away on one side to accommodate the monstrous *Bella Vista* hotel. More spectacular still is the beach to the north, a kilometre-long sand bar that slows the progress of the River Veleka towards the sea. Framed by low green hills, it's one of the most beautiful spots on the Black Sea coast and is the kind of place that attracts younger, liberal-leaning Bulgarians – bathing nude here will hardly raise an eyebrow.

There are four daily buses from Ahtopol to Sinemorets, although it's possible to walk the 6km that separates the two if you're not weighed down with luggage. Almost all the houses in Sinemorets offer **rooms** – just ask around or knock on a few doors. There are a few modern **hotels** to choose from: the *Villa Philadelphia* (Ⓣ0550/66106, Ⓦwww.villaphiladelphia.com; ❸) is a comfortable, modern place with Internet access which arranges guided birdwatching tours of the Strandzha Nature Park (see opposite), while the *Sinyata Akula*, otherwise known as the *Blue Shark* (Ⓣ0550/6623; ❶), is a well-regarded family **pension** with TV and fridge in every room. Closer to the beach are the *Domingo* (Ⓣ0550/66093, Ⓦwww.casadomingo.info; ❸) and studio apartments (❺). *Zafo Camping* (Ⓣ0550/66141) towards the end of ulitsa Botamyata has clean double bungalows for 24Lv, while *Bella Vista* offers all-inclusive accommodation to package tourists for 129Lv per person. *Blue Shark, Domingo* and *Zafo* have their own **restaurants**, while at the bottom of town looking out over the sea is *Home Bar Koraba*, perfect for outdoor evening drinks.

From Sinemorets one bus a day covers the 10km south to the village of **Rezovo** on the Turkish border – passports are checked upon entry - though it's *not* possible to cross the frontier here. The *Panorama* **restaurant** here has a terrace offering sweeping views of the Turkish coastline and can arrange **private rooms** (❶) in the village if you intend to stay, but there's not much to keep you here once you've climbed down the steps to the river borderline and seen the national flags on either side.

The Strandzha Nature Park

The interior west of the south coast is dominated by the wooded **Strandzha Nature Park**, a region of plateaux and hills interrupted by rift valleys, and watered by the Ropotamo and Veleka rivers. It's a captivating area of untouched forests, thick with beech, alder, elm and the ubiquitous Strandzha oak, and would be perfect hiking territory were it not for the fact that distinct paths are few; though good maps of the area are available from the **Strandzha Nature Park Administration** in Malko Tûrnovo (see overleaf). It is also home to significant early Bronze Age **dolmens**, known locally as dragons' dens, which can be located through the **Historical Museum** in Malko Tûrnovo (see overleaf).

The most direct route into the region **from Burgas** is via a minor road (served by four buses a day from Burgas' Avtogara Zapad) which works its way over the western shoulder of the Strandzha massif before arriving at Malko Tûrnovo, 10km short of the Turkish border. **From the south coast**, the main E87 highway dives inland from Tsarevo towards Malko Tûrnovo, passing some of the region's most picturesque villages on the way – although this route is only served by three buses a week from Burgas' Avtogara Yug. If you want to explore the Strandzha in depth, you definitely need your own transport.

South from Burgas

Immediately south of Burgas the main inland route to Malko Tûrnovo begins to ascend through wooded hills, passing a sequence of rustic, half-abandoned villages. Fifty-three kilometres out of town, at the village of **ZVEZDETS**, a minor road forks left towards **Petrova Niva**, a hilltop overlooking the river Veleka, which serves as a popular spot for picnics and short hikes. Bulgarian insurgents met here in 1903 to launch the **Preobrazhenie Uprising** against the Turks (so called because it was launched on *Preobrazhenie* – Transfiguration – an important Orthodox holy day falling on August 6). The event is still marked by an annual *sûbor* or "gathering" on the weekend nearest to *Preobrazhenie*, which involves folk music, feasting and dancing.

Continuing along the main route from Zvezdets, a right turn after 10km leads to the tiny village of **BRÛSHLYAN** (all Malko Tûrnovo buses from Burgas Zapad call in here), site of the Strandzha's best-preserved ensemble of traditional peasant houses and an architectural reserve - it's a charming spot imbued with rural calm. The village is centred on the sunken church of **Sveti Dimitûr**, built, according to Ottoman restrictions, behind a wall high enough to render it inoffensive to any passing Muslim. Call in at the mayor's office (*kmetstvo*), opposite, to obtain the key for the restored **church school** (*kiliino uchilishte*) next door, a small room where the better-off village children once sat on goatskin rugs and wrote on wax tablets, erasing their work by holding the tablets up to the heat of the nearby fireplace. There's a small **ethnographic collection** inside the *kmetstvo*, showing the woollen cloaks once worn by Brûshlyan's menfolk – predominantly herders who wintered their flocks on the shores of the Aegean to the south. At least eight old houses offer **accommodation**: *Seeka Yankova*

(☎05952/4929) has rooms (❷) and can also arrange food for guests; *Gergana Nakova* guesthouse (☎05952/4144; ❹) has more comfortable rooms. Two **restaurants** serve decent Bulgarian fare.

Inland from Tsarevo

The other main route into the region, the E87, heads inland from Tsarevo, winding its way slowly over the hills. The first village of any note is **BÛLGARI**, renowned for the still-practised custom of *nestinarstvo* or **fire dancing**. Traditionally associated with the feast day of SS Konstantin and Elena (which falls on May 21 in most parts of Bulgaria, but is celebrated here on June 3 and 4, or the nearest weekend), the ritual involves initiates falling into a trance and dancing on hot embers, to furious bagpipe and drum accompaniment. The secret lies in the low thermal conductivity of the embers, whose heat is transmitted slowly enough for the walkers to avoid injury by moving at a fast pace. Preparations for the fire-dancing last all day, with icons of the saints paraded round the village, and the inevitable sacrifice of sheep prior to communal feasting. The local **bar** behind the church sells basic provisions and can direct visitors to several houses in the village that offer **private rooms** with meals included, one such is the homely *Gerjikovi* (☎055069/597; ❶).

From Bûlgari, a minor road heads off towards **KOSTI**, another bucolic spot lying 7km south, on the banks of the River Veleka. There's a wealth of (unmarked) hiking paths heading up and down the river, with the most inviting being the eight-hour trek downstream to Sinemorets (see p.434). A **restaurant** on the vast main square serves simple dishes and is frequented by inebriated locals most of the time. The best **accommodation** is just off the main road into Kosti at the renovated stone house owned by Sasho Pankovski (☎055069/546; ❶) with small but comfortable rooms. Back on the main road, **GRAMATIKOVO** lies midway between Bûlgari and Malko Tûrnovo, offering a smattering of traditional buildings and a **Nature Museum** (Mon-Sat 9.30am-5.30pm) covering the history of forestry in the region. Several **restaurants** cluster around the main square, and the municipality office (Mon-Fri 9am-12.30pm & 1.30-5.30pm; ☎05958/266) can arrange **private rooms** in the village.

Malko Tûrnovo and the border

All roads in the Strandzha lead to **MALKO TÛRNOVO**, a former copper-mining town lying in a bowl surrounded by hills. It's a quiet place where tourism was never encouraged in the past due to the proximity of the border. A small collection of National Revival buildings huddles above the main square, three of which together serve as a **Historical Museum** (Mon-Fri 8am-noon & 1-5pm, weekends by appointment; 4Lv; ☎05952/2998), including regional archeological discoveries such as a pair of early Iron Age clay idols, and historical, ethnographic and icon collections. With advance notice the museum can arrange trips to the nearby **Mishkova Niva complex** consisting of a megalithic grave site and a temple to Apollo; it can also provide information about the numerous hard-to-reach Thracian, Roman and prehistoric sites that are scattered throughout the locality. The **Strandzha Nature Park Administration** (*Upravlenie na naroden park Strandzha*; Mon–Fri 9am–5pm; ☎05952/2896), in a marked office block just off the main square at Yanko Maslinkov 1, is the place at which to book **private rooms**, and there are a couple of **cafés** and a **restaurant** around the square.

Travelling on from Malko Tûrnovo **by car**, traffic at the frontier is pretty light, but clearing Bulgarian customs can still involve lengthy queuing. Things can be even more time-consuming on the Turkish side, where you'll have to wait behind files of bus passengers in order to buy an entry visa, which will cost £10 for UK citizens, and US$10 for US citizens.

It's impossible to predict how long it will take to cross the border **by bus**. Malko Tûrnovo is overrun with Bulgarians, Romanians and Ukrainians on the way to Istanbul (many carrying holdalls stuffed with goods they hope to sell on Turkish markets), and their baggage gets a thorough going-over by officials on both sides. Bus passengers will probably be stuck here all night, but the wait is worthwhile – the descent into Turkey through the scrub-covered southern slopes of the Strandzha is highly scenic.

Travel details

Trains

Burgas to: Karnobat (14 daily; 45min–1hr 30min); Kazanlûk (2 daily; 3hr 15min); Plovdiv (5 daily; 4hr 30min); Sliven (2 daily; 1hr 30min–2hr 30min); Sofia (7 daily; 6hr 30min); Stara Zagora (5 daily; 3hr).
Varna to: Dobrich (1 daily; 2hr 45min); Karnobat (2 daily; 3hr–3hr 30min); Plovdiv (3 daily; 6–7hr); Ruse (3 daily; 4hr); Sofia (6 daily; 8–9hr).

Buses

In addition to the services below, there are regular private buses (which set off when there are enough passengers) linking Varna with Albena, Balchik and Burgas; and Burgas with Sunny Beach, Sozopol, Kiten and Tsarevo.
Ahtopol to: Burgas (4 daily; 2hr 15min); Sinemorets (3 daily; 15min); Sozopol (3 daily; 1hr 30min); Tsarevo (5 daily; 20min).
Albena to: Balchik (every 20min; 30min); Dobrich (every 30min; 40min); Golden Sands (every 15–30min; 30min); Varna (every 30min; 30min).
Balchik to: Albena (every 20min; 30min); Dobrich (every 40min; 1hr); Durankulak (Sat & Sun only 1 daily; 1hr 20min); Kavarna (8 daily; 30min); Shabla (1 daily; 1hr); Varna (hourly; 1hr 30min).
Burgas *Avtogara Yug* to: Ahtopol (5 daily; 2hr 15min); Nesebûr (every 40min; 50min); Obzor (1 daily; 1hr); Pomorie (every 30min; 20min); Primorsko (7 daily; 1hr 20min); Ruse (3 daily; 4hr); Sofia (8 daily; 6hr 30min); Sozopol (every 30min; 50min); Sunny Beach (hourly; 45min); Tsarevo (hourly; 2hr); Varna (1 daily; 3hr). *Avtogara Zapad* to: Malko Tûrnovo (4 daily; 2hr).
Durankulak to: Balchik (3 daily; 1hr 20min); Kavarna (2 daily; 50min); Shabla (4 daily; 20min).
Golden Sands to: Albena (every 15–30min; 30min); Sveti Konstantin (every 10–30min; 20–25min); Varna (every 10–30min; 30min).
Kavarna to: Balchik (every 30min; 30min); Bûlgarevo (5 daily; 20min); Dobrich (hourly; 1hr 30min); Durankulak (2 daily; 50min); Kamen Bryag (1 daily; 40 min; Mon-Fri only); Shabla (4 daily; 30min); Varna (hourly; 2hr).
Kavatsite to: Sozopol (hourly; 15–30min).
Malko Tûrnovo to: Brûshlyan (4 daily; 20min); Burgas *Avtogara Zapad* (4 daily; 2hr).
Nesebûr to: Burgas (every 40min; 50min); Pomorie (every 40min; 30min); Sofia (7 daily; 6hr 30min); Sunny Beach (every 15–20min; 15min).
Obzor to: Burgas (1 daily; 1hr); Sunny Beach (1 daily; 25min); Varna (7 daily; 1hr 30min).
Pomorie to: Burgas (every 30min; 20min); Nesebûr (every 40min; 30min); Sunny Beach (every 40min; 30min).
Shabla to: Balchik (4 daily; 1hr); Durankulak (2 daily; 20min); Kavarna (4 daily; 30min); Krapets (1 daily; 15min).
Sofia *opposite Central Station* to: Burgas (4 daily; 6hr 30min); Sozopol (2 daily; 7hr 15min); Varna (5 daily; 8–9hr).
Sozopol to: Ahtopol (1 daily; 1hr 30min); Burgas (every 30min; 50min); Dyuni (hourly; 20min); Kavatsite (hourly; 15min); Kiten (hourly; 45min); Primorsko (hourly; 30min); Sofia (4 daily; 7hr 15min).
Sunny Beach to: Burgas (every 30min; 45min); Elenite (hourly; 20min); Nesebûr (every 15min; 15min); Obzor (6 daily; 25min); Pomorie (hourly; 30min); Sveti Vlas (hourly; 10min); Varna (7 daily; 2hr 10min).
Sveti Konstantin (Druzhba) to: Golden Sands (every 10–30min; 20–25min); Varna (every 10–30min; 25min).
Tsarevo to: Ahtopol (5 daily; 20min); Burgas (hourly; 1hr 10min); Kiten (8 daily; 20min); Kosti (2 daily; 40min); Resovo (1 daily; 1hr); Sinemorets (4 daily; 35min); Sozopol (1 daily; 40min); Varvara (1 daily; 15min).

Varna to: Balchik (hourly; 1hr 30min); Burgas (hourly; 3hr); Byala (1 daily; 1hr 20min); Dobrich (every 30min; 50min); Golden Sands (every 20–30min; 20min); Kamchiya (2 daily; 50min); Kavarna (10 daily; 2hr); Obzor (hourly; 1hr 30min); Ruse (3 daily; 4hr); Shabla (5 daily; 2hr 30min); Shumen (4 daily; 2hr); Silistra (6 daily; 3hr); Sunny Beach (hourly; 2hr 10min); Sveti Konstantin (every 10–30min; 25min); Veliko Tûrnovo (7 daily; 4hr).

Flights

Burgas to: Sofia (1–2 daily; 1hr).
Varna to: Sofia (2 daily; 1hr).

International trains

(mid-June to mid-Sept only)
Varna to: Budapest (3 weekly; 24 hr); Bucharest (3 weekly; 8hr); Kiev (3 weekly; 36hr); Minsk (1 weekly; 4 days); Moscow (3 weekly; 36hr); Prague (3 weekly; 36hr); Rostov (1 weekly; 3 days).

International buses

Burgas to: Istanbul (4 daily; 6hr).
Varna to: Athens (2 weekly; 24hr); Istanbul (4 daily; 8hr); Kiev (2 weekly; 26hr); Odessa (2 weekly; 30hr); Paris (2 weekly; 36hr); Rome (2 weekly; 30hr); Thessaloniki (2 weekly; 12hr).

International boats

Varna to: Odessa (2 weekly; 9hr).

Contexts

Contexts

The historical framework

National history is a serious business in a country that was virtually effaced for five hundred years – when this part of the Ottoman Empire was referred to by Westerners as "European Turkey". Since the Liberation in 1877–78, successive regimes have tried to inculcate a sense of national pride among their citizens, emphasizing historical continuity between the modern state and the medieval Bulgarian empires of the past.

Neolithic beginnings

Despite several Paleolithic finds in the caves of the Balkan Mountains, the early inhabitants of the Bulgarian lands don't really enter the limelight of history until the sixth millennium BC, when the Balkans were a major centre of the so-called **Neolithic Revolution**. This came about when Stone Age hunters began to be replaced by a more settled, agricultural population – probably the result of a wave of migration from the Near East. This sudden flowering of organized culture is best observed at the recently excavated Neolithic village at **Stara Zagora** (see p.317), famous for its decorated pottery, clay figurines and fertility symbols. By the fourth millennium BC mining and metallurgy took off in a big way: copper and gold objects found in the **Chalcolithic necropolis** near **Varna** (see p.391) show that the Balkan peoples were developing smelting techniques independently of the civilizations of the Near East.

Chalcolithic culture went into decline at the end of the fourth millennium BC, a process hastened by a worsening of the climate. Civilization in the Bulgarian lands was revitalized by the arrival of newcomers from Central Europe, bringing with them the metalworking techniques of the **Bronze Age**. By the end of the second millennium BC these migrant groups, together with the original tribes of the eastern Balkans, were coalescing into an ethnic and linguistic group subsequently known to history as the **Thracians**.

The Thracians

Ruled by a powerful warrior aristocracy rich in gold treasures, the ancient Thracians inhabited an area extending over most of modern Bulgaria, northern Greece and European Turkey. Close ethnic links with their neighbours in both the Danube basin to the north and in Asia Minor to the east placed them at the centre of an extensive Balkan–Asian culture. Despite their subsequent absorption by a whole host of invaders and their eventual assimilation by the Slavs, the Thracians are regarded as one of the **bedrock peoples** of the Balkans whose ethnic stock (though much diluted) has endured – and the present-day Bulgarians are proud to claim them as ancestors. We're largely dependent on ancient Greek authors – notably Herodotus, Xenophon and Strabo – for knowledge of the Thracian world. Herodotus, in a famous passage you'll see quoted in museums throughout Bulgaria, claimed that the Thracian population was "greater than that of any country in the world except India", and would have been a force to be reckoned with had it not been for their tribal disunity.

Although the Thracians were admired for skills such as archery and horsemanship, many of their **customs** seemed slightly barbaric to their southerly neighbours. Certain tribes practised polygamy, others allowed their young women unlimited sexual freedom before marriage, while tattoos for both males and females were *de rigueur* in most areas. Strabo relates how one group of Thracians was nicknamed the *Capnobatae* (literally the "smoke treaders"), suggesting that they burned hemp seeds indoors and got high on the fumes. Dope-crazed hopheads or not, the Thracians practised an ecstatic, **orgiastic religion**, honouring deities closely linked with the Greek god Dionysus. Themes of death, rebirth and renewal figured highly in their religious rites, providing a corpus of belief from which the Greeks borrowed freely – most notably in the case of the legendary Thracian priest-king **Orpheus**.

Greeks, Persians and Macedonians

Certain Thracian tribes developed close links with the **Greek colonists** who began settling the Black Sea coast from the seventh century onwards. The Greek presence turned the Black Sea into an extension of the Mediterranean world, and while bounteous harvests of wheat and fish were shipped southwards to the Aegean to feed cities like Athens, exquisite sculpture and pottery came in the other direction, enriching the culture of the eastern Balkans.

The **Persians** invaded the area in the late sixth century BC, disrupting the lively system of trade that linked the Black Sea Greeks with the Thracians inland. However, their departure allowed the emergence of powerful Thracian tribal kingdoms such as that of the **Odrysae**, which brought stability to the region in the mid-fifth century BC and allowed Greek–Thracian mercantile contacts to flourish anew.

The Odrysae briefly threatened to become the nucleus of a powerful Balkan empire, but this role was taken up a century later by the neighbouring **Macedonians** under Philip II – who invaded Thrace and founded Philippopolis (present-day **Plovdiv**). It took Philip and his son Alexander the Great (who marched to the Danube in 335 BC) a lot of time and men to subdue the Balkans, but their empire (under Alexander's successors the Antigonids) proved lasting. It was during this period that the Thracian interior was opened up fully to the ideas, goods and culture of the Hellenistic world, and the **tombs** of local Thracian rulers (most notably those at **Kazanlûk**; see p.310) were sumptuously kitted out with Greek-inspired frescos and luxurious furnishings.

Rome and Byzantium

The **Romans** became the dominant power in the region after their defeat of Macedonia in 168 BC, but it took almost two centuries for the empire to subdue the Thracians, who were in constant revolt. It wasn't until about 50 AD that the conquerors were finally able to carve out secure administrative units, creating the province of **Thrace** to the south of the Balkan range and **Moesia** to the north. Using slave labour, the Romans built garrisons, towns, roads and bridges across their domain, and conscripted many Thracians into their legions.

Military strongholds and neighbouring civilian settlements sprang up along the **Danube frontier** (relics of which can today be seen in the museums of Vidin, Pleven and Sofia), while prosperous new towns like **Nicopolis ad Istrum** (near Veliko Tûrnovo; see p.243) commanded the trade routes inland.

Many of the old Greek towns along the coast continued to thrive, and although they now hosted a population of mixed Greek and Thracian descent, Greek language and culture remained dominant throughout the region.

From the third century onwards the empire's contraction and decline was hastened by recurrent invasions of the Danubian provinces by the Goths (238–48), Visigoths (378), Huns (447) and other so-called **barbarians** – civilization in Moesia and Thrace suffered greatly as a result. However, the division of the empire into two parts, with **Byzantium** inheriting the mantle of Rome in the east, meant that the authorities in nearby Constantinople could (for a while at least) concentrate their military resources more effectively here.

Both the Danubian frontier and the stronghold of Thrace were reinforced by Emperor **Justinian** in the sixth century, allowing urban life in the region a brief reprieve. Both Philippopolis (Plovdiv) and **Serdica** (Sofia) flourished during his reign. Even under Justinian, however, the **sklaveni** (ancestors of the Balkan Slavs) found a way of breaching the empire's defences, and indulged in big looting trips into Thrace in the 540s. By the seventh century, increasing numbers of Avars and **Slavs** were crossing the river with impunity, leaving the Byzantines with little choice but to allow them to settle and employ them as irregular frontier troops.

Slavs and Bulgars

The **Slavs** who migrated into the Balkan peninsula from the late fifth century onwards were one of the indigenous races of Europe, the distant forebears of the Russians, Poles, Czechs, Slovaks, Slovenes, Croats and Serbs – and, of course, the Bulgarians. Many of them came in the wake of the Avars, a warlike Central Asian people who briefly forged a Central European empire in the sixth century and press-ganged the Slavs into their all-conquering armies. However they got here, the Slavs who settled south of the Danube soon began to outnumber any remaining Thracians in the area and established a linguistic and cultural hegemony over the region.

The Slavs were later to fuse with a new wave of migrants, the warlike **Bulgars**. These mounted nomads, possibly originating deep in Central Asia, swept down towards the Balkans after being driven out of "Old Great Bulgaria" – a swath of territories over which they briefly ruled lying between the Caspian and the Black seas. They were a Turkic people, ethno-linguistically akin to the Huns, Avars and Khazars. Under pressure from the latter, the Bulgars began a great **migration** into southeastern Europe, where the largest group (some 250,000 strong) led by **Khan Asparuh** reached the Danube delta around 680 and shortly afterwards entered what would soon become Bulgaria.

The First Bulgarian Kingdom

Theophanes the Confessor records that in 681 the Byzantine emperor Constantine IV was forced to recognize the independence of a "new and vulgar people" north of the Balkan range. Asparuh's new **Bulgar Khanate**, subsequently known as the *Pûrvo Bûlgarsko Tsarstvo* – the **First Bulgarian Kingdom** – was centred at **Pliska** and ruled over a Danubian state that stretched from the

Carpathians in the north to the Balkan Range in the south. Although the Khanate was very much reliant on Slav strength, the Bulgars – whose society was geared to movement and war – definitely provided the impetus for its expansion over the next 150 years.

The Khanate – and the growth of Christianity

The Khanate's growth was greatest during the reign of **Khan Krum** "the Terrible" (803–14), who collected goblets fashioned from the skulls of foes, and pushed his boundaries as far as the Rila Mountains in the west and the Rhodopes in the south. Finally, having conquered all that he could, **Khan Omurtag** (816–31) signed a thirty-year treaty with the Byzantine Empire, and in the ensuing peace the Bulgar state was increasingly opened up to Byzantine culture. The most obvious manifestation of this process was the decision of **Khan Boris** (852–89) to adopt Orthodox **Christianity** as the official state religion in 865. The move was a pragmatic one, recognizing that a rapprochement with Byzantium was in the First Kingdom's long-term diplomatic interests, but Boris' son **Simeon** feared that the Orthodox Church could be used as a vehicle for Byzantine interests in Bulgaria: he therefore established a separate **Bulgarian Patriarchate**, thus ensuring the Bulgars full ecclesiastical autonomy.

The **majority Slav population** over which the Bulgars ruled was largely Christianized well before 865, and Boris' decision to adopt the new religion bolstered the growing influence of the Slavs in the Bulgar state. Many Bulgar nobles agitated for a return to **paganism**, and their defeat only served to confirm the gradual eclipse of the Turkic culture of the original Bulgars – although the name of the former ruling class has been perpetuated in the name **Bulgaria**.

Language and the Cyrillic alphabet

The position of Slavs in the Bulgarian kingdom was also enhanced by the decision to adopt the **Slav tongue** (rather than Greek) as the official language of the Bulgarian Church. The Byzantines themselves were eager to promote this, as they thought that their missionaries, armed with a Slavonic translation of the Gospels, would be able to go forth and convert the entire population of Central and Eastern Europe. Thessaloniki-based missionaries **Cyril and Methodius** began the job of creating an alphabet suited to the needs of the Slav language, initially opting for a rune-like script subsequently known as Glagolitic. However, the task was completed by their disciples **Kliment** and **Naum**, who named the script (still used in varying forms by the modern Bulgarians, Serbs, Ukrainians and Russians) **Cyrillic** in honour of their mentor.

Zenith and decline

Armed with the Cyrillic alphabet, Bulgaria became the main centre of **Slavonic culture** in Europe. The "golden age" of literature and arts coincided with the reign of **Tsar Simeon** (893–927), whose defeat of the Byzantine army at Aheloi in 917 allowed the annexation of sizeable chunks of Macedonia and Thrace, and the haughty claim to be "Tsar of all the Bulgarians and Byzantines".

But the tsars' perennial exactions and wars bred discontent with the feudal order. Thus arose the **Bogomils**, a sect whose "heretical" doctrines amounted to a rejection of Church and state, which took fright wherever Bogomilism appeared in the Balkans, and in France and Italy where like-minded movements emerged during the twelfth and thirteenth centuries.

Besides such conflicts, the reigns of Petûr I (927–69) and Boris II (969–71) were also marked by increasingly violent conflicts between the nobility, or **bolyari**. Byzantium, too, posed a constant threat, and an invasion by Prince Svyatoslav of Kiev gave the Byzantines the pretext they needed to launch a full-scale onslaught. Bulgaria was reduced to a rump, known as the **Western Kingdom**, governed from Ohrid in Macedonia. **Tsar Samuil** was partly successful in restoring the old kingdom until the Byzantine emperor Basil Bulgaroctonos – the "**Bulgar-Slayer**" – defeated his army at Strumitsa in 1014 and blinded the 14,000 prisoners taken. Samuil died of horror after seeing the maimed horde fumbling its way into Ohrid.

Following Ohrid's capture in 1018 the whole of Bulgaria fell under **Byzantine domination**. As a result, the Orthodox Church was largely Hellenized, and Bulgarian architecture and art were increasingly influenced by Byzantine styles. The authorities in Constantinople visited savage repression upon heretics like the Bogomils, and retaliated violently to various eleventh-century rebellions. However, their power didn't extend to protecting the local populace against marauding **Magyars** and **Pechenegs**, the latest group of warlike migrants from Central Asia, who plundered south of the Danube in the eleventh and twelfth centuries.

The Second Kingdom

In 1185 the *bolyari* Petûr and Asen led a successful popular uprising against Byzantium, proclaiming the **Second Kingdom** in Veliko Tûrnovo, henceforth its capital. Byzantine forces under Emperor Isaac Angelus confidently expected to be able to crush the rebel state at birth, but after two attempts in 1187 and 1190, were finally forced to accept Bulgarian independence. Asen's brother and successor **Tsar Kaloyan** (1197–1207) extended Bulgaria's borders further, recapturing Varna and parts of Macedonia and Thrace from Byzantium. However, it was the **fall of Constantinople** to the **Crusaders** in 1204 that gave the Second Kingdom the chance it needed to consolidate and grow. Exiled Byzantine aristocrats, having established statelets in Epirus and Nicaea, proceeded to make war on both each other and the Crusaders' self-styled **Latin Empire of the East**. Tsar Kaloyan sought to exploit this fragmentation of Byzantine power in the Balkans, dreaming of one day setting up a Slav–Greek empire of his own.

Kaloyan succesfully negotiated **union with the Catholic Church** in 1204 in the hope that the pope would support Bulgarian expansion, although at grass-roots level Bulgaria's Church remained Orthodox in all but name. Widely admired in his own time (the name *Kaloyan* was derived from the Greek for "John the Handsome"), Kaloyan was also mercilessly cruel, notoriously razing Plovdiv to the ground and flaying its leading citizens alive in 1205, and hostile chroniclers were subsequently to dub him *Skiloyan* – "John the Dog".

Kaloyan inflicted a stunning defeat on the Latin rulers of Constantinople in 1205, capturing Emperor Baldwin and holding him prisoner in Tûrnovo (see p.250). Before he could take advantage of this success, however, Kaloyan was murdered in a palace coup – as were almost all of Bulgaria's thirteenth-century tsars. A period of anarchy ensued under Tsar Boril before **Ivan Asen II** (1218–41) could restore order and continue the expansion of Bulgaria's frontiers. His victory over Theodore Comnenus of Epirus at **Klokotnitsa** in 1230 won him territories from the Adriatic to the Aegean, and ushered in an era of prestige and prosperity that marks the zenith of medieval Bulgaria's development. Ivan Asen also brought an end to the union with Rome, allowing a vibrantly Orthodox, Bulgaro-Byzantine culture to flourish.

The Mongols

This period of plenty was cut short by an unexpected disaster. After 1240 **Mongol hordes**, fresh from their campaigns in Central Europe, withdrew through Serbia and Bulgaria, desolating the countryside. The ensuing chaos provided the Byzantines with an opportunity to win back some of the ground they had lost in the plain of Thrace.

One batch of Mongols – subsequently known as the **Tatars** – settled in southern Russia and the Crimea, whence they mounted continual raids on the lands bordering on the Black Sea. The presence of this powerful and unpredictable warrior-state on its northeastern borders considerably weakened Bulgaria's freedom of manoeuvre – perpetually threatened by enemies on both sides, the Second Kingdom increasingly had to compromise with its neighbours in order to avoid their wrath.

The late thirteenth century

The latter half of the thirteenth century saw a return to internecine feuding and punitive taxation, producing a **peasant rebellion** that led to the crowning of **Ivailo the Swineherd**, whose brief reign (1277–80) was largely devoted to fighting off the Tatars. Referred to as "the Cabbage" by Byzantine historians eager to accentuate his humble origins, Ivailo was a messianic figure who mobilized a hitherto docile peasantry by claiming to have been inspired by miraculous visions. Despite early successes against the Tatars, Ivailo was incapable of meeting the aspirations generated by his rebellion, and the Bulgarian nobility mounted a counter-coup. Ivailo fled to the court of the Tatar khan Nogai expecting to secure an alliance that would return him to power, but was instead put to death.

He was replaced by the first of the **Terterids**, a dynasty whose only remarkable tsar, Todor Svetoslav (1300–21), succeeded in making peace with the Tatar khans. By threatening to secede from the kingdom, the feudal ruler of Vidin, **Mihail Shishman**, managed to have himself crowned tsar in 1323, inaugurating the new **Shishmanid dynasty**. However, Mihail was fatally wounded at the battle of Velbûzhd (modern Kyustendil) in 1330, when the Bulgarian army was smashed by that of **Serbia** – by now the ascendant power in the Balkans.

Ivan Aleksandûr – and the Turkish conquest

During the reign of Mihail's successor, **Ivan Aleksandûr** (1331–71), Bulgaria almost regained the prosperity and level of civilization attained during Asen II's time, with literature, sculpture and painting displaying a harmonious fusion of Bulgarian and Byzantine styles. However, the rest of the fourteenth century was a confused story of disintegration and decline. Overpowerful *bolyari* asserted their autonomy from Tsar **Ivan Shishman** (1371–96), weakening the central authority of the kingdom just when it was needed to organize resistance to a new threat: the **Ottoman Turks**.

Possessing a disciplined war machine and superior numbers, the Turks proved unstoppable; mutual distrust between Balkan and Byzantine rulers prevented any meaningful concerted action against the invaders, and the defeat of a powerful Serbian army at **Kosovo** in 1389 effectively sealed the fate of the whole Balkan peninsula. Most of Bulgaria had been overrun by 1393 and the anti-Turkish **crusades** of 1394 and 1444 failed to reverse the situation. With the fall of Constantinople, last bastion of the Balkan Orthodox world, in 1453, any remaining hope of outside help against the Turks disappeared for good.

"Under the yoke"

It's estimated that almost half of Bulgaria's population was massacred or enslaved and transported to another part of the empire within a few years of the Turkish conquest, whose long-term effects were equally profound. The **Ottoman Empire** not only isolated Bulgaria from the European Renaissance, but imposed and maintained a harsher system of **feudalism** than had previously existed. Muslim colonists occupied the most fertile land and prosperous towns, while the surviving Bulgarians – mainly peasants – became serfs of the Turkish *Spahis* (land-holding knights), who gouged them for their own profit and for numerous state taxes. In northern Bulgaria and the Rhodopes some Bulgarians succumbed to forced **Islamization** and, as converts (*pomaks*), gained rights denied to the Christian *Rayah* or "Herd", notably exemption from the hated **blood tax** or *devshirme*, whereby the oldest boys were taken from their families and indoctrinated before joining the elite Ottoman janissary corps.

The Turks looted monasteries and subordinated the native **Orthodox Church** to the Patriarchate of Constantinople, which imposed Greek bishops and ignorant, grasping clergy on the faithful. Worst of all was the perpetual insecurity, for Bulgarians were raped and robbed by Turkish troops or "visiting" dignitaries, cheated by tax collectors and Greek merchants, and had no way of getting **justice** through the Ottoman courts.

Ottoman power in Bulgaria was repeatedly challenged by popular **rebellions**, which tended to break out whenever Turkish armies were beaten back by those of their European neighbours. Austrian and Moldavian advances encouraged an uprising in Tûrnovo in 1598, and the successful Austrian and Polish campaigns of the 1680s led to widespread revolt throughout northern Bulgaria. For the most part, however, life under Ottoman rule settled down to something approaching normality in the seventeenth and eighteenth centuries. Highland settlements such as Koprivshtitsa, Elena and Kotel were accorded privileges and allowed to accumulate wealth through trade, merchants sank their money into the renewal of churches, and the *devshirme* system gradually withered away. It was only with the disintegration of Ottoman provincial government in the late eighteenth century, and the emergence of the rapacious Turkish bandits known as the **kûrdzhali**, that the idea of Turkish rule as something fundamentally unjust and corrupt once again gripped the popular imagination. The partiality of the Ottoman legal system was one reason why many Bulgarians took to the forests to became **haiduti**, or outlaws.

Meanwhile, spiritual and artistic values predating the conquest were nurtured in the **monasteries**, which remained important repositories of Slav learning at a time when regular parish priests conducted services in Greek only. After the sixteenth century, the Bulgarian monasteries had restored contacts with **Russia**, a newly resurgent and rapidly expanding Orthodox power which came to be viewed as the great hope of the subject Christians of the Balkans.

The National Revival

The role of Bulgaria's monasteries in preserving ancient traditions ensured that memories of the medieval empire never died out altogether. Interest in Bulgaria's past began to express itself with the publication (outside Ottoman territory) of a *History of Bulgaria*, written by Peter Bogdan Bakshev, seventeenth-century Catholic bishop of Sofia, and a *History of the Serbs and the Bulgarians*, written by Hristofor Zhefarovich a century later. However, neither of these had the impact of **Paisii of Hilendar**'s *Slav-Bulgarian History*, written in 1762. Circulated in manuscript form (because the Greeks who controlled the Church wouldn't countenance the printing of Bulgarian-language texts), Paisii's work inspired a generation of nationalists, and became the spiritual cornerstone of the Bulgarian renaissance, the **National Revival**.

The material base for such an upsurge in national feeling was provided by the economic changes of the nineteenth century. Bulgaria was increasingly supplying the Ottoman Empire with wool, cloth and foodstuffs, giving rise to a prosperous **mercantile and artisan class** based in the towns and villages of both the Balkan Mountains and the Sredna Gora. Economic development speeded up after the Crimean War, when Turkey's French and British allies demanded that the Ottoman Empire should be opened up to Western European trade.

Bulgaria's cultural reawakening expressed itself in protests against the **Greek Church**, which controlled all ecclesiastical affairs in the country and ran most of the schools. The Greeks opposed Bulgarian efforts to establish churches and schools of their own, and **riots**, in which the local Greek priest was chased out of town, were a not uncommon feature of mid-nineteenth-century life.

Community leaders had to bargain hard with the Ottoman authorities in order to gain concessions on the issue of Bulgarian-language schooling, but by the 1840s Bulgarian **education** was beginning to take off. The growing middle class endowed schools offering a modern, secular education; in addition, there were *chitalishta* or "reading rooms" – cultural centres that offered courses for adults. The campaign for church autonomy was rewarded in 1870, when a decree from the sultan permitted the foundation of the **Bulgarian Exarchate** – a semi-independent institution nominally subject to the Greek Orthodox patriarch of Constantinople, but capable of enforcing use of the Bulgarian language in churches and church schools. This emboldened the Bulgarians to extend their struggle further into the political sphere.

Whereas their elders had sought reforms, "second generation" nationalists increasingly pursued Bulgarian independence through armed struggle, and émigrés in the Serbian capital Belgrade, led by **G. S. Rakovski**, began organizing a **Bulgarian Legion** in 1861. Its members fought alongside Serbia in its wars with the Ottoman Empire, while other Bulgarian exiles formed *cheti* or armed groups that raided Turkish-controlled territory from sanctuaries in Serbia and Wallachia.

The revolutionary underground

The *cheti* received little support from the Bulgarian peasantry, however, and their unpopularity convinced **Vasil Levski** and the Bucharest-based **Bulgarian Revolutionary Central Committee** (**BRCK**) that a mass uprising could only be inspired by an indigenous **revolutionary underground**, which they set about creating. Levski himself led the way, travelling the length and breadth of the country in order to establish clandestine revolutionary cells: Levski and the other agents charged with setting up the BRCK network were henceforth known as the **apostles** due to the almost evangelical nature of their work. Levski himself was captured and executed in 1873, a setback that nevertheless provided the liberation struggle with its first great martyr, inspiring idealistic and patriotic youngsters everywhere to rally to the cause.

The April Rising

The culmination of the BRCK's organizational efforts was the **April Rising of 1876**, which after exhaustive (but, as it turned out, insufficient) preparation was launched in the Balkan Mountains and the Sredna Gora – a heroic attempt answered by savage Ottoman reprisals, which took an estimated 29,000 Bulgarian lives.

The "Eastern Question"

Despite these valiant efforts, the fate of Bulgaria didn't really rest with the Bulgarians themselves. The gradual stagnation of Ottoman power in Europe had raised the problem – dubbed the "**Eastern Question**" by contemporary politicians and journalists – of who would profit from the empire's demise. The main contenders in the area were Austria–Hungary and tsarist Russia, the latter nursing a long-standing ambition to extend its influence as far south as Constantinople and thereby gain control of the Bosphorus. Both the French and the British were horrified by the prospect, and tended to support Turkey in order to frustrate Russian expansion. The British establishment was notoriously hostile to any Bulgarian aspirations that involved Russian backing, with Queen Victoria herself remarking that the Bulgarian people "hardly deserved the name of real Christians". In the cynical environment of Great Power diplomacy, the aspirations of the nationalities languishing under Ottoman rule counted for little.

The Russians exploited the ideology of **Pan-Slavism** – the belief that Slav peoples everywhere should be freed from foreign domination and united under the authoritarian guidance of the Russians – in order to stir up anti-Ottoman sentiment in the Balkans and exert control over the liberation movements thus produced. It was therefore taken for granted by Russia's opponents that any future Bulgarian state would merely be a vehicle for the Balkan ambitions of its big Slav brother. However, the Western powers found it difficult to give the Turks their unqualified support: public opinion in the West was often deeply sympathetic to the demands of the Ottoman Empire's Christian subjects – of which Russia fancied itself to be the protector.

Russian troops had temporarily expelled the Ottomans from parts of Bulgaria during the 1810–11 and 1828–29 **Russo-Turkish wars**, but were consistently unwilling to provoke the Western powers by pressing their advantage in the region too far. Britain and France had even laid siege to Russia's Black Sea ports in the **Crimean War** of 1854–56 in order to demonstrate their support for the Ottoman Empire – which they hoped would survive in its present form if only they could persuade it to introduce "reforms".

The War of Liberation

In 1876, however, the **massacres** that followed the April Rising sent a wave of revulsion throughout Europe, and the Russian army prepared to teach the

Turks a lesson. The British and French, faced by an angry public enraged by tales of Ottoman **atrocities** against Bulgarian civilians, were no longer in a position to back the Turks. The British tried to diffuse the situation by bringing the Turks to the negotiating table, but after assenting to the **Constantinople Conference** in November 1876, the Ottoman government rejected its draft proposals for an autonomous Bulgarian province.

The Russians were initially cautious about embarking on a war with Turkey because they feared an armed response from Austria. By the time the Constantinople Conference broke up, however, the Russians had reached a secret agreement with the Austrians; promising them Russian support for their claim to Bosnia-Herzegovina if they remained neutral in any Russo-Turkish conflict. Free to act, the Russian Tsar Alexander II (subsequently known to Bulgarians as **Tsar Osvoboditel** – the "Tsar-Liberator") declared war on Turkey in April 1877.

Romanians and Bulgarian volunteers fought alongside the Russians in the 1877–78 **War of Liberation**, which would have been a total rout had the Turks not fought belated rearguard actions at the siege of Plevna (modern-day Pleven) and the battle of the Shipka Pass.

The defeated Turks signed the **Treaty of San Stefano** in March 1878, recognizing an independent Bulgaria incorporating much of Macedonia and Thrace. This so-called "**Big Bulgaria**" was too much for the Western powers to swallow, and was promptly broken up by the speedily summoned **Congress of Berlin** (July 1878). The outcome of the Congress reflected the desire of British prime minister Benjamin Disraeli to "keep the Russians out of Turkey, not to create an ideal existence for Turkish Christians". Macedonia and southern Thrace were returned to the Turks, and the rest of Bulgaria was split into two chunks: land south of the Balkan Mountains became **Eastern Rumelia**, an autonomous province of the Ottoman Empire; while land to the north became an independent **Principality of Bulgaria** owing nominal suzerainty to the Turks and paying annual tribute to the sultan.

From Independence to World War II

In the immediate post-Liberation years, attempts to build a stable **democracy** in the principality were hampered by continuing Great Power interest in Balkan affairs. The Russians still regarded Bulgaria as a potential instrument of tsarist policy, provoking tension between pro- and anti-Russian elements within the country itself.

Russian advisers were responsible for drafting an autocratic constitution for the fledgling state, but this was rejected by the Constituent Assembly which met at Tûrnovo in 1879. Dominated by the Liberal Party (in which many leading lights of the liberation struggle were gathered), the Assembly drew up the so-called **Tûrnovo Constitution**, which envisaged a single chamber parliament elected by universal male suffrage. This went down badly with Bulgaria's newly chosen prince, the autocratically minded Alexander Battenberg (Aleksandûr Batenberg to the Bulgarians) – a German aristocrat who had served with the Russian army during the War of Liberation. The prince suspended the constitution and convened a special assembly in the Danubian town of Svishtov – which he blackmailed into voting him emergency powers by threatening to abdicate if they refused. To the new Russian tsar, Alexander III (Alexander II had been murdered in March 1881), however, the German-speaking prince was a living reminder of Russia's humiliation at the Congress of Berlin. Eager to forge alliances with those in Bulgaria who were suspicious of Russian influence, Aleksandûr accepted a partial return to democratic government in 1883.

Unification – and the Serbo-Bulgarian War

Many of the Liberal politicians who fled Aleksandûr's so-called **personal regime** ended up in Eastern Rumelia, which since 1878 had been ruled by local governor-generals eager to advance the Bulgarian cause in the region, despite its continuing status as a province of the Ottoman Empire. Growing popular agitation for **unification with Bulgaria** culminated in an uprising within Eastern Rumelia and the declaration of union in September 1885; a *fait accompli* that Turkey accepted after much sabre-rattling.

Serbia, offended that changes of Balkan borders could be made without its permission, and afraid that Bulgarian unification would be followed by territorial gains elsewhere, launched a punitive attack on Bulgaria – in the ensuing **Serbo-Bulgarian war of 1885** a ramshackle Bulgarian army successfully routed the Serbs at Slivnitsa.

International intrigue

More serious, however, was the displeasure expressed by Russia at Bulgaria's failure to consult its big Slav cousin on the issue of unification. In a **turn-around of international attitudes**, Bulgarian expansion was now opposed by the Russians, because they were constrained by an agreement with Germany and Austria promising to preserve the status quo in the Balkans. The British, slowly becoming aware that Bulgaria wasn't necessarily the subservient Russian creature they had feared it to be, responded to Bulgarian unification with glee. The Russians withdrew their advisers and troops from Bulgaria, expecting the principality to collapse. When this didn't happen, pro-Russian officers in the Bulgarian army deposed Prince Aleksandûr and spirited him out of the country in 1886, before themselves falling victim to a counter-coup organized by leading Liberal politician **Stefan Stambolov**. Stambolov secured Aleksandûr's return, but the fawning way in which Aleksandûr attempted a reconciliation with the Russian tsar enraged Stambolov, and the prince's position became so untenable that in September 1886 he was forced to abdicate. The Russians prepared to mount a takeover of Bulgaria but misjudged local opinion, parliamentary elections producing an anti-Russian, pro-Stambolov majority. Acting as the head of a **Council of Regents**, Stambolov attempted to sever the Russian connection entirely by realigning Bulgaria's foreign policy with Austria and Germany, and inviting the Habsburgs' favourite German toff **Ferdinand of Saxe-Coburg-Gotha** to become the new monarch.

Stambolov, however, had to initiate a repressive regime in order to get these changes accepted by the country, and an **uprising by Russophile army officers** in 1887 was mercilessly suppressed. Stambolov's **dictatorship** lasted until he was ditched by former protégé Ferdinand in 1894. Ferdinand sought a rapprochement with Russia, and set about creating a more **absolutist monarchy**. Stambolov, the only politician with the stature to challenge the court, was killed by Macedonian terrorists – possibly with Ferdinand's connivance – in 1895.

The Balkan wars

By 1900 growing turmoil in the Ottoman Empire left the Great Powers of Europe increasingly unable to control events in the region – however desperate they were to do so – giving the small states of the Balkans more room for independent action. Ferdinand exploited the chaos created by the **Young Turk** revolution in July 1908 to declare Bulgaria's full independence from Ottoman suzerainty, crowning himself **tsar** in the same year. Political crisis in the Ottoman lands meant that the future of **Macedonia and southern Thrace** was once more back on the agenda, and Bulgaria and its neighbours began discussing ways of driving the Turks from the area for good.

The **First Balkan War** of 1912 gave Bulgaria the chance it had been waiting for to try and reclaim some of the territories taken away by the Congress of Berlin. In alliance with Serbia and Greece, Bulgaria launched an attack on Turkey, coming within a whisker of capturing Istanbul. Bulgarian forces were so confident of capturing the city that Ferdinand ordered his state carriage to be sent to the front line so that he could enter the city in triumph – ultimately, bad weather and a cholera outbreak saved the Turks from defeat. Bulgarian troops succeeded in occupying the Pirin region of eastern Macedonia, but found that the Serbs and the Greeks had beaten them to the rest. Unable to agree on an equitable division of the spoils, the former allies fell out, Greece and Serbia defeating Bulgaria in the **Second Balkan War** of 1913.

Bulgaria was forced to renounce claims on the bulk of Macedonia and surrender the southern Dobrudzha to Romania, but still managed to finish the Balkan Wars with a positive balance. Allowed to keep the Pirin, it also obtained Thracian lands in the south, including access to the Aegean Sea at the port of Dedeagach (now the Greek town of Alexandroupolis).

World War I

Following the outbreak of **World War I**, much of Bulgarian opinion sided with the Entente Powers of Britain, France and Russia, largely due to ties of Slavic kinship with the Russians and a common dislike of the Turks. However, the Entente's commitments to Bulgaria's major Balkan rival, Serbia, dissuaded Bulgaria from joining the alliance. Instead, German promises to restore **Macedonia** persuaded King Ferdinand and prime minister Radoslavov to enter the war on the side of the Central Powers.

Hoping to gain large amounts of territory at very little human cost, Bulgaria waited until September 1915 before joining the action, with Radoslavov confidently boasting to his compatriots that it would all be over by Christmas. Three years of agony ensued: anti-war politicians like the leader of the Agrarian Party, **Aleksandûr Stamboliiski**, were jailed; and countless thousands of Bulgarians were dispatched to die in the trenches and mountains of Macedonia.

1918–1944

With the country bled white, Bulgaria's army collapsed beneath the Allied offensive along the Salonika front in September 1918. Deserting soldiers hoisted red flags and converged on Sofia, soon to proclaim the "**Radomir Republic**", while the cabinet declared an **armistice** and released Aleksandûr Stamboliiski, hoping to avert a revolution. Though the mutineers were swiftly crushed, Ferdinand was forced to abdicate in favour of his son, **Boris III**, leaving Stamboliiski's **Bulgarian Agrarian National Union** or **BZNS** the most powerful force in the country.

The Agrarians emerged as the largest party in the 1919 election – the general desire for radical change was reflected in the fact that the Communists came second – and Stamboliiski became prime minister of a country whose wartime allegiance the Allies punished by the **Treaty of Neuilly** (1919). Under its terms, Bulgaria was bound to pay crippling war reparations, Romania reoccupied the southern Dobrudzha, Yugoslavia claimed most of Macedonia, while southwestern Thrace – and with it, access to the Aegean – went to Greece.

Unlike previous governments, the **Agrarians** favoured the countryside rather than the towns, exalting "peasant power" to the dismay of Bulgaria's traditional elite. The bourgeoisie became alarmed by Stamboliiski's dictatorial radicalism, and nationalists everywhere were outraged by his attempts to build peaceful relations with neighbouring Yugoslavia – a policy that entailed renouncing Bulgarian claims on Macedonia. Bulgaria had been flooded with Macedonian refugees since the end of the war, many of whom owed their allegiance to the **Internal Macedonian Revolutionary Organization**, or **IMRO** – a group committed to liberating Macedonia from Yugoslav control and therefore implacably opposed to Stamboliiski's new direction in foreign policy.

The 1923 Coup

In June 1923, right-wing military officers supported by IMRO gunmen staged a bloody **coup d'état** against the Agrarians, assassinating Stamboliiski in the process. The reactionary "**Democratic Concord**" coalition under Aleksandûr Tsankov assumed power, which it monopolized until 1931. Having failed to come to Stamboliiski's aid in June, the **Communists** staged a hastily planned **uprising** in September 1923, provoking the army and police to savage repression and anti-Communist terror. The Communist Party was banned, and many of its leaders who fled to the Soviet Union later perished during the Stalinist *Ezhovshchina*, or "Great Purge".

The 1930s

The 1930s were a time of stagnation and political unrest, epitomized by the murderous feuds within IMRO. The June 1931 election brought to power a left-of-centre coalition, the "People's Bloc", but faced by the constraints of the **Great Depression**, the new government was unable to carry out its radical social programme. Economic slump provoked an increase in political extremism, which mirrored the growth of authoritarianism elsewhere in Europe. The Communists re-emerged in the shape of a front organization, the **Bulgarian Workers' Party**, banned by the government in 1932; while Aleksandûr Tsankov made up for the demise of the Democratic Concord by forming the Hitler-inspired **National Socialist Movement**.

Disintegration of the body politic encouraged the **Military League** to assume power in May 1934 in a coup inspired by the ideas of **Zveno** (Link), another elitist organization whose programme included the customary hotch-potch of militant left- and right-wing ideologies. Parliament was dissolved, all parties were abolished and IMRO was brought to heel: Bulgaria was "depoliticized". But in government the League proved as faction-ridden and ineffectual as its civilian predecessors, and after November 1935 **Tsar Boris III** established his own **dictatorship**, periodically erecting a parliamentary facade.

World War II

Nazi Germany's economic penetration of the Balkans during the late 1930s provided the Third Reich with considerable influence over Bulgaria and its neighbours, and despite the country's declaration of neutrality on the outbreak of **World War II**, Bulgaria inexorably succumbed to the Reich, which required it as a "land bridge" which German troops could cross in order to mount the invasion of Greece. In return for Hitler's offer of Macedonia, Boris committed Bulgaria to the Axis in March 1941, although he baulked at declaring war on the Soviet Union due to Bulgaria's traditionally good relations with the Russian people (it was long believed that Boris' death, following a visit to Berlin, was the result of Nazi poisoning, although a team of pathologists examining the tsar's heart in 1991 finally put an end to these rumours).

Many Bulgarian Communists exiled in Moscow returned home to foment resistance, but Bulgaria's wartime **partisan movement** was a relatively small affair. However, the Communists did manage to infiltrate and manipulate other opposition groups, combining them into the **Fatherland Front** (*Otechestven Front*) in 1942. Events moved towards a climax with the Red Army's advance and Romania's escape from the Axis in August 1944. On September 8 the USSR declared war and crossed the Danube; that night, junior officers acting with the connivance of the minister of defence, Gregoriev, seized strategic points in Sofia, while partisan brigades swept down from the hills. This virtually bloodless putsch was repeated across Bulgaria the next day, making September 9 **Liberation Day**.

The People's Republic

After September 9, the **Bulgarian Communist Party** emerged from two decades of clandestine existence to become the leading political force in the country. Initially their radicalism was hidden behind the ostensibly moderate **Fatherland Front government** led by political veteran Kimon Georgiev, principal architect of the 1934 coup. However, the Communist Party's domination of the Front was never in doubt. Manipulating the ministries of Justice and the Interior to cow right-wing collaborators, and driving the left and centre parties into opposition by repeated provocations, the Party increased its membership from 15,000 to 250,000 in six months. Dominant in government, they then staged a referendum on the **monarchy**, abolished it, and proclaimed the **People's Republic** on September 15, 1946.

Now controlled by **Georgi Dimitrov**, **Vasil Kolarov** and **Anton Yugov**, the state apparatus was turned against the opposition. Many of the political parties left outside the Communist-controlled Fatherland Front had boycotted Bulgaria's first postwar elections in 1945, convinced that the presence of the Red Army on Bulgarian soil would intimidate voters into backing the Front.

A more organized campaign was mounted for the general elections of October 1946, producing a parliament that included a small but vociferous number of anti-Communist MPs. The opposition centred around the Agrarian party or **BZNS**, heir to the popular radical tradition of Stamboliiski, and leaders of peasant resistance to enforced collectivization of the countryside. The Communists claimed that they were traitors sabotaging the economic recovery of the nation: hundreds of BZNS party workers were purged and their leader, **Nikola Petkov**, was hanged for "treason" after a show trial in 1947. Other parties outside the Front were snuffed out at the same time. The same year, Bulgaria acquired the new "Dimitrov" **Constitution** (modelled on the USSR's) and the **nationalization** of 2273 enterprises struck the "bourgeoisie" a mortal blow.

The following year saw a power struggle within the Party, largely over **economic links with the Soviet Union** and **relations with Tito's Yugoslavia**. The Tito–Stalin row of 1948 and Yugoslavia's subsequent expulsion from the Soviet camp gave Communist leaders everywhere the chance they needed to get rid of comrades who they found troublesome. Moscow-trained cadres targeted "home-grown" Communists – that is those who had chosen to remain in the country during the interwar years rather than flee to the USSR – in an attempt to settle old scores.

Some of the more patriotic Bulgarian Communists criticized the terms of Bulgaro-Soviet trade (eighty percent of Bulgaria's tobacco crop was purchased at below market prices and then undersold abroad), leaving themselves open to accusations of nationalism at a time when blind loyalty to the Soviet Union was the order of the day – as good a reason as any to launch a purge of "Titoists". Ten ministers, six Politburo members (including **Traicho Kostov**, shot after renouncing his "confession" to having been a fascist spy since 1942) and 92,500 lesser Party members were arrested or dismissed in the purge of 1948–49, while the nation was paralysed by **police terror**. Stalinism pervaded Bulgaria, and for his total sycophancy the Party leader who succeeded Dimitrov, **Vûlko Chervenkov**, was dubbed "little Stalin".

The era of "Socialist Construction"

With opposition both outside and inside the Party effectively crushed, the government could embark on the transformation of Bulgaria into a modern industrial state. Average Bulgarians, however, gained little from the first **Five-Year Plan**, though this gave a great boost to heavy industrial production (up 120 percent from 1949 to 1955). While factories mushroomed, workers were expected to meet ever-rising production targets, and consumer goods and foodstuffs grew increasingly scarce. Agricultural production remained at roughly its 1939 level, despite an increase in the population and Bulgaria's acquisition of the grain-producing southern Dobrudzha. Unlike elsewhere in Eastern Europe, there were few large estates to be expropriated – on the contrary, economists bemoaned the mass of smallholdings and the individualism of their owners.

Following the **death of Stalin** (1953), Moscow gradually withdrew support from hardliners in the satellite states, and advocates of less spartan policies replaced them. In Bulgaria, Chervenkov lost the position of Party Secretary (1954) and prime minister (1956) to **Todor Zhivkov** and Anton Yugov. The separation of these offices reflected the Kremlin's new policy of "collective" leadership, and Bulgaria's dutiful purge of "anti-Party" elements in 1957 followed their example by avoiding bloodshed. China, however, seems to have inspired Zhivkov's sudden announcement of the "**Big Leap Forward**" in October 1958, whereby the economy aimed to fulfil the Five-Year Plan in three years, and smallholdings were pooled into 3290 **collective farms**. Industrial dislocation was considerable, but the effect on agriculture was mitigated by the private plots that peasants were allowed to retain.

The Zhivkov era

For much of the **Zhivkov era**, Bulgarian conformity to Soviet wishes became a cliché of East European politics, with the country jokingly referred to – even by Bulgarians themselves – as the sixteenth republic of the USSR. However, this pliability did have its advantages: Bulgaria obtained cut-price Soviet oil, electricity and raw materials, and was relieved of the duty of hosting significant Soviet garrisons.

With access to education and employment consistently denied to people who failed to conform, most Bulgarians had no choice but to grudgingly accept rigid Party control of public life, although this passivity was made easier to bear by the Communist system's achievements in the social sphere. Given adequate food, guaranteed work, schooling and medical care, and the prospect of an apartment in the future, people were generally prepared to tolerate low wages, shortages of consumer goods and the lack of many liberal freedoms.

The West's image of Bulgaria under Zhivkov was almost wholly negative, coloured by the country's slavish adherence to Soviet foreign policy, and the fearsome reputation of the *Dûrhavna Sigurnost* or **DS**, the state security police. The assassination of dissident writer **Georgi Markov**, who died after being stabbed by a poison-tipped umbrella on London's Waterloo Bridge in 1978, gave the Bulgarian security services a reputation for subterfuge and cruelty. Subsequent allegations that the DS had abetted a **plot to kill Pope John Paul II** in 1981 suggested that Bulgaria did the kind of dirty work with which not even the KGB would wish to soil its hands.

However, it was the Party's manipulation of **nationalism** that seemed to Western eyes to be the most distasteful aspect of the regime. On the surface, attempts by the Party to present socialist Bulgaria as a homogeneous national state, the logical culmination of centuries of struggles for freedom, seemed to start off innocently enough. Vast amounts of money were spent on the monuments and festivities celebrating the **1300th anniversary of the founding of the Bulgarian state** in 1983, and resources were channelled into the restoration of historical monuments associated with Bulgaria's past greatness.

However, there wasn't much room in Zhivkov's Bulgaria for people of different ethnic origin. Ever since the 1950s smaller minorities like the Vlachs (see p.202) and Islamized Gypsies had been encouraged to drop their traditional names and adopt Bulgarian ones. The campaign moved on to the **pomaks** (Muslim Bulgarians) in the 1970s, and to the million-strong **Turkish minority** in the 1980s. Those who refused to Bulgaricize their names were refused work, housing, or worse still, sent to concentration camps such as Belene and Lovech. Opposition to the **name-changing campaign** sparked violence in 1984, and led to a mass exodus of Bulgarian Turks in summer 1989, provoking outrage from human rights groups across the world. All this led to a further deterioration of relations between Bulgaria and the outside world – even Bulgaria's socialist allies were increasingly embarrassed to be associated with it.

The demise of the Communist regime

Bulgaria's socialist economy was beginning to stall well before the emergence of **perestroika** in the Soviet Union began to raise fundamental questions about the continuing viability of the whole system. Summer droughts in 1984 and 1985 had harmed agriculture and reduced hydroelectric power (which usually accounts for much of Bulgaria's supply) at a time when Soviet oil supplies were cut back, causing widespread energy shortages. Prices skyrocketed with hardly any corresponding wage increases, and for the first time in many years a note of testiness entered Bulgaro-Soviet relations.

As Gorbachev increasingly toyed with the idea of wide-reaching reform in the USSR, the hardline leaders of his Soviet bloc allies became more and more of an embarrassment. Zhivkov was particularly unpopular with the new Soviet leadership, not least because they found his anti-Turkish policies repugnant. Aware of this, high-ranking Bulgarian officials began jostling for position in preparation for the day when they could (perhaps with Gorbachev's backing) oust their ageing leader. However, they had to wait until the end of the decade for their opportunity to do so.

The July Conceptions

The Bulgarian Communist Party's initial reaction to Gorbachev's innovations was predictably cautious, and it wasn't until July 1987 that Zhivkov announced the **July Conceptions**, an attempt to give the Party a patina of *perestroika*-esque credibility. Although it promised decentralization of state-run businesses and democratization of Party structures, it was difficult to find examples of these fine-sounding commitments ever being carried out.

By January 1988 Bulgarians were being allowed to form private firms providing that they employed no more than ten people, and the government increasingly advocated a departure from rigid state planning and a tentative move towards **market economics**. Enthusiasm for political change continued to be lukewarm, however, and for some time Bulgarians moved in a strange political limbo, where talk of *glasnost* and *perestroika* was officially sanctioned, but any practical application of them merely invited the usual hassles from the security police.

Protest

Ecological protesters from the city of **Ruse** were the first independent citizens to organize themselves into pressure groups outside Party control in spring 1988. Encouraged by their example, intellectuals in Sofia formed the **Club for the Support of Glasnost and Perestroika** in November of the same year, an organization that united both dissidents and moderate Party members, but the Club's supporters were subjected to petty harassment, denied meeting space and forbidden to use photocopiers.

The Communist Party itself was split between those around Zhivkov who favoured caution, and those eager to rush ahead with political change. Throughout 1989 opposition organizations like **Podkrepa**, the new independent trade union federation formed in February 1989, and **Ecoglasnost**, a green pressure group (which did much to unite disparate strands of the opposition around a cause which they could all share), were allowed to operate after a fashion, but their members never knew from one day to the next what the precise limits to their political freedom were. As the year progressed Zhivkov attempted to win support by stoking up nationalist fervour, with renewed repression of Bulgaria's Turks. The resulting **mass exodus** of Bulgarian Muslims into neighbouring Turkey merely served to convince many in the country that the Communist regime had finally lost all legitimacy to rule.

The fall of Zhivkov

In October 1989 Sofia's police were still beating up members of Ecoglasnost with impunity on the capital's streets, but in the end the forces of conservatism were overtaken by events. On **November 10, 1989** (the day after the Berlin Wall came down), reformers within the Party seized their chance and called a meeting of the Central Committee, which forced Zhivkov's resignation. The former dictator was arrested on charges of inciting racial hatred and, soon afterwards, embezzling state funds; new Party leader **Petûr Mladenov** promised free elections, market reforms and an end to the corruption and gangsterism of the past. Opposition leaders took advantage of the new atmosphere to form the **SDS** or Sûyuz na demokratichnite sili (Union of Democratic Forces) on December 7, an impressive assemblage of dissidents, greens and human-rights activists which non-Communist Bulgarians everywhere pressed forward to join.

Post-Communist Bulgaria: a slow start

The reformist wing of the Bulgarian Communist Party had obviously thought that by ditching Zhivkov and committing themselves to the idea of a multiparty system, they stood a good chance of being perceived as the authors of democratic change, thereby winning back the trust of the populace. Initially, however, their strategy ran into trouble. Throughout December 1989 the Bulgarian parliament was regularly under siege from protesters demanding a speeding up of democratic reforms, most notably the abandonment of the Communist Party's **leading role** in society, hitherto enshrined in the constitution. The Party was also under pressure from its own hardliners, who tried to sabotage democratization by organizing **nationalist demonstrations and strikes** throughout the country in protest at the government's retreat from Todor Zhivkov's anti-Turkish policies.

In 1990 the dismantling of Communist power structures began in earnest. Separation of party and state was symbolized when Petûr Mladenov became state president and relinquished the Party chairmanship to **Aleksandûr Lilov**, previously the victim of one of Zhivkov's purges. Former hardliners were removed from government, Mladenov's protégé **Andrei Lukanov** became prime minister, and the Party itself changed its name to the **Bulgarian Socialist Party (BSP)**.

Multiparty elections were called for **June 1990**, too early for either the BSP or the opposition SDS to establish themselves as credible democratic movements. The BSP, despite verbal commitments to democratic socialism, still included far too many dyed-in-the-wool Communists for people to take its new identity seriously; while the SDS, a loose coalition of newly formed parties and citizens' pressure groups, could agree on little save for a hatred of Communism and a desire to speed up market reforms.

Public uncertainty over the economic changes proposed by the SDS played into the hands of the BSP, which garnered 45 percent of the vote and an absolute majority in the Veliko Narodno Sûbranie or **Constituent Assembly**. Much of this success was attributed to the conservative nature of the Bulgarian countryside, where the Socialist Party machine was far more effective in reaching potential voters than its cash-starved opponents. The other main beneficiary of the poll was the **Movement for Rights and Freedoms** – Dvizhenieto za prava i svobodi or **DPS**. Formed to protect Bulgaria's Muslims, the DPS gained solid support from the country's Turks and pomaks, giving it 23 MPs in the new chamber. However, Bulgaria's urban population had voted en masse for the SDS, and many suspected that the BSP's majority had been artificially inflated by **vote rigging**.

The summer of 1990 – and after

The SDS leadership was split on the issue of whether to accept the election result or stage some kind of protest, but the potentially volatile nature of Bulgarian society persuaded them to refrain from anything that might provoke violence. Nevertheless, **discontent** smouldered on throughout June, with regular street demonstrations in the capital, and student-manned **barricades** going up outside Sofia University. Frustration at the BSP's victory boiled over with the discovery of an old **video tape** that showed President Mladenov threatening to use tanks against opposition demonstrators in Sofia the previous December. Mass meetings called for his resignation, a demand echoed by Socialist Party members themselves.

Mladenov bowed to pressure and resigned on July 7, but this only encouraged further demonstrations by opposition groups dissatisfied with the slow pace of change. In Sofia, university lecturers and students established the "**City of Truth**" – a tent settlement near the mausoleum of Communist Bulgaria's founder, Georgi Dimitrov – to demand a removal of all former Communist MPs and a speeding-up of the criminal proceedings against Todor Zhivkov. Similar "cities" soon sprang up in provincial capitals. In the meantime, **conservative forces** egged on by hardline Communists continued to protest against the new freedom accorded to Bulgaria's ethnic Turks, outraged by the thought that national unity might be compromised by the presence of Turkish deputies in parliament.

By the time the Constituent Assembly convened in Veliko Tûrnovo in mid-July, political authority within the country was in a serious state of disintegration, prompting dark rumours of a return to hardline government with possible help from the military. The Assembly's first and most urgent task was to elect a new president who could somehow hold the country together. After more than a month of deadlock, the Assembly awarded the presidency to the leader of the SDS, **Zhelyu Zhelev**, a respected dissident academic who had been sent into internal exile by the former regime for writing a book entitled *What is Fascism?* – a work that embarrassed Bulgaria's erstwhile rulers by demonstrating the similarity between both left- and right-wing forms of totalitarianism.

Zhelev faced a potentially dangerous breakdown in public order almost immediately upon his election. A decision by parliament ordering the removal of Communist symbols from all public buildings was interpreted by the Sofia mob as an invitation to **set fire** to the Socialist (Communist) **Party headquarters** – where a big red star was prominently displayed – on August 26. Zhelev denounced the vandals, and things began to calm down.

Plummeting confidence in the socialist system had, however, produced a crisis in the Bulgarian **economy**. The cabinet of BSP prime minister Andrei Lukanov courted the likes of Robert Maxwell in an attempt to attract foreign investment into the country, but unwillingness to adopt necessary market reforms soon led to the government's collapse. Made nervous by a nationwide wave of **strikes** and **student protests**, the socialist-dominated Assembly consented to the formation of an all-party **coalition government** in December 1990. Stiff medicine was applied to the Bulgarian economy with the **liberation of prices** in February 1991. Subsequent massive inflation and high interest rates caused bankruptcies, growing unemployment and widespread **social misery**.

October 1991 and after

As the **elections of October 1991** approached, Bulgarian society appeared to be as divided as at any time in its history. The most visible results of post-Zhivkov change – rising prices, declining social services and the ostentation of those who grew fat on the proceeds of private enterprise – were an affront to people on fixed incomes, especially pensioners and employees of ailing state firms. The BSP tapped these resentments by proposing a slowed-down model of economic reform and the retention of some measure of state planning. For the SDS and other non-socialists, however, Bulgaria's salvation depended on a total **purge of Communist influence**, and the wholesale adoption of a **free market** – whatever the social cost.

In the end the elections were a **close-run thing**. The SDS received 34 percent of the vote; the BSP 33 percent; and the DPS held the balance of power with 7.5 percent. Despite the narrow margin of victory, the result was hailed as a turning-point in Bulgarian history by the BSP's opponents – but claims that Bulgarian socialism had been finally laid to rest proved to be premature.

The new government of prime minister **Filip Dimitrov** initiated a crash programme of economic reform, removing barriers to foreign investment, speeding up the **privatization** of state-run firms, and establishing the ground rules for *restitutsiya* or "**restitution**" – the process by which property and land nationalized by the Communists could be reclaimed by its former owners. Public spending was slashed and wages in the state sector were held down, producing much social hardship and polarizing the country even further. The winter of 1991/92 was characterized by extensive **power cuts**, after former Soviet republics began to demand hard currency for the electricity they used to supply so cheaply.

The first challenge to the post-socialist order came in the **presidential elections** of January 1992, when Zhelyu Zhelev only narrowly beat off the challenge of BSP-sponsored candidate Velko Vûlkanov. As well as pointing to declining living standards, Vûlkanov had exploited growing unease about alleged "Turkish" influence in Bulgarian affairs resulting from the DPS's central position in political life.

Failure to win an **outright majority** in October 1991 had left the SDS dependent on the support of the predominantly Turkish DPS in order to remain in government. However, the Dimitrov government's reluctance to give aid to the economically depressed tobacco-producing regions of the south – where much of the DPS's bedrock support comes from – soon led to a split.

Without DPS support Dimitrov lost a parliamentary vote of confidence in December 1992, and President Zhelev called upon economist Lyuben Berov to form an administration of non-party technocrats. Although Berov promised to continue the market reforms of the SDS while trying to limit their more socially harmful consequences, it was clear that Bulgaria's push towards capitalism had been put on hold.

Towards the winter of discontent

The next parliamentary **elections**, in **December 1994**, resulted in a crippling defeat for the SDS and handed an absolute majority in the National Assembly to a rejuvenated BSP. Led by the young and popular Zhan Videnov, the BSP was by now an odd grouping of genuine social democrats, old-style Communists and out-and-out careerists, supported by industrial workers, pensioners and rural Bulgarians bewildered by the changes of the last few years. The BSP continued the cautious policies of the Berov government, indexing pensions and industrial wages to the rate of inflation and devaluing the lev in the hope of kickstarting Bulgaria's moribund economy with an export boom.

Privatization of Bulgaria's state-owned industries moved at a snail's pace, prompting the government's critics to claim that most big enterprises were being run down prior to being sold off cheaply to former Communist functionaries. Indeed, the relationship between Bulgaria's emerging business class and the old political elite raised a few eyebrows. Considerable popular resentment was directed towards members of the old regime who were able to build up sizeable reserves of hard currency in foreign bank acounts in the late 1980s, and then return to buy into the country's economy.

Ultimately, though, the Videnov administration was brought down by its own economic incompetence. Market reforms ground to a standstill, and all levels of the economy became infected with corruption – often with government connivance. BSP elder statesman Andrei Lukanov – who had himself become a byword for shady dealings – was gunned down by mystery assailants in October 1996 for threatening to blow the whistle on government corruption. As **winter 1996** approached, foreign investors fled the country, the lev plummeted against the dollar, and food shortages re-emerged. With the government unable to meet its foreign debt repayments, and unwilling to introduce the economic austerity programme demanded of it by the IMF, Videnov resigned in December, ushering in a period of acute instability.

The BSP had already lost the initiative following the presidential elections of November 1996, when Zhelev had been replaced by the SDS lawyer **Petûr Stoyanov**. However they still tried to cling to parliamentary power, refusing to yield to opposition demands for fresh elections. With the economy getting worse, a wave of anti-government demonstrations swept the country, and with SDS-inspired crowds mounting an assault on parliament in mid-January 1997, the BSP finally threw in the towel. A caretaker administration under Stefan Sofianski (the popular SDS mayor of Sofia) took over, and a general election was called for the beginning of April. The SDS won by a landslide, with suave technocrat **Ivan Kostov** becoming prime minister.

Another false dawn

Bulgaria's **economy**, however, had been left in such bad shape by the departing administration that the new government had little choice but to swallow the medicine offered by the IMF – by now the real power in Bulgarian affairs. An economic austerity programme was introduced, and inflation was brought under control by pegging the lev to the Deutschmark. The privatization of state-controlled industries was speeded up once more, but this only led to renewed accusations that enterprises were being sold off cheap to government supporters, with the officials responsible for negotiating the deals pocketing hefty commission fees. A series of much-vaunted **anti-corruption drives** aimed to restore public confidence in big business, but often had the opposite effect – those under investigation invariably tended to be linked to the BSP, while SDS supporters escaped scrutiny.

Although unable to control the struggles for power and status within governmental ranks, Ivan Kostov himself was widely respected – especially by Western observers – for his largely successful efforts to stabilize government finances. However, he was a bad communicator, and his long-term vision of a slow but steady return to economic growth cut little ice with the majority of the Bulgarians, who continued to eke out a living on meagre wages.

The return of the king

With the lack of any real improvement in living standards, support for the Kostov government simply withered away. Only in the relatively prosperous SDS strongholds of Sofia, Plovdiv and Varna was there any remaining enthusiasm for his unexciting political platform of fiscal prudence. However, the BSP, still tainted by the economic incompetence of the Videnov years, was badly placed to profit from widespread disillusionment with the SDS – leaving a political vacuum ready to be exploited by a new and unexpected force.

Ever since 1990, the idea of a return to the **monarchy** had occasionally been floated by those disillusioned with Bulgaria's frequently unstable post-Communist political setup. The Madrid-based **Tsar Simeon II**, who had been chased out of the country by the Communists at the age of nine, was in regular contact with Bulgarian politicians throughout the 1990s, but initially showed little real interest in coming back. He revisited Bulgaria for the first time in 1996, and made it clear that he considered the stage-managed referendum which had turfed him out fifty years earlier to have been illegal. However, he wisely refrained from outright political involvement at a time when most mainstream Bulgarian voters still saw the SDS as the force of the future. By the turn of the millennium, however, events were inexorably moving in his favour. Tired of investing their hopes in successive governments that failed to deliver, ordinary Bulgarians needed a figurehead who could restore some level of confidence in the country. They were joined by many educated, professional Bulgarians who traditionally voted for the SDS, but felt betrayed by its descent into corruption and place-seeking.

Simeon's backers formed a new political organization, the **National Movement of Simeon the Second** (*Natsionalnoto Dvizhenie Simeon Vtori*; or **NDSV**), and prepared to fight the parliamentary elections of June 2001 with Simeon himself heading their list of candidates. Simeon adapted to this new role with an impressive display of *noblesse oblige*, proclaiming that Bulgaria was in a mess, and that he as a simple patriot would do his best to sort things out if that was what people wanted. This went down a storm with the electorate: having lived in exile for the last 55 years, Simeon was perceived to be untainted by the corruption endemic among Bulgaria's political elite, thereby offering the kind of moral rectitude that other national figures lacked. Simeon himself kept his cards close to his chest, studiously avoiding the question of whether he was using the parliamentary elections as a platform from which to regain his throne.

Simeon's programme differed little from the package of budgetary restraint and market reforms offered by other parties, but his promises to stamp out corruption struck a popular chord. In the event the NDSV won a landslide, securing 43 percent of the vote as against the SDS's 18 percent and the BSP's 17 percent. Commanding 120 places in the 240-seat Assembly, Simeon struck a deal with Ahmed Dogan's DPS (which won its customary seven percent share of the vote) to ensure an absolute majority. Reserving the post of prime minister for himself, Simeon assembled a cabinet which included figures from across the political spectrum, as well as young financial experts who had been lured away from highly paid banking jobs abroad by the possibility of forging high-profile political careers at home.

Sitting president Petûr Stoyanov was politically damaged by the scale of the SDS parliamentary defeat, and decided to stand in the **presidential elections of November 2001** as an independent, depriving himself of an effective campaigning machine. After a remarkably low turnout, Stoyanov was pipped at the post by the BSP's **Georgi Pûrvanov**.

The political present

The government of Simeon – still known officially by his family name of **Simeon of Saxe-Coburg-Gotha** (Simeon Sakskoburgotski in Bulgarian) even though many of his supporters refer to him simply as "The Tsar" – continued the work of its SDS-led predecessor, pursuing financial stabilization policies advocated by international organizations such as the IMF and the EU. As with previous administrations, however, popular support for Simeon ebbed away as voters realized that their living standards were not going to improve with any great speed, and the NDSV received a paltry seven percent of the vote at the local elections of 2003. Simeon himself was increasingly seen as the grey tool of his ministers rather than as the charismatic saviour people had hoped for.

With the class-based BSP and ethnic-Turkish DPS remaining the only political parties capable of commanding a solid electorate, Bulgarian politics are entering another fluid and unpredictable phase. The SDS is still powerful in the big cities, but elsewhere the centre-right is as fragmented as ever, with a host of minor parties – often tied to a particular leader rather than a coherent set of policies – jostling for attention.

Bulgaria's position in the world

After November 1989 Bulgaria was eager to be accepted as a political and economic partner of the Western world, but found progress frustratingly slow on both counts. The series of wars in the former Yugoslavia provoked a muddled response from a Western community unable to decide what its precise interests in the Balkans were, and the cultivation of Bulgaria as a useful ally in the region only ever proceeded in fits and starts. On the economic front, the Yugoslav conflict severed Bulgaria's land links with central Europe, isolating the country from trade; while the appetite for corruption and fiscal incompetence displayed by successive Bulgarian governments provided potential Western investors with another reason for giving the country a wide berth.

Membership of **NATO** and the **EU** have been the main planks of Bulgarian foreign policy ever since the early nineties. Progress on both counts was sporadic in the extreme up until the early 2000s, when the possibility of renewed stability in the former Yugoslavia and the continuing weakness of Russian power suddenly opened up new opportunities for the countries of southeastern Europe. Bulgaria was admitted to NATO in April 2004, and accession to the EU – notwithstanding last-minute hiccups – is envisaged for 2007. These developments have made it much easier for young, educated Bulgarians to travel and work abroad, producing a migratory tide which can only increase once the country becomes a full EU member. With birth rates plummeting at home, and Bulgarians in their twenties and thirties seeking a new life abroad, demographic impoverishment could well be the biggest challenge facing the country in the future.

The Macedonian question

The name "Macedonia" is a geographical term of long standing, applied to an area that has always been populated by a variety of races and cultures. For centuries an area of discord between Balkan peoples, it's currently divided between three states – Bulgaria, Greece and the Republic of Macedonia – each of which has deep-seated historical reasons for regarding the Macedonian name and the Macedonian heritage as something exclusively its own. Bulgaria went to war over Macedonia three times in the early twentieth century, only to end up on the losing side on each occasion. As a symbol of the nation's unfulfilled destiny in the Balkans, Macedonia continues to occupy an important place in the Bulgarian psyche.

Historical Macedonia

The original **kingdom of Macedonia**, which reached its zenith in the fourth century BC under Philip II and Alexander the Great, was governed by Greek-speaking kings and inhabited – from what historians can gather – by a predominantly Greek-speaking population. Its early borders spread from Mt Olympus in the south to the upper Vardar basin in the north, and it was this core area that provided the basis for the subsequent **Roman province of Macedonia**, although the region was carved up into different administrative units during the Byzantine period. The name Macedonia faded from people's consciousness

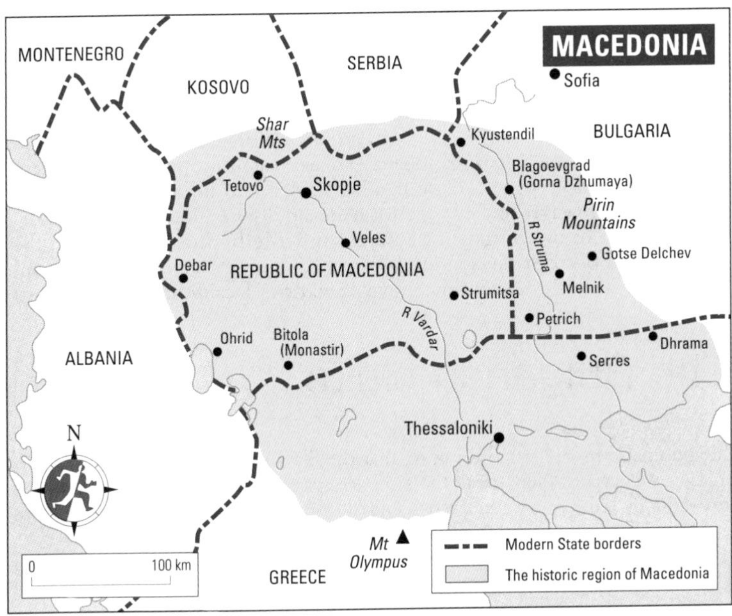

during the Middle Ages, only to be resurrected from the Renaissance onwards by West European geographers and diplomats eager to give the area a convenient geographical label. The ethnic composition of the area was in any case constantly changing (in ancient times Greeks lived cheek-by-jowl with Thracians and Illyrians, and from the sixth century onwards they were increasingly joined by **Slavonic tribes**), so there was never really any ethnic or political continuity between the Macedonia of the ancients and the Macedonia of the modern era.

Under **Ottoman rule** Macedonia was known officially as the "**Three Provinces**", with administrative centres at Thessaloniki, Skopje and Monastir (present-day Bitola in the Former Yugoslav Republic of Macedonia). At the beginning of the twentieth century, Macedonia was one of the most cosmopolitan regions of the empire, peopled by Slavs, Greeks, Turks, Albanians and Jews. Cities like Thessaloniki were centres of **revolutionary intrigue**, rocked not only by the increasing national consciousness of the subject peoples of the empire, but also by Turkish reform movements that hoped to liberalize the archaic institutions of the Ottoman state.

In the late nineteenth century the newly independent **nation-states** of Greece, Serbia and Bulgaria each coveted Macedonian territory, but their claims were complicated by the confused ethnic map of the area. The races who lived here didn't inhabit clearly defined geographical units: towns with predominantly Greek or Turkish populations were often surrounded by exclusively Slav or Albanian rural areas. To make matters worse, people were also divided along **religious lines**. Local Slavs who had converted to Islam in the fifteenth century (known hereabouts as *pomaks*, *torbeshes* or *poturs*, they're still very much in evidence) often identified with Macedonia's Turks and Albanians more strongly than with the Christian Slavs. It's not surprising, therefore, that the Greek, Albanian and Slav **armed bands** that roamed the countryside in the early years of the twentieth century were often implacably opposed to each other – each fighting for a "Free Macedonia" that would exclude the national aspirations of its rivals.

Education was one way in which the struggle for the allegiances of the Macedonian people was waged. By raising money to establish schools in the area, Bulgarian, Serb and Greek cultural societies could impose modern **literary languages** on people whose patchwork of regional dialects had hitherto confused their sense of ethnic belonging. Macedonia's Slavs, who were concentrated in the north of the region, but also formed substantial communities in the south along the Aegean seaboard, spoke a language grammatically very close to Bulgarian, but local dialects often shaded into neighbouring Serbian. Both states were eager to claim the Macedonian Slavs as their own, provoking the formation of the Bulgarian **SS Cyril and Methodius Society** and the Serbian **Society of St Sava** in the 1880s, both of which intended to carry out educational work throughout the province and win local hearts and minds.

The Bulgarian claim

It's axiomatic to Bulgarian thinking that the Slavs who inhabit Macedonia are, in fact, Bulgarians. They speak the same language (or at the very least, a dialect exceedingly close to it), and are descended from tribes that came to the Balkans at around the same time.

In the medieval period Macedonia was closely linked to Bulgaria, thus bolstering the latter's **historical claims** to the area. Northern Macedonia was conquered by the Bulgar khans in the ninth century, and remained within the orbit of the First Bulgarian Kingdom until 1218, when the western Macedonian town of **Ohrid** – by that time the Bulgarian capital – finally fell to the Byzantines.

Under the Second Bulgarian Kingdom (1185–1396) things were more confused, with the emergent power of **Serbia** increasingly extending its influence in the area in the 1300s. The central Macedonian town of Skopje was briefly the capital of the greatest of medieval Serbia's rulers, **Tsar Dušan**. The feudal princedoms into which Macedonia fragmented immediately before the **Ottoman conquest** are claimed by both Serbian and Bulgarian historians as their own; and the Macedonian-based **Krali Marko**, a semi-legendary figure who fought vainly to stem the Turkish advance, is a popular figure in the folk literature of both countries – an example of how modern ideas of ethnicity don't always conform to the complex racial mix which prevailed over much of medieval Europe.

Under Turkish rule links between Bulgaria and Macedonia remained strong. The needs of Bulgaria's Christian population were served by the **Archbishopric of Ohrid**, a town which became synonymous with Bulgarian spirituality and learning, until the Church was eventually placed under the jurisdiction of Constantinople in 1767.

During Bulgaria's nineteenth-century **National Revival**, Bulgarians and Macedonians shared a common upsurge in Orthodox culture and art. Woodcarvers from **Debûr** in west Macedonia, an area famed for its craft traditions, worked in churches throughout Bulgaria. Bulgaria's struggle to free ecclesiastical affairs from the control of the Greek Patriarchate was accompanied by assumptions that any future Bulgarian Church would extend to cover the Orthodox Slavs of Macedonia as well. When the Ottoman authorities acquiesced to the creation of an autonomous **Bulgarian Exarchate** in 1870 they included within it much of central Macedonia, and promised that it would have jurisdiction over any other areas where at least two-thirds of the population voted to join. Those around Skopje, Ohrid and Bitola did so – a move regarded by the Bulgarians as an implicit recognition of their claims to the region.

Bulgarian designs on Macedonia found a powerful sponsor in the shape of **tsarist Russia**. After the Russo-Turkish War of 1877–78 the Ottomans agreed to the creation of an independent Bulgarian state, which included the lion's share of Macedonia, at the **Treaty of San Stefano**. This didn't just antagonize the many non-Slav nations who lived within the borders of this so-called "Big Bulgaria" – it also struck fear into the hearts of the European Great Powers, who saw the new country as a vehicle for Russian ambitions in the Balkans. The subsequent **Berlin Congress** promptly returned Macedonia to the Turkish Empire, on the condition that the Ottoman authorities carried out a vague programme of "reforms". The Bulgarians have always regarded the Berlin Congress as a cynical move to frustrate their legitimate national aspirations, and the desire to regain control of Macedonia was a recurring theme in Bulgarian politics in the decades that followed.

Macedonian revolutionary politics: IMRO

Whatever the peoples of Macedonia felt about the idea of being incorporated into a "Big Bulgaria", most of them were pretty unhappy to find themselves once again languishing within the borders of the decaying Ottoman Empire. The ensuing frustration helped to fuel a growing **Macedonian separatist movement**, characterized by a plethora of clandestine groups who specialized in terrorist action and political assassination. Most influential of these was the Vûtreshnata Makedonska revolutsiyonna organizatsiya or **Internal Macedonian Revolutionary Organization** – more commonly known by the acronym of VMRO or **IMRO** – founded in Thessaloniki in 1893 by schoolteachers **Gotse Delchev** and **Dame Gruev**.

Inspired by Bulgarian freedom fighters like Vasil Levski and Hristo Botev, and adopting the "Liberty or Death" slogan beloved of Bulgarian insurgents, IMRO clearly saw themselves as the inheritors of the **Bulgarian revolutionary tradition**. Although IMRO's early leaders undoubtedly considered themselves to be ethnically Bulgarian, none of them thought that Macedonia's interests would be served by straightforward incorporation into Bulgaria.

Delchev, a committed republican, was disillusioned by post-Liberation Bulgaria's degeneration into monarchical dictatorship, and saw the creation of an **autonomous Macedonia** within some future **Balkan federation** as the best possible antidote to the wave of authoritarianism then sweeping the infant nation-states of the region. Together with other IMRO leaders, Delchev also suspected that the idea of a separate Macedonian entity was more likely to win support from Europe's Great Powers – who were for once united in their suspicion of Bulgarian expansionism in the area.

Delchev and Gruev therefore set about creating a clandestine organization within Macedonia itself in order to ensure the movement's independence from Bulgarian government interference. However, many of the **Macedonian emigrants** who found refuge in Sofia after the Berlin Congress began to look towards the Bulgarian state as their most likely means of liberation. In the 1880s and 1890s up to a third of Bulgaria's army officers and civil servants were from Macedonia, and links between government circles and Macedonian émigré organizations were strong. Most influential of the Macedonian organizations within Bulgaria was the **Supreme Macedonian Committee** (whose members came to be known as the *vûrhovisti*, or **Supremists**), a Sofia-based group that worked closely with the Bulgarian court. Jealous of IMRO's influence within Macedonia itself, the Supremists set out to gain control of the Macedonian freedom movement for themselves.

Supporters of both IMRO and the Supremists began to infiltrate each other's organizations, and Macedonian activists became increasingly **split** – between those who saw Macedonia as an entity in its own right and those who favoured its incorporation into Bulgaria. These two strands in the Macedonian revolutionary tradition were exploited by future Bulgarian and Yugoslav governments, each eager to secure historical legitimacy for their diametrically opposed policies in the region.

The Ilinden Uprising

IMRO leaders particularly resented incursions by Supremist-sponsored armed bands into Ottoman territory. Ill-starred adventures such as the **occupation of Melnik** in 1896 and the attempted **uprising** in **Gorna Dzhumaya** (now Blagoevgrad) in 1902 merely served to provoke Ottoman repression and hamper the work of the underground IMRO network within Macedonia. Fearful that a reform programme forced on Turkey by the Great Powers might take the limelight away from the revolutionary movement, IMRO opted to launch a premature and hurriedly planned uprising. Leaders like Delchev were against the idea, but were outmanoeuvred by elements of IMRO allied to the Supremists.

Named **Ilinden** (St Elijah's Day) after the day on which it was launched – August 2, 1903 – the uprising was centred on the town of Krushevo high in the mountains southwest of Skopje. Intended as a beacon of hope to the surrounding populace, the so-called **Krushevo Republic** fell in a matter of weeks.

Fierce Ottoman reprisals followed, and surviving IMRO members retreated into despair and impotence. Gotse Delchev had been killed three months before the uprising in a chance run-in with police, and Dame Gruev fell three years later in an isolated guerrilla action. IMRO itself was increasingly divided into left- and right-wing factions. The left, led by **Yane Sandanski** (after whom one of Bulgaria's Pirin towns is named), argued that the movement had to stop being an exclusively Slav organization and seek alliances with Macedonia's other ethnic groups, while the right sought better relations with the Bulgarian government. Sandanski, who ordered the murder of one of IMRO's most flamboyant leaders Boris Sarafov, found his ideas rejected by the majority, and was himself assassinated by IMRO rivals in 1915. With the bitter failure of Ilinden still hanging over IMRO, power increasingly passed into the hands of the right wing of the organization.

From the Balkan Wars to World War II

In the aftermath of Ilinden, Serbian organizations had taken advantage of IMRO's failure by flooding the area with cultural workers and priests. The government in Sofia increasingly sought a rapprochement with Serbia in order to preserve what was left of Bulgarian influence in Macedonia. Planning a joint attack on Turkey, the two states agreed in March 1912 to split Macedonia between them, with Bulgaria being promised the west-central portion around Bitola and Ohrid. Greece joined the alliance soon afterwards, and in the **First Balkan War** of 1912, Greek and Serbian troops occupied most of Macedonia, while the bulk of the Bulgarian army was tied up fighting the Turks in the east. The Serbs were particularly unwilling to give up any portion of land thus acquired: the creation of an independent state of Albania had frustrated Serbian dreams of westward expansion, and so Macedonia – renamed "**South Serbia**" by government propagandists – became the new target of Serbia's imperialist ambitions.

Bulgaria protested, but its attempt to drive its erstwhile allies from the region in the **Second Balkan War** of 1913 ended in defeat. The subsequent carve-up of the historic province created divisions that endure to this day. The Bulgarians were allowed to keep the eastern part, known as **Pirin Macedonia**; while **Aegean Macedonia**, comprising the port of Thessaloniki and its hinterland, fell to Greece; the Serbs grabbed **Vardar Macedonia** to the north and west, including the towns of Skopje, Bitola and Ohrid. Each of the three states regarded their newly acquired inhabitants respectively as Bulgarians, Greeks or Serbs – expressions of any other ethnic identity were either ignored or suppressed.

After a brief period of Bulgarian occupation during World War I, predominantly Slav-populated Vardar Macedonia ended up in a Serb-dominated **Yugoslav state** that had no place for a separate Macedonian identity. Serbian administrators, priests and schoolteachers descended on the region to run local affairs, and Serbian settlers were encouraged to grab land vacated by emigrating Turks. In Greek-controlled Aegean Macedonia, many Slav communities moved north into Bulgaria during the interwar years, thus consolidating Greek ethnic dominance of the region.

Bulgaria found itself **diplomatically isolated** after 1918, and therefore unable to press any claim to the Macedonian territories of which it felt unjustly deprived. However, a resurgent IMRO, sustained by the refugees who poured into Bulgaria to escape Serbian rule in Vardar Macedonia, put pressure on politicians to take a tough line on the Macedonian question. The presence of such a vociferous (and heavily armed) Macedonian lobby, with strong clandestine networks in both Sofia and the Pirin town of Petrich, was a serious threat to internal stability at a time when Bulgarian governments were eager to build bridges with their Balkan neighbours.

IMRO in the interwar years

Years of guerilla struggle in the Balkans had turned IMRO into a disciplined revolutionary force, and armed bands continued to harry the Yugoslav authorities in Vardar Macedonia from their sanctuaries in the Pirin. The organization also carried out **terrorist attacks** in Bulgaria itself, occupying Kyustendil in 1922 in protest against the government's pro-Yugoslav policies, and threatening the lives of political opponents. Bulgarian nationalists initially thought that they could use IMRO as a private army, enlisting their support to topple the Stamboliiski regime in 1923. However, successive governments regarded IMRO as an obstacle to good relations with Yugoslavia and Greece and worked to neutralize its influence.

In Moscow the newly established Communist International, or **Comintern**, saw IMRO as a potential partner, imagining that the creation of a revolutionary situation in Macedonia would be a prelude to the toppling of reactionary regimes throughout the Balkans. Discussions in Moscow and Vienna in 1924 led to the **May Manifesto**, a document calling for cooperation between IMRO and the Comintern signed by IMRO leaders **Todor Aleksandrov**, **Aleksandûr Protogerov** and **Petûr Chaulev**.

Communist strategy for the Balkans, however, envisaged the creation of a free Macedonia – not its incorporation in an enlarged Bulgarian monarchist state – and therefore ran counter to the wishes of many of IMRO's right-wing, pro-Bulgarian activists. Aleksandrov and Protogerov bowed to pressure by disowning the Manifesto, launching a purge of "socialist" elements from the organization, and expelling Chaulev. However, Aleksandrov was still regarded as a traitor by more-reactionary IMRO colleagues, who had him assassinated in August 1924.

Confined to "exile" in Pirin Macedonia and unable to find a proper role for itself, IMRO spiralled downwards into **self-destruction**. In July 1928 veteran leader Protogerov was shot on the instructions of fellow Central Committee member **Ivan Mihailov**, a particularly ugly piece of internecine strife from which the organization never recovered. Mihailov went on to run IMRO like a mafia boss, liquidating opponents and funding arms purchases by trading in opium grown in the valleys of the Pirin Mountains.

By the 1930s IMRO had become completely ineffectual as a Macedonian liberation movement. Its last great act of wanton terrorism came in 1934, when – in a plot hatched with Croatian fascists – Yugoslav **King Alexander** was shot dead in Marseille by Macedonian Vlado Chernozemski (and in a staggering display of bad taste, a street has been named after Chernozemski in modern-day Blagoevgrad). As far as the Bulgarian government was concerned, IMRO was by now simply a **criminal organization** that needed to be eliminated – a task carried out the same year when troops were sent into the Petrich region to destroy the IMRO network.

The demise of IMRO meant that, for much of the interwar period, the denizens of Vardar Macedonia were left without any effective political leadership, and had to endure **Serbian repression** alone. This led many young intellectuals in Vardar Macedonia to find solace in the ideology of **Macedonism** – which held that the Macedonian Slavs should not aspire to inclusion in the Bulgarian nation, but should aim for separate statehood within something approximating Gotse Delchev's original idea of a Balkan confederation. Many saw Macedonism as an ideology invented by the Serbs in order to break the unity of Bulgarians and Macedonians, but it did attract some notable adherents: former IMRO member Dimitûr Vlahov, who had been involved in the preparation of the May Manifesto in 1924, emerged at the head of pro-Comintern "**United IMRO**" which agitated for the formation of an autonomous Macedonia separate from Bulgaria. Vlahov's organization was never very popular within Macedonia itself, but it helped to keep autonomist traditions alive – something that Yugoslavia's Communists were subsequently to exploit.

The Socialist Republic Of Macedonia

With the outbreak of **World War II** Bulgaria was invited to occupy Macedonia in return for supporting the Axis powers. Having endured two decades of heavy-handed Serbian rule, the locals greeted the Bulgarian army with open arms, but the imposition of a military government – often staffed by officials with little knowledge of the area – soon led to disillusionment.

Eager to exploit the rumbling discontent, Yugoslav Communist and partisan leader **Josip Broz Tito** sent his able sidekick **Svetozar Vukmanović Tempo** southwards to help organize a Macedonian resistance movement, which would act in concert with the Yugoslav partisan army. Not all the local Communists agreed with Tito's avowed aim of creating a Macedonian republic within a federal Yugoslavia, and a purge of "Bulgarophiles" – who included Macedonian party boss Metodije Šatorov Šarlo – had to be carried out.

The success of Yugoslavia's partisans in combating Nazi aggression gave them an enormous amount of prestige among fellow Communists after the war, and their Bulgarian comrades were very much the junior partners in an unequal relationship. Tito hoped that the creation of a Macedonian republic would be a good way of enticing Bulgaria into a Balkan federation that he himself could then dominate.

The Bulgarian leadership felt obliged to open negotiations on the subject of a **merger between the two countries**, not least because the idea had the backing of Stalin, although they were suspicious of Tito's ambitions. Most importantly, they feared that any Macedonian component of a future federation would seek to remove the Pirin region from Bulgarian control, thus weakening their own power and importance. For the time being, however, the laws of Communist solidarity decreed that such reservations had to remain unvoiced:

Bulgaria recognized the right of the Macedonians to have their own republic, and de facto recognized the existence of a Macedonian nationality – something that all previous Bulgarian governments had refused to do.

Plans for Bulgarian–Yugoslav union ultimately came to nothing, and Bulgaria retained the Pirin region, but the inhabitants of the Pirin were from 1945 onwards accorded the status of a **national minority**, and positively encouraged to declare themselves as Macedonians – not Bulgarians – in state **censuses**.

Greece's rulers, on the other hand, were horrified by the creation of the Yugoslav Republic of Macedonia. The government in Athens feared that the Greek Communists, currently waging a guerilla war in the north of the country, had come to a secret agreement to turn over parts of Aegean Macedonia to the Yugoslavs in the event of a Communist victory. It became apparent that the Greek Communists were themselves divided on the issue, and such plans came to nothing. However, the Greeks have accused Yugoslav Macedonia of harbouring **territorial pretensions towards Aegean Macedonia** ever since.

Forming a Macedonian nation

Having established the Socialist Republic of Macedonia, and having won from the Bulgarians an admission that such a state had the right to exist, the Yugoslav authorities set about building a Macedonian **national identity**. Most important was the creation of an official **written language**, which was based on a dialect far enough removed from literary Bulgarian to be just about credible as a separate tongue.

Leaders of the original, autonomist IMRO – most notably Gotse Delchev – were elevated to the status of national heroes in order to provide the new republic with **historical legitimacy**. The Macedonian Empire of Alexander the Great was claimed as the state's ancient precursor, and pro-regime academics argued that although Alexander may have been Greek-speaking, he belonged to a distinct Macedonian race whose bloodlines had been preserved through intermarriage with the Slavs.

Although Yugoslavia's federal constitution permitted the republics a certain degree of autonomy, Tito's League of Communists ensured that manifestations of national feeling were never allowed to get out of hand. Macedonians who advocated outright independence or, worse still, expressed overly warm feelings towards neighbouring Bulgaria, were swiftly silenced. In **1967**, however, the Communist authorities supported the local clergy in the establishment of an autonomous **Macedonian Orthodox Church** (ecclesiastical affairs in the republic had hitherto been under Serbian jurisdiction). This was a typical example of Tito's management of Yugoslavia's nationality problems: throwing a concession or two to the Macedonians was a good way to prevent the Republic of Serbia from becoming too cocky.

In Bulgaria, worsening relations with Yugoslavia following the **Tito–Stalin split of 1948** produced a turnaround in official policy towards the Pirin Macedonians. Initially they continued to be classed as an ethnic group in their own right, with the Bulgarians demonstrating to Yugoslavian Macedonians that they would be treated with sympathy should they ever choose to rebel against the benighted Tito regime. By the early 1960s, however, Bulgaria's rulers were increasingly keen to emphasize the ethnic homogeneity of the Bulgarian nation. The authorities henceforth refused to issue personal identity documents to inhabitants of the Pirin region who failed to declare themselves as Bulgarians, and the version of history taught in schools once again drove home the message that the true boundaries of the Bulgarian people extended from the Black Sea in the east to Ohrid in the west.

In Yugoslav Macedonia, the change in Bulgarian attitudes assisted the process of nation-building. By playing on people's fears of Bulgaria as an expansionist power, the authorities succeeded in uniting people around a sense of regional Macedonian pride.

The 1990s and onwards

With the collapse of Communism throughout Eastern Europe and the disintegration of the Yugoslav state, the unresolved ethnic problems of the Balkans were once more up for grabs. Initially, however, the Yugoslav Republic of Macedonia entered **the 1990s** as one of the more stable states in the region, moving quietly towards independence in a manner devoid of drama or bloodshed. Democratic elections in November 1990 brought a broadly nationalistic selection of political parties to the fore, but a full declaration of independence didn't come until April 1992, even though the Yugoslav Federation had ceased to function a long time before then. Bulgaria recognized the infant state at once, but objections by **Greece** prevented the European Community and other Western powers from doing the same.

The ostensible reason for Greek intransigence was the **name** of the republic: seeing as much of northern Greece went under the same title – and had done so since before the days of Alexander the Great – how, insisted the Greeks, could a foreign state call itself "Macedonia" and thereby usurp the rich heritage that went with it? Lurking behind this objection lay Greek concern over the future of remaining pockets of Slavs (the so-called "**Slavophone Greeks**") who still lived in Aegean Macedonia. The presence of a newly independent Macedonian state threatened to reawaken demands for minority rights in northern Greece, perhaps calling into question the unitary nature of the Greek state. The Greeks invited their northern neighbours to rename their state Vardar Macedonia or Skopje- Macedonia, but despite EC mediation no compromise was reached. Certain **symbols** adopted by the republic led to increased Greek disquiet. A picture of the **White Tower**, a famous landmark in Thessaloniki, found its way into Skopje's official publicity literature; while a **sun motif** previously associated with the empire of Philip II and Alexander became the centrepiece of the Macedonian flag. Both cases suggested that the Republic of Macedonia nursed territorial pretensions far beyond its current borders, although this was strenuously denied by the authorities in Skopje.

Macedonia's relations with the outside world were only normalized in 1993, but official diplomatic **recognition** came with a price: in order to avoid inflaming Greek sentiment, the republic was forced to call itself the **Former Yugoslav Republic of Macedonia** (**FYROM**), a rather clumsy title which has only recently gone out of usage. A Greek trade blockade of Macedonia initiated in early 1993 was called off two years later when the Macedonians promised to change the design of their national flag.

Macedonians and Albanians

The biggest threat to the republic's stability came from the presence of a large **Albanian minority** in western Macedonia. Though ethnic Albanian MPs occupied a quarter of the seats in the Macedonian Assembly, many members of the Albanian community felt that they weren't getting a fair deal from the infant state. The Macedonian constitution specifically identified the state with the Macedonian nation, something that was regarded as discriminatory by all other ethnic groups living there. There were also rumblings of discontent over the lack of any opportunities for higher education in the Albanian language. Attempts to set up an independent Albanian university in the west-Macedonian town of Tetovo were suppressed by the authorities in 1994, and tensions in the town remained high throughout the 1990s.

To make matters worse, the average Macedonian in the street rarely took Albanian grievances seriously: although the migration of Albanians into western Macedonia had been going on for many centuries, most Macedonians thought of them as recent arrivals who didn't have the right to the land that they were living on. The fact that Albanians had a much higher birth rate than Macedonians was popularly perceived as a cunning strategy to take over more of the country, rather than as a consequence of backwardness, poverty and patriarchal traditions.

The crunch for Macedonian–Albanian relations came in 1999, when a **NATO air campaign** secured the withdrawal of Yugoslav forces from the Yugoslav province of **Kosovo**, whose population is predominantly Albanian. Kosovo borders on northwestern Macedonia, and links between the Albanians on both sides of the frontier have always been strong. Encouraged by the reassertion of Albanian rights in Kosovo, Albanian radicals in Macedonia now thought that they could do the same. From March 2001, Albanian insurgents operating out of Kosovo started crossing the mountainous border into Macedonia, beginning a guerilla war with the Macedonian authorities. The fact that Western forces – which were nominally in control of Kosovo and its borders – did nothing to prevent the Albanian insurgents, enraged the Macedonians, leading many to think that the West had given up on Macedonia and was actively encouraging its dismemberment.

Having learned something from the decade-long cycle of post-Yugoslav wars, the Albanian insurgents in Macedonia used the same tactics as the Serbs in Croatia ten years earlier: gaining control of areas where their own kin were in the majority, driving out other ethnic groups in order to make the region ethnically pure, and using the language of intransigence to freeze out moderate, conciliatory politicians. In the end, and despite atrocities committed on both sides, an all-out war between Albanians and Macedonians never materialized. By signing the **Ohrid Accords** in **August 2001**, Macedonian leaders gave in to certain Albanian demands (a change to the wording of the constitution, more autonomy for Albanian-populated areas), in the hope that this would save the territorial integrity of the country. The Albanian insurgents agreed to give up a proportion of their weapons – a largely cosmetic exercise which left the bulk of their arsenal untouched.

The main obstacle to implementation of the Accords came from disagreements over new local government boundaries, which threatened to create ethnically homogenous Albanian areas closed to central government influence. An attempt by Macedonian nationalists to force a referendum on the issue was foiled in autumn 2004, and the local elections of March 2005 passed off largely without incident.

Bulgarian responses

Despite **recognizing the Republic of Macedonia** and offering it economic and political support, the Bulgarian government has always stopped short of recognizing the existence of a Macedonian nation. Successive Macedonian governments have come to live with this, even though they regard it as another example of Bulgarian arrogance.

Most Bulgarians living in the Pirin region continue to see themselves as Bulgarians first, and Macedonians second. One organization, the Obedinenata makedonska organizatsiya (United Macedonian Organization) or **OMO-Ilinden** campaigns for recognition of Macedonian nationhood and autonomy for the Pirin region, but can only boast a few hundred supporters. Far more influential is the VMRO-Sûyuz na makedonskite druzhestva, or **IMRO-Union of Macedonian Societies**, which (rather fraudulently) claims descent from the original IMRO. The VMRO-SMD is generally sympathetic towards the infant Republic of Macedonia, but refuses to believe that the Macedonians themselves are anything other than Bulgarians – an attitude which leaves most people in Skopje apoplectic with rage, but goes down rather well in Bulgaria. Feeding off the militant heritage of the original IMRO, the VMRO-SMD is metamorphosing into a radical right-wing party with neo-fascist leanings, and shows increasing ambitions to become a major player on the Bulgarian political stage.

Bulgaria's minorities

Despite a proud Slavonic heritage forged through centuries of national struggle, Bulgaria is far from being an ethnically homogeneous state. As well as Vlachs, Armenians, Jews and Karakachani, the country contains about a million Muslims (many of whom are ethnic Turks), and more than half a million Gypsies.

Muslims

Bearing in mind that Islam is associated with the Ottoman Empire, under which Bulgarian Christians languished for five hundred years, it's not surprising that Bulgaria's Muslims have on occasion been regarded as a threat to national unity and have suffered state repression as a result.

During the 1980s Todor Zhivkov's Communist regime attempted to **forcibly integrate** Muslims into mainstream Bulgarian life by pressing them to abandon their traditional culture and **adopt Slavonic names** – attracting widespread international outrage in the process. Democratic changes after November 1989 brought an end to such blatant abuses of human rights, but the question of interethnic relations remains a touchy subject for all concerned.

Origins

Some sources estimate that Muslims constituted up to a third of Bulgaria's population on the eve of the Liberation. Many of them fled in the wake of the Ottoman collapse, but the descendants of those who stayed are scattered throughout the country. Today, the heaviest concentrations of Muslims are found **near the Turkish border** around Kûrdzhali, Harmanli and Haskovo; near the towns of Shumen, Razgrad, Tûrgovishte and Isperih in **the Rhodope mountains**; **northwest of the Balkan range**; between Burgas and Varna on the **Black Sea coast**; and north of Varna in the **Dobrudzha**.

During the 1980s Bulgarian historians argued that almost all of the surviving Muslims were descended from **ethnic Bulgarians** who adopted the religion, and in many cases the language, of their Ottoman conquerors in the fifteenth century. That said, however, it is known that a constant stream of **settlers** came from Asia to Europe in the wake of the Ottoman advance, and it's impossible to believe that their bloodlines are not in some way preserved in the Muslim communities of the Balkans.

Many of Bulgaria's 745,000-strong **Turkish population** are likely to be descended from **Yörük tribespeople**, nomadic sheep-rearers from central Anatolia who were introduced to the Balkans by the Turkish sultan in order to guard the frontiers of his European domains. These newcomers put down roots throughout Bulgaria, especially in lowland regions where the native Christian population was either wiped out or put to flight.

Tatars had been frequenting the Dobrudzha and the Black Sea coast since the thirteenth century, and their Islamic religion and Turkic language made them natural allies of Bulgaria's Ottoman conquerors. Their numbers were augmented in the nineteenth century by refugees fleeing from Turkey's wars with tsarist Russia. Large numbers of Crimean Tatars were settled here in the 1850s, but they found it hard to adapt to a sedentary lifestyle, continued to practise nomadism, and in lean years pillaged Christian and Muslim farmers alike. Similarly unruly were the **Circassians**, also refugees from the tsarist empire, who were given lands along the southern banks of the Danube. The Circassians were recruited as irregulars by the local Ottoman gendarmes, and soon earned a reputation among the local Bulgarians for arbitrary cruelty. Both Tatars and Circassians were gradually assimilated by the more numerous Turks, and soon lost many of their specific racial characteristics – nowadays, Dobrudzhan Tatars are usually referred to as Turks by the local Bulgarian population.

Some fifteenth-century Bulgarians **renounced Christianity** in favour of Islam. It's unclear whether these conversions were forced, or whether landholding peasants willingly adopted Muslim ways in order to retain their privileges under a new regime. In many cases village priests went over to Islam and took their flock with them, despairing at the way in which Balkan Christianity had collapsed so quickly. Subsequently known as **pomaks** (derived from the word *pomagach*, or "helper" – they were viewed as collaborators by their Christian neighbours), about 300,000 of these Slavic Muslims still live in compact communities throughout the western Rhodopes. Under the Ottoman Empire, *pomak* irregulars were often used by the authorities to police the local Christians. It was a *pomak* leader from Dospat, Ahmed Aga Barutanliyata, who was allegedly responsible for the **Batak** massacre in 1876 (see p.368).

Muslims under the modern Bulgarian state

Muslims tended to occupy a privileged position under Turkish rule, and fear of Bulgarian reprisals caused many of them to flee during the War of Liberation in 1877. The Turkish Muslim population of Sofia, for example, evacuated en masse in 1878, and most of their mosques were either demolished or put to other uses. The Bulgarian government undertook to preserve the religious rights of Muslims that remained, paying for the upkeep of surviving mosques and providing Turkish-language teaching in some schools. Numerous cases of **revenge** did occur, with ethnic Turks being burned out of their villages by irate Slavs, but few of these incidents are documented.

During the **interwar years** Muslims were left largely unmolested by the state, although several Turkish settlements were awarded Bulgarian names in the 1930s – the northwestern town of Tûrgovishte, Eski Dzhumaya until 1934, is one example. Local government officials habitually doled out Slavonic names to ethnic Turks when registering births, although there was no consistent, government-sponsored campaign to do so.

The Soviet-inspired **constitution of 1947** paid lip service to minority rights, although Bulgaria's Communist bosses seemed eager to facilitate **emigration** of Muslims to Turkey during the immediate postwar years. Around 155,000 Turks departed between 1949 and 1951, and were followed by a second wave in the late Sixties. The early years of the **Zhivkov regime** were characterized by attempts to encourage Turks to join the Party and participate in Bulgarian political life. In 1964, Todor Zhivkov made a much-publicized speech calling for an improvement of Turkish-language schooling and a widening of minority cultural activities, but with hindsight this appeared to be the swan song of Bulgaria's enlightened nationality policy rather than the herald of some new dawn.

Turning Muslims into Bulgarians

Educational facilities for ethnic Turks were being wound down by the late 1960s, marking a radical change in the government's attitude towards Bulgaria's minorities. From now on the emphasis was to be on outright **assimilation**. Bulgaria's atheist leaders were frustrated by the way in which Turks and *pomaks* clung to religious traditions – of all the country's inhabitants, the Muslims were the most impervious to the propaganda of secular education – and began to wonder whether they could ever be turned into loyal citizens of the socialist state.

To make matters worse, Muslim fertility was increasing at a time when the Bulgarian birth rate was in decline. Anxieties about Bulgaria's changing demography were coupled with the Party's growing exploitation of **nationalism**. The Zhivkov regime was eager to camouflage its subservience to the Soviet Union by posing as the guardian of patriotic values, and the ideology of the integral-nation-state – in which there was little room for ethnic minorities – began to brush aside the proletarian internationalism of Marx and Lenin.

The *pomaks* were the first to experience the effects of the **name-changing campaign**, which aimed to coerce the bearers of traditional Islamic names into adopting Bulgarian alternatives. Beginning in 1971, official ceremonies took place in villages throughout the western Rhodopes, in which *pomaks* were awarded fresh identity papers bearing their new Bulgaricized names. The vast majority had little choice but to accept them without complaint, as any dissent was harshly dealt with. Riots in Pazardzhik, in which two Communist Party officials were reportedly killed by an angry mob, resulted in mass arrests and deportations. Opposition to the campaign in the Gotse Delchev region led to a military clampdown, accompanied – it is alleged – by public hangings of *pomak* leaders.

The unexpected strength of resistance probably led to a lull in name changing over the next decade, but **the winter of 1984** saw the full force of the campaign directed against Bulgaria's ethnic Turks. This time the campaign was accompanied by a full-scale attack on Muslim traditions. Mosques were closed down or demolished, local religious leaders were replaced with Party stooges, circumcision was discouraged, and use of the Turkish language in public places was forbidden. The speed and ferocity of the campaign was surprising, but it was part of the Communist mentality to believe that wholesale social change could be achieved through administrative decisions from above. The Party leadership had been shaken by events elsewhere in the Balkans – in Yugoslavia, the emergence of Muslim Albanian sentiment in Kosovo posed a threat to that state's continued existence – and Zhivkov obviously wanted to deprive Bulgarian Turks of their ethnic identity before they developed separatist aspirations of their own.

The campaign, going under the sanitized name of the *Vûzroditelniyat protses* or "**Regeneration Process**", was presented to the Bulgarian public as another glorious chapter in the country's progress towards national rebirth. Sycophantic academics were employed to argue that the Turkish minority had in fact been Bulgarians all along: forcibly Islamized in the fifteenth century, they were merely fulfilling their destiny by adopting Bulgarian names and returning to the fold. Repressive aspects of the campaign were often conducted under the smokescreen of social progress. Well-intentioned Bulgarians were led to support the measures against the Turks when it was argued that Muslim women, denied access to educational and career opportunities by the bonds of patriarchal society, would benefit from forced assimilation.

The campaign met with **fierce resistance** from the Turks themselves. Numerous demonstrations in towns in the Kûrdzhali district ended with security forces firing on angry crowds; and eight civilians were shot dead during one peaceful protest in Momchilgrad in December 1984. Such events soon attracted the attention of human rights organizations abroad, but the regime turned a deaf ear to foreign criticism. The government turned the crisis to its own advantage, garnering domestic support by accusing Amnesty International and the Western press of participating in a plot to destabilize socialist Bulgaria.

Summer 1989: the "Great Excursion"

With the Zhivkov regime increasingly relying on nationalist excesses in order to distract attention from the Communist system's failings, anti-Turkish policies were stepped up in the **spring of 1989**. This time the action moved on to Bulgaria's northwest, where strikes and demonstrations in the Razgrad area gave vent to Muslim anger.

Growing numbers of Turks sought to emigrate rather than change their names, and the Turkish government declared its willingness to accept as many Bulgarian Muslims as wanted to leave. Sofia called Turkey's bluff by issuing passports to any Muslims requesting them, and by June 1989 the Bulgarian–Turkish border was jammed with people trying to leave, many taking their entire worldly possessions with them. Official sources claimed that the crowds gathering at the frontier were "tourists" (*ekskurziyanti*) taking advantage of the new freedom of travel, unintentionally providing the phrase by which 1989's exodus of Turks came to be known – the *golyama ekskurziya* or "**Great Excursion**".

Between May and August up to 300,000 Turks and *pomaks* crossed the border. Initially Turkey promised to provide sanctuary to Bulgaria's entire Muslim population if necessary, but by August the flood of refugees was placing impossible strains on the Turkish economy. There was insufficient accommodation or work for the newcomers, many of whom were housed in tent cities along the border, and the special treatment accorded to them (however meagre it may have been) was resented by local people. Many *ekskurziyanti* were beginning to return home after a couple of months, dismayed by Turkey's inability to provide them with a life better than the one they had left. Turkey had in any case **closed the border** by the end of August, unable to take any more.

The Great Excursion was beginning to have serious consequences for Bulgarian society. Whole areas had been depopulated, and entire towns and villages deprived of highly trained professional people like teachers and doctors. Most importantly, the economically vital **tobacco crop**, traditionally concentrated in areas of Muslim settlement, lay unharvested in the fields. Urban Bulgarians were organized into work brigades and sent to the countryside to save the crop – for many of them, this was their first experience of the havoc wrought by Todor Zhivkov's nationality policies.

Inspired by the progress of *glasnost* in the Soviet Union, Bulgarian intellectuals were increasingly eager to join persecuted Turks in denouncing the totalitarian nature of the state, and organizations like the **Independent Committee for the Defence of Human Rights** brought leaders of both groups together for the first time. Sharing a common hatred of Communism, Bulgaria's ethnic Turks and urban liberals seemed to be at the start of a fruitful political friendship when the Zhivkov regime came to an end on November 10, 1989.

The post-Zhivkov era

Muslims themselves responded to the demise of totalitarianism by reclaiming their culture. *Pomaks* took to the streets of Gotse Delchev to demand the right to wear *shalvari*, the baggy trousers banned during the dark days of the name-changing campaign; nowadays traditional dress is worn with pride, even by westernized younger women, in many parts of the Rhodopes. The Turkish language – and Turkish music – were loudly flaunted in those areas where ethnic Turks lived; and attendance at the local mosque once more became *de rigueur* for respectable members of the community.

Much of this provoked a conservative backlash, and in 1990 protestors tried to prevent newly elected Turkish MPs from taking their seats in the Grand National Assembly in Veliko Tûrnovo. Originally, ethnic Turk leaders had joined the main opposition coalition, the SDS, but personality clashes within the movement had persuaded them to form a political party of their own in early 1990. Named the "Movement for Rights and Freedoms" – Dvizhenieto za prava i svobodi or **DPS** – the party was led by **Ahmed Dogan**, a former university lecturer imprisoned by the Zhivkov regime for his opposition to the name-changing campaign.

The DPS made every effort to present itself as a multiracial human rights organization, although it was clear that most of its supporters were Turks and *pomaks*. Bulgaria's Muslims voted *en bloc* for the DPS in June 1990, leaving its critics to claim that the Movement would lead to the ghettoization of the country's minorities, not their rehabilitation into national life. Others feared that the DPS's monopolistic hold over the Muslim population, especially in the Kûrdzhali area where ethnic Turks form a majority, would lead to demands for regional autonomy and, eventually, outright secession. Fear that the DPS was an exclusively Turkish national party which owed its allegiance to Ankara rather than Sofia seemed to unite both the BSP, which was heir to Zhivkov's Communist–nationalist tradition, and those on the right of the SDS, who were busy reviving a much older, conservative–nationalist tradition. Both strands of opinion argued that the DPS's dominance over Bulgarian Muslims would also lead to the gradual Turkification of Bulgaria's *pomaks*, who would slowly lose their Slavonic roots.

The political present

Fears of the DPS's intentions have remained a constant theme in Bulgarian politics ever since. However the position has been complicated by the fact that inconclusive election results have often left the DPS holding the balance of power in parliament, and successive administrations on both left and right have been forced to cultivate DPS support in order to remain in office. The SDS government of Filip Dimitrov needed Dogan as an ally after coming to power in the **October 1991 elections**, but his radical economic programme involved cutting subsidies to the tobacco-producing areas of Bulgaria where DPS support was most concentrated – the DPS withdrew its support for Dimitrov, who was promptly replaced by an administration favoured by the BSP. The fact that the DPS could make and break governments in this way provoked profound misgivings in nationalist circles, who argued that Bulgaria's experiment with democracy had merely served to create a "Turk-dominated" parliament.

In all of Bulgaria's **post-Communist elections** (in 1991, 1994, 1997 and 2001), the DPS has consistently won a 7–8 percent share of the vote, confirming its status as the only effective political voice for Muslims in the country. The party has established a firm hold on the Turkish- and *pomak*-inhabited areas of Bulgaria – a development which, by excluding other political forces from those regions, has had a largely negative effect on any attempts to cultivate a liberal–democratic ethos among the inhabitants. With such an unwavering bedrock of support behind him, Ahmed Dogan has retained his position as one of the key political power-brokers of the post-Communist era. He was one of the first party leaders to develop ties with the former king, **Simeon of**

Books

There is more writing on Bulgaria than you might initially imagine – though, as a rule, it appears more in books on the Balkans as a whole rather than forming the central subject of either travel writing or fiction. Sadly, much of it is no longer in print. What follows is a collection of books about the country either currently in print, or out of print (o/p), and available in larger libraries or specialist secondhand bookstores. Titles marked ★ are particularly recommended.

Travel books and general accounts

Frank Cox *Bulgaria* (o/p). The *Morning Post*'s Bulgaria correspondent during the Balkan Wars, Cox was impressed by a well-organized country that seemed to have imposed order on this hitherto chaotic corner of southeastern Europe. He found Sofia rather staid though, commenting that "the system of partial seclusion of the womenfolk kills all social life, and the absence of a feminine element in the restaurants and other places of social resort deprives them of all convivial charm".

Lovett Fielding Edwards *Danube Stream* (o/p). This book on the Danube and its influence on southeastern Europe is chiefly interesting for its account of life amongst the polyglot boat-people. Includes descriptions of Vidin, Lom and Ruse, but otherwise only marginally relevant to Bulgaria.

Leslie Gardiner *Curtain Calls* (o/p). East European travelogue of 1960s vintage, the last six chapters of which deal with Gardiner's experiences in Bulgaria – including a slow-burning flirtation with his Balkantourist guide, Radka – recounted in an amusing style.

Jeremy James *Vagabond* (o/p). Recounting a voyage on horseback from Bulgaria to Western Europe in 1990, James' book offers a convincing picture of rural life in the Balkans of today. The author seems especially at home in Gypsy culture – a milieu that other travellers rarely get to grips with.

Stowers Johnson *Gay Bulgaria* (o/p). More earnest than Newman and prosier than Savas, Johnson voyaged by Dormobile across Bulgaria just before the country became a tourist destination, which constitutes the book's main attraction. Achieved brief notoriety in the 1990s when a British newspaper declared it one of the least-borrowed books in public library history.

Claudio Magris *Danube*. This highly praised account of the Danubian countries interweaves history, reportage and high-brow literary anecdotes in an ambitious attempt to illuminate their cultural and spiritual backgrounds. Only one section is devoted to Bulgaria, naturally enough, but the rest is a fascinating read.

Bernard Newman *The Blue Danube* (o/p); *Bulgarian Background* (o/p). The latter is marginally more lively – and contains a lot more about Bulgaria – than Newman's earlier book, relating his epic bicycle ride alongside the Danube. Solid stuff, but hardly riveting.

S.G.B. St Claire and Charles A. Brophy *Residence in Bulgaria* (o/p). These two former British army officers lived in a village south of Varna in the late 1860s, returning to write a book on a country "which although but five or six days distant from England, is as little known as the interior of Africa". Their account is largely pro-Ottoman and anti-Bulgarian, although their characterization of the Bulgarians as a surly bunch who overcharge foreigners will be familiar to those holidaying on the Black Sea coast today. Worth tracking down for the folkloric anecdotes alone.

George Savas *Donkey Serenade* (o/p). Savas did his travelling on foot along the backroads of Bulgaria, accompanied by the roguish ex-IMRO fighter Vasil. Rather twee, but includes a couple of fine Bulgarian poems and the odd notable vignette.

Guide books

Peter Carney and Meri Anastassova *Bulgaria: the Mountain Resorts* (Bulgaria). Useful guide to the highland regions, written by a Sofia-based team and full of insightful nuggets. On sale from bookshops and kiosks in Bulgaria, as are the same authors' *Bulgaria: Sofia and Plovdiv* and *Bulgaria: the Black Sea Coast.*

Julian Perry *The Mountains of Bulgaria.* No-nonsense practical guide to trekking routes in the Balkan, Rila, Pirin and Rhodope ranges, written by an experienced trek leader. A good investment if you're planning a major hiking expedition.

History, politics and sociology

Amnesty International *Bulgaria: Imprisonment of Ethnic Turks* (o/p). Reports on the forced "assimilation" of Bulgaria's largest minority group during the 1980s, using documentary, eyewitness and hearsay evidence.

J. D. Bell *Peasants in Power* (o/p). Before, during and after World War I, the Agrarians were the largest radical opposition party in Bulgaria and the "Greens" of southeastern Europe. Bell discourses on the brief period of Agrarian government and their charismatic leader, Stamboliiski, in a scholarly but uninspiring manner.

Stephen Constant *Foxy Ferdinand* (o/p). Readable and impeccably researched biography of Bulgaria's unlamented tsar, who privately referred to his subjects as *mes bufles* – "my buffalos". Deals candidly with Ferdinand's bisexuality – a subject that contemporary Bulgarian historians still shy away from.

★ **R. J. Crampton** *A Short History of Modern Bulgaria.* Probably the definitive work on the subject: an informed, well-balanced and easy-to-read account widely available from bookshops and public libraries. Especially good on the intrigues of Bulgarian political life after the Liberation.

★ **John V. A. Fine** *The Early Medieval Balkans: a Critical Survey From the Sixth to the Late Twelfth Century.* Up-to-date and sophisticated analysis of the formation of Slav states in southeastern Europe, revealing just how formidable an entity the First Bulgarian Empire actually was. Contains revealing ruminations on the true nature of the Bogomil heresy (see p.252).

Isabel Fonseca *Bury Me Standing.* Part travelogue, part social enquiry, presenting a sympathetic description of contemporary Gypsy life in Eastern Europe. The one chapter on

Bulgaria concentrates on the town of Sliven, where Gypsies and ethnic Bulgarians are more integrated than anywhere else in the country.

★ **Misha Glenny** *The Balkans: Nationalism, War and the Great Powers, 1804–1999.* Wide-ranging history written in breezy accessible style – but backed up with prodigious research. The narrative zooms around from Croatia to Constantinople and all points between, but just about everything you ever wanted to know about the region is in here somewhere.

Richard C. Hall *The Balkan Wars.* Good academic history of the cycle of wars which engulfed the region in 1912–13, providing the curtain-raiser for World War I. Packed with insights into the national rivalries which still plague the region to this day.

R. F. Hoddinott *The Thracians* (o/p). Thorough introduction to the Bulgarians' ancient antecedents, although descriptions of archeological evidence are sometimes a bit too technical for the lay reader.

Dennis P. Hupchik *The Balkans: From Constantinople to Communism.* Accessible widescreen narrative which functions well as a general introduction to the main themes of Balkan history.

★ **Machiel Kiel** *Art and Society of Bulgaria in the Turkish Period.* Pretty much the definitive work on the development of churches, monasteries and religious painting between the fourteenth and nineteenth centuries. Kiel adopts a refreshingly even-handed approach to both Bulgarian and Ottoman sources, debunking the national myth-making perpetrated by both sides.

Elizabeth Kwasnik *Bulgaria: Tradition and Beauty* (o/p). The catalogue to an exhibition that toured several provincial museums in the UK, with essays on carpet-weaving, traditional costumes and rural celebrations, accompanied by excellent colour pictures.

D. M. Lang *The Bulgarians* (o/p). Traces the Bulgars from Central Asia until the Ottoman conquest, neatly complementing Macdermott's history (see below). Illustrated.

Mercia Macdermott *A History of Bulgaria, 1393–1885* (o/p); *The Apostle of Freedom* (o/p); *Freedom or Death* (o/p); *For Freedom and Perfection* (o/p). Written sympathetically and with obvious enjoyment – all in all, probably the most engaging histories of Bulgaria in the English language. The last three are biographies of famous nineteenth-century revolutionaries – Vasil Levski, Gotse Delchev and Yane Sandanski – which, despite being tinged with hero worship, are impeccably researched and eminently readable.

Georgi Markov *The Truth that Killed* (o/p). Disillusioned by constraints on his literary career in Sofia, Georgi Markov defected for a new life in England, where he began broadcasting for the BBC World Service. Both autobiographical and a sermon *à la* Solzhenitsyn, this book apparently so enraged the Politburo that they ordered his murder. Jabbed with a poison-tipped umbrella on Waterloo Bridge, Markov died of a rare fever a few days later.

★ **Mark Mazower** *The Balkans.* Masterful, readable study which tackles the broad sweep of Balkan history in thematic rather than narrative style. Displaying even-handed empathy for the peoples who actually live in southeastern Europe, Mazower avoids many of the cliches and preconceptions that tend to mar other writings on the subject.

Dimitri Obolensky *The Byzantine Commonwealth*. Classic work on the spread of Christianity and Byzantine culture in the Balkans during the Middle Ages; it's particularly good on the medieval Bulgarian church.

Duncan M. Perry *Stefan Stambolov and the Emergence of Modern Bulgaria*. A political rather than personal biography of the most talented and charismatic of Bulgaria's post-Liberation politicians, which makes a good introduction to the period as a whole. The same author's *The Politics of Terror: the Macedonian Revolutionary Movements 1893–1903*, is a thorough and readable account of the genesis of IMRO.

Hugh Poulton *The Balkans: Minorities and States in Conflict* (o/p). Exhaustively researched compendium on the national minorities of Bulgaria and its neighbours.

Steven Runciman *History of the First Bulgarian Empire* (o/p). Though long out of print, this is the classic account of the rise and fall of Bulgaria's first medieval kingdom, by a respected scholar of Byzantine and Balkan history.

Claire Stirling *Time of the Assassins* (o/p). *Readers' Digest* bankrolled Stirling's hunt for the "Bulgarian Connection" whereby Mehmet Ali Agca's attempted murder of the pope in 1981 was stage-managed by the KGB, and her tendentious account is couched in the *Digest's* breathless right-wing house style. Similar assertions are made in *The Plot to Kill the Pope* by **Paul Henze** (o/p). In an earlier book, *The Terror Network* (o/p), Stirling accused Bulgaria of smuggling arms and narcotics into Turkey.

E. P. Thompson *Beyond the Frontier* (o/p). Heartfelt account of the Allied mission to aid Bulgarian partisans in World War II, led by the author's brother Major Frank Thompson.

Tzvetan Todorov *The Fragility of Goodness*. Bulgaria's Jews were saved from the Holocaust during World War II, largely as a result of popular pressure on Bulgaria's pro-German government. This book offers a thought-provoking account of this unique episode in European history, and asks what it is that encourages ordinary members of the public to embark on altruistic protests.

Maria Todorova *Imagining the Balkans*. Seminal work of cultural theory which argues that the concept of the Balkans – as an unstable and backward area populated by crazy people – was largely the invention of Western travellers and writers who aimed at the promotion of exotic images rather than real understanding. A stimulating read.

Fiction and poetry

Blaga Dimitrova (trans Brenda Walker and Belin Tonchev) *The Last Rock Eagle*. Bulgaria's most popular contemporary poet, Blaga Dimitrova was a prominent anti-Communist in the late 1980s, and served briefly as vice-president in 1992–93.

Georgi Gospodinov *Natural Novel*. Fragmented, postmodern novel from one of Bulgaria's leading contemporary poets and critics, with entertaining prose-morsels addressing subjects as diverse as life on Sofia's housing estates, the sources of literary inspiration, and the importance of the toilet in the domestic life of extended families.

Nikolai Haitov *Wild Tales*. Short stories set in the rural communities of the Rhodope Mountains, from a popular contemporary Bulgarian author.

Lyubomir Levchev (trans Ewald Osers) *Stolen Fire*. Levchev was a Central Committee member and president of the Writers' Union under the old regime, but despite occasional flashes of ideological content most of his work is unashamedly personal and emotional.

★ **Geo Milev** (trans Ewald Osers) *Roads to Freedom*. Milev's death at the hands of the reactionary Tsankov regime in 1925 made him into one of socialist Bulgaria's favourite left-wing martyrs, but it's often forgotten that he was a ground-breaking modernist poet who borrowed from expressionism and other Western styles.

John Naughton (ed) *The Traveller's Literary Companion to East and Central Europe* (o/p). The Bulgarian section of this book, written by Sofia-based critic Belin Tonchev, contains an excellent overview of Bulgarian literary history, accompanied by extracts from the works of major Bulgarian authors.

Viktor Paskov *A Ballad for Georg Henig* (o/p). Acclaimed Bulgarian novel of the 1980s, recounting, in mildly Kafkaesque manner, the story of an elderly Sofia violinmaker who has somehow managed to be overlooked on all official state records.

Belin Tonchev (ed) *Young Poets of a New Bulgaria*. A collection of more than twenty poets, mixing those who did well under the old regime with those who suffered for their anti-Communist convictions. Other anthologies published by Forest/Dufour are *Poets of Bulgaria* and *The Devil's Dozen*, a collection of women poets, including work by Blaga Dimitrova.

Yordan Yovkov (trans John Burnip) *The Inn at Antimovo and Legends of the Stara Planina* (o/p). Twentieth-century novelist Yovkov was born in Zheravna in the eastern Stara planina (the Balkan Range), and this collection of short stories recalls the atmosphere of small-town life under the Ottoman occupation.

Bulgaria in foreign literature

★ **Boris Akunin** *Turkish Gambit*. Genteel espionage novel in which tsarist-era civil servant Erast Fandorin unearths a double agent at the heart of the Russian general staff. Set in Bulgaria during the Russo-Turkish War of 1877–8, this is a satisfying holiday read.

★ **Julian Barnes** *The Porcupine*. Political satire centring on the trial of deposed Communist dictator Stoyo Petkanov – a fictional character based on Bulgaria's Todor Zhivkov. A telling account of how democratic revolutions can soon degenerate into cynicism and disillusionment.

★ **Malcolm Bradbury** *Rates of Exchange*. Comic novel recounting the misadventures of an English academic sent by the British Council to lecture in the imaginary Communist state of Slaka, loosely based on countries like Bulgaria. As a Westerner's view of the absurdities of life under Communism, it's extremely funny. The same author's *Why Come to Slaka?* (o/p) was a less successful send-up of the kind of propagandist tourist literature published by Communist states before 1989 – although anyone with experience of Bulgaria in those days will find it curiously familiar.

Robert Littel *October Circle* (o/p). Cold War thriller concerning a group of young Bulgarian Communists who fall foul of the regime in the aftermath of the Warsaw Pact's 1968 invasion of Czechoslovakia. Breezy, undemanding, and with plenty of local colour.

Cuisine

Dan Philpott *The Wine and Food of Bulgaria* (o/p). Marrying coffee-table values with practical, easy-to-follow recipes: an essential buy if you want to tell your *kebapche* from your *kavarma*.

Bulgarian music

Until very recently all aspects of Bulgarian musical life, from musicological research to composition and teaching to recording and broadcasting, were under the control of the state. Although this helped to preserve the music and encourage certain developments, it also introduced distortions and affected the natural growth of the music. This has led to the paradoxical situation that the beautiful recordings of the Women's Choir of RTV Bulgaria, sold in the UK under the title of "Le Mystère des Voix Bulgares", were thought of here as folk music, when they are in fact postwar pieces by the country's leading modern composers. On the other hand, the band of Ibraim (Ivo) Papazov is seen as that of a unique Balkan jazz genius – when he is actually the most remarkable representative of a movement that managed to flourish outside official encouragement or censorship. Both are products of the postwar era and examples of growth from village roots, yet are utterly different in aesthetic and ideology.

Open throat

There is something about Bulgarian music that at once proclaims itself: both its matter and manner are powerfully individual. To the Western ear one of the most immediately recognizable characteristics is the vocal timbre of such singers as Nadka Karadzhova, Yanka Rupkina and Konya Stojanova, a rich, direct and stirring sound, referred to in the West as "**open-throated**". In fact the throat is extremely constricted and the sound is forced out, which accounts for its focus and strength and which allows the complex yet clean ornamentation that is such a striking feature of this style of singing. The only songs that the villagers dignified with the name of "folk songs" are the slow, heavily ornamented solo songs that are particularly the province of women. These used to be sung at the social events called *sedyanki*, evenings when unmarried women would gather together to sew and embroider, gossip and compare fiancés, or at the table on the occasion of various parties of one sort or another. Songs for dancing, or for various rites, were seen as being "practical" or "useful", and weren't felt quite worthy of being called music. The ornamentation, although subtly varied with each performance, was always considered a vital part of the tune, and the only time you will ever hear a song without such decoration is when the singer is too old to manage it.

Much Bulgarian music, both sung and played, was performed with no harmony, or with (at most) a simple drone like that of a bagpipe. Nonetheless, in some districts a most extraordinary system of **polyphonic performance** grew up. In the Shop area near Sofia, women in the villages of Plana, Bistritsa and others sing in two- and three-part harmony, though not a harmony that Western ears readily recognize, as it is full of dissonances and tone clusters and decorated with whoops, vibrati and slides. The singers themselves say that they try to sing "as bells sound". In the Pirin district, in the southwest, the villagers sometimes sing two different two-voiced songs with two different texts simultaneously, resulting in a four-part texture. This polyphonic style of performance is normally the domain of women, although in Pirin men also sing in harmony, but with a different repertoire and in a rather different and simpler style.

The **rhythmic complexity** of Bulgarian music is also striking and, for the Hungarian composer and collector of folk songs **Béla Bartók** (1881–1945), the discovery of these irregular rhythms was a revelation. The most widespread is probably the *Ruchenitsa* dance, three beats arranged as 2 2 3, closely followed by the *Kopanitsa* (2 2 3 2 2). More complex patterns like 2 2 2 2 3 2 2 (*Bucimis*) or 3 2 2 3 2 2 2 2 3 2 2 (*Sedi Donka*, also known as *Plovdivsko Horo*) are also common. These patterns, foreign to us, are ingrained in the Bulgarian people, who snap their fingers in such rhythms while waiting for a bus or hanging around on the corner of the street.

Though Bulgaria is a small country, there are several clearly defined regional styles: the earthy, almost plodding dances from Dobrudzha, in the northeast, are quite different in character from the lightning-fast dances of the Shop people, while the long heart-rending songs from the Thracian plain contrast with the sweet and pure melodies from the northeast. In the remote mountains of the Rhodopes, in the south, occasionally you can still hear the distant sound of a shepherd playing the bagpipe to his flock of a summer evening, and in the villages or small towns of the valleys groups of people sing slow, broad songs to the accompaniment of the deep *kaba gaida*, a large, deep-voiced bagpipe.

Ritual music

The yearly round of peasant life was defined by the rhythm of the seasons, sowing and harvest, and many of the **ancient rituals** intended to ensure fertility and good luck still survive, though more as a folk tradition than in the belief that they will produce any kind of magical effect. All these customs, such as *Koleduvane*, which normally involves groups of young men going in procession around the village and asking for gifts from the householders; *Laduvane* at New Year; and *Lazaruvane* on St Lazarus' Day in spring (the most important holiday for the young women, when they take their turn to sing and dance through the streets) have particular songs and dances connected with them. The songs are usually simple, repetitive and very old. The most startling of these rites, *nestinarstvo* – from the villages of Bulgari, Kondolovo and Rezovo in Strandzha – has died out in its original form, when its exponents would fall into a trance and dance on hot coals to the sound of bagpipe and drum to mark the climax of the feast of SS Konstantin and Elena, but it's sometimes presented at festivals and folklore shows. The wild stirring music remains the same.

These days the two most important rites of passage in Bulgarian life, be they in the country or in the town, are **getting married** and **leaving home** to do military service. Both occasions are marked by music. Every aspect of a wedding – the arrival of the groom's party, the leading out of the bride to meet it, the procession to the church and so on – has a particular melody or song associated with it. The songs sung at the bride's house the night before the wedding are by no means joyful celebrations of marriage: on the contrary, they are the saddest songs in the whole body of Bulgarian music, because the bride is leaving home, never to return to her parents' house.

Parties to see the young men off to the army are more cheerful. In the town the family of the recruit hires a restaurant and a band, normally some combination of accordion, keyboard, electric guitar, clarinet/saxophone and drum kit, which plays a haphazard mix of folk, pop and other melodies, and the guests eat, drink and dance. In the country the feast is often held in the evening and outdoors. In the village of Mirkovo the guests are entertained by a little band of two clarinets, trumpet and accordion, who play the slow melodies called *na trapeza* (at the table) while the guests eat. Later the young soon-to-be soldier is led round and presented with gifts of money, flowers or shirts. (**Shirts** in fact play a great role in Bulgarian folk life. At weddings each member of the party wears a handkerchief pinned to their breast, but the more important relatives are permitted an entire shirt, sometimes still in its cellophane wrapping.)

After all the food has gone, the band strikes up a set of local dance tunes, and everyone rushes to join in a *horo* whose leader capers and leaps while flourishing an enormous flag on a long pole. Dancing is very popular, especially among villagers; and at the end of a festival or similar event, if the band starts to play a bit for pleasure you can see people – from grannies to young children – literally racing across the grass to join the circle.

In most of the country the bands for weddings and so on are made up of modern, factory-made **instruments** often amplified, but around the town of Yambol in the east, many people prefer the old folk instruments and if they can afford it, will even hire a band from Sofia to come and play them.

Bands and instruments

Traditional bands almost invariably consist of *gaida* (bagpipe), *kaval* (end-blown flute), *gadulka* (a bowed stringed instrument) and *tambura* (a strummed stringed instrument), sometimes with the addition of the large drum, the *tapan*. They were always common throughout the country, but when after World War II the state founded its own ensembles for folk songs and dances, these instruments were the ones chosen to make up the huge orchestras thought necessary to accompany them. As a result they have undergone certain developments and refinements to aid reliability of tuning and tone, while some players have brought their skill to a quite unbelievable peak of virtuosity.

The **gaida** is maybe the most famous of all these instruments, although it's fairly simply made: a chanter for the melody, a drone and a mouth-tube for blowing, all attached into a small goatskin that acts as a reservoir for air. It's capable of a partly chromatic scale of just over an octave, and in the hands of a master such as Kostadin Varimezov or Nikola Atanasov the wild sound has an astonishing turn of speed and rhythmic force. These players also have the ability to use the possibilities that the *gaida* has for rich ornamentation to perform beautiful versions of slow songs and other *na trapeza* melodies. In the Rhodopes the huge, deep-voiced *kaba gaida* accompanies singing or plays dance music, sometimes alone and sometimes in groups of two, three, four or even more. There is one group called rather literally *Sto kaba gaidi* (One Hundred *kaba gaidi*), and although this could be thought excessive the sound is undeniably impressive.

Like the *gaida,* the **kaval** was originally a shepherds' instrument, and some of its melodies, or rather freely extemporized meditations on certain motifs which are specific to it, go by such names as "Taking the herd to water", "At noon", "The lost lamb". The modern *kaval* is made of three wooden tubes fitted together, the topmost of which has a bevelled edge that the player blows against on the slant to produce a note. The middle tube has eight finger holes and the last has four more holes that affect the tone and the tuning. They are sometimes called **Devil's holes**: the story goes that the

Devil was so jealous of the playing of a young shepherd that he stole his *kaval* while he was sleeping and bored the extra holes to ruin it. Of course, they only made the instrument sound sweeter and the Devil was, as usual in folk tales, discomfited once more.

The school of *kaval*-playing led by Nikola Ganchev and Stoyan Velichkov that has grown up since World War II is extremely refined and capable of all manner of nuances of sound. The sound is sweet and clear (the folk say "honeyed"), the low (*kaba*) register is rich and buzzing, and in the last ten years or so someone (possibly Nikola Kostov) invented a new technique called *kato klarinet* (clarinet style) where the instrument is played as though it were a trumpet, producing a sound very like the low register of the clarinet.

The **gadulka** is a relative of the *rebec*, with a pear-shaped body held upright on the knee, tucked into the belt or cradled in a strap hung round the player's neck. It has three, sometimes four bowed strings, and as many as nine sympathetic strings that resonate when the instrument is played, producing an unearthly shimmering resonance behind the melody. The *gadulka* is unbelievably hard to play – there are no frets and no fingerboard, the top string has to be stopped by fingernails and the whole thing keeps wriggling out of your grasp like a live fish. This makes the *gadulka* players' habit of showing off by playing virtuoso selections from the popular classics both startling and irritating. Mihail Marinov and Atanas Vulchev are among the older players of note, and Nikolai Petrov is one of the younger generation.

The **tambura** is a member of the lute family, with a flat-backed pear-shaped body and a long fretted neck. Its original form, found in Pirin and in the central Rhodopes, had two courses of strings, one of which usually provided a drone while the melody was played on the other. These days the common form of the instrument has four courses tuned like the top four strings of a guitar, and in groups it both strums chords and plays melodies.

Around the end of the nineteenth century factory-made instruments like the accordion, clarinet and violin appeared in the country and were soon used to play dance music and to accompany songs. Modern **accordion style** was pretty much defined by **Boris Karloff** (no relation to the horror-movie star) who wrote a number of elegant tunes – "Krivo Horo" in particular – that have become standards. More modern accordionists worthy of note are the Gypsy **Ibro Lolov** (sometimes known as Ivo as a result of the programme of Bulgarianization of names of Turkish origin under the Zhivkov regime; see p.477), Traicho Sinapov and Kosta Kolev, also well known as a composer, arranger and conductor who plays in a very unique style which contrasts in its restraint and care with the high-speed acrobatics of some of the younger players. By far the most brilliant of these is **Petar Ralchev**, a Thracian, who unlike some of the speed-merchants combines new ideas with a lot of taste and, more importantly, a lot of soul.

State control

The extent to which music was controlled by the former Communist government and how far the musicians themselves were able to escape this control is an integral part of the development of music in Bulgaria. In the early Fifties the Communists set up the **State Ensemble for Folk Songs and Dances** under the leadership of **Philip Kutev** (sometimes spelt Koutev), an extraordinarily talented composer whose style of writing and arranging became the model for a whole network of professional and amateur groups across the country. His great gift was the ability to take the sounds of village singers, drone-based and full of close dissonances but essentially harmonically static, and from this forge a musical language that answered the aesthetic demands of Western European concepts of form and harmony without losing touch with the particularly Bulgarian feeling of the original tunes. If you compare his work with the attempts of earlier arrangers to force the tunes into a harmonic system which they really didn't fit, his success is as obvious as their failure. This is what you hear on the "Le Mystère des Voix Bulgares" recordings, and from the Trio Bulgarka and the instrumental group Balkana.

It is impossible to overestimate the tight grip that the state had on every aspect of life, and this is as true of music as of anything else. What began as a praiseworthy attempt to preserve and enrich folklore became a straitjacket to which all musicians had to conform or else stop working as musicians. It reached even such ridiculous extremes as prescribing a certain percentage of Russian songs to be played in the course of an evening's entertainment in a restaurant, say, to demonstrate the eternal friendship of the Bulgarian and Soviet peoples. And you couldn't ignore this insanity, because there were people around whose job it was to make sure that you were complying. One musician told with rage how he had had to audition all his new songs and dances to a committee that he called "The Committee of Pensioners" before he was permitted to perform them on the radio. If they were "not Bulgarian enough" then permission was refused. Even if it was granted, then the style of performance had to be acceptable. "Once they told me that I was playing too fast, and that Bulgarian music is not played so fast. This was a tune that I myself had written, it was I that was playing it, and I am a Bulgarian musician. How should they tell me the way to play my own song? But they could. I tell you, Bulgarian music used to be behind closed shutters – but now the shutters have been opened."

This doesn't mean that the people working in the field of folklore were all apparatchiks or that they failed to produce beautiful music. The network of regional professional ensembles fed by a stream of talent trained in special schools set up to teach folk instruments and folk singing meant that time, money and opportunity were available for people to develop the approved language in their own way, and many composers – among them **Kosta Kolev** and Stefan Mutafchiev and Nikolai Stoikov with the "Trakiya" ensemble in Plovdiv – created their own individual styles. The mass-production of cheap folk instruments under the Communist regime, and the encouragement shown to amateurs, also managed to keep music alive in the villages. Unfortunately, this was at the cost of alienating many people, particularly young city-dwellers, by insisting on such propagandist drivel as "Mladata Traktoristka" (The young girl tractor-driver) and referring to them as "contemporary developments in folk creativity".

Another crucial factor in the growth and encouragement of Bulgarian music is the series of regional competitions and festivals held around the country. The **Koprivshtitsa festival** (see p.291), is particularly important, not merely because of its size (there are literally thousands of performers bussed in from all over the country) but because it is the only one devoted to amateur performers. Practically the only recordings of genuine village music that the state record company, Balkanton, has ever released were made here: *Koprivshtitsa '76* and the double album *Koprivshtitsa '86* are among the most beautiful and valuable recordings of Bulgarian songs and dances ever made.

Wedding bands

The **wedding bands** are a fascinating example of the formerly "underground" folk music that is currently an extremely important part of Bulgarian musical life. Unlike the musicians mentioned above, who were approved by the state (though none the worse for that), they existed outside the framework of official music-making, hired to play at weddings, the seeing-off of recruits and various village festivities. Because they did not have to conform to the Communist idealization of the people and the people's music in order to record or get on the radio, they were free to experiment with new instrumentation, fusing folk instruments such as the *gaida* and *kaval* with electric guitar, synthesizer and kit drums, rock and jazz rhythms, and foreign tunes. As the recording industry in Zhivkov's Bulgaria didn't allow the formation of a commercial style like that of the Yugoslav folk-based pop music, they simply took those songs straight across, learning them from radio broadcasts picked up from over the frontier (or from pirate cassette tapes) and performing them to a public that responded to their directness and energy. It was only in the mid-1980s that officialdom realized the existence of this music, and through the efforts of some quite brave and far-seeing musicologists was persuaded to recognize them as worthy of public support and recording. A tri-yearly festival was set up in the town of **Stambolovo** (hence their alternative name *Stambolovski orkestri*) which presented them in perhaps a somewhat bowdlerized form – they were subjected to the "assistance" of approved musical directors – but the Balkanton record *Stambolovo '88* gives a very good impression of the amazing revelation of this kind of previously unsuspected music.

Ivo Papazov is the best known of these musicians in the West, thanks to the work of Hannibal Records, who managed to record him with his electric band after a long struggle with the bureaucracy. His flirtations with jazz following his work in the late Seventies and early Eighties with the Plovdiv Jazz-Folk Ensemble are maybe less successful than his startling transformations of traditional Thracian music, but some of his most intriguing achievements lie in the performance of **Turkish music**. He is of Turkish origin, and even in the period just prior to the fall of the Zhivkov regime when the very existence of a Turkish minority in Bulgaria was denied, you could get home-made recordings of Papazov playing Turkish melodies with a typical small band of the type common today in Istanbul. His second Hannibal release, *Balkanology*, begins with a Turkish dance and also includes Macedonian and Greek material. Papazov's most recent release *Fairground/Panair* (2003) by Bulgarian label Kuker has a very heavy jazz influence.

Many bands now employ the new freedoms in all kinds of ways. Bands like Kanarite and Vievska Folk Grupa and the hugely popular singers **Slavka Kalcheva** and **Todor Kozhuharov** all employ fresh interpretations of traditional Bulgarian music. Many bands and singers have made commercial recordings, others are still only to be heard live or on poor-quality home-made tapes sold in the markets of the small towns where they live.

New sounds

It is not only the *Stambolovski orkestri* who have been pushing back the boundaries. Some of the bands that play purely traditional instruments have been experimenting. Black Crown records in the UK released a record of the band Loznitsa called *Moods*, featuring both the old master of the *gaida* **Nikola Atanasov** and the *kaval* player Georgi Zhelyazkov: it's a good representation of the new trend. Particularly worth investigating is the work of the *kaval* player **Teodosii Spasov** who has not only recorded a very beautiful and practically avant-garde folk album, *Dûlûg Pût* (*The Long Road*) in collaboration with composer Stefan Mutafchiev, but also played to great acclaim with the well-known Bulgarian jazz pianist Milcho Leviev in his first concert in Sofia after twenty years' exile. Spasov's subsequent albums *The Sand Girl*, *Welkya*, *Beyond the Frontiers*, *Titla* and *Nestardartni Standarti* represent a successful folk-jazz fusion from one of Bulgaria's most exciting young players.

Modern Bulgarian music is currently experiencing a commercial boom. During the 1990s Bulgarians took to a new form of music which mixes Balkan folk motifs with Western and Oriental pop – **popfolk** (commonly referred to as **chalga**). Popfolk is heard everywhere and is big business, complete with video clips, catchy-but-disposable songs and teenybopper starlets. Amidst all this, two (Gypsy) *chalga* performers stand out: the strong voice of **Sofi Marinova** and Bulgaria's most controversial, gender-bending phenomenon **Azis**.

The past few years have seen Bulgarian Romany music make a mark for itself outside of the country. Leading the way, former *chalga* singer **Jony** Iliev has taken Gypsy roots music out of the *mahala* and onto the world stage, sticking to acoustic instruments while producing a modern sound.

While the wedding bands have been able to hook onto popfolk's success, the old network of folklore festivals that had kept traditional music alive in the past now struggles to find sponsorship and an audience. Many younger folk musicians have abandoned roots music to work in popfolk, leaving traditional folk music in the hands of an older generation who aren't always open to ideas of innovation and development. The best hope for the survival of folk as a living musical form lies with ground-breaking figures such as Teodosii Spasov, - who enjoys something akin to mass popularity in Bulgaria, the New Age artists **Isihia** (see discography) and the ever-popular wedding bands.

Discography

The best place to find Bulgarian music is, of course, Bulgaria, especially since some of the most interesting labels are not easily available outside the country. Balkanton, the one-time state record company, still has an enormous amount of wonderful material – it's hard to go wrong with them if you stick to the folk side of things, but not much is available on CD. And keep an eye open for productions by the more modern Kuker and Gega records as well; although hard to get hold of they hardly ever put a foot wrong. Popfolk and wedding band music is easily available at the many CD shops and market stalls throughout Bulgaria but hardly found abroad. However, you should be able to get hold of most of the recordings below without too much trouble.

Various

Anthologie de la Musique Bulgare Vols. 1–5 (Le Chant du Monde LDX 274970, 274975, 274977, 274979, 274981). Recorded by an ethnomusicologist on several field trips through the length and breadth of the country, and including styles that are often passed over, this is undoubtedly the most comprehensive survey of folk and traditional music available.

Song of the Crooked Dance (Yazoo 7016). Vintage recordings of songs and instrumentals, well chosen and well remastered. There are some breathtaking performances here and a wealth of material, mostly of village music, all with excellent notes.

Two Girls Started to Sing (Rounder #1055). Amateur recordings of village musicians made by an enthusiast from the USA, perhaps a little ragged but a wide-ranging and effective selection.

Vocal Traditions of Bulgaria (Saydisc CD-SDL 396). A lovely selection of songs by professional and amateur performers taken from the radio archives, displaying enormous authority and covering the whole country. Once again though, the emphasis is on the village rather than the town.

Individual artists

Azis *Na Golo* (Sunny Records, Bulgaria 2003). To experience the *chalga* superstar at his best, go for this camp classic. Azis's Gypsy roots, Bollywood-flavoured vocal acrobatics and shuffling of Balkan melodies gives the listener an aural sugar rush. Huge fun and the sound of modern Bulgaria at play.

Balkana *The Music of Bulgaria* (Hannibal HNCD 1335). The Trio Bulgarka are joined here by members of the Trakiiskata Troika and friends in the first major project by a Western label to record material afresh rather than pick over the archives. Both a historic step and a fine recording, it came as a revelation when it was first released in the mid-1980s.

The Bisserov Sisters *Three Generations of the Bisserov Sisters* (PAN Ethnic Series 2080). Although the Bisserov Sisters have been performing professionally for a long time, they remain very close to their roots. At their best when singing local music to their own accompaniment of *tarabuka* drum and long-necked tambura lute, as here, they can also cover other material.

Bûlgari *Bulgarian Folk Music* (Latitudes LAT 50613). Bûlgari have taken the small-band folk-instrument tradition and pushed it to the limits – fast, intricate and harmonically interesting, they are probably the best of this particular bunch at the moment, although this recording finds them a little on the staid side.

The Bulgarian Voices Angelite *Melody Rhythm and Harmony* (Jaro 1993–2). The amoeba-like development of Bulgarian female choirs, splitting, reforming, changing directors and record companies, with legal action always lurking in the background, is not easy to disentangle. The particular incarnation known as Angelite ("The Angels") is caught here live on a double CD – there are fine performances of all the old favourites, and the instrumental playing is immaculate.

The Bulgarian Voices Angelite *Mercy for the Living* (Jaro 4220–2). A CD dedicated to performances of Orthodox Christian religious music, ranging from reconstructions of medieval chant to big nineteenth-century compositions by Bulgarian and Russian composers, and providing an excellent introduction to this very rich, if specialized, field.

Folk Scat *Folk Scat* (Nomad NMD 50310). An unexpected delight – this is a recording of a remarkable vocal quintet who take folk material, and mix in slightly jazzy harmonies and rocking Balkan rhythms. Not only great fun, it's beautifully performed and produced.

Yildiz Ibrahimova *Balkanatolia* (Universal/Virginia, Bulgaria). Impressive exercise in jazz-folk fusion from a well-regarded ethnic Turkish singer. The album features a brace of Bulgarian folk songs, alongside Turkish traditional material from both Anatolia and the European side of the Bosphorus. Only occasionally marred by showy excursions into jazz extemporization, this is on the whole a sparkling collection characterized by Ibrahimova's obvious feeling for the material.

Jony Iliev *Ma Maren Ma* (Asphalt Tango). Amazing Bulgarian Roma roots music straight from the poor Gypsy quarter of Kyustendil. Jony sings the Balkan blues and his family band plays with real fire.

Isihia *Isihia* (AveNew, Bulgaria). A beguiling mixture of folklore, electronica and Orthodox church-style chanting which recalls the ethereal, ethnic-influenced soundscapes of Western groups like Dead Can Dance. A young outfit from Sofia, Isihia take their name from the fourteenth-century monastic movement of the hesychasts (see box on p.259), a clear statement of their enthusiasm for all things medieval, Bulgarian and mystical. One for the chill-out generation rather than the purists.

Kanarite *Izbrano – chast 1* (Payner PNR 2412830 –49). A collection of the best numbers by Bulgaria's most popular and successful wedding band. This album covers most styles of wedding music found throughout Bulgaria.

Le Mystère des Voix Bulgares *Le Mystère des Voix Bulgares* (Disques Celliers CD 008). Cellier's groundbreaking release of what he had trawled from the state archives remains one of the best available. There isn't much more to say.

Le Mystère des Voix Bulgares *Ritual* (Elektra Nonesuch 7559-79349-2). Although this could be described as "more of the same", it's a very good same, and includes interesting arrangements of songs from Bulgaria's Sephardic Jewish tradition.

Ivo Papazov *Fairground/Panair* (Kuker, Bulgaria). After a 13-year recording break, Ivo Papazov's latest album showcases his mix of Bulgarian wedding music with Eastern-Bloc jazz elements that often overtake and dominate. Overall, Papazov's wedding music style is very "Eighties" (his prime years), but a BBC World Music award testifies to his appeal to the Western audience.

Philip Koutev Ensemble *Philip Koutev Ensemble* (Gega New GD 119). Koutev was a brilliant arranger and composer, and his ensemble was the vehicle for displaying his ideas. This recent CD of mostly old favourites show that they have lost none of their magic, and at least some ears will find the clean and well-balanced modern sound an improvement on their reverb-drenched earlier recordings.

Theodosii Spassov *Fish are Praying for Rain* (Traditional Crossroads TCRO 4298). Spassov's collaboration with a jazz pianist and drummer is either a fascinating exploration of the boundaries or an egregious example of a dog walking on its hind legs, depending on taste. In any case, it can't be ignored. If you are lucky enough to come across his 1986 collaboration with composer Stefan Mutafchiev on Balkanton, *The Long Road*, try that for a bit more experimentation with a bit less self-indulgence.

Theodosii Spassov and Nikola Iliev *Na Trapeza* (Gega New GD 207). Spassov is undoubtedly the finest and most startling player of the notoriously intractable shepherd's flute, the *kaval*, and here he is joined by clarinetist Iliev in an extraordinary mixture of spontaneous invention and amazingly disciplined unison playing. A fine disc.

Trakia Folk Ensemble Plovdiv *Grozdana* (Gega New GD 228). The Trakia Ensemble was always the most experimental and exciting of the large-scale regional ensembles, and the spanking performances and sweeping orchestral and choral arrangements, leavened by a couple of tracks in which the instrumentalists get a chance to cut loose, show it at its best.

Trio Bulgarka *The Forest is Crying (Lament for Indje Vojvoda)* (Hannibal). For many people the Trio Bulgarka remain the best vocal group to come out of Bulgaria. The three soloists manage to blend their highly individual voices beautifully, and they had the cream of composers and arrangers writing for them.

This article – an edited extract from *The Rough Guide to World Music* (Rough Guides, 1999) – was researched and written by **Kim Burton** and updated by **Nick Nasev**.

Language

Language

Language

Bulgarian is a South Slavonic tongue closely related to Slovene and Serbo-Croat, and more distantly to Russian, which most Bulgarians learned at school before 1989. Since then, English language studies have become increasingly popular, but you'll still find that English is widely understood only among young people and urban professionals, or in the ski and beach resorts favoured by British holiday-makers. Those who acquire some Bulgarian will find that even the smallest effort reaps great rewards.

Two widely available **self-study courses** offering an accessible introduction to the everyday language are *Colloquial Bulgarian* (Routledge) and *Teach Yourself Bulgarian* (Hodder & Stoughton), both of which are accompanied by optional cassettes. *Learn Bulgarian*, an interactive DVD published by Eurotalk, doesn't get much beyond basic phrases but is perfect for getting children – and linguistically jaded adults – up and running. Once in Bulgaria itself, you'll find an increasing number of Bulgarian-English **dictionaries** and phrase books at bookshops and street stalls.

The Cyrillic alphabet

Most signs, menus and so on are in the **Cyrillic alphabet**, but along highways you'll also see signs in the Roman alphabet. For easy reference in the course of this guidebook, you'll find **town names** boxed in both alphabets at the beginning of each chapter. And note that at train stations, the Roman version won't be visible before the train pulls out unless you sit up front.

There are different ways of **transcribing** Cyrillic into Latin script (for example, "Cherven Bryag" or "Červen Brjag" for ЧЕРВЕН БРЯГ; "Tûrnovo" or "Turnovo" for ТЪРНОВО) but – with a few notable exceptions like "Bulgaria" and "Sofia" instead of "Bûlgariya" and "Sofiya" – we've tried to adhere to the following system. This shows Cyrillic characters in capital and lower-case form, with their Roman transcription and a roughly equivalent sound in English.

It's useful to know that putting the word *da* before **verbs** makes an infinitive (*iskam da kupya*, "I want to buy"); while *ne* is used to form the negative (*ne iskam*, "I don't want"). Use of the particle *li* turns the sentence into a question – *imate li …?* is "do you have …?"

А а	a as in bad
Б б	b as in bath
В в	v as in vat
Г г	g as in gag
Д д	d as in dog
Е е	e as in den
Ж ж	zh like the 's' in measure
З з	z as in zap
И и	i as in bit (or 'bee', at the end of a word)
Й й	i 'y' as in youth
К к	k as in kit
Л л	l as in like
М м	m as in met
Н н	n as in not
О о	o as in got (never as in go)
П п	p as in pot

Р р	r as in rasp	Ш ш	sh as in dish
С с	s as in sat	Щ щ	sht like the last syllable of sloshed
Т т	t as in tap	Ъ ъ	û like the u in but
У у	u as in rule	Ь ь	(this character softens the preceding consonant)
Ф ф	f as in fruit	Ю ю	yu as in you
Х х	h as in loch (aspirated)	Я я	ya as in yarn
Ц ц	ts as in shuts		
Ч ч	ch as in church		

In practice there are the odd exceptions to this pronunciation: Bulgarians pronounce ГРАД (town) as "grat" instead of "grad", for example. But the system generally holds good and if you follow it you'll certainly be understood.

The most important thing is to work on the **pronunciation** of certain sounds (Ж,Х,Ц, Ч, Ш, Щ, Ъ, Ю and Я in the alphabet) and attuning your ear to Bulgarians' throatily mellow timbre. Most Bulgars sway their heads sideways for "**yes**" and nod to signify "**no**", but a few do things "our way", increasing the possibility of misunderstandings which can leave both parties floundering through *da*s and *ne*s.

Bulgarian words and phrases

Basics

dobâr den	Hello/Good Day	**molya – izvinete**	please – excuse me
dovizhdane	Goodbye	**blagodarya** (or **merci**)	thank you
Govorite li angliiski/ nemski/ frenski?	Do you speak English/ German/ French?	**nyama zashto**	you're welcome
		kak ste?	how are you?
		kakvo ima?	what's up?
da – dobre	yes – OK	**zdravei**	hi!
ne	no/not	**lek den!**	have a good day!
ne vi razbiram	I don't understand		

Requests

Imate li…?	Have you got…?	**Kûde moga da si kupya …?**	Where can I buy …?
Staya s edno leglo/dve legla	a single/double room	**Smetkata, molya**	The bill, please
Kolko se plashta na vecher za leglo?	How much for the night?	**Kolko?**	How many/how much?
		Daite mi… molya	Please give me …
Mnogo e skûpo	It's too expensive		
Nyamate li poevtina staya?	Haven't you a cheaper room?		

For more on accommodation and eating see p.49 and p.52.

Reactions

dobro, loshe	good, bad	**moe, nashe, vashe**	my/mine, ours, yours
skûpo, evtino	expensive, cheap	**kakvo?**	what, which?
trudno, interesno	difficult, interesting	**kak?**	how?
hubavo, spokoino	beautiful, calm	**tova, onova**	this, that
golyamo, malko	big, little/few		
novo, staro	new, old		
rano, kûsno	early, late		
toplo, studeno	hot, cold		

NB. If you're uncertain about a noun's gender it's easiest to give the qualifying adjective or pronoun a neuter ending (as above).

Signs

vhod, izhod	entrance, exit ВХОД, ИЗХОД	**pochiven den**	day off ПОЧИВЕН ДЕН
otvoreno, zatvoreno	open, close ОТВОРЕНО, ЗАТВОРЕНО	**pochivka**	pause/lunch break ПОЧИВКА
svobodno, zaeto	vacant, occupied СВОБОДНО, ЗАЕТО	**na remont**	closed for repairs НА РЕМОНТ
vhod svoboden	admission free ВХОД СВОБОДЕН	**vnimanie**	attention/danger ВНИМАНИЕ
		pusheneto zabraneno	no smoking ПУШЕНЕТО ЗАБРАНЕО

Getting about

tuka	here	**Spri!**	Stop!
tam	there	**Ima li vrûzka za...?**	Are there connections for...?
Kak moga da otida do tam?	How can I get there?	**tryabva li da se prehvârlyam?**	Do I need to change?
S koi avtobus moga da otida v tsentra?	Which bus to the centre?	**Molya, zapazete mi...**	Please reserve me...
Tozi li e avtobusût za...?	Is this the bus for...?	**dve legla/mesta**	two sleepers/seats
Tozi li e vlakût za...?	Is this the train to...?	**Na koi kolovoz se namira vlakût za...**	Which platform for the ... train?
Za kûde pûtuvate?	Where are you going?		
Blizo li?	Is it near?		
Na koya spirka da slyaza za...?	Where do I get off for...?		

See p.44 for more help with transport.

Time and dates

Kolko e chasût?	What's the time?	**tazi sedmitsa**	this week
Koga?	When?	**ot … do …**	from … until …
dnes, utre	today, tomorrow		
(za)vchera	(the day before) yesterday	**Yanuari**	January
		Fevruari	February
sutrinta	in the morning	**Mart**	March
sled obed	in the afternoon	**April**	April

Mai	May	**vtornik**	Tuesday ВТОРНИК
Yuni	June	**sryada**	Wednesday СРЯДА
Yuli	July	**chetvûrtûk**	Thursday ЧЕТВЪРТЪК
Avgust	August	**petûk**	Friday ПЕТЪК
Septemvri	September	**sûbota**	Saturday СЪБОТА
Oktomvri	October	**nedelya**	Sunday НЕДЕЛЯ
Noemvri	November		
Dekemvri	December		
ponedelnik	Monday ПОНЕДЕЛНИК		

Numbers

edin, edna, edno	1	**sedemnaiset**	17
dve, dva	2	**osemnaiset**	18
tri	3	**devetnaiset**	19
chetiri	4	**dvaiset**	20
pet	5	**dvaiset i edno**	21
shest	6	**triiset**	30
sedem	7	**chetiriiset**	40
osem	8	**petdeset**	50
devet	9	**shestdeset**	60
deset	10	**sedemdeset**	70
edinaiset	11	**osemdeset**	80
dvanaiset	12	**devetdeset**	90
trinaiset	13	**sto**	100
chetirinaiset	14	**petstotin**	500
petnaiset	15	**hilyada**	1000
shestnaiset	16		

Useful slang terms

Borets (pl. bortsi)	Literally "wrestler"; strong man employed by gangsters	**Mente**	Fake (as applied to cigarettes, designer clothes, watches, etc).
Chenge	Policeman, "cop"	**Mutra (pl. mutri)**	Gangster (literally "thick-necked")
Gadzhe	Girlfriend or boyfriend		
Krûchma	Literally "tavern"; a real dive.		

Bulgarian food and drink terms

Basics

Imate li...?	Do you have...?
Az sûm vegetarianets/ vegetarianka	I am a vegetarian
Ima li postno yadene?	Do you have any vegetarian dishes?
Ima li neshto bez meso?	Do you have anything without meat?
Molya, donesete mi/ni...	Please bring me/us....
Listata	the menu
Smetkata, molya	The bill, please
Dve biri	two beers
Nazdrave!	Cheers!
Hlyab	bread хляб
Kifli	rolls кифли
Kiselo mlyako	yogurt кисело мляко
Maslo	butter масло
Med	honey мед
Mlyako	milk мляко
Piper	pepper пипер
Sol	salt сол
Yaitse	egg яйце
Zahar	sugar захар

Appetizers, soups (supi) and salads (salati)

Bob	spicy bean soup Боб
Bulyon	consommé бульон
Chorba	broth, thick soup чорба
Kyopolu	aubergine, pepper and tomato salad кьополу
Lyutenitsa	piquant sauce of red peppers and herbs лютеница
Postna supa	vegetable soup постна супа
Salata shopska	mixed salad, topped with grated cheese шопска салата
Shkembe chorba	tripe soup шкембе чорба
Tarator	yogurt and cucumber soup таратор

Meat (meso)

Drebolii	giblets дреболий
Ezik	tongue език
File	fillet филе
Gyuvech	meat and veg stew baked in a pot гювеч
Imam Bayaldi	stuffed aubergines (lit. "the Imam burst") Имам Баялди
Kare	fillet or loin chop каре
Kebapcheta	grilled, sausage-shaped meatballs кебапчета
Kyufteta	meatballs кюфтета
Mozûk	brains мозък
Musaka	moussaka мусака
Pûrzhola	grilled cutlet пържола
Pileshko	chicken пилешко
Ptitsi	poultry птици
Salam	salami салам
Shishcheta	lamb or pork shish kebabs шишчета
Slanina	bacon сланина
Svinsko (s kiselo zele)	pork свинско (and sauerkraut) (с кисело зеле)

Terms

cheverme	barbecue чеверме	**pûrzheno**	fried пържено
divech	game дивеч	**pecheno**	roast печено
na skara	grilled на скара	**zadusheno**	braised задушено

Fish (riba)

Byala riba	pike perch бяла рива	**Lefer**	bluefish лефер
Chiga	sterlet чига	**Midi**	mussels миди
Esetra	sturgeon есетра	**Palamud**	tuna паламуд
Haiver	roe хайвер	**Pûstûrva**	trout пъстърва
Kalkan	turbot калкан	**Sharan**	carp шаран
Karagyoz	Black Sea herring карагьоз	**Skumriya**	mackerel скумрия
Kefal	grey mullet кефал	**Som**	sheatfish сом

Vegetables (zelenchutsi)

Chesûn	garlic чесън	**Pûrzheni kartofi**	chips/french fries пържени картофи
Chushki	peppers чушки	**Praz**	leeks праз
Domati	tomatoes домати	**(Presen) luk**	(spring) onions (пресен) лук
Gûbi	mushrooms гъби	**Sini domati**	aubergines сини домати
Grah	peas грах	**Spanak**	spinach спанак
Karfiol	cauliflower карфиол	**Tikvichki**	courgettes тиквички
Kartofi	potatoes картофи	**Zelen fasul**	runner beans зелен фасул
Krastavitsa	cucumber краставица		
Luk	onions лук		
Maslini	olives маслини		
Morkovi	carrots моркови		

Fruit (plodove) and cheese (sirene)

Chereshi	cherries череши	**Vishni**	morello cherries вишни
Dinya	watermelon диня	**Yabûlki**	apples ябълки
Grozde	grapes грозде	**Yagodi**	strawberries ягоди
Kaisii	apricots каисий	**Kashkaval**	hard, Edam-type cheese кашкавал
Krushi	pears круши	**Pusheno sirene**	smoked cheese пушено сирене
Limon	lemon лимон	**Sirene**	salty, feta-type cheese сирене
Malini	raspberries малини		
Praskovi	peaches праскови		
Slivi	plums сливи		

Drinks (napitki)

Goreshti napitki	hot drinks горещи напитки	**Sok portokal**	orange juice сок портокал
Kafe	espresso кафе еспресо	**Aperitivi**	aperitifs аперитиви
Neskafe	instant coffee нескафе	**Rakiya**	brandy ракия
Chai	tea чай	**Vino**	wine вино
Bezalkoholni napitki	soft drinks безалкохолни напитки	**Shardone**	Chardonnay Шардоне
Voda	water вода	**Bira**	beer бира
		Nalivna	draught наливна

Glossary

Alafranga Term for the combination of native woodwork and textiles with Western fashions in nineteenth-century interior design (from *à la française*); or painted niches and walls in National Revival-style houses.

Banya Public bath or spa.

Bashibazouks Murderous bands of *pomaks* (see below) and Turks, employed to punish rebellions against Ottoman rule.

Bey Turkish provincial governor.

Blato Marsh or reed-encircled lake.

Bolyarin Medieval Bulgarian nobleman (a bolyarka is a noblewoman).

Caravanserai Hostelry for merchants in Ottoman times.

Chardak Balcony or porch.

Charshiya A bazaar or street of workshops, once a typical feature of Bulgarian towns.

Cherga Handwoven rug. With a simpler design than a kilim, and often taking the form of a long thin runner.

Cherkva Church (see also *Tsûrkva*).

Cherno More Black Sea.

Cheshma Public drinking fountain.

Cheta Unit of resistance fighters or guerillas.

Chetnik Member of a cheta.

Chiflik Farm, or small administrative unit in Ottoman times.

Chorbadzhii Village headmen (literally, "soup makers") or rich landowners; also pejorative term for those who collaborated during the Ottoman occupation.

Dere Stream.

Dupka Hole, den or cave.

Dvorets Palace.

Dzhamiya A mosque (also spelt *Djami* or *Dzhamija*).

Esonarthex Short porch before the narthex of a church.

Ezero Lake.

Firman Sultan's seal of authorization.

Gora Forest, hill or mountain (Sredna Gora – Central Range).

Grad City or town. The oldest quarter is often known as the *Stariya grad* or the *varosh* (see opposite).

Gradina Garden.

Guber Fleecy rug.

Hadzhi Man who has made the pilgrimage to Mecca (if a Muslim), or to Jerusalem (if a Christian).

Haiduk Outlaw, bandit.

Haidutin Outlaw, freedom fighter. Plural: haiduti.

Hali Market hall.

Halishte Soft blanket or fleecy rug.

Han Inn or caravanserai.

Hisar Fortress.

Hizha Hikers' hostel or mountain hut.

Igumen Father-superior of a monastery.

Izvor A spring.

Janissaries Elite military fighting corps raised from foreigners whom the Turks abducted during childhood (under the hated *devşirme* system, and indoctrinated with fanatical loyalty to the sultan.

Kûrdzhali Turkish outlaws, particularly active in the late eighteenth and early nineteenth centuries.

Kûshta House.

Kaza Small Ottoman administrative unit.

Khan (or *Han*) Supreme ruler of the Bulgar tribes and, later, the first Bulgarian state; the title is of Central Asian origin.

Kilim Woollen carpet, featuring a complex central design within a border.

Kitenik See *Guber*.

Kobilitsa Yoke used for carrying buckets.

Koleda Christmas.

Koledar Christmas carol singer.

Komitadzhi Another word for *Chetnik* (see above).

Konak Headquarters of an Ottoman *chiflik* or region; including the governor's residence, a garrison and a prison.

Korso Evening promenade.

Kozek See *Guber*.

Kozyak Goat-hair rug.

Krepost Fortress.

Kuker Mummer; a man dressed in carnival costume to celebrate winter nearing its end, a ceremony that usually takes place in January, although in some areas it is associated with the beginning of Lent.

Kvartal Suburb.

Kvartira Room (*chastni kvartiri* – private rooms).

Liberation, The The attainment of Bulgaria's independence from Ottoman rule, following the Russo-Turkish war of 1877–78.

Magistrala Main highway.

Mahala Quarter or area of town, often occupied by a particular ethnic or religious group (*tsiganskata mahala* – the Gypsy quarter).

Malko Small, little or minor (Malko Tûrnovo –Tûrnovo Minor).

Manastir Monastery.

Minder Couch or seat built into a room (plural, *minderi*).

Mogila Burial mound.

Most Bridge.

Naos Innermost part of an Orthodox church.

Narthex Entrance hall of Orthodox church.

National Revival Nineteenth-century upsurge in Bulgarian culture and national consciousness. Sometimes called the Bulgarian renaissance.

National Revival Style Architecture developed during the eighteenth and nineteenth centuries, characterized by the use of oriels and decorative features such as carved wooden ceilings, stylized murals and niches. Best seen in Koprivshtitsa, Tûrnovo, Tryavna and Plovdiv.

Nos Cape.

Odyalo Blanket.

Oriel Angular or curved bay window projecting from the upper floor of a house.

Osvobozhdenieto The Liberation (see above).

Pametnik Monument or memorial.

Pût Road.

Pazar Market.

Peshtera Cave (see also *dupka*).

Planina Mountain.

Ploshtad (Pl.) Town square.

Pomaks Bulgarians who converted to Islam during the Turkish occupation, or their descendants; mainly resident in the Rhodopes.

Pop Orthodox priest.

Prohod Mountain pass.

Prolom Gorge or defile.

Rayah (or *Raya*) "The Herd", as the Ottomans called and treated the non-Muslim subjects of their empire.

Reka River.

Sûbranie Parliament, assembly

Selo Village.

Shose Avenue or highway.

Sofra Low table with a circular top of copper or brass.

Survakar Boy who goes from house to house wishing people a happy new year by hitting them on the back with a *survaknitsa*.

Survaki New Year.

Survaknitsa Decorated twig borne by a *survakar*.

Sveti (Sv.) Saint; blessed or holy. *Sveta* is the feminine form: *Sveta Bogoroditsa* is the Holy Virgin; *Sveta Troitsa* is the Holy Trinity.

Tekke Dervish lodge.

Tell Mound of earth left by successive generations of human settlement. Tells in the Plain of Thrace provide evidence of Bulgaria's Neolithic and Bronze Age inhabitants.

Thracians Inhabitants of Bulgaria during the pre-Christian era.

Tsûrkva Church.

Turbe Small Islamic mausoleum.

Turisticheska Spalnya Tourist hostel, providing cheap dorm-type accommodation.

Ulitsa (Ul.) Street.

Varosh Central quarter of old Balkan town.

Vûzrazhdane National Revival (see above).

Velikden Easter.

Veliko Great (Veliko Tûrnovo – Great Tûrnovo).

Vilayet Large Ottoman administrative unit; province.

Voyvoda Leader of a *cheta*.

Vrûh Summit or peak.

Yazovir Reservoir, artificial lake.

Acronyms

BKP Bulgarian Communist Party.

BSP Bulgarian Socialist Party (successor to the BKP).

BZNS Bulgarian Agrarian National Union.

DPS (Dvizhenieto za prava i svobodi). The Movement for Rights and Freedoms – a party supported by Bulgarian Muslims and ethnic Turks.

DS (Dûrzhavna Signurnost). State security police under the Communists.

IMRO (Internal Macedonian Revolutionary Organization). Macedonian separatist organization, predominantly terroristic from 1893 to 1934. In Bulgarian it's VMRO – Vûtreshnata Makedonska Revolutsionna Organizatsiya.

NDSV (Natsionalnoto Dvizhenie Simeon Vtori). The National Movement of Simeon II: the political platform created to support Simeon of Saxe-Coburg-Gotha in the general elections of 2001.

SDS (Sûyuz na demokratichnite sili). Union of Democratic Forces – a coalition of right-of-centre forces.

Rough Guides

advertiser

...music & reference

Jordan
Kenya
Marrakesh DIRECTIONS
Morocco
South Africa, Lesotho & Swaziland
Syria
Tanzania
Tunisia
West Africa
Zanzibar

Travel Theme guides
First-Time Around the World
First-Time Asia
First-Time Europe
First-Time Latin America
Skiing & Snowboarding in North America
Travel Health
Travel Online
Travel Survival
Walks in London & SE England
Women Travel

Restaurant guides
French Hotels & Restaurants
London Restaurants

Maps
Algarve
Amsterdam
Andalucia & Costa del Sol
Argentina
Athens
Australia
Baja California
Barcelona
Berlin
Boston
Brittany
Brussels
Chile
Chicago
California
Corsica
Costa Rica & Panama
Crete
Croatia
Cuba
Cyprus
Czech Republic
Dominican Republic
Dubai & UAE
Dublin
Egypt
Florence & Siena
Florida
Frankfurt
Greece
Guatemala & Belize
Iceland
Ireland
Kenya
Lisbon
London
Los Angeles
Madrid
Mallorca
Marrakesh
Mexico
Miami & Key West
Morocco
New York City
New Zealand
Northern Spain
Paris
Peru
Portugal
Prague
Rome
San Francisco
Sicily
South Africa
South India
Sri Lanka
Tenerife
Thailand
Toronto
Trinidad & Tobago
Tunisia
Tuscany
Venice
Washington DC
Yucatán Peninsula

Dictionary Phrasebooks
Czech
Dutch
Egyptian Arabic
European Languages (Czech, French, German, Greek, Italian, Portuguese, Spanish)
French
German
Greek
Hindi & Urdu
Hungarian
Indonesian
Italian
Japanese
Mandarin Chinese
Mexican Spanish
Polish
Portuguese
Russian
Spanish
Swahili
Thai
Turkish
Vietnamese

Music Guides
The Beatles
Bob Dylan
Cult Pop
Classical Music
Elvis
Heavy Metal
Hip-Hop
Irish Music
Jazz
Music USA
Opera
Reggae
Rock
Sinatra
World Music (2 vols)

Film Guides
Comedy Movies
Ganster Movies
Horror Movies
Sci-Fi Movies

Reference Guides
Books for Teenagers
Children's Books, 0–5
Children's Books, 5–11
Conspiracy Theories
Cult Fiction
Cult Football
Cult Movies
Cult TV
The Da Vinci Code
Ethical Shopping
iPods, iTunes & Music Online
The Internet
James Bond
Kids' Movies
Lord of the Rings
Macs & OSX
Muhammad Ali
PCs and Windows
Pregnancy & Birth
Shakespeare
Superheroes
Unexplained Phenomena
The Universe
Weather
Website Directory

Football 11s Guides
Arsenal 11s
Celtic 11s
Chelsea 11s
Liverpool 11s
Manchester United 11s
Newcastle 11s
Rangers 11s
Tottenham 11s

Also! More than 120 Rough Guide music CDs are available from all good book and record stores. Listen in at www.worldmusic.net

small print and

Index

A Rough Guide to Rough Guides

In the summer of 1981, Mark Ellingham, a recent graduate from Bristol University, was travelling round Greece and couldn't find a guidebook that really met his needs. On the one hand there were the student guides, insistent on saving every last cent, and on the other the heavyweight cultural tomes whose authors seemed to have spent more time in a research library than lounging away the afternoon at a taverna or on the beach.

In a bid to avoid getting a job, Mark and a small group of writers set about creating their own guidebook. It was a guide to Greece that aimed to combine a journalistic approach to description with a thoroughly practical approach to travellers' needs – a guide that would incorporate culture, history, and contemporary insights with a critical edge, together with up-to-date, value-for-money listings. Back in London, Mark and the team finished their Rough Guide, as they called it, and talked Routledge into publishing the book.

That first *Rough Guide to Greece*, published in 1982, was a student scheme that became a publishing phenomenon. The immediate success of the book – with numerous reprints and a Thomas Cook Prize shortlisting – spawned a series that rapidly covered dozens of destinations. Rough Guides had a ready market among low-budget backpackers, but soon also acquired a much broader and older readership that relished Rough Guides' wit and inquisitiveness as much as their enthusiastic, critical approach. Everyone wants value for money, but not at any price.

Rough Guides soon began supplementing the "rougher" information about hostels and low-budget listings with the kind of detail on restaurants and quality hotels that independent-minded visitors on any budget might expect, whether on business in New York or trekking in Thailand.

These days the guides – distributed worldwide by the Penguin Group – offer recommendations from shoestring to luxury and cover more than 200 destinations around the globe, including almost every country in the Americas and Europe, more than half of Africa, and most of Asia and Australasia. Our ever-growing team of authors and photographers is spread all over the world, particularly in Europe, the USA, and Australia.

In 1994, we published the *Rough Guide to World Music* and *Rough Guide to Classical Music*, and a year later the *Rough Guide to the Internet*. All three books have become benchmark titles in their fields – which encouraged us to expand into other areas of publishing, mainly around popular culture. Rough Guides now publish:

- Travel guides to more than 200 worldwide destinations
- Dictionary phrasebooks for 22 major languages
- History guides ranging from Ireland to Islam
- Maps printed on rip-proof and waterproof Polyart™ paper
- Music guides running the gamut from Opera to Elvis
- Restaurant guides to London, New York and San Francisco
- Reference books on topics as diverse as the Weather and Shakespeare
- Sports guides from Formula 1 to Man Utd
- Pop culture books from *Lord of the Rings* to Cult TV
- World Music CDs in association with World Music Network

Visit **www.roughguides.com** to see our latest publications.

Rough Guide credits

Text editor: Ann-Marie Shaw
Layout: Amit Verma
Cartography: Animesh Pathak
Picture editor: Jj Luck
Proofreader: David Price
Editorial: **London** Kate Berens, Claire Saunders, Geoff Howard, Ruth Blackmore, Gavin Thomas, Polly Thomas, Richard Lim, Clifton Wilkinson, Alison Murchie, Sally Schafer, Karoline Densley, Andy Turner, Ella O'Donnell, Keith Drew, Edward Aves, Nikki Birrell, Helen Marsden, Joe Staines, Duncan Clark, Peter Buckley, Matthew Milton, Daniel Crewe; **New York** Andrew Rosenberg, Richard Koss, Steven Horak, AnneLise Sorensen, Amy Hegarty, Hunter Slaton
Design & Pictures: London Simon Bracken, Dan May, Diana Jarvis, Mark Thomas, Harriet Mills, Chloë Roberts; **Delhi** Madhulita Mohapatra, Umesh Aggarwal, Ajay Verma, Jessica Subramanian, Ankur Guha
Production: Julia Bovis, Sophie Hewat, Katherine Owers
Cartography: **London** Maxine Repath, Ed Wright, Katie Lloyd-Jones; **Delhi** Manish Chandra, Rajesh Chhibber, Jai Prakash Mishra, Ashutosh Bharti, Rajesh Mishra, Jasbir Sandhu, Karobi Gogoi
Online: **New York** Jennifer Gold, Suzanne Welles, Kristin Mingrone; **Delhi** Manik Chauhan, Narender Kumar, Shekhar Jha, Rakesh Kumar, Lalit Sharma, Chhandita Chakravarty
Marketing & Publicity: London Richard Trillo, Niki Hanmer, David Wearn, Demelza Dallow, Louise Maher; **New York** Geoff Colquitt, Megan Kennedy, Milena Perez; **Delhi** Reem Khokhar
Custom publishing and foreign rights: Philippa Hopkins
Manager India: Punita Singh
Series editor: Mark Ellingham
Reference Director: Andrew Lockett
PA to Managing and Publishing Directors: Megan McIntyre
Publishing Director: Martin Dunford
Managing Director: Kevin Fitzgerald

Publishing information

This fifth edition published August 2005 by
Rough Guides Ltd,
80 Strand, London WC2R 0RL
345 Hudson St, 4th Floor,
New York, NY 10014, USA
14 Local Shopping Centre, Panchsheel Park,
New Delhi 110017, India.
Distributed by the Penguin Group
Penguin Books Ltd,
80 Strand, London WC2R 0RL
Penguin Putnam, Inc.,
375 Hudson St, NY 10014, USA
Penguin Group (Australia)
250 Camberwell Road, Camberwell,
Victoria 3124, Australia
Penguin Books Canada Ltd,
10 Alcorn Avenue, Toronto, ON,
M4V 1E4 Canada
Penguin Group (New Zealand),
Cnr Rosedale and Airborne Roads,
Albany, Auckland, New Zealand

Typeset in Bembo and Helvetica to an original design by Henry Iles.

Printed LegoPrint S.p.A.

534pp includes index
A catalogue record for this book is available from the British Library

ISBN 1-84353-457-6

1 3 5 7 9 8 6 4 2

Help us update

We've gone to a lot of effort to ensure that the fifth edition of **The Rough Guide to Bulgaria** is accurate and up to date. However, things change – places get "discovered," opening hours are notoriously fickle, restaurants and rooms raise prices or lower standards. If you feel we've got it wrong or left something out, we'd like to know, and if you can remember the address, the price, the time, the phone number, so much the better.

We'll credit all contributions, and send a copy of the next edition (or any other Rough Guide if you prefer) for the best letters. Everyone who writes to us and isn't already a subscriber will receive a copy of our full-colour thrice-yearly newsletter. Please mark letters: "**Rough Guide Bulgaria**" and send to: Rough Guides, 80 Strand, London WC2R 0RL, or Rough Guides, 4th Floor, 345 Hudson St, New York, NY 10014. Or send an email to **mail@roughguides.com**.

Have your questions answered and tell others about your trip at **www.roughguides.atinfopop.com**.

Acknowledgments

Jonathan would like to thank Mihaela & Matt, Lyuba, Desislav, Krasimir, and Iva & Tomi in Karlovo. Thanks also go to Annie Shaw for unflagging enthusiasm and encouragement. **Matt and Mihaela** would like to thank Yana Stamenova and Emil Mihaylov for their working holiday; Emil and Rositsa Nikolovi for supporting us throughout; Eli Kachunova for providing a pile of information; Yutaka Ban, Evgeni Kolev, and Ivailo and Maria Yordanovi for their faultless hospitality; and thanks to Jonathan Bousfield for getting us involved in the first place.

Thanks also go to Geoff Howard for editorial support and Claire Saunders for her eagle-eyed way with an en-dash.

Readers' letters

Thanks to the following readers who took the time to write in with their comments and suggestions (and apologies to anyone whose name we've misspelt or omitted).

Alex Andrew, Adrian Banfield, Hugh Bayley, Chris Bell, Rev. J. Noel Burke, Rosemary Capel, Robin Castle, Anna, Ben, Linda & Joern Clarke Janssen, Thomas Collett, Alison & Chris Coote, Adrienne Dahl, Paula Davis-Larson, Bart Desschans, Carolyn Draper, Gerald Fimberger, Peter Gurney, Alan Hickey, Christian Imdorf, Alistair Johnson, Graham Jones, David King, Hamish Kirk, Robert Phillips, Rani, Sonia Smith, Dave Thompson, Emily Thompson, D. Tootall, Jeffrey Walter, Vern Warkentin, Abi Weeds, Tony Woodbury, Milena Yaneva, Andreas Zahner.

Photo credits

Cover credits

Main front picture: Alexsandûr Nevski Church © Powerstock
Small front top picture: Swallowtail butterfly © Alamy
Small front lower picture: lacework © Corbis
Back top picture: Black Sea coast © Picturescolourlibrary
Back lower picture: Veliko Tûrnovo © Alamy

Title page

Rainbow over Mesta valley © Gregory Wrona

Full page

Rooftops, The Rhodopes © Gregory Wrona

Introduction

Fishing boat, Varna © Nick Chaldakov/Alamy
Horse and cart © Kyle Clapham
Bar in Plovdiv © Gregory Wrona
Communist Party medals © Earl Young/ Robert Harding
Rose petals © Robert Harding
Hikers in the Pirin Mountains © J. Worker/ Sylvia Cordaiy
Zurna players, Pirin Sings Festival © Jon Bousfield
Autumn forest, Rila Mountains © Kyle Clapham
Troyan Monastery © Richard Watkins
Man tending geese, Dobrudzha © Gregory Wrona

Things not to miss

01 Sunflower field © Staraplanina © Gregory Wrona
02 Fresco, Bachkovo Monastery © J. Hall/Trip
03 Vasil Levski Statue, Sofia © Richard Watkins
04 Ski lifts and skiers, Mount Vitosha © Chris Taykor/Sylvia Cordaiy
05 Trigrad Gorge © J. Hall/Trip
06 Freedom Monument, Shipka Pass © Boiko Kalev
07 Yoghurt and banitsa © Gregory Wrona
08 Aleksandûr Nevski Church after the Easter service © Dimitar Dilkoff/Reuters
09 Animal figures made from beaten gold © Archivo Iconografico, S.A./Corbis
10 White stork © Bill Coster/NHPA
11 Rila Monastery © Edmund Nagele
12 Church detail, Nesebûr © Gregory Wrona
13 Fresco depicting family tree of Christ, Church of the Nativity, Arbanasi © Jos. F. Poblete/Corbis
14 Restaurant band, Bansko © Robert van der Heuvel
15 Kukeri, Eleshnitsa © Jon Bousfield
16 The Whore of Babylon fresco, Rila © Jon Bousfield
17 Sozopol, Old Town © Gregory Wrona
18 Sinemorets, Black Sea © Gregory Wrona
19 Beachfront bar, Varna © Jon Bousfield
20 Virgin Mary icon © Travel Bulgaria
21 Veliko Tûrnovo on banks of River Yantra © Rolf Richardson/Robert Harding
22 Thracian Tomb, Kazanluk © T. Wellbelove/Trip
23 Koprivshtitsa © J. Love/Trip
24 Belogradchik © Adam Woolfit/Robert Harding
25 Lazaruvane, Sofia © Jon Bousfield
26 Houses in Plovdiv © Eye Ubiquitous/ Corbis
27 Eroded sandstone pillars, Melnik © J. Worker/Sylvia Cordaiy
28 Tombul Dzhamiya, Shumen © Avistra
29 Aleksandûr Nevski Church, Sofia © Kyle Clapham
30 Shiroka Lûka street © Richard Watkins

Black and white photos

p.78 Guards of the Presidential Office in Sofia © Rochaphoto/Alamy
p.106 Apartment building, Sofia © Kyle Clapham
p.124 Train to Bansko © Gregory Wrona
p.157 Shepherd © Kyle Clapham
p.176 Belogradchik Rocks © Sandro Vannini/ Corbis
p.217 Rock Church, Ivanovo © Sandro Vannini/Corbis
p.244 The Varosh quarter, Veliko Tûrnovo © C. Bowman
p.286 Gypsy family on the road © Stoyan Nenov/Reuters/Corbis
p.307 Kazanluk shoe shop © Richard Watkins
p.328 The Last Judgement (fresco at Bachkovo) © T. Wellbelove/Trip
p.356 Roman stadium, Plovdiv © Gregory Wrona
p.382 Old Town and harbour, Nesebûr © Gregory Wrona
p.416 Docked boats at sunset, Nesebûr © C.Bowman/Robert Harding)

Index

Map entries are in colour

Q

R

S

INDEX

T

V

INDEX

W

Y

Z

Map symbols

Maps are listed in the full index using coloured text

Main road
Minor road
Underpass
Steps
Path
Railway
River
National border
Chapter division boundary
Wall
Bridge
Point of interest
Airport
Tram/Bus stop
Church (regional maps)
Monastery
Mosque
Synagogue
Museum

Pass
Mountain peak
Mountain range
Cliff
Cave
Ski area
Accommodation
Restaurant
Tourist office
Telephone
Post office
Stadium
Building
Church (town maps)
Cemetery
Park
Forest
Beach

НЕДЕЛЯ 25/06/06

софия 23:10

3 legla